GP&GR 1845 No. 1-3 | GP&GR 1846-1850 class '4' | CR 1849

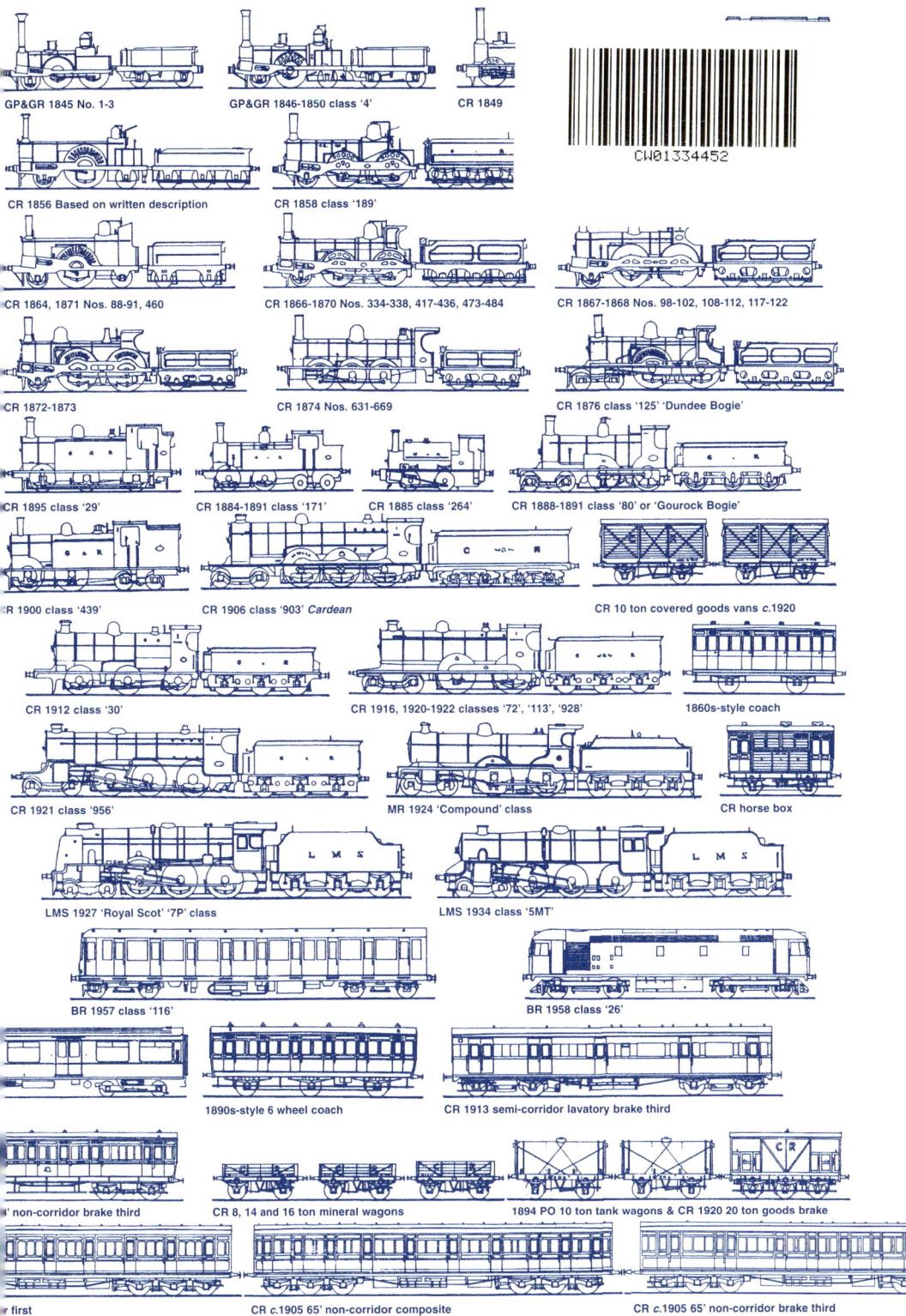

CR 1856 Based on written description | CR 1858 class '189'

CR 1864, 1871 Nos. 88-91, 460 | CR 1866-1870 Nos. 334-338, 417-436, 473-484 | CR 1867-1868 Nos. 98-102, 108-112, 117-122

CR 1872-1873 | CR 1874 Nos. 631-669 | CR 1876 class '125' 'Dundee Bogie'

CR 1895 class '29' | CR 1884-1891 class '171' | CR 1885 class '264' | CR 1888-1891 class '80' or 'Gourock Bogie'

CR 1900 class '439' | CR 1906 class '903' *Cardean* | CR 10 ton covered goods vans *c.*1920

CR 1912 class '30' | CR 1916, 1920-1922 classes '72', '113', '928' | 1860s-style coach

CR 1921 class '956' | MR 1924 'Compound' class | CR horse box

LMS 1927 'Royal Scot' '7P' class | LMS 1934 class '5MT'

BR 1957 class '116' | BR 1958 class '26'

1890s-style 6 wheel coach | CR 1913 semi-corridor lavatory brake third

non-corridor brake third | CR 8, 14 and 16 ton mineral wagons | 1894 PO 10 ton tank wagons & CR 1920 20 ton goods brake

first | CR *c.*1905 65' non-corridor composite | CR *c.*1905 65' non-corridor brake third

Caley to the Coast

or
Rothesay by Wemyss Bay

by
A.J.C. Clark

THE OAKWOOD PRESS

© Oakwood Press & A.J.C. Clark 2001

British Library Cataloguing in Publication Data
A Record for this book is available from the British Library
ISBN 0 85361 580 2

Typeset by Oakwood Graphics.
Repro by Ford Graphics, Ringwood, Hants.
Printed by Canbrian Printers Ltd, Aberystwyth, Ceredigion.

All rights reserved. No part of this book may be reproduced or transmitted in any form or by any means, electronic or mechanical, including photocopying, recording or by any information storage and retrieval system, without permission from the Publisher in writing.

Arrivals for steamers at Wemyss Bay station. *Watt Library, Inverclyde Council*

Title page: The ivy is now well-established on Wemyss Bay station, and taxis and a charabanc await the train. The picture may have been taken around 1920. *G.E. Langmuir Collection*

Published by The Oakwood Press (Usk), P.O. Box 13, Usk, Mon., NP15 1YS.
E-mail: oakwood-press@dial.pipex.com
Website: www.oakwood-press.dial.pipex.com

Contents

	Foreword *by Cyril Bleasdale*	4
	Acknowledgements	5
Chapter One	From Glasgow to Wemyss Bay	7
Chapter Two	From Wemyss to Bute	37
Chapter Three	Geography, Geology and History	51
Chapter Four	The Development of Land Transport	64
Chapter Five	Personalities	71
Chapter Six	Building the Line and Constructing the First Wemyss Bay Station	79
Chapter Seven	Maintenance of the Line - Engineers' Reports	125
Chapter Eight	Managing the Railway	131
Chapter Nine	Boats on the Clyde and the Steamer Traffic	147
Chapter Ten	Clyde River Traffic	177
Chapter Eleven	The Kirk Upset and the Perils of Travel	183
Chapter Twelve	Caledonian Railway Rolling Stock	192
Chapter Thirteen	Running the Railway	205
Chapter Fourteen	The Second Wemyss Bay Station and Other Works	217
Chapter Fifteen	From Caley Times to British Rail	255
Chapter Sixteen	Restoring Wemyss Bay Station	267
	Driving Forward *by Malcolm Reed*	288
Appendix One	Chronology	289
Appendix Two	Noteworthy Personalities on the Local Scene	294
Appendix Three	Fares Compared	298
Appendix Four	Land Purchase and Other Agreements	300
Appendix Five	The Specification for the 1903 Wemyss Bay Station	302
Appendix Six	Marshalling of Trains for use on the Wemyss Bay and Gourock Routes	309
Appendix Seven	A Selection of Engines known to have run on the Greenock and Wemyss Bay Lines	310
Appendix Eight	A Selection of Paddle Steamers known to have visited Wemyss Bay and some other vessels	314
	Selected References	317
	Index	319

Foreword

My immediate attraction to Caley to the Coast began in the late 1960s when I first travelled over the route, and on arriving at Wemyss Bay, the remarkable station struck me as being something well out of the ordinary, both in its functionalism and in its simple and compelling design.

Archie Clark has reminded us of the personalities who made their own contributions to the railway and to the community it serves. On returning to Scotland as the Director, ScotRail in 1990, I was saddened to see the dereliction, and the real possibility that Wemyss Bay station would be demolished or at best left to decay. It was when I was in the United States that I met an American who recalled a journey - and the station. This conversation focussed my determination to bring together those who might contribute to restoring the station to its former grandeur. The result was that with many parties involved we had an agreed plan to find the funding. The restoration of the station proved much more difficult and more costly than had been anticipated. The tough environment had almost made restoration impossible, but the will to see the job done as intended remained.

I recall only too well listening to Glasgow families who went via the Caley to Rothesay for their holidays and today I can only hope that those who travel over the route will share our pride in having a beautiful station to meet them as they arrive.

Of course there is much more than Wemyss Bay station to the line and we all owe a great debt to Archie for his research into the early history, and once having read this book, we will see the railway in a more informed and interesting way. I would like to add my own thanks, not only to Archie for his inspiration to produce this book, but also to those who have contributed directly and indirectly, to this enjoyable read.

Cyril Bleasdale
Director General of the Chartered Institute of Transport
(formerly Director, ScotRail)

Wemyss Bay station around 1910 where a liveried 0-6-0 'Jumbo' waits at platform 3 as its train empties. Note the gas lamps and the apparent necessity to fence off the vegetation in the centre of the concourse.
Alan Brotchie Collection

Acknowledgements

This book has been many years in the making. If I could list all who contributed, it would be lengthened by the equivalent of the telephone directory for a small town. I hope I will be forgiven for some pruning by thanking those whose contribution, however small it may have seemed, helped to complete part of the jigsaw.

Thanks are due to the many in ScotRail who showed an interest and allowed me access to their records, to Murdoch Nicholson and Ian Gordon of the Mitchell Library in Glasgow where many an hour was spent pouring over records and photos, to Don Martin of the William Patrick Library in Kirkintilloch who look after J.F. McEwan's voluminous manuscripts, to Mrs Couperwhite, librarian at the Watt Library in Greenock, to Ian MacLaggan for introducing me to records held in the Bute Museum, to the helpful staff of the Scottish Record Office, the Cunningham District Council library, the Largs Museum and the National Railway Museum in York, to Tom McGhie, one time ScotRail's Archivist and latterly keeper of the records of the Caledonian Railway Association, to Tom Osborne, Tarmac Construction's Site Manager with whom I shared a cabin and the problems of construction, to Frank Chandler who lived in Pier House below the station clock tower and provided me with local knowledge, to Ian B. Smith whose marvellous collection of picture postcards, unpublished manuscript, photographic and other records of the Wemyss Bay line helped clarify many details, to Hamish Stevenson for allowing me to use pictures from his superb collection of photographs, to Alan W. Brotchie who permitted me to use photos from his collection and to David Thomson whose employment on site on Fridays allowed me to do much investigative work. Just as I thought no more pictures would appear, Andrew Swan produced some astonishing photographs which just had to be included – my thanks to him. I am very grateful to Cyril Bleasdale and Dr Malcolm Reed who so willingly agreed to introduce and to add the closing paragraphs to this work and to Professor Dugald Cameron, until recently Director of Glasgow School of Art, who allowed me to use his paintings on the jacket of this book.

To those who read and corrected parts of the text, Tommy Thomson of ScotRail - my 'Client' during the reconstruction works, John Hume, Principal Inspector of Historic Buildings in Historic Scotland, to John Spencely of Reiach and Hall, and to my father-in-law, Owen J. Beilby who not only checked the section on steamers but undertook the task of reading and commenting on the entire text, I offer my thanks.

Finally to my long-suffering wife Susan who allowed me to use the computer when I should have been mowing the grass - you'll be glad it's finished.

Archie Clark
Currie

Note: To equate costs of the time to recent values, the original cost may be followed by an approximately equivalent value at 1997 thus '1s. [*£2.10]' means an item costing one shilling in 1865, other things being equal, would have cost about £2.10 in 1997.

Approximate imperial and metric linear measurement equivalents

Imperial	Metric	Imperial	Metric	Imperial	Metric	Imperial	Metric
1 in.	25 mm	2 ft	610 mm	5 yds	4.570 m	100 yds	91.450 m
3 in.	75 mm	3 ft	915 mm	10 yds	9.150 m	200 yds	182.900 m
6 in.	150 mm	10 ft	3.050 m	20 yds	18.300 m	500 yds	457.200 m
9 in.	230 mm	50 ft	15.250 m	30 yds	27.450 m	1,000 yds	914.400 m
12 in.	305 mm	100 ft	30.500 m	50 yds	45.700 m	1 mile	1,609.350 m

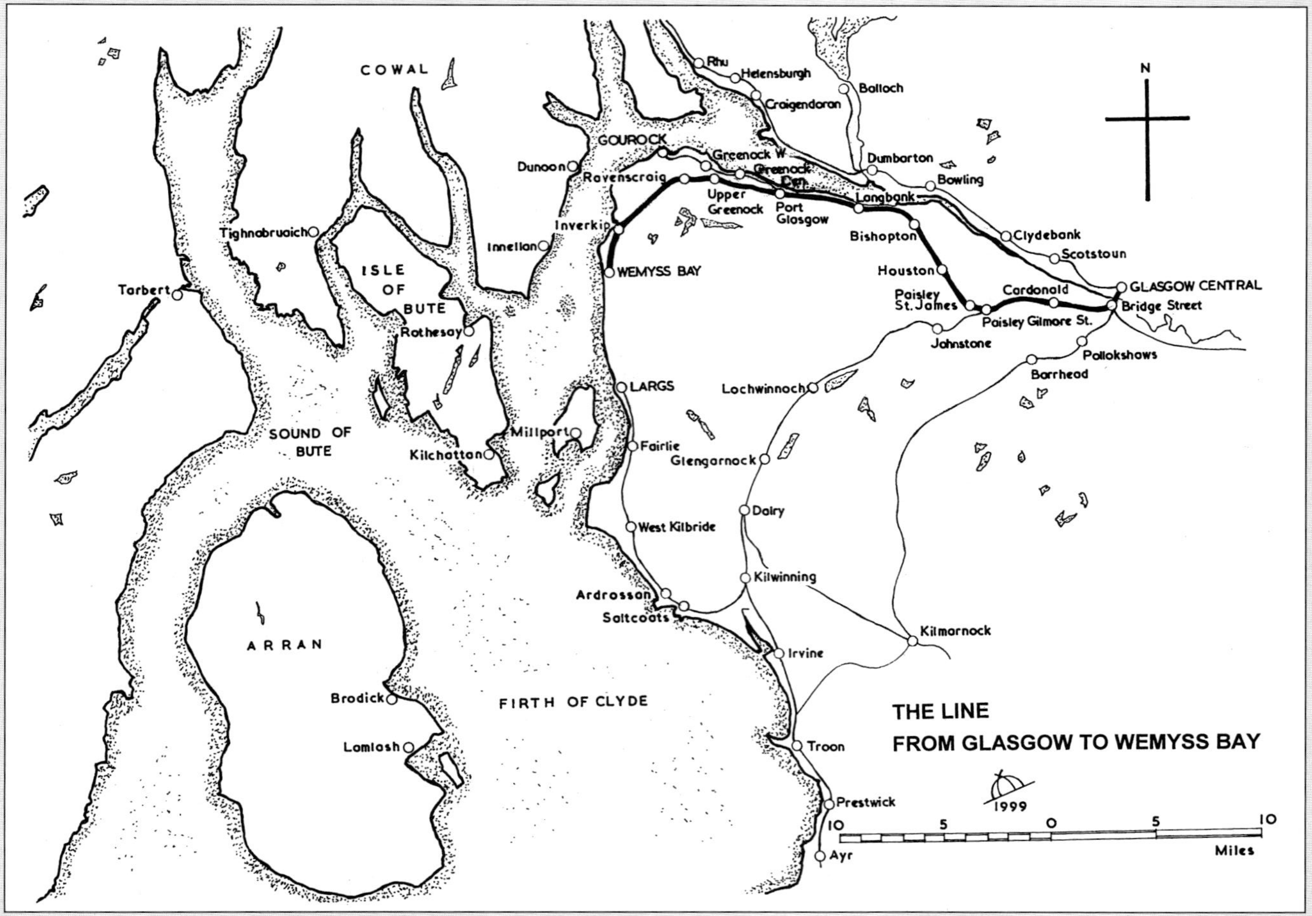

THE LINE
FROM GLASGOW TO WEMYSS BAY

Chapter One

From Glasgow to Wemyss Bay

Hurrah for the summer holidays! Pa sporting his second best cloth cap, Ma with an impossibly large hat wearing an austere dress that floated across the ground, little sister Doris in a momentarily clean dress and me, with my peaked school cap and already dirty short trousers, had arrived in the marvellously huge new Glasgow Central station. But, so it seemed, had every other Glasgwegian. There was not even enough space for me to get sparks off the new studs on my shoes. Was everybody else taking the 'Trades' in Rothesay too? Pa consulted the big destination board at the side of the 'concourse', checked his fob watch and said, 'Quick, Platform 10.' We soon found we weren't pushing through the crowd but being swept along with it. We were lucky this year. We found a compartment near the engine. Ma kept a seat for Pa and me as we went to admire the locomotive. Maybe not as spectacular as the big 'Dunalastairs', the '812' class 0-6-0s were surprisingly fast and handsome in their Caley blue livery, hissing steam, radiating suppressed heat, oil and that glorious smoky smell that Ma complained she couldn't wash out of my clothes. The fireman was busy shovelling coal into the roasting firebox while the engine driver oiled some hidden shaft. The penalty for spending too long looking at the locomotive was that Pa had to squeeze into the space Ma had managed to keep for him and I had to stand or sit on his knee all the way to Wemyss Bay.

Three generations later, the station is still well used. The atmosphere is cleaner with only an occasional whiff of diesel amidst the electric trains. Thus it was in 1993 and 1994 when as Resident Architect on the Wemyss Bay station restoration project, I commuted to the coast.

Four railway companies built the line over 25 years from Glasgow to Wemyss Bay:

1. the Caledonian Railway Company across the Clyde to Bridge Street station;
2. the Glasgow and Paisley Joint Railway (G&PJR) from Bridge Street station to Paisley Gilmour Street, servicing the Glasgow, Paisley, Kilmarnock and Ayr Railway and the Glasgow, Paisley and Greenock Railway;
3. the Glasgow, Paisley and Greenock Railway (GP&GR) from Paisley via Port Glasgow to Greenock; and
4. the Greenock and Wemyss Bay Railway Company (G&WBR) from Port Glasgow to Wemyss Bay.

The Joint Railway was built in 1840, followed by the GP&GR in 1841, the G&WBR in 1865 and the Caledonian's cross-Clyde section in 1879. From 1850, the G&PJR was jointly run by the successor Caledonian Railway Company and Glasgow and South Western Railway (G&SWR).

The Caledonian Railway Company worked the line from Glasgow to Wemyss Bay from the outset, providing a competitive edge to the Greenock line, conveying passengers by train and steamer to destinations across the Clyde to Bute and the West. In 1923, the line became part of the London, Midland and Scottish Railway (LMS) until it was nationalised under British Railways in 1948. Latterly it was operated by ScotRail.

Plan and Gradient Profile
Glasgow to Gourock and Wemyss Bay

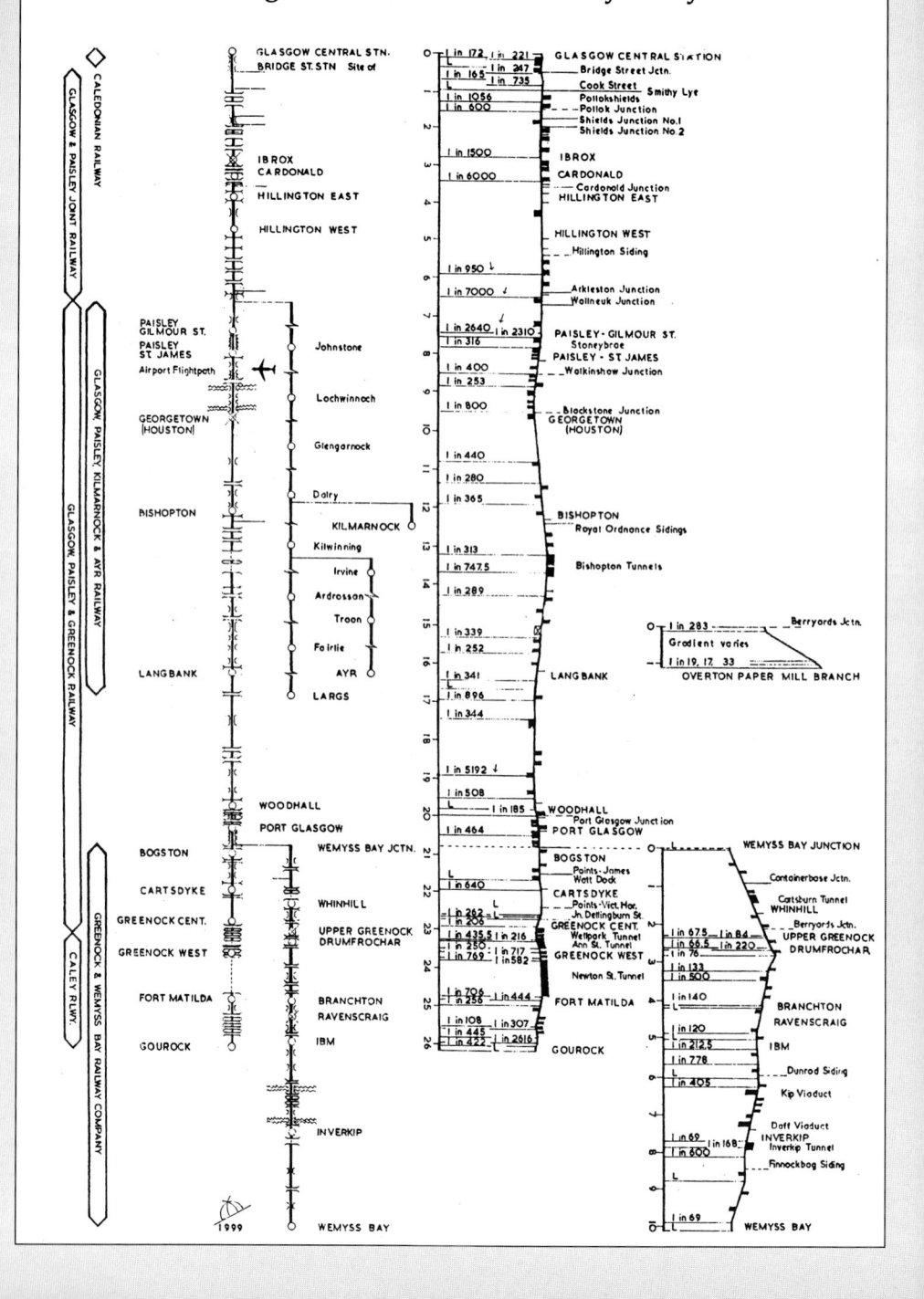

Crossing the Clyde in 1995 - the main line south deviates to the left, the line to Paisley, Ardrossan, Largs, Greenock, Gourock and Wemyss Bay bends to the right.   *Author*

Fairburn 2-6-4T No. 42262 running backwards on the 10.30 am Glasgow to Wemyss Bay train at Smithy Lye in February 1964.   *Hamish Stevenson Collection*

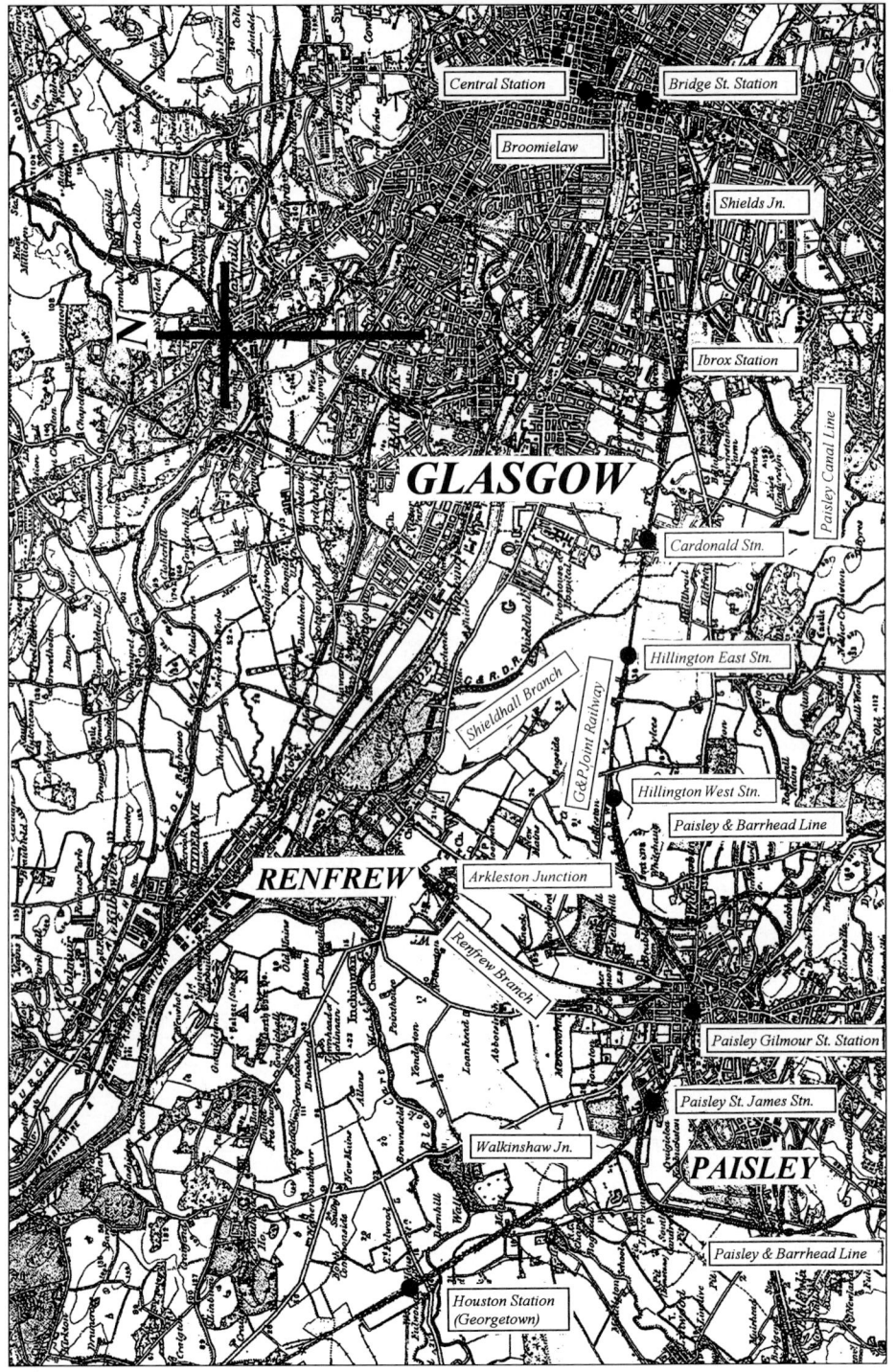

The line from Glasgow to Houston. 1902 OS plan. *National Library of Scotland*

Glasgow to Paisley

Outwith the holidays, the number of travellers were fairly consistent with the November 1993 details below.

At Central Station, I joined the 7.35 am to Wemyss Bay with about 60 others. The 3-car train set was made up of 1960s style stock, without toilets, stopped at all stations and was scheduled to do the trip in 57 minutes. It usually departed on the heels of the Greenock and Gourock train from either platform 9 or 10 (11, 12 or 13 in the 1930s) ahead of another 3-car train.

Once the train was given the 'off', it rapidly reached the 20 mph limit over the Clyde bridge. Downstream in winter, I could see the twin red, white and black stacks of the PS *Waverley* alongside the Broomielaw. Sometimes the train snaked across and back over the multiplicity of tracks leading out of Central, bringing us close to main line locomotives, parked on the bridge beside the former Bridge Street station, waiting their turn.

At Port Eglinton Junction, the West Coast Main Line forks left and the Clyde 'coast' route curves westwards to the right. The triangle between the rails contains the signalling centre for much of South-West Scotland, built on the site of a Caledonian Railway gasworks. The goods sheds on the left are where the Cook Street workshops of the Glasgow, Paisley, Kilmarnock & Ayr line was. Parked at the edge of the little used railway yard was the railing vehicle used to load cars into motorail vans.

To the north are white-painted workshops built about 1841 by P.& W. McOnie and once used as marine engineering shops by James Howden & Co. In this vicinity, from about 1810 till the 1980s, much of the world's sugar machinery was made, not surprising as Greenock was home to several refineries, including one at Upper Greenock (latterly owned by Tate & Lyle) whose sidings provided a significant tonnage on the Wemyss Bay line. In 1862, there were 15 sugar refineries in Greenock, reduced to 13 in Greenock and Port Glasgow around 1900, and to only two by 1957. Latterly, the trade all went by road. In 1995, Tate & Lyle announced its intention to close its Greenock plant and subsequently dismantled the works.

The line continues past a succession of nondescript industrial buildings beyond which the original cable power station of the Glasgow Subway (1896) can be seen and beyond that, Scotland Street School, one of Charles Rennie Mackintosh's best-known works.

The slight downward grade from 1 in 90 after Port Eglinton Junction reduces to 1 in 600 as the train passes the site of Shields Road station. On the left, between Pollock Junctions East and West, is Shields Depot, built to service electric stock. Trains to Paisley Canal diverge here. On the right is Kinning Park, with the 1872 Vulcan Tube Works and the works of P. & W. MacLellan, once noted for railway rolling stock and bridges. By this time, the line is almost level at 1 in 1500. The train next passes the site of Ibrox station which served Rangers' football stadium, and the route of the Govan branch.

Approaching Cardonald, on the left is an apparently modern factory bearing the name Howden. In fact this is a new façade on a large single-storey shed built during World War I as the Cardonald shell-filling factory where shell casings made in west of Scotland factories were completed. Clearly visible is the M8 motorway flitting from one side of the line to the other.

The first stop is Cardonald station, two strips of platform that used to contain four lines. Only the outer two 'slow' lines remain. A most exposed halt with the most rudimentary of bus shelters imaginable. Two people left the train, and four entered. On the right at Cardonald Junction immediately after, a short line goes northwards to Shieldhall distribution centre.

At one mile intervals on the slight 1 in 950 upgrade are the uninspiring stations of Hillington East and Hillington West. Five passengers left and seven joined. Bordering the south lineside are the back gardens of a council house estate, followed by multi-storey blocks on a patch of green. On the north side is Hillington Industrial Estate, laid out in the late 1930s to bring industry to the depressed Glasgow area. Its largest works was built as a shadow factory for Rolls-Royce aero engines and still makes parts for aeroplane engines. In March 1994, ScotRail put up a 'to let' sign over the boarded up station at Hillington West though its hidden potential has yet to be revealed.

Ibrox station in February 1967. The station, signal box and the line to Govan on the right have disappeared.
Hamish Stevenson Collection

Hillington West station looking east towards Cardonald in June 1964.
Hamish Stevenson Collection

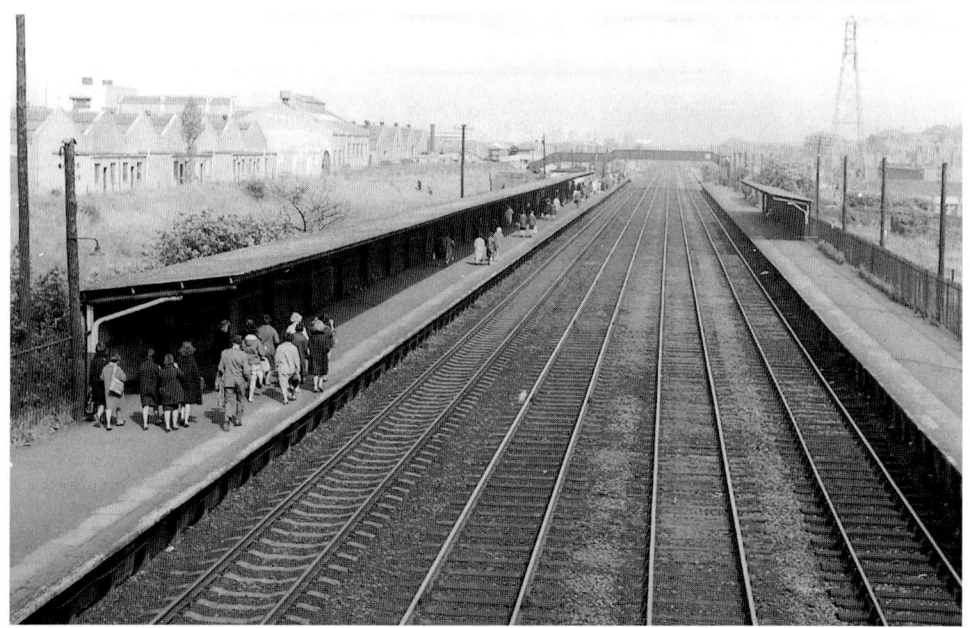

FROM GLASGOW TO WEMYSS BAY

Fairburn 2-6-4T No. 42241 bound for Glasgow at Hillington West in July 1965.
Hamish Stevenson Collection

Between Hillington West and Paisley Gilmour Street, the line is almost level. To cope with increasing traffic, two more tracks were added in the 1880s to produce the longest stretch of four-line track in Scotland. This required the 209 yard long Arkleston tunnel to be opened out in 1883 to form a cutting. Prior to the £6½m electrification of the line in 1966-67 [*£65m], most of the Glasgow to Paisley section was reduced back to two tracks and resignalled. The short buffer of land between Hillington West and Arkleston cutting is optimistically designated Green Belt. (In 1930, the 'country' started at Cardonald.)

The train now approaches Paisley with the abandoned Renfrew branch to the right and the short-lived Paisley and Barrhead District Railway on the left. On the left are St Mirin's Roman Catholic Cathedral (built in 1930-32 to the designs of Thomas Baird) and the Clark Town Hall (designed by W.H.Lynn of Belfast and built in 1879-82). Beyond one can glimpse Paisley Abbey, founded in 1163 by Walter FitzAlan of Shropshire, High Steward to David I. Only the nave survived the Reformation reasonably intact; the rest was rebuilt between 1888 and 1928 when Paisley was the world centre for sewing thread manufacture. The line curves high over the River Cart, carried by an 85 ft-span bridge, the first of a long series of arches that carry the line well above street level.

Paisley Gilmour Street station has been described as the busiest station in Scotland outwith the main line stations in Glasgow and Edinburgh. Two pairs of rails are separated by an island platform, trains to Ayr, Largs and Kilmarnock taking the southern side while trains to Wemyss Bay, Greenock and Gourock use the northern platforms. Thirty-five people disembarked here and a similar number took their vacated seats. This, at least is a building of character. It is not the first station constructed for the Glasgow and Paisley Joint line, but the original Tudor frontage survives, as does much of the viaduct carrying the line. Most of what remains was completely rebuilt by 1888 with four platforms instead of two.

Arkleston Junction looking towards Paisley, June 1966. *Hamish Stevenson Collection*

Paisley Gilmore Street looking west in 1956. The Gourock/Wemyss Bay line is to the right of the central island. *W.A.C. Smith*

On the line to Port Glasgow - looking west to Paisley
St James signal box in January 1956.   *W.A.C. Smith*

The next section of the line to Greenock, opened on 29th March, 1841 by the Glasgow, Paisley and Greenock Railway, provided direct access for Glasgow folk to the steamers that plied the Clyde estuary. It was one of the first railways in Britain to offer cheap fares for excursionists. It was built against severe opposition from Glasgow merchants who had a virtual monopoly of transport down the Clyde, little traffic being conveyed by road. As a consequence, though there was a fair amount of support from Renfrewshire, the Greenock promoters had to look farther afield for finance to build the line. To encourage English investors at a time of commercial difficulties, they replaced Thomas Grainger, their perfectly competent Scottish engineer, with Joseph Locke, who was well-known on the English scene. It was very costly to construct, influential landowners seeking to screw every penny they could out of the company. Where contemporary land costs on other lines amounted to about 13 per cent of the total capital cost, the GP&GR cost over 18 per cent. When the line was constructed, the train reduced the 2½ hour boat trip from Greenock to Glasgow to an hour. The line was taken over by the Caledonian Railway in 1847.

Paisley to Port Glasgow

Leaving Gilmour Street, the train travels westwards down the 1 in 316 and 1 in 400 grades over the 28-arch viaduct through Paisley centre. On the left beyond the station is the ridge known as Oakshaw, displaying some of Paisley's finest buildings. These include the former Gaelic Chapel (1793) and the High Church (now Oakshaw Trinity - built between 1754-6, its 1770 steeple undergoing repair in 1994). Also visible are the Coats Observatory (1884 - Architect John Honeyman) and the former John Neilson Institution (1849 - Architect Charles Wilson), recently converted into flats after a long period of disuse.

The line crosses Underwood Road on an early and highly-skewed 3-span bridge. On the left is St. James's Church, a notable Gothic Revival building of 1880 by the Edinburgh Architect, Hippolyte Blanc.

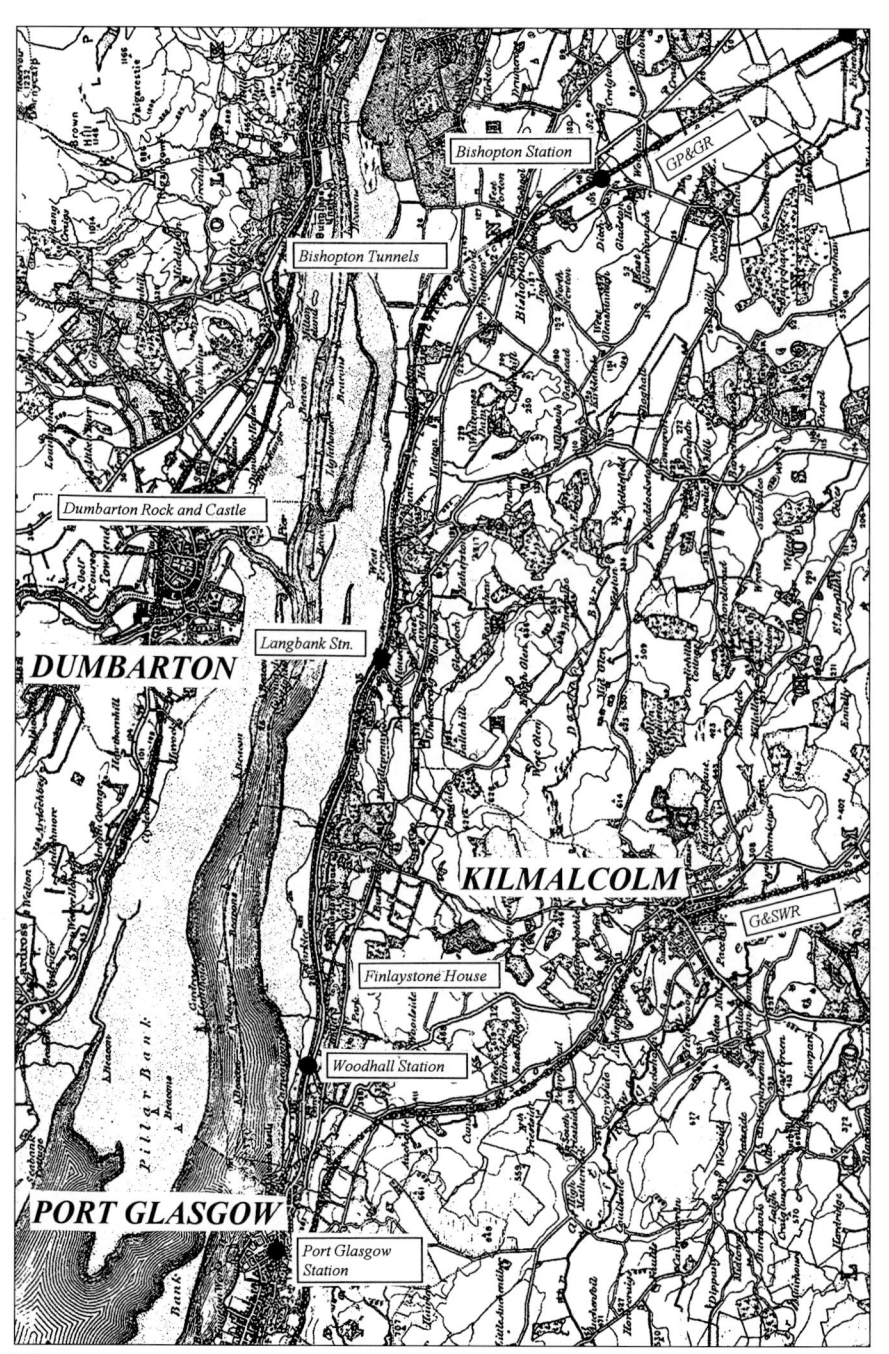

Bishopton to Port Glasgow. 1902 OS plan. *National Library of Scotland*

Georgetown station in January 1959 (now demolished). W.A.C. Smith

Paisley St James station is the next stop. It is just as bleak as Cardonald. Only three people boarded the train while one left. Visible here was the neglected Art Deco cigarette factory (1936-38) designed by Paisley Architect James Steel Maitland.

On the south side immediately beyond the down platform, a line was built in the early part of the 20th century which curved away south to Barrhead. Originally intended to carry passenger traffic, in fact it never did so; by the time the line was constructed, the electric tram had wrested away the commuter traffic.

Shortly after Paisley St James, we run alongside the motorway and pass under the flightpath into Glasgow airport - there is usually a plane arriving or departing. Sometimes one can spot their lights in the sky as they line up to land. Meanwhile, some cars race the train - and usually win, even though the train's maximum speed is 75 mph. The line drops slightly on the long straight section past the site of Georgetown station before inclining up at 1 in 440, 1 in 280 and 1 in 365 to Bishopton. According to J.F. McEwan, Georgetown signal box and its extensive sidings were laid down for use by the nearby ordnance factory in 1916. In 1919, the Caley undertook to maintain and work the sidings for the Government. Until fire-less engines were used, an 0-4-0 saddle tank and an 0-6-0 tank engine were allocated this duty. The station was called Houston till 1925 (leading to confusion with a similarly-named station on the nearby G&SWR line) and comprised a wooden shed with no goods facilities, built to remove opposition from a local landowner. The station closed in 1959 and no longer exists.

Before Bishopton, there was a 20 ft deep cutting, removed in 1915. On the left immediately after there is a glimpse of the Royal Ordnance factory, which made explosives in both World Wars and at 1999, was still manufacturing them. A bricklayer who worked there told me that there are all sorts of buildings on the site, some of which were just locked up once their function had been completed. So long have they been closed up that people have forgotten what their purpose was.

18 CALEY TO THE COAST

Bishopton railway station looking towards Gourock in Caledonian Days.
J.L. Stevenson Collection

Looking to Bowling near Bishopton tunnel.
Author

FROM GLASGOW TO WEMYSS BAY

Girder Bridge between Bishopton and Langbank. *Author*

The pretty little Bishopton station is the only surviving Glasgow, Paisley and Greenock Railway station, modernised in recent years within the original shell. On either side of it are large car parks, partly associated with the utilitarian buildings of the Ordnance factory. Here ten left while 15 people boarded the train.

The train climbs the 1 in 313 grade past the empty weed-strewn sidings beside the Ordnance factory and enters the Greenock line's major engineering work - two curving tunnels cut through exceptionally hard whinstone rock. Sometimes the rate of cut was only 6 inches a day. They are 330 yards and 350 yards long respectively, unlined and separated by a short deep cut 70 feet deep - as a result they were locally known after the contractor as 'Femmister's E'en' (eyes). Hundreds of men were engaged for years, using over 300 tons of gunpowder to blast their way through, but such were the difficulties that the line was nearly a year late in opening. Purchase of the ground for the tunnels was very costly. The land owner, Lord Blantyre, nearly prevented the line from proceeding, forcing surveyors off his property and taking his opposition to the House of Lords. Eventually, he settled for a very generous £10,000 [*£350,000] and his legal expenses, insisting that spoil be carted away from the *ends*, fearing that if a central drift was permitted, the excavated material would not be removed. Working their way through nearly 1,700 yards of cutting either side of the tunnel, on its own, prolonged completion. In 1841, Locke commented that 'I have never met with fewer facilities than were granted at Bishopton, and scarcely ever known more concessions made, nor greater compensation given, than have been made by this Company to the owner of the land there'. The cutting on the 1 in 289 descent west of the tunnels is spanned by an unusual and elegant cast-iron pipe bridge.

The line swings round to follow the southern bank of the Clyde. In clear weather, there are magnificent views across to the Kilpatrick Hills and beyond and by the opposite waterside one often sees the thin orange line of a train. The growing expanse of visible river makes it feel as though one has *really* entered the west - the air seems different. On our side, a longish stretch of the M8 motorway runs along the coast beside the mirror-flat wide river on the approach to Langbank station. On dark mornings, there is a continuous stream of white and

Above: Langbank station in Caley days.   *J.L. Stevenson Collection*

Right: The disused Greenock Ropeworks.   *Author*

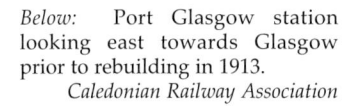

Below: Port Glasgow station looking east towards Glasgow prior to rebuilding in 1913.
  Caledonian Railway Association

red lights as commuters hurry past. Opposite is the oil depot at Bowling with the unmistakable bulk of Dumbarton Rock poking out of the water, sheltering an almost invisible castle. The rock was the headquarters of the Britons of Strathclyde, an independent kingdom until about 1015 AD. Most of the surviving buildings on the rock date from an 18th century re-fortification. Left of the rock is the red brick bulk of Hiram Walker's whisky distillery, an early example (1937-8) of inward investment by a Canadian company. In the river are the stone markers on the 'Lang Bank', a 'training wall' built in 1773 to clear a channel by natural scour; over the next two centuries, the once fordable river was steadily deepened till it could take vessels 1,000 feet long and over 80,000 tons displacement. Langbank village stretches along the lineside affording good views of the Clyde. There was a time when the Glasgow Paisley and Greenock Railway Co. sought permission to operate wagon ferries across the Clyde between Langbank and Dumbarton to capture some of the bleaching, printing and dyeing trade that had built up in the Vale of Leven opposite, however this came to nothing.

Meanwhile, the train has steadily descended the 1 in 340 grade, bending round over the girder bridge above the old A8 road which runs back to Bishopton. At Langbank station, only one person left while two entered. People have lived here for centuries - an Iron Age 'crannog', a homestead on an artificial island, was located hereabouts and the Romans built a number of fortlets on the hills overlooking the Clyde. Only very occasionally have I seen vessels on this stretch of the river - the majestic PS *Waverley*, the odd foreign frigate making a courtesy visit or the mundane grey sludge vessels on their daily trip from Glasgow.

The line is nearly level between Langbank and Port Glasgow. On the near river bank, rows of wooden posts mark the ponds where imported timber was seasoned before being used in ship building. High up on the left one glimpses Finlaystone House, the home of the MacMillan family, constructed about 1500 (remodelled between 1898-1903 by J.J. Burnet) and visited by John Knox. Nearby is Broadstone House (1869-70 by David Bryce), built for one of the Birkmyres of the Gourock Ropeworks. These stately homes contrast with the harled tenements for Port Glasgow shipyard workers on the right at Woodhall, our next stop, where the houses look like barrack blocks. The station opened in September 1945. Nobody left the train and only one person joined it. During my trips in 1993-1994 many of the windows were boarded up while children played on the streets and on the workmen's scaffolds. This is an area where the overhead lines were damaged on more than one occasion while I worked on the Wemyss Bay station project, resulting in passengers being bussed to Gourock, delaying arrival in Glasgow by an hour.

Up to the time when electrification effectively made the line passenger only, there were up to 20 goods trains a day on this line carrying minerals and steel plate. The decline of the sugar industry, steel manufacture and shipbuilding has seen a matching reduction in railway traffic.

On the right beyond Woodhall is the site of Lamonts' Castle shipyard. This is followed by Newark Castle, built in 1484 and much enlarged between 1597-99, with Fergusons' shipyard behind it. The sale of land at Newark Castle in 1668 to Glasgow merchants allowed the construction of the deep water harbour at Port Glasgow. Now Fergusons' is the only shipbuilding yard on the Lower Clyde. Next on the right is a large red and white brick block, the last surviving part of the Gourock Ropeworks, which relocated here in 1851. This block was built in the 1860s as a sugar refinery. It is listed category A and awaits new use.

Further on, again on the right, is the steeple of the Port Glasgow Town Buildings (built 1815 - Architect David Hamilton), a symbol of municipal pride reflecting Port Glasgow's notable achievements in shipbuilding. On the right at Port Glasgow station, the next stop, can be seen the town centre as remodelled by the Lithgow shipbuilding family.

This is Shaw Stewart country. Much of the branch line from Port Glasgow to Wemyss Bay was built on land purchased from Sir Michael Robert Shaw Stewart. His elder sister Jane was responsible for building the large St Mary's Episcopal Church in Port Glasgow. This building was replaced by the present St Mary the Virgin in the 1980s, the site being converted into a roundabout to serve the gods of the car.

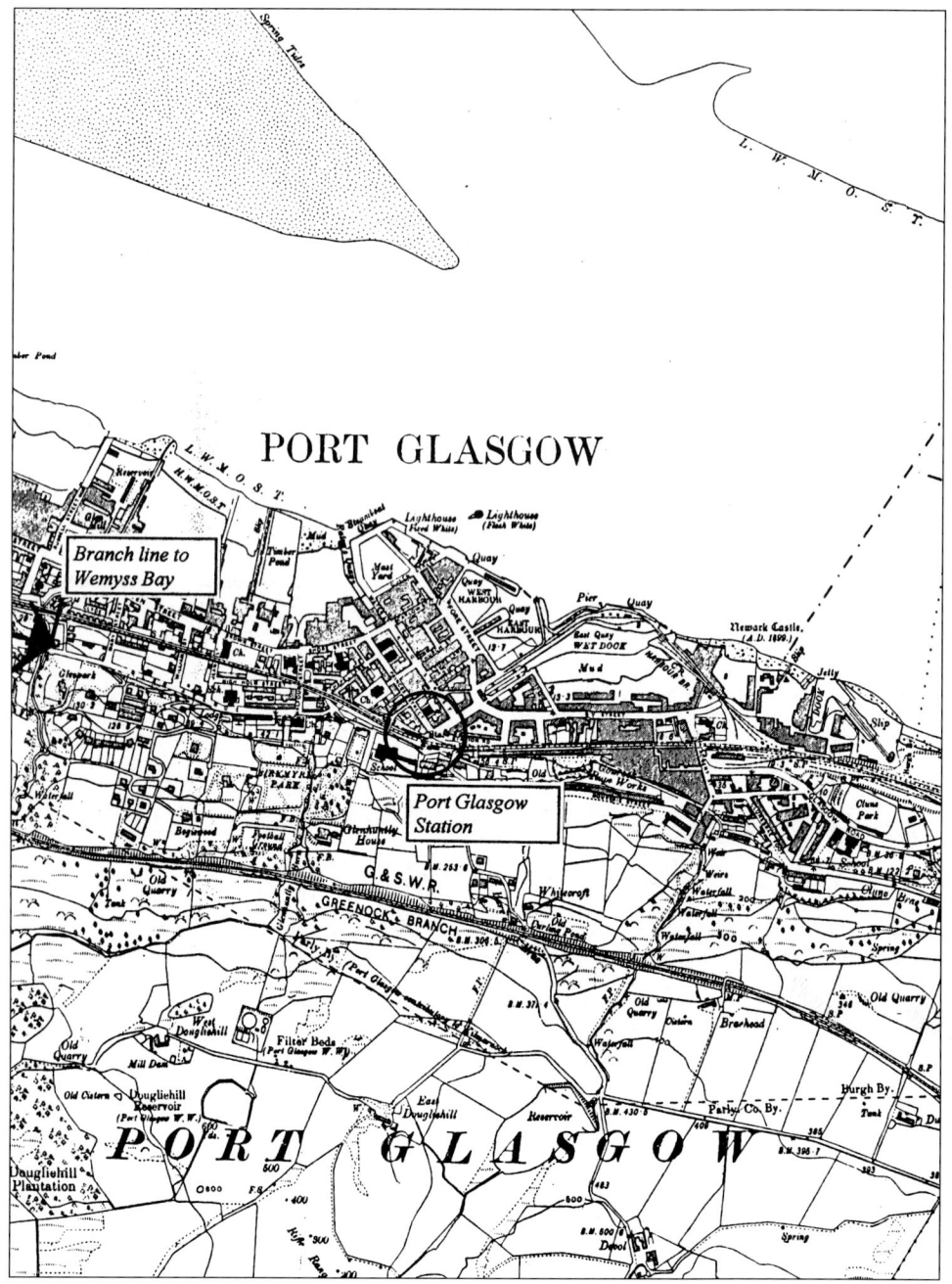

Port Glasgow station, Glasgow, Paisley & Greenock Railway. 1915 OS plan.
National Library of Scotland

FROM GLASGOW TO WEMYSS BAY

Port Glasgow station looking towards Gourock. *Hamish Stevenson Collection*

Port Glasgow station was reconstructed in the late 1880s when the line was extended from Greenock to Gourock. In 1911, according to J.F. McEwan, pressed by the local authority, the Caley rebuilt the station. In 1930, it had a bay, now disappeared, on the down side for Gourock and Wemyss Bay trains. In 1993, only three people left the train and only four joined.

Port Glasgow to Wemyss Bay

This is where the Greenock conurbation begins. On the left beyond the station is the disused 1774 Newark Church and on the right the vacant site of Scott-Lithgow's Glen Yard, a sad reminder that even this highly successful company, which in 1952 was in seventh place as ship builders *world wide*, could not survive against overseas competition to build ships for our island nation. Its landmark Goliath crane was installed in 1971 to facilitate production of very large tankers, built in halves and joined after launching. In July 1997 an attempt was made to demolish the crane using explosives; this only blew off one pair of legs. The crane dominated the foreshore for another month, as a tripod, till its remaining support was blown up.

Just after the station, the Gourock line continues straight and level past the shipyards down to Bogston station, while ours twists left at Wemyss Bay Junction and climbs steeply uphill at 1 in 67½. This is the start of the Wemyss Bay line and a stiff test for steam engines hauling heavy trains.

Greenock lies spread out to the north. In the 17th and 18th centuries, it was the Clyde's most important port and developed industries associated with maritime activity - shipbuilding, ropemaking, sailmaking, cooperage, marine engineering and sugar refining. To the north beyond the junction to Gourock, there are views of the Kingston Shipyard, the Clyde Dry Dock (1960-64) and the Great Harbour (1880-onwards) - never completed.

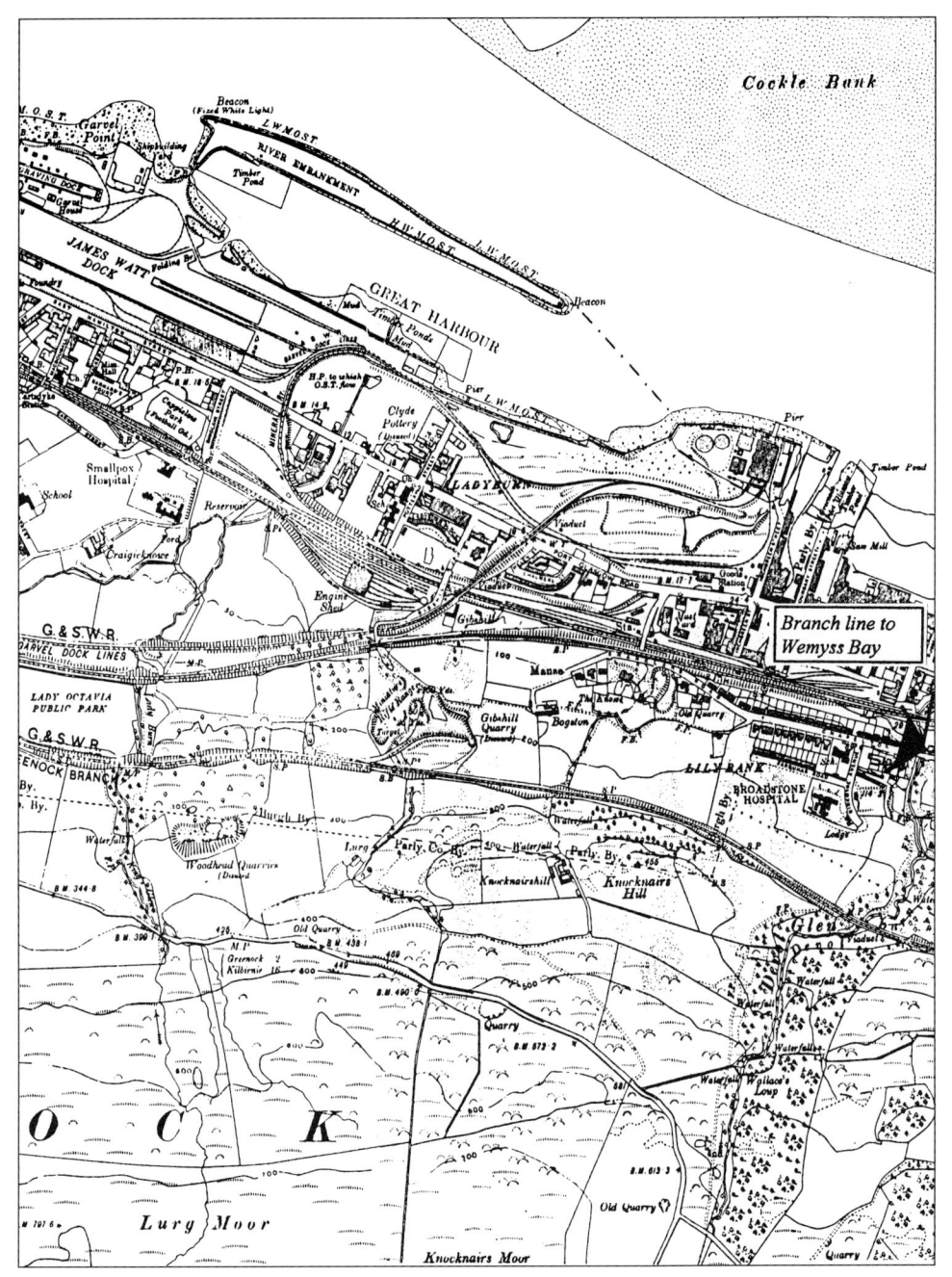

Young & McCall 'Greenock' contract (5¼ miles). Wemyss Bay Junction with Glasgow, Paisley & Greenock Railway. 1915 OS plan.
National Library of Scotland

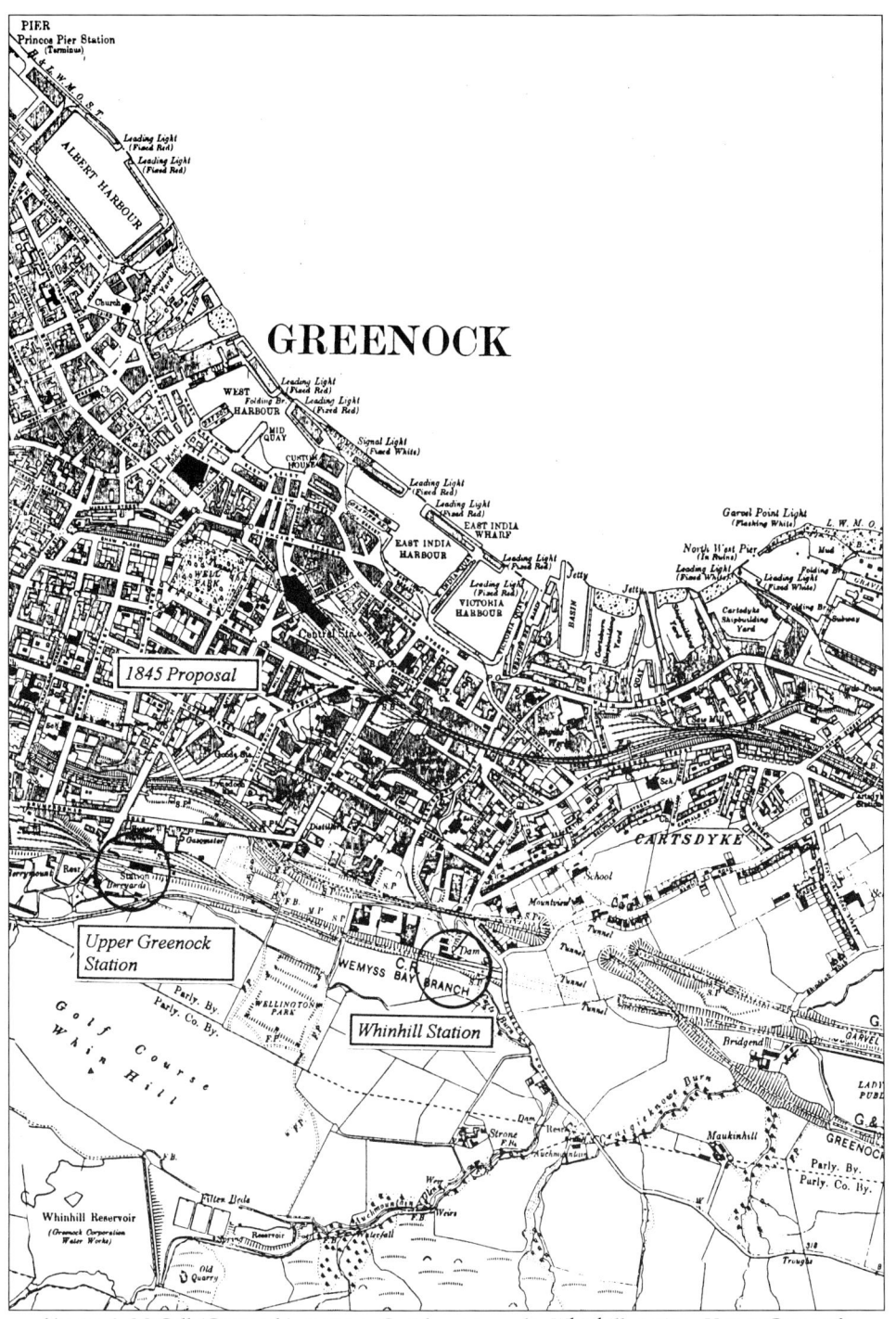

Young & McCall 'Greenock' contract. Cartsburn tunnels, Whinhill station, Upper Greenock station. 1845 proposed line to Gourock and Largs. 1915 OS plan. *National Library of Scotland*

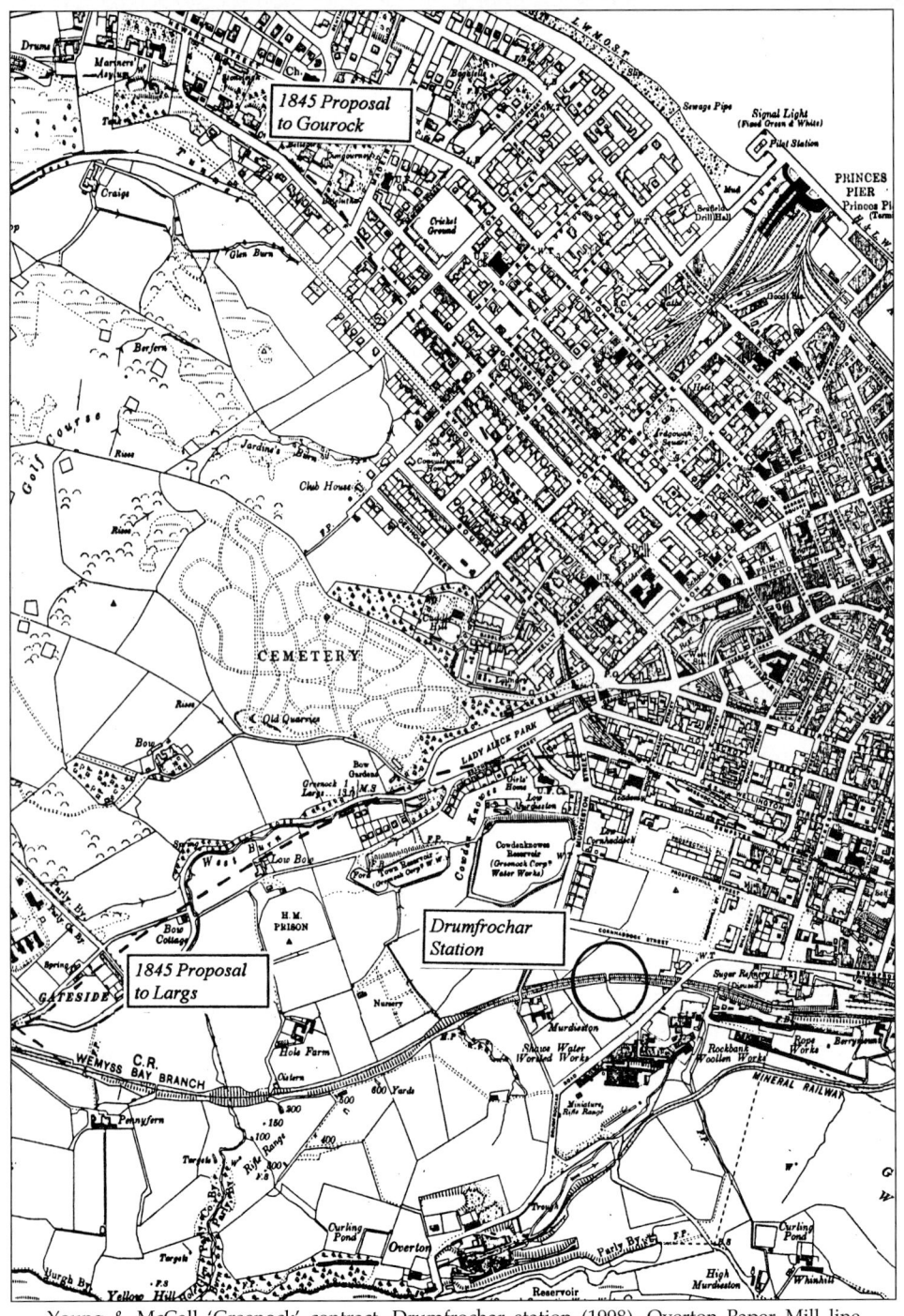

Young & McCall 'Greenock' contract. Drumfrochar station (1998), Overton Paper Mill line (1889). Proposed 1845 lines from Greenock to Gourock and Largs. Connection of proposed 1882 extension to Gourock. 1915 OS plan.

National Library of Scotland

FROM GLASGOW TO WEMYSS BAY

Port Glasgow station looking east in July 1954, still showing decorative valances.
Hamish Stevenson Collection

In 1893, the Caledonian Railway Company absorbed the Greenock and Wemyss Bay Railway Co.'s track from Port Glasgow to Wemyss Bay and between 1899 and 1903 widened parts of the originally single-track line. The doubled railway line opened on 1st June, 1903, allowing the immediate acceleration of services to Rothesay and Millport. (One trip on the Glasgow Central to Rothesay run - train and ferry - took only 75 minutes.) The line reverted to single track on electrification in 1967.

The train continues uphill through the 310 yds-long Cartsburn tunnel to Whinhill station - where high tenements dominate the hillside. Only one person got on here, but four left the train. If the driver releases his brakes before he puts on forward power, he slips backwards as the gradient is 1 in 66½, the steepest on the line. Nearby downhill is the large red brick Roman Catholic church by Gillespie, Kidd & Coia (1951-55). A little further on is a viaduct on the former G&SWR line to Greenock (Princes Pier), with views beyond to the tower of the Municipal Buildings (1879-86 - by H. & D. Barclay) and the Victoria Harbour (1846-1850 - by railway engineer Joseph Locke). Still climbing, we pass the site of Berryards Junction where the 'puggie line' constructed about 1889/90 ran up a 1 in 17 gradient (part graded as steeply as 1 in 13!) to the Overton Paper Mills sidings. The locomotive used on this line was a diminutive 0-4-0 saddle tank which was limited to pushing two trucks. Around 1900, the branch was recorded as being quite busy. On the short level stretch immediately beyond was the site of Upper Greenock station. The line reaches its apex just before Drumfrochar station, beside Lemmon Street - a tight little halt on a curve in a cutting (opened by Strathclyde Passenger Transport (SPT) in May 1998). It then descends to Branchton on a succession of grades - 1 in 193, 1 in 500 and 1 in 140. In so doing, it passes the junction, proposed in 1882 but never built, for a line from Pennyfern to Gourock Pier.

Branchton station is a characterless halt where seven people got off and five primary school children got on. In the 1950s, there was so much pressure on the local buses at peak hours when shipyard and factory workers travelled to work that consideration was given to

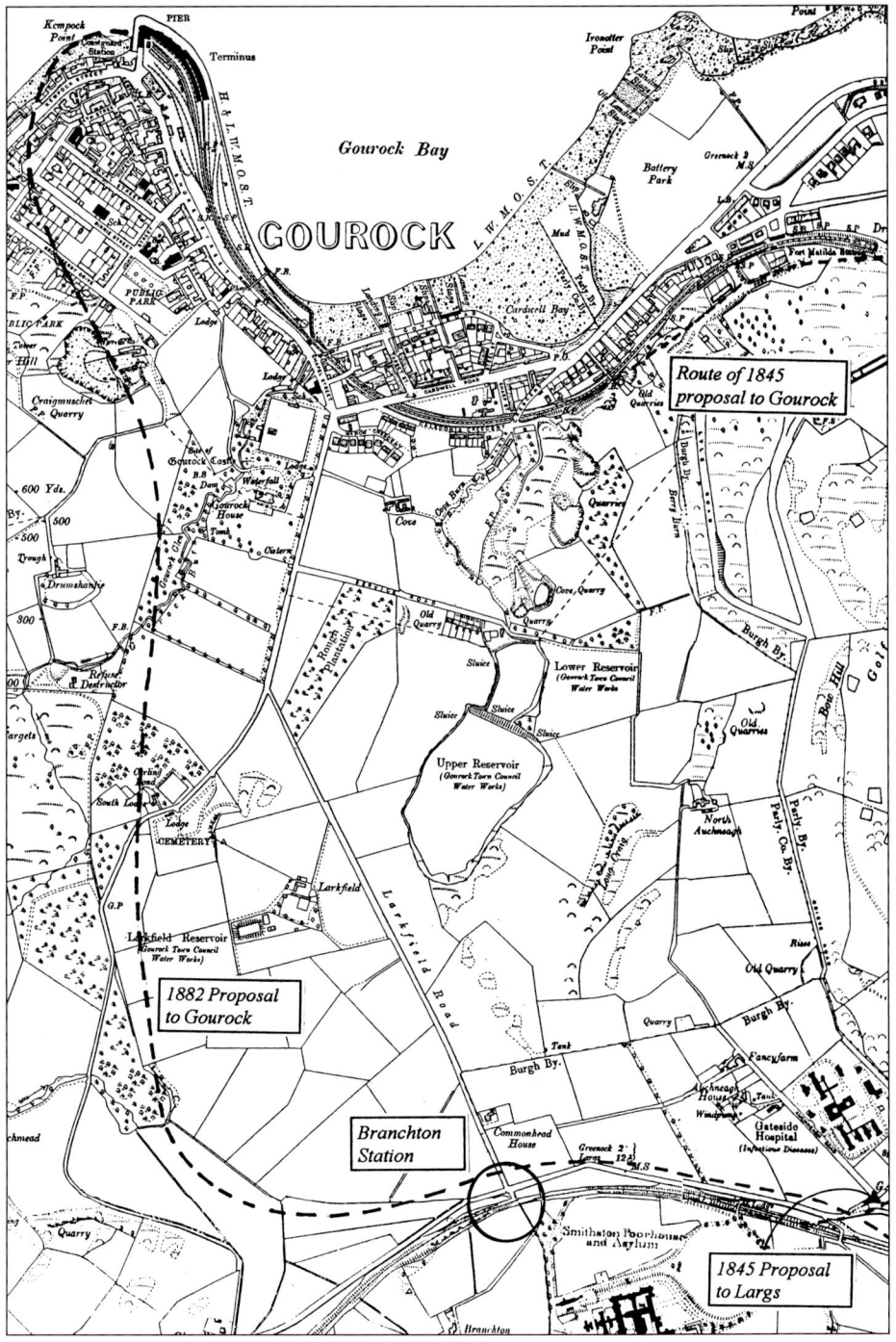

Young & McCall 'Greenock' contract. Branchton station. Variation to built route for 1845 proposed line to Gourock. Proposed 1882 extension to Gourock from Wemyss Bay line. 1915 OS plan.

National Library of Scotland

225 tonne Goliath crane at the Scott Lithgow yard, Port Glasgow, in 1955.   *Author*

reopening Ravenscraig station just west of this point. Branchton was built instead, though the subsequent closure of the shipyards and the ubiquitous car have lessened its need. The original 1960s brick building is boarded up and looks distinctly sad while a plastic 'bus shelter' provides nominal protection from the west winds. The next mile or so of line is nearly level, with a slight uphill incline past the site of Ravenscraig station, closed in 1944.

At the far side of Greenock, just beyond Glenburn Primary and Greenock High School, the huge IBM complex spreads out up the Spango valley. Architect and Engineer colleagues of mine in Robert Matthew Johnson-Marshall and Partners designed most of these works, commencing with the Materials Distribution Centre in 1981 and concluding with five manufacturing buildings in 1986. The difficult ground bearing problems required deep piling. IBM's new electronic industry grew as shipbuilding declined. Hopefully the community will not become as dependent on computing as it was on shipbuilding. Forty people got off at the private IBM station, the largest number on the whole trip. Westwards is Ardgowan, once the home of Sir Michael Robert Shaw Stewart on whose land this part of the line runs. The house was visible in 1865, on a terrace in the centre of a wide natural amphitheatre. Now it is surrounded by mature trees. Within the grounds is a square tower fortress temporarily held by 'Southern invaders'. The lands were given to ancestors of the Shaw Stewarts by King Robert III in 1404.

Out of sight above and to our left is the Greenock Cut, a remarkable aqueduct designed by Robert Thom for the Shaws Water Company, fed from Loch Thom and several small reservoirs. Early in the 19th century, Greenock suffered a water shortage for consumption and to power the mills. Sir Michael Shaw Stewart engaged Robert Thom, who had done similar work on Bute for the Marquess of Bute, to improve Greenock's water supply. The Loch Thom dam and the aqueduct were built between 1825 and 1827. The 'Cut' is like a small canal and

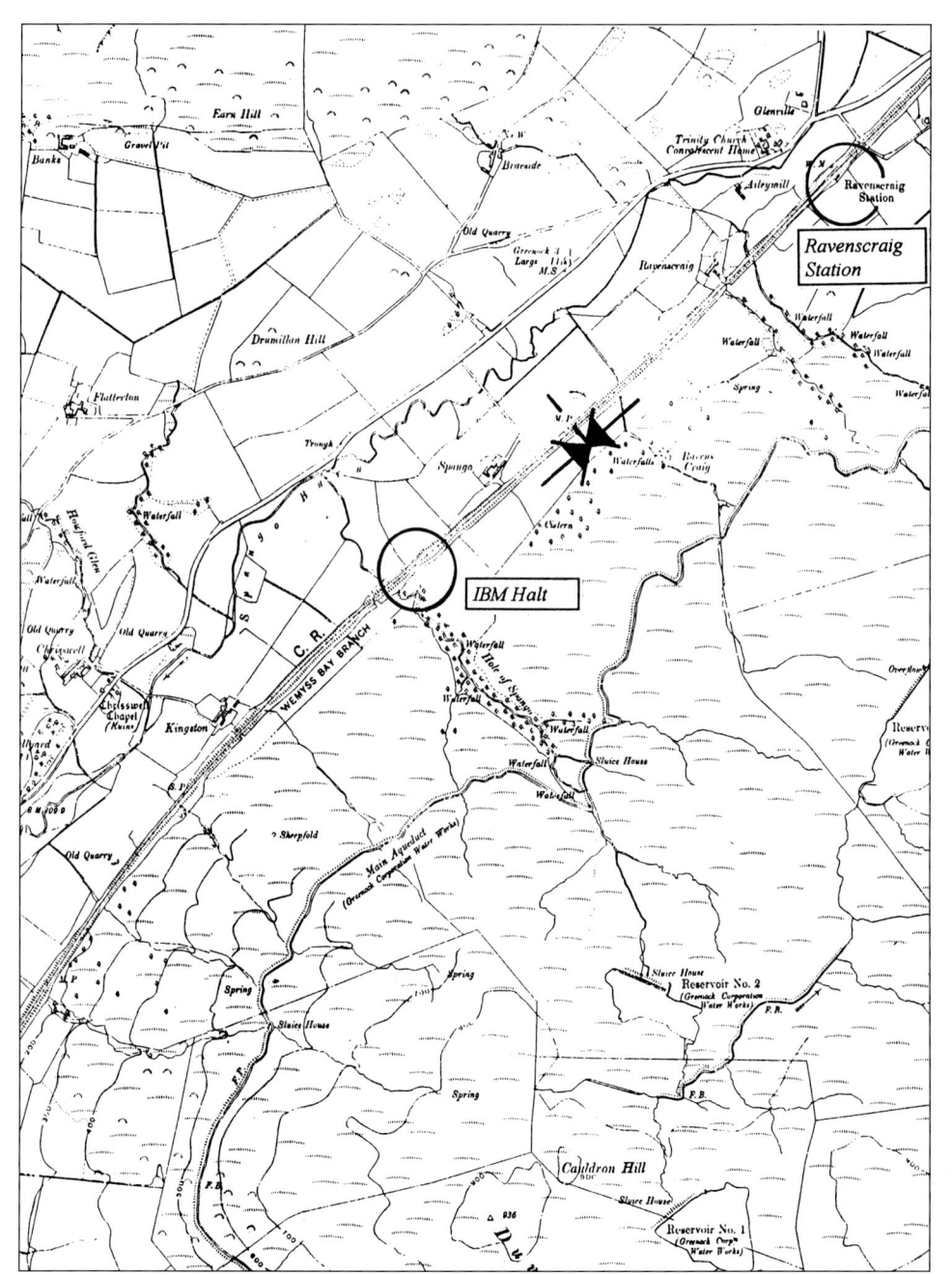

Young & McCall 'Greenock' contract, A. & K. McDonald 'Inverkip' contract (4 miles), Ravenscraig station, IBM station. 1915 OS plan. *National Library of Scotland*

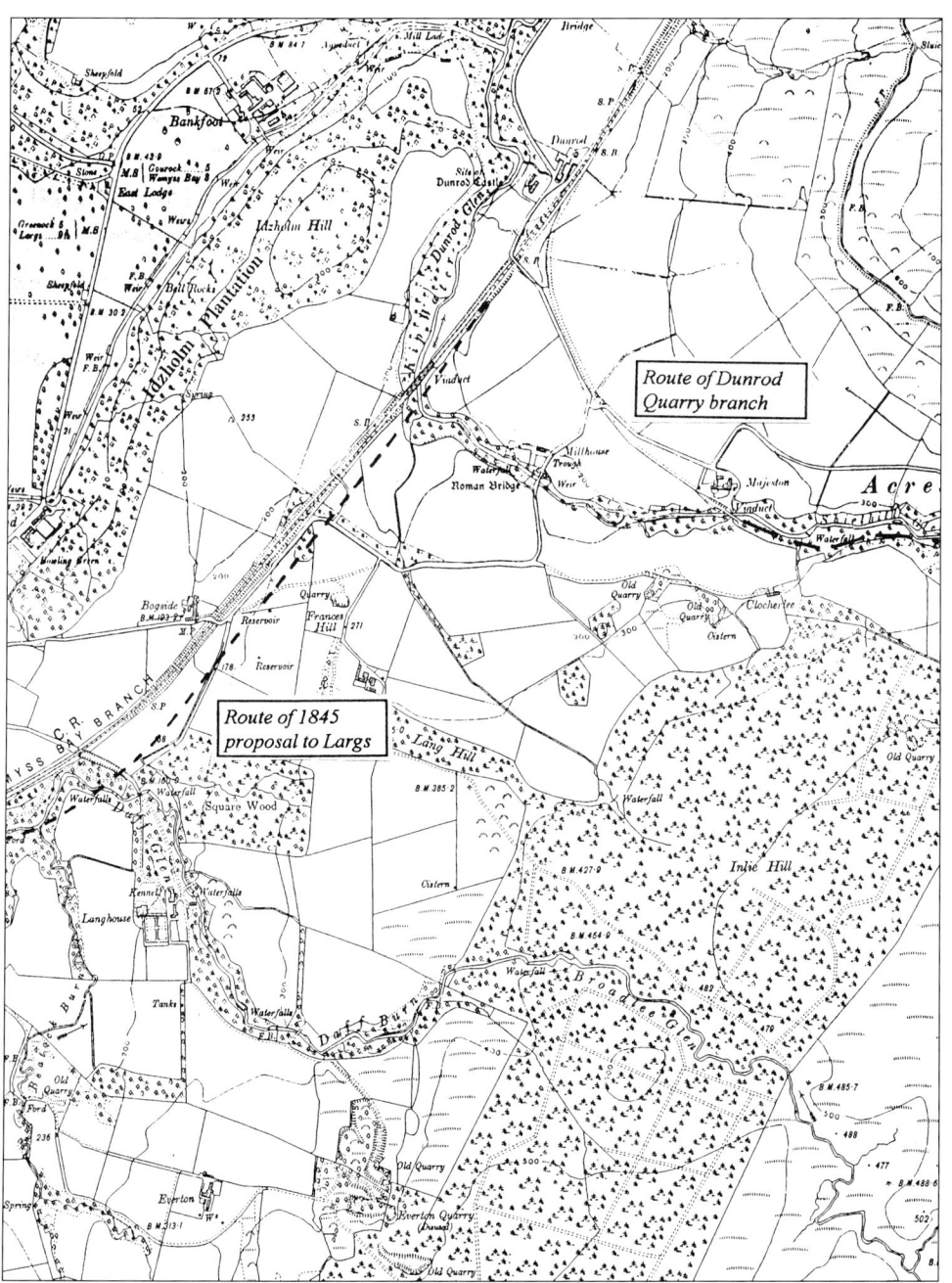

A. & K. McDonald 'Inverkip' contract. Dunrod Quarry branch, Kip and Daff viaducts. Variation to built route for 1845 proposed line to Largs. 1915 OS plan. *National Library of Scotland*

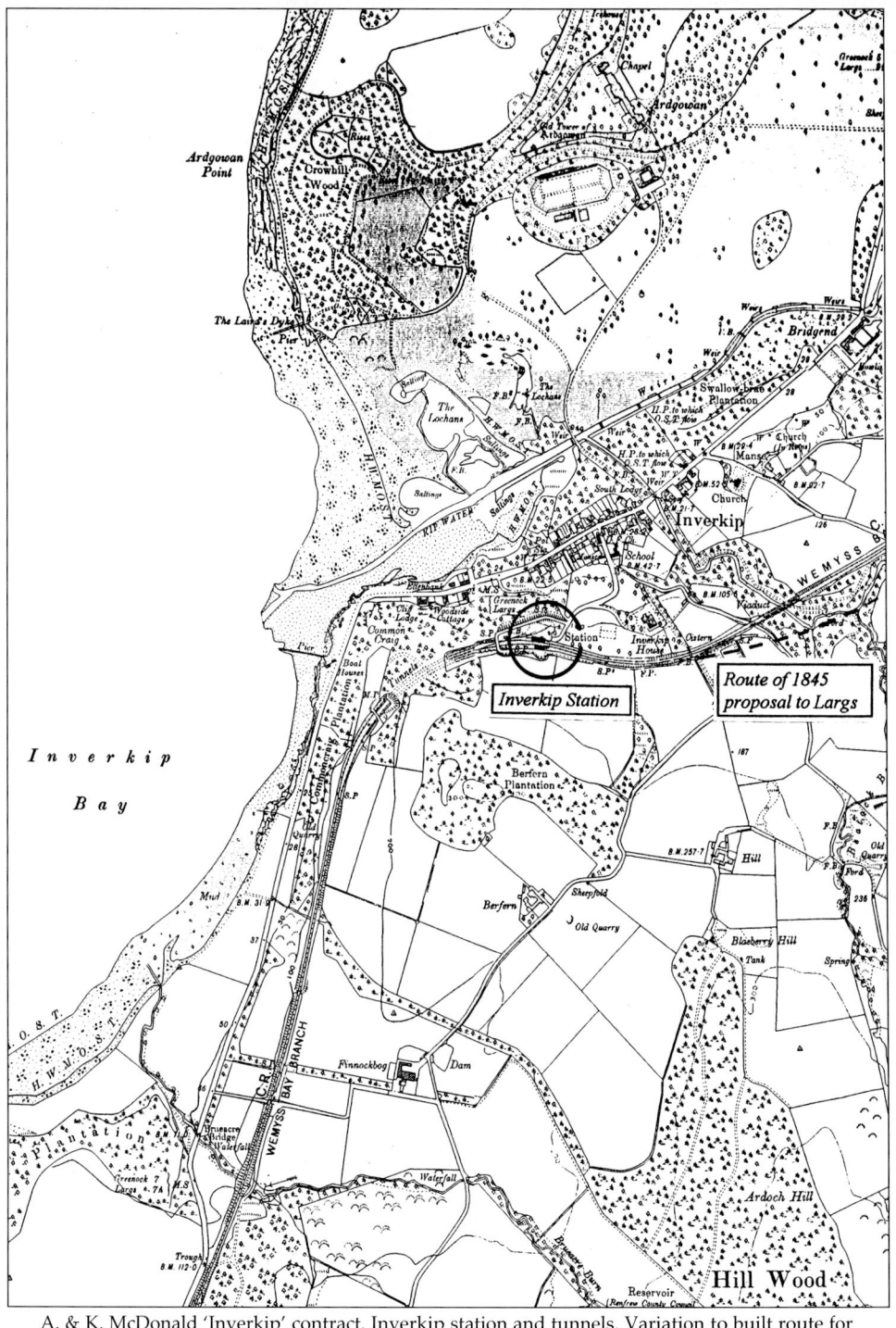

A. & K. McDonald 'Inverkip' contract. Inverkip station and tunnels. Variation to built route for 1845 proposed line to Largs. 1915 OS plan

National Library of Scotland

Fairburn 2-6-4T No. 42216 on a Glasgow to Wemyss Bay train in June 1964.
Hamish Stevenson Collection

over its 5 mile length, falls only 30 feet. At its opening Baillie Leitch sailed its entire length in an iron boat. In a series of 19 steps, each marked by a water-wheel powered mill, 2,000 hp was made available. The Cut was used till 1971 when it was replaced by a 1¼ mile tunnel from Loch Thom to a dam at Overton. There are splendid views from the path alongside the Cut over the Clyde to Helensburgh and the Kyles of Bute.

On to Dunrod Siding where quarry trucks once brought a substantial amount of mineral traffic to the line. A set of overhead warning bells either side of the farm crossover indicate roughly where the siding joined the line. There is a passing loop here. Prior to electrification in 1967, when the line from Upper Greenock to Dunrod was single track, the tablet for that section used to be collected at Dunrod signal box, built on the south side of the line. The signalman (and his dog) would stand on the platform to receive the tablet before the train entered the double track section to Wemyss Bay.

The line now rises at 1 in 405 before descending sharply at 1 in 69 to Inverkip. Mr Martin, the factor to Sir Michael Shaw Stewart, lived in a house built on the north side of the railway.

Inverkip station, replaced in 2000 by a perspex box, was sadly run-down. Rebuilt in 1903 simultaneously with Wemyss Bay station, it was closed by 1993. Beyond and far down below, the 700 berth marina is just visible. The Branchton school children reminded me of E. Nesbit's *Railway Children* as they vied with one another to operate the door controls - except they didn't wear Edwardian costume. Outside, they stood and exchanged waves with the driver as he sounded his horn before entering the 200 yard Inverkip tunnel where, the story goes, the Royal train was occasionally parked during the last war. Initially there was one tunnel, then a second was driven. Trains use the original, the other being partially blocked up.

After the tunnel, the line bends round on the level, past the site of Finnock bog siding, to look down on the Clyde and the massive bulk of Inverkip oil-fired power station with its single chimney, smokeless and lifeless. The Architects for this project, completed for the South of Scotland Electricity Board in 1980, were also Robert Matthew Johnson-Marshall and Partners. Planned when oil was cheap, it has rarely been used. Only once did I see a tanker alongside the jetty, although I was told the vessel had been brought across for repairs before

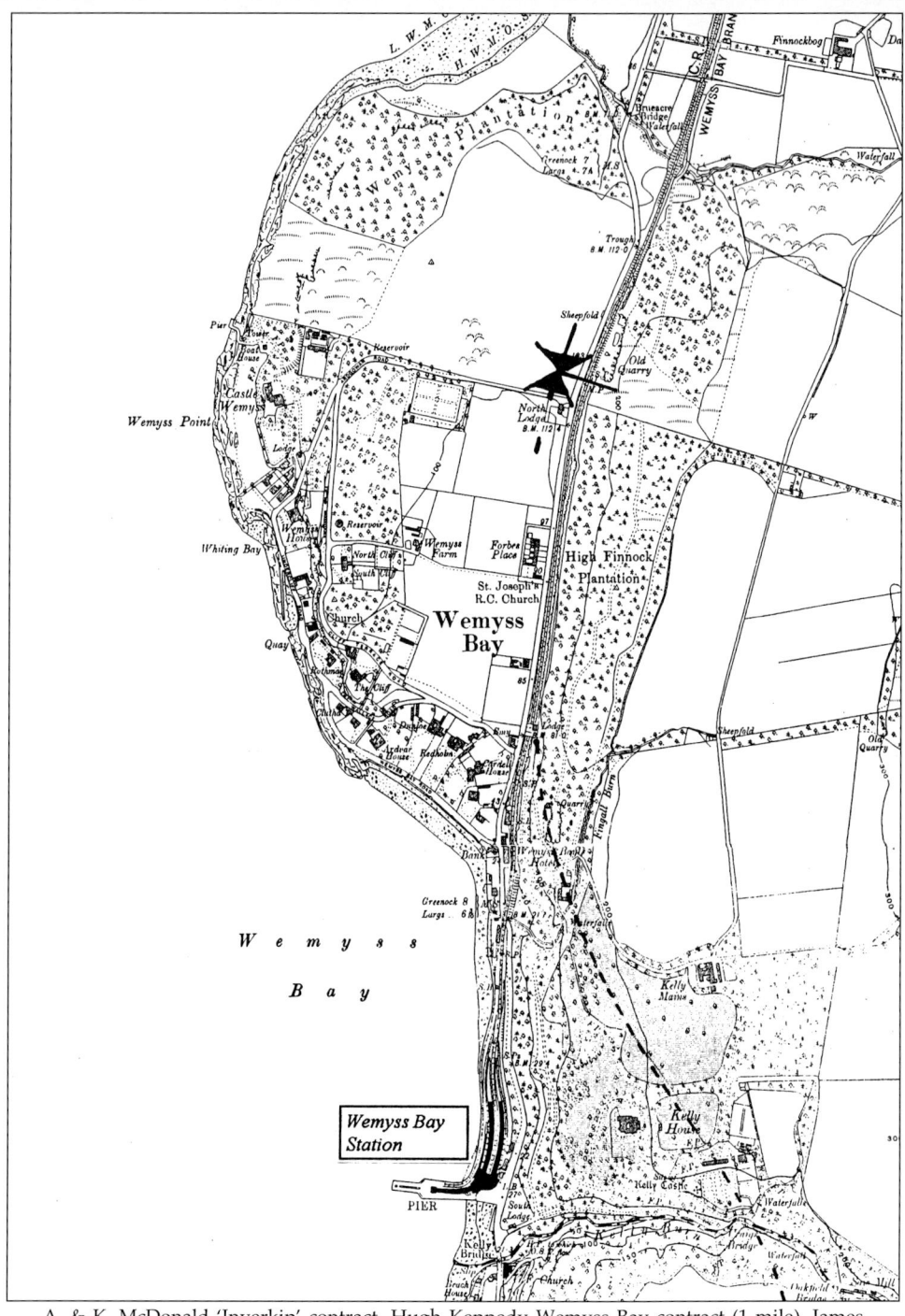

A. & K. McDonald 'Inverkip' contract, Hugh Kennedy Wemyss Bay contract (1 mile), James Young pier contract. Deviation of proposed 1845 Greenock to Largs railway. 1915 OS plan.

National Library of Scotland

Above: Walking the Greenock Cut.
Author's Collection

Left: The Dunrod signalman (and his dog) collect the train tablet from the driver of the Wemyss Bay bound train in January 1965. *J.L. Stevenson Collection*

Right: Inverkip power station. *Author*

Fairburn 2-6-4T No. 42055 on a special from Glasgow Central station to Wemyss Bay in July 1961.
Hamish Stevenson Collection

returning to its long-term anchorage in Loch Striven. Occasionally, the dark shadow of a nuclear submarine sailed up river, preceded by a small guard vessel visible beyond by its pronounced white wake.

But then there was a different atmosphere - like the excitement experienced when nearing a much desired holiday destination. The line descends at 1 in 69 to Wemyss Bay station and the sea. Even after all these days travelling, there would still be pleasure seeing the new day opening up in front of me. The ferry from Rothesay could be observed turning round to back up against the car ramp against the backcloth of the widening Clyde with Bute directly opposite. And in a moment, the train would squeal its way round the sinuous curve down platform 2 to the buffers to discharge its 20-odd remaining passengers, several of whom took the ferry for Rothesay. One could imagine the station in its heyday when holiday crowds left the train and guided by the carefully curved platforms and walkways, would move through the flower-decked concourse down the covered ramp flanked by its gaily painted paddle-box decorations, to the pier and the waiting steamer.

Thus ended my journey on a route built in sections over 30 years. The original 'basic' two-platform terminus of 1865 was replaced in 1903 by the present elegant five-platform station designed by Donald Matheson and James Miller, built largely on reclaimed ground. It was once described as one of the most distinctive stations on the former Caledonian system 'in that great attention has been paid to artistic aspects'. The landmark clock tower stands above the curved red roofs of the station buildings, visible from land and sea.

From our Edwardian forebears to the present day, the bright open station is not just a place to pass through - it is a symbol of the uplifting freedom that comes with the happy anticipation of a holiday across the Clyde.

Chapter Two

From Wemyss to Bute

Passengers on the train may have noticed the car ferry approaching Wemyss Bay pier, turning south before backing into its berth to face back to Rothesay across the Clyde. They leave the train and either proceed directly down the pier ramp to the ferry or go to the Caledonian MacBrayne (CalMac) office in the station concourse to collect their tickets. In years gone by, they might have seen the advertisement painted on the wall above and beside the bookstall extolling the attractions of the Glenburn (Hydropathic) Hotel in Rothesay, only just visible during the restoration work carried out in 1993-94.

Reaching the pier, they may see the heaving line thrown as the *Jupiter* reverses, adjustments being made by the bow thrusters. The main ropes are hauled to the bollards as the boat pulls itself back to the ramp and in to the south side of the pier.

Four CalMac vessels may be seen on the Wemyss Bay to Rothesay run: the MVs *Pioneer*, *Saturn*, *Jupiter*, and *Juno*. The fleet has red chimneys with black caps, white superstructure and black hulls. The 67m *Pioneer* has two reasonably tall stacks at the sides of the vessel, just aft of amidships. She was built for the short sea crossing to Islay and can take 273 passengers and 30 cars whereas the other vessels were built for the Clyde crossings. The latter are of similar size, with squat stacks and slightly different mast configurations, each capable of taking 36 cars and 694 passengers.

At Wemyss Bay, disembarking passengers walk down the long gangway that has been winched up to the ship's side, while the cars, lorries and buses are guided to the stern of the vessel and the lowered folding ramp.

Once all are discharged, the Bute-bound vehicles are immediately loaded - nose forward and round to the side ramp doors. In a surprisingly short time, the vessel is ready, the ramp raised, lines retrieved and coiled up on the ship, and the *Jupiter* is under way, the powerful thrust of its propellers throwing up a heavy froth as it gathers way into the Firth.

Ahead and to the right extends the Cowal peninsula, the lighthouse at Toward Point marking its southern extremity, Dunoon spreading out along the shoreline further north. Beyond Dunoon, the Holy Loch has dug an invisible inlet where the Firth of Clyde bends eastwards at the Tail o' the Bank to work its way past Gourock, Greenock, Port Glasgow and further upstream, Dumbarton and Glasgow. Just at the curve in the river, Loch Long can be seen coming in from the north. Up river, there is quite a bit of activity as the red-hulled craft of Western Ferries compete with the larger CalMac boats. Sometimes sailing boats emerge from the crowded marina at Inverkip, just beyond the concrete stack of the power station, to try the water. Meanwhile a hopeful seagull keeps effortless pace behind the upper saloon on the port side, gently rising, falling and side slipping without moving its wings.

As we cross the shipping lanes, the Kyles of Bute (Kyles means 'narrow crossing place') show that the land ahead is separated from the mainland by water - on clear days it is possible to see the small CalMac ferry at Colintraive making its 4 minute crossing to Bute as our ferry passes the end of Loch Striven. Getting nearer, we pass the stubby little Toward Lighthouse. Shortly after appears the large gothic mansion called Castle Toward, built in 1820 by Kirkman Finlay (one time Lord Provost of Glasgow) and subsequently inhabited by his son, Alexander Struthers Finlay MP, an early director of the Wemyss Bay line. Presently we can distinguish Port Bannatyne on the north shore opposite Rothesay. Bute becomes an entity and while it does not have many obvious features beyond its rocky slopes and occasional forests (Windy Hill to the north is only 912 feet high), we can see the rolling lands which have been cultivated for thousands of years. The island is just 15 miles long by 3-5 miles in width.

PS *Duchess of Montrose* berths at Wemyss Bay pier. In the foreground, a gentleman appears to be fishing while the presence of Kelly House through the smoke dates the picture to some time prior to 1913. *Andrew F. Swan Collection*

Looking across the Firth of Clyde from Wemyss Bay to Dunoon and the hills of the Cowal peninsula. *Author*

Wemyss Bay pier and station in August 1994. *Author*

The CalMac car ferry *Saturn* (1977) departs from Wemyss Bay for Rothesay in 1993. *Author*

Wemyss Bay pier in August 1994. *Author*

Inverkip power station with Toward lighthouse on the Cowal peninsula in August 1994.
Author

The CalMac car ferry *Saturn* (1977) on its way to Rothesay about to cross the wake of the *Caledonian Isles* (1993) in 1993. The *Caledonian Isles* is used on the Ardrossan to Brodick crossing.
Author

The *Jupiter* turns in towards Rothesay, its church spires giving added character to the community arranged round the harbour bay. At one time, there were at least 12 different churches in the town. While now Gaelic is not spoken, up till 1918 one church still catered for the ancient language.

The ferry turns and docks alongside the pier and the passengers depart. Those in need of 'spending a penny' can inspect the splendidly refurbished Victorian 'period' toilets on the quayside before going on to admire the graceful Art Nouveau style iron and glass Winter Garden built in 1924, where people could sit indoors and listen to the top Music Hall entertainers of the day. In 1937, the Pavilion was erected to provide a dancehall, concert hall and restaurant.

Bute has a lot to offer the holidaymaker who likes walking, history and just watching the boats go by. But the islanders dependent upon the tourist are not so fortunate. Relying almost entirely upon a holiday trade that lasts from June to the end of August, existence for many over the remaining nine months is largely dependent upon a 'good season'. While agriculture, sheep and dairy farming has at times done well with increasing yields over the century, the island has to export its produce and is therefore utterly dependent upon road vehicles and a reliable ferry service.

There is substantial evidence that Bute has been occupied at least since the Mesolithic period (4000 BC). Standing stones, cists and burial grounds are dotted all over the island. In the earliest days, the middle of the island was less inhabited, being largely forested and boggy. Over the centuries, maritime travellers moving north made this their home, bringing trade and new ideas to the cultivated sea frontage. Amongst these incomers were early Christian settlers. In the south of the island, St Blane, who had been born in Bute, set up a monastery at Dunagoil in the 6th Century, the remains of which still exist.

Restored Victorian toilets on Rothesay pier in August 1994. *Author's Collection*

The Glenburn Hotel as viewed across Rothesay Bay. *Author*

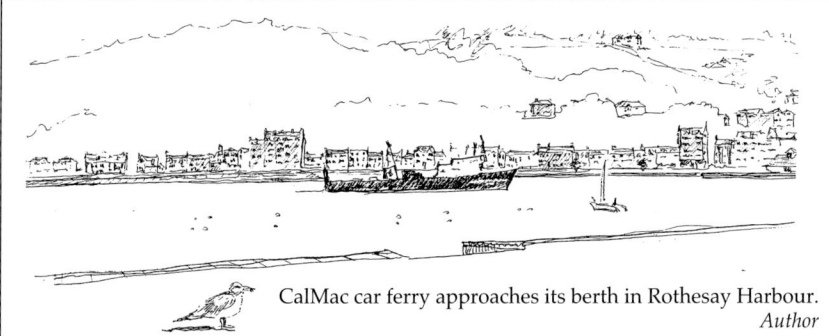

CalMac car ferry approaches its berth in Rothesay Harbour. *Author*

The CalMac shipping office on Rothesay pier. *Author*

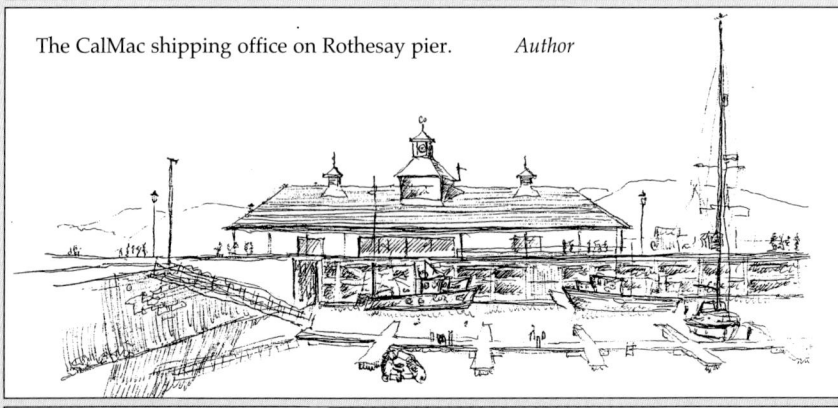

New Farm, Isle of Bute with the mainland beyond. *Author*

Rothesay Castle

The remains of Rothesay Castle are low lying, once on the coast but now 75 yards from the sea. In 1263, the Vikings under King Haco of Norway took the castle after a fierce struggle, though many of their boats were wrecked on the Cowal shore in a wild storm. Later that century, the castle was retaken by the Scots. Then the English stormed the fortress in the 14th century. When they were thrown out by a mob of local men, Edward III, King of England laid the island waste.

King Robert II of Scotland (1316-1390) subsequently lived in the circular moated castle, as did his son Robert III (1337-1406). It was the latter who appointed his son David Duke of Rothesay, a title currently held by HRH Prince Charles. Rothesay became a Royal Burgh when Robert III granted it its charter in 1400. On Robert's death, the Stewards of Bute became keepers of the castle. The present Lord Bute is still Keeper of the Castle.

Rothesay Castle has seen other visitors - James V visited it in 1530 and 1534. In the 17th century, Cromwell's men, who were garrisoned there, commenced destroying its defences, a task completed in 1685 when the Duke of Argyll burnt it down. The Bute family moved to the Mansion House in High Street (built in 1681). The family name Steward changed to Stewart and then to Stuart. Round about 1817, the 2nd Marquess of Bute employed a large number of men to clear up the area around Rothesay Castle. In 1872, the 3rd Marquess cleared the moat and did some restoration work on the castle walls. In 1900, he restored the Great Hall in the barbican.

The ruins of Rothesay Castle in the centre of the town are surrounded by a moat originally at sea level. The extension of the town frontage on reclaimed land has subsequently isolated the castle from the Firth.
Argyll & the Islands Enterprise

Rothesay Castle, Isle of Bute.
Author

Mount Stewart House, Isle of Bute.
Author

Mount Stuart House

Early in the 18th century, the 2nd Earl of Bute moved out of Rothesay to Mount Stuart, in the south of the island where he built his new residence in 1719. His son was James Stuart, 3rd Earl of Bute, who on being appointed Prime Minister by George III in 1761, was described by Bishop Warburton as 'a very unfit man to be Prime Minister of England. First he is a Scotchman, secondly, he is the King's friend and thirdly he is an honest man'. A later heir to the estate, the 2nd Marquess of Bute made a fortune through building Cardiff docks. His son, the 3rd Marquess of Bute was a remarkable and very learned man, believed to be the richest person in Britain. When his residence at Mount Stuart burnt down in 1877, he engaged the Architect Robert Rowand Anderson to erect the stupendous red sandstone pile that forms the present day Mount Stuart House, a building constructed on a scale to match a major public building in the centre of a great city. It is now a money earning tourist attraction on the island. At times the present Marquess of Bute lives there.

Rothesay Harbour and Ferries to Bute

A port existed at least as far back as 1584 (and probably very much earlier) though the present harbour and pier have their origins in the 30-year construction of a 300 yds-long by 10 yds-wide pier begun in 1752. Initially the principal uses for the pier were for fishing and commerce, the harbour being crammed with small 'herring busses' while steam puffers off-loaded clear of the paddle steamers.

In the 17th century, the main ferries were from Scoulag, four miles south of Rothesay, to Largs on the mainland, and from Rothesay to Ardyne at the southern end of the Cowal peninsula. To the north was the short Colintraive ferry. Over the years, many piers and quays were built round the island but only those at Rothesay and Rhubodach are now used by ferry boats.

Industry

In 1779, a thriving cotton industry developed - the first in Scotland. The arrival of a steam engine in 1800 boosted production but owing to competition from Lanark and the cost of coal, several mill owners were bankrupted and the mills closed. The Marquess of Bute encouraged Robert Thom (1775-1847), an engineer and proprietor of the Rothesay Cotton Works, to develop water power (*see Chapter One*). This the latter did by 6-7 miles of 'cuts' and aqueducts whereby he connected a number of burns to discharge into a heightened Loch Fad, conduiting the outfall to the mills thereby providing clean and cheap power. It is rumoured that he incurred the Marquess's displeasure by reducing the water supply to Mount Stuart by his actions. By 1820 there were five mills operating in Rothesay; in 1840, the cotton mills employed over 350 people. There was also a rope works and tileries at Kingarth near Kilchattan Bay in the south of the island, making and exporting large numbers of tiles and bricks. The cotton industry declined till by 1880 there was only one - now long disappeared.

Rothesay's fishing industry prospered at the end of the 18th century and was still doing well in the middle of the 19th, boats landing catches taken in the Kyles of Bute, from Loch Fyne and further afield - from the north of Scotland and around Ireland. As on the east coast of the Clyde opposite, there was fishing for salmon. A second stone quay was constructed at Rothesay between 1785 and 1790. This was L-shaped to provide a protected basin with the existing quay. But neither was well-constructed. When the steamboats arrived, the quays were found to be inadequate. From 1822, they were rebuilt and extended eastwards to form Inner and Outer harbours.

Redundant brick-built works, Rothesay, Isle of Bute. *Author*

Rothesay Harbour probably taken during Fair Week around 1900. The big RMPS *St Columba* (1878) lies at her berth as the PS *Duchess of Rothesay* (1895) approaches. The *Marchioness of Bute* (1890) is at the north end with the *Marchioness of Lorne* (1891) behind her.
McLean Museum & Art Gallery, Inverclyde Council

Rothesay

Rothesay's frontage is built on ground used between 1839 and 1872 for boat building and as a graving slip. Part of this area, in front of Rothesay Castle, is on reclaimed land susceptible to flooding in the January neap tides. These sites were incorporated into the promenade which had been built adjacent in 1869. The steady decline of the fishing trade from 520 sailing skiffs in 1861 to about 50 motor vessels in 1935 coincided with an increase in holiday traffic resulting in the pier being again extended in 1867 and 1899 to take the larger steamers. Nowadays, there are more pleasure craft than commercial boats.

Rothesay became a highly popular holiday resort. In 1851, its population was just over 7,000, in 1901 about 9,300. As the population increased, the town climbed up the hill and water shortages had to be made good by new systems served from two more lochs on the small island. In the summer, Rothesay's population would treble. But the development of the tripper trade corresponded with the decline of indigenous industry. From the beginning of the steamer era, boats plied between Glasgow and Rothesay. Later, with the introduction of railways and steamers to Greenock, Gourock and Wemyss Bay, quick crossings could be made across the Clyde. There were also sailings by steamers from Craigendoran pier on the north side of the river to Dunoon and Rothesay. Ferry services or excursion boats provided links with piers on Bute - Kilchattan Bay, Craigmore - and elsewhere - to Kames, Ormidale, Innellan, Kilcreggan, Kirn, Largs, Millport and Ayr. Rothesay pier was a stopping off point for boats sailing through the Kyles of Bute to Tighnabruaich and Loch Fyne.

Before the arrival of the telegraph on the island in 1864, prosperous merchants who could not afford to be long away from their businesses in Glasgow had already bought estates on the island and built themselves holiday homes where they could live in style with their servants, horses and the yacht in the bay. The better off might rent a house for a month in the summer and the husband commute daily to Glasgow by the fast ferry and train service. At the end of the 19th century, cheap travel saw tourists flocking to the island. Whole families, including their servants, would come down for the summer and stay in the grand houses erected round the town. In 1890, the Glenburn opened as a Hydropathic Hotel and if guests did not enjoy their cold bath there, they could always go and bathe in the sea or travel round and round on the magnificent steam merry-go-round, to popular tunes played on the organ.

From the middle of the 19th century, the bulk of holidaymakers were from working class homes. Whole families would crowd into single rooms in the tenements and boarding houses in Rothesay. It is said that accommodation became so short that landladies would mark out in chalk the areas where people should sleep, rubbing out the chalk lines and moving them closer to squeeze in another paying guest. For those that could not find a room for the night during the Glasgow Fair fortnight, their canopy for the night might be the Skeoch Woods.

With the vast numbers of foot passengers descending on the island, a thousand at a time, there was a need to transport them quickly away from the pier area. The Rothesay Tramways Co. Ltd was formed in 1879 to provide a horse drawn tramway from Guildford Square to the front at Port Bannatyne. So keen were the councillors to see the system in use that it started running on 27th May, 1882 before it had been passed by the Board of Trade. This incurred the displeasure of Major General Hutchinson, who when he arrived, assembled the council in front of him. 'There was one speech, and the General made it'. He then insisted that the party walk the length of the line with him ahead of a tram. Satisfied, the party boarded the tram and returned. However, the cars were 5 inches too wide, a minor matter solved by sawing off 2½ inches from the footboard on each side. In service, the trip was scheduled to take half an hour from end to end, though one horse, aware that it was time for his nosebag when he reached the end of the line, could do the trip in 10 minutes flat. In the first six months, the four cars travelled over 60,000 miles and carried more than 290,000 passengers.

In 1902, the Rothesay Tramways Company replaced the horse-drawn vehicles with electric traction. In 1905, the service was extended to Ettrick Bay. The trams were cheap and well-used

Rothesay harbour in 1998. *Author*

Fernerey on Bute in September 1999. The glazing conceals a large sunken rock garden containing a wide variety of ferns collected from all over the world. *Author*

House in Rothesay designed by Alexander (Greek) Thomson (1817-1875) as at September 1999. Thomson was a prominent Architect on the Glasgow scene, probably best known for his churches in St Vincent Street and Caledonia Road. *Author*

Guildford Square, Rothesay taken about 1907. Electric trams replaced horse-drawn in 1905. Note the number of horse-drawn carriages waiting for custom and the complete lack of cars.
Ian B. Smith Collection

CalMac shipping office on Rothesay pier.
Author

however not even the 'toast racks' (two trams that were entirely open) could survive the development of the motor coach and the trams ceased to run after 1936. Petrol-engined vehicles appeared first in 1905, and after World War I, visitors could hire a motor boat for 6d. [* 50p] to go round the Bay instead of taking a rowing boat.

The place was crowded with holidaymakers, swarming like bees off the steamers. Rothesay centre was so full of people, trams and hired bikes that the Editor of the *Rothesay Chronicle* was driven to comment that 'Mankind is divided into two classes: those who ride bicycles and those who dodge them'. Royalty visited Rothesay too. In 1920 the *Britannia* and *Victoria and Albert* sailed into the resort and King George V entered the sailing regatta during the Fair Fortnight.

The island did its duty during World War II, providing a temporary home for evacuees from the big cities, a billet for Poles, Canadians and British soldiers while Commandos trained out of sight on Inchmarnock island, west of Bute. In Rothesay Bay sheltered the submarine mothership *Cyclops* and a little flotilla of submarines. There was even a decoy village constructed on the north of the island. Although there never was a railway (except for the tram lines and a track along the shore to carry building materials to construct Mount Stuart House), there was nevertheless a Railway Convalescent Home at Ascog for British Railways' employees, the only one in Scotland.

Chapter Three

Geography, Geology and History

While there have been established communities along the eastern bank of the Clyde for centuries, from Largs in the south northwards round the 'tail o' the Bank' to Greenock, the community of Wemyss Bay only appeared on the maps comparatively recently. Johan Blaeu's 1654 *Atlas Novus* does not mention Wemyss Bay, though lesser places, many now gone, feature across the countryside, indicating an extensive though scattered community. Readers wishing to study the area in detail are recommended to consult W. Smart's book, *The Story of the Parish Consisting of Skelmorlie and Wemyss Bay*, on which this chapter is largely based.

By 1796, John Ainslie's *Map of the County of Renfrew* showed both Wemyss Bay and Wemyss Point (on the Finnock - or Finnoch - estate), but no *place* of that name. In 1826, Thomson's plan of Renfrewshire still does not admit to the existence of a hamlet at Wemyss Bay. So when did Wemyss Bay village appear?

Geologically, the Shore Road area between Wemyss Bay and through Skelmorlie is a 'raised sea beach', bearing traces of shells and other marine objects from the time before the land rose above sea level. Parts of Bute are of similar origin. The district lies on part of the old Red Sandstone Band, estimated at over 1,000 feet thick providing a number of local quarries with stone for some of the more prestigious buildings, possibly even for the original Wemyss Bay station and its approaches. (Most of the present station's stone is more likely to have come from Dumfriesshire.) There are also large areas of igneous rock, the hard black volcanic bands contrasting with the softer red sandstone. 'Often', Smart wrote, 'the red sandstone, which is very old, cracked along fissures, sometimes many miles in length, and molten lava has walled up and solidified. Being harder, they have worn better and stand up like black walls contrasting with the red sandstone'. The hardness of the volcanic stone caused great problems when carving out parts of the railway line.

It is hardly surprising to learn that the area around Skelmorlie Castle at one time had but few trees and that there was little vegetation between Knock and Kelly. That has now changed - there is an abundance of softening greenery.

There have been settlements in this area for thousands of years. The inhabitants included the Picts, Scots and Britons. Roman fortlets were sited along the hill route from the south round to Bishopton: a couple of miles east of Skelmorlie, at Lurg Moor above Greenock and near Bishopton. Roman patrols crossed the Clyde (or Clotta, meaning warm and sheltered) on forays to the north. Roman coins and tiles have certainly been found in Largs and it is believed the Romans erected villas along the coast from Kelly Burn (at the boundary between Wemyss Bay and Skelmorlie) southwards to Irvine.

There is also evidence that Celtic Lake dwellers as well as English and Scandinavian invaders lived hereabouts.

The area is believed to have been occupied by the Damnii, (or Damnoniia), the most powerful and civilised of the Celtic tribes. They were Britons and spoke Gaelic, but owed allegiance to the Welsh Kings. They exerted an influence on events stretching from Perthshire to the Devon-Cornwall peninsula. It is possible, according to Collins *County Geography of Ayrshire*, that these ancient Britons worshipped Baal, god of Fire and the Sun, on the 'Serpent Mound' at the south end of Skelmorlie beside Skelmorlie Water at Meigle Bay. Long before the Roman invasion, they hunted and herded their flocks on the hills above Skelmorlie and Largs.

The history of the area is rich with names learned at school. The first is a doubtful reference to Caractacus (or Carractacus). When the Romans invaded Britain in the first century AD, they captured Caractacus, who was a leader of some prominence, and took him to Rome. It has been suggested that following a pardon because of his great courage he was 're-established in part of his Kingdom comprising Brigantia, Kyle and Cuninghame', though there is some debate as to the truth of this.

The Damnonii were still there after the Romans left and after an invasion by the Scots of Kintyre. They became Christians and joined with other Britons to form the kingdom of Strathclyde, whose capital was Alclot (Alclwyd or Alclyd) - the 'rock of the Clyde' - now known as Dumbarton. Strathclyde stretched as far as Cumberland and Westmorland and suffered attacks from Saxons, Danes, Picts and Scots. In the 9th century, to provide themselves with greater protection, the Damnonii formed an alliance with Kenneth MacAlpin, King of the Scots of Dalriada ruler of Pictland. By the middle of the 11th century, the Welsh influence over this area ceased as Anglo Saxon gradually replaced Gaelic. In the 13th century, William Wallace, the son of a Renfrewshire knight, made his mark.

The Principal Estates

North of the Kelly Burn as far as Inverkip was originally known as Finnock, the Bay area being Low Finnock. Low Finnock abounded in springs, being described as 'Spouty Ground'. At one stage, the lands belonged to the Stewarts of Bute, descendants of John Stewart, son of King Robert II (1316-90). Another John Stewart, a son of King Robert III (1337-1406), purchased Ardgowan (north of Inverkip) in 1404. The present incumbents, the Shaw Stewarts, are his direct descendants.

James III (1460-88) granted James Bannatyne, who likewise is believed to be descended from a Bute family (*vide* Port Bannatyne north of Rothesay), the wooded lands at Kelly on the north bank of the Kelly Burn. (Kelly and Kelburn are derived from 'Coil' meaning a wood.) The Bannatyne family held the estate till the end of the 18th century, during which time Kelly Castle was erected on the cliff overlooking Kelly Burn. The building ceased to be inhabited after a fire in 1740.

From the 11th to the 15th century, Skelmorlie was Cuninghame (or Cunninghame) country, though at some stage an older family, the Foresters (or Fosters) appear to have been local landowners. By the end of the 18th century, the name Fosterland had disappeared, all that remained being a smallholding called Fosterby, near Skelmorlie Water. That name has now gone.

Over the centuries, the estate was split up, large parts being acquired by the Montgomeries. The direct Cuninghame line ceased with the death of John, the 15th Earl, in 1796, though reorganisation of local government in 1975 revived the name for Cunninghame District for the area south of Kelly Burn.

The Montgomeries were Normans, tracing their lineage back to William the Conqueror. The first to establish himself in the Clyde area was Robert de Mundegumbri, first laird of Eaglesham, in the 12th century. Later, the family extended their holdings to include Renfrew and Bute, North Skelmoirluy being acquired in 1453. The Montgomeries and the Cuninghames had a long history of strife, especially after James II passed the office of Hereditary Bailiff from the largely Protestant Cuninghames to the Royalist Montgomeries in 1448.

The Montgomeries were active in national politics and events. In 1507, Hugh Montgomerie was created first Earl of Eglinton by King James IV. 'George Montgomery of Largges' commanded 5,000 soldiers against the English army of Henry VIII in 1545. Sir Robert Montgomerie, a particularly fierce soldier who continued the family feud against the Cuninghames, nevertheless became patron of the Old Parish Church of Largs where he built the renowned Skelmorlie Aisle. His beautiful wife Margaret suffered fatal injuries remonstrating with a horse which had thrown her at the Colm Fair. He died in 1651.

Other distinguished Montgomeries followed. These included Sir Robert, Governor of the garrison in Northern Ireland and his uncle Sir Hugh, the 6th and last Baronet of Skelmorlie, Provost of Glasgow and Glasgow's MP, as well as being a Commissioner of the 1707 Treaty of Union. Marriage later brought the Skelmorlie estate into the hands of the Eglintons.

From about 1600, the great estates were subdivided, parts held at various times by the Earl of Glasgow, the Brisbanes, the Montgomeries, the Cunninghames, the Crawfords, the Bannatynes and the Wallace family.

The lands at Knock (between Skelmorlie and Largs) were granted to Hew Frazer by King Robert III in 1402. John, one of his sons, married an heiress, believed to have been Isobel, daughter of Sir David Weemes of Weemes in Fife. The Frazers held the estate till 1647 when it was sold to Sir Robert Montgomerie of Skelmorlie. The old red castle of Knock (which still exists) was recorded as a ruin in 1775.

The Decline of the Agricultural Workforce

By the 17th century, most people living on the coast from Gourock to Largs would have been relatively poor estate workers or fishermen, living in dry stone or turf houses, possibly with their cattle. Social life revolved around the church. They took life seriously - according to Smart, the last witch in the west of Scotland was burned in 1662 at Inverkip. Until the 19th century, local people worshipped some distance away - in Largs to the south or at Inverkip 'Auld Kirk' to the north. The latter also served Greenock. Even at 1811, the New Parish Church at Largs was still used by Skelmorlie people five miles to the north.

Between Greenock and Largs, there were a large number of small townships or shepherds' cottages, some quite far inland. A few names that featured in Blaeu's *Atlas Novus* of 1654 are recognisable today. The Clyde is the 'River of Clyd' or the 'Fyrth of Klyd'. The Cumbraes were the 'Kumbra Isles'. Grinok (Greenock), Gourok (Gourock), Ardgawan, (Ardgowan), Innerkyp (Inverkip), Over Fennock (Finnock) and Fennockboig, Kelly and Kelliback, Barfarn (Berfern), Langhous (Langhouse), Daff, Brigend and Dunrod north of the Kelly Burn and North Skelmoirluy, South Sckelmorly, Knock and Lairgs (Largs) to the south are still recognisable place names. As industrialisation developed especially where good harbours, water and steam power existed, many of the isolated houses or villages disappeared from the maps.

The 18th century saw the rise of an industrial population matched by a decline in agrarian workers. Small crofts were absorbed into larger units; people moved from the land into the town. Little communities emerged at Finnock, Kellybridge and Skelmorlie (at Meigle) and the landward population fell - for example, in the Parish of Inverkip, it reduced from 1590 in 1755 to 1280 in 1790/5. By 1871, the decline had reached the point where there were only 637 souls in Inverkip. Likewise the Parish of Largs diminished from 1164 to 1025 in the same period.

Agriculture remained the chief occupation between Largs and Greenock. Local farms supplied Greenock and other towns nearby with cattle and dairy products. The main industry was weaving, particularly silk for the mills of Paisley. There was some fishing, especially for herring and salmon. The annual June 'Colm' Fair held in Largs on St Columba's Day regularly drew over 100 boats from the west coast into Largs Bay, but gradually the importance of the fair diminished as roads improved and pedlars travelled to the country shops. There was little manufacturing because of the expense of coal for fuel.

In 1740, there were no habitations in Low Finnock, near Whiting Bay (at the north end of Wemyss Bay).

As overseas trade developed in the 18th century, so prosperity came to the west coast. Wealthy traders and shipbuilders built grand houses along the edge of the Clyde, at Rothesay, Dunoon, Wemyss Bay and Skelmorlie. Among these was John Wallace of Neilston and Cessnock, a descendant of Sir William Wallace and a successful West Indian merchant, who acquired Kelly in 1792. The following year, he built an impressive white mansion on the high ground overlooking the road, south of the present railway bridge. But even in 1835, Skelmorlie still contained thatched cottages inhabited by the Kelly workmen.

With industrialisation, the less well-off benefited too. People now came during the summer months from many places to Innerkip (Inverkip), Gourock and along the shore betwixt the two places, to drink and bathe in the salt water for their various ailments. The health and leisure industry was beginning to develop.

Wemyss and Skelmorlie

For centuries, Gaelic was the native language. Some believe that Wemyss (alternatively spelt Wemys, Weyms, Weems or Weemes) could be derived from 'Uaimh', the Gaelic for a cave. The Scots equivalent of the word was 'Weem', which means a cave, earth house or an Iron Age underground drystone storehouse. The Picts, who inhabited this part of the country are known to have used such structures which would give credence to this view. A 15th century marriage connection to the Wemyss of Fife seems an unlikely origin for the name.

A more colourful explanation is that the name came from Robert Wemyss, an old fisherman who lived in the mid-1700s at what was sometimes called 'White Week' (meaning a cleft in the hill) or 'Kelly Bay'. The story goes that three men hired a boat from Bob Wemyss and in explaining where they had got their catch, described the area as 'Bob Wemyss' Bay'.

Weems Point was certainly marked on Watt's survey of 1734 while an isolated 'Fisher's House' (possibly where Bob Wemyss lived) is shown nearby on a plan of 1740. Whiting Bay appears on various maps as a minor indentation just south of the Point. By 1796, John Ainslie's map of Renfrew described the south facing bay where Wemyss Bay Road has been constructed, reaching round to Fingal Burn, as 'Wemyss Bay', but there was no sign of a village below the house of Kelly. However, development of the bay was now imminent.

The name Skelmorlie may derive from the Gaelic, to describe a sheltered space between rocky headlands. 'Sceiligmor' is Gaelic and Irish for 'a great rock', which might represent the Knock (hill). Up to the second half of the 19th century, the place name 'Skelmorlie' related only to lands round the Castle, the shore part being known as Kelly Bridge at the end of the 18th century.

The Wemyss Bay and Skelmorlie communities meet at the Kelly Burn, in Strathclyde. However Skelmorlie is in the parish of Largs in Ayrshire and Wemyss Bay is in the parish of Inverkip in the County of Renfrew. To make matters more confusing, ecclesiastically, Skelmorlie and Wemyss Bay are in the *Quoad Sacra* Parish of Skelmorlie (i.e. one that deals only with spiritual matters), within the Parish of Largs, but in the Presbytery (administrative district) of Greenock.

Developments Between 1800 and 1860

Wemyss Bay - 'New Glasgow'

During the first 60 years of the 19th century, there were major changes, first at Kelly in Wemyss Bay, then in Skelmorlie and later in the old Estates. Up till the mid-19th century, heather, shrubs and trees covered the land at Wemyss Bay down to the Firth. There was salmon fishing off Ardgowan where salmon nets extended into the Clyde at North Bay, Whiting Bay and Weyms [sic] Bay, as the inner part was now called. The few local buildings included Kelly House, a fisherman's cottage near the point, Weyms Cottage at Middle Lodge, an hotel and a few other small buildings near South Lodge, one of which may have belonged to a local smuggler. A gravel beach swept round to the mouth of the Fingal Burn by the present railway bridge. The attractive bathing bay, north of the Kelly Burn is now largely under the station buildings.

John Wallace's son Robert, the first MP for Greenock, inherited the Kelly estate in 1803. He enlarged Kelly House and by a complicated series of transactions with local landowners - notably the Earl of Glasgow and the Earl of Eglinton - increased the size of the policies, consolidating them along the Bay into upper Skelmorlie as far as Auchendarroch. The estate continued to Shore Road, including the area of Beach House, but the Earl of Eglinton retained the main road to Kelly Quay.

By the 1840s, it took roughly two hours to travel from Wemyss Bay to Glasgow, four hours to Edinburgh and 24 hours to London. The trip to London involved using the ferry from Wemyss Bay to Ardrossan, and another ferry to Liverpool where the traveller could catch his train to London. It was anticipated that once the line from London had been built to Glasgow, the journey between Wemyss Bay and London would reduce substantially, to 15 hours. A further acceleration was expected when the proposed (1845) Greenock to Largs line 'which would pass near to Wemyss Bay' was constructed. That line, however, was never built.

Against this background, Wallace saw an opportunity to develop his assets. Plans of 1835 and 1845 show the area from Fingal Burn northwards round the coast to Castle Wemyss laid out as a 'Marine Village'. There would be nearly 200 houses, a couple of hotels, cottages, shops, a school, three churches and a Post Office. The estate was to be laid out with ornamental gardens and recreational facilities would include a bowling green, curling pond and quoiting ground. There would be hot baths, reading and billiard rooms and on the front, a harbour, steamboat quay and a bathing area. Materials would be unloaded at the pier in Whiting Bay (at the north end of Wemyss Bay) beside the Episcopal Church. A start was made and by 1812, four nearly identical 'elegant mansions' on the north side of 'Weemes Bay' were let out to wealthy Glasgow merchants for sea bathing, the location therefore becoming known as 'New Glasgow'.

Wallace's grand ideas, which according to Smart included a 'New Town of Brisbane' for Largs (1845), overstretched him and he had to sell Kelly. He moved to Forbes Place, named after his father-in-law, Sir William Forbes, Bart., of Craigievar in Aberdeenshire. However, he had prepared the way for Wemyss Bay to be 'put on the map'.

The new owner of Kelly was an Australian named Mr Alexander. After only a few years, he was declared bankrupt, whereupon his creditors divided it up, selling Kelly to James Scott and lands at Wemyss Bay to Charles Wilsone Broun.

Wilsone Broun was a merchant in Glasgow and a Justice of the Peace in Renfrew. He sold off the plots proposed by Wallace for feuing, and for his own use, built Wemyss Castle (designed by Robert Billings) overlooking Whiting Bay. By 1855, the first Valuation Roll showed that 20 out of the 36 buildings in 'New Glasgow' were owned by Charles Wilsone Broun, James Scott of Kelly, James Harvey (a distiller) and James Wallace.

An indication of the lifestyle can be gleaned from the Charter granted to Bruce Richardson to build Ivybank - he was allowed to place a bathing machine on the beach, to land coal and manure and to anchor pleasure boats in the Bay, so long as there was no interference with Mr Broun's rights to the Salmon Fishing. There was no consistency of building style. As a local guide described the place in 1857, 'some of the specimens at Wemyss Bay are sufficiently pretty and tasteful, others are abundantly fantastical, while in several instances there is plainness even to a fault. The latter . . . seem to have been erected before the prevailing mania for quaintness commenced'. The Guide had the following comments to make on 'modern architecture' - 'There is no end of cottage designs now-a-days, and every particular laird seems resolved to have something decidedly original in the construction of his own domicile'. Architectural criticism is nothing new!

Financial problems forced Wilsone Broun to sell and after falling into the hands of a couple of builders, John Burns - who later became Lord Inverclyde - bought Castle Wemyss in 1860 and rebuilt it in 'hard-edged' baronial style. Until its demolition, the castle, described as 'a symbol of 19th century industry and enterprise', was the most significant pile at Wemyss Bay.

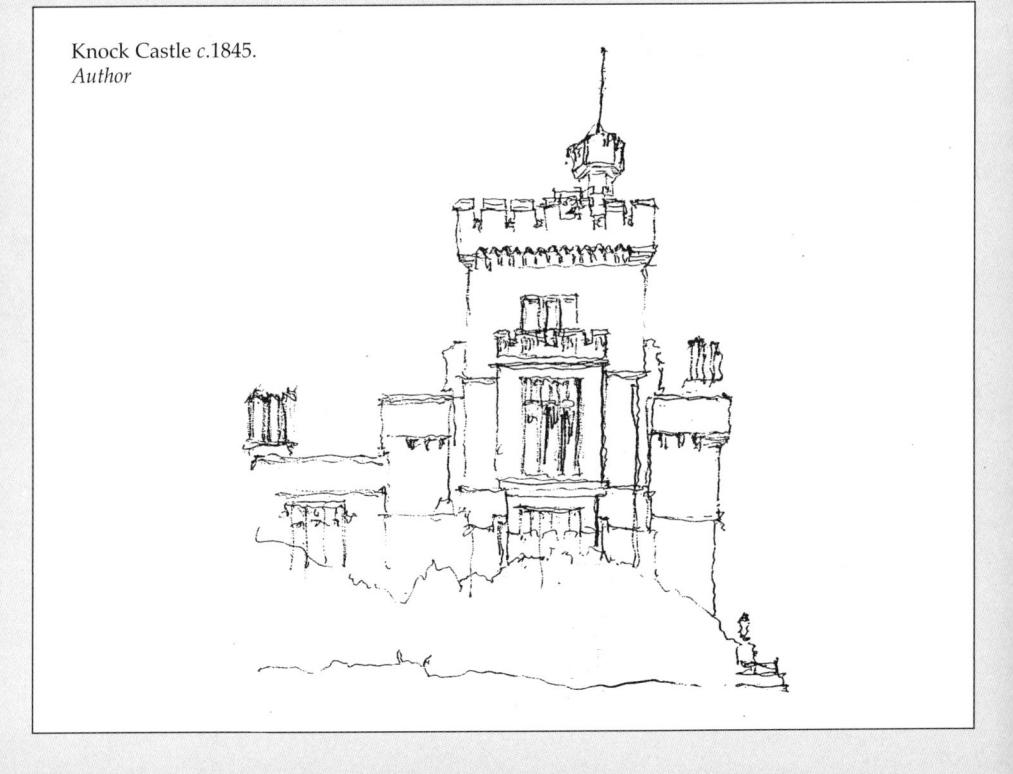

Skelmorlie Castle 1502 with Victorian additions.
Author

Knock Castle *c.*1845.
Author

Skelmorlie

In the early 1800s, James Montgomerie of Wrighthill, MP for Ayrshire, lived at North Skelmorlie. He was directly descended from George, first laird of Skelmorlie. The property was owned by the 13th Earl of Eglinton, known as the 'Tournament Earl' because he hosted a spectacular event at Eglinton in August 1839 which lasted three (very wet) days and cost a fortune.

The prominent property owners in Skelmorlie about this time included the Earl of Eglinton and Winton, the Earl of Glasgow, Sir Thomas Brisbane, Robert Wallace MP, Archibald Campbell (a descendant of the Bannatynes), Wallace of Kelly, Christopher Scott of Greenock, John Wilson, Robert Steele, William Stewart, John Lang and John Lane.

At 1820, Kelly had the best natural woodlands in the area and Skelmorlie had not started to develop. By the 1830s, the buildings comprised the ancient Skelmorlie Castle, farm dwellings, a few thatched cottages and the Toll-bar sited where the Post Office was to be found in 1895. The first villa built in Skelmorlie was Beach House, constructed by George Arbuthnot in 1844, a son of Lord Provost William Arbuthnot of Edinburgh and father-in-law of John Burns. In 1865, Beach House appears to have been owned by Mr Ronaldson, a Wemyss Bay Railway Company Director.

About 1850, John Wilson sold the old red Castle of Knock to Robert Steele, a Greenock shipbuilder who built the present castle while keeping the old. Skelmorlie village effectively dates from about this period, houses being constructed from the locally available red sandstone. At that time, the combined population of Wemyss Bay and Skelmorlie was about 300.

Local Industry

By 1860, quarrying for whinstone and sandstone was an important industry, two quarries in Kelly being marked as 'old'. Beithglass was the largest remaining but there were others on Shore Road near Heywood, south of Kelly Burn, and elsewhere. There were more in Wemyss Bay near Wellesley House and in the railway cutting in Kelly.

The 'Exclusive' Developments between 1860 and 1900

'God made the country, man made the cities and the railways made the suburbs'

The early part of the 19th century had seen great industrial development. Coal seams were opened up and iron ore mined in Renfrewshire and Ayrshire. Steam power was harnessed, providing an answer to the urgent need for transport. Co-incidental with the early railway developments, the failure of the Irish potato crop in 1846-47 drove many Irishmen and their families to the new factories and on to the railways as cheap labour. They came across looking for work and food, packed in as 'human ballast' in the holds of returning collier ships. Fifteen years on, these immigrants formed a substantial population and had the resources for an annual holiday back in their 'mother country' or to get away from the crowded sulphurous towns to the fresh air of the west coast. It is questionable whether the railways would have developed so rapidly or prosperity been so quickly achieved if that labour force had not been available in such quantity at that time.

The Glasgow-Greenock railway was opened in 1841. But until 1865, Wemyss Bay and Skelmorlie people depended on the steamship services operating from Meadow Place in Skelmorlie and Whiting Bay in Wemyss, the Largs steamer to Glasgow calling at Wemyss Bay and other piers on its five hour journey up the Clyde. The Wemyss Bay railway was to reduce the journey to the City to a little over an hour. One suspects that the hoards of trippers on the line might not have been entirely welcome to the owners of the big houses, but at least they would

Castle Wemyss (now demolished) in Wemyss Bay. Photo pre-1908. *Alan Brotchie Collection*

be gone with the steamers. The compensation was that Wemyss Bay was becoming a more desirable place in which to live as feus were let to those who could afford the increasing land cost.

Between 1860 and 1970, Wemyss Bay did not alter much, but Skelmorlie did. Both places catered for the well known and the well off. In 1867, Dr (Paraffin) Young purchased Kelly House which he later enlarged. The Kelly estate was subsequently sold to the shipbuilder Alexander Stephen in 1889. He demolished the house and built the third and last Kelly House in 1890 to the designs of William Leiper. Another notable local personage was Mr Martini, the Danish Consul for Glasgow, who in 1879 was living in an 'elegant Gothic structure of red sandstone' created by Mr Burnet of Glasgow above Ferncliffe in Wemyss Bay, adjacent to the 'English' Episcopal Church.

John Burns, (Lord Inverclyde) entertained many famous people at Castle Wemyss and on his yachts *Mastiff* and *Capercailzie*, the latter being a sizeable boat and one of many similar to be seen in the vicinity. So great was the wealth in this area, that the entrance gates became known as the 'Golden Gates' and the Clydesdale Bank opened a branch in the Lodge, remaining there till World War I to provide wages for domestic staff and yacht hands. There was also a Post Office (under Greenock) with money order, savings bank and telegraph facilities. (In 1888, there were three collections and deliveries per day.) The Inverclydes held the estate till 1957 when Alan, Lord Inverclyde, died.

In Skelmorlie, George Elder acquired the new Knock Castle around 1860. It passed to Mr F.G. MacAndrew in 1897, whose son, Lord MacAndrew of the Firth of Clyde, was MP for the area for over 20 years, from 1935 to 1959, and latterly Deputy Speaker. Skelmorlie Castle, previously the home of the Montgomeries, passed to the Earl of Eglinton who held it from 1876-80. It was occupied by John Graham of Glasgow between 1852 and 1890. In 1856 he rebuilt the castle and later added a mansion house where he displayed a noteworthy art collection. The castle was subsequently tenanted by Mr W.A. Coats of J.P. Coats (threadmakers) of Paisley.

The 1860s saw house building in Montgomerie Terrace and Eglinton Terrace, on the lower part of the hill above Shore Road in Skelmorlie. By 1879, a crescent was well under way above Eglinton Terrace. A Guide of the period indicates that the area was definitely exclusive - feu contracts generally forbade the erection of a house of less than a certain value, and not more than one house was permitted per feu.

In 1868, Dr Ronald Currie, a pupil of Professor Joseph Lister, erected the 50-bedroom red sandstone Hydropathic in Skelmorlie. This was built in Scottish Baronial style on a cliff 100 ft above sea level and commanded magnificent views across the Firth. (A Guide of about 1888 mistakenly described it as 'Wemyss Bay Hydropathic' though it seems that Wemyss Bay and Skelmorlie were effectively one community.) In 1875 Dr Currie added Turkish and Salt Water Baths, water being pumped from the Clyde at 1,000 gallons/hour to supplement a 'chalybeate spring' (i.e. water impregnated with iron salts). The Clyde must have been much cleaner then for the water to be regarded as a supplement to health. The establishment provided a source of employment and attracted a great number of people. Dr Currie lived in Skelmorlie till his death in 1923. About 1940 the Hydro constructed a car park on the shore and installed a lift from it up the cliff face. Both Hotel and lift have since disappeared.

Prestigious developments brought about a rise in property values. A house that sold for £280 [*£10,500] in 1857 before the railway arrived, in 1877 sold for £1,400 [*£55,000]. By 1864, there were only about 20 people living locally who were 'eligible' as electors. With the railways, more feus came on the market, prices rising from about £8 per acre to between £15 and £35 an acre. The population of upper and lower Skelmorlie rose dramatically - in 1871, there were 404 residents, by 1881, 757 and by 1891, 951. Skelmorlie became popular as an élite summer resort, or *the* place to live in. In 1875, the *Largs Advertiser* was advising its readers that Mr Innes had purchased the 'extensive and beautiful feuing grounds of Annatyard, and the operations are expected to begin early next year.'

Pastoral Needs - Wemyss Bay and Skelmorlie

By 1850, developments in the area pointed to the need to establish a new chapel. After some number crunching between the Revd Brown of Inverkip and the Revd Kinross of Largs (the former including 40 summer visitors in his total of 304 souls and the latter making 350 by adding the crew of a yacht lying off Skelmorlie), in 1855 work commenced building a chapel. Skelmorlie Parish Church opened as the Kellybridge Chapel of Ease in 1856 (though somewhat south of Kelly Burn), under its first minister, the Revd Walter Little Gilmour Boyd. By 1860, the Chapel had not only been enlarged but the Parish boundaries had been established to include the estates of Kelly and Castle Wemyss, encompassing both Skelmorlie and Wemyss Bay. The organ by Connacher & Co. of Huddersfield, was installed in 1865 and was one of the first used for public worship in Scotland. The disapproval of some of the parishioners was evinced in that this, the *South Church*, was also known as 'Boyd's Theatre'. Boyd died in 1872. In 1891, the elders approved plans by the Glasgow Architects, Honeyman & Keppie, to enlarge the Church.

In 1869, steps were taken to provide a permanent place of worship for the Skelmorlie Union Church, a joint congregation superintended by the Free Church and the United Presbyterian Church. Hitherto, worship had taken place in a timber hut brought over from Kilcreggan, sited in Wemyss Bay where Pearson's Garage now is (adjacent to the station) and seating up to 250 people. The Revd John Boyd was ordained in 1871 to the new charge, called the Wemyss Bay and Skelmorlie United Presbyterian Church. In 1874, having purchased land beside Kelly Bridge from Dr James Young of Kelly, a Church was erected in white stone with a spire 115 feet high and a capacity for 370 worshippers. In 1878, this, the *North Church* was closed for extensive repairs, including installing an organ. Further ground was purchased from Dr Young and the Church Hall was erected in 1886 to the plans of Glasgow Architect A. Lindsay Miller. In 1897, the Church was extended to the plans of Mr Leiper, Skelmorlie Quarry stone being used for the inside pillars. In 1900, the Church was renamed the Wemyss Bay and Skelmorlie United Free Church.

On 13th October, 1929, the Parish and United Presbyterian Churches were merged into the Church of Scotland, the North Church then being renamed the North Church Skelmorlie and Wemyss Bay. Among its distinguished ministers was Donald Caskie, OBE, minister of the Scots Kirk in Paris. Sadly, having stood for 100 years, the church was dismantled, leaving only the hall, since converted into a dwelling.

In 1879, George Burns of Wemyss House built the white sandstone Episcopal Church in the grounds of Wemyss Castle at Whiting Bay. It was designed by Mr James Salmond of Glasgow who had also prepared the plans for Wemyss House next to the 'jaggedly gothic' Ferncliffe (Architect J.T. Rochead, c. 1860). The Church was used till 1956 but has since been demolished. It possessed a peal of eight bells and followed the Church of England liturgy, rather than that of the Episcopal Church of Scotland. The clergy were selected by Mr Burns from England and Ireland to preach during the summer.

In 1876, the 'Concrete Chapel' was erected by the Misses Stewart of Ashcraig at Meigle. By 1912, it was recorded as being a Mission Hall but was later converted into a house. There was a thriving Roman Catholic population as well. St Joseph and St Patrick's Chapel was constructed in red sandstone in 1901 to designs by Pugin and Pugin, though worshippers had met in temporary buildings on the site for at least 15 years previously.

Local Industry and Entertainment

By 1875, the Skelmorlie and Wemyss Bay Gas Co. was in operation and two years later 20 gas lamps had been erected. (Gas lighting was replaced by electric in 1912.)

Quarrying declined and ceased in Wemyss Bay in 1879, though the Skelmorlie Quarry remained open. The friable local red sandstone used for much of the new building often ended up being painted white - in the 1870's, Kelly House was so treated - and by 1900, many more were similarly decorated.

Between 1876 and 1880, the local Skelmorlie tradesmen included joiners, a baker, boot and shoemakers and a piermaster. Captain Alexander Campbell, Captain of the Wemyss Bay steamers also lived there. In addition to the post office, the Clydesdale bank and an hotel, at various times, there was a blacksmith, a builder, coal merchants, grocers, gardeners and fruiterers, an ironmonger, plumber and a milliner.

In summer at the end of the 19th century, there was bathing and tennis; in winter, curling and skating. There was a lot to see on the Clyde, and seats were installed in 1882 along the Shore Road for those who wished to sit and gaze. In 1889, a reading room and a games room for billiards and table-tennis was opened and within a few years, a golf club and bowling club had been inaugurated.

August 1890 saw the Caledonian Steam Packet Company organising 'The most magnificent display of fireworks ever exhibited in Scotland', Messrs. Brock of London providing the gunpowder and the 'pyrotechnists'. The woods of Kelly (hardly a safe location) were lit up for the entertainment of 10,000 people on seven of the most popular boats on the Clyde: the *Duchess of Hamilton* 'lit up throughout by electricity', the PS *Marchioness of Bute*, the year old PS *Caledonia* and PS *Galatea*, the *Madge Wildfire*, the *Meg Merrilies* and the *Ivanhoe*. The *Greenock Telegraph & Clyde Shipping Gazette* recorded that the illuminated *Duchess of Hamilton* looked like a street afloat. While waiting for all the boats to arrive, the spectators admired the effect of the searchlight on the yacht *Katoomba* and picked out Kelly House which appears to have been floodlit. The uncertain weather became unpleasant half way through the 'chromotropic' display, dampening the spirits and the powder, however the transport arrangements by train and boat worked to perfection.

From 1900 to World War II

Wemyss Bay and Skelmorlie reached a peak of affluence and splendour at the turn of the century. As one contemporary account stated, 'It was too exclusive for day trippers who, "looking for bands and coloured minstrels", merely passed through *en route* for Rothesay'.

Wemyss Bay station was demolished and the present, much larger building constructed in 1903-4 to cope with the tripper trade. In keeping with developing technology Robertson Anderson and Connor built a garage in the 1920s, now taken over by Pearson, and on the opposite side of 'Station Square', shops were constructed.

Up until World War II, the big houses 'mostly of a superior class' were only occupied during the summer months - and then generally by the city merchants and county magnates who owned them. In 1921, the population of Wemyss Bay and Skelmorlie was 1,500, but only 900 of these were permanently resident. In 1915, Knock was bought by John Dunn, a Glasgow tobacco merchant. The Knock estate was sold in 1934 to David Sloan of Alexander Sloan & Co., a Glasgow furniture firm. Some families had houses elsewhere and life in the Bay centred round the yacht or the house parties. An article appearing in The *Railway Magazine* in 1926, written by 'Indicator' stated that throughout a large part of Scotland, families moved to their summer quarters at the end of the month, staying for one, two or three months. People with business interests in Glasgow could commute to the city under 'the very favourable season-ticket arrangements or week-end facilities' offered by the LMS and LNER in Scotland. This necessitated additional trains.

Smart records that leisure activities now included whist drives, dances, billiards, table tennis, badminton, carpet bowls, golf and bowling. Indoor tennis was played at Castle Wemyss and the other activities at the Hydro, the Workman's Rest and the Athletic Association's hall at Annetyard. In 1912, the old reservoir at Annetyard was used for curling, skating being popular up to the 1930s.

An early picture of the revamped Wemyss Bay station taken from a picture postcard stamped 'Skelmorlie - May 30th 1910'. Apart from the interesting collection of carriages - only one of which has two horses - note that there is no landscaping at all, that the timberwork on the gables is all different and that the window sashes have different numbers of panes.   *Alan Brotchie Collection*

In May 1913, the tenant of Kelly House left to live in Largs. The house lay empty but on 4th December, caught fire. It took an hour for the fire brigade to come from Johnstone, too late to save the building. As the suffragettes were currently particularly active, there was a strong suspicion they had been involved. (It was reported that 'two muddy and dishevelled women who boarded a train at Fairlie shortly after the fire had started looked suspiciously like the culprits'.) The value of the estate, put at £70,000 [*£3.1m] before the fire, plummeted to £27,000 afterwards. The shell was demolished in 1940, and home guard defences erected on the site.

In April 1925 after a night of exceptionally heavy rain, the 3.5 million gallon Skelmorlie lower reservoir burst its banks. The torrent that flowed down the Halket Burn caused five deaths and extensive damage. Glengyron lost some outhouses, Invereoch suffered more damage and further down Birchburn Cottage was demolished killing three children. (The cottage was occupied by Mr Dallas the coalman, who also stabled the station horses.) The Hydro was extensively damaged. Two people were drowned when water poured in the back door of their home and out the front. One man escaped by climbing a tree. The road above Stroove was cut 12 ft wide by 40 ft deep and the Shore Road was blocked by debris. Fishing boats from Largs unsuccessfully dragged the sea for bodies. Over the weekend, sightseers gathered, but could not get away because there were no Sunday trains. At the time, the County Council was negotiating to purchase the reservoir from the Eglinton estate. It subsequently took over the Waterworks and built a new reservoir, opened in October 1928. According to Smart, when the top reservoir beside the golf course was drained, 10,000 golf balls were found - a testament to the popularity of the game!

The cascade of water from the collapsed reservoir down to Shore Road was not the only occasion when the road has been blocked. There have been occasions when the low lying road between Largs and Wemyss Bay has been flooded - the Clyde after all is tidal. During winter, snow too has halted through traffic.

Kelly House built 1890 to designs by William Leiper was burnt down in 1913. The photograph was taken *c.*1908. *Alan Brotchie Collection*

Annetyard and Beithglass farms have been absorbed into Skelmorlie. Most obviously, Castle Wemyss and Kelly House have been dismantled. At the start of World War I, Sir Michael Hugh Shaw Stewart allowed Ardgowan (north of Wemyss Bay) to be used as an auxiliary hospital. To the south, the abandoned Brisbane House was blown up by Commandos during World War II. The local electric power station and the gas works have come and gone.

In May 1941, the German Air Force carried out two damaging raids on Greenock. On the 6th, 50 bombers attacked the town and the next night between 250 and 300 more dropped incendiaries, high explosives and parachute land mines. Dellingburn power station was reduced to half capacity. Nearly 10,000 homes were damaged, 1,000 being completely destroyed. 280 people were killed and more than 1,200 injured. Over 800 Greenock people are known to have been evacuated to Skelmorlie and Wemyss Bay, though the actual number was probably much higher. Many stayed. By 1946, the population of Skelmorlie reached 1,540 and many were living in very poor conditions. Housing became a major concern.

In February 1940, King George VI and Queen Elizabeth stayed overnight in Wemyss Bay, and in 1947 passed through the station to inspect the Home Fleet, spread out across the Clyde. A previous recent recorded visit by royalty was when Edward VII passed through and admired Wemyss Bay station.

Post War Development

After the war, many grand houses were demolished or converted into flats. Meigle, Skelmorlie, Wemyss Bay and recently Inverkip have seen an enormous growth in 'affordable' housing. Caravan parks, especially that at Kelly, bring a substantial number of people to the area during the tourist season - by car. Kelly estate might have been converted differently; in the *Glasgow Herald* of 23rd May, 1947, the following item appeared: 'Greenock Corporation yesterday approved the recommendation of the Joint County Committee that the proposed new hospital for Renfrewshire should be established on the Kelly estate, Wemyss Bay. Baillie McLaren said that the site had room for extension, belts of trees which added to the shade and an admirable view over the firth.' The hospital was built in Greenock.

When the Montgomerie family left (the 18th Earl of Eglinton spent his early life at Skelmorlie Castle), the Castle became a company HQ. The north wing was rebuilt after a major fire in 1959. Later the Castle was restored into a house, for use by their Chairman.

In 1951, there was little recorded local industry, work being of a maintenance character or seasonal. Local people were described as: 'the very rich, the not-so-rich and the others', reportedly with uneasy relations between the groups. There were 150 children attending the primary school, but older children had to go to Largs and Greenock. The churches were still active, the North Church having 280 members, Skelmorlie South Church 350, while smaller numbers supported the Roman Catholic faith, the Scottish Episcopal Church and other persuasions. For the younger generation, there were the church based Youth Club and Scout Troop.

In 1967, the Hydro closed for the winter and never reopened. Television arrived and many sporting and other shore-based recreational activities departed. As with other late twentieth century communities, huge changes in living, working and leisure patterns have removed the appearance of permanence as characterful stone building has been replaced by lighter modern budget construction.

Chapter Four

The Development of Land Transport

Roads

> *One day through the primeval wood,*
> *A calf walked home, as good calves should,*
> *But made a trail, all bent askew,*
> *A crooked trail, as all calves do.*

After 40 lines describing how the meandering calf created the track that became a lane then a road and finally the main street 'of a renowned metropolis', the anonymous author concluded that as a result, 'A hundred thousand men were led, by that one calf, near three centuries dead'.

Blaeu's 1654 *Altas Novus* depicted the towns and estates that made up Scotland. One of the few routes shown described a 'Way to Glasgow' from Paisley through Hillingtoun, but until the 18th century, the only 'engineered' roads connecting communities were those constructed by the Romans. There were tracks, like those created by the calf, but these were poorly maintained and generally unsuitable for wheeled traffic. Under an Act of 1669, workers had to devote six days a year repairing roads, but this did not keep them in order. In bad weather they could be impassable. Sheriffs and Justices of the Peace were authorised to decide on repairs, organise labour and exact tolls. The poor state of the highways encouraged the more remote and inland communities to be largely self-sufficient. With transport improvements, they were able to buy a wider range of materials of better quality - and enabled to sell produce to townships further away. How far habits have now changed is clear when local shops often sell little more than convenience goods (papers, confectionery, tobacco) while bulk grocery purchases and consumer durables (furniture and carpets) are made many miles and an hour's drive away in and around Glasgow.

The 1707 Act of Union produced trading opportunities, especially in the tobacco, cotton, mahogany, sugar and rum industries, Strathclyde and Glasgow merchants growing rich as a result. The increase in trade demanded better and faster transport. Even in the 1740s, in Glasgow goods were carried by pack horse or hauled on a horse-drawn sledge while personal transport (for the better off) was by sedan chair. Outwith the city, travel was dreadfully slow. In 1748, it took Provost Andrew Cochrane of Glasgow and two magistrates *12 days* to reach London, via Edinburgh. Heavy loads were impossible by land - the most a horse could pull was about 6 cwt (about one third of a tonne).

Incredible as it seems, before 1709, the mail between Edinburgh and Glasgow, 44 miles apart, was carried by one man, on foot. After that date, he was provided with a pony. Before 1749, mail to Glasgow from the South came on horseback, directed through Edinburgh. In 1747, the Edinburgh and Glasgow Caravan Company ran a twice-weekly service between the cities for 5s. [*£18.75] single, taking nine hours. In 1763, the new coach service between Glasgow and Greenock also took nine hours.

Poor roads hampered development. Heavy goods could only be carried over short distances. After heavy rain, pack roads became so ill-defined that travellers even lost their way. Until the middle of the 18th century, the only regular means of goods transport was by the cadger - a rider on horseback with creels carrying goods and letters. Thus conurbations like Glasgow, Paisley and Greenock could not get the coal and agricultural produce they needed to expand. Sometimes canals provided an answer - especially for transporting coal, steel and lime, but they required level routes through the hilly country. As coal came to be mined further away from where canals could be driven, so short feeder railways linked the pits to the waterways. Then the railways bypassed the canals so avoiding double handling yet taking bulk shipments closer to the user. Thus evolved the cheaper, faster and more flexible railway system (a railway cost a third of what a canal cost). But only the roads could be used to convey passengers, local transport and small items.

Turnpike trusts began with one in Midlothian in 1714. The first Turnpike Act for Ayrshire, whose most northerly coastline township was Skelmorlie, was passed in 1767 and authorised the construction of new roads, the formation of a governing body and the charging of tolls. One of the roads defined under this Act ran from Saltcoats, by Largs to Kelly Bridge and was completed in the 1780s.

The trustees tended to be men of substance - landowners, advocates and merchants who had a personal interest in creating roads. The Cunninghames and Montgomeries (including Hugh Montgomerie of Skelmorlie, 12th Earl of Eglinton) were also represented. The clerks and treasurers appointed to manage the roads were usually local government officials. Surveyors were employed to inspect all roads, tunnels, causeways, pavements and arrange compensation for the landowners through whose property the new roads ran. They had to inspect and make good defective highways and bridges and organise labour squads. In 1787, John Loudon McAdam, an engineer and one of the Ayrshire Trustees, considered that the expertise of the road surveyors needed improving too. It was he who introduced the tarmacadam road surface.

Prior to the evolution of a national transport system, it was cheaper to send goods by water. Adam Smith (1723-1790) calculated that while it would take six weeks for a round trip from Leith to London both by road and by sea, to convey 200 tons would require either one ship with a crew of six to eight men or 50 road wagons each requiring two men and eight horses (i.e. 100 men and 400 horses). As late as 1780, there was no proper road out of Greenock to the East. Small wonder the sea was the busiest thoroughfare and that the major towns were those accessible by water.

In 1790, a new road connected Glasgow to Port Glasgow. By 1791, wheeled transport was in general use, the turnpike roads allowing horses to pull up to 30cwt (1½ tons) - several times more than previously.

In 1800, Glasgow to Greenock by stage coach took 3½ hours for 5s. inside, or 3s. outside [*£6.90 and *£4.15p]. Around 1835, before the railways appeared, the journey from London to Glasgow had come down to about 44 hours on horseback, post-chaise or stage coach with 'as many changes of horses'. In 1812, there was one daily coach between Glasgow and Paisley; by 1830 this had risen to 27 a day.

By 1836, Greenock Carriers operated a coach from Inverkip to Largs, mainly carrying mail. C.J.A. Robertson (*The Origins of the Scottish Railway System*) records that the appearance of the paddle steamer had driven 'all the previous twenty-four stage-coaches off the road' between Glasgow and Greenock and the trip now took 2½ hours for 1s. [*£1.90]. Not surprisingly, the number of passengers carried increased enormously - to about 750,000.

John Ainslie's map of 1796 shows Wemyss Bay connected to the highway system. Roads in the vicinity of Wemyss Bay, Finnock, Inverkip, Gourock and Greenock were constructed to a higher standard than those connecting the communities over the hills. The road through Wemyss Bay was a section of a 'new' route being built between Glasgow and Port Patrick, part of which, dating from the 1780s, ran the full extent of the parish. The road building programme included the Shore Road which would give easier access to Largs than the hill road by Auchendarroch, Annetyard and Skelmorlie Castle. The cost of upkeep of the turnpike road between Skelmorlie and Largs was defrayed by tolls collected at the 'Toll bar' at Kelly Quay Cottage (at Kelly Burn). In the 1780s, a coach and six cost 8s. [*£21.70], a wagon and six, 12s. [*£32.60] and a drove of sheep, 10d. [*£2.25].

In 1803, Sir John Shaw Stewart realigned the River Kip while bringing the turnpike road through the Kip valley to Greenock. By 1835, a large network of improved roads had been built. Those that could avoid paying the tolls, inevitably did, so making maintenance of some roads very difficult. The advent of the railways meant that these roads had to be subsidised to cover the cost of repair. They therefore fell into disorder as evidenced in the following letter in the *Glasgow Herald* dated 28th February, 1865:

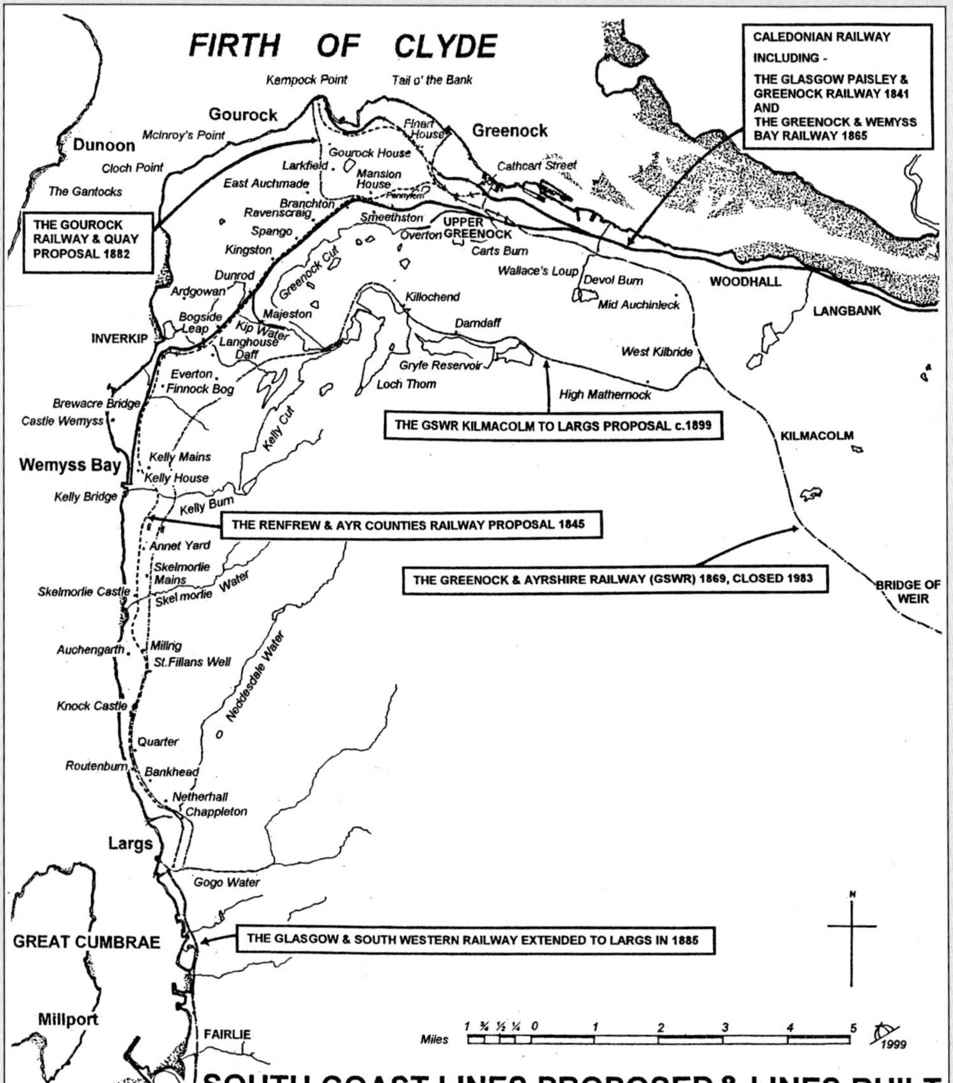

SOUTH COAST LINES PROPOSED & LINES BUILT

THE DEVELOPMENT OF LAND TRANSPORT

Sir - I am reluctantly compelled to complain about the impassable state of the road between Inverkip and Wemyss Bay, especially since the thaw. Last evening, in coming from Greenock to Largs, I found the road at the place referred to so dirty and narrow that I would never have got my horse and cart through but for the assistance of some railway navvies.

'I am aware that the state of the road is greatly aggravated, if not altogether caused, by the railway operations on the line of the Wemyss Bay Railway; but surely the road trustees are bound to see that the road is kept passable for carriages, etc. while they levy toll dues.

Wm. Crawford, Carrier

In 1865, the Roads (Scotland) Bill was going through committee to put Scotland's roads under a uniform system of management and control. With the passing of the Roads and Bridges (Scotland) Act in 1876, turnpike trusts were abolished and responsibility for roads was passed to county boards, but it was 1883 before this was achieved in Ayrshire.

By 1905, there were many in Wemyss Bay who could afford the much prized motor car. Horse troughs were replaced by petrol pumps. But even though Paton the butcher and Ure Young the baker ran around in petrol-driven delivery vans in 1916, horses were still used many years after. Mr Dallas, the coalman, is recorded as stabling the station horses in 1925. In the 1930s, the roads were cluttered with cyclists as well as cars.

There was a scheme to link Wemyss Bay to Largs, Inverkip and Gourock by tramcars, but this came to nothing. Charabancs operated between Station Square and Largs - in 1914, they made five runs a day at 6d. [*£1.10] each way. Later the LMS operated chocolate and cream coloured buses between Greenock and Largs in competition with Dunlop's red buses.

Railways

North Lanarkshire's production of pig iron rose from 22,800 tons in 1800 to nearly 40,000 tons in 1830 and then dramatically to 564,000 tons in 1848, putting great pressure on the transport system. Growth was not steady - there were some exceedingly difficult years in the 1840s when many iron works closed.

Timber waggonways using longitudinal rails had been used from the 17th century to transport heavy loads over short distances but the voracious appetites of the industrial era demanded heavier and more robust rails and greater haulage capacity. Using a waggonway, about 1810 a single horse could pull 8 tons, 25 times more than its predecessor on the road 40 years before. By the early 1820s steam locomotives were reckoned as more profitable than barges or trains drawn by horses as they could pull more and move faster. They could attain 10 mph, though 20 mph was considered to be their limit.

Greenock-born James Watt (1736-1819), who developed the steam engine into a practical source of power, suggested a canal connecting London and Edinburgh to transport goods in large quantities. This was not an unreasonable suggestion as canals had been developed to the extent that one horse could tow between 30 and 45 tons. But by 1824, when most of our surviving canals had been built, Robert Stevenson, a prominent Glasgow engineer and lighthouse builder, saw bulk transport as favouring the railway. By the early part of the 19th century, the transport revolution saw bulk goods being carried by rail rather than over water.

Railway development was beset by financial problems. The boom years for the railways - 1824-26, 1833-1837 and 1844-1847 - reflected a buoyant economy. But there were other years, such as 1842, when businesses toiled to survive, when a severe decline in trade, falling prices and a shortage of money, caused many railway schemes to be put 'on hold'. This was not helped by the way finance was raised for new development. Lack of trade and thereby the monies available for investment dogged the development of the railways. For example in 1862, the Caledonian Directors complained that the sluggish trading market was affecting their operations.

Costing Railways could not be described as an exact science. Engineers could price physical structures with some accuracy but unforeseens frequently lifted the estimates of the earliest railways by substantial amounts. Invariably, the promoters had to issue more shares because they had underestimated land acquisition costs, miscalculated the price of construction, or paid inadequate regard to the purchase of rolling stock, working expenditure and traffic revenue. For example, the Kilmarnock and Troon (1812) cost 50 per cent more than estimated. However, the Wemyss Bay branch appears to have been priced more realistically, only exceeding its cost limit by about 5 per cent, though that was 30 per cent more than the first concept figure. New railways would be proposed when there was general optimism in the country and investors would then promise fixed sums. But after the protracted (and costly) Parliamentary processes, the country might be in depression and money not so readily available when construction began and the calls were made against the promised finance. Early investors tended to be those who lived locally but when railway shares seemed like a promising investment, outsiders subscribed to the proposals and expected a good yield. Being less committed to local needs but more to a good return, withdrawal of their support could jeopardise a project.

The Glasgow Paisley and Greenock Railway

Lines to Glasgow, like the Glasgow, Paisley, Kilmarnock and Ayr (GPK&A) railway, were often financially supported by City merchants intent on expanding their trade, but the Glasgow Paisley and Greenock Railway (GP&G) (1841) was not. Glasgow merchants who had invested in shipping would not support what looked like a rival. Back in 1802, Greenock Town Council suggested to the Glasgow magistrates that a waggonway between the two communities would bring great benefits. Goods transported by waggonway would arrive in less than half the time it took to bring a boat up the Clyde, besides boats were also subject to grounding and affected by fog. But the Glaswegians remained aloof. Only one Glasgow merchant of any substance was to support the railway, and he only because toll charges on the river were unacceptably high. The bulk of the investment for this line came from England (nearly 40 per cent) and local (Renfrewshire) merchants. To attract the English investor, giving him confidence in the competence of the proposals, the GP&G appointed the successful English engineer, Joseph Locke. A prominent fundraiser was Patrick Maxwell Stewart, MP for Lancaster and brother of Sir Michael Shaw Stewart, 6th Baronet and MP for Renfrewshire. Maxwell Stewart (d.1846) was Chairman of the London and Westminster Bank (which had interests in the Caledonian Railway), Chairman of the Greenock Railway and was active on the Boards or committees of the other railways which were to form the line to Greenock.

The Greenock to Glasgow line opened on 30th March, 1841 (the first train taking 65 minutes for the journey), but most transport, especially heavy goods, still went by water. Within three years, the number of people travelling by boat and train was over 920,000, but two thirds went by train, the journey taking only an hour. Removal of passenger tax on the railways meant that the lowest fare on the railway had dropped to 1s. from 1s. 6d. [*£2.12 from *£3.19], the boat fare being forced down to 8d. [*£1.42].

Land acquisition for the GP&G Railway was unusually costly. In 1837, Sir John Maxwell of Pollok demanded (and received) payment at the level he expected to get for selling it for the houses he said he proposed to build there. In the case of the Wemyss Bay line, most subscribers seem to have been people who lived reasonably nearby and saw some benefit in the line crossing their land.

Whereas railway development had been driven by the need for volume goods conveyance, people soon realised that they could visit places they had previously only dreamt about, very quickly, and cheaply, something that the canals and roads of the time were incapable of doing. This 'liberation' changed the habits of centuries for country and urban dwellers alike. Many people now had sufficient spare money to spend on a holiday away from the stench of the big cities. As Joseph Grainger stated to a Select Committee in 1839, 'Whenever a cheap, safe, expeditious and comfortable means of conveying passengers has been established, either upon land or water, the increase in travelling has in almost every instance far exceeded what could reasonably have been anticipated.' The opening of the Glasgow-London railway in 1848 enabled holidaymakers to arrive on the doorstep to the Highlands in large numbers since Glasgow was now only 13 hours away from the English capital. By 1865, Queen Victoria, referring particularly to the lines round London, observed that the railways had 'succeeded in securing the monopoly of the means of travelling of almost the entire population of the country'.

While the Glasgow, Paisley and Greenock Railway had been conceived to carry goods mainly from seagoing ships into central Glasgow, it had no difficulty attracting huge numbers of passengers. With its large population of Highlanders, driven south following the Jacobite Rebellion, and Irish seeking work, Glasgow was a most unhealthy place - crowded, insanitary and with a high level of poverty. People, keen to get away to cleaner climates, could now do so either by the cheap passenger carrying paddle steamers on the Clyde or the railways. The lower the fares, the more could be carried - and competition drove down the fares.

The Greenock and Wemyss Bay Railway Line

The Greenock and Wemyss Bay Railway Company (G&WBR) completed the 10 miles of line from Port Glasgow in 1865, but from the start, the Caledonian Railway Company ran the trains. The original plan was to build a station on land owned by Major General Swinburne and connect with the steamer services at Whiting Bay but, before construction began, it was decided to extend the line to near Kelly Burn on the Ayrshire boundary.

The line was different to the earliest lines: it deliberately set out to capitalise on the mood of the masses to travel. It was not conceived to carry goods. Its main *raison d'être* was to convey people from Glasgow and Paisley to the steamboat which was to take them to resorts across the Clyde. It was crucially important that the line, the trains and the steamers worked efficiently and punctually. The G&WBR was very sensitive to anything that could affect its operation - it had to attract custom from competing railways in the centre of Glasgow (including the Caledonian Railway), run the fastest trains possible and make connection with a closely-scheduled and efficient steamer service. That it succeeded was largely due to its energetic secretary James Keyden, who was quick to deal with running problems and to anticipate the future needs of the line. Had it failed, the Caley and the steamboat companies could have survived, but not the G&WBR.

Until 1885, Fairlie was the nearest station to Largs. Fairlie got its railway in 1880, (the pier connection was formed in 1882) and the Largs line was only completed in 1885. So passengers for Largs and Fairlie had to take the train to Wemyss Bay then travel by the Millport steamer for the next few miles down the coast. Proposals to link Largs to Wemyss Bay along the shore were thwarted by local landowners. An alternative route to Largs from Kilmacolm (south of Port Glasgow) via Upper Skelmorlie and the Brisbane Glen ran up against severe constructional problems and objections from landowners and was finally abandoned in 1899.

In May 1885, Murray's Diary showed that the Wemyss Bay line had still to reach its full potential. The journey time to Glasgow Bridge Street was just over an hour for 3s. 6d. return first class and 2s. third class [*£8.35 and *£4.75] - though Central Station had been opened by this time. By contrast, in 1898, the Caley scheduled some trains to travel between Glasgow and Gourock in only 32 minutes, a time sometimes bettered to the discomfort of the passengers.

As the railways expanded, the public depended on them more and more. Yet they had virtually all been financed privately. Government money was only forthcoming when there was a perceived national or military requirement or a safety failure. In the 1830s, some had advocated a national railway system while others saw competition keeping prices down; in March 1865 the *Glasgow Herald* referred to a strong public aversion to Government ownership of the lines arising from the nationalisation clause in the 1844 Regulation of Railways Act becoming operative. In 1888, the House of Commons debated a motion that Government acquire the lines, causing W.E. Gladstone to reflect that when he was at the Board of Trade in 1841, before the Caley was formed, the debate then was whether there could be more than one railway into Scotland. By 1888, not only were there two main lines across the border but they were carrying enormous amounts of freight and passengers. An unimaginable transformation had taken place affecting the life and prosperity of the nation.

Wemyss Bay line upgraded

Early in the 20th century, the Wemyss Bay railway was reconstructed from Port Glasgow, and Wemyss Bay station was replaced in 1903 'and became one of the most beautiful and best kept in the country, the floral decorations receiving praise from King Edward VII himself.' Trains were more frequent and faster - return to Glasgow 3s. 1st class, 2s. 2d. 3rd class [*£7.40 and *£5.35] the express taking less than 50 minutes, as good as the 1995 schedule for electric traction.

Tripper trains were not limited to running between Glasgow and the Clyde ferry terminals. In 1926, 'Indicator' writing in the *Railway Magazine* recorded that one could catch the 6.55am from Edinburgh (Princes Street) and be in Gourock by 9.00 am. (I am told that after the direct east-west coast trains were removed from the timetable, coaching stock was rostered so that a train starting the day on a west coast route might later appear on a Glasgow Central to Edinburgh service. However the July 1913 Caley instructions for Marshalling of Trains does not appear to indicate this was normal procedure.)

'Indicator' also noted that there were at least four distinct divisions of traffic to be catered for.

Firstly, during the summer months there was a considerable amount of daily business travel between the Clyde resorts and Paisley and Glasgow, involving inward journeys in the morning and return services in the late afternoon or early evening;

Secondly, there was a large amount of week-end traffic requiring outward services on Friday or Saturday afternoons, with provision for return on Monday mornings in time to commence business in Glasgow by about 10 am;

Thirdly, there was an extensive day-trip traffic outwards from Glasgow in the morning, returning in the evening; and

Fourthly, general holiday traffic involving both inward and outward journeys on Saturdays.

He noted that there was a fifth class: one where trains were frequently required (but not generally announced) on the first of the month, to cater for the general practice throughout a large part of Scotland of changing living quarters at the month's end. Family parties would travel to their summer quarters at the end of the month, remain there for one, two or three months, while those members who were engaged in business travelled to or from Glasgow under the attractive season-ticket arrangements or week-end facilities offered by the LMS and LNER in Scotland. Thus there was a general interchange on the first of each month, often necessitating additional and relief trains beyond those applying throughout the remainder of the month. While it was an important factor in the railway arrangements, it was met by scheduling relief boats and trains without public announcement.

Against this general background, competition developed from road traffic. From about 1918, small consignments delivered to railheads were transported by lorries and vans to the locality. It wasn't long before the roads took traffic off the rails; by the 1920s and 1930s, many motor vehicles released from wartime service appeared on the public highway. In 1928, the number of vehicles registered in Renfrew County numbered about 6,700, a figure which was to nearly double by the end of World War II. The LMS acquired buses to compete against this new threat to the railways, however the 'new society' where most people have a car, has meant that the railways now need to try new initiatives to attract people back to the trains.

Chapter Five

Personalities

Before embarking on the story behind the development of rail and steamer traffic through Wemyss Bay, let me add colour by giving some details of the main participants and local worthies. The list includes people prominent in various walks of life as well as the 'ordinary' folk who are essential characters in the historical backdrop. They are included here because without them, the story would be incomplete.

The Great and the Braw

Sir Michael Robert Shaw Stewart of Greenock and Blackhall (1826-1903) - 7th Baronet, traced his ancestry back via Sir John Stewart of Auchengowan, Blackhall and Ardgowan to Robert de Bruis (*c*.1090-1140). The Stewart family changed its name to Shaw Stewart when Sir John Shaw Stewart, 4th Baronet, inherited the lands of Easter and Wester Greenock on the death of his great uncle Sir John Shaw about 1752. Sir Michael Robert Shaw Stewart inherited the title at the age of 10 on the death of his father, Sir Michael Shaw Stewart MP for Lanarkshire (and later, Renfrewshire). His mother closed Ardgowan and took her six surviving children to her mother in London. Sir Michael joined the Life Guards when he was 19, resigning when he reached his majority, to return to run his estate from Ardgowan. In 1852, Sir Michael married Lady Octavia Grosvenor, a daughter of the 2nd Marquess of Westminster, and subsequently gifted land and resources to establish Wellington Park, Wellpark and Whinhill Braes in Greenock and to help establish Greenock Infirmary. In 1856, Henderson designed an Episcopal Chapel at Ardgowan, appropriately consecrated to 'St Michael and All Angels'. (The chapel fell out of use in 1983 and in 1998 the building was 'consolidated' into a ruin.) Between 1855 and 1865, he was MP for the County of Renfrewshire. He was Lord Lieutenant for Renfrewshire between 1868 and 1903 and Honorary Colonel of the 1st Battalion of the Argyll and Sutherland Highlanders.

Sir Michael's mother, the Dowager Lady Shaw Stewart, bought shares in the fledgling Glasgow Paisley and Greenock Railway in 1841. It is not clear whether Sir Michael ever acquired shares in railway stock on his own account. In his booklet on the origins of the Caledonian Railway, George Graham, the Caledonian Railway Company's first Engineer, refers to Robert Farquhar Shaw Stewart - Sir Michael's youngest brother - being elected a Director of the Caley in January 1864, a position he held till his resignation in March 1868. R.F. Shaw Stewart is recorded as attending meetings when matters relating to the Wemyss Bay line were discussed.

One of Sir Michael's sisters, Jane Catherine (b.1821), assisted Florence Nightingale in Scutari in 1852, at the beginning of the Crimean War. She was also responsible for building St. Mary's Episcopal Church in Port Glasgow.

At least till the early part of the 19th century, the Shaw Stewarts were involved in trading, to the Baltic and to Tobago in the West Indies. Sir Michael was a major landowner, the chief superior of Greenock and part of Port Glasgow. His agents were regularly involved in correspondence with the Greenock and Wemyss Bay Railway Company on such subjects as the purchase of land between Greenock and Ardgowan, and at Upper Greenock station, the provision of a private loading platform at Inverkip, a siding for mineral extraction near Dunrod, the unacceptability of fencing with barbed wire along the lineside where his cattle could be damaged and compensation for the disturbance of game during the doubling of the railway line.

Ardgowan House, the home of the Shaw Stewarts as pictured in 1998. *Author*

Replica African hut built on Dr James Young's Kelly House estate in 1875.
Alan Brotchie Collection

On his death, his staff numbered 33 male servants and his movable assets included nine 4-wheeled carriages, and six carriages 'with less than 4 wheels'.

He was followed by his eldest son - *Sir Michael Hugh Shaw Stewart* of Carnock in Stirlingshire and Ardgowan (1854-1942) - 8th Baronet, who was a Captain in the 4th Battalion of the Argyll and Sutherland Highlanders. He was much travelled - to the Cape, Tasmania, New Zealand, China and Canada. Like his father, he was a keen huntsman and features latterly in connection with reinstatement of grounds following the upgrading of the Wemyss Bay line in 1906. He married Lady Alice Emma Thynne, daughter of the Marquess of Bath. He was MP between 1886 and 1906 for the East Division of the County of Renfrew, a constituency that included Polmadie, Eaglesham, Cathcart and Stirling.

Sir Hugh gifted four acres at Battery Park at Fort Matilda to Greenock Town Council for recreational use, despite being offered more for industrial purposes. In 1914, he loaned Ardgowan to the Government for use as an auxiliary hospital, his wife, a keen Guider, acting as Commandant.

Sir Hugh and his wife died in 1942 - both are buried at Inverkip. His nephew, Walter Guy Shaw Stewart, 9th Baronet (d.1976), succeeded him. The succession continued with Euan Guy Shaw Stewart (d.1980) and the title is currently held by Sir Houston Mark Shaw Stewart (b.1931), 11th Baronet. Sir Houston's son Ludovic Houston was born in 1986.

Locally prominent personages included the following: *Robert Wallace* (1773-1855) - who became the first MP for Greenock in 1832 and helped achieve the Penny Postage. He claimed descent from Sir William Wallace. His father was a wealthy West India Merchant who owned Kelly estate, among others. Robert held various posts in his life - minister of the Church of Scotland, Professor of Church History, Editor of *The Scotsman* and barrister at law. In May 1834, the *Scots Times* published his proposals to develop Wemyss Bay as a holiday resort and watering place. He also had an interest in creating a new town at Brisbane in Largs in 1845 - this proposal was not pursued. Financially overstretched, he sold Kelly and retired to Greenock.

James Scott of Kelly - was one of the original directors of the Greenock and Wemyss Bay Railway Company in 1861. He was also a Justice of the Peace. His estate was sold to Dr James Young in 1867.

Dr James Young (1811-1883) - was the Glasgow scientist who discovered paraffin oil and started the world's first commercial oil works at Bathgate in Lothian in 1851. In his youth, he received some education at night school while working as a joiner during the day. He continued at Anderson's College in Glasgow (where he met the explorer and missionary David Livingstone) before moving to University College London to study industrial chemistry. His friend Dr Livingstone laid the foundation stone for Young's Addiewell works in 1864. Dr Young was visited by George Graham, the Caley's Chief Engineer, at Limefield shale works the same year. Dr Young was the founder of the world's first chair of applied chemistry in Glasgow in 1871.

At his own expense, he fitted out an expedition to track down Dr Livingstone. An African hut was built for Dr Livingstone at Limefield House, Polbeth, West Lothian by Dr Young. He purchased Kelly Estate in 1867, a year before the death of his wife Mary. His admiration for Dr Livingstone (who frequently stayed at Kelly House) was displayed in his trim 10 acre garden by another replica African hut (rectangular on plan, with low eaves and thatched pitched roof and walls) built by Livingstone's servants, Susi and Chuma in 1875. His yacht *Nyanza* was named in Livingstone's honour. Young was responsible for the erection in 1879 of the Mossmain statue to Livingstone, now repositioned at Glasgow Cathedral. Young died in 1883 and was buried in the nearby churchyard at Inverkip. A large memorial stone records his death and that of his wife; two sons are buried alongside.

Other people who visited or lived in the area

The short length of coastline from Wemyss Bay south to Largs has seen many who distinguished themselves in public life. Among them, *Sir Hugh Skelmorlie* - the 6th and last Baronet of Skelmorlie was Provost of Glasgow, Glasgow's MP, and a Commissioner of the Treaty of Union (1707). *General Sir Thomas Mcdougall Brisbane* (b.1773) - who died at Brisbane House near Largs in the 1860s, achieved fame as an astronomer, was Governor General of New South Wales (1821-1825), serving with distinction in the West Indies and in Europe. He was on friendly terms with Arthur Wellesley (later Duke of Wellington). The parliamentarian the *Earl of Shaftesbury* (1801-1885) who campaigned for fairer working conditions, spent five or six weeks in the Bay every summer for 14 years. *Lord Inverclyde* included him as a guest at Castle Wemyss. *Sir William Pearce* - MP for Govan in 1885, lived locally in the villa called Cardwell. *Robert Steele* - a Greenock shipbuilder acquired the red Castle of Knock in 1850 and built the present castle, retaining the old. *Professor Thomson* - probably Allan Thomson, a professor of anatomy who rendered assistance at an accident at Wemyss Bay Station in 1865 - lived at Muirsland (renamed Moreland) and is believed to have opened the local school in 1866.

The local cast included *John McConnachie* of Carradale who used to smuggle whiskey at night from an illegal still on Arran in the mid-18th century, storing his supplies in a bothy at Skelmorlie Castle to be delivered under cover of darkness. *William Watson* - an engineer who fought for the Confederate Army in America, built three houses in Skelmorlie that he named after battles in which he had fought - Oakhill, Pea Ridge and Beechgrove. Then there was *Duncan Grant* - carrier, who was to be found at Wemyss Bay station in the 1870s.

Personalities directly involved with the railway and the steamboats

Railway development throws up the same names in widely scattered places. I have pulled together a few facts about some of the people connected with the Wemyss Bay line, the Caledonian Railway and its associated steamboat company, to help describe their careers and where known, their approach to life.

In this story, one of the most significant was *James Keyden* (1807-1887), a well-known Glasgow solicitor and property speculator, who at his death was principal of Keyden, Strang and Girvan at 186 West George Street, Glasgow.

Keyden's father the Revd James Keyden, minister of Keir Parish in Dumfriesshire, his grandfather William Keyden, and his uncle Theodore Edgar Keyden were ministers in the established Church. James Keyden broke the mould by becoming a solicitor while his younger brother William practised as an accountant in Glasgow.

James was born on 4th March, 1807, a year after his father married Helen Grierson. In 1825, he was apprenticed to Lachlan Lumsden and William Shortridge. In 1830, he became a Writer in Strang and Yuille's office in Glasgow before becoming a partner, the firm being renamed Strang, Yuille & Keyden in 1831. He was admitted to the Faculty of Advocates in 1836 and in the same year, he married Esther Cauvin. Over the next few years, he lived at several addresses before moving to Torwood House at Row (now called Rhu), Helensburgh which was to be his domicile, except for a few years around 1870 when he lived with his wife and three grown-up sons, James, Theodore and Philip, at Craigend Castle, Milngavie.

The firm was renamed Strang, Keyden and Sons in 1859 when James Keyden (junior) was taken into the practice. Following the death of the senior partner in 1863 the firm was again renamed, emerging as Keyden, Strang and Keyden in new premises at 186 West George Street. George Yuille Strang-Watkins (hyphenated through marriage to a Shropshire heiress), lived with his brother Robert Strang at Kilmory, a substantial house on the Shore Road in Skelmorlie. He was much engaged in Parliamentary business promoting Railway Bills and may have been involved in the approvals process for Keyden in London. George Strang-Watkins and Keyden's son Theodore practised as accountants and sharebrokers in Strang & Keyden, (possibly a separate division of the practice). The arrival of the railway at Wemyss Bay occurred simultaneously with a rapid rise in property values, no doubt anticipated by those established in Skelmorlie before 1865! In 1870, the firm was renamed Keyden Strang and Girvan, the name it retained till 1899 when it was changed to Keyden, Strang & Co.

From 1861 till his death on 31st May, 1887 at the age of 80, Keyden acted as Company Secretary to the Greenock and Wemyss Bay Railway Co. Both he and his son *Philip Grierson Keyden* who was taken into the partnership on the death of his father, maintained a vigorous correspondence with the Caledonian Railway, often to the latter's discomfort.

Keyden was involved in other speculative ventures. He was a promoter of the Glasgow, Dumbarton and Helensburgh line (1858), built by the Glasgow Dumbarton and Helensburgh Railway Co. and absorbed into the North British in 1865. His company was also associated with the Crofthead & Kilmarnock Extension Railway proposals (1865) and the Busby Railway Co. (1866) on the south side of Glasgow. Around 1870 he was pressing the North British Railway Company to build a railway between Glasgow and Dumbarton engineered by Charles Forman, with a passenger station at Sauchiehall Street. The NB did not pursue the idea when they priced the land and related it to the likely returns.

He was also influential in the development of the Blane Valley Railway. It is recorded that the idea of promoting the Strathendrick and Loch Lomond Railway, which would have been a westward extension to Aberfoyle and Inversnaid of the Blane Valley Railway along the east shore of Loch Lomond, was first mooted in his office in 1879. Keyden's optimism was not borne out by results; poorly financed with quite inadequate returns, he promptly proposed another line, the Milngavie, Strathendrick and Port of Monteith Railway which would have cut across the country served by the Blane Valley line. The Blane Valley Directors were appalled and sacked Keyden, their Secretary, he duly recording his dismissal in the Minute Book. In his entry, he added that he was resigning to meet the wishes of the Board and would require the usual payment in lieu of notice, which he was advised was a year's salary. One can guess what the Board's response was.

James Keyden's death was announced in *The Evening Times* and *The Glasgow Herald*. He was highly respected and locally known as a supporter of many benevolent and charitable institutions. An elder of the West Free Church, Helensburgh (now the West Kirk of Helensburgh), 'he took a warm and kindly interest in the welfare of the working classes at Row, and, when at home, conducted a weekly religious service in the village, and also lent any who were desirous of improving their minds the use of valuable and instructive works'.

His estate was valued at about £19,400, making him nearly a millionaire at present day values [*£985,000]. His executors included his three surviving sons: James, Philip and Theodore Edgar Keyden as well as Philip Grierson (Advocate in Edinburgh - presumably a relative from his mother's side) and his partner James Girvan. A year earlier, his sister Helen had died in Stirling, leaving estate worth nearly £16,400 [*£800,000].

Keydens maintained their links with the railway world after James's death. According to J.F. McEwan, in 1891, Formans and McCall engineered the Lanarkshire and Dumbartonshire Railway, which once opened, was run from Keydens' office. In 1892, the Caley engaged them to prepare documents to oppose the G&SW Railway Bill for an extension to Largs. The work cannot have been especially demanding as the proposed route above and behind Wemyss Bay and Skelmorlie could hardly have been profitable, and besides the G&SW had reached Largs from the South in 1885.

On the death of the other two partners, George Strang-Watkins and James Keyden (jun.), for a short time, Philip was sole partner. The last of the Keydens, he died on 3rd December, 1915. The name still exists, following amalgamation with two old established firms in 1994 to form Borland Montgomerie Keyden.

James Keyden was assisted on many projects by *James Richardson Forman*, CE (1822-1900) - a Scots Canadian, who was involved in most of the important railway engineering projects in the west of Scotland. In 1780, James Forman's parents emigrated from Coldstream in Berwickshire to Nova Scotia. He came to Scotland in 1841 and joined the engineering office of Robert Hazelton Robson. In 1845, Robson sent him to supervise the construction of the Wilsontown Morningside and Coltness railway, east of Glasgow. This was followed by his appointment as manager of the General Terminus Railway (1848) (where coal carried by various railways was emptied into cargo vessels from quays on the south bank of the Clyde in Glasgow) and an appointment as Government engineer for his native province of Nova Scotia. Six years later, in 1860, he returned to Glasgow and entered into partnership with Robson and David McCall, the firm being renamed Robson, Forman and McCall, civil engineers, at 133 West Regent Street. In 1871, the partnership, renamed Forman & McCall in 1868, moved to 160 Hope Street.

James Forman was the Greenock and Wemyss Bay Co.'s first Engineer, from about 1860 to early 1869. He was also associated with the Milngavie (1863), the Blane Valley (1866) and Greenock & Ayrshire (1869) railways as well as civil engineering constructions such as Greenock Water Works. In January 1860, it appears he was engaged by Rothesay Town Council to advise on how to improve the town's water supply. His interests extended into the commercial world and included the chairmanship of the Aberfoyle Slate Quarries Co. Ltd as well as directorships of other companies. For his last 20 years, he lived in Ratho (near Edinburgh) where he served on the Parish Council and chaired the School Board. He died at his home, Craigpark, on 8th July, 1900 at the age of 78, one of the oldest members of the Institution of Civil Engineers to which he had been elected in 1866. In an obituary notice, the *Glasgow Herald* respectfully timetabled the conveyance of his coffin from Ratho station to the Necropolis in Glasgow.

James Forman had five daughters and four sons, one of whom, *Charles de Neuville Forman* (1852-1901), became an energetic partner in the practice. He made a name for himself as a persuasive contestant in Parliamentary committees, notably as an expert witness and for the obtaining of an Act for the construction of the Clyde, Ardrishaig and Crinan Railway, though the line was never built. Born in Glasgow, he served a pupilage in his father's firm before gleaning experience under James Deas, the Engineer to the Clyde Trust during the building of the Queen's Dock. In 1876, he returned to Forman and McCall and the following year was assumed into the partnership, the firm being renamed Formans & McCall. Charles was responsible for the construction of the Lanarkshire and Ayrshire Railway (1890), the West Highland Line to Fort William (1894) and was associated with the Invergarry & Fort Augustus Railway (1903) in the hope that it would make the connection to Inverness. He was also involved with the Lanarkshire and Dumbartonshire Railway (1904). A notable achievement in its day was his supervision of the construction of the Glasgow Central Railway, completed in 1896 though authorised in 1888. He died aged only 48, in Switzerland, where he had been recuperating, less than a year after his father.

Formans and McCall were associated with Crouch and Hogg (established in 1863) from the mid-1930s, being absorbed into the latter company in 1949. Crouch and Hogg exist as Crouch Hogg Waterman.

The Caledonian Railway depended heavily on their Chief Engineer - *George Graham*, MICE (1822-1899) - who had been born into a family of tenant farmers in Hallhills, Dumfriesshire. He originally worked as a joiner, cabinetmaker and mechanic to a local piano and organ builder. In 1839, he started work as an apprentice in Robert Napier's in Glasgow on the engines for the first Cunarders, but left 'ill, exhausted and depressed' in 1843 to run the family farm. In 1845, he joined Joseph Locke, the engineering consultant responsible for the Caledonian line between Carlisle and Glasgow. Perhaps as a result of support from the local laird, J.J. Hope Johnstone of Raehills (at one time MP for Dumfries), who at the time was Chairman of the Caley, the following year saw him representing the Caley's interests before a Commons Private Bill Committee. He worked as a surveyor for a short time for I.K. Brunel but returned to work on the Caley line. On 10th September, 1847, Graham drove the first passenger train between

Beattock and Carlisle. According to J.F. McEwan, the Caledonian Directors intended to terminate his employment at the end of June 1849 as part of an economy move, but pressure from the engineering department, no doubt accompanied by a reminder to the Directors that the line would require maintenance throughout its life, changed their minds.

He was Engineer-in-Chief of the Caledonian Railway from August 1853 to 30th June, 1899, (he died on the day of his retirement after a long period of ill-health when he only went into the office for occasional committee meetings). He was a very shy person, uncomfortable when giving evidence before committees. He often visited Innellan when on holiday. Certainly in his earlier years, Sunday was a day of rest when he would go to Church, even when he was down in London on business. He was a regular at Park Church in Helensburgh. His churchgoing activity was broken for some time in the spring and summer of 1861 when he damaged his arm sufficiently badly to be off work. His 1884 plans for extending the line from Greenock to Gourock via Newton Street tunnel, the longest in Scotland at 1 mile 350 yards, allowed the Caledonian to dominate the Clyde pleasure traffic.

In 1888, he wrote a private work on the origins of the Caledonian Railway. He was elected a Member of the Institution of Civil Engineers in 1889.

Other people of note who make an appearance in this story include:

Thomas Hill - Deputy Chairman then Chairman of the Caley between 1868 and 1880, who died in April 1888 after nearly 32 years on the Caley Board. He was much involved in the running of the Wemyss Bay line.

Archibald Gibson (1819-1890) - who was born in Edinburgh where it was his parents' intention that he should go into law, but by 1846, he had become Assistant Secretary of the Manchester Sheffield & Lincolnshire Railway. In February the following year, he joined the Caledonian Railway in Edinburgh as Assistant Secretary and bookkeeper. He was promoted to Secretary of the Company in August 1852, the position he held till his death.

James Thompson - JP and Deputy Lieutenant of the County of the City of Glasgow and of Lanarkshire, was born in 1834 and went to school in Carlisle. In 1848 he entered the Goods Department as a junior clerk. By 1852, he was chief clerk there and four years later, chief clerk in the goods manager's office. In April 1865, he was transferred to Edinburgh as assistant district officer and less than a year later, was promoted goods manager of the Western and Southern districts. After further promotion to general goods manager of the whole system, he was appointed General Manager of the Caledonian Railway in 1882 and knighted in 1897 in Queen Victoria's Jubilee Honours list. He won a seat on the Board in 1900 on his retiral. According to J.F. McEwan, in 1903, shareholders questioned how he could act as Chairman of the Caledonian Railway and the rival James Dunlop and Co. (bus company) at a time when the railways were struggling to return a profit. He continued to serve the company till his death in June 1906.

Captain James Williamson, (1851-1919) - was the successful Clyde skipper of his father's boat, the *Sultana* (built 1868). He was appointed first marine superintendent of the Caledonian Steam Packet Company Ltd in 1889 at the age of 38, and served 30 years with the company till his death. His book, *The Clyde Passenger Steamers* details the development of the Clyde passenger trade to 1904.

On the construction and management side of the Wemyss Bay and Caledonian Railways, the following had important parts to play: *Mortimer Evans*, CE, of 97 West Regent Street, Glasgow who followed James Forman as the Wemyss Bay Co.'s second engineer, superintending the line from early 1869 to the end of 1881. Evans is also listed in the Glasgow Postal Directory as a land surveyor. His successor, *Thomas Weir*, working from the same address, was the Wemyss Bay Co.'s engineer from the end of 1881 to September 1887. *T.O. Niven* CE of 131 West Regent Street, Glasgow was the Wemyss Bay Co's last engineer, from September 1887. *Henry Ward* - joined the Traffic Department of the Caledonian Railway in 1847 and was appointed general superintendent in 1857. He died in office on 26th March, 1881 and was succeeded by Irvine Kempt (Sr) who between 1882 and 1891, also acted as Assistant General Manager to James Thompson.

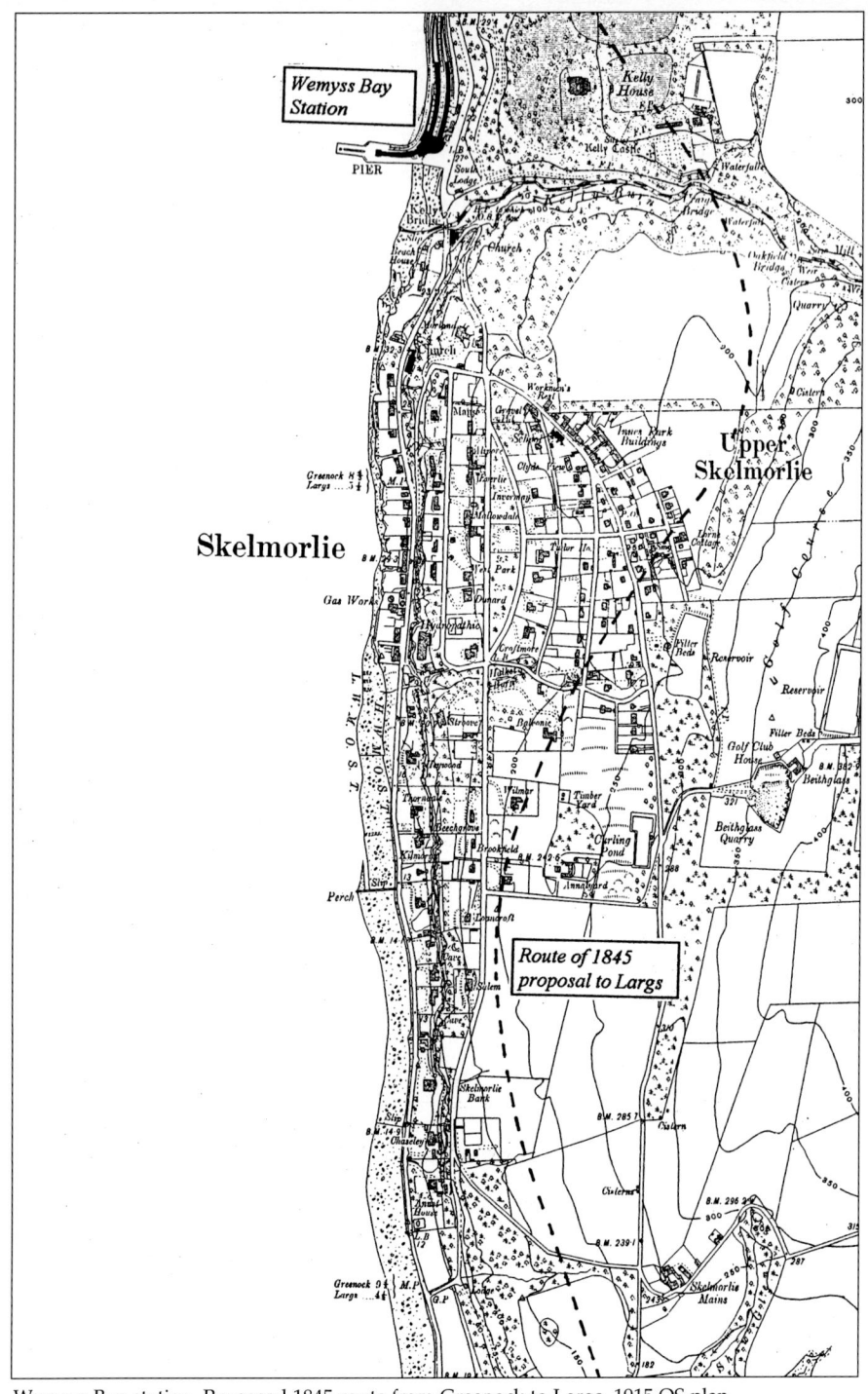

Wemyss Bay station. Proposed 1845 route from Greenock to Largs, 1915 OS plan.

National Library of Scotland

Chapter Six

Building the Line and Constructing the First Wemyss Bay Station

First Lines - The Glasgow, Paisley and Greenock Railway

We think of the Wemyss Bay line as part of the 'natural' route from Glasgow to Rothesay but this was not always the case. The line from Glasgow to Paisley (the Glasgow and Paisley Joint Railway) came into use in July 1840. Late in May 1840, the *Glasgow Herald* announced that eight passenger vehicles had been delivered, including three 'elegant' first class coaches at £480 [*£16,400] each (weighing between five and six tons apiece). By 4th July, 15 coaches were ready, with more to follow, and three locomotives had been delivered, 'via Lancaster'. The first train with its 300 invited guests left Glasgow from King Street, near the unfinished Bridge Street station on Monday 13th July, 1840, pulled by 2-2-0 tender locomotives, *Hawk* and *Zamiel*. It comprised 19 coaches and took 20 minutes to reach Paisley, a journey which stopping trains now do in 15. The trip back was rather faster - just under 15 minutes - marred by a slight collision with a locomotive that had been left on the line. Typical of the time, the locomen involved were summarily dismissed. The line began service the next day.

Nearly a year later, the line was completed from Paisley to Greenock. It opened on Tuesday 30th March, 1841, a week before Bridge Street station came into use. Two 12-coach trains hauled respectively by *Lucifer* and *Zamiel* and *Witch* and *Eagle*, made their way down to Greenock. According to J.F. McEwan, one of the returning trains had only one locomotive and ran out of steam in Bishopton tunnel. On completing their run, the crew was dismissed 'for carelessness'.

Management of the line between Bridge Street and Paisley Gilmore Street was complicated as it was run by a joint line committee from the Glasgow, Paisley, Kilmarnock and Ayr Railway and from the Glasgow, Paisley and Greenock Railway, later by their respective successors, the Glasgow and South Western Railway and the Caledonian Railway.

Proposal to extend the GP&GR south to Largs

With the GP&GR up and running, Greenock businessmen conceived the idea of extending the line from Greenock to Largs. According to J.F. McEwan, in September 1845, several Glasgow, Paisley and Greenock Railway Directors issued a Prospectus for the Renfrew and Ayr Counties Railway. The Parliamentary notice dated 15th October, 1845 indicates that a great deal of work had been done by Neil Robson as Engineer and A. McFarlane as the surveyor proving the line. Solicitors had been appointed - Robert Lamond of 29 St Vincent St Glasgow and Messrs Graham Moncrieff and Weems of Westminster. The Book of Reference contained the details of over 600 properties that would have been affected. The principal feu superiors were Sir Michael Shaw Stewart and Lieutenant General Duncan Darroch, others being the Shaws Water Joint Stock Company, the Earl of Glasgow, the Earl of Eglinton and Winton, Robert Wallace and Sir Thomas McDougall Brisbane.

The line was intended to branch off the GP&G just east of Cathcart Street station, continue westwards for a mile then split - with a branch just over two miles long to a quayside position on the west side of Gourock Bay while the main line diverged southwards to Largs. The destination and much of the route of the Gourock branch were similar to the line eventually installed many years later, though much less expensive. The maximum gradient would have been 1 in 85.

The route to Largs was just short of 15 miles and would have followed most of the present day Wemyss Bay route from Branchton station. The chief difference was that the line would have travelled inland from Inverkip at a height of several hundred feet above sea level, passing through the Kelly Estate east of Kelly House, swinging further east to cross the Kelly Burn then continuing downward via Annetyard and Skelmorlie Castle. It would then have proceeded near the coastline to Largs.

The major works would have been a 600 yard tunnel under Lynedoch Street as the line diverged from the GP&GR, a 440 yard tunnel at Inverkip, a 122 yard viaduct at Skelmorlie Glen 102 ft high above the Kelly Burn and a 460 yard tunnel as the line approached Largs. The steepest gradient proposed was 1 in 60, just where the line would have connected to the GP&GR. But due to lack of support, the proposal was abandoned later that year.

Considering the time and money spent preparing the submission, I suspect that the support came from Greenock and Largs as they had more to gain than those whose land the line would have crossed. The route of the line high above Wemyss Bay would not have helped sell off the feus which Wallace had defined in his 'Marine Village' to the north of the bay and there would have been little benefit to the farmers. Had the line been built, Wemyss Bay would have been little more than a suburban halt, the Millport trade being fed from Largs and the Rothesay route being serviced from Gourock. The grand proposals for a 'New Glasgow' would not have got beyond pipe dream stage. The concept of a connection to Largs was to resurface several times in the next 50 years.

Connections to the South and a line to Wemyss Bay

The main lines from Glasgow and Edinburgh to Carlisle to provide a direct connection to London were as yet unbuilt. On 31st July, 1845, an 'Act for making a Railway from Carlisle to Edinburgh and Glasgow and the North of Scotland to be called "The Caledonian Railway"' received the Royal assent. Promoting the Bill through Parliament alone cost about £75,000 [*£3m]. The line cost of £2.1m [*£85m] was to be raised by selling 42,000 shares at £50 [*£2,000] each. It opened in February 1848.

Shortly before, on 9th July, 1847, an Act was passed to amalgamate the existing Glasgow, Paisley and Greenock Railway with the Caledonian Railway. This line was of particular significance to the Caley, providing an already well-used extension to the Caley line, giving access to the GP&G railway workshops in Greenock, Greenock harbour and steamboat quay and thus the Clyde steamer services.

Over the next decade, business on the GP&G (now the Caley line) proved profitable. Simultaneously, Wemyss Bay was developing into a desirable resort. While some businessmen continued to promote a rail connection between Greenock and Largs, others thought differently. The argument that is regularly offered for building the Wemyss Bay line is that it provided the shortest route to Rothesay for the rapidly growing tripper trade. I believe there was another reason: people will not live in a place which is not easily accessible so developers like Wilsone Broun would face an uphill task selling a large number of feus that could only be reached by an indifferent turnpike road. The trick was to discover how to make Wemyss Bay a magnetic attraction.

The realisation that Rothesay was significantly nearer Wemyss Bay than to either Largs or Greenock gave the proposers the argument they needed - by providing a pier where passengers could step off the train virtually into the boat (unlike Greenock where passengers had to walk through an undesirable part of the town), a low level station could simultaneously encourage the purchase of valuable feus. Largs was still not accessible by rail so a steamer linking Wemyss Bay to Largs and Millport would still shorten the time of passengers to these and other watering places. The sale of prestigious housing sites would allow those eminent in public life to travel more rapidly and comfortably to Glasgow and

London. Clearly a station above Wemyss Bay or Skelmorlie would be less suitable than a station a few hundred yards away, level with where people lived. Perhaps it was significant that Wilsone Broun, financially straitened and selling off parts of his estate, was an early Director of the Greenock and Wemyss Bay Railway Company.

From notes prepared by J.F. McEwan, about 1858, parties interested in building a line from Greenock to Wemyss Bay approached Robson's practice, (now Robson and McCall) and asked them to review the 1845 plans. The intervening years had seen quite an expansion of Greenock and therefore it was not possible to propose the same connection to the former GP&GR line. This time there was plenty of encouragement and finance would not be wanting.

On October 9th 1860, Lt Col Salkeld (Chairman of the Caledonian Railway) and nine fellow Directors (including Thomas Hill, a subsequent Chairman of the Caley who was to be much involved in the running of the Wemyss Bay line) had before them a letter from Mr George C. Bruce seeking the Caley's support to the building of a railway line to Wemyss Bay. The Caley Directors declined to support the venture 'in the meantime'. It is unclear whether Mr Bruce was speaking as an individual or represented a group, nor is it clear whether he was the civil engineer whom the Caley later approached regarding an extension of the Wemyss Bay line. However, the seed was sown and shortly afterwards we find others prepared to sink money into the venture.

Office bearers of the Greenock and Wemyss Bay Railway Company

In 1861 the promoters of the line to Wemyss Bay, undeterred by the Caley's initial reaction, engaged James Keyden, of Keyden, Strang and Keyden, solicitors in Glasgow, to act as Secretary to the Greenock and Wemyss Bay Railway Company. James Forman, CE, a partner in Robson, Forman & McCall in Glasgow was appointed as the line's Engineer. This was by no means the only railway these two had worked on - or were to work on in the future. They set to with energy. These and other officials later working for the G&WBR mostly worked in Glasgow about 10 minutes' walk away from each other and from the Caley offices.

On 9th May, 1861, Robson Forman and McCall published the Prospectus for the 'Proposed Greenock and Wemyss Bay Railway'. They estimated its length at 9½ miles and on the basis of it being 'comparatively free from engineering difficulties', put its cost at £100,000 [*£3.94m]. The promoters were clear who would use it. The Prospectus continued, 'The district abounds in eligible sites for Villas, which will become valuable if the Line is made, while the large and important district below Wemyss Bay, and the Towns and Villages on the Frith [sic] of Clyde, including Rothesay, Innellan, Largs and Millport will also be greatly benefitted by the undertaking. It will give another outlet for the large and rapidly increasing population of Glasgow.' Somewhat hopefully, it suggested that it would provide '. . . a convenient outlet for the people of Greenock to places on the Frith [sic].' There was no mention of any goods traffic. As other lines along the Clyde had proved profitable, so also should this proposal. Citing four successive years of rising returns on the GP&G Railway (taken 14 and more years' earlier!) and giving some questionable figures based on the previous 2½ years' experience of the Helensburgh line - which Secretary Keyden used regularly (having been instrumental in setting it up) - the promoters predicted that the receipts on the Wemyss Bay line would be at least as good as those on the Helensburgh line. Indeed, 'The distance to the Terminus at Wemyss Bay is so much further from Glasgow than Helensburgh, that it would be more difficult for other means of communication to compete for its traffic.' Producing another red herring that the Helensburgh line was handicapped by having to compete with the adjacent Forth and Clyde Canal, the Prospectus failed to mention the rather more direct and co-ordinated rail and ferry competition already established at Greenock. It estimated the returns at £14,820 [*£580,000] pa, which, after deducting 50 per cent for working expenses, left a balance of £7,500 to pay interest on a capital outlay of £100,000.

Whether the promoters envisaged the line might eventually be extended the few miles to Largs, is not clear at this stage.

The committee of management (or provisional Directors) who set up the Greenock and Wemyss Bay Railway Company were James Scott of Kelly, James Lamont of Knockdow, Alexander Struthers Finlay MP (for Argyle) of Castle Toward, and Alexander Ronaldson merchant in Glasgow (all of whom were to be provisional Directors of the Wemyss Bay Steamboat Co.). They were joined by Charles Wilsone Swinfen Broun of Swinfen Hall, Staffordshire and Robert Macfie of Airds. Lamont lived at the south end of the Cowal peninsula, was at one time a prospective MP for Bute, later Chairman and major shareholder of the G&WBR and it seems an inveterate litigant. In 1865, Ronaldson appears to have lived at Beach House in Skelmorlie.

Later Greenock and Wemyss Bay Railway Co. Directors included James Stewart of Garvocks (a merchant in Greenock and sometime MP), Messrs Robert Towers (1865), G.Fyffe Christie W.S., Hugh Brown, Stewart Jamieson, David Carrick R. Buchanan of Drumpellier and John Campbell, Merchant, of Inverardoch, near Doune. David Dunn of Annet House, Skelmorlie was a Director in 1874, and others were James William Turner, W.S., of Greenock (who had been involved with the Glasgow, Paisley and Greenock Railway from its inception till its takeover by the Caley), Robert Maclean (died 1887), Robert Lockhart Alston of Newfield (22 Forsyth Street, Greenock), Charles Magnay (Sunnyside, Caterham and Director of the Phoenix Fire Office in London) and Thomas Spark Hadaway (a merchant at 134 Bath Street, Glasgow).

The first Directors named in the subsequent Act were James Scott, Alexander Finlay, Alexander Ronaldson and James Stewart, who were obviously men of substance as they each had to put £500 [*£20,000] into the company.

The Caley agrees to proceed

On 20th August, 1861, a meeting of Caledonian shareholders was advised that Messrs Keyden and Forman had indicated that the promoters were prepared to proceed with their plan to construct a railway if the Caledonian would subscribe a third of the capital cost of £110,000 [*£4.3m]. The Caley Board postponed making a decision. At this time, the Caley shareholders seemed to spend most of their time proposing new lines and amalgamations and considering the likely dividends. Then on 8th October, they approved a proposal following a meeting of Board members with four of the six promoters - Messrs Scott, Finlay, Lamont and Brown - Keyden and Forman being in attendance.

The proposal briefly confirmed the technical requirements, and how the line was to be funded:

1. the Caley would pay £30,000 of the £110,000 cost;
2. if the cost exceeded £120,000 [*£4.725m], the excess would be borne by the promoters or others, not the Caley;
3. if it cost less than £120,000, the Caley's contribution would be proportionately less;
4. the line would be built single but with sufficient land to allow for doubling, overbridges being made double width, (according to J.F. McEwan, substantial increases in land prices since 1858 caused the company to look for savings, but the purchase of land for doubling shows the company was confident of success);
5. the worst gradient should not exceed 1 in 70;
6. the Caley would work the line 'in perpetuity' at no less than 50 per cent of the traffic receipts.

Keyden replied directly after the meeting, accepting the Caley's decision with minor amendments. On 25th October, 1861, George Graham, the Caledonian Railway Company's

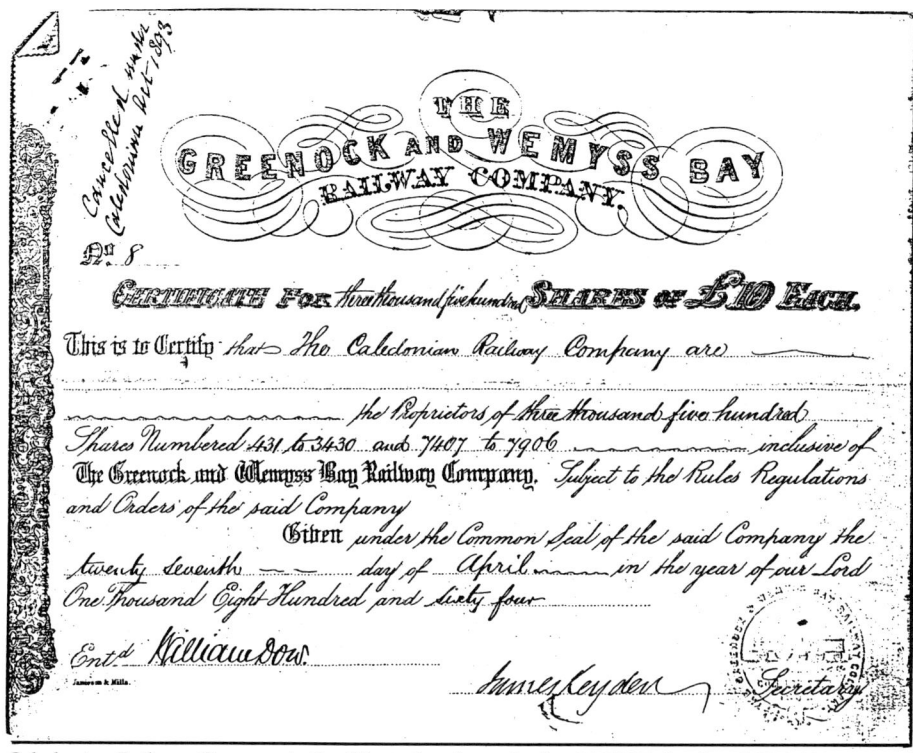

Caledonian Railway Company's Certificate for shares in the G&WBR Co. dated 27.4.1864, signed by James Keyden.
Scottish Record Office Ref.BR/CER(3)2/1-38

Chief Engineer, went to Greenock and then on to Wemyss Bay with Christopher Johnstone (General Manager of the Caley) and Thomas Hill, and spent the afternoon looking at the proposed route for the Railway to Wemyss Bay. This appears to have been the first official visit by Caledonian officials to consider the possibilities 'on the ground'. The proposals had now been agreed by both parties. The first hurdle was over.

A Schedule containing the names of the landowners, reputed owners, lessees, reputed lessees and occupiers was drawn up, the route surveyed, test borings made, land costs assessed and drawings and estimates prepared. The Caledonian Railway Co. stipulated that rails would be 75 lb. weight per lineal yard, 24 feet long, fish jointed on larch sleepers. Sleepers at joints would be 12 in. x 6 in. deep and 10 in. x 5 in. elsewhere, not more than 3ft from each other. (By way of comparison, in 1907, the Caley was using creosoted Baltic redwood or Scotch fir sleepers 9 ft long by 10 in. x 5 in. thick spaced at 2 ft 8½ in. except at fishplates where they were spaced at 2 ft 2½ in.) Timber bridges would not be allowed unless they were carrying private roads over the railway and the Caley demanded that stations, station masters' houses, platelayers and gate keepers' cottages, goods sheds, engine sheds, water tanks connected to a permanent water supply, sidings, loading banks, 'turning tables', station cranes, weighing machines, stationery, signals, wires and telegraphic apparatus be provided to the satisfaction of its Engineer before the line was opened to traffic. This Schedule was attached to the 1862 Act for the line.

After the line was opened to traffic, the Greenock and Wemyss Bay Company was required under the Contract to maintain the 'buildings, works and conveniences therewith' in good order to the satisfaction of the Caley Engineer or a competent neutral engineer. Should the line justify further development, the cost would be shared between the parties.

For its part the Caley agreed to provide the necessary rolling stock 'and plant of every kind' to run the line. They would appoint and pay all agents, officers, bookkeepers, booking and other clerks, servants, porters, line superintendents and others working either in the stations or looking after the line's accounts in its Glasgow office. It would also bear the loss and damage arising from defective plant or 'mismanagement in the working of the line'. This arrangement seemed to work satisfactorily except for a lapse in 1886 when the Wemyss Bay Directors objected 'very much' to their servants being obliged to *work* the signalling apparatus - quickly resolved following a sharp letter to the Caley's solicitor.

The agreement required that the G&WBR appoint and pay a Secretary, treasurer and any other officers needed for their part of the undertaking including engineers to look after the pier and maintain the line. It had to pay for line and building maintenance costs and 'all Public and Parish burdens including Poor's Rates, County Rates, Prison Assessment and Taxes generally', Government Duty on passengers (prior to 1844, a serious imposition on early Scottish lines), feu duties and land lease payments chargeable on the railway and pier. Out of the remaining monies, 25 per cent (one fourth - about which more would be heard) would be passed to the Caley, proportional to its financial contribution to the works.

In the first year, there would be at least three passenger and one goods train each way per day between Glasgow and Wemyss Bay, the Caley deciding the timetable. The Caley would collect the revenues due for use of the Railway and Pier and produce monthly accounts, stating the amount due to the Directors of the Greenock and Wemyss Bay Railway Company.

The Joint Management Committee would comprise three persons named by the Board of Directors of the G&WBR but the Chairman would be one of the Caledonian Railway's nominees, though without a casting vote, no doubt recognising that the Caley was the smaller contributor. Where the committee was equally split, the matter would be referred to arbitration.

On Saturday 22nd March, 1862, George Graham, Christopher Johnstone and Thomas Hill took the train down to Greenock and drove to Wemyss Bay to look at the site of the proposed railway terminus. Very shortly after, on 31st March, 1st and 2nd, April 1862, the contract was signed by James Scott of Kelly and Alexander Ronaldson (as provisional Directors of the Greenock and Wemyss Bay Railway Company Committee of Management), James Keyden, and by the Caledonian Railway Company Directors Thomas Hill, John Ross (a Glasgow merchant) and by Archibald Gibson, the Secretary of the Caledonian Railway Company.

Much later, in October 1874, it was recorded in the Minutes of the Joint Committee of the Caledonian and G&WBR companies that the Rules and Regulations applicable on the Wemyss Bay line were the same as those applying on the Caley system.

There had been a pier for steamers in Whiting Bay, just north of Wemyss Bay. Built about 1845, it was blown down in 1856; the reconstructed pier was blown down on 31st December, 1865 and not rebuilt. It seems the new pier was never conceived as being so closely linked with the station that travel between train and boat would be minimal. If it had been, the pier would have been lengthy and probably parallel to the shore. The need for vessels to approach, dock and steam away rapidly with the minimum of manoeuvring was not as critical as at Rothesay or Greenock where there was real competition. Besides, as proved to be the case with a later landlord of Kelly, the local property owners would have been unhappy with this arrangement as such a pier would have affected the amenity of the Bay, allowing less room for mooring their yachts. The first published plan of the pier was therefore designed to project at right angles to the shore at the northern end of the Bay.

First Developments

The next stage was to prepare a Bill to put before Parliament. Mr Mackay, the Caley's legal adviser, reported that Keyden 'did not understand that the Caley should pay no part of the Parliamentary expenses in the event of the Bill being lost.' (The Bill was to stipulate that win or lose, the Caley would not be required to pay any contribution towards the legal expenses of promoting the Bill through Parliament.) Mackay was instructed to advise Keyden that the Caley would part with no cash till the promoters had spent £20,000 [*£800,000] of their own money.

The draft Contract was prepared. The Caley would work the line for 50 per cent of the gross amount earned on the railway and pier, 'but not to maintain the line for that', nor would it increase its share to £40,000. Once receipts exceeded £8,000 [*£315,000] per annum, provided the Caley received not less than £4,000, it would be content with a 45 per cent return (up to £12,000, according to one newspaper). On a query from Keyden, the Caley said it would not accept that George Burns, a co-founder of the Cunard line, should have an interest in the Pier tolls. Perhaps they feared Burns might introduce steamers and undermine the joint undertaking. In March 1862, Keyden confirmed that his promoters would be proceeding with the Bill.

The Caledonian shareholders' meeting on Friday 7th March, 1862, was momentous. Lt Col Salkeld was in the chair. 'The Directors [of the Caledonian Railway] have agreed to aid in the promotion of a Bill for a line from the Greenock Section to Wemyss Bay, a rising watering place on the Clyde, and a convenient point for the arrival and departure for Steamboats to and from other places on the river. The [Caledonian Railway] Company are to subscribe £30,000 towards the capital and are to work the line in perpetuity on fair terms. The remainder of the Capital will be provided by gentlemen locally interested in the measure.' This last sentence is significant. Railways were often constructed using capital provided by remote investors whose interest was simply financial return - and who were therefore more prone to shift their investment to some more lucrative venture. Local people who had the wherewithal generally committed themselves more deeply and therefore the Caley was at less risk from investors wanting to withdraw.

The Bill sought permission from Parliament to make and maintain a railway,

> ... and all proper works and conveniences connected therewith commencing by a junction with that part of the undertaking of the Caledonian Railway Company known as the Glasgow Paisley and Greenock Railway at or near a point in the parish of Port Glasgow between the point where that Railway is carried across Mary Street of Port Glasgow and the point where the said Railway is carried across the stream called Devol Burn or Devol Glen Burn and terminating at or near a point in the Lands of Wemyss in the Parish of Innerkip and Sub-division Parish of Skelmorlie about half a furlong [i.e. 110 yards] westward from the point of junction of Cliff Terrace Road with Wallace Road.

The promoters applied for permission to build a pier 85 yards long jutting into the sea from the Lands of Wemyss about 165 yards south-west of the end of the line, nearly opposite Major General Swinburne's house (Villa Clutha) on the north side of the Bay. Road works were required to link up with the Greenock to Kelly Bridge turnpike road. The pier was to be parallel sided but generously wide to cater for the expected crowds. (The promoters were to modify their proposals twice before deciding to site the pier near its present location further south near the Kelly Burn, jutting out at right angles to allow up to five vessels to be moored at the height of the season - two on either side of the pier and one across the end. Even so, vessels had to perform some tight turns to draw alongside the quayside.)

The detailed design required some changes. The Caley accepted Mr Forman's proposal for a bridge instead of a level crossing at Bogston - for which they would contribute £200 [*£8,000]. But the Wemyss Bay terminus was too high - Mr Scott of Kelly (one of the Wemyss Bay Directors) asked that the line be constructed no higher than 6 ft above the road level and that trains should stop at Kelly Avenue. He was tactfully advised that these matters would be subject to further discussion.

ANNO VICESIMO QUINTO & VICESIMO SEXTO

VICTORIÆ REGINÆ.

****

Cap. clx.

An Act for making a Railway from the *Glasgow, Paisley, and Greenock* Railway to *Wemyss Bay* in the County of *Renfrew,* and a Pier and Roads in connexion therewith; and for other Purposes.
[17th *July* 1862.]

WHEREAS the making of a Railway from the *Glasgow, Paisley, and Greenock* Railway, which forms Part of the Undertaking of the *Caledonian* Railway Company, to *Wemyss Bay,* with a Pier at *Wemyss Bay,* and Roads connecting the said proposed Railway and Pier with each other and with the Turnpike Road from *Greenock* to *Kelly Bridge,* all in the County of *Renfrew,* would be of great local and public Advantage: And whereas the Persons hereinafter named, together with others, are willing, at their own Expense, to carry such Undertaking into execution, and it is expedient that they should be incorporated for that Purpose: And whereas the said proposed Railway and other Works may be beneficially worked in connexion with the Railways of the *Caledonian* Railway Company, and that Company are willing to work the same, and it is expedient that Provision should be made for that Purpose, and also with regard to the Interchange of Traffic on the said respective Lines of Railway: And whereas the *Caledonian* Railway Company are desirous and it is expedient that they should be enabled to subscribe to the proposed Undertaking, and to take and hold

[*Local.*]   25 *K*   Shares

The Act which authorised the construction of the line from Port Glasgow to Wemyss Bay.
Scottish Record Office Ref.AP(S)/51

One might observe that the Caley's reference to Wemyss Bay as 'a rising watering place' was somewhat wide of the point. The sands were limited, Dr Currie's Hydropathic had yet to be built, and the main objective was to speed the journey to Rothesay.

The Working Agreement

Matters moved swiftly. The contract whereby the Caley operated the line on behalf of the Directors of the Greenock and Wemyss Bay Railway Company was drawn up between the 31st March and 2nd April, 1862, the first of many needed to allow the line to be constructed and managed. It reveals that the sites of the terminus and pier as described in the Bill awaiting consideration by Parliament were being reappraised. The contract confirmed that the Caledonian Railway would contribute towards the capital cost of building the railway and would work the railway, charging agreed levies on the line and pier.

In April, the draft Bill suffered many alterations at the hands of Lord Redesdale. The Caley Board was concerned that the redrafting would give the Board of Trade the power of decennial revision of the Working Agreement, but clearly felt that as it was being referred to the Committee on Unopposed Bills, even though some steamboat owners objected to the railway as likely to put them out of business (and the Clyde trustees being found ineligible to make representations), it was best to accept the amendments.

There was another slight hiccup. On 23rd May, 1862, with Thomas Hill (Deputy Chairman) in the chair, the Caledonian shareholders approved the Bill then before Parliament 'intitled "An Act for making a Railway from the Glasgow, Paisley and Greenock Railway to Wemyss Bay, in the County of Renfrew, and a Pier and Roads in connection therewith, and for other purposes".' However, three shareholders, John Cameron, David Cross and David Sloan, dissented to the approval, 'unless a clause is inserted therein expressly restraining and prohibiting the [Greenock and Wemyss Bay Railway] Company and the Caledonian Railway Company from owning, hiring or subsidising Steam or other vessels or for affording any preference or partiality directly or indirectly to any vessel resorting to the pier referred to..over those belonging to the general trade'. Perhaps these gentlemen were also shareholders in steamboat companies and didn't want to see their investment devalued. No such clause was inserted.

The Act of Parliament of 1862

Matters moved smoothly on and the Greenock and Wemyss Bay Railway Bill was incorporated under Act of Parliament dated 17th July, 1862, 'An Act for making a Railway from the Glasgow, Paisley, and Greenock Railway to Wemyss Bay in the County of Renfrew, and a Pier and Roads in connexion therewith; and for other Purposes', the short title being 'The Greenock and Wemyss Bay Railway Act, 1862'. The company was to be domiciled in Glasgow.

The Act named the subscribers as James Scott, Alexander Struthers Finlay, Alexander Ronaldson, James Stewart, David Law and George Martin who together with the other subscribers and Corporations would be incorporated by the name of 'The Greenock and Wemyss Bay Railway Company' with a common seal and the power to purchase, acquire and hold land and heritages for the purposes of the undertaking. Thus, with share capital set at £120,000 [*£4.85m], to be raised by 12,000 shares of £10 [*£400] each, the development could commence. £90,000 [*£3.63m] would be raised by the Directors, £30,000 [*£1.21m] by the Caley. (A share certificate dated 27th April, 1864 reveals that the Caley purchased 3,000 shares at a comparatively early stage and made a further purchase of 500 shares later.)

The company could borrow up to £40,000 [*£1.6m]. Ordinary meetings had to be held at 6-monthly intervals, eight shareholders forming a quorum, their aggregate shareholding amounting to not less than £3,000 [*£120,000]. Five Directors, each with a minimum

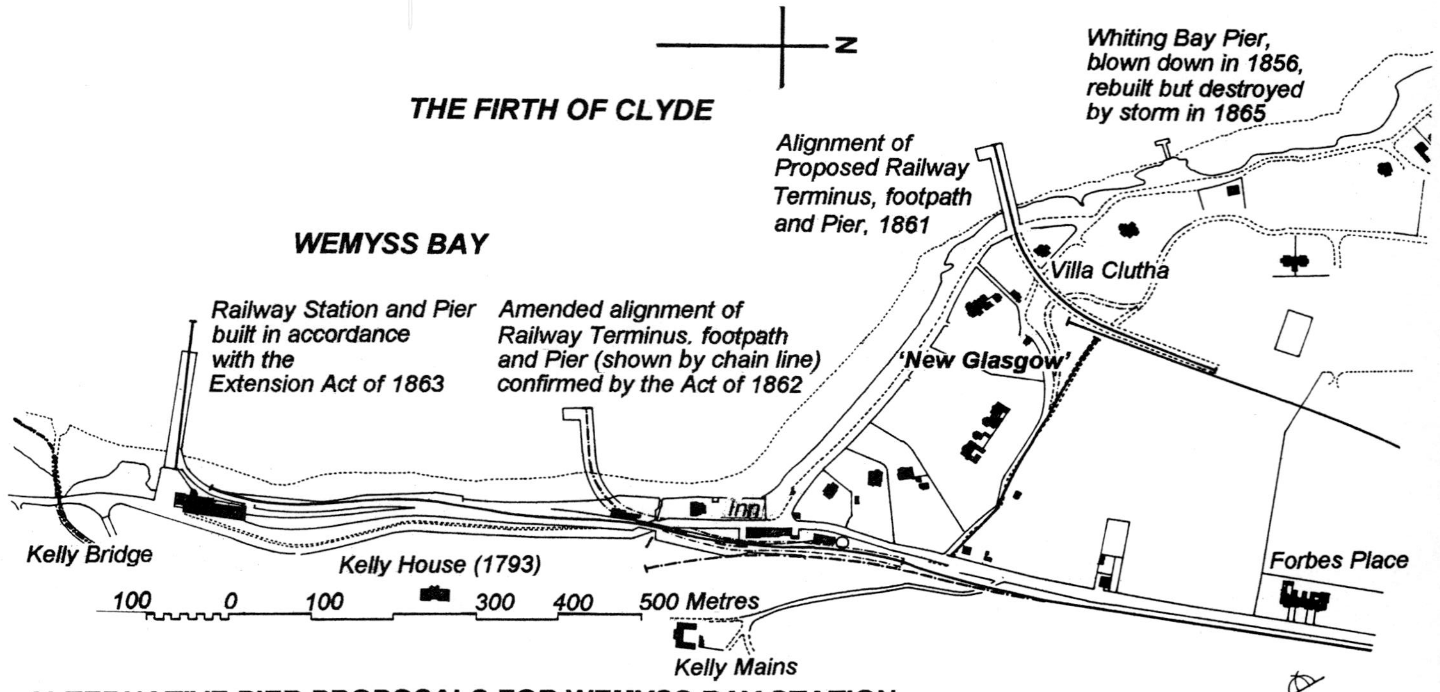

ALTERNATIVE PIER PROPOSALS FOR WEMYSS BAY STATION

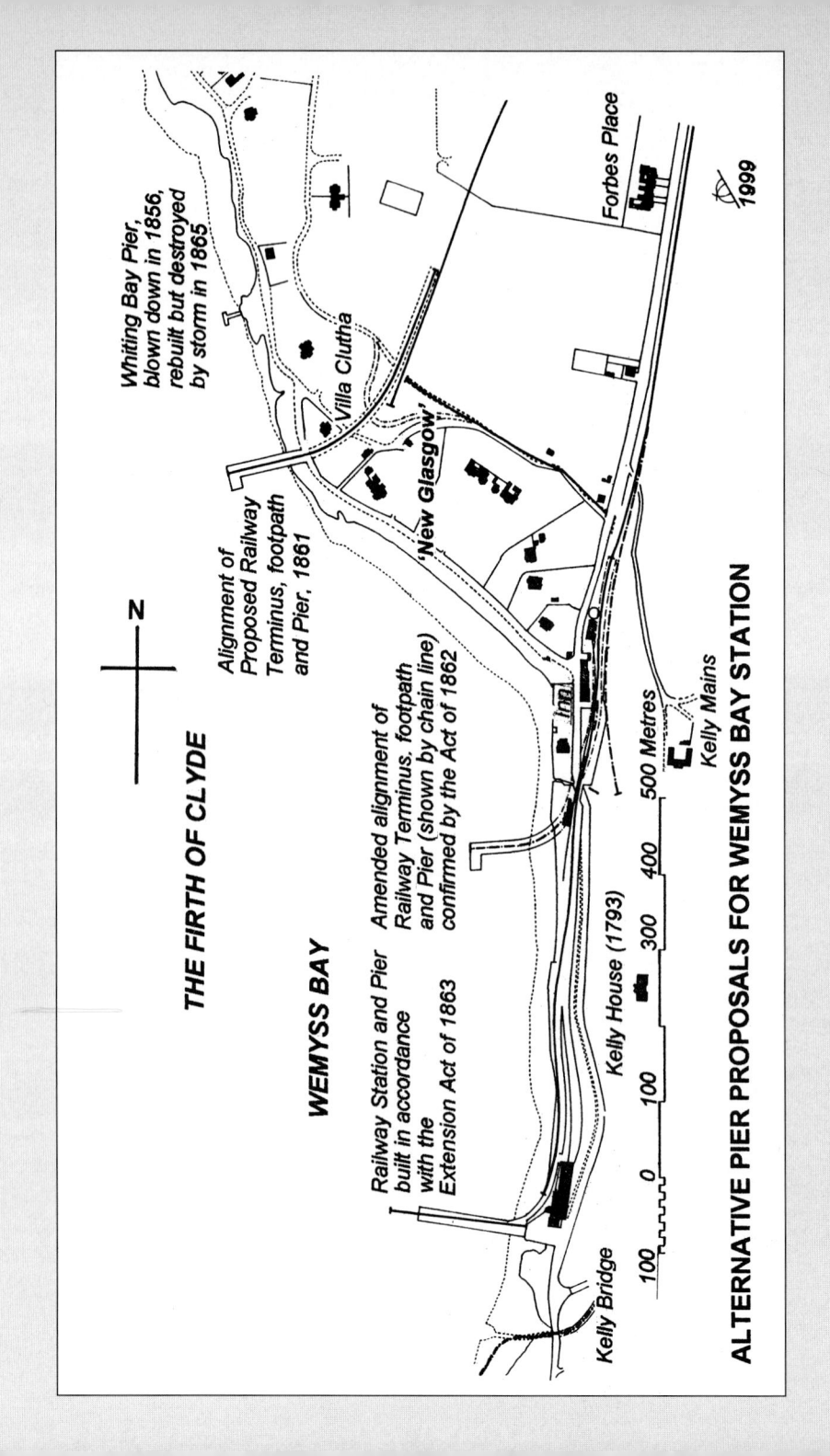

shareholding of 50 shares were to be elected, though the number could be reduced to three - and two Directors would be sufficient for a quorum.

The original plans and sections prepared by Robson Forman and McCall, bearing the names of landowners, had been deposited for public comment 'in the Office of the principal Sheriff Clerk of Renfrewshire' in November 1861. These showed the Wemyss Bay terminus sited as described above at the *north* end of the Bay, a quay curving out into the water 200 yards or so from a small jetty. The station was shown in the middle of 'New Glasgow', at some height above the adjacent houses and would have involved a 300 yard walk to the boat. No railway was shown on the pier. In addition, positioning the station 375 yards from the turnpike road required a new carriageway. Clause 21 of the Act then referred to a change of plan made after the submission of the Bill to Parliament. At the end of March 1862, a deviation route was drawn up showing the line taken 185 yards (170m) south of the 'Inn' (the Wemyss Bay Hotel). From this point, a 'new road' would curve round, cross the Inverkip road, and lead passengers to a pier at the *north-east* end of the Bay. The pier would extend into the sea about 130 yards. The travel distance for passengers was much the same, and again, no line was shown going on to the pier. Clause 22 of the Act confirmed this amendment.

Clause 22 confirmed the start point at Port Glasgow and stated that the line would terminate 'at or near a point on the Lands of Kelly in the Parish of Innerkip and Subdivision Parish of Skelmorlie, about Three-Quarters of a Furlong South-eastward from the Inn at Wemyss Bay, and on the East Side of the turnpike road leading from Greenock to Kelly Bridge'. But this was not the last word on where the station was to be.

A noticeable difference between the Bill and the Act was that the allowance for deviation from the notional construction line for the pier was significantly greater in the abandoned proposal, which suggests that there was considerable opposition from local residents who would have had their view across the Clyde blocked out, by the fishermen whose nearby salmon nets extended into the sea and by the yachting fraternity who would have lost berthing space for their boats. But it is possible that developments at Skelmorlie were now more imminent than a 'Marine Village' on the north side of Wemyss Bay.

The junction with the Glasgow, Paisley and Greenock railway was to be to the satisfaction of the Caledonian Railway's Engineer. The Caley would install the signalling and engage the necessary staff who would work 'under the exclusive control and regulation of the Caledonian Railway Company', the cost being paid by the G&WBR.

The Act sounded rather Gilbertian respecting the seaward works: the pier was to be constructed by the company 'only on such a line as the Lord High Admiral of the United Kingdom of Great Britain and Ireland, or the Commissioners for executing the Office of Lord High Admiral, shall previously approve of'. Various clauses in The Harbours Docks and Piers Clauses Act, 1847 also applied.

From the passing of the Act, the company had four years to construct the railway, pier and alterations to the roads - in other words, everything had to be complete by 16th July, 1866. (It was in fact completed a year earlier.) The Act referred to the agreement between Sir Michael Robert Shaw Stewart to allow the railway to pass through his estates of Greenock and Ardgowan.

The Act fixed various maximum rates by rail per mile, for example (figures in brackets are charges for using company vehicles as against private owners'):

For all dung, compost, lime and limestone -	½d. per ton	(1½d.)	[*25p]
Coal, building stone, bricks, slates, sand -	1½d. per ton	(2½d.)	[*42p]
Sugar, grain, timber -	2½d. per ton	(4d.)	[*67p]
Cotton, fish, merchandise -	3½d. per ton	(5½d.)	[*93p]
Non-rail Carriages	up to 1 ton - 6d.		
Passengers	each 2d.	(4d.)	[*67p]
Horses, cattle	each 2d.	(4d.)	[*67p]
Calves, Sheep	each 1d.	(2d.)	[*34p]

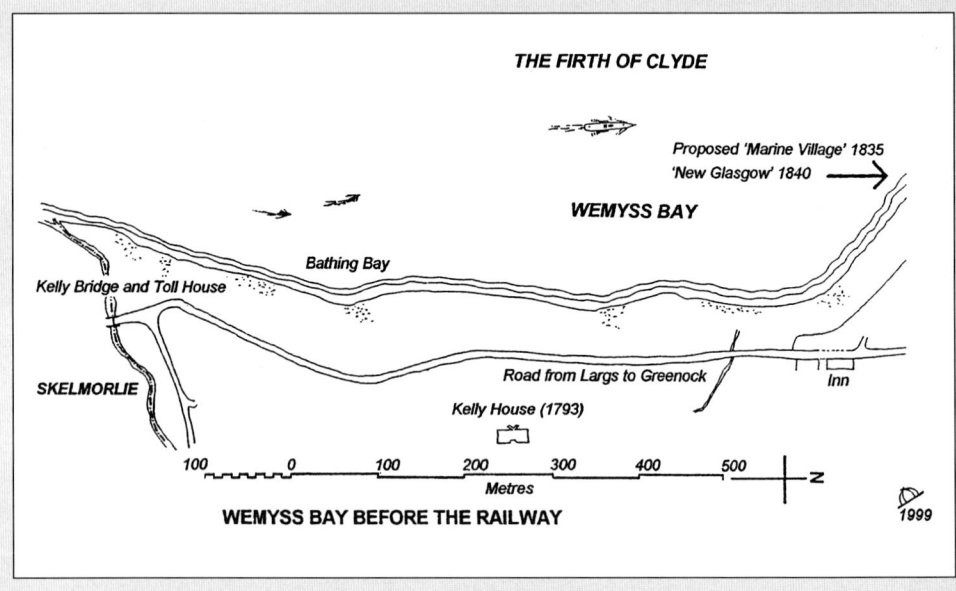

WEMYSS BAY BEFORE THE RAILWAY

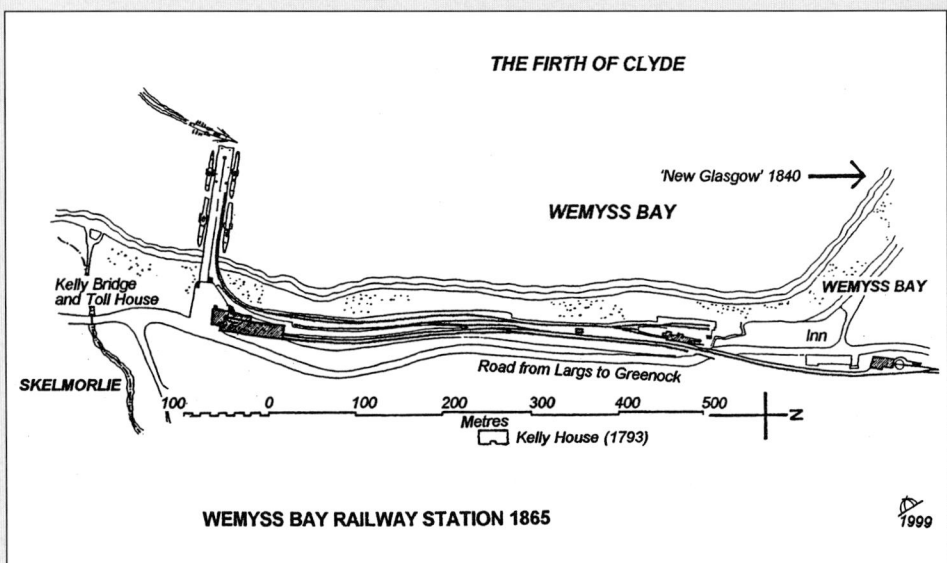

THE FIRTH OF CLYDE

Proposed 'Marine Village' 1835
'New Glasgow' 1840 →

WEMYSS BAY

Bathing Bay

Kelly Bridge and Toll House

SKELMORLIE

Road from Largs to Greenock

Kelly House (1793)

Inn

100 0 100 200 300 400 500
Metres

1999

WEMYSS BAY RAILWAY STATION 1865

THE FIRTH OF CLYDE

'New Glasgow' 1840 →

WEMYSS BAY

Kelly Bridge and Toll House

SKELMORLIE

Road from Largs to Greenock

Kelly House (1793)

WEMYSS BAY

Inn

100 0 100 200 300 400 500
Metres

1999

In addition, a charge of up to 1*d*. per mile was chargeable for each passenger or animal or ton of goods. The normal maximum charges for express and ordinary trains, inclusive of carriage and locomotive charges, would be 3*d*./passenger/mile for first-class carriage (luggage allowance 112 lb.), 2*d*./passenger/mile for second-class carriage (luggage allowance 100 lb.) and 1½*d*./passenger/mile for third-class carriage (luggage allowance 60 lb.). Special train charges were subject to charge under the maximum scale.

The company was permitted to add on a charge for loading, covering and unloading goods at terminal stations where the Company provided this service ('terminals'). Samples of these charges, were:

For all dung, compost, lime and limestone -	2*d*. per ton per mile	[*34p]
Coal, building stone, bricks, slates, sand -	2*d*. per ton per mile	[*34p]
Sugar, grain, timber -	3*d*. per ton per mile	[*50p]
Cotton, fish, merchandise -	4*d*. per ton per mile	[*67p]
Non-rail Carriages up to 1 ton -	6*d*. per ton per mile	[*99p]
Horses, each -	4*d*. per mile	[*67p]
Cattle, each -	2*d*. per mile	[*34p]
Calves, Sheep, each -	¾*d*. per mile	[*13p]

Parcels from small packages up to 500 lb. weight were chargeable on a sliding scale - from 3*d*. to 6*s*. [*50p to *£12] each maximum. Heavier items would be charged on a ton per mile basis.

Then there were maximum charges for the conveying of people, animals and goods using the pier. These varied from 3*d*. [*50p] per person, 8*d*. [*£1.35] per ton for dung, coal and stone and 1*s*. [*£2] for sugar and cotton to 1*s*. 6*d*. [*£3] for carriages over a ton weight. The charge for horses was 8*d*. each, cattle 3*d*. each and calves and sheep 1*d*. each. Berthing charges amounted to ¾*d*. per registered ton on each arrival and departure but if the vessel remained longer than 4 hours in any 24 hour period, the boat owners would be charged 4*d*. per registered ton. If goods required to be craned or weighed on the pier, the company could levy rates from 6*d*. per ton upwards.

Provision was made for the Board of Trade to review the traffic and working Agreement between the Directors of the G&WBR and the Caledonian Railway at 10 year intervals.

The levies outlined in the contract would generally be the same as described in the 1845 Caledonian Railway Act (except for small parcels and terminals), or as subsequently fixed and regulated by a Joint Committee of the Greenock and Wemyss Bay Railway Directors and delegates of the Caledonian Railway.

So, before the first sod of earth had been cut, a substantial amount of money had been spent setting up a provisional committee, surveying and designing the line, agreeing land purchase arrangements, advertising the project, holding meetings, and paying the preliminary and Parliamentary expenses. The Parliamentary procedures had to be carried out in accordance with Standing Orders and involved attending committee meetings on the merits of the Bill, modifying the proposals in the light of objections and then submitting the Bill for Parliamentary approval. Such approval commonly cost about 2.4 per cent of the authorised share capital. Having to modify the proposals, for example to acquire additional borrowing powers - which many railways had to because they had accepted their over-optimistic engineers' estimates or had not included for the unexpected - could mean a further round of Parliamentary proceedings (as the G&WBR found to its cost), thereby pushing up the 'unrecoverable' costs.

The Parliamentary solicitors were Graham, Weems, Graham and Wardlaw of Westminster. It was crucial to the success of a project that people with Parliamentary expertise were engaged where an Act of Parliament was necessary to enable the company to acquire the necessary land (unless it could be secured privately).

Building the line commences and the Extension Act of 1863

Inevitably more money was needed to cope with the proposed changes. In September 1862, Mr Forman sought £9,000-£10,000 [*£360,000-£400,000] extra to extend the line at Wemyss Bay, the Caley being asked to contribute a third. At the end of September, George Graham went to 'Greenock and Weems Bay' [sic] where he, Christopher Johnstone and Thomas Hill looked at the site of the proposed extension before lunching at Kelly. There must have been some indecision on the benefits·of the extension as Keyden later asked the Caley to obtain an opinion from Mr Blyth (an eminent railway engineer) on the merits of the alternative termini. The Caley did not oblige but made allowance for some additional expense. In October 1862 they declined another request from Keyden for more money to enable the Cartsburn tunnel to be made double width. But in June 1863 they relented, offering £7,600 [*£315,000] for doubling the tunnels on the line 'provided the Wemyss Bay Company will pay 4 per cent on the above sum until the whole line be doubled'. The Wemyss Bay company were very reluctant, but eventually an agreement was worked out.

The line and pier were originally programmed to be complete and ready for traffic by 1st June 1864. The bulk of the work was constructed by the undernoted contractors:

Messrs *Young & McCall* for the first 5¼ miles of line from Wemyss Bay junction half-a-mile west of Port Glasgow station to Spango Farm (which we shall call the 'Greenock' contract for want of a name);
Messrs *A. & K. McDonald* for the next 3¾ miles (the 'Inverkip' contract.);
Mr *Hugh Kennedy* for the last portion of the line including the station, engine house and 'turning table' (the 'Wemyss Bay' contract);
Mr *James Young* of Sunderland for the Wemyss Bay pier contract.
Four other contractors' names have survived -
Messrs *James Goodwin & Co.*, Ardrossan and Messrs *Stewart* of Kilmarnock for the iron girders for the bridges and the Daff and Kip viaduct steelwork;
Messrs *Stephen & Sons*, Darlington Works, Southwark, London, for the signals;
The Railway Company for the rails and chairs for the permanent way.

The appointed contractors employed Irish labour for navvying work, although it has been suggested that Scottish labour was also extensively used. The 'first turf' was cut in November 1862, a short distance from Brigend House which had been occupied by Thomas King, Esq., writer, Greenock for many years. Brigend House was sold to the G&WBR when the ground was surveyed and later disposed of to Mr McCall, the contractor for the adjacent stretch of line.

The onset of a 'rigorous winter' delayed real progress till early 1863 and shortly after work was well under way, it was found that owing to the unexpectedly difficult character of the cuttings and formation of the embankments, it was going to be impossible to finish the line on time. The company therefore 'spontaneously' granted an extension of time to the contractors. What with the emergence of other serious problems, the original 19 month contract took a further year to complete.

During the time the 1862 Bill was making its way through Parliament, it was decided that certain amendments were needed. On 7th April, 1863, the Caledonian shareholders unanimously approved the changes and the amending Bill then going through Parliament.

The amendments were incorporated in an Act of Parliament dated 8th June, 1863, 'An Act for making an Extension of the Greenock and Wemyss Bay Railway, in the County of Renfrew, and a Pier in connection therewith, in lieu of the Pier authorised by 'The Greenock and Wemyss Bay Railway Act, 1862'; and for other purposes' - the short title being the 'Greenock and Wemyss Bay Railway Extension Act, 1863'. The Act allowed the extension of the line southwards across the land of James Scott of Kelly, one of the Directors, to about a furlong north of Kelly Bridge, the pier being likewise relocated. This reduced the distance travellers had to walk between train and boat to about 220 yards and additionally a goods line would run on to the pier. Other amendments required that the company 'shall exhibit upon the pier every night, from sunset to sunrise, such light or lights, . . . for the guidance of vessels, as the Board of Trade may require' and the deletion of the reference of road access to the station - no longer needed as the station would be built alongside the turnpike road. The Act allowed the company to raise a further £30,000 [*£1.24m] for the undertaking, (£5,000 of which would be contributed by the Caley) and borrow up to a further £10,000.

Meanwhile, some time in 1863, James Keyden was appointed Secretary of the Wemyss Bay Steamboat Company.

Quite some time after work commenced, in May 1863 the Caley authorised a first instalment of £7,600 [*£315,000]. In July, George Graham 'drove to Wemyss Bay' from Greenock, no doubt by horse and carriage. (It is an interesting reminder of a bygone age to note that the railway Engineer's expenses included payment for a 'coachman and tolls' when being driven near Moffat that year.) By August 1863, the Board had paid another £13,502 5s. 7d. [*£560,000], and George Graham recorded that he had again inspected the Wemyss Bay line.

The Caley Board was informed at its August 1863 meeting that the line to Wemyss Bay was in progress and that an Act had been obtained for the short extension to the line. But the Caley Directors were not satisfied with the depth of the report and asked Mr Graham for a more detailed résumé 'on the model of the Lockerby [sic] report.'

The next payment of £13,333 6s. 8d. [*£567,000] by the Caley was made in January 1864. (This included £3,333 6s. 8d. of the £5,000 authorised under the Greenock and Wemyss Bay Railway Extension Act.) In May 1864, Keyden requested £200 [*£8,500] from the Caley for the work at Bogston Bridge, but Mr Graham reported that work was as yet incomplete. Payment was certified a year later. The Caley's final payment of £11,666 13s. 4d. [*£497,000] was made in July 1864. The line cost about £155,000 [*£6.6m] to build.

Acquiring land for the line

The Greenock and Wemyss Bay Railway was constructed mostly on land acquired from Sir Michael Robert Shaw Stewart Bart., small parcels being obtained from Duncan Darroch of Gourock, James Scott of Kelly and a number of others. The majority of land transactions were agreed in 1862 and early 1863 though sometimes land purchase took years to sort out.

Prior to 1867, James Scott, proprietor of Kelly acquired a right of access to over seven acres of ground by the shore, on the other side of the line from his estate. Mr Scott was one of the original Directors of the G&WBR and the Agreement, drawn up in May 1862 with two of the other provisional directors, Alexander Finlay MP and Alexander Ronaldson, allowed the track to cross his land, subject to height and width requirements, to a point 'at or near the inn or hotel' on the plans. The line was to be to the south of the turnpike road. The Agreement stated that the land to be taken should allow for a line of double track and that Mr Scott should be able to have a siding running into any quarry he desired to make off the line - but only one siding would be allowed at any one time. The fledgling company would have to construct three bridges to permit access to the Kelly estate. For this, the G&WBR would pay £10,000 [*£403,000] for the land, payable in company stock. Two of Strang, Keyden and Sons clerks witnessed the signatures.

As I previously mentioned, the Greenock and Wemyss Bay Railway Extension Act of 1863 brought the line to 150 yards short of the Kelly Burn on the Ayrshire boundary, making the proposed new railway more accessible to people in Skelmorlie. This involved bridging the turnpike road - by a bridge of a character and style to the satisfaction of Mr Scott. The revised alignment was shown on plans prepared by Robson, Forman & McCall. The Agreement pointed out that the conveyance related only to that which Scott had a right to as part of the shore 'belonged to the Crown as part of the alvens of the Firth of Clyde'. The G&WBR had right to any rocks on the surface, but not to any minerals under the same, though how Mr Scott was to access them was not described. Mr.Scott also held to himself fishing rights, timber felled on 'his' land and the exclusive right to the removal of gravel from the shore. Further, the amenity of Kelly House was not to be affected by the railway. The Agreement also covered the appearance of any buildings erected on railway ground and the provision of evergreens positioned wherever Mr Scott required. The cost of this extra land was £5,000 [*£207,000], £2,000 being paid in stock of the company.

Other kinds of Agreement were necessary, for example that with the Shaws Water Joint Stock Co. (formed in 1825) to allow the railway to cross an aqueduct serving Greenock's mills and residences, at a point near Upper Greenock station.

In 1852, prior to the appearance of the railway, Sir Michael conveyed to the Provost, Magistrates and Town Council of Greenock land known as Wellington Park. As this would be bisected by the railway, the G&WBR laid out replacement land provided by Sir Michael and arranged to build a footbridge to link the two parts, though it would seem, not before 1869. In March 1866, after the Greenock and Wemyss Bay line was established, the railway company entered into working Agreements with the Wemyss Bay Steamboat Company, Gillies & Campbell and with the Caledonian Railway Company.

A particularly long drawn out settlement remaining unconcluded for years, related to the feu charter respecting Darroch's land beside the turnpike road at Ravenscraig. Keyden wrote to his Edinburgh solicitors, Messrs Skene Edwards and Bilton of 21 Hill Street in May 1886 and again in September. By this time the line had been in use for 20 years! In October 1886, Keyden wrote with a touch of asperity to Skene Edwards, 'As your vacation is now over, and the Court has set down again, may we request you to prepare the feu contract between Major Darroch and this Company - our directors are blaming us for the delay'. Later, he asked Skene Edwards for a plan so that he could 'reconcile the quantity of land with the feu duty paid' - from 1866. As no plan appeared, Weir was asked to prepare a drawing to enable the feu disposition to be checked. Keyden then found the company had been overcharged 15s. 4½d. [*£33] a year since 1862. The matter dragged out; Skene Edwards referred to a letter from the line's Engineer way back in April 1867 but were reluctant to show it to Keydens, who could not find their copy. Then Keyden's dropped their claim to recover the overpayment to 5s. 3d. per annum. In the end after considerable correspondence, Keyden's sent Skene Edwards £55 4s. 6d. [*£2,750] to conclude the transaction.

(In 1903 Skene Edwards and Carson lodged a claim respecting land at Ravenscraig purchased for the widening of the line. This was rather more speedily resolved - for £85 [*£4,200].)

Other land transactions were still being questioned 20 years after the line opened. In October 1885, Keyden wrote to John Macdougal, WS in Greenock, that the G&WBR should not have paid for Ardgowan Estates' land over Inverkip tunnel; also, less of Sir Michael's land had been used for Upper Greenock station than was covered in the Agreement. The feu contracts and dispositions for this last item were still being processed a year later. In November 1886, Keyden wrote to Mr T.S. Hadaway, a G&WBR Director, outlining the land transactions being negotiated. Thirty poles (somewhat over 900 square yards) had been acquired for sidings for Alex Scott and Sons' Sugar Refinery at Berryards in Greenock and 33 poles had been bought from the Greenock Water Trust plus eight poles where the line crossed their aqueduct. In the muddle of who owned what, it seems that Sir Michael had been paid feu duties for land he did not actually own! It took some time to recover the monies inadvertently paid to him.

Some idea of the proportions of land purchased can be gauged by the feu duties paid. For example, in 1886, this amounted to £192 3s. 9d. [*£9,450] to Mr Darroch and £937 8s. 3d. [*£46,000] to Sir Michael Shaw Stewart and £1 12s. 10d. [*£80] to a third party.

BUILDING THE LINE

The 'Greenock' Contract

On 30th March, 1865, the *Glasgow Herald* described in detail the landscape and the construction problems experienced. The writer extolled the attractions of the line, the delightful country, the suitability for the tripper trade and the potential for house building. He commenced his narrative at Port Glasgow station which he described as a 'neatly kept station, with its trim little garden, arranged in the most tasteful order'. Half-a-mile west at what was then the pretty Devol's Glen at the extremity of the town, the new line branched uphill where 'an extensive signal establishment, having all the latest appliances for effectively signalling approaching trains' had been built. (One of several high waterfalls in the glen is called 'Wallaces's Loup', reputed to have been jumped on horseback by the 'hero of Scotland' as he escaped his pursuers). The first 2½ miles of line rise 210 feet at the steep gradient of 1 in 66½ - 1 in 67½ causing the contractors, Messrs Young & McCall to lay a double line of rails for about 300 yards at the bottom 'to give greater security for the shunting of trains', the remainder being built as single with provision for doubling.

The line proceeded through Bogston Farm, Gibb's Hill Farm, Fence Wood Farm and after crossing the Lady Burn, through Brigend (or Bridgend) Farm from where the Clyde and Tail o' the Bank could be seen along with the Cardross shore. In the distant background he saw the peaks of Benlomond and The Cobbler. To the north and north west he observed Helensburgh and Rosneath and the rugged range of mountains known as 'Argyll's Bowling Green' at the south end of Loch Goil where it joins Loch Long. Further uphill the line passed Brigend House in front of which he noted a large mound of earth, the remains of the castle of Easter Greenock owned by the Crawfords till 1669 when it was transferred to Sir John Shaw of Greenock. Wester Greenock Castle, owned by the Shaws, was incorporated into a mansion house on a prominent elevation above the town of Greenock.

Just beyond Brigend is the cutting where the 'first turf' was cut. 310 yards in length, 50 feet deep, it provided a severe challenge to the navvies, being mostly composed of bastard freestone of great hardness. A whin dyke about 20 feet, thick running at an angle through it, just made it more difficult. Later the Greenock & Ayrshire Railway crossed over this section of line on a 1 in 70 grade. The cutting was immediately followed by the straight 285 yds-long Cartsburn tunnel through Barwharly Hill on Mr Crawford's estate where two-thirds of the rock was bastard freestone and the remainder blue till, of great tenacity. Hundreds of men were engaged night and day at the cutting, to finish it on time. The tunnel was lined out in brick bonded with Arden lime and Roman cement and faced with hewn freestone at both ends. The line continued over the innocent Cartsburn, whose swollen channel discharged 18.7 million gallons of water on to Cartsdyke, once a small riverside community, killing about 40 people and causing great damage to houses and mills, when the Whinhill reservoir burst in November 1835. The writer noted that this industrious part of Greenock was generally covered by clouds of dense smoke. (Plans of the time show flour and rice mills, sugar refineries, iron foundries, a rivet manufactory, tannery, chemical works, potteries, saw mills and a brick and cement works all within a mile of one another. A little farther away were a carpet factory and a cotton spinning works.)

The next portion was constructed mostly across Shaw Stewart land. After Strone Farm, the line rose through the extensive Wellington Park, gifted by Sir Michael Shaw Stewart to Greenock in 1852. The predations of both the G&WBR and the G&SWR Greenock and Ayrshire line were forcing Greenock Corporation to look for substitute recreation space. Berryards Farm followed then a stretch of level line through Greenock station which was sited on the south side of the line at the top of Lynedoch Street, immediately behind the Drumfrochar Road Sugar Refinery occupied by Messrs Anderson, Orr & Co. A stone station house was attached but the goods depôt proposed on the north side had yet to be built.

The next mile or so provided different problems. Greenock was largely powered by water stored uphill and delivered by the Shaws Water Company so the conduits crossing the line had

Interior of the original Wemyss Bay station looking south showing the covered platform and seaward-facing accommodation. Note the preponderance of advertisements. The Sunlight soap advertisement indicates that it was taken after 1893 - probably 1900. *Ian B. Smith Collection*

The original Wemyss Bay station with work under way on the roof, probably about 1902.
Andrew F. Swan Collection

BUILDING THE LINE

to be maintained in service as the line was built. New water courses were formed under the line or the water was siphoned overhead. At Murdieston farm, the writer observed the Greenock Cemetery 'recognised as one of the most beautiful places of sepulture in the kingdom' which included the monument to James Watt. At this point, town gave way to a 'magnificent pastoral landscape'. Uphill was the Shaws Water Company's Works through which water from Loch Thom flowed to Greenock's mills past the Everton Paper Mill (later Overton). In the valley were two large reservoirs, one owned by the town and the other in process of being conveyed to the Corporation. Hole Farm followed, the railway then crossing the estate of Mr Darroch of Gourock. More whin rock was experienced at Penny Fern (or Farm) and Fancy Farm. The line then skirted the base of a hill on Branchton Farm and ran alongside the Greenock to Inverkip turnpike road. Next came a view of the attractive Glen of Inverkip before arrival at Ravenscraig station which the writer thought ill-placed to serve Gourock, two miles north. Shortly after the station the line passed through a cutting to emerge at Spango Farm.

The 'Inverkip' Contract

Messrs A. & K. McDonald continued the line over the next 3¾ miles, through Kingston Farm to Dunrod Farm where the contractor had some difficulty stabilising the embankment. Beyond the farm steading was constructed a siding with a crane for use by local farmers. Two high viaducts followed - the first of four spans over the River Kip, about 76 feet high, the second of five spans 90 feet above the wooded defile through which the Daff trickles down its lovely valley. All the spans were constructed of wrought-iron girders 55 feet each, made by Messrs Stewart of Kilmarnock. The viaducts are separated by cuttings through hard freestone on Bogside Farm and Leap Farm and at the time the line was constructed, it was possible to see the westward shore of the Clyde including the Bullwood and Innellan while near the line was Langhouse mansion, the residence of James McFie of Airds. By this time, the line was falling at 1:70 towards Wemyss Bay. Inverkip station followed, the *Glasgow Herald's* writer commenting that he knew little of the history of the place except that witches once seemed to abound in the area and when apprehended and sentenced were subjected to a painful death.

Inverkip station was built somewhat uphill of the village. Just west a cutting about 250 yards long and 45 feet deep was made through 'pudding stone' and whinstone. This led directly into the 180 yds-long Inverkip tunnel cut on a curve through the whinstone and old red sandstone of Common Craig Hill. The tunnel was lined like Cartsburn tunnel. The line now sloped down southward with a broad view of the 'Frith', through Berfern Farm, Finnoch Bog Farm and Brueacre (or Brewacre) Farm.

The 'Wemyss Bay' Contract

More whinstone was experienced in Hugh Kennedy's contract, part of which included a cutting up to 35 feet deep, parallel to the turnpike road and 1¼ miles long, formed through old red sandstone and whinstone. There was a siding, cranes and a smithy in a widened part of the cutting. At the south end was built a wide bridge 95 feet long to take the road to Kelly House, then the residence of James Scott. The gradient on this contract was 1 in 70, falling towards Wemyss Bay. The writer commented that the house had an elevated view of the Firth but little pretensions to architectural elegance.

A large water tank, engine shed and 'turning table' were built about half-a-mile north of the station. Then followed an interesting detail: a ticket platform built north of the turnpike road bridge to allow tickets to be collected, presumably to ensure there were no free rides and to avoid holding up passengers as they hurried down to the steamers. Tickets were later collected at Inverkip.

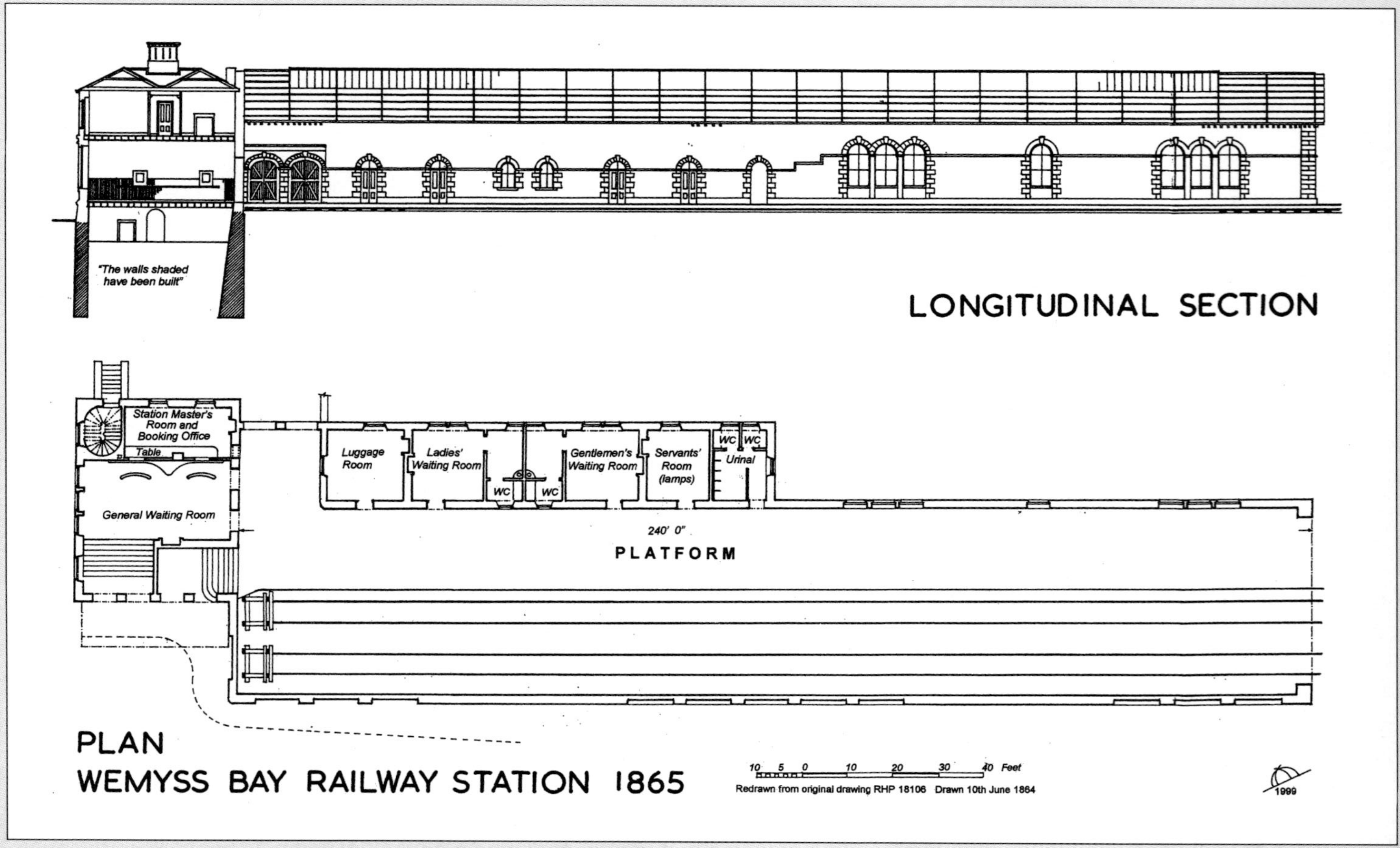
"The walls shaded have been built"
LONGITUDINAL SECTION
Station Master's Room and Booking Office
Table
General Waiting Room
Luggage Room
Ladies' Waiting Room
WC
WC
Gentlemen's Waiting Room
Servants' Room (lamps)
WC
WC
Urinal
240' 0"
PLATFORM
PLAN
WEMYSS BAY RAILWAY STATION 1865
10 5 0 10 20 30 40 Feet
Redrawn from original drawing RHP 18106 Drawn 10th June 1864
1999

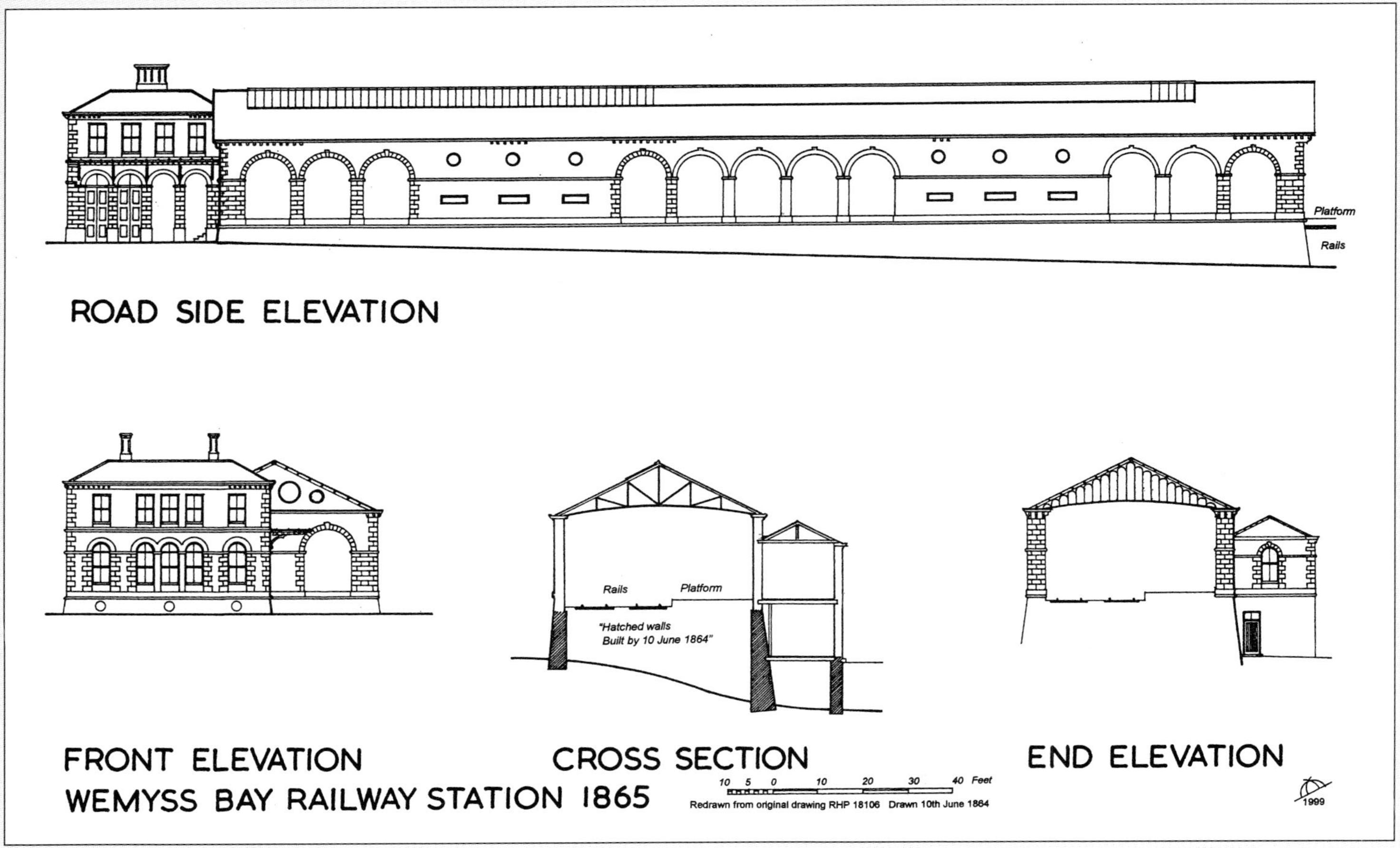
Platform
Rails
ROAD SIDE ELEVATION
Rails
Platform
"Hatched walls
Built by 10 June 1864"
FRONT ELEVATION
CROSS SECTION
END ELEVATION
10 5 0 10 20 30 40 Feet
WEMYSS BAY RAILWAY STATION 1865
Redrawn from original drawing RHP 18106 Drawn 10th June 1864
1999

The original Wemyss Bay station entrance as viewed from the south. The entrance and station offices are on the ground floor with the station master's house above. The trainshed with its single platform on the west side abuts the entrance canopy.

Caledonian Railway Association Collection

Wemyss Bay pier looking towards the original Wemyss Bay station with Kelly House behind. Note the lifeboat suspended above the pier. Behind it, coal is being bagged on a trailer from a coal truck. Taken about 1900.

Ian B. Smith Collection

Meanwhile a handsome station 'like a gentleman's mansion house' had been constructed at Wemyss Bay. Original drawings indicate that the station was constructed in two phases, the foundations 'by 10th June, 1864' presumably under the main civil works 'package'. The square Georgian style two-storey stone station house had windows on the ground floor with rounded upper sashes while the smaller first floor windows were rectangular sash and case. The entrance to the booking hall below was through openings on the east (road) side. A light canopy - subsequently deepened by a fretted valance projecting into the infill panel on the gable of the station shed - provided some cover (a protection not matched on the exposed seaward side). Above the entrance was the station master's house. On the west side, a two-storey block entered along its length from the platform at first floor level, provided waiting rooms, 'dressing rooms', toilets and refreshment rooms, as well as the bookstall (latterly let to John Menzies of Glasgow and Edinburgh); below were the various station and pier staff offices and stores. The 'train shed' covered the two tracks, only one of which had a platform. The shed had an 'iron' roof with glazing along the length of the ridge capping. It was 31 feet high, covering the first 240 feet or so of the 502 feet platform. A later plan shows the booking office relocated to the end of the platform, a refreshment room occupying most of the ground floor below the station master's flat.

By the end of March 1865, a 'back shunt' had been formed on the seaward side northwards from the station towards the turnpike bridge where the goods sheds were being built. This low level line ran back southwards and on to the pier and as the writer said, 'Invalids can thus be conveyed alongside the steamboat if necessary, without leaving the railway carriage'.

The Pier Contract

The timber portion of the pier was built by Mr Young of Sunderland and commenced at the low-water mark. It was 500 feet long by 50 feet broad, with a central palisade for the protection of passengers during stormy weather. The pier was made of greenheart timber, planked with red pine.

The Navvies

Seemingly late in the day, the Rev. Walter Boyd is recorded as organising special meetings in 1865 for workmen on the line. With heavy construction work substantially complete and therefore the workforce run down to a minimum, one would not have expected 'special meetings' at this stage. Possibly several workers, having spent a year or more in a camp in the area had moved into the community when the camp closed and the bulk of the workforce dispersed. It is likely that the line opened before work was finished and that some workers stayed on to help run the railway.

Many of these men may well have come from Ireland and as the works at Wemyss Bay would have retained a sizeable workforce for some time, quarrying stone, blasting through the hillside, tunnelling, laying the elevated track and building the station, it would be surprising if a camp had not been set up beside the line. A convenient spot would have been about a mile up from Wemyss Bay station, beyond Forbes Place, at a spot where workmen were near Kelly Quarry, a major rock cutting, and not far from Inverkip tunnel a mile further up. The Ordnance Survey Map of the period shows 'Cranes' and a 'Smithy' in this vicinity, though these features disappeared later. It is unlikely that the gentility would have been too keen to share their pleasant places with what were often regarded as rumbustious ruffians. It is hardly evidence, but the Roman Catholic chapel to St Joseph and St Patrick, built many years later at Forbes Place where there was only a handfull of houses, might have been constructed near a temporary chapel used by the railway builders. The fact that two saints'

Approach to Wemyss Bay station with goods trucks in front of the goods shed to the left, the signal box somewhat north of the line linking the westward station platform to the low level line. This link line commences about the fifth post south of the signal box. Taken about 1900.
Ian B. Smith Collection

The first Wemyss Bay station from near the signal box with headshunt and line to the pier on the right - about 1900. *Ian B. Smith Collection*

names are used suggests an amalgamation of two congregations implying that the patron saint of Ireland came supported by an Irish cast - and stayed after they had left.

That there was a camp in this vicinity is revealed in a short piece in the *Glasgow Herald* as the line neared completion. Saturday morning was pay day, after which the navvies would descend on Gourock, Greenock or Port Glasgow to get intoxicated. Fights broke out and some spent the night in police cells. One night, a 60-year old drunk labourer, a widower from Ireland, who resided in one of the temporary huts erected on the opposite side of the turnpike road from the 35 foot deep cutting '. . . which begins Mr Kennedy's contract on the Wemyss Bay Railway . . .', was found dead having fallen off a narrow gangway. The 'bridge', used by navvies employed on the railway, was protected by a rail on one side only '. . . unsafe for a sober man - much worse for the intoxicated'.

George Graham appears to have left the Caley's supervision to Henry Ward, their General Superintendent, and to the permanent site staff, these being (at least at the end of the works) Mr Sloan the resident engineer and Mr Speed the inspector of works. During 1864 and 1865, Graham visited the line only four or five times, though there is evidence that he paid trips to Greenock in 1864 to see work in progress and have a (rare) meeting with Sir Michael Shaw Stewart, (though this seems to have been regarding work between Port Glasgow and Greenock). Once he went down to look at the 'new junction for Weemys [sic] Bay line'.

The line for sale

In March 1865, the *Glasgow Herald* commented that the proliferation of lines constructed by different companies served no purpose other than to injure a rival, without materially benefiting the proposer. Referring to shareholders, it stated that 'they will discover too soon the truth that the glories of war between railways, as between nations, must be paid for in very hard cash indeed'. The words mirrored the situation on the Wemyss Bay line where despite the ultimate cost not being very far above the projected figure, nevertheless some Directors were feeling stretched. In November 1864 Mr Scott of Kelly, and again in December 1865, Messrs Scott, Lamont, Christie and Stewart approached the Caley Board with a view to the Caley buying them out.

In February 1866, *Engineering* magazine reported that a large number of projects had been dropped, partly because of the high bank rate and the great demand for capital. In the same month, Archibald Gibson reported to his Board following a meeting he had had with Mr Ronaldson, another of the Wemyss Bay Directors. Possibly because of the difficult trading conditions then prevailing, the line was for sale to the Caledonian, 'for 20s. in the pound, payable without interest'. The Caley Board decided to postpone making a decision. They too were finding trading difficult and had to curtail expansion due to 'the great panic of 1866'.

Railway promotion was much more difficult. In June 1866, *Engineering* reported that Lord Redesdale proposed a change to Standing Orders in the House of Lords 'to throw out all railway bills which are not brought forward upon actually subscribed capital with a deposit laid down'. The magazine commented that this would virtually stop all railway building; that capital was now no longer freely available for railway undertakings and that railway shares were as hazardous as those of any other undertaking. The magazine lamented that those venturing into railways had to sink large sums of money over an extended period [in surveys, legal preparation and Parliamentary expenses] without guarantee that they would be allowed to continue, whereas others could invest and immediately recoup where they did not have to obtain an Act of Parliament. Parliamentary and legal costs alone amounted to about 5 per cent of the capital expenditure.

The Greenock and Wemyss Bay shareholders remained unhappy with their investment. In September 1869, Mr Strang offered the company to the Caley at a time when things looked bleak. In October 1870, the Caley declined the proposed terms. Again, in February 1871, the Caley declined to purchase the line. In 1873, Swinfen Broun offered his shares to the Caley, but once more, they were not accepted, even though the Caley had recently been buying up the company's shares.

In December 1884, Mr Lamont offered his shares to the Caley and received the same response he had in 1865. The shareholders probably also felt that as the history of the Caley was punctuated by the takeover of small companies, it was only a matter of time before they were bought out.

The promoters of the railway expected their investment to reap dividends from the tripper trade and from the development of Wemyss Bay as a desirable place to live. But until the line was established, people were not willing to build houses. Had they built houses before the line arrived, they would have had to commute using the turnpike road which was in poor condition in places partly caused by the railway works. Encouragingly, shortly before the line opened, the *Glasgow Herald* commented that 'notwithstanding this railway having been constructed through the districts of Inverkip and Wemyss Bay, few additional villas are in course of erection. No doubt much convenience will be experienced by gentlemen having villas in the district'. It concluded by wishing the Wemyss Bay company 'every speed and large half-yearly dividends'.

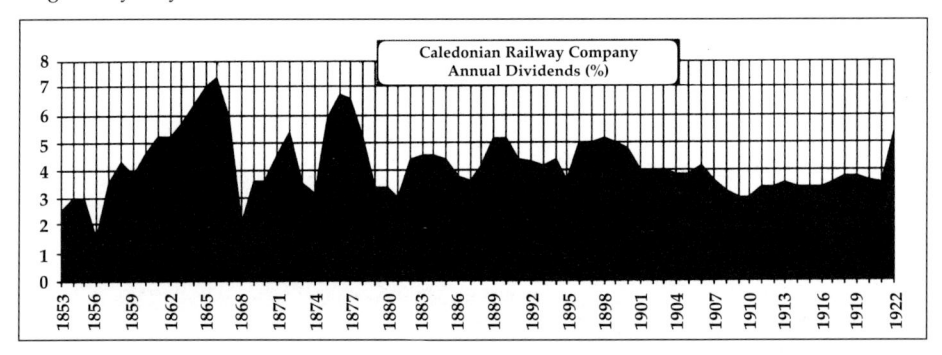

Caledonian Railway Company Annual Dividends (%)

It was 16 years after the initial shareholders invested their capital before the company paid its first dividend of 5½ per cent - in 1878. It is therefore no surprise that they tried so many times to dispose of their shares. The public's attraction to railways has rarely been matched by financial return of like proportions. However, an indication of the railway's improving fortunes is revealed in the pier dues collected:

1870/71 - £47 10s.   [*£1,870]   for 407,985 passengers [approx. *0.46p/passenger]
1880/81 - £624 9s. 4d. [*£26,225]   for 770,632 passengers [approx. *3.4p/passenger]

The Caley's finances were also steadily improving. Between 1881 and 1890, dividends were generally 4 per cent or better, peaking at 5 per cent in 1890. The share price rose to £108 [*£4,600] in 1882 before declining to £96 [*£4,875] in 1887 then rising to £131 [*£6,450] in 1890.

The railway commences operations

On 11th April, 1865, the Joint Committee of the Wemyss Bay Railway met in Glasgow under the chairmanship of Thomas Hill, his Caley colleague Andrew Buchanan and the Wemyss Bay Directors, James Scott, A.S. Finlay MP and Robert Towers. In attendance were James Keyden (Secretary of the Greenock & Wemyss Bay Railway Company) and Messrs Knight and Christopher Johnstone (General Manager of the Caley).

In the early years, the Joint Committee was attended by the following:

Caley members
Thomas Hill, Andrew Buchanan, John Cowan, Irvine Kempt, James Smithells (General Manager of the Caley after Johnstone)

Greenock & Wemyss Bay Directors
James Scott, A.S. Finlay MP, Robert Towers, James Stewart, Alex Ronaldson, G. Fyffe Christie, Hugh Brown, Stewart Jamieson, James Lamont

Officials
James Keyden as Secretary of the G&WBR (till his death in June 1887 when his son Philip Grierson Keyden succeeded him); Archibald Gibson (Secretary to the Caledonian Railway Co) Secretary of the committee to April 1871 when he was succeeded by James Grahame of St Vincent Place; J.R. Forman, CE (the Wemyss Bay Co.'s Engineer to early 1869);
Mortimer Evans, CE (the Wemyss Bay Co's Engineer for 12 years after J.R.Forman to the end of 1881);
Thomas D. Weir, CE (the Wemyss Bay Co.'s Engineer for 5½ years after Mortimer Evans - to September 1887);
T.O. Niven, CE (the Wemyss Bay Co's Engineer from September 1887);
Messrs Knight, Johnstone and Murray.

The meeting on 11th April decided that the line would open for passenger traffic on Monday 15th May, 1865. Four passenger trains were to be run each way during May, the service being increased to six trains in each direction from 1st June:

From Glasgow *(down)*   9.00 am, 11.00 am, 3.00 pm, 5.00 pm
From Wemyss Bay *(up)*   8.30 am, 9.30 am, 4.00 pm, 6.00 pm

However, the *Glasgow Herald* of 12th May, 1865 advertised the four trains each way to run at entirely different times, adding that all first and third class carriages had seats (in contrast to some of those on the Greenock line which did not). The fares would be:

Glasgow by rail to: Wemyss Bay	*First* 2s. single 3s. 6d. return	*£4.15 *£7.25	*Second* 1s. 6d. single 2s. 9d. return	*£3.10 *£5.70
Wemyss Bay by boat to: Innellan, Rothesay, Toward, Largs, Millport	*Cabin fare* 4d. single 6d. return	*.70p *£1.05	*Steerage fare* 2d. single no return fare	*.35p
Glasgow via Wemyss Bay to: Rothesay, Toward, Largs and Millport Innellan Arran Tarbert and Ardrishaig (Loch Fyne) Kyles of Bute	*First with Cabin* 2s. 4d. single 3s. 9d. return 2s. single 3s. 3d. return 3s. single 5s. return 3s. 6d. single 6s. return 2s. 9d. single 4s. 6d. return	*£4.80 *£7.75 *£4.15 *£6.75 *£6.20 *£10.35 *£7.25 *£12.45 *£5.70 *£9.35	*Third with Cabin* 1s. 9d. single 3s. return 1s. 6d. single 2s. 6d. return 2s. 6d. single 3s. 9d. return 2s. 6d. single 4s. return 2s. single 3s. 3d. return	*£3.65 *£6.20 *£3.10 *£5.20 *£5.20 *£7.75 *£5.20 *£8.30 *£4.15 *£6.75

The Steamboat company would receive a third of the fare of each passenger travelling from Glasgow or Paisley via Wemyss Bay and onward by steamer and half the fare for those travelling from Greenock.

The time had come for the Directors to travel the line. The *Glasgow Herald* reported that on Thursday 13th April, 1865, '. . . the first locomotive engine, to which was attached a first class carriage, passed over the Greenock and Wemyss Bay Railway, from the junction at Devol's

Location Plan

PLAN 1 — Railway Station
PLAN 2 — Goods Shed
PLAN 3 — Engine Shed

PLAN 1   Station and Pier

Refreshment Room
Booking Office
Waiting Rooms, etc.
STATION
PLATFORM
Staff Box
10 MP
Ordinary Spring Tide
Flt Line
RAILWAY COMPANY'S BOUNDARY
PUBLIC ROAD
wall
TP, SP, Disc

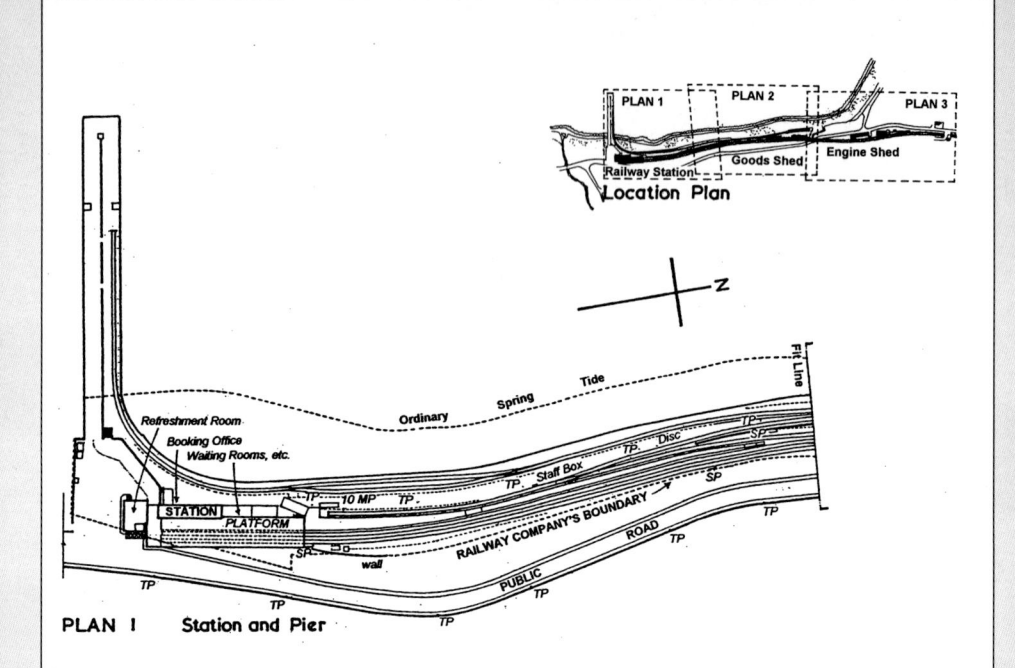

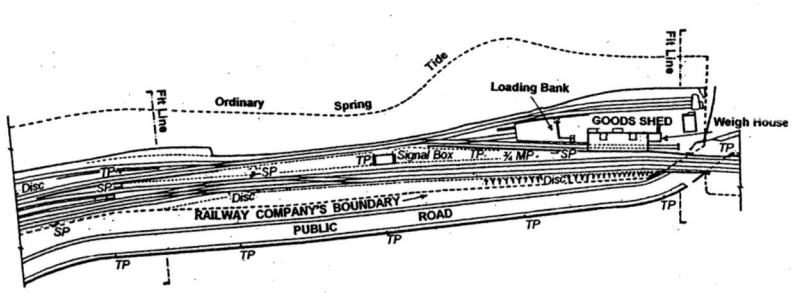

PLAN 2   Goods Shed

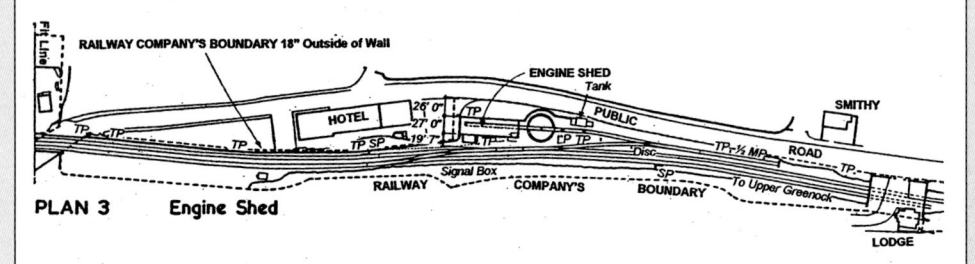

Loading Bank
GOODS SHED
Weigh House
Signal Box
¾ MP
Ordinary Spring Tide
Flt Line
RAILWAY COMPANY'S BOUNDARY
PUBLIC ROAD
TP, SP, Disc

PLAN 3   Engine Shed

RAILWAY COMPANY'S BOUNDARY 18" Outside of Wall
ENGINE SHED
Tank
HOTEL
26' 0"
27' 0"
19' 7"
SMITHY
Signal Box
RAILWAY COMPANY'S BOUNDARY
PUBLIC ROAD
½ MP
To Upper Greenock
LODGE
Flt Line

WEMYSS BAY RAILWAY STATION AND APPROACHES
1865 – 1903

0 50 100 150 200 250 300 350 400   Feet

Redrawn from original drawing No. 1536 RHP 86556

1999

Glen to the terminus at Wemyss Bay. The inspection was an unofficial one. In the carriage were several of the Directors, Mr Ward, the manager, and other officials of the Caledonian Railway'. The Government Inspector, Captain Reid, RE, visited the line on 27th April. According to J.F. McEwan, the Certificate permitting the line to operate stated that the line was to be worked by one engine in steam at all times till a passing loop was formed. As no passing loop was made in the days when the Greenock and Wemyss Bay company operated the line, trains could run very late when a steamer was delayed (a frequent happening) and thereby lose their path to Glasgow, especially on the busy stretch from Paisley. Also, a train bound for Wemyss Bay could not enter the branch at Port Glasgow till the up train had passed it. Naturally, passengers complained.

The line opens

In April 1865, Mr Ward told the Caley Board that houses were urgently needed for station staff at various stations along the Wemyss Bay line - the Caley passed the request to Keyden, though whether this was a previously unforeseen requirement or a comment on late completion is unclear. A fortnight before the line opened, George Graham 'went early to Greenock and drove to Wemyss Bay and walked over part of the Wemyss Bay line'. A few days later, the *Glasgow Herald* recorded that 12 trucks carrying 75 tons of Caithness pavement were sent down to Wemyss Bay - the pressure was on to finish. On Thursday 11th May, 1865, Graham 'went on the Wemyss Bay line with Mr Ward', just prior to the opening. There is no record of him attending the formal opening of the line - in fact, his diary states that on Friday 12th and Saturday 13th he was either in Glasgow or on site at Wishaw.

> Yesterday, [reported the *Glasgow Herald* on Saturday 13th May], a special train, consisting of thirteen carriages, ran along this line to the terminus and back to Greenock, containing nearly 600 excursionists, kindly invited by the contractors and resident engineer of the Wemyss Bay Railway to a trip on the new railway prior to its opening on Monday first for general traffic. The morning was most auspicious, and all along the line of railway numbers of people had assembled to give a passing cheer. The Greenock station was gaily decorated with flags, and the large and respectable company who assembled on the platform gave evidence of the satisfaction they felt . . . Shortly after twelve o'clock the train started, the crowd of people assembled to witness the departure lustily cheering as the carriages moved off. At the several stations along the route numbers of friends joined the train . . . Arriving at Wemyss Bay, ample refreshments were provided for the large party. Mr Adams' celebrated quadrille band was in attendance, . . . the younger portion of the excursionists joining in the dance, which was formed on the pier . . . The scenery along this line can hardly be equalled in the West of Scotland.

The train returned at 5.30 pm. There was no mention of the steamer connection to Rothesay.

I suspect that this 'first train' carried those most intimately involved in the line's construction - the contractors, the men who had formed the cuttings, tunnels and stations, the navvies, rock blasters, masons, carpenters, wrights, their friends and families. It was, after all, a railway for the people's pleasure. A second train had been arranged for the Directors and their friends for the following day.

At first sight the list of those travelling on the Directors' train seems deficient. Unlike the previous train, it ran between Glasgow and Wemyss Bay. One might have expected local landowners to have been included - notably Sir Michael Robert Shaw Stewart MP and Duncan Darroch of Gourock, the shareholders, the Directors of the G&WBR (especially Alexander Finlay MP who was active on the Boards of both the railway and steamboat companies), James Keyden the Secretary of the line and James R.Forman, its Engineer. There is no mention of the Caledonian Railway Company's Secretary, Archibald Gibson, or their Chief Engineer, George Graham. One might have anticipated that the captains of the Wemyss

Wemyss Bay station pier about 1900 with the Millport berth on the left separated from the Rothesay berth by a wind shield. Note the signal kiosk to regulate steamboat arrivals, gas lighting and gangways.
Ian B. Smith Collection

Rear ramp with railed off walkway alongside coaling line which runs on to the Wemyss Bay station pier. Note the proliferation of advertisements and the trucks at the end of the line with a Rothesay steamer at the opposite berth. The pier lifeboat is just to the left of the detached truck. Probably taken about 1900.
Ian B. Smith Collection

Bay Steamboat Company boats, *Largs* and *Kyles*, would have been offered places on the train as part of the line's *raison d'être* was to carry steamboat passengers.

The explanation for their absence was probably because just as the line was about to open, the Caley was fighting a proposal by the Glasgow and South Western Railway to construct a line from Greenock to Howood to bring Ayrshire's iron and coal traffic to Greenock, in direct competition with the Caley's established line. William Johnstone CE, the General Manager of the G&SWR even indicated that their proposed line might be connected to the G&WBR line 'at a small expense'. It is therefore likely that the Caley with its Greenock line and the Wemyss Bay Company with its new line, would have been very concerned about this threat to their investment and would have been following events closely in the Committee Rooms of the House of Commons. This appears to be confirmed as George Graham noted in his diary that he took the 5.50 pm train to London on Monday 15th 'to attend committee on Parliamentary Bills'. He was not a great committee man and the fact that he made one of his rare trips south of the border indicates the serious nature of the G&SWR proposal. James Forman was certainly there - as Engineer for *both* lines!

On Monday 15th May, 1865, the *Glasgow Herald* ran a long article entitled 'Wemyss Bay Railway':

> On Saturday [it commenced] a second pleasure trip was made along this interesting line of railway, the excursionists in this instance being the Directors and a select party of friends. The Glasgow portion of the company left Bridge Street Station shortly before nine in the morning accompanied by the band of the 19th L.R.V. [Lanarkshire Rifle Volunteers] whose services had been bespoken for the occasion. The train, consisting of brand new first class carriages and forming by the way an excellent sample of the Wemyss Bay rolling stock, arrived in due time at Greenock, where the number of excursionists received a considerable accession. A pleasant ride, affording at intervals charming glimpses of rural scenery, and towards the close a magnificent view of the Firth of Clyde, brought the party to Wemyss Bay about two minutes after ten - the journey from Glasgow, including several stoppages, having been got through in an hour and a quarter.
>
> At the railway pier, the handsome and commodious steamer *Kyles* was in waiting, with steam up, to convey the excursionists to sea. The embarkation was speedily effected, and after some little delay, due apparently to the shipment of commissariat stores, the vessel started for the Kyles of Bute. [The *Kyles* had only completed its test runs a few days before.]

The writer then noted in his pocket book the great and the braw, without, unfortunately describing their connection with the railway. One assumes that where the parties were not obviously guests, they were probably people of influence, people whose land the line now crossed or shareholders. Included on the list were local Bailies, four of the six original Directors of the G&WBR and the Steamboat company, some Caley Directors and officials, and merchants who may have supplied goods for the line.

He continued: 'The morning was dull, and a cold wind blew from the north west, so that those who had brought thick shawls and greatcoats found reason to congratulate themselves on their foresight'. The party then adjourned to enjoy the 'creature comforts' provided below, as they sailed on to pick up more passengers from Rothesay before proceeding through the Kyles of Bute and on to Arran. As they coasted towards Lamlash Bay, 'luncheon was served in sumptuous style' while the hired band played on, a feature not uncommon on excursion boats even in the 20th century.

On they steamed to Millport and Largs before heading back to Wemyss Bay. However, as they had time to kill before the train was due to take them back, they headed off to Innellan, returning to board the train about five pm.

The writer concluded,

> The Wemyss Bay Railway and steamers . . . will today, for the first time, be placed at the disposal of the public. The line, so far as through traffic is concerned, may be regarded as completed, only

a few details connected with the stations and sidings remaining to be carried out. Of the three steamers intended to ply in connection with the train, two, namely the *Kyles* and the *Largs*, are ready for the reception of passengers. The company is thus in a position, at the outset, to offer a very large instalment of the accommodation which their enterprise is calculated to afford.

The *Kyles* would run westwards to Toward, Rothesay, Colintraive and Tighnabruiach. The *Largs* would go south to Largs, Millport, Invercloy and Lamlash. Glasgow to Rothesay would take 1 hour 50 minutes and Millport would be reached in 2 hours 15 minutes. 'Where time is money' the new railway line would be much appreciated.

Carefully(?) juxtaposed directly below this flowing piece was a letter:

Sir - I observe in the advertisement of the Wemyss Bay Steamboat Company (Ltd) that in the sailings commencing today (Monday 15th May) no provision is made for accommodation to Innellan, much to my surprise and disappointment . . . I subscribed for a few shares when the Wemyss Bay Railway Company was first spoken of principally on the representation that it would afford a speedy communication to Innellan. [There must have been a minor hitch as Innellan featured on the original - and later - timetables.]

Having advised the paper that people would therefore patronise the rival service from Greenock, he went on to complain about the high fares on the Wemyss Bay Railway. Comparing fares from Glasgow to Wemyss Bay unfavourably with the fare to Greenock, he feared the railway company would fail to make adequate profits. I suspect he was not among those invited to the opening ceremony. As time would tell, he was also right about the fares. The company made every effort to jack them up.

The completion of the station saw the introduction of an omnibus service with William Orr of Main Street, Largs offering a morning and evening connection between Largs and the Wemyss Bay trains as well as the hire of horses and carriages. The *Glasgow Herald* was enthusiastic about the steamers, 'Such a fleet of splendid steamers as are now plying, and about to ply on the river this season, has never been equalled'.

In September 1865, the Caley shareholders learned that the Wemyss Bay line had already carried considerable passenger traffic. However the goods and minerals accommodation had yet to be provided.

Line Management

The next meeting of the Joint Committee noted a request by Miss Reid and Mr Cuthbert for accommodation in the station to serve refreshments. (Presumably, this was the same Miss Reid who ran a refreshment room at Bridge Street station between 1855 and 1858.) Following an earlier request, the bookstall was offered to Mr Gunn, however he seems to have declined as in June 1865, a tender submitted by Mr Simpson to operate the bookstall was accepted, the rent being payable quarterly, in advance. At the same time, the Committee decided to allow people free access to the pier, probably because it would have been difficult to stop them. The meeting decided to charge all steamers using the pier 1*d*. [*17p] / registered ton per call, up to a limit of £1 [*£41.45] / ton per annum for the limited company's boats. To boost traffic, tickets for the boat and train trip would be on sale at Rothesay, Innellan, Millport and Largs quays.

Trade did not develop sufficiently to justify the Caley putting on the originally proposed six trains from 1st June; but a 5th train was added each way for the summer period.

An early rockfall and a tunnel collapse coupled with staff inexperienced in single line running and steamboats that drifted from their timetables produced an unreliable service. Underpowered locomotives with poor brakes that had to slow down at passing places made matters worse. On 7th July, 1865, part of the wall in the Finnoch cutting broke away, leaving 70 tons of spoil on the line.

BUILDING THE LINE

It took several hours to clear the debris and reconstruct the line. George Graham and Henry Ward went down 'to look at a Railway Rock Cutting where a rock had fallen in', and finding builders constructing a wall (presumably unfinished original work), Mr Ward said he was dissatisfied with the state of the line: trains were not running to time which he seemed to attribute to the steepness of the permanent way. Anyway, he resolved to test the gradients. At the end of July, George Graham revisited Wemyss Bay with his Directors, presumably to take a view on the line.

September's dusky hours revealed a lack of lights on the pier. The Caley instructed the G&WBR to fit lights, and reluctantly the latter agreed, as long as they were not fixtures.

The over ambitious steamboat operation, connecting to Lamlash, Rothesay, Port Bannatyne, Innellan, Dunoon, Tighnabruiach and Ardrishaig contributed to the poor performance of the railway line. Boats did not run punctually so train connections were frequently delayed. The trains then ran so late that they missed their time slots on the Caley line from Wemyss Bay Junction to Paisley and consequently ran late into Bridge Street station. This meant that trains leaving Glasgow became further delayed - and worse, passengers unwilling to wait three hours for the next connection, used the existing Greenock service instead - and wrote caustic letters to the press about hour-long delays. Following a barrage of correspondence, in June 1865 the *Glasgow Herald* advised the steamboat operators that they should consider getting vessels which could meet the schedule.

Two proposals of significance were aired at the Joint Committee's meeting on 12th September, 1865. Presumably because of co-ordination problems between the Caley and the boat company, Mr Scott for the G&WBR proposed that the company apply to Parliament in the next session for powers to own its own steamers. The Caledonian Board undertook to consider this and reply.

A line to Largs and Ayrshire?

The first proposal to extend the former GP&GR line to Largs may have been abandoned, but not the idea. Work on the Wemyss Bay line was well in hand when in October 1863 Mr Mansfield Grieve (I assume this reference in the Caledonian Minutes of Directors and Committees may relate to Provost James J. Grieve, then Provost of Greenock) submitted a printed circular to the Caley Board suggesting the line be continued to Largs. It seems that Forman & McCall had updated the 1845 proposals as they submitted a Prospectus at the same time. Greenock could see advantages (bringing dairy products from Largs, for example) but at a time of financial difficulty, the Caley was not prepared to pursue the suggestion. The Board took no action.

In July 1864, Mr Grieve repeated his request for a line to Largs and received a similar response from the Caley Board. But later that year, an exchange of correspondence between Keyden and Gibson revealed a perceived threat from the G&SWR who, according to Keyden were 'going for a line to Largs'. As mentioned above, the G&SWR intended to enter Greenock by way of the Wemyss Bay line connected to their Ayrshire lines. In August 1864, Gibson confirmed to Keyden that the Caley was not proposing to extend the Wemyss Bay line to Largs and later wrote to Keyden presuming that the Wemyss Bay company would petition against the Greenock and Ayrshire Railway Bill proposed by the G&SWR. The Wemyss Bay Directors *did* oppose the Bill - after all, had the G&SWR been allowed to link into their line, most of the G&WBR's investment might well have been lost. The Caledonian fought the Bill vigorously as they already had a profitable trade with Greenock and did not intend to lose out to the G&SWR.

Yet the Caley seem to have been somewhat two-faced. In January 1865, as the Wemyss Bay line neared completion, we find the Caledonian Board asking Mr Bruce, CE, for a report on extending the Wemyss Bay line along the coast to Largs. Mr G. Cunningham, a prominent railway engineer, was engaged and did some groundwork, including plotting a route along the shore and having preliminary discussions with the feuars. Bruce reported back to the Board within a couple of weeks, offering two routes.

It seems the preferred scheme was to branch off the track north of Wemyss Bay, pass to the seaward side of the station then go *under* the pier approach before travelling along the shore. It would then cross to the other side of the road (which would have to be raised). Thereafter, making use of several short tunnels, it would alternate between the seaward and landward sides of the Wemyss Bay-Largs Road, terminating in a station 'north of Nelson Street, Largs, west of the junction of Wilson Street and Nelson Street'.

The Caley put the proposals to the G&WBR Directors, offering liberal assistance if they were prepared to go for the extension. Keyden indicated that his Board would not entertain the idea. But the Caley, encouraged by Mr Grieve, instructed their legal adviser Mr Mackay, to prepare a Bill for the Largs extension for the next Parliamentary session. However, Mr Scott, the Chairman of the G&WBR, firmly told the Caley that his Board would *not* entertain the proposal. The Caley withdrew the Bill.

It is in any case hard to imagine how such a scheme could be proposed when the clearance under the pier would have been minimal and where the road through Skelmorlie, which would have been level with the track, is liable to flooding in bad weather. I presume the other option was to revert to the 1845 scheme where the railway completely bypassed Wemyss Bay and would have taken the tripper trade on down to Largs, to the benefit of Largs and the detriment of those who had invested so much in the station and pier at Wemyss Bay. (A third possibility would have been to rebuild the station as a through station.)

A few months later, just when the Wemyss Bay Railway opened, the Caley was fighting the Greenock and Ayrshire Railway Bill (engineered by Forman and McCall) in Parliament - and losing. Edward Blyth, CE, for the Caledonian, claimed that the proposed 1 in 70 gradients, three tunnels and tight turns, would create operational problems. But on 13th May, 1865, the *Glasgow Herald* reported that all the vessels in Greenock harbour were decorated with flags, rejoicing that the preamble to the Bill had been proven. But at least the Greenock and Wemyss Bay Directors had seen off the proposed link to their own investment.

Fifteen years later, the Caley Board had another proposal on the table, this time it seems from the G&WBR, which indicates a surprising change of attitude. But relations between the two companies had deteriorated to such an extent that the Board perfunctorily decided to have nothing to do with them. An early proposal was resurrected, bypassing Wemyss Bay, and was reported thus in the *Largs and Millport Weekly News* of 3rd November, 1883: 'Mr Turner, solicitor from Greenock, [presumably the later G&WBR Director] explained scheme of a direct railway via Inverkip'. The Greenock and Wemyss Bay Railway Company had long been in contemplation and he said things should get a move on. The proposed line would branch off from the Wemyss Bay line about 1 mile east of Inverkip, entering the Bay of Largs beside the manse, the line then extending to the pier. There would be a station at Upper Skelmorlie [which would have enabled the inhabitants of this developing area to commute north and south]. The journey from Glasgow to Largs would be shorter by 5 miles [*sic*] than extending the G&SWR route by Fairlie and Ardrossan, more picturesque and only take an hour. Largs would then be as busy in winter as it was in summer and more people would go to Millport. He said that the G&WBR was favourable to the new scheme, but the Caley was 'not sufficiently far forward for their consideration'. The resolution 'that this meeting cordially approves of the proposal to erect a direct railway to Largs and pledges itself to do everything in its power to forward the scheme' was carried unanimously.

Largs, through the auspices of the Glasgow and South Western Railway, eventually got its line in 1885. Had the Caley and the G&WBR not been at loggerheads throughout the previous 20 years, Largs would have been about 35 miles from Glasgow instead of 42 and better connected to the prosperous towns of Greenock and Port Glasgow. It would also be true to say that Wemyss Bay would probably never have developed as a ferry terminal, losing out to Largs and Greenock. Quite why the G&WBR were allegedly so keen on the extension is not easy to understand as Wemyss Bay station would have lost most of its clientèle. Perhaps with the passage of time, and different Directors, new opportunities made the extension idea viable.

BUILDING THE LINE

In 1899, the Caledonian Railway Company under the Caledonian Railway (General Powers) Act of 1899, obtained permission to increase the capacity of Wemyss Bay station. Round about the same time, the G&SWR proposed yet another connection to Largs. The route proposed would run between its line at Johnstone and Largs station and would have allowed them to make a connection between Greenock and Largs but at considerable cost and questionable benefit. Travelling at high level, the line would have skirted the north and west sides of Loch Thom before continuing well inland to drop down to Annatyard on its way to Largs. It would have entirely missed Wemyss Bay. It does not seem to have been a serious proposal, rather a 'spoiling motion' to delay the progress of the Caley's Bill. There even appears to have been another variation that would have seen the G&SWR make use of the Caley's (singled) line between Upper Greenock and Dunrod, thereby cutting the cost of building four miles of new railway line.

And a line to Gourock?

In October 1863, Mr Forman presented plans to the Caley proposing that the Greenock and Wemyss Bay line be extended north to Gourock. Keyden wrote on Christmas Day 1863(!) suggesting the Caley subscribe £5,000 [*£207,000] to the Wemyss Bay company's £20,000 [*£830,000] for the Gourock extension. The Caley remitted the proposal to a committee. I suspect that the route would have been similar to the 1845 plans, but leaving the Wemyss Bay line at Upper Greenock station and running on the surface all the way.

In March 1866, six months after the Caley raised the idea of extending the Wemyss Bay line to Largs, it was promoting a Bill to extend *its* line to Gourock, 'a favourite Clyde watering place', and to acquire the pier. In April 1868, we find Keyden proposing a branch line to Gourock on terms that the Caley was not prepared to entertain. The Wemyss Bay company repeated its proposal in September 1870, but the Caley was not interested.

In June 1872, the Caley instructed Mr Cunningham to plan a route to Gourock, though whether this was to be an extension of the Caley's line from Greenock or from the G&WBR's line is not clear. The idea of a branch to Gourock was repeated in 1882 with what seems to have been a joint proposal by the G&WBR and the Caley to build a three-mile-long line from Pennyfern, off the Wemyss Bay line, to Gourock Bay. The line was to be graded at 1 in 70 over most of its length and involved deep cuttings on either side of a 850 yds-long tunnel, a bridge over the horse tramway on Shore Street and a station and quay built on reclaimed land where the present station now stands. The Book of Reference for the Gourock Railway & Quay Bill stated that an hotel was to be built near Kempock Point. Nearly 200 properties were affected, many of them owned by Duncan Darroch (an earlier Duncan Darroch, a successful West Indian merchant, had acquired the estate of Gourock in 1784). The cemetery administered by the Parochial Board of the Parish of Inverkip was mentioned, its 'occupier' (a somewhat unfortunate legal description) being named as Horatio Renaud Babington Peile. The solicitors were once again Keydens, Strang & Girvan but the Engineer was John Strain of Glasgow with W.A.Loch retained as Parliamentary Solicitor. With the exception of the tunnel, this route would have been comparatively easy to build as much of it would have been in open country and would have cost far less than the Caley eventually spent by 1889, drilling a tunnel under Greenock. The timing of the Bill suggests that this was a 'fall-back' proposal in case the Caley's other Bill to extend its line from Greenock Central under the town to Gourock should fail in favour of the G&SWR's rival proposals. In the event, the G&SWR proposals were rejected and the Caley built its line to Gourock under the centre of Greenock.

The first year

Following 5 months' of summer operations, train times were adjusted for the winter months, starting in October 1865 as follows:

| From Glasgow | *(down)* | 8.40 am, 11.15 am, 4.10 pm, 5.45 pm |
| From Wemyss Bay | *(up)* | 8.50 am, 12.30 pm, 5.30 pm, 7.15 pm |

A month later, the Caley announced that the last up and down trains were to be discontinued - only three trains would run each way. The Caley, perhaps reflecting on the poor performance to date, (some of it their fault) said they could not run the number of trains the Wemyss Bay Railway Company wanted. But they could put more trains on if the line, or a portion of it, was doubled.

About this time, arrangements were made with Mr.Burckhard, the Surveyor of Mails, to carry mail by train and by Captain Rankin's Wemyss Bay boats. The proceeds would be split, two-thirds going to the railway, the remainder to the boat company.

Mr Ward reported to the Joint Committee that certain works were incomplete. At Wemyss Bay, the horse and carriage loading bank, and a cattle loading pen and sidings by the water, were unfinished and he proposed to move the through crossing in the station 'further east'. Inverkip needed a horse and carriage loading bank while completion of the sidings was awaited both there and at Upper Greenock. At Dunrod, a coal depôt and a cattle loading pen were to be formed. All stations were to get weighing machines.

At the Joint Committee meeting on 27th February, 1866, not for the first time, and by no means the last, the Wemyss Bay Railway Company expressed the desire to increase fares. The Caley thought this would hurt traffic and the matter was set aside, for the moment. Between 1865 and 1870, railways generally were feeling the pinch and the Caley was probably stretched having purchased or being in the course of acquiring other railway companies. Anything that might reduce trade was to be avoided.

Instead, the Caley wanted to increase business on the line. There already existed a system, on their line and others, whereby people building on new plots could acquire Villa Tickets entitling the ticket holder, but not his family, to travel free for a period of five years or more. This scheme was agreed in May 1866 for houses begun after the passing of the Wemyss Bay Act in July 1862.

There were complaints from the public - the Revd Walter Boyd of the South Church in Skelmorlie and others criticised the running of the refreshment room. While the meeting considered that there was no foundation to the complaint, they decided that smoking was to be prohibited immediately and no spirits would be sold at the station rooms as from the next Whitsunday.

The second year

June 1866 must have been a good month as there was a strong plea for a further platform at Wemyss Bay station. But the committee did not possess the resources to provide one. The following month, Keyden asked what the Caley would charge for maintaining the line. A particular concern was 'watching the rock cutting', for which the G&WBR was charged the tidy sum of £182 16s. [*£7,100] the following month. Presumably this referred to the possibility of more rock falls at the Finnoch cutting.

Back at Port Glasgow, there was a need for a goods and minerals siding. It was agreed that the G&WBR would provide this.

In October 1866 it was determined that the Caledonian Railway Company's share of receipts beyond Wemyss Bay would be:

BUILDING THE LINE

	First		Third	
Caley share of rail fare	1s. single	*£1.95	8d. single	*£1.30
	1s. 6d. return	*£2.95	1s. return	*£1.95
Caley share of pier dues	2d. single	*.33p	1d. single	*.15p
	3d. return	*.50p	2d. return	*.33p

The minor shareholders of the G&WBR must have felt they were getting a poor return on their investment. Against strong representations by the Caley, as from 1st January, 1867, with some exceptions, fares would generally rise by about 15 per cent:

Glasgow and Paisley by rail to:	First	First Previously	Third	Second Previously
Ravenscraig	2s. single		1s. 4d. single	
	3s. 4d. return		2s. return	
Inverkip	2s. 2d. single		1s. 8d. single	
	3s. 10d. return		2s. 5d. return	
Wemyss Bay	2s. 4d. single	2s. single	1s. 9d. single	1s. 6d. single
	4s. return	3s. 6d. return	2s. 6d. return	2s. 9d. return
Glasgow or Paisley via Wemyss Bay to:	First	First Previously	Third	Third Previously
Rothesay, Toward, Largs	2s. 8d. single	2s. 4d.	2s. single	1s. 9d.
	4s. 3d. return	3s. 9d.	3s. return	3s.
Innellan	2s. single	No change	1s. 6d. single	No change
	3s. 3d. return		2s. 6d. return	
Fairlie and Millport	2s. 10d. single	2s. 4d.	2s. 2d. single	1s. 9d.
	4s. 6d. return	3s. 9d.	3s. 3d. return	3s.

One can understand why the Caley was upset; such increases tend to drive traffic away and the November addition of 4d./ton for carrying coal to all stations on the Wemyss Bay line was unhelpful. Looking for further revenue, the G&WBR was trying to extract £100 [*£3,900] from the Postal Service instead of the present £50-52 per annum.

In October 1866, Sir Michael Shaw Stewart asked the Caley Board if they would build a single line from Dunrod siding to Clocherlee on the Kip Burn for quarrying purposes. The Board agreed and in January 1867 the Joint Committee arranged to provide second-hand sleepers, chairs, spikes, keys and rails to allow the quarry owner at Dunrod to transport stone, a major commercial earner for the G&WBR. Sir Michael got the Caley to agree that when the line was worn out, they would renew the rails, chairs and sleepers. A weighing machine for loaded stone wagons was added at a cost of £100 [*£3,750] in 1868. The quarry was tenanted by two firms, Jamieson and Coghill. In August 1868, Mr Martin, Sir Michael's Agent, arranged with Mr Smithells, the Caley's General Manager that the Caley would send a specially-built locomotive (believed to have been ordered from Barclay of Kilmarnock) to work the line. This could not be provided immediately. After a brief period when horses were proposed to work the top of the line, a direct approach from Sir Michael saw the Caley release an engine and driver from traffic pending the appearance of the new locomotive. The agreement between the Caley and Sir Michael was that Mr Conner, the Caley's locomotive superintendent, would provide an engine to operate the branch conditional on Sir Michael guaranteeing to pay £500 [*£18,750] for a year's working. Smithells spent a year trying to extract payments from the tenants, eventually drawing the gruff response from Mr Jamieson that the £500 would be derived from the traffic receipts at the year's end (definitely not Smithells' understanding) and that the Caley was to blame as they had made 'the greatest bungle of the business that ever was heard of'. Adjustment of the tonnage rate seems to have resolved the problem.

Early in February 1867, the Joint Committee was considering an extension to the station at Upper Greenock. The expected cost (excluding land) would be £7,000 [*£260,000], the Caley providing the money and the Wemyss Bay railway feuing the land from Sir Michael Shaw Stewart. It took nine months and a change of plan before an additional track was authorised for £974 13s. 4d. [*£36,500].

There was more discussion on rates to be charged, this time on freight. It was decided that mineral rates would be as at Lower Greenock station - a terminal rate (the sum payable to the line owner for loading or unloading) of 4½d. per ton to both the Wemyss Bay and the Caley railway companies, taken off previous deductions calculated on distance travelled. Terminals on goods brought from the Caledonian Railway after deducting cartage should be equally divided; terminals on minerals would go to the G&WBR.

Prior to the holiday season, there is a reminder of the nature of the trade: '*Weight of Luggage allowed - Passengers on Wemyss Bay Steamers*'. The Steam Boat Company representatives undertook to hold the Railway Company 'skaithless [i.e. not financially liable] in the event of claims being made by passengers who may be charged for their luggage on board the boats'. The Wemyss Bay Railway Company raised the possibility of increasing the use of the pier for steamboats to Dunoon, but the Caledonian Railway Company were not keen on the idea, presumably because it would divert existing trade from Greenock.

After two years, the steamboat clerks were feeling cramped but were given short shrift when they asked if they could use part of the station master's house. Small additions included the provision of a crane and 'lift' at the pier, the Caley and the G&WBR sharing the £150 [*£5,600] cost.

The third year

But the train service was not fast enough. The G&WBR asked it to be accelerated to 60-70 minutes to Bridge Street. The service must have been slow indeed, justifying Mr Finlay's complaint of delayed trains to the Board. The Board agreed, but they would not put on extra trains.

The G&WBR's finances were stretched. Keyden wrote to the Caley in August 1867 seeking its share of the revenue to the end of May 'without deduction of charges for old rails and telegraph'. The Caley was quite prepared to pay but would retain the amount due for rails and telegraph.

A year later, in April 1868, the Joint Committee was faced with a problem when Dr Young, the new proprietor of Kelly, threatened to cut off the water supply from the Kelly Burn. Initially, the Committee decided to discuss permanent supply arrangements with Dr Young but then Mr Forman obtained permission to pipe water from the Bruacre Burn on Sir Michael's property to the engine shed at a cost of £137 14s. [*£5,150]. (As the line developed, so did the thirst of the engines till it was necessary to pipe a supply into the station. In February 1882, the Caley rejected the G&WBR's request to pay half the cost of extending the pipe from the engine shed to the station, no doubt on the basis that it was a G&WBR responsibility under the Schedule in the 1862 Act.) In April 1868, Miss Reid's contract to run the refreshment room was extended for another year.

The fourth year and later

The Joint Committee meeting on 28th May, 1868 saw the G&WBR suggesting that the Caley introduce 3rd class carriages without seats, an idea that took nearly a year to be rejected. Perhaps the inspiration came from the G&SWR where it was said the trains to Ayr had 3rd class 'without seats, simply because were they otherwise, those who took the 2nd class would crowd into them'. It was a general concern of the railway companies serving the Clyde that many people able to afford 1st or 2nd class fares liked to travel in the 3rd class open carriages. The railways, of course, lost out. This was reminiscent of proposals by the GP&GR in 1844 to remove the roofs of the seatless third class carriages to force those who could pay more into the better accommodation - hardly an appreciation of the needs of those whose spending power had forced the introduction of an especially low fare. (The Caledonian later had a 'Special Instruction' stipulating that on corridor coaches the doors between third and first class coaches be locked to prevent third class passengers entering 'upper class' coaches - unless they were going to the Dining Car!)

In August 1868, another train was added, all trains connecting with the boats:

| From Glasgow | (down) | 8.25 am, 10.10 am, 2.45 pm, 4.10 pm, 6.00 pm |
| From Wemyss Bay | (up) | 8.45 am, 10.00 am, 11.35 pm, 4.10 pm, 5.30 pm |

In November 1868, Keyden asked the Caley to provide a movable crane or a shunting engine for Upper Greenock station. The Caley said that the G&WBR should provide the engine, which seems odd when the operating Agreement was for the Caley to run the railway. Perhaps the Caley thought that the G&WBR was trying to wriggle out of its responsibilities for a fixed crane, which the latter would have had to provide under the Agreement.

In November 1866, the Caley's General Committee had considered a request from Mr G.Y. Strang for help to erect a gas works at Wemyss Bay. The Committee was not inclined to subscribe, but would 'take gas when ready'. It seems a little surprising that in 1869 Mr Keyden was discussing the cost of installing gas lighting with the gas company (presumably a forerunner to the gas works established in 1875 below Skelmorlie Hydropathic), when it was more expensive than oil. The lighting had probably been oil-fired initially but as gas lighting was brighter and cleaner, it would have enhanced the gloomy station. Pressure may have come from the Caley as its records for December 1869 show it wanted gas lighting at its own Langbank station as well as at Wemyss Bay.

In 1869, Mr Forman, the G&WBR's Engineer, left the company and was succeeded by Mr Mortimer Evans. Whether Mr Forman's departure was amicable is not known, but the Finance Committee minute of 5th January, 1869 asked for an explanation of a 'claim' from Forman and McCall for £250 [*£9,600] - equivalent to a whole year's wage bill for the G&WBR's staff on the line.

Mr Evans's period of notice was 3 months. In the legal agreement drawn up by Keyden, Strang and Keyden, he was employed to perform all engineering work, including superintending the maintenance of the railway and the pier, stations and sidings, paying men, keeping books and preparing weekly accounts for the Directors. He was supposed to live at Wemyss Bay, the not exactly generous fee of £250 being expected to cover the wages of all assistants, clerks, etc. whom he employed. Like the Secretary of the company with whom he was in close communication, he maintained an office in Glasgow, but probably lived elsewhere.

It may be observed that Mr Evans and *his* immediate successor, Mr Weir, belonged to a different company. It is quite possible that the Caley had not forgiven Forman and McCall for supporting the Greenock and Ayrshire Railway in its bid to bring competing trade to Greenock, and remarks by independent surveyors checking accounts for work on the Dunrod branch suggest that accounts submitted by contractors were passed by Forman & McCall without adequate verification.

The first meeting Mr Evans attended, with 15 others, was on 19th May, 1869. The meeting decided to run seven trains down from Glasgow and six back up. How this worked in practice is not revealed, but presumably one of the trains to Glasgow had arrived at Wemyss Bay as two shorter trains.

The proposed schedule was as below, trains marked† having a boat connection for Millport, Largs and Rothesay.

From Glasgow   *(down)*   8.35 am†, 11.30 am†, 12.40 pm, 2.45 pm, 4.10 pm†, 6.00 pm†, 7.10 pm
From Wemyss Bay *(up)*   7.40 am, 8.45 am†, 10.00 am, 11.35 am†, 4.10 pm†, 7.10 pm

In 1869, the Joint Committee briefly flirted with the idea of allowing Messrs Langland's Liverpool steamer to load passengers at Wemyss Bay for Ireland but nothing came of the proposal. In the same year, the Steamboat Company failed, seriously affecting the railway Directors. The G&WBR wrote suggesting terms to the Caley for the purchase of the railway. The Caley Board enquired about the financial position of the company. According to J.F. McEwan, the G&WBR was simultaneously having discussions with the G&SWR to form a junction to its line at Upper Greenock. (The Caley objected and the proposals fell through.)

In 1870, the Joint Committee squabbles on the fare structure became noisier. Mr Stewart for the G&WBR 'insisted' on a more favourable division of receipts. Without this concession, it could not agree to the lower fares the Caley wanted. The Caley responded by saying that under the Working Agreement, it was entitled to 52½ per cent of the gross receipts, before heavy interest charges on outlay were deducted. It reckoned that the 47½ per cent which the Agreement allocated to the Wemyss Bay company was more than the latter was entitled to. Attempting to ease the deteriorating situation, the Caley reluctantly agreed to make an exception for the division of 4th class fares - 5¼d. to the Caley and 6¾d. to the Wemyss Bay Co.. They also acceded to the G&WBR's request for a 50-minute express - one each way. But shortly after, we find Mr Stewart protesting at the withdrawal of express trains.

Mr Jamieson, a lessee of the Dunrod quarry, was dissatisfied too. In July 1869, he demanded more trucks failing which he would have to lay off some of the 100 masons in his employ. Smithells arranged with Mathieson to make good the shortfall. The following year Jamieson complained again, claiming that he was provided with insufficient wagons for stone cartage. The General Manager was asked to give this his immediate attention. Smithells checked and found that 60 wagons were in use for the Dunrod quarries, which should have been ample if properly deployed. Mr Jamieson was therefore himself to blame for their inefficient use. (Dunrod Quarry seems to have been working till at least the mid-1880s. The story goes that its closure was precipitated by the failure of three railwaymen, two of whom were fishing the Kip Burn while the third 'looked after' the engine. The brakes were not properly applied and the loaded train moved off downhill. By the time it reached the main line, its momentum caused a spectacular pileup.)

But there was a brighter side. May 1870 also saw new second class carriages running on the line.

Rows between the Railway Companies

A year later, they were still grumbling. In April 1871, Mr Smithells considered the high fares charged by the G&WBR was the main cause 'of want of better success'. Mr Stewart countered that the lack of an express service was hindering trade. Mr Smithells responded by saying that on his own initiative, and for the betterment of the Wemyss Bay Railway Co., he had instructed the train to stop at Inverkip because of complaints from that community. The Wemyss Bay representatives were also upset by the decision of the Caley Directors to terminate from 1st May the existing arrangements regarding through booking, through rates and division of receipts from passengers. Matters were coming to the boil. A week later, the Caley retreated, postponing revising the booking procedures, but stating that they still intended to revise the fare structure. This did not satisfy the G&WBR. Before the month was out, it decided it had no alternative but to seek arbitration on the fare scales for the Wemyss Bay line.

BUILDING THE LINE

Two weeks later, the Joint Committee met to discuss freight rates on the understanding that they would not interfere with the Caley's charges. By the end of November 1871, Mr Cowan of the Caley and Mr Stewart had failed to reach agreement on freight charges. Mr Stewart again questioned why express trains should stop at Inverkip. Had not the Caley agreed to accelerate certain trains to 55 minutes, yet the quickest trains to date had been 65 minutes?

The year 1872 did not start off any better as the two sides bickered over coal rates. The G&WBR subsequently took the matter to an arbiter who settled the rates, but not to the G&WBR's satisfaction.

On 22nd February, Mr Stewart vented his anger on the Caley, carefully minuted on four foolscap pages. It was being high-handed in disregarding the Wemyss Bay Railway Company's need for higher fares, especially as the Caley had raised fares on its own line 'to such a rate as practically debars the public from the use of the Wemyss Bay line'. That was particularly galling to the G&WBR which had shortened the route from Glasgow to Rothesay and Largs and other places by four miles.

The Caley proposed that the G&WBR sort out its Season Ticket charges for its length of line while the Caley did the same for its portion of the route from Glasgow and add the two together - but the Wemyss Bay Railway Co. was opposed to this. It must have been a long meeting.

A further seven pages were added, with the Caley's response. The new arrangements introduced from 1st February, 1872 followed the arbiter's decision which had fixed the Wemyss Bay company's rates, and these, added to the Caley's own rates, formed the new through rates. The Caley claimed its own rates were the lowest in Scotland and 30 per cent lower than those on the Wemyss Bay line. Furthermore, the Wemyss Bay company's contention that the Caley's rates on the Greenock line were excessive was because of the G&WBR's extraordinarily high rates having to be applied on top of the Caley's own fares. The Caley protested as the largest shareholder of the line and stated that the action of the Wemyss Bay Railway Co.'s Directors would ruin the traffic.

The row rumbled on. Mr Hill, now Chairman of the Caledonian Railway Company, said the Caley might take the matter of season ticket charges to an arbiter. Mr Stewart said that the arbiter had already decided the level of charges.

While the arguments were going on behind closed doors, the people of Wemyss Bay, Skelmorlie, Largs, Fairlie, Millport and Rothesay petitioned the Joint Committee about the fares. Simultaneously a deputation of Innellan residents claimed that passengers were being driven away by the high fares on the line. This suggests that the Wemyss Bay line was well used.

Going to law

As the railways mushroomed, so also did the fortunes of the legal profession. The Caley and the G&SW Railway were often to be found locked into legal squabbles, notably over the use of Bridge Street station in Glasgow. And what happened in Glasgow was mirrored at Wemyss Bay. The following gives an idea of what the Caley was up against.

In November 1867, Keyden wrote to the Caley saying that his Directors 'resolved to give a Parliamentary Notice' for a junction between the G&WB Railway line and lines to Greenock and Ayrshire, which is odd as the G&WBR was initially quite opposed to the idea - perhaps it reckoned this trade would do *it* no harm. No response is recorded from the Caley, though it would have seen that the Glasgow and South Western Railway would then have access to Greenock from the south, affecting its own Greenock investment. In November 1870, Mr Hughes, the Wemyss Bay station master, reported to the Caley Directors that surveys were apparently being carried out for a junction which would make the connection. Three weeks later, the Caley acted to oppose the Bill being prepared by the G&WBR. In January 1871, the G&WBR asked the Caley for its support but instead the Caley decided to oppose and by March 1871 had mustered sufficient support to have the Bill killed by the Standing Orders Committee of the House of Lords. Thirty years later, the Caley firmly opposed a G&SWR attempt to obtain a similar foothold.

February 1871 saw the Caley in dispute with the G&WBR over the amount due to it, claiming that from 1867, the Wemyss Bay company, while certifying that monies were due to the Caley, had failed to pay. The Caley was now owed a substantial sum.

In April 1871, the Caley Directors noted that an Interdict presented to the Sheriff by the Wemyss Bay company in respect of third class fares to Upper Greenock station had been suspended. At the time, the G&WBR was locked into a protracted dispute with the Caley about the fares generally. The line was still seven years off producing its first dividend and some Directors were clearly feeling the pinch - had they not just recently again tried to sell the line to the Caley?

The Caley minute book for July 1871 records that the Lord Ordinary ruled in favour of the Caledonian regarding suspending the Interdict. The Wemyss Bay Directors promptly appealed to the Inner House. A few days later, the Caley Directors noted with satisfaction that the Inner House had ruled in their favour in two appeals raised by the G&WBR. The House ordered that fares from Wemyss Bay to Upper Greenock be the same as to Greenock.

In August 1871, the Caley and the G&WBR were again in arbitration. This time, the Lord Ordinary Interlocutor ruled against the Caley. The Caley instructed its legal advisors, Messrs Hope and Mackay, to appeal. In October 1871, Mr Kerr reported the draft findings of the Dean of Faculty in the arbitration. It did not favour the Caley. Mr Kerr was instructed to lodge an objection.

Perhaps in an attempt to get rid of the prickly Wemyss Bay Directors, in January 1872, the Caley Board decided to consider any proposal the former might offer for an amalgamation - no doubt thinking that buying them out would be cheaper and less distracting in the long run.

More legal action followed regarding fares. The Sheriff Substitute ruled one way, then the Sheriff ruled the other. Frustrated, the Caley Directors 'resolved to advocate the case to the Court of Session'. They then tabled their intended train fares.

The Caley had had enough. On 19th March, 1872, the Directors,

> ... resolved that, inasmuch as we cannot work in amity with the Wemyss Bay in regard to rates, we now decide on acting on our own responsibility alone - and we direct our Manager to fix such rates for the coming season as he sees to be most to our advantage, with due regard to the rights of the Wemyss Bay Company, without further communication with that Company. It is recommended that the rates via Wemyss Bay should be fixed at such rates as will give to this Company their share of the through return fare - 2s. 2d. for 1st Class, 1s. 1d. for 2nd class.

The following week, the proposed fares from Glasgow to Rothesay via Wemyss Bay were submitted 'in proof' and 'very carefully considered'. Fares were adjusted to avoid traffic being driven off the Wemyss Bay route. The Caley Directors then unanimously adopted the table of fares.

But the Wemyss Bay Directors were still proving difficult. In April 1872, Keyden wrote saying that his Directors were applying to the Board of Trade to have the 1862 Working Agreement revised. However, the Board of Trade said they had no jurisdiction under the 1862 Greenock and Wemyss Bay Act to revise the Agreement between the two companies. Meantime, the Caley instructed Messrs Kerr and Graham to check the state of the line. They had some reason to do so for a petition had been sent to the Wemyss Bay Directors 'as to the alleged dangerous state of the permanent way'. The Caley's engineers checked it and reported in October 1872 that the line 'was not unsafe for the speed of the trains on it.' But it cannot have been too good because less than two years later, the matter was raised again.

In June 1872, the G&WBR was back offering terms for amalgamation with the Caley, but these were not acceptable to the Caledonian Directors.

The legal process surrounding the fare structure was still not concluded. In July 1872, the Inner House favoured the Caley on the subject of fares but the Court of Session ruled in favour of the Wemyss Bay company. The Caley decided to appoint the Lord Advocate to appeal against the latter's ruling. The Caley was even prepared 'to take the legal opinion of eminent English Counsel on the Wemyss Bay case' though it is hard to see what that would have achieved.

BUILDING THE LINE

The Caley Directors searched for a different approach. In August 1872, the Chairman, Thomas Hill, was authorised to draw on the Commercial Bank of Scotland for money to acquire shares in the G&WBR, at or under par. Keyden probably guessed what they were up to; in October 1872, he again offered the line for sale and again his offer was rejected. The Caley stopped purchasing shares later that month.

By September 1872, the Caley was prepared to go to the House of Lords against the little company over the non-payment of its net fourth. It engaged English Counsel to advise on whether an Appeal should be made to the Lords. However, the dispute seems to have been pushed to one side - for the moment.

Business Improves

In July 1872 the Caley decided to provide another platform at Wemyss Bay, the railway companies sharing the £79 [*£3,000] cost.

Sugar refining in Greenock had developed from small beginnings in the 1760s, when merchants began trading to the West Indies, to the point when by 1872, 250,000 tons were being produced annually, greater than any other area outside London. In February 1873, Scott and Son's Sugar Works at Upper Greenock advised the Joint Committee that as previously arranged with the G&WBR, they had built sidings within their own grounds. They asked the railway to fulfil its side of the bargain by installing points to allow their traffic on to the line. The Committee arranged for the work to be done, the £906 [*£33,000] cost being shared equally between the G&WBR and the Caley. In 1882 under Mortimer Evans and again in 1887, under Mr Niven's direction, additional accommodation was provided for Scott's, the cost being shared between the railway companies and Scotts.

Sugar was classified as 1st class goods. The G&WBR noted that terminal charges for such cargo at Leith, Granton and places in England amounted to 4s. per ton, however, agreement was reached that the terminal charge on the Wemyss Bay line for sugar to and from Leith and Granton would be 2s. 6d., presumably because loading and unloading would take place on private sidings. One suspects that the agreement was quietly worked out by the officers on both sides without the assistance of their Directors.

Better signalling and more business

As traffic increased, the signalling system needed upgrading. Although the block system, whereby signals prevented trains from entering occupied sections of line, had been used in parts of Britain since the 1850s, the Wemyss Bay branch only had a telegraph to advise on train movements. More passenger and goods traffic required a better method of working than the time interval system still common on a number of railways. Accordingly, in November 1873, the Caley and the G&WBR decided to introduce the Block system on the line, sharing the cost between them.

The two companies appear to have been unable to resolve matters relating to fares and charges to each other's satisfaction, or perhaps the G&WBR suspected it was being short-changed by its big partner. Anyway, in November 1873, it decided to go to arbitration once again, this time on coal rates. The Caley must have been constantly irritated by its small companion, but rather than go to arbitration, on Christmas Eve, they proposed a compromise on coal rates - the G&WBR would get the entire increase on the cost of coal transported to them. The G&WBR appear to have been content with its Christmas present.

The line continued to pick up new business. In January 1874, Sir Michael Shaw Stewart asked for more sidings. The additional traffic had another effect - accelerated wear on the rails. In May 1870, the G&WBR had asked the Caley if it would maintain the line. In

September 1872, when the two companies were locked into a series of legal battles, the Caley offered to maintain the line at cost price, the cost being retained out of gross receipts. The G&WBR, suspicious as ever, declined.

The condition of the line was giving cause for concern. In March 1874, the Caley, unhappy with its Chief Engineer's report, asked for more detail. The G&WBR must also have been worried for they again asked the Caley for their terms to maintain the line. The Caley said they would do it at cost, but to its own standard, and if the G&WBR didn't like it, the Board of Trade would adjudicate. Five months later, the Caley repeated its offer. The ever sensitive G&WBR replied that the Caley should charge on the basis of the average cost of the Caley network. So the G&WBR continued to maintain its line, though Keyden tried again (unsuccessfully) in February 1876 to get a better deal out of the Caley.

The fortunes of the line were affected by the G&SW Railway charging very low fares to Princes Pier in 1876 and 1877. But the fare cutting stopped when they found they derived no benefit. The Wemyss Bay line increased in popularity. On 7th April, 1877, the first issue of the *Largs and Millport Weekly News* looked forward to improvements at Wemyss Bay:

> Every passenger who has had the misfortune to meet an opposing crowd of passengers on the narrow platform of this station, striving to reach a train or pressing out to get on a steamer will be glad to know that there is some prospect of improvement in this respect for the coming summer. The Railway Company, we understand propose either laying down an additional platform so as to arrange for arrival or departure trains, or enlarging the means of reaching and leaving the present branch line which runs round to the pier and by making a proper branch road for passengers round the side of this line, relieve the great pressure hitherto experienced on the platform during the summer months.

The paper noted that the company intended to resume the summer traffic to Arran and through the Kyles of Bute, and with the 'splendid new steamer' *Lord of the Isles*, there would be considerable pressure to improve passenger facilities.

In June 1880, Mr Graham expressed concern at the condition of the line in Mr Evan's charge. Jointly they inspected the line but two weeks later, they had not reached any agreement. Two members of the public wrote to the Board of Trade about the state of the viaducts. Keyden again instructed Evans to meet Graham but still they disagreed. Each side proposed an intermediary, but as the Caley would not accept the G&WBR's suggestion, Major General Hutchinson of the Board of Trade was called in instead.

The winter of 1881/1882 hit the railway hard. On 22nd/23rd November, 1881, the sea wall was badly damaged during a storm and rail access to the pier and goods shed was cut off. Repair works were not completed by the end of the year and the pier sustained more damage in the severe storms of January 1882. On 24th January, the Caley's Traffic Committee noted that 25 wagons had been lost when part of an embankment at Wemyss Bay was washed away. Fifteen of these belonged to the Caley, two to the North British Railway Co. and eight to traders. The Caley decided to charge the G&WBR demurrage (i.e. an amount payable for failure to load or discharge within an agreed time) at the rate of 3s. [*£6.40] per wagon per day until they could be restored to use. Keyden said that repairs would be put in hand immediately. By April 1882, the pier had still not been rectified to the Caley's satisfaction and its Board of Directors decided that if Mr Graham was unsuccessful in getting the G&WBR to put matters right, it would have to approach the Board of Trade. Two months later, Mr Graham was asked to report on the state of the Wemyss Bay platform.

The Caley found the small company more than just a minor irritation. The G&WBR was frequently successful in its legal battles with the mighty Caley. On balance, they seem to have won more cases than they lost at Arbitration, with the Railway Commissioners, the Court of Session and the First Division. On one occasion alone, it cost the Caley £500 [*£20,000] in legal expenses, for no gain whatsoever. In October 1882, the Caley Board advised the G&WBR that if certain (unspecified) defects were not quickly rectified, it would notify the Board of Trade. It seems the Board of Trade required work to be carried out at Upper Greenock, to which both companies contributed half.

But the Wemyss Bay Directors were still not getting the returns they wanted. In October 1882, Keyden wrote to the Caley Board advising that the 'open and floating debts' due by his company now amounted to £22,496 14s. 9d. [*£958,000]. The G&WBR proposed to take powers to raise the sum by shares and borrowing. The Caley enquired about the company's assets, stating firmly that it would not allow the money to be raised by mortgage, however it shortly consented to an amended Bill. In June 1883 Keyden wrote to the Board proposing that the amount to be raised should be £30,000 [*£1.3m], to pay off the debts and provide accommodation at Upper Greenock and elsewhere.

The line's financial problems affected the level of maintenance. In April 1884, Mr Graham expressed concern to his Traffic Committee, saying that the Caley might have to make a direct approach to the Board of Trade 'again' unless the work to the track was carried out 'at once'. The subsequent Report from the Board of Trade showed that the line was not up to standard and the Caley was forced to carry out remedial work, advising the G&WBR that the cost should be regarded as a loan.

Considering the companies were dependent upon each other one might have expected more co-operation. The G&WBR probably felt it had to fight its corner hard because, while it was becoming more successful, it was small compared to the Caley and no doubt aware the Caley could switch more trade to Greenock. In 1884, the Caley sought permission to extend its line to Gourock, which was a clear threat to a small company which could not get its trains over the Clyde, as its competitors could.

The Caley meantime probably saw that the G&WBR was still the most convenient line for conveying passengers to Rothesay and places further south - and at a time when finances were strained, it did not make sense to enlarge its operation out of Greenock. Besides as majority shareholder, it was well aware of the finances of the little company and no doubt considered that it could buy it out when the time was right.

A successful end to the G&WBR - The Caley takes over

The year 1890 was a busy one. River traffic from the Broomielaw had declined significantly whereas rail traffic had grown. The *Glasgow Herald* reported that the Fair Saturday trains to Wemyss Bay were so well patronised that the two afternoon trains had to be duplicated, one having to be run in three sections and the other in four, while a further two specials were dispatched in the evening. Not surprisingly, the heavy demand increased the pressure on facilities at Wemyss Bay. The *Glasgow Herald* reported that the pier at Wemyss Bay station had been rebuilt, though during the reconstruction, extensive damage was suffered from a fire. (Until a further rebuild in 1988, some of the charred beams were still visible.) As in the original pier, there was a solid central division, with openings along its length and a small square piermaster's hut at the seaward end. The walls were covered with advertisements for Pears, Veno's and Lifebuoy soaps, *The Mail* and *Weekly Mail*, Bovril, Fry's Cocoa, Haig's GlenLeven Whisky, Corry & Co's Aerated Waters, and was surmounted by gas lamps and boards advertising the Hydropathic Hotel. Outside the hut was a lifebelt beside a typical Victorian weighing machine. The hut itself had windows on three sides, that on the south side having a counter sill. The door was on the east side and the hut was heated by a cast-iron stove.

On 6th October, 1890, the Caley Board decided to apply to Parliament to absorb the Wemyss Bay company. But it was three years before they received permission. Meanwhile, Wemyss Bay trains had access to Central Station and business improved.

The Greenock and Wemyss Bay Line becomes part of the Caley System

On 6th December, 1892, the Caley Board considered their officers' report concerning the Greenock and Wemyss Bay Railway Absorption Bill. The Board resolved to ask Parliament for authority to raise £176,895 [*£8.7m] in Caledonian stock for the shareholders, borrowing powers, and the power to substitute Caledonian Debenture stock for Wemyss Bay Debenture stock, to the sum of £10,170 [*£500,000].

On 27th July, 1893, the Caledonian Railway Act, 1893, 'An Act for enabling the Caledonian Railway Company to widen the Dalmarnock Branch Railway across the River Clyde ... for amalgamating the Greenock and Wemyss Bay Railway Company with the Caledonian Railway Company for extending . . . [and] for enabling the Caledonian Railway Company to raise additional money and for conferring further powers on them with respect to their undertaking and for other purposes', was passed, finally allowing the Caley to absorb the little company. The Act referred to the Caley's obligations under the Acts of 1862 and 1863 that had seen them invest £35,000 in the line and the later addition of a further £15,482 'for works and improvements'.

Clause 19 of the 1893 Act stated:

As from and after the first day of August one thousand eight hundred and ninety-three (which date is in this Act referred to as 'the date of amalgamation') and subject to the provisions of this Act the Wemyss Bay Company shall be and is hereby dissolved except for the purpose of winding up their affairs and the undertaking of the Wemyss Bay Company subject to the contracts obligations debts and liabilities affecting the same except so far as otherwise provided by this Act shall be and is hereby as from and after that date amalgamated with the undertaking of the Company and shall form part of that undertaking.

This pompous bit of legal jargon was followed by Clause 20 which stated that: 'As from and after the date of amalgamation the agreement scheduled to and confirmed by the Wemyss Bay Act of 1862 shall cease to have effect'.

Thus the Wemyss Bay line ceased to have an identity of its own. Constructed with a share capital of £150,000, with its various additions, it was valued in January 1894 at over £185,294 [*£9.4m] when amalgamated into the Caledonian. In January 1894, the value of the shares of G&WBR stock held by the Caley was put at £134,731 10s. 8d. [*£7.1m].

On 2nd January, 1895, the Caledonian Railway Company recorded that Keyden Strang and Girvan had handed over books, papers, etc. to the Caledonian Railway for the period from 27th August, 1887 to 24th October, 1893 - and were paid £80 'law charges'. So ended the Greenock and Wemyss Bay Railway Company.

At the end of 1915, the Caledonian Railway Company listed the total capital outlay for the railway and pier as £465,153 [*£16.3m] and the station master's and the other two houses at £1,340 [*£47,000]. Taking their whole enterprise into account, the Caley's capital outlay was a staggering £56m [*£1,960,000,000], the Wemyss Bay portion accounting for a tiny 0.8 per cent of all the Caley's stock.

Chapter Seven

Maintenance of the Line
Engineers' Reports

Every six months, the G&WBR line's engineer produced a report for the Directors of the company. These had to be set out in accordance with the format and at the frequency dictated by the Regulation of Railways Act, 1868. Those produced by Mortimer Evans, CE, between 31st January, 1878 and January 1882 provide an insight into the fortunes of the line.

For the half-year to 31st January, 1878 Mr Evans had this to record:

Pier - a considerable portion of the planking had been renewed at a substantial cost. Heavy wear was due to barrow wheels.
Sea Wall - a small portion had been repaired.
Stations & Bridges - The station roof at Wemyss Bay had had its lead flashing lengthened 'and it now effectually prevents the rain blowing in by the south west winds'. [Whether the lead had been dislodged is not recorded.]

Mr Evans went on to comment on the passenger receipts: 'I find the Caledonian Company earn 52.83d. [per passenger per train mile] while the Wemyss Bay earn the enormous sum of 104.94d. or almost double the Caledonian, notwithstanding the low fares on the Wemyss system'. Goods amounted to 65.55d. to the Caledonian and 238.96d. to the Wemyss Bay Company.

Rents at Wemyss Bay
Station Houses	£ 20	*£800
Refreshment Room	£ 40	*£1,600
Advertising	£ 15	*£600
Bookstall	£ 10	*£400
Coal Stances	£ 6	*£240
Capt. Campbell for offices & stores	£150	*£6,000

The Caledonian Railway Company paid no rent for the double-stalled stable behind the station. Mr Evans suggested they should be charged £10.

Permanent Way - 100 tons of rails had been bought to replace 80 tons which had become worn out over the last half year. (This was to be a constant cause for concern. Mr. Evans's track diagrams clearly revealed the condition of the lines along the length of the branch.) It is curious to note that 35 years earlier, chairs and rails cost more than twice as much. He then added his proposed budget for the next six months.

Expenditure for the next half year
Rails - 50 tons @ £6.6/- [*£250] per ton (£315)		
less 50 tons old rails @ £3 [*£120] per ton (£150)	£165	*£6,660
750 Chairs (21t 5cwt) @ £5 [*£200] per ton	£106	*£4,280
1,000 Sleepers @ 4/- [*£8] each (In 1864, they cost 2/10d [*£6] each)	£200	*£8,080
Keys	£ 8	*£320
Spikes and Bolts	£ 20	*£810
Ballast	£ 20	*£810
Repairs to Stations	£ 20	*£810
Paint	£ 40	*£1,620
Telegraph poles, insulators, etc.	£ 30	*£1,210
Wages	£700	*£28,260
Total Budget for next half year	£1,309	*£52,860

Mr Evans had obtained estimates for certain works needing doing on the line:

Viaducts
Estimated repairs to Inverkip viaduct		£ 49 17s. 4d.	[*£2,000]
Estimated repairs to Dunrod viaduct		£ 41 13s. 0d.	[*£1,680]

Another point he noted, presumably because he thought it had a significant effect on receipts and the condition of the line, was that about 8,600 tons of sandstone, including 710 tons from the G&WBR property, had been taken from Kelly Quarry in the last half year. Probably all this went over one of Henry Pooley's weighing machines, for which the line had to pay £5 8s. for adjustments.

Daff viaduct in 1999. The line is now carried on the piers built in 1902 when this section of line was doubled. The original viaduct was removed in 1966-1967, though the piers remain.				*Author*

MAINTENANCE OF THE LINE : ENGINEERS' REPORTS

	£	s.	d.	
Line Maintenance Cost				
Line maintenance costs arose from general repairs, ironmongery (unspecified), wages, rails, sleepers, fishplates, carriage of goods and slag, etc..	1,515	6	6	*£61,200
Block Telegraph by E.G.Bartholomew and Co. and connecting rods supplied by George Urie	42	5	0	*£1,700
Total Expenditure for the half year passed	1,557	11	6	*£62,900

He then detailed the receipts, apportioning them between the two railway companies, revealing how much more dependent the Wemyss Bay line was on the passenger traffic than on goods. His analysis is interesting as he compared it to the much larger Caledonian Railway.

	Caledonian Railway		Wemyss Bay Railway	
Receipts for the half year				
Passengers	£469,179	*£18.95m	£8,529	*£344,000
Goods	£925,449	*£37.37m	£6,223	*£251,300
Total	£1,394,628	*£56.32m	£14,752	*£595,300
Miles maintained	785.5		10.08	
Receipts/mile:				
Passengers	£ 618.5	*£25,000	£846.1	*£34,150
Goods	£1,220.1	*£49,250	£617.3	*£24,900
Receipts/train mile:				
Passengers	52.83d.	*£8.90	104.94d.	*£17.80
Goods	65.55d.	*£10.90	238.96d.	*£40.40
% of Receipts:				
Passengers	33.6%		57.8%	
Goods	66.4%		42.2%	
Expenditure for maintenance:	£152,284	*£6.15m	£1,959	*£79,000
Expenditure/mile maintained:	£200	*£8,080	£194	*£7,830

He also noted briefly that half the receipts on the steamboats to Innellan, Rothesay and Largs went to the G&WBR, the remainder going to the Caledonian Railway Company.

Mr Evans disposed of used steel rails to P. & W. MacLellan, Mersey Steel and Iron Company, the Steel Company of Scotland and John Harrison and Company. These companies melted the old rails down and made new ones to sell back to the railway companies. Mr. Evans considered that a rail was 'done' or worn out when it had lost 6.3 per cent of its weight. Not all the old rails were sold. Some were used for sidings at Kennedy's works, Finnock Bog, at Smithston, and at Wemyss Bay for coal and alteration works.

The report concluded with a description of the freight traffic over the line, showing that the company could not have survived on passenger traffic alone. His reports over the next four years showed the considerable expenditure needed to keep the line operational.

The pier, not yet 15 years old, now needed almost constant repairs - 2,700 sq. ft of the best pitch pine was followed 6 months later by renewal of a further 1,153 sq. ft of 3 in. decking. Two and a half years later, 1,800 sq. ft of deck and 1,250 sq. ft of joisting were renewed and only six months after that a further 3,190 sq. ft of 4 in. pitch pine planking was required. The Engineer recorded that, at the beginning of January 1882, the pier had suffered severely in a storm which had stripped a large area of planking, destroyed the yacht stairs (made from discarded timbers less than four years previously to allow landing from small boats) and damaged the stones under the higher part of the pier. Most of the planking had been recovered and used for patching but decayed joists urgently needed replacing.

The sea wall appears to have caused little problem till November 1881 when it was badly damaged in a storm 'which entirely cut off the access by rail, both to the Pier and Goods shed' and cost £108 5s. 4d. [*£4,600] to make good. But the severity of the storm two months later 'completely destroyed the restored work together with a further portion of the wall itself' resulting in a further £453 4s. 5d. [*£19,300] being spent to allow the wall to be 'even temporarily secured'. Repairs to the sea wall and replanking part of the platform was not completed till mid-1882.

In 1878, Wemyss Bay station platform had to be renewed in asphalt as 'the original asphalt floor was not good being far too thin besides being made with soft stone'. As the horse used for pulling the luggage trailer had been largely responsible for the wear, the Caledonian Railway Company should bear part of the cost. Further repairs were carried out in 1886.

Mr Evans commented that the houses occupied by the engine driver (3 apartment), porter (2 apartment) and the 'very fine' station master's house (4 bedrooms and an elegant drawing room) yielded only £20 in rent whereas letting off the cellars of these houses to Captain Campbell of the steamboat company yielded £21 [*£850]. There is a hint of poor workmanship with the appearance of dry rot in the engine driver's house and the need for repairs to the station roofs and gutters.

The bridges had been allowed to deteriorate. The viaducts required about £100 [*£4,000] spending on the longitudinal timbers to support the chairs and rails. In 1878, painters gave a much needed first repaint to the woodwork on the bridges. The bridge over the turnpike Road near Wemyss Bay was to be painted in 1882 'before the brackets for carrying the new water pipes are fixed'. 1881 saw a new water supply taken to Wemyss Bay station, presumably to cater for larger engines hauling more frequent trains. In October 1885, Thomas Weir, Mr Evans' successor, was instructed by Keydens to obtain the sanction of the Board of Trade for repairs to the planking of the Inverkip and Dunrod viaducts. One suspects Keyden was reluctant to authorise expenditure on these high viaducts, passed by the Board of Trade only five years earlier.

On the request of Horatio Peile, Sir Michael Shaw Stewart's factor, Mr Evans also inspected the timber viaduct over the Kip, on the Dunrod branch, and indicated that while generally sound, rot eradication repairs were necessary. This little private branch appears to have had further sidings added by McQueen & Harvie in 1867. According to an independent firm of surveyors, their engineers, Forman and McCall, seemed to have over certified the work by 25 per cent.

Rules 48-49 required that 'The foreman platelayer ... shall ... report particularly on the state of Inverkip & Cartsburn tunnels and of the rock cutting at Kelly & Cartsburn tunnels, etc, to ensure they are kept in good order, inspected weekly by the head inspector and 'brick by brick' under Rule 50'. The tunnels appear to have caused few problems but occasional work was needed to the rock cuttings at Upper Greenock and at the entrance to Inverkip tunnel.

The permanent way was a constant headache. In July 1878, Mr Evans reported that it had deteriorated by 14 tons and that it would be necessary to purchase 100 tons of new rails and 2000 sleepers. Six months later, action had been taken and he could report that the 'Rail Road' was in better condition with a larger percentage of the rails better than half worn. 50 tons of rails and 1000 sleepers (at 3s. 6d. [*£7.35] each) would be needed in 1879.

By July 1879, a third of the line had been lifted and relevelled from 1 in. to 6 in.; within the next six months, Mr Evans expected to have half the line relaid. One wonders how the railway could have been allowed to deteriorate by so much.

In his July 1879 report, Mr Evans proposed a new chair to carry the rail. The Caley had stopped using its previous chair for 75 lb. rails. The new chair gave about double the bearing of the old one and should extend the life of the sleepers (now costing 4s. [*£8.75] each) which had been damaged due to the old chair's small bearing area and the increased weight of the engines in use. The Anderston Foundry Co. were prepared to convert the old chairs to the new for £1 [*£44] per ton. Evans intended to replace 2,000 chairs each half year and renew the road at about 1 mile/annum over 10 years. The improvements would result in less labour costs for surfacemen and therefore a reduction in labour costs.

Track weight had increased considerably since 1831 when the Garnkirk line used fish-bellied rail supported in 8lb. cast iron chairs at 3 ft centres. On the Caley-owned lines, 75 lb.

rails (the type originally laid by the G&WBR in 1862) had been superseded by 80 lb. rails. In 1886, the Caley changed to 90 lb. rails in 46 lb. chairs for main lines, 80 lb. being retained for branch lines. (Progressively heavier trains saw 95 lb. bullhead rail used, superseded from 1948 by the 109 lb. flatbottom section used in modern continuously welded track.) This corresponded with an increase in locomotive weight. In 1846, the heaviest engines were about 19 tons. When the Wemyss Bay line opened, the heavier engines weighed about 35 tons. Around 1879, when Mr Evans was making his report, the heaviest engines were a little over 40 tons and by the end of the century only about 10 tons heavier. (The biggest increase in locomotive weight occurred in the early years of the 20th century. When the present station opened, the heaviest engines were 73 tons but the Pickersgill Wemyss Bay tank engines of 1917 were 91 tons - among the heaviest ever to run on British rails.)

Points were another area of concern. Mr Evans though was persuaded that the new Williams Patent Points would improve matters and save the company money. The Williams Railway Patent Point was duly installed at Dunrod for £387 11s. [*£17,000] and over the next 10 years at various places along the line but having chalked up an unenviable record of derailments, it was replaced, having cost a lot of money and a great deal of worry.

Rail realignment was carried out at the rear of the Wemyss Bay Hotel where it crossed the Kelly Turnpike Road at a cost £23 11s. 4d. [*£1,000] and steady progress was made on the permanent way: another 2,375 sleepers, 4,350 of the new heavy chairs, 1,000 yards of drain pipe and 1,449 tons of slag ballast had been installed by July 1881. Work done on the wet cuttings which had 'given great trouble for many years' was expected to much reduce the degree of maintenance required. But the replacement seemed never ending. By January 1882, another 300 new sleepers and 600 new chairs had been fitted and yet 50 tons of rails, 700 sleepers and 1,400 new chairs would be needed for the next half year - and the ballast required attention.

Minor repairs costing £7 0s. 4d. [*£300] were carried out to the turntable at Wemyss Bay and £60 [*£2,550] was allocated for new signalling by Stevens.

Gas fittings were installed in 1881 by Henry Carson, presumably at Wemyss Bay station, (possibly upgrading an earlier installation following Mr Keyden's meeting with the gas company in 1868) and the Post Office erected a wire from Upper Greenock station to a pole opposite Wemyss Bay Post Office.

One is left with the impression that dealing with 15 years of increasingly heavy usage had been a struggle. While many materials had survived well, the same did not apply to the track and pier which had to cope with mechanical wear and tear and the elements on a very exposed coastline. However the company seem to have carried out regular maintenance and improvements as necessary.

More income was being generated from the refreshment room, advertising and from the bookstall. In July 1878, Mr Evans noted that 'the Wemyss Bay is almost the only line just now shewing a traffic increase'.

Receipts taken in the years 1878 to 1881 showed that the Caley earnings were roughly in the ratio of £1 for passengers to £2 for goods, whereas the G&WBR earnings were the opposite way about:- better than £2 for passengers to £1 for goods. In 1879, Mr Evans observed that the Caley engines had to run eight times the distance on their own line to earn the equivalent amount on the Wemyss Bay railway, confirming a publicly held view that the Wemyss Bay Directors were greedy.

Revenue on the line fluctuated seasonally - in the August 1881 to January 1882 period the fall off in passenger receipts was about 30 per cent from the previous six months, though there was a 22 per cent increase in goods receipts. The goods traffic figures for the period show that for most categories, more goods were carried (especially coal) in the August to January period than between February and July. The overall receipts for these periods were £16,200 [*£690,000] (January 1881-July 1881) and £13,500 [*£575,000] (August 1881-January 1882). Train mileage (February 1879-July 1879) was 19,082 for passenger traffic and 6,130 for goods. As befits a branch line, proportionately less was spent by the G&WBR than the Caley on maintenance (approximately 10 per cent of receipts).

Summary of the goods & mineral traffic over the railway (tonnage)

Period From	To	Coal	Stone	Other minerals	Sugar	Beet sugar	Other goods
Aug. 1877	Jan. 1878	47,905	22,723	6,478	8,322	2,979 *	5,336
Feb. 1878	Jul. 1878	48,256	15,350	6,092	5,924	2,776	4,708
Aug. 1878	Jan. 1879	53,709	9,991	5,147	6,324	7,308	4,441
Feb. 1879	Jul. 1879	50,853	6,510	5,116	5,964	4,058	4,254
Aug. 1880	Jan. 1881	53,050	4,976	5,928	5,608	8,935	5,151
Feb. 1881	Jul. 1881	48,121	5,687	5,765	6,984	7,797	4,516
Aug. 1881	Jan. 1882	52,302	6,436	7,533	6,479	12,686	4,717
Average		50,599	10,239	6,008	6,515	6,648	4,860

* Beetroot sugar was only carried from November but became the second largest load carried on the rails.

The extension of Kelly siding in 1878 does not seem to have led to an overall increase in stone transported from Kelly Quarry. However it will be observed that the new siding installed at Scott & Son's Sugar Works at Upper Greenock in 1881 coincided with a substantial increase in sugar beet goods carried that year. (Scott and Son's works was connected to the G&WBR line in 1873.) Its successor, Tate & Lyle, closed the factory in 1997 with the loss of 190 jobs.

At monthly intervals, Keyden acknowledged receipt of payments from the Caley to the G&WBR for traffic on the line, after the Caley deducted its expenses. Here is a sample. It clearly shows the highly seasonal nature of the line and a remarkable consistency between consecutive years.

	1885 £ s. d.		1886 £ s. d.		1887 £ s. d.	
January			763 8 7	*£37,550	817 0 6	*£41,500
February			566 15 10	*£27,900	655 9 8	*£33,300
March			709 16 1	*£34,950	771 0 2	*£39,200
April			1,131 9 1	*£55,700	1,276 3 8	*£64,850
May			1,283 15 6	*£63,200	1,123 13 4	*£57,100
June			1,403 3 6	*£69,050	1,381 3 1	*£70,200
July			2,327 8 1	*£114,550	2,244 18 9	*£114,050
August	1,867 16 2	*£89,150	1,941 2 4	*£95,550	1,794 9 2	*£91,200
September	1,182 10 7	*£56,450	1,219 19 4	*£60,050	1,166 5 9	*£59,250
October	805 16 10	*£38,450	769 9 6	*£37,900	786 1 4	*£39,950
November	750 14 0	*£35,850	742 3 10	*£36,550	633 1 1	*£32,150
December	653 8 2	*£31,200	705 12 4	*£34,750	605 0 8	*£30,750

Every so often, the railway had to swallow hard and accept that they would not get their money back. In February 1887, Keyden wrote to Weir that the Caley could not collect payment from the British Asphalt Co. 'as they had given up business months ago'. Also in 1887, a certain building contractor, Mr Wagham, who had premises in central Glasgow, was unable to pay a bill of just under £20 [*£1,000]. Philip Keyden suggested that Mr Niven, the line's new Engineer, should 'buy' cement off him, even if it was not immediately needed, in order to reduce the amount owed. One suspects that Mr Keyden was unaware of cement's limited shelf life.

In another case, Thomas Edmiston owed the G&WBR just over £6 [*£300] for an old weighing machine. The company sought payment and then suggested he paid half meantime. Edmiston replied that he wished he could comply, but was currently unable to. Keyden sought Weir's advice - should he take proceedings? Eventually it was decided to do so and a Post Office Order for 2s. 4d. was sent to the Sheriff Clerk Depute in Greenock to commence proceedings. However, Edmiston was not to be found. The Post Office could not serve the documents as Edmiston had 'left'. Keydens later wrote to Edmiston's solicitor saying they would be prepared to accept payment by instalment. The records are silent on what happened next - if anything.

Chapter Eight

Managing the Railway

Letters were used as freely as we use the telephone. As the telephone was invented in 1876 it was several years before it was usefully available. Only in 1888 do we find P.G. Keyden starting to use the 'phone; Sir Michael Shaw Stewart did not have one installed at Ardgowan till 1900. The postal system was reliable, as evidenced by a letter written by James Keyden just before Christmas 1886 asking Mr Weir to call round 'tomorrow morning'. Another asking the publisher of the *Scottish News* to advertise the half-yearly meeting of the company in Keyden's offices 'tomorrow' shows that the letter could be almost as efficient as our fax machine. A daily exchange of correspondence between Glasgow and Edinburgh on the subject of land at Ravenscraig Station shows an efficient service which did not need to rely on first and second class postal systems or couriers. When passes were requested from the Caley for the G&WBR's Directors or employees, the Caley would almost invariably forward them the next day. There is little evidence that telegrams were much used.

Both James and Philip Keyden were efficient servants to the company. The surviving letter book shows them to have been diligent in directing the business.

The line's Engineers operated competently and seldom needed a reminder from the Secretary, who acted as intermediary between the Directors, the Caley management and the public. One senses that the Engineers generally had a good working relationship with the Secretary. Philip Keyden, who had only been Secretary for a short time, was clearly upset to learn from a Director that Mr Weir was contemplating leaving. Was it true?, he asked Weir in August 1887. Weir immediately confirmed this to be so - he had been offered a post abroad. Keyden looked for a successor and shortly wrote to Mr Lamont, the Chairman with four names: William Roger of Greenock - unlikely because he 'is now a very rich man, and would not be in the least likely to accept the position' (which probably says as much about the emolument as it does of the man); Charles Lindsay, recommended by Mr Weir but discounted by Keyden as being a surveyor and not a railway engineer; T.O. Niven, who had previously worked 10-12 years with Forman & McCall and was recommended by David McCall (from the same firm as J.R. Forman, the company's first Engineer) and James Bulloch, a young engineer with James Young & Co., contractors. Weir said he was quite prepared to work full time with his successor if he could leave by 8th September, but if this were not acceptable, he would have to decline the post offered him. Lamont was sympathetic to Weir. As Keyden said in his letter of 12th August to Weir, his Chairman was unwilling to injure Weir's professional career - he 'has always had a friendly feeling towards you'. Weir could leave on 7th September, but Keyden would be obliged if he would help his successor prior to that date and attend the AGM on 21st September. Weir accepted these conditions.

On 17th August, Keyden offered the job to Mr Niven, CE, starting on 8th September. He was expected to reside at Wemyss Bay. The overlap Weir saw as necessary was not going to happen.

Line Management

Water Supply. Though the line was opened for service in May 1865, no arrangement seems to have been made to supply water for the engines for in April 1868, we find J.R. Forman seeking permission from Sir Michael Shaw Stewart's agent to run a 3 inch diameter pipe from Brueacre Burn to supply water for the engines and the station houses at Wemyss Bay. Mr M.J. Martin, Sir Michael's agent agreed but pointed out that the company would be charged a 'nominal rent' of 10s. [*£20] per annum and would have no title to be provided with water.

Large volumes of water were needed by the locomotives. Exact quantities are not known but a letter from Mr Peile of the Lower District Committee of the County Council of Renfrewshire to the Caley dated 1st June, 1897 quoted rates of 5d. [*£1.10] per 1,000 gallons for the first 3 million gallons, 4½d. per 1,000 gallons for the next 4 million gallons and 4d. per 1,000 gallons for any quantity thereafter, with a minimum supply of 7.5 million gallons [*min. charge £7,600].

Lamps & Weighing Machines. One senses that it was only the approach of the dark winter nights that forced the company to instal lamps. The matter was raised in September 1865 and the G&WBR installed fittings in the stations, and with some reluctance on Wemyss Bay pier. Presumably oil fittings were used as gas was not initially available. In November 1871, the Caley decided to purchase a platform weighing machine for Wemyss Bay station as the G&WBR refused to pay its half of the £13.10s. [*£530] cost. In 1883 the bookstall there was let to the Misses Dickson for a yearly rent of £35 [*£1,500].

Upper Greenock Station. In October 1885, John Young of Grahamshill, Airdrie built a goods station at Upper Greenock. After various remedial works had been done, James Thompson, General Manager of the Caley, wrote to Keyden in October 1886 stating that the sidings and roads at Upper Greenock were in a very unsatisfactory condition and that work should be put in hand straight away as winter would see heavy stone traffic using the line. Also, the exterior lamps could not be lit. Keyden forwarded the letter to Weir to action.

Temporary Sidings. Occasionally, temporary sidings were built for use by building contractors. During the widening of the line between Port Glasgow and Upper Greenock in 1900, Robert McAlpine was allowed to build a temporary line. Likewise, Loudon and Inglis formed a temporary siding in connection with their 2-year contract to construct Greenock Combination Hospital.

Stables at Wemyss Bay. The Caley approached the G&WBR in March 1886 to see if they would build a stable at Wemyss Bay. Mr Keyden wrote to Mr Thompson accepting the proposal provided the Caley footed the bill, adding a dig about the falling off of trade. Having just received the February traffic receipts, Keyden was writing with feeling. Mr.Weir advised Keyden that a two-stall stable with hay loft over would cost £200 [*£9,800]. As the G&WBR was not bothered how it looked, Keyden wrote to Thompson in August that a stable at the south end of the goods shed 'of any description they please' would be approved by the G&WBR provided the Caley removed it when asked. The Caley contracted the work to Mr Robb, who built it for less than £40.

Sheep Cartage. In October 1886, Hugh Crawford, who presumably was a farmer, wrote to Mr Keyden querying the cost of transporting sheep. He intended to send 13 score lambs (260) from Lochgilphead to over-winter near Wemyss Bay. He mentioned that he had been charged 10d./score [*£2] the previous year where other piers only charged 4d./score. He would be better off landing them at Greenock and *driving* them to Wemyss Bay. What he eventually did, is not recorded.

Old Rails. Keyden maximised the company's resources by selling off worn out material - even sacks and a weighing machine. In December 1885, he disposed of 43 tons of old chairs (less 5 per cent for loss of weight) to the Anderston Foundry Co. of Glasgow at 55s. 6d. [*£130] per ton. However payment was not always readily forthcoming. In October 1886, he was chasing John Fairlie of Waterloo Street for a long overdue account of £241 18s. 11d. [*£11,500] for old rails. Sleepers also found a home - though what the Commissioners of Police at Port Glasgow found to do with 700 old sleepers, bought at the bargain price of £10 4s. 2d. [*£490] (3½d. each when they had probably cost 4s. each new), is left to the imagination.

Passes. Keyden periodically obtained annual passes for named parties from the Caley. Used passes had to be returned. For example, in January 1886 he applied for Mr Weir's assistants, James Rae (a telegraph linesman) and James McCluskey. In February, Keyden requested a pass for John Russell, contractor, between Glasgow and Wemyss Bay, so that he could repair the platform there, and in September, for a 1st class pass for William Duncan, contractor, to repair the sea wall. At the end of 1886, Keyden sent out first class passes for use on the line to Robert Maclean, Banker in Greenock, J.W. Turner WS in Greenock, and Messrs Hadaway, Lamont and Magnay, Mr Weir and his two assistants, with the request that they return their expired ones. Directors' passes were not restricted to the G&WBR line. Keyden also sought and obtained passes for certain Directors to travel on other lines - Mr Alston for example needed one to travel from Cathcart St station into Central Glasgow. Philip Keyden also wrote to John Morton, General Manager of the G&SWR asking whether he would provide passes for the G&WBR Directors on their metals. Mr Morton was not forthcoming so Keyden pointed out that G&SWR Directors' passes entitled them to ride on the G&WBR line; but it was some months before the rival railway company provided the passes. The Directors of the G&WBR and Mr Weir were also favoured with passes for the steamers.

Parcels. The Caley was quite happy to arrange for parcel delivery from certain stations, free of charge. In the centre of Glasgow, there were six deliveries during the day for distances up to 2 miles from Glasgow Central. Gourock, Greenock and Port Glasgow had four deliveries covering most of the town, Inverkip had two deliveries daily up to a maximum of 28 lb. It therefore seems a little odd that there was a charge for delivering to Wemyss Bay, made even more surprising as the cost of delivering passenger train parcels to Rothesay was substantially less than to Wemyss Bay.

The Jacomb Award. In July 1884 the Caley Minute Book records that Mr Jacomb, a Board of Trade appointed engineer, had adjudicated on the condition of the track. The line urgently needed relaying. The Caley Board agreed 'to adopt the suggestion of Mr Jacomb, but it must be made clear that the money is an advance, to be repaid, and not a contribution, and that this must not be pleaded as a precedent'. By December 1885, the work had cost £773 5s. [*£33,800], the Caley paying half. Over the next six months it cost another £728 18s. 11d. [*£31,900], of which the Caley would pay a third. The G&WBR made its first repayment of £333 6s. 8d. [*£14,600] to the Caley in October 1886. The company must have been struggling at the time as Keyden had made arrangements to borrow 'a few thousands at Martinmas' - which fortunately did not prove necessary.

Widening the Line. Keyden wrote to Mr C. McCulloch, Town Clerk at Greenock, in January 1886 to have the legal agreement with the Water Trust for piping water over the line modified as the G&WBR was contemplating doubling the line, which 'may be carried out before very long'. The Town Clerk demanded that the company pay £25 [*£1,250] for widening a bridge owned by the railway. Keyden asked him to reconsider, reminding the Town Clerk that Greenock had long known that the line would be doubled, and had not objected before. The pipeline would be rerouted on land the Railway had purchased from Sir Michael Shaw Stewart which would be transferred to the Water Board. The Town Clerk stood firm, stating that the line had been built single whereupon Keyden replied that many of the bridges had been built double. Keyden paid up, though he did not see why the company should. In March 1886, Mr J. Martin Hardie of the Smithston Asylum, requested permission to survey the Branchton bridge with a view to laying a sewer across it. Keyden granted the request. In May, Keyden sent a cheque to Mr Hardie for £7 9s. in payment for damages sustained by his staff extinguishing a fire at Smithston bridge. The cause of the fire was not explained.

Private Transport. In 1883, a horse loading bank at Inverkip was reconstructed using local stone. Mr Horatio R.B. Peile, writing as Factor to Sir Michael Shaw Stewart from the Mansion House, Greenock, sought permission to use the siding there to load Sir Michael's passengers and carriages. Sir Michael owned a large number of carriages and had a sizeable establishment. Keyden replied that Sir Michael's horses and carriages could be loaded there, but only on the *down* line (i.e. to Wemyss Bay). Passengers and servants would have to board at Inverkip.

The 1902 Appendix to the Working Time Table states that private carriages and horses could be loaded or unloaded at Glasgow Central, Paisley (Gilmour Street), Bishopton, Greenock Central, Gourock, Inverkip and Wemyss Bay. Judging from the number of loading points, this was a not uncommon practice before the advent of good highways and reliable road vehicles.

Refreshment Room. In March 1871, James Keyden asked the Caley Board if they would be prepared to allow the gentlemen's waiting room to be used as an additional refreshment room. It is not clear whether the Board decided to concur in this request. In February 1887, Keyden wrote to Archibald Gibson, Secretary of the Caledonian Railway, saying that he understood the Caley would soon be advertising that the refreshment room at Wemyss Bay station was to let - without even allowing the tenant to apply for a spirits' licence. Keyden said that his Directors would not allow the refreshment room to be let 'without the tenant being allowed to apply for the usual licence'. He claimed that elsewhere on the Caley, for example at Glasgow and Gourock, the refreshment rooms were licensed. He added that the G&WBR was intending to reorganise the refreshment room so that it could get trade from passers-by on the road as well as the railway patronage. He advised the Caley that if they withheld approval, they would be held liable for any loss sustained and he asked them to think again. But the Caley, ignoring the wishes of the G&WBR, advertised the premises at the end of February, without making any reference to a spirits' licence.

A flurry of correspondence followed. Keyden had a meeting with Gibson. Gibson said the Caley would not prevent John Hughes, the present licensee, from seeking an application for a licence - but the Caley would oppose it. (The patrons at Wemyss Bay seem to have been a special case.) The Caley said it was worried about the effect of spirits on its drivers and guards. If the refreshment room was reorientated, it would be no better than a public house and the Caley would oppose that. Keyden sought the views of Hadaway and Turner, then in London lobbying to allow the G&WBR access into Central Station. Mr Turner successfully negotiated the G&WBR case. Next month, Mr Weir made preparations to alter the refreshment room layout along the lines proposed by the G&WBR, Mr Hughes bearing the cost. In mid-March 1887, Keyden wrote to James Thompson, General Manager of the Caledonian Railway, saying that Mr Hughes was prepared to increase the rent he presently paid from £70 to £100 [£*5,100] if he obtained the spirits' licence, on the basis that he was granted a 5-7 year lease, adding that he was 'glad to hear that his offer has been accepted'.

An odd twist to the story suggests that it was Keyden who was forcing the pace. A few days later, Keyden asked Hughes to call to discuss the matter, and encouraged him to make application for a spirits' licence. But Hughes was a slow mover. A week later, he had done nothing. In mid-April, Keyden wrote to James Turner saying that the refreshment room's lease would be sent down for Hughes to sign. He mentioned that Hughes seemed apprehensive about obtaining a licence and that he had suggested he test local feeling in the time honoured manner of getting a petition together. Two months later the lease was still not signed. In September 1887, Philip Keyden wrote to Mr Hughes noting that he was about to seek an extension of the wine and beer licence for the new bar. Keyden asked him to apply for a spirits' licence for the *whole* premises - saying he was prepared to help procure it if necessary. However, no amount of pushing was going to get Mr Hughes to apply for that spirits licence. In September, Philip Keyden seems to have finally noted that Hughes was not going to make any application.

The Glasgow Terminus

Bridge Street station on the south side of the Clyde soon became the terminus for the Caledonian in Glasgow. It was built on a brick viaduct which has survived subsequent extension and was formally opened on 6th April, 1841, a week after the line between Glasgow and Greenock was completed. John Miller was the Engineer, James Collie the Architect, John Buchanan the contractor. According to J.F. McEwan, the classical entrance portals were from a former Weslyian chapel built in 1813, built as grandly as the narrow frontage on Bridge Street allowed. Behind, the iron-framed 'train shed', as the station was described, was a somewhat gloomy enclosure - all-over roof glazing only made its appearance later in the century.

The station provided a Glasgow terminus for passengers travelling to London. Initially, their 24-hour trip (which it must be remembered was faster than anything previous), saw them embark on the 4.00 pm for Ardrossan where they would arrive at 6 pm. They then transferred to the steamer *Fire King* for the 13-hour overnight sail to Liverpool. From Liverpool, a 9-hour train journey brought them into London. The completion of the Caley line from Carlisle to Glasgow in 1848 finally linked London to Glasgow by rail.

In an article in the *Glasgow Herald* of 15th February, 1898, a writer commemorating the Jubilee of the Caledonian Railway wrote:

> It is just 50 years today since the Caledonian Railway was opened to the public throughout its entire length between Glasgow, Edinburgh and Carlisle . . . The inauguration of the line was unostentatious . . . because the country had not then recovered from the great commercial panic which made the late autumn months of 1847 long memorable. Many commercial firms had failed in the months of September and October; and a number of banks had suspended payment . . . But the crowds that assembled at various points in the neighbourhood of the line to see the Directors' train pass testified to the deep interest that was felt in the new railway, by means of which passengers would be enabled to travel between Glasgow and London without break of journey. Many of them had probably read with much astonishment and some incredulity a few days previously the official announcement that on and after the 1st of March express trains would run between London, Edinburgh and Glasgow in 13 hours!

While the first trains ran a cautious timetable, they were a good 11 hours better than anything previous. The idea of travelling by train and boat to London soon became a thing of the past.

By 1847, Bridge Street was handling 1 million people in a cramped 0.75 acre site. In 1851 the station had four lines linked by eight turnplates. In 1863, William Johnstone and George Graham submitted a report recommending purchasing adjacent property to allow the station to be enlarged to take the traffic from the proposed Wemyss Bay and Bridge of Weir lines. The Board decided against extending the station. But traffic continued to increase.

In 1866, a year after the Wemyss Bay line opened, the Caley, in common with other burgeoning railway companies, was proposing construction projects totalling over £6.6m [*£260m], including a £2m [*£79m] station in the heart of Glasgow. But the boom collapsed and the Caley postponed its ambitious plans. Things improved in the early 1870s. In 1873 the Caley presented a Bill to Parliament to construct a much needed station on the north of the Clyde accessed through Bridge Street station. But this scheme was dropped. The Board of Trade claimed that a serious accident at Bridge Street station in 1873 was the result of 'the traffic having outgrown the possibilities of the station'.

Bridge Street station was under the joint management of the G&SW Railway Co. and the Caledonian, competitors and uneasy bedfellows. It was clearly too small for the competing companies. W.M. Ackworth, in *The Railways of Scotland*, published in 1890, recorded that:

> In all, 11 trains, and 13 boats in connection, run for the accommodation of passengers leaving Glasgow in the half hour after 4 o'clock. On Saturdays, the whole of this elaborate mechanism begins to work some two hours earlier. Needless to say, it has also to be set in motion every morning to get people up to business by half-past nine; while on Mondays, in particular, the crush is so tremendous that a special relief service has to be organized in front of the ordinary daily service. Even so, the train booked to leave Gourock at 8.30 has sometimes had to be despatched in 4 portions.

He added:

> . . . though the Wemyss Bay line looks on paper far and away the best to Rothesay, it has been seriously handicapped by the use of a much less convenient station in Glasgow. However, last autumn [1889] it [the Wemyss Bay branch] was bought by the Caledonian...and it is understood that next summer will not only see its service much improved but also its trains admitted in Glasgow into the 'Central', a station which is - what Central Stations by no means always are - honestly entitled to its name.

According to J.F. McEwan, around 1898, the Wemyss Bay train was accelerated so that Rothesay was 78 minutes from Glasgow.

Wemyss Bay - The longest line but the shortest time

Glasgow to:	Caledonian via Gourock (minutes)		G&SWR via Greenock (minutes)		North British via Craigendoran (minutes)		Caleodonian via Wemyss Bay (minutes)	
	Up	Down	Up	Down	Up	Down	Up	Down
Innellan	85	77	85	70	94	90	70	65
Rothesay	105	97	105	95	114	110	80	80
Train Time:	40	40	45	40	37	37	50	50
Railway Distance travelled	26¼ miles		25½ miles		22½ miles		30½ miles	

The G&SWR began to develop the St Enoch station nearby, (mooted in 1866, opened 1876), on the north side of the river. The Caley offered to share the cost but drew back when the G&SWR (supported by the Midland, its English counterpart) said it would cost the Caley £500,000 [*£20m]. By the early 1880s the Caley, at G&SWR insistence had had to spend £150,000 [*£6m] enlarging Bridge Street station while the G&SWR made plans to expand St. Enoch. Included within the Bridge Street station works was a new block of offices (reconditioned about 1990) designed by James Miller (unrelated to John Miller, the original Architect). The station now included an area originally occupied by a goods station, and an area to the south. The last part of the original Bridge Street station buildings disappeared in the late 1960s.

Parliamentary permission was obtained under the Caledonian Railway (Gordon Street, Glasgow, Station) Act 1873 (modified in 1875) to build a station on the north of the river. The Clyde was bridged between 1876 and 1878 and the first Caley Central Station (Gordon Street station) built by Watt & Wilson, was opened in December 1879. In 1878, Watt and Wilson began construction work on the building (originally intended as offices for the company) designed by Sir Robert Rowand Anderson that became the 400 room Central Station Hotel. Completed in 1883, it opened in 1885, after the installation of electric lighting.

The building of the station was costly: two lines led Central bound trains, including those from London, through the north end of Bridge Street station, over four tracks across the Clyde (the Clyde Trustees had imposed a width limitation) to eight short, narrow platforms in the new station, erected on arches over the surrounding ground and constrained between Gordon Street and Argyle Street. By 1880, Central handled 173 trains daily and 4,750,000 people per annum. The Caley soon discovered its new terminus was too cramped and lack of sidings meant that one of the lines across the bridge had to be used for parking carriages.

The Wemyss Bay Directors seek access to Central Station

Meanwhile, James Keyden had been busy writing to the Caley Board seeking permission for Wemyss Bay trains to run right through to Central. He rejected the terms offered by the Caley in June 1879 and asked for better. In April and again in July 1880, Wemyss Bay residents petitioned the Caley for access to Central. With the G&SWR offering a competitive service from St Enoch station on the north of the Clyde connecting with boats at Princes Pier in Greenock, the public had a choice of route to Rothesay. The convenient new station contrasted markedly with the cramped arrangements at Bridge Street - and the G&WBR felt the result.

In 1882, the opening of the line to Fairlie Pier gave the G&SWR the edge on traffic to Millport. While the G&SWR line was distinctly longer than that to Wemyss Bay, the sea crossing was very short and St Enoch station provided the direct access across the Clyde denied the G&WBR. The Directors of the Greenock and Wemyss Bay Railway Company maintained pressure on the Caley to allow their trains into Central. Again in June 1883, the Caley Minute Book records Keyden's request that Wemyss Bay trains be allowed into Central Station. The Wemyss Bay Directors were no doubt aware of the Caley's intention to extend its line to Gourock and that by running a train from Glasgow Central to a ferry at Gourock, the Caley could strangle the Wemyss Bay Company. Matters were not helped by the indifferent performance of Captain Campbell's steamers.

On 12th August, 1886, at the height of the tourist season, Keyden wrote to James Thompson, the Caley's General Manager, voicing the displeasure of his Directors and the irritation of passengers that Wemyss Bay trains were still excluded from Central Station. The Caley was asking too much for the Wemyss Bay trains to be allowed access and consequently, if it continued in this manner, the G&WBR would make an application to the railway Commissioners to be dealt with in a manner similar to its competitors.

As if to emphasise the point, the same day he wrote another letter to James Thompson asking the Caley to retain the 8.15 pm down to Wemyss Bay and the 9.30 pm up as they had been very popular. Keyden's Directors further noted that Sunday services had been successful on the Caley and G&SWR lines to Greenock. Could the Wemyss Bay line also have Sunday services? In October, they were still making the same request, and objecting to the reduction in the evening services.

At the end of August 1886, Keyden wrote to Mr Lamont, Chairman of the G&WBR, suggesting that as the G&WBR was getting a splendid share of the traffic to the coast, that it might be imprudent to insist on equal right of access to Central Station as the Caley might say that the railway already got too much of the proceeds. (It *was* doing rather well - the July returns were 66 per cent up on the previous month.) Passengers could walk through Bridge Street station into Central for a penny ('and sometimes this is not charged'). Keyden offered to have a chat with Mr Thompson and suggest that the Wemyss Bay passengers pay an additional penny for the privilege of being deposited in Central Station.

A few days later, Keyden wrote to Lamont saying that Thompson thought the penny ticket impractical. Keyden had proposed to Thompson that the G&WBR line be charged the same as the Cathcart line, and had left him to think it over.

Nothing happened. The Directors of the G&WBR decided to force the issue. On 15th December, 1886, Keyden wrote to Messrs Gordon Pringle Dallas & Co., W.S. of 3 Queen Street in Edinburgh:

> Dear Sirs - I beg to subjoin an excerpt from the Minutes of my Directors requesting you to take proceedings to obtain for this company admission to the Caledonian Company's Central Station, and I shall be glad to receive any writ which you propose to serve upon the Caledonian Company and to give you all necessary information to enable you to proceed.

On 23rd December, having notified the Caley of his intentions, at the instigation of Gordon Pringle Dallas & Co., Keyden sent a letter to Andrew Beveridge in Westminster 'proving service of the application by this Company to the Railway Commissioners' for permission to access Central Station.

The Directors were becoming more concerned that their line was being treated as a side issue by the Caley as they concentrated on winning more of the Greenock clientèle. With Campbell's steamboats in decline, the G&WBR needed access to Central Station to prevent its enterprise foundering. In a letter in January 1887 to Mr T.J. Gordon, of Gordon Pringle Dallas, who was temporarily staying in the Scottish Club in Piccadilly, Keyden expressed his concern that Caley passengers from Gourock would get direct access to Central Station, but the G&WBR's passengers would not. To strengthen the chances of success, more support was needed. Keyden thought he had found an ally. He wrote to ex-Provost Sommerville of Port Glasgow:

Dear Sir - Mr J.W. Turner, Writer, Greenock, informs me that you are a Director of the Cathcart Railway and that this railway has access to the Central Station of the Caledonian. Also, that you are of opinion that the Wemyss Bay passengers should get access to the Central Station, and that even without any extra payment. I have written to Gordon, W.S. Edinburgh who is acting for the Wemyss Bay Company in a case which they have brought before the Railway Commissioners to compel access to the Central Station, and told him what I understood you were prepared to say. You will hear from him or me upon the subject immediately.

The same day, he wrote to Mr Gordon reckoning that Mr Somerville would make an 'excellent witness' in their case, however, Mr Somerville's evidence was not called. Perhaps if Mr Somerville had been present, things might have been different.

In February 1887, Messrs Todd, Simpson and Marwick W.S., of 116 George Street Edinburgh, wrote to Keyden offering to give the G&WBR access to Central Glasgow by a new city and suburban line which was being contemplated. Keyden sought details and when these arrived he confirmed his interest. But nothing developed, and the G&WBR were left trying to get into Central over the Caley's line.

On 8th February, 1887, Messrs Gordon Pringle Dallas wrote to Mr Thompson saying that the G&WBR was prepared to pay the extra to get its passengers into Central Station. The Caley Board replied that the Railway Commissioners had backed them up by confirming that the Caley had no obligation to provide the G&WBR access to Central. Mr Thompson wrote,

> I have to state in the first place, that under existing circumstances and the crowded state of Central Station during the busy hours in the morning and afternoon, and considering the character of the Wemyss Bay traffic and trains and the extent of Station accommodation they require, my Directors regret that at present they are quite unable to admit the Wemyss Bay trains.
>
> And as regards the remuneration proposed, it is so very inadequate - in no case more than ¼*d*. per passenger - that we could not entertain the proposal, even if the accommodation at the station were such as to enable us to admit the Wemyss Bay trains.

But the door wasn't *quite* closed. Thompson defined the charges the Caley would levy per passenger if and when they were in a position to accept the Wemyss Bay trains. This varied from 1*d*. [*20p] for a third class single to 4*d*. [*84p!] for a first class return - in *addition* to the existing rates.

Late in February 1887, Keyden wrote Gordon Pringle Dallas advising that their application had failed. He observed that this could have a serious affect on the company if the Caley's Gourock trains got into Central but those on the G&WBR's branch did not. Keyden kept up the pressure on the Caley. He asked for a meeting with James Thompson to discuss terms for running trains into Central. He recognised that the Caley's present terms were too onerous and that litigation was costly. In July 1889 his son Philip Keyden again wrote to ask if the Caley were ready to work the Wemyss Bay trains into Central Station, but I have found no reply to this enquiry.

The precipitate withdrawal of Captain Campbell's Wemyss Bay fleet in April 1890 hastened the complete takeover of the management of the steamers by the Caley. By good fortune the Caley had two new boats available for immediate use. On 1st May, 1890, the Caley put its newly-built boats, the *Caledonia* and *Galatea* on the Wemyss Bay service to fill the gap, and now as it was in its interest to make a success of the line, they allowed the Wemyss Bay trains access to Central Station as from that date. Whether by accident or design, the Caley was now in complete control of the Wemyss Bay enterprise.

By 1888, Central handled 300 trains a day and 9,250,000 people. A ninth platform was added in 1889, bringing the aggregate platform length to 1,530 yards. But there were severe operational problems. To ease matters, the Caley acquired property round the station to allow it to expand. Eventually it accumulated enough to more than double its floor area, including a wide access over the Clyde permitting three times as many tracks to cross the river. The number of trains being handled grew to 486 in 1897, by which time passenger numbers had reached 15,750,000.

Looking some years ahead, the subsequent enlargement and reconstruction of Central Station and the building of a second Clyde bridge alongside the existing (1901-1906) involved intricate underpinning and foundation work in ground lying between the underground railway and the River Clyde, (with foundations taken down 45 ft below street level) the whole costing about £500,000 [*£25m]. Quicksands had to be overcome and, together with underpinning hundreds of buildings and dealing with old sewage systems along the route of the underground lines, the engineers under Donald Matheson, first as Resident Engineer for the Central Low Level lines then as Engineer-in-Chief of the Caledonian Railway, were not short of challenges. Where the station crossed Argyle Street, there was a level below the street where the Caley ran trains on the Central Underground Railway. Further south, to provide the required headroom under the 110 ft wide bridge over the Clyde, the rails had to be raised by up to 3 ft, necessitating raising the old bridge. Altogether 13 lines of rails were laid over the two bridges to serve the new station.

The new Central Station (1901-1906) was a 'far-sighted' design. Current station trends laid emphasis on terminal stations as the 'gateway' to the city, with the result that entrance portals were grand and dominating, while inside a generous space was set aside for the 'concourse' - Central Station, the nearby St Enoch and Queen Street stations demonstrate this trend. Central was enlarged to provide 13 platforms at the upper level (total length 2,910 yards and four below, with flow patterns based on Donald Matheson's studies of American practice. Matheson once stated, 'In planning, the probability of crowding and the tendency of people to spread like flowing water and travel along the line of least resistance was kept in view. It was therefore thought desirable to have curved building lines and rounded corners not only in the concourse, but also in the subway and elsewhere in the station, and this idea was maintained throughout'.

The station covered 14,000 sq. yds against the previous 6,250 sq. yds with a much enlarged concourse area of 3,000 sq. yds against the 550 sq. yds before. Platform width increased from 15 ft to 23 ft. The main departure platforms to the south extended to 900 ft x 30 ft wide and there was one platform 1,000 ft long, 33 ft wide where two trains could be dealt with simultaneously, the permanent way being laid out so that the rear train could depart ahead of the front. South of the cab rank above the Broomielaw, was a special double-sided platform for fish, fruit and milk vans so that they were kept separate from passenger traffic. All but this last platform had hydraulic buffers. Bridge Street station ceased to be a passenger station. In its place there were eight running lines and nine carriage sidings.

The Architect who assisted Matheson design this great glass terminus was James Miller, and the same pair, employing the same philosophy, were responsible for the Wemyss Bay terminus at the other end of the line, rebuilt about the same time. Both Central and Wemyss Bay stations had island platforms where a double line of columns down the platforms allowed Matheson 'to form three avenues for traffic - the central avenue for the wheeling of luggage and an avenue on either side for passengers'. In 1899, over 23 million passengers used Central Station's high and low level platforms. The construction of the second (i.e. current) Central Station was carried out by Mr, later Sir, John Wolfe Barry as consulting engineer, following his considerable experience of constructing underground railways in London. In 1907, the Rowand Anderson designed Central Station hotel was extended southwards along Hope Street to Miller's designs. Miller also designed the 7-storey Caledonian Chambers in Union Street on the opposite side of the station (built 1901-1903). This building, which included shops at pavement level, provided office and other railway accommodation. Originally, the street entrances were more obvious by the canopies that projected well out over the pavements. The *porte cochère* where taxis set down their passengers, is not original. Internally, the buildings of the first Central Station were replaced with structures that encouraged free movement of people. However the old clock was retained. Elsewhere there were attractive features - wrought-iron railings, gates, signs, an enormous destination board; 'everything', observes John Paton, 'that today is plain and functional was treated as an object of art'.

In the summer season, in the years up to World War I, Central handled up to 30 trains a day to the coastal resorts at Gourock, Wemyss Bay and Ardrossan, generally from the west side platforms Nos. 10-13.

Further extension of platforms 1, 2 and 11 shortly before World War II was provided for sleeping cars. With electrification, the station was 'cleaned up' with the removal of the old clock, the ornate ironwork at the platform entrances (though some still remains on isolated platforms), the ground floor building frontages and the exterior verandas. In 1974, Central Station was handling over 82,500 passengers per day and 963 trains. In the 1990s, alterations and new buildings reverted to Miller and Matheson's free-flow principles.

The Clyde Navigation Act 1887

In the next chapter we will learn that Captain James Williamson, first marine superintendent of the Caledonian Steam Packet Company, had been influential in getting signals erected at pier ends to regulate steamer berthing. In January 1886, anticipating the 'Bill of the Clyde Trustees', Keyden wrote to T.S. Hadaway suggesting that the Caley should pay half the cost of erecting the new signalling apparatus and that a small charge be levied on steamers to pay for operating the signals.

Early in February, what seemed like a good idea that should not have cost much to implement, saw Keyden writing to George Jackson of the Caley to say the G&WBR would probably lodge a similar objection to the Caley opposing the Bill. The matter continued, with Keyden sending Messrs Currey & Spens, Parliamentary Agents in London an impression of the G&WBR's seal, to be attached to the petition being presented by the Caley agent against the Clyde Navigation Bill.

But at the end of March, Keyden had to write to his Chairman, James Lamont, to say that the Clyde Navigation Bill had been passed.

Accidents, Incidents, the Williams Patent Points and other problems

On 6th October, 1874, the Caley's traffic committee learned that there had been a landslip at an embankment near Inverkip viaduct that day. There was a surprising delay in Mr Graham reporting back to his Caley Directors - in fact, nearly four weeks later, the Directors were talking about getting an independent engineer to inspect the line, even though the G&WBR seemed happy that Graham check it out himself. When two more weeks had passed without a report, the Caley Directors instructed Mr Graham to produce one 'at once'. Two days' later, he sent in his report. Within a week, the necessary works had been done.

On 12th October, 1875, there was a partial collapse of the Cartsburn (or Ingleston) tunnel near Upper Greenock station. The tunnel was not reopened till 5th November due to a serious collapse of the waterlogged roof. By this time, Wemyss Bay was so fixed in people's minds as the terminal for Rothesay that instead of taking the Greenock ferry, travellers walked uphill from Cathcart Street station to Upper Greenock, where they boarded the train that had been trapped on the Wemyss Bay side.

Mr Evans' July 1879 report to his directors indicated that in the 14 year life of the railway, points had caused a lot of trouble. He referred to the number of facing points that inevitably occur when a line is subjected to two-way traffic.

> I have however had my attention lately drawn to a system of points and crossings, (the invention of a Mr Williams) which entirely does away with the damage to which the ordinary

points and crossings are subject, and while allowing every facility for shunting while the points and crossings are in use, will leave the main line absolutely intact at all times when the points and crossings are not in use for shunting purposes.

As the advantages of this system appear all but invaluable for a single line such as the Wemyss Bay, I determined to give the system a trial, and I am glad to say with complete success, and our Engine drivers appear unable to speak too highly in their favour . . . I estimate their introduction will save the Company a very considerable amount in this department.

Mr Evans was evidently approached while the Williams Railway Patent Point was being developed. Its inventor, Richard Price Williams CE, did not lodge his provisional specification for 'Improvements in Apparatus forming the Junctions with Railways of Branch Lines, Sidings, and Crossover Lines' with the Commissioners of Patents till November 1880. The patent, No. 4477 of that year, was confirmed in May 1881 which suggests that by that time, it had been perfected. Five pages and two drawings described how it worked. Alas for Mr. Williams, the problems it caused led to complete removal by 1889.

The idea behind the points was quite clever. If the main running line could be left intact, without breaks for switching to another track, there should be less chance of accidents arising. Mr Williams stated: 'I lay the fixed rails of the branch line where the train enters upon the branch at a somewhat higher level than the main line, and I provide movable rails or pieces which can be brought into position to form inclines leading from the main line rails to the branch'. Two pairs of moving rails were therefore introduced. When a train was diverted off the main line on to a branch, the two sets of tapered rails lying outside the running rails would be drawn inwards to rest on top of the running line, providing a ramp to lift the wheel flanges above the top of the main line. The other set of rails would simultaneously move in a manner similar to conventional points to marry up with the raised portion. Where the branch rail crossed over the running rail, the line was split into two, one each side of the main line. These would lie parallel to the main line except when vehicles were being worked on to the branch when their ends would be brought together, resting on the running line.

Major Marindin, inspecting officer for the Board of Trade, approved it for the main line, but had doubts about its operation. Williams Patent Points were installed first at Dunrod in 1881 then at Upper Greenock and Berryards in 1884. In the latter case, the inspector, Major-General Hutchinson, observed that the crossing seemed to work a good deal under the wheels of wagons. The Board of Trade only sanctioned their use for a six-month experimental period at Upper Greenock, requiring any derailments to be reported to them.

There *were* derailments. These were initially attributed to bad wagons: private owners were not as concerned about the state of their rolling stock as the railway operators who generally had a good maintenance record. Between August 1884 and January 1885, there had been seven derailments. A string of modifications were made to the points at Upper Greenock, where the majority of derailments occurred to the wagons of the Ferniegair Coal Company. The reasons for failure are not known.

The points were blamed for at least two accidents at Upper Greenock station. In January 1886, Keyden sent T.D. Weir, Mr Evan's successor, a report from the Board of Trade with copies of the accident reports. There were at least four further accidents attributed to the points there. In the same month, the Board of Trade report of an accident at Berryards on 4th January was passed to Mr Weir. The Board requested information on the cause of several accidents at the patent crossings. Berryards saw no less than four due to the points. A few days later, on 22nd January, 1886, Keyden wrote to the Assistant Secretary of the Railway Department of the Board of Trade, forwarding Mr Weir's report on the accidents.

Early in 1887, the Board of Trade recommended to a reluctant G&WBR that they replace the points. The Board sent Major-General Hutchinson and Major Marindin to meet Mr Weir on site to discuss the problem points in February 1887. On 12th March, 1887 Keyden wrote to James Thompson enclosing a copy of a letter from the Board instructing the removal of the

Apparatus Forming Junctions with Railways of Branch Lines, &c.

A.D. 1880, 2nd November. N° 4477. WILLIAMS' SPECIFICATION

The Williams Patent Points.

Mitchell Library

Patent Points, adding that the G&WBR 'repudiate all responsibility for any loss or damage which may be occasioned by their removal and the substitution of ordinary points'. Simultaneously, he wrote to the Assistant Secretary of the Railway Department at the Board of Trade claiming that their removal would 'materially increase the risk of accidents to passenger trains'. One detects Keyden was annoyed that the appearance of the Board of Trade was because the Caley (presumably irritated by the increasing frequency with which it had to re-rail its engines) had approached the Board direct. Normal procedure was for the Caley to write a report to the G&WBR which would go to Mr Weir before being forwarded to the Board of Trade. Keyden hoped he could get the Board to reverse their decision by sending on a copy of Weir's report and getting the Board to give him a hearing. However Mr Turner, WS, a Director of the G&WBR, probably sensing that the Patent Points were not going to last much longer, sent Keyden a telegram advising him to withhold Weir's report till the G&WBR received a favourable reply from the Board. Nearly two months later, the Assistant Secretary to the Board of Trade, Courtenay Boyle, asked for details on five accidents that had happened at the Patent Points since mid-January. Keyden promptly replied. The Board relented - only the Upper Greenock points needed replacing - the others would be reviewed in six months.

It seems that it was only after the Caley pointed out that the private owner wagons which allegedly were to blame successfully negotiated all the other points on the Caley system that the G&WBR eventually saw the light and arranged for their progressive removal.

The Williams Company did not survive long. On 4th March, 1886, Keyden wrote to Mr Weir enclosing a copy of a letter from Mr. Watson, the liquidator of the Williams Railway Patent Point Co., requesting payment of £100 [*£4,900] outstanding to the company. However, Keyden was not going to pay until the liquidator removed a cabin and other materials left behind at Inverkip.

One of Philip Keyden's first actions following his father's death in 1887 was to write to Mr A.Williamson, Secretary of the Railway & Electric Appliances Company Ltd who had taken over the assets of the Williams Company and had an office nearby in West George Street. Keyden would not pass the account pending final approval of the Board of Trade to use the Williams Patent Points 'which were supplied by your company'. Keyden required them to remove the points at their expense, immediately. Two weeks later, he advised his Board that two sets of Patent Points would be removed on two successive weekends as implementation of the Board of Trade's requirements could not be further delayed. The bill would be sent to the Railway & Electric Appliances Company Ltd.

The G&WBR decided to get rid of all the points as soon as possible. By 2nd July, 1887, Philip Keyden had advised Mr Williamson that four had been removed. The Dunrod points were apparently replaced early in 1888, but those at Berryards lingered on till 1889. In the end, Keyden's settled the Railway & Electric Appliances Co. account for £130 [*£6,400]. The cost of changeover was minimal as the Upper Greenock No.6 points cost £3 5s. 4d. [*£160] to convert. One wonders why it was not done much earlier.

At Dunrod, there had been at least 10 incidents in 1886-1887 alone. One instance did not appear to be related to the points as the offending wagon mounted the rails some distance away. In February 1887 the Caley sought interest from the G&WBR on materials supplied to the Dunrod branch. Keyden responded that with no traffic on the line they were hardly entitled to payment.

In April 1886, Keyden wrote to Mr Weir about an accident to Mrs Bisset, whose solicitor was seeking £50 [*£2,500] in damages. There is a note of scepticism in his suggestion that 'perhaps we should send a doctor to see her'. Following Dr Douglas's report, the directors authorised £30. This was rejected by Mrs Bisset's lawyer, who raised the amount to £100 and advised that he was taking the claim to court. However, after a second opinion, it appears the claim was settled for £35 [*£1,700].

In July 1886, Keyden had cause to write to Mr Hadaway in response to a request to remove a 'jagged wire' erected along the top of a fence beside the railway at Spango Farm. A second letter to Mr Weir instructed him to 'get it right', i.e. removed, as Sir Michael Shaw Stewart objected as it could damage cattle. In August, Mr Keyden wrote to Mr John MacDougal, Sir Michael's legal agent in Greenock, to say that barbed wire was generally acceptable and besides, it was on the railway side of the fence! Two years later, the company received a complaint from Greenock Football Club, who for reasons one can only imagine, objected to barbed wire at the side of its pitch.

September 1886 saw Keyden reject a claim for damages following the death of three of Messrs J. Bostock and Co.'s lambs which had strayed on to the line. Mr Hadaway, an active director of the G&WBR, promptly asked Keyden to get Weir to check the state of the fences - in case an action was brought. A year later, Messrs Bostock received the same response.

Strikes in the mining industry and on the railways had a disruptive effect between 1888 and 1894. The poorer quality coal available resulted in the evaporative rate for one locomotive class dropping 25 per cent, from 8 lb. to 6 lb. of steam per pound of coal. A protracted colliery strike in 1912, resulted in some conversions to oil. Inflation also affected profitability; in 1906, according to J.F. McEwan, the cost of locomotive coal rose between 10 per cent and 23 per cent, from 7s. 6d. [*£19.70] to between 8s. 3d. and 9s. 3d. [*£24.30] a ton.

It was common for railway employees to work excessively long hours, a stated cause for a number of railway accidents. In 1883, the railwaymen went on strike for a 9-hour day for all men except signalmen, pointsmen, pilotmen and shunters for whom 8 hours was requested. The Caley refused claiming that this would be impractical, insisting on 10 hours. The Caley was prepared to reduce the 12-hour day for mineral brakesmen - but their pay would be affected in consequence. In 1919, Government introduced, with little consultation, a requirement that the working day be restricted to 8 hours. This satisfied neither party - the employers because it obliged them to employ more people and the workforce whose take home pay was reduced *pro rata*.

Reorganisation of local government did not just happen in the 20th century. James Keyden had his problems too. With Parliamentary boundary changes, local authority boundaries and responsibilities changed also. All sorts of rates were payable - Poor and School rates, Water rates, Police rates due in the burgh of Greenock as well as Police rates for other parts of the line, registration and other assessments. In October 1886, he wrote to Thomas D. McMurrich, Collector in the Town Assessment Office in Greenock asking which Acts, national and local, determined the Police and other assessments imposed on the line. The same month he asked how Thomas Burton, the Greenock Collector of Poor Rates made up his valuation as it did not tally with other estimations. In November, another letter to McMurrich observed that the Wemyss Bay line was assessed differently to the Caley. Next day, he wrote to Mr W. Munro, the Assessor of Railways and Canals at 63 Castle Street, Edinburgh, giving him his assessment of the appropriate rates for the stations and the line within the Greenock 'catchment' area - viz. £2,176 [*£112,000]. Munro agreed with Keyden so the latter wrote to McMurrich requesting him to correct his figures. But Inland Revenue could not be avoided. In January 1887, Keyden sent them £263 8s. 7d. [*£13,400] relating to income tax on the company's profits.

On 30th December, 1886, Keyden informed Weir that the sanitary inspector threatened to prosecute 'about the nuisance at Inverkip'. The 'nuisance' was that the drains did not work. Early in the New Year, Keyden asked the sanitary inspector to suspend action as his Engineer had been asked to deal with the problem. But a month later, Keyden wrote another stalling letter to James Tyre, the sanitary inspector, saying that the problem was going to be removed 'immediately'. April revealed that either the work was more complex than originally envisaged or had taken second place to more pressing business. In July, the sanitary inspector again requested action. But action was slow - it seems it only commenced late in August.

The 1890s

In December 1890, the National Telephone Company asked the Caley's Traffic Committee if they could place a telephone exchange in the station master's house at Wemyss Bay, 'to be attended to by the Station Master's wife or family'. The committee agreed, for a charge of 20s. [*£50] pa for the house room, and 1s. pa 'for every wire led up to or attached to the building'. There is no record of Mrs Robison being consulted, or what remuneration she received.

The Caley reminded passengers in its May 1891 timetable that 'Heavy luggage may not be taken by the Steamers in connection with any particular trains, but may be sent by a succeeding steamer'. No doubt Glaswegians going 'doon the watter' had their own ideas of what heavy luggage meant and doubtless it did not coincide with the railway company's interpretation. In 1893, the Caley discontinued second class bookings - the last on its system.

Once again, the running of the 'refreshment room' was upsetting local people. In March 1892, Mr R. Hunter Craig submitted a letter and a 'memorial from residents of Wemyss Bay' requesting that the sale of alcohol be discontinued. The Caley Board declined to alter 'at present'. After all, they got more rent from licensed premises.

Small alterations continued at Wemyss Bay to the turn of the century. £30 [*£1,500] in 1892 to provide an office, and in 1897, £7 10s. [*£400] to paint the refreshment rooms and £50 [*£2,600] to combine two gateways to the pier into one. This last item had been deferred from 1890 and presumably was needed because of the large numbers of passengers using the pier at peak periods. The steps between the station and the pier were replaced by a ramp in 1894.

But by this time the station was long overdue for a major revamp. In 1900, one writer described it as the worst railhead on the Clyde.

Wemyss Bay station in 1900 showing the island platform extending beyond the trainshed.

J.L. Stevenson Collection

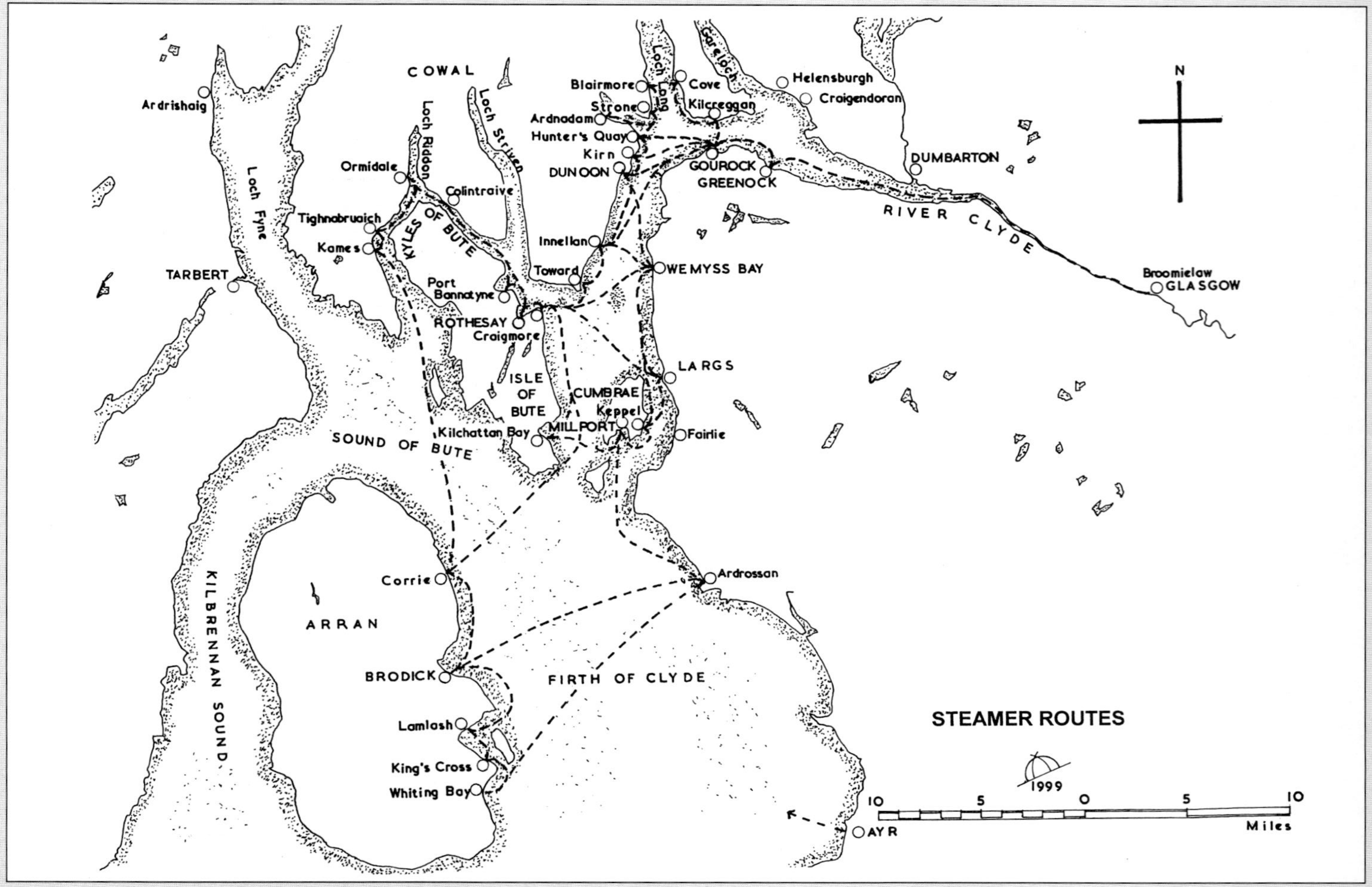
N
COWAL
Ardrishaig
Loch Fyne
TARBERT
Loch Riddon
Loch Striven
Ormidale
Colintraive
Tighnabruaich
Kames
KYLES OF BUTE
Port Bannatyne
ROTHESAY
Craigmore
ISLE OF BUTE
Kilchattan Bay
SOUND OF BUTE
Blairmore
Strone
Ardnadam
Hunter's Quay
Kirn
DUNOON
Innellan
Toward
Loch Long
Gareloch
Cove
Kilcreggan
Helensburgh
Craigendoran
GOUROCK
GREENOCK
DUMBARTON
RIVER CLYDE
Broomielaw
GLASGOW
WEMYSS BAY
LARGS
CUMBRAE
Keppel
MILLPORT
Fairlie
Ardrossan
Corrie
ARRAN
BRODICK
Lamlash
King's Cross
Whiting Bay
KILBRENNAN SOUND
FIRTH OF CLYDE
AYR
STEAMER ROUTES
1999
10 5 0 5 10
Miles

BOATS ON THE CLYDE AND THE STEAMER TRAFFIC

The *Passat* of the New Zealand Shipping Company at Yorkhill Quay in June 1935 with a Clyde Ferry crossing nearby. *John A. Smith Collection, Mitchell Library*

The Stinking River

As Glasgow grew during the 19th century, so people sought relief from the unhealthy disease-ridden overcrowded city. Over the winter of 1848-49, the nightly death-cart wheeled away those who had succumbed to the cholera epidemic. The upper reaches of the Clyde stank abominably, especially in hot dry weather, as the Clyde was the recipient of untreated sewage. (It was not till 1890 that Glasgow Town Council decided to proceed with a 'sewage precipitation scheme' for the east end of the city. It took five years to improve the nauseous atmosphere.) In 1865, a leader in the *Glasgow Herald*, calling for the removal of a weir above Hutchesontown bridge said: 'At present the water in the harbour is generally as stagnant as was the untroubled pool of Bethesda and the impurities which it receives make it as black as ink, as thick as gruel and, when stirred, of a most unlovely odour . . .'

In 1831, Glasgow's population topped 200,000; by 1850, it was about 300,000, by 1871, nearly 500,000 and by 1900, it had reached 750,000. The population density in Central Glasgow rose from 50 to 94 per acre between 1841 and 1871. The steamboat allowed those with even limited resources to get away, and many did. The Glasgow to Rothesay paddler was well patronised with local holiday makers and their luggage, taking the bracing air accompanied by the steady thump of the paddles, music from a harmonium, and a trail of smoke. Now English tourists arrived on the new railway to enjoy scenic Scotland from the decks of the steamers. The tonnage of vessels reaching Glasgow increased - between 1870 and 1880, it rose by 230 per cent, resulting in the construction of miles of new wharves and docks.

Steamboat Travel

Until the railway appeared, the preferred form of transport was the steamboat. There were piers at Whiting Bay in Wemyss (described by Hugh Macdonald in 1857 as 'the neat little wharf at Wemyss Bay') and at Meadow Place in Skelmorlie, below the Hydropathic. The Meadow Place building had a wooden 'walk-through' shed at its landward end. This pier, dismantled in the 1870s, was used by private yachts mooring for fresh water. The Pier House at Whiting Bay was likewise made of wood, but looked more ecclesiastical with a tall beehive vent at one end. It was destroyed in a gale in the autumn of 1865.

The Glasgow steamer commenced at Largs, calling at Wemyss Bay, Greenock, Dumbarton, Erskine Ferry, Cartsmouth and Renfrew. It took 5 hours for the whole journey and cost 7s. 6d. [*£15] cabin fare. It left Largs at 8.00 am and returned at 5.30 pm - rather inconvenient for holidaymakers looking for a summer residence. The railway time from Glasgow to Wemyss Bay cut this to an hour-and-a-quarter, for a fare of only 2s. 9d. [*£5.70]. The steamer schedule changed when trains started running to Wemyss Bay.

As if to mark Wemyss Bay out, when Queen Victoria made her first trip up the Clyde in August 1847 with Prince Albert and her entourage, a salute was fired from Kelly House. The *Glasgow Courier* added that the echo from Major Darroch's guns blazing away from *his* 'fort' on Kempoch Hill above Gourock could be heard for miles around. The Queen had arrived in the royal (steam) yacht *Victoria and Albert* on her way to holiday north of Fort William. There was fog on the river and celebrations had to be postponed for a day. However, as the Lord Provost and magistrates of Glasgow were to meet her on the *Thetis* steamer opposite Wemyss Bay, after she had transferred to HM screw tender *Fairy*, a messenger was dispatched by rail from Greenock when the fog showed signs of lifting. The train took 43 minutes to reach the City. It was a great occasion with upwards of 25 steamers bedecked with flags while the shoreline for miles around the Tail o' the Bank was lined with her subjects. According to the *Glasgow Courier*, the Queen visited Gourock, Dumbarton and Rothsay Bay [sic] in the *Thetis* before travelling north through the Kyles of Bute. Two years later, the Queen sailed up to Dumbarton on the royal yacht and having declined to travel by rail from Greenock, completed her journey to Glasgow in the *Fairy*. There she stayed less than three hours before boarding her train for Perth and Balmoral.

Other craft

In the first quarter of the 20th century, there were at least half-a-dozen ocean going yachts of up to 800 tons in Wemyss Bay, including Lord Inverclyde's 450 ton yacht *Beryl*. John Burns, whose father George was a founder member of the Cunard Steamship line in 1839, entertained famous personalities on his yachts *Mastiff* and *Capercailzie*, the latter described as a 'landmark' in the Bay.

The Royal Clyde Yacht Club Regatta drew huge crowds, big yacht racing being especially popular in the 1890's. Gourock and Largs developed as yachting centres and holiday resorts, and several marinas (including one at Inverkip) have appeared over the years round the coast from Gourock southwards. The popularity of sailing created other problems as steamer skippers hired out their best boats for the regattas leaving inferior vessels to cope with the normal service. This was demonstrated by an enraged Mr Thomson of Kilchattan Bay who wrote in July 1894: 'Do the Caledonian Co. think that the visitors to Kilchattan are a lot of tramps? Coming down last Saturday on the 2.40 pm train to Wemyss Bay, the passengers to Kilchattan were bundled into a dirty tug boat which was unfit for service. I do not intend ever coming again per Wemyss Bay, neither do the rest of my fellow travellers'. He concluded by commending the G&SWR route via Fairlie 'Where the passengers are never so treated'.

Rowing boats were regularly hired from Alexander Currie on Skelmorlie beach or from A. & W. Towers at Springbank. On 30th April, 1900, the *Greenock Telegraph and Clyde Shipping Gazette* recorded one such hire which had tragic consequences for two Greenock men.

A number of workmen belonging to the east end of the town travelled as usual on Saturday afternoon from Upper Greenock Station to Wemyss Bay for a few hours fishing on the firth. Among them were James McAulay, caulker and Robert Anderson, caulker. On arriving at their destination about four-o-clock, they hired a boat at Skelmorlie, where both men were well-known to the boat hirers. A high gusty wind prevailed, and the water on the firth was very rough. As the two men were well acquainted with the handling of boats, the weather conditions did not deter them from proceeding to the fishing grounds. While on the way out, the boat was observed either to founder or capsize by some pedestrians on the Skelmorlie Road. The boat disappeared and McAulay and Anderson were not seen again.

In the early part of the 20th century, James Hunter built ships' lifeboats in Skelmorlie. New Regulations on lifeboat provision following the 1912 *Titanic* disaster caused this trade to develop to such an extent that boats were sent by rail to John Brown, G. & J. Burns, Cunard and Harland & Wolff. The Caley paddle steamers had a third lifeboat added by 1914.

In the days of sail, good fishing in Loch Fyne and round Bute led to the introduction of 'herring-screws', fast small single-screw steamers which were common on the Clyde taking fish to the railheads. Between 1927 and 1933, Wemyss Bay played its part. Boats fished by moonlight or under arc light, offloading at Rothesay whence their catches were transported to Wemyss Bay to be entrained south to the London market. Though there were some good catches just prior to World War II, by 1945 local herring and the industry had all but disappeared. Few boats now fish the Upper Clyde.

Paddle Steamers on the Clyde

In 1801, William Symington built the steam driven paddle boat *Charlotte Dundas* to tow barges along the Forth and Clyde canal. While mechanically sound, the vessel could not prove herself due to opposition from vested interests 'concerned' about damage to the canal banks. In 1812, John Wood of Port Glasgow (on what was till the late 20th century, Lithgow's yard) built the 25-ton 3 hp 4-paddle steamer *Comet* for Henry Bell. At 45 ft long, it was the first commercial steamship and conveyed passengers from Glasgow and Greenock to Bell's baths at Helensburgh. On a trial trip between Glasgow and Greenock, the *Comet* took 3½ hours against the fly boats' 10-12 hours. (Fly boats were small vessels driven by sail and oar taking up to 40 passengers and goods. Their irregular schedule could see them take four hours down stream or up to 1½ days upstream - passengers sometimes being decanted to help push the boat through shallow water.) The *Comet* was uneconomic because of her small size, but the idea caught on. By 1816, 20 bigger steamships were plying their way across the Clyde to schedules that sailing boats could not match.

In 1817, shortly after the inauguration of steamboats between Glasgow and Rothesay, Captain Johnson on the Dumbarton-built *Rothesay Castle* did the run in 4 hours, averaging 9½ knots. (The maximum speed of the vessel was 12 knots.) In 1861, another *Rothesay Castle*, skippered by Captain Simon, took 2 hours 28 minutes, an average of over 15 knots. At the height of the steamer era, passenger steamers were known to achieve a racy 22 knots. The surviving paddle steamer *Waverley* (1947) can reach 15 knots, about the speed of the Caledonian MacBrayne motor ferries between Wemyss Bay and Bute. This may seem as surprising to us now as was the speed of only 18 knots to people in 1895, attained by the *Duchess of Rothesay*. One local paper, comparing performance with vessels in 1861, commented, 'It is rather curious that the highest speed of river steamers should be . . . at the same level it was a generation ago, while the speed of both channel and ocean steamers has increased to such a marked extent'.

The first 78 Clyde steamships were made of wood, the 1831 steamer *Fairy Queen* being the first iron ship.

The Railways link up with the Steamers

On 30th March, 1841, one of the earliest railways in Scotland, the Glasgow, Paisley & Greenock Railway, opened from Bridge Street station in Glasgow to Greenock Cathcart Street. The GP&GR, in furthering its aims to develop trade to Clyde Coast resorts, acquired an interest in the Bute Steam Packet Company in the same year. This company owned two 1835 wooden paddle steamers built by John Wood of Port Glasgow, the *Maid of Bute* and the *Isle of Bute*.

At this time, the principal steamboat operators were the Glasgow Castles Steam Packet Company (sailing between Glasgow and Rothesay, the Kyles of Bute and ports on Loch Fyne), the Helensburgh and Gareloch Company and D. & A. McKellar who ran steamers to Largs, Millport and Arran. When the GP&GR brought the railway to Greenock, these companies inaugurated direct sailings between Glasgow and Gourock, forcing the Bute Steam Packet Company to replace its wooden hulls with three iron paddle steamers. In 1844, Barr and McNab of Paisley built the *Pilot* and the *Pioneer* for the company, now owned by the GP&GR, and completed the trio with the *Petrel* in the following year.

These ships proved very successful, but in 1846, they were sold to G. & J. Burns when the GP&GR disposed of its maritime interests. Messrs. Burns' trade included sailings from Glasgow to Belfast and to Liverpool. In 1845 Burns took control of the Glasgow Castles Steam Packet Company and hence became involved in the Clyde steamboat trade. In 1848, having purchased the Castles Company, they disposed of their Firth of Clyde trade to David Hutcheson and Company in 1851. (Hutcheson's business was subsequently acquired by David MacBrayne Ltd.)

The railways offered cheap rapid travel to Glaswegians away from the smelly city. Simultaneously the Clyde steamer trade increased during the 1850s, paddle steamers got faster and consequently coastal resorts such as Kilcreggan, Cove, Blairmore, Dunoon and Rothesay expanded, Rothesay being the most popular. The Caledonian Railway Co., which had taken over the GP&GR in 1851, entered the steamship trade to encourage the use of their railway. Consequently, a separate entity, the Railway Steamboat Packet Company, was formed to operate the service. In 1852, it commenced sailings with the new iron paddle steamers *Gourock* and *Osprey*, adding the *Eva* and *Glasgow Citizen* the following year. However, this venture came to an end in 1854 when the Caley, like its predecessor, surrendered its steamboat interest to others, though it still sold tickets for the combined rail and steamer trip.

So popular were the paddle steamers that their captains were accused of overloading their boats. The *Glasgow Herald* reported a meeting in January 1865 when George Barber, Surveyor to the Board of Trade, spoke to the owners and masters of the larger steamboat companies, asking them to take steps to prevent overcrowding. Even the more responsible companies were reluctant to take action, and Mr Barber's suggestion that only ticket holders be allowed on the boats (as was successfully done elsewhere) was met by a comment from David Hutcheson that this would be 'excessively offensive' and from David MacBrayne that they would not allow 'exceptional overcrowding'. One captain claimed that notwithstanding a sheriff's ruling that boats must not be overloaded, James Gilchrist, the Caley's agent at Greenock who had a remarkable influence on the steamboat companies, insisted that the boats had to take people who had bought through railway/steamer tickets. The *Glasgow Herald* continued to push the matter, observing that some people even sat on top of the paddle boxes. In March 1865, it printed a long letter from Mr Barber to Sir Archibald Alison, Bart, Sheriff of Lanarkshire, that repeated his recommendations to the steamboat companies, including the advice 'that no passenger is allowed to sit or stand on the paddle boxes while the wheels are in motion'. The following day, an editorial in the *Glasgow Herald* thundered that overcrowding could not be disputed, adding, 'Is it natural or reasonable that men, women, and children, out for a holiday, or in pursuit of business, pleasure or recreation, should be packed together in immovable masses, for hours, like negroes during the middle passage?' (Slavery, abolished in Britain only 30 years earlier, was only then coming to an end in America.) The *Herald* somewhat unrealistically suggested that steamer captains should charge more if the problem was lack of profit.

The steamboat captains linked the problem of overcrowding with aggressive drunks. More effective policing (by others of course) was needed to prevent them boarding. In the 1870s, a partial solution was found with 'teetotal' boats.

Paddle steamers were fast and manoeuvrable and could operate in shallow water - consequently, some were sold at great profit to run the blockade during the American Civil War of 1861-3. The loss of over 100 of these between 1861 and 1864, including the best, newest and fastest vessels on the Clyde, seriously affected the steamship fleet. Therein lay the overcrowding problem. In 1861, 33 Clyde steamers were licensed to carry 22,890 passengers. In 1863, the 20 boats left could only carry 73 per cent of that total. However, the profits made by selling vessels on allowed bigger and better ships to be constructed. Traffic on the Clyde steadily increased.

The development of the Wemyss Bay Tripper Traffic

By the 1860s there was a regular steamer trade from Glasgow to Rothesay. With a stop at Gourock, it was fast, taking 2½ hours for the entire journey. But the steamer owners found the railway companies dictating the division of the fare. In 1860, one steamboat owner, claiming that the cost of the ticket barely covered his operating expenses, attempted to form a 'combine' of Clyde passenger steamer owners to strengthen their negotiating position. The lack of response from his fellow captains resulted in all control of fare setting being lost to the railways.

The Greenock businessmen who conceived the idea of a line to Wemyss Bay thought they could capture a substantial amount of the Glasgow tripper trade going 'doon the watter' to Rothesay by offering an even quicker service. Not surprisingly, the steamer companies saw the proposed line as a threat to their livelihood at a time of reduced river traffic. The building of the *Largs* and *Kyles* for the Wemyss Bay traffic to Rothesay, Largs and Millport, heightened their concern. The year after the Wemyss Bay line opened, the G&SWR reacted by running 12 new steamers from Greenock. It has been said that the survival of the up river steamboat trade for the next few years was mainly due to the initial poor co-ordination and management of the Wemyss Bay railway and its associated steamboat companies. Matters would have been worse had the McKellar fleet on the Millport station not been obsolete. When the Wemyss Bay railway and steamboat companies finally got themselves sorted out, the additional five rail miles compared to its (then) rival Greenock was more than compensated by a reduction in the sailing distance of 8½ miles, as shown below.

Glasgow Via	To	Rail miles	Steamer miles	Total
Greenock	Rothesay	25½	15¼	40¾
Gourock	Rothesay	26¼	13	39¼
Wemyss Bay	Rothesay	30½	6¾	37¼

The Wemyss Bay Steamboat Co.

In November 1863, James Keyden, as Secretary of the Wemyss Bay Steamboat Company, discussed arrangements for the steamboat service with the Caley Board. On 23rd December, 1863, the *Glasgow Daily Herald* published the Prospectus of the Wemyss Bay Steamboat Company (Limited). This stated that the company was being set up with a capital of £40,000 [*£1.66m], in 4,000 shares of £10 [*£415] each. Several Directors were also on the Board of the Greenock and Wemyss Bay Railway Company - Alexander Finlay, MP, of Castle Toward, James Scott of Kelly, James Lamont of Knockdow and Alexander Ronaldson of Glasgow. The Board also included Colin George Campbell of Stonefield and John Malcolm of Portalloch. The Glasgow brokers were listed as Messrs James Watson & Smith, Aitken and Mackenzie, Kerr Anderson & Brodie, and Robert Strang of 57 St George's Place. The interim Secretary was James Keyden of 186 West George Street, Glasgow.

The advertisement continued: 'The line of railway now in course of construction between Port Glasgow and Wemyss Bay imperatively demands the establishment of Steamers between Wemyss Bay and Largs and Millport and also to Innellan, Rothesay, Kyles of Bute and Ardrishaig and other places in the West of Scotland'.

As the railway would convey passengers from Glasgow to Wemyss Bay in an hour, Rothesay and Ardrishaig would then be within 1½ and 4 hours of Glasgow respectively. The venture was expected to be remunerative as the population of Argyle was steadily increasing and by way of example, the advertisement stated that the Lochlomond Steamboat Company already paid dividends of 10 per cent and the Castle Steam Packet Company had paid dividends of 7½ per cent before the company was wound up, all the capital being returned to the shareholders. Interested people were invited to invest capital quickly as boats had to be built.

The Wemyss Bay Steamboat Company Limited was duly incorporated under the Companies' Act 1862 on 29th April, 1864 with James Keyden as Secretary. (Two sources have stated that an Act was passed in May 1863 or in 1864 authorising the formation of the company, however, I have been unable to confirm this.) The document of incorporation included as its objects the 'conveyance of Passengers, Goods, Cattle, and other Articles in Steamships or Boats between such places as the Directors of the Company may from time to time determine'. The company was authorised 'to enter into such Contracts, Agreements and Arrangements with Railway Companies, Steamboat Companies and Steamboat owners, and others, for carrying out the purposes of the Company . . .' and the Directors were empowered to borrow money 'upon the Security of the Vessels and other Property of the Company'. By January 1868, it had 77 shareholders of £10 shares - some with one share, but several had 50 or 100.

Three steamers were built: the aforementioned *Largs* and *Kyles* in 1864 and the *Bute*, a sister to the Kyles, in 1865. For a short time prior to the (delayed) opening of the Wemyss Bay line, the Wemyss Bay Steamboat Company ran from the Broomielaw to Largs and Millport. In March 1865, 'A would be visitor' complained about the inadequate steamer service to Largs and Fairlie: 'that fine little steamer called the *Largs*' had been withdrawn some time before the Wemyss Bay line was due to open and he implored the prospective railway operators not to forget those wanting to go to Largs. The Steamboat Company took note and in March 1865 advertised its intention to put the *Largs* on the Glasgow to Millport run with the *Kyles* and an un-named new steamer (the *Bute*) on the Rothesay station early in May, coinciding with the opening of the line. When trains started to run to Wemyss Bay station in 1865, the Wemyss Bay Steamboat Company commenced sailing from the adjacent new pier.

These new vessels each had two funnels, two-cylinder oscillating engines and haystack boilers. The *Largs* was the smallest, flush-decked, intended for the Largs and Millport run. The others had small deck saloons fore and aft and were designed for the Rothesay traffic. Illustrations of the Wemyss Bay pier in 1875 show berths for up to five vessels - two each side and one across the end. Until the end of the 20th Century, Millport and Rothesay were the principal destinations. However, the initial service proved unsatisfactory with poor timekeeping caused by what J.F. McEwan described as an impossible schedule (the boats could not achieve the 20 knots expected of them), and the *Kyles* and *Bute* were sold for service on the Thames. One might feel sorry for Robert Lees, appointed Superintendent Engineer of the Steamboat company just before the railway opened, when the *Kyles* was completing its speed trials, the *Largs* was being taken off its Glasgow, Largs and Arran run, and only two months after the *Bute* was launched.

The initial routing saw the *Largs* operating to Largs, Millport on Cumbrae and Lamlash on Arran - an extended service that proved to be unreliable and unremunerative with boats regularly arriving late at Wemyss Bay. To improve timekeeping, the Arran stop was dropped but the losses continued.

In June 1865, barely a month after the railway opened, Mr Scott, one of the Wemyss Bay Steamboat and Railway Company Directors, asked whether the Caley would lend the Steamboat company £5,000 [*£200,000] at 5 per cent. The Caley did not feel so inclined. A month later, Mr Strang (presumably Robert Strang, one of the Steamboat company brokers) asked the Caley for £10,000. Again, the Caley declined. A few days later, the Caley Board learned that Captain Rankin had replaced Mr Wright as manager of the Steamboat company.

The Steamboat company's troubles continued. G&WBR Director Fyffe Christie and Keyden sought 'pecuniary aid' from the Caley, the Board's minutes of 22nd August, 1865 recording 'but they got no encouragement to expect it'. On 7th December, 1865, Keyden advised the Caley that the steamers would be withdrawn by the end of the year unless a more favourable arrangement could be arrived at with the railway company. James Gilchrist, the Caley's Greenock agent, attempted to resolve some of the problems but was only partly successful due to antagonism from the Steamboat company's Directors. The steamers continued, but not without objections. In July 1866, Sir Alexander Maitland complained that the luggage charges were excessive.

The G&WBR depended for its survival on the trains run by the Caley and the boats operated by the Steamboat company. (Incidentally, the Caledonian Railway Company was not allowed to operate shipping services till 1890.) But strained relations between the G&WBR and its partners hindered development of the Wemyss Bay routes to Rothesay, Millport and Largs. The Wemyss Bay Steamboat Company purchased the *Victory* (1863) and the *Argyle* (1866) from Captain Duncan Stewart, but even with these more economical vessels, the service would not break even. This was not entirely the fault of the steamboat owners as early trains were underpowered, late as a result, and cancellations did not aid profitability.

In February 1868, James Smithells, the Caley's General Manager, reported that the Steamboat company wanted a £1,000 [*£37,500] subsidy. He was instructed to 'decline'. Keyden repeated the request in March and in June 1868 to allow the Steamboat company to reduce its debt to the bank. The Caley was unmoved: 'decline, having no power to advance money as requested'. By November, the Steamboat Co. owed the Caley over £1,500; the Caley insisted on early settlement. On 17th December, 1868, we learn that the Steamboat company owed £1,810 [*£68,000] to the Caley. It was unable to pay because the Bank held the boats as security. The Caley asked the Company to pay weekly while it sorted itself out. Somehow the Steamboat company continued into the new year but on 20th February, 1869, Keyden wrote that the bank required a personal guarantee of the bank's debt on the Steamboat Co. and that 'the Company will have to be wound up failing some means of carrying it on be devised'. The Caley was not disposed to be helpful: 'decline to interfere beyond ranking as creditors' and as a result, the Steamboat company failed. The boats were put up for sale but did not find a purchaser.

Captains Williamson, McLean and Buchanan were invited to call at Wemyss Bay to take up the Rothesay service, and with Gillies and Campbell, Graham Brymner & Co. to call at Wemyss Bay on their Glasgow, Greenock and Millport run. This proved unsatisfactory, partly because of the poor service provided and partly because some captains thought they could now bring about the collapse of the objectionable Wemyss Bay operation if they refused.

Gillies and Campbell

The success of the Wemyss Bay railway line demanded that the steamboat service worked efficiently. It seems that James Gilchrist was instrumental in bringing about a solution by introducing Captain James Gillies and his son-in-law Captain Alexander Campbell to the Wemyss Bay Steamboat Company's Directors. Gillies had worked for the Largs Steamboat Company from whom he bought the PS *Venus*. Captain Campbell had sailed the Clyde then joined the Anchor Line. He later became captain of the Wemyss Bay steamers, operating from Meadow Place in Skelmorlie. Following the Steamboat company's failure, the G&WBR found that Gillies and Campbell provided a better service than their competitors.

On 2nd August, 1869, the G&WBR contracted Gillies and Campbell to run the Wemyss Bay Steamboat Company between Wemyss Bay pier and Largs, Fairlie and Millport till 31st July,

A photograph of Wemyss Bay station pier taken between 1872 and 1877. At the end is PS *Lady Gertrude* (built 1872), PS *Argyle* (1866) on the north (*right*) berth, with the single funnel *Lancelot* (1868) and PS *Largs* (1864) on the Rothesay side. Note the temporary lack of advertisements on the screen between the berths and the fixed crane beside the railway.

McLean Museum & Art Gallery, Inverclyde Council

1870. The boats included Captain Gillies' *Venus* as well as the *Largs* and *Argyle*, purchased from the liquidators of the Wemyss Bay Steamboat Co. Ltd for £5,100, [*£201,000] £5,000 being borrowed from the National Bank of Scotland. The G&WBR had to provide a guarantee of £2,000 [*£79,000] to the Bank for the loan. By reducing the fares from Glasgow to Rothesay and to Largs and Millport to 2s. 6d. [*£4.92], traffic increased enormously. Except for a 3-month break in 1880-81, Gillies and Campbell ran their 'white funnel' fleet continuously till May 1890 when the newly formed yellow funnel fleet of the Caledonian Steam Packet Company took over.

Between November and February, the last connection was with the 2.45 pm from Glasgow. During the rest of the year, connections had to be made with the 8.45 am up (to Glasgow) and the 4.10 pm down. The steamboat portion of the fare from Glasgow or Paisley to the 'parts aforesaid' was 7d. [*£1.15] per passenger (single) or 1s. 2d. [*£2.30] (return) while the fare from Wemyss Bay was 6d. and 1s. [*98p and *£1.96]. Two-fifths of the goods fare went to the steamboat company, the remainder to the railway companies. The Caley sold through tickets at Largs, Fairlie and Millport. Pier dues were 10s. [*£20] per ton per annum. No doubt because of the previous unhappy experience with the Steamboat company, the Joint Committee required accounts to be made up fortnightly. There was a penalty clause of £100 [*£4,000] if either side failed to perform.

The *Venus* was to be used only on the Wemyss Bay run, though it was accepted that a stand-in would be required on occasion. The G&WBR would not allow Gillies and Campbell to run their boats between Glasgow and Wemyss Bay or between Glasgow and Largs, Fairlie, Millport, Innellan (south of Dunoon on the Cowal peninsula), Toward or Rothesay without permission. Any dispute would be referred to John Burns of Castle Wemyss who would act as sole arbiter.

In 1872, the Wemyss Bay fleet was augmented by the flush deck *Lady Gertrude*. Her career ended on the rocks at Toward pier in 1877 when she failed to engage reverse in heavy weather. In 1874, the *Venus* was scrapped and replaced the following year by the *Lancelot* (1868).

There are few references in the Minutes of the Railways' Joint Committee to the steamboat operation. One survivor is a three-year agreement, reached in August 1874, which determined the income distribution between the G&WBR and Alexander Campbell, 'Steamboat Owner, Millport', from 27th September 1874 to 31st December, 1877, 'or any time thereafter on 3 months' notice'. The rates Captain Campbell would receive would be reduced to 5d. [*80p] per passenger, single, 10½d. [*£1.68] return. The G&WBR would provide porters and secure the steamers' ropes. Pier dues would be £300 [*£11,500] pa and the Rothesay boat had to connect with the 8.30am train from Wemyss Bay to Glasgow and the 4.10 pm from Glasgow, while the Largs/Fairlie/Millport service had to connect with the 2.20 pm train from Glasgow. Once again, John Burns would be the sole arbiter in the event of a dispute. A further Agreement was ratified in December 1877.

In 1877, the engine salvaged from the *Lady Gertrude* was fitted into the *Adela*, built by Caird & Company (who the same year built the 'very fast' steamer *Sheila* for the Wemyss Bay/Rothesay service). Apparently the engine from the *Lady Gertrude* would stick in top dead centre. Travelling slowly, the *Adela* experienced problems more than once when she was temporarily left without steerage, which may explain why the *Lady Gertrude* foundered.

Competitive routes to Rothesay

By 1877, passengers leaving Glasgow St Enoch station on the G&SWR 4.05 pm for Greenock Princes Pier could take Captain Williamson's steamer *Sultana* (built 1868) and be in Rothesay at the same time as those who had taken the 4.10 pm from Bridge Street to Wemyss Bay. The Caley accelerated the service, running a fast train at 4.35 pm to Wemyss Bay, only stopping at Port Glasgow to collect tickets. This enabled a quicker transfer of passengers between train and the *Sheila* at Wemyss Bay, the journey from Glasgow to Rothesay taking only 80 minutes. The two paddle steamers arrived virtually simultaneously at Rothesay's Craigmore pier, and left together. Between 1877 and 1878, competition was fierce, but the larger and newer *Sheila* was not as quick as her older and smaller rival. There was another result: the up river steamers finally lost out.

In 1879, paddle steamers berthing at Wemyss Bay included the *Lancelot*, *Sheila* and the *Lady Kelburne*. In October that year, fog, not an unusual hazard on the Clyde, was so dense that steamers had to be guided to the pier by ringing the church bells.

In 1880 friction between the Wemyss Bay Railway Co. and Gillies & Campbell's Wemyss Bay Steamboat Company resulted in other steamers, including the *Lord of the Isles* and the *Ivanhoe*, being allowed to use the Wemyss Bay pier also. It was feared that sailings would not match the train times, but this did not happen. However, Gillies & Campbell's service ran another 10 years though the last five years saw increasingly strident calls by the G&WBR for its replacement.

Captain Campbell withdraws the boats

In August 1881, Captain Campbell requested a review of the fare apportionment for his boats. In November, presumably for want of a reply, he asked if his Agreement was to be renewed. On 23rd November, 1881, Archibald Gibson, the Caley Secretary, wrote back:

> I am directed to reply to your letter of 18th instant. As you are aware, the action taken by this Company last season in the interest of the public, for the purpose of retaining your steamer on the Wemyss Bay route, has not been allowed by the Wemyss Bay Company to pass unchallenged, and has in fact landed this Company in litigation and trouble. Under these circumstances, and the Wemyss Bay Company not having indicated their willingness to reconsider the position they took up, this Company are not prepared at present to renew the Agreement to which your letter refers.

Shortly before Christmas 1881, disgruntled, Captain Campbell responded that he would withdraw his four boats from the Wemyss Bay station from 1st January, 1882. He offered them to the Caley but the latter would not buy them. The Caley wrote to the G&WBR advising them of the service curtailment and advertised the discontinuance of the boat service. According to J.F. McEwan, on New Year's Day 1882, the Wemyss Bay station manager called his Chairman as no boats had appeared. He in turn contacted the Caledonian chairman and in consequence, passengers for Rothesay were re-routed via Greenock. The residents of Millport and Rothesay, appealed to the Caley and the G&WBR. On 14th January, 1882, *The Buteman* carried a letter which put the blame squarely on the shoulders of the G&WBR, stating that it exhibited 'the Directors of the Wemyss Bay Railway in a very unlovely light'. It added that on a second class return fare of 2s. 6d., the Wemyss Bay Directors wanted 1s. 8½d. for the rail fare from Wemyss Bay to Port Glasgow (20 miles), that the steamboat only received 8½d. and the Caley received 1d. for the 40 mile trip up to Glasgow! Another article in the paper described a meeting of islanders with the Caley where the latter said the fault lay not with them or the steamboats but with the Wemyss Bay Directors. (No-one seems to have questioned the Caley's 'take' of only 1d. The Caley did not mention that of the Wemyss Bay's 1s. 8½d., they received nearly half, or that as shareholders, they might expect a dividend.) *The Buteman* concluded that 'if the Wemyss Bay Railway Directors can afford to have no return for the capital invested in their line, the public must look about for some other way of getting to and from Rothesay, and when they find this . . . it would be a good return for the indifference of these Directors never to travel by Wemyss Bay if they can help it'.

The Board of Trade wrote to the Caley expressing concern at the suspension of the Coastal traffic from Wemyss Bay, but did nothing to bring the parties together.

The G&WBR remained obdurate. Keyden wrote to the press suggesting that the steamers should be doing quite well from the trade the line brought them and therefore the blame lay with the Steamboat company. He added that as the G&WBR had no Act of Parliament empowering it to own or work steamers, complainers ought to direct their attention elsewhere. This brought forth a detailed cutting reply by D.M. Nelson in the *North British Daily Mail* of 2nd March, 1882 reminding the Wemyss Bay Directors that it was the strength of the Caley and the willing friendliness of the Steamboat company that had allowed the Wemyss Bay Railway to survive. He indicated that the present Directors of the railway company lacked the wisdom of their predecessors and prophesied that with the 'prohibitive' fare structure, the Caley might seek powers to take over 'this small, obstructive and impracticable railway, which without regard to public interest or convenience, has simply entrenched itself behind its statutory powers . . . It will speedily receive that death-warrant as an independent company which it has so ostentatiously coveted'. A week later, Mr Nelson followed this up in *The Glasgow News* with copies of letters from MP's whose support for his views was roughly proportionate to the distance of their constituencies from the action.

The G&WBR advertised for a steamboat company to resume the services and must have received a response because, in mid-March 1882, Keyden wrote to the Caley proposing an Agreement with Messrs Williamson to provide ferry services 'via' Wemyss Bay. The Caley was not inclined to proceed on this basis. Instead, the Caley Directors made another approach to Captain Campbell. Campbell responded that he was prepared to resume the service to Innellan, Toward, Rothesay, Largs and Millport if the Caley would agree to through booking *at the former rates*. The Caley agreed, asking him to recommence on 22nd March. They then wrote to Keyden saying that Williamson's proposals were unacceptable and that they had approved Captain Campbell's imminent resumption of the service. Uncharacteristically, Keyden's response is not recorded. A little later, the Caley allowed the Frith of Clyde Steamboat Company's PS *Ivanhoe* to enjoy the same terms as Captain Campbell on excursion trips from Wemyss Bay pier to the Kyles of Bute and Arran.

It appears that with both boat and rail costs rising, only the trains received additional fares. According to J.F. McEwan, the slower all-the-way boats from Glasgow to Rothesay and Millport cost as much as the train fare from Glasgow to Wemyss Bay. As a result, Captain Campbell was losing out to the all-the-way boats. Thus it seems that while the G&WBR attracted the bad press, the fact that Captain Campbell was prepared to restore traffic at the previous rate suggests that he speculated that the pressure the railway company was under would help him negotiate a better deal before the start of the next season. He probably also found it impossible to sell his boats in the 'off' season so his heavy overheads left him no choice but to resume - and hope. The G&SWR had a similar problem which was resolved by the Caley and the G&SWR agreeing to raise the steamer fare portion of the journey.

In 1882, Gillies and Campbell sold the *Sheila* to the North British Steam Packet Company, replacing her with Seath and Steele's Glasgow to Ayr steamer, *Bonnie Doon* (1876). Two years later, the Wemyss Bay company acquired the *Arran* (previously called *Dunoon Castle*, known at one period as a 'Sunday Breaker') from Messrs Hill of Fairlie.

David MacBrayne

In 1879, David MacBrayne purchased the well-established firm of David Hutcheson & Co. Meanwhile, Captain Campbell's operation had deteriorated. In June 1885, Keyden wrote to the Caley Board objecting to Campbell's Agreement being continued beyond the year end. In July, at the height of the holiday season, Keyden wrote that Campbell's boats were 'insufficient'. The Caley was unimpressed; it did not consider itself bound to give notice of termination of the Agreement at the Wemyss Bay company's request. Captain Campbell then made a proposal to the Caley for continuing the service. Correspondence followed between James Thompson, General Manager of the Caley and Keyden culminating in a letter from Keyden's of 22nd December, 1885, saying that David MacBrayne was interested in running a steamboat service, but not in competition with Captain Campbell. According to Keyden, MacBrayne was 'the best man in Scotland' to work the Wemyss Bay traffic. Campbell's steamers were slow, obsolete and needing repair; he had 'sacrificed the interests of the railway for his excursions'. Clearly, Keyden saw Campbell's steamboat activities coming to an end and one guesses that MacBrayne's interest might have been 'encouraged'.

Following a request from Thompson for more details, on 9th January, 1886 Keyden confirmed MacBrayne's interest in taking over the existing steamboat traffic on the same terms as Campbell. However, MacBrayne, if offered the contract, would like a 'friendly arrangement' with Captain Campbell. Keyden asked Thompson to take the matter up with his Board so that he could discuss the outcome with the G&WBR Directors thereafter, obviously thinking that the MacBrayne proposal could not be bettered.

Later the same month, Keyden wrote to Thompson to say that MacBrayne was prepared to discuss 'differences' with Mr. Thompson or with the Caley Chairman. But on 20th February, Keyden was stung into writing to Thompson. The Caley Directors had decided to continue the contract with Campbell. The Directors of the Wemyss Bay Railway were surprised at the 'high handed' action of the Caley in allowing Campbell's steamboat contract to continue, without first telling the G&WBR. Keyden did not mince his words to the General Manager of the mighty Caledonian. He reminded Thompson that negotiations had been proceeding 'with a steamboat owner of undoubted position who was ready to conclude a Contract, delaying only for your comment'. Captain Campbell had conducted his company unsatisfactorily and as a result, traffic had fallen off. The G&WBR reserved the right to take whatever action was necessary to protect their interests.

The Steamer Service deteriorates

Keyden wrote again to Thompson in May, reiterating the G&WBR's objection to extending Captain Campbell's contract for another five years as his steamers were unfit for the traffic. Keyden observed that Campbell wanted to do excursions to Arran with his fine new steamer, the PS *Victoria* (1886), which he claimed conflicted with the Agreement that Wemyss Bay Company steamers be used on the Rothesay, Largs and Millport runs. (This was the last vessel built for the Wemyss Bay company, constructed shortly after the introduction of smart new trains on the Wemyss Bay line. The boat had a simple diagonal two-cylinder engine and an early electric light installation. She received her pennant from the Queen.) Keyden was well aware of the G&SWR competition on the Greenock to Rothesay run and was sensitive to losing more trade. But Murray's Diary for July showed some improvement in the connections. Meanwhile, Keyden wrote to T.S. Hadaway and others, inviting them to the *Victoria's* trial trip on Tuesday 29th June, 1886, connecting with the 10.30 am from Glasgow and the return train at 5.35 pm.

PS *Victoria* (1886) operated by Gillies & Campbell on the Wemyss Bay ferry crossing. This vessel was fitted with an early electric generator. *McLean Museum & Art Gallery, Inverclyde Council*

On 2nd December, 1886, Keyden wrote to Thompson drawing his attention to the frequent breakdown of Campbell's boats 'this season'. For example, on 28th October, the *Lancelot* broke down returning from Rothesay, delaying the connecting 11.55 am train by 24 minutes. Keyden said his Directors wanted Campbell's contract rescinded 'in consequence of the quality of his boats'.'

In April 1887, Keydens wrote to Thompson about an accident to the PS *Argyle* on 11th April, reported in the next day's newspapers. The steamer had broken a float on one of her paddles on the 6.45 pm run from Rothesay and was immobilised in the Bay for an hour while temporary repairs were effected. The boat was crowded and some people, feeling unsafe, demanded to be put ashore on Bute. Keydens held the Caley responsible for any loss or damage they incurred as the Caley had ignored the G&WBR's advice to get rid of Campbell and his boats.

Nothing happened. Keyden asked Weir for background information on how often the PS *Victoria* had been diverted from her regular traffic then informed the Caley's General Manager that from 16th to 20th July, 1887, at the very height of the season, PS *Victoria* had been removed from the Wemyss Bay run for excursions from Glasgow to Ayr calling at Rothesay, Largs and Millport, making no connection at all with Wemyss Bay. In June, she was used during the 'Jubilee Holiday in Glasgow' for excursion traffic to Campbelltown 'via Wemyss Bay', which must have been supremely annoying to Rothesay travellers, and during the Royal Northern Regatta, she ran as Club Steamer for two days. Keyden's Directors protested most strongly that Campbell was operating contrary to his Agreement. The summer service had been very erratic - up to 20 minutes late - and the public was dissatisfied that the *Victoria*, his best vessel, had been replaced by the *Argyle*, a worn out, dirty boat. Keyden sought action from the Caley so he could report that steps were being taken to improve matters. At the end of August, Keyden sent a clipping from the *Herald* dated 15th August to James Thompson about an accident to another of Campbell's boats, the *Adela*. Keyden insisted that the performance of Campbell's steamers be advised to the Caley's Board; the replacement boats Campbell used included the notoriously slow PS *Dandie Dinmont*.

The squabble continued. In August 1888, Philip Keyden wrote to the Caley complaining about the Wemyss Bay steamer service. In December 1888, Captain Campbell, no doubt realising that he would get no consideration from the G&WBR in seeking a better return, once more proposed that the Caley buy his boats. The Caley declined.

Meanwhile, the Caley had developed plans for its own operation at Greenock. As its previous efforts to manage a steamboat service in the early 1850s and in 1870 had been unsuccessful, it was reluctant to get its fingers burnt. In August 1888, it tried to interest the main steamboat owners to run boats from the Gourock pier they hoped to open in 1889. But the steamer companies wouldn't play - perhaps because they felt Captain Campbell's efforts had been damaged by a lack of Caley support in the Wemyss Bay enterprise or because the outlay for new boats on this scale would have been excessive. Few steamboat operators had the resources to provide the size of fleet needed by the Caledonian. The Caley decided to provide the service themselves and acquire four steamers.

The Competition - The Greenock and Gourock Ferry Service

In 1869, the G&SWR through its subsidiary the Greenock and Ayrshire Co., opened a line directly to Greenock Princes Pier. Getting to their boats was easy by comparison with the Caley whose passengers, decanting from Greenock Cathcart Street station to walk through East Quay Lane, - a narrow vennel, ankle-deep in muck in bad weather and possessing a 'malodorous atmosphere' - would reach Custom House Quay to find they often had to clamber over one vessel to reach their own. According to J.F. McEwan, the local council while encouraging the G&SWR, vacillated over improving access arrangements suggested by the Caley and refused to allow a coach to be used because of the narrowness of the lane. The mass stampede for the boats (5 minutes was allowed for the transfer) could only have pleased the manufacturers of carbolic soap.

At the time, the Caley while recognising public demand, was strapped for cash and unable to react beyond purchasing Gourock Harbour, three miles west of Greenock, with a view to recovering lost trade. But they also acquired properties round the G&SWR establishment in Greenock thus making it difficult for their rival to expand. After all, the Caley was experiencing competition from the G&SWR which was attempting to wrestle trade away from Wemyss Bay by extending its line northwards from Fairlie to Largs.

In 1884 the Caley eventually obtained Parliamentary approval to extend its railway to Gourock Pier. The line would run from Greenock Cathcart Street station (now Greenock Central) by a tunnel which opened out briefly at Greenock West, then on to Fort Matilda station where it would reappear to run round Cardwell Bay to Gourock station, parallel to Gourock pier. The Caley even considered forming docks in Cardwell Bay to receive the increasingly large ocean liners. Its proposal was rejected by the river authority which was making arrangements to further deepen the Clyde up to Glasgow.

In 1886, work started at each end of the Gourock extension. Difficulties experienced constructing the 1 mile 350 yds-long twin-track Newton tunnel under Greenock, the longest main line tunnel in Scotland, prevented the line from opening till 1st June, 1889. The pier station, built on reclaimed land using spoil from the tunnel workings, came into use in 1887. Passengers were allowed two minutes to transfer from boat to train. (They were not allowed to take luggage, a common feature on day excursion traffic. Luggage had to be forwarded in an earlier train.) Cathcart Street station was subsequently dismantled and replaced by Greenock Central. The extension of the line cost £620,000 [*£30.5m], an enormous sum to pay for a three-mile advantage over the steamer competition. Newton tunnel provided a potent reminder to holidaymakers of what they were escaping from; it could be pretty unpleasant. *Variorum*, writing in the *Greenock Telegraph* of 4th January, 1897, said 'Passengers complain of the disagreeable odour which assails the nose in the long stretch of tunnel between Greenock West and Fort Matilda. Is the ventilation up to the mark?'

The formation of the Caledonian Steam Packet Co.

In March 1889, the Caledonian Railway (Steam Vessels) Bill was introduced, supported by various local authorities who wanted an improved service, including Rothesay and Dunoon, but it was rejected after protests from ship operators, including David MacBrayne, William Buchanan and M.T. Clark who claimed with some justification that a virtual monopoly of steamboat services would result. The Caledonian then formed the Caledonian Steam Packet Company Ltd (CSP), incorporated on 7th May, 1889 - a syndicate of Caley shareholders with Lord Breadalbane (a Caledonian Director) as Chairman. This enabled the Caley to get round the restrictions preventing them from owning and operating steamers on the Clyde. Shortly afterwards, the *Meg Merrilies* (1883) and *Madge Wildfire* (1886), which the Caley had bought from Captains Peter and Alexander Campbell (two of the most successful local boat owners) were transferred to the new organisation. These the Caley added to the PS *Galatea* (1889) built by Messrs Caird of Greenock and the smaller PS *Caledonia* (1889) constructed by John Reid and Co. of Port Glasgow. The Caley had ordered these vessels back in November 1888 as part of what now looked like a covert operation to take over the Wemyss Bay service.

Their first marine superintendent was Captain James Williamson. His father Captain John Williamson owned the 'Turkish' fleet - the paddle steamers *Sultana*, *Sultan* and *Viceroy*. These boats were based at Port Bannatyne on Bute and operated out of Greenock. James Williamson was a skilful captain when there were fewer restrictions to cramp a racing skipper's style. During most of the period when he had been a skipper, 'Somehow . . . there seemed to be great necessity - or it may have been great temptation - to relieve the monotony of ordinary plain sailing, the consequence being a weekly or bi-weekly invitation to make explanation to the River Baillie, to the tune of £5 [*£200] per visit'. He recalled that he received one of these

The *Marchioness of Lorne* (1891) tied up at Wemyss Bay pier around 1900.
Watt Library, Inverclyde Council

regular summonses to appear on the day of his marriage, however, 'the good old Baillie cancelled the appointment and the 'fiver' was expended on the youthful skipper's honeymoon'. Before he joined the CSP, for nine seasons he ran the teetotal boat *Ivanhoe* with considerable success.

Back in 1885, Capt. Williamson suggested to the Board of Trade that the Clyde Pilot Board arrange for pier signals to be erected to reduce the hazards occasioned by boats racing to tie up first, especially at single berth piers. This was a bit rich as Williamson was one of the offenders. Monday morning traffic was always heaviest, with several boats vying for the limited berthing space. As boats came in, the passengers would rush to the train where they would be whisked up to Glasgow. The skipper who managed to berth first would enable his passengers to reach the big city half an hour ahead of the boat that berthed last. On one occasion, when three boats were jockeying to be first at the pier, Captain Williamson slipped in ahead of them in the *Sultana*. The 'fiver' it cost was no doubt amply compensated by the increased patronage it bought. Under the Clyde Navigation Act of 1887, powers were granted to the Clyde Pilot Board to erect pier signals; these became operational in March 1889.

May 1889 saw the opening of the new Gourock pier and apparently Dugald Drummond, the Caley locomotive superintendent drove the first train on 1st June. With nearly 30 trains each way and a running time to Glasgow Central station of about 40 minutes, the Caley attracted traffic away from the G&SWR at Princes Pier, though one wonders whether passengers were treated to a 'rough ride' to meet the timetable! The CSP, the subsidiary company in which the Caledonian Railway had a controlling interest, began services with the *Meg Merrilies* and the *Madge Wildfire* and the chartered *Ivanhoe*. The addition of the new boats, *Caledonia* and *Galatea* immediately diverted a large part of the G&SWR's trade and allowed *Ivanhoe* to be put off charter. Other companies used the pier too. The smartness of the CSP boats and their good timekeeping attracted custom. The Caley laid out extensive sidings at Gourock station to store trains. The effect was that the competing railways had to accelerate their timings. Other fleets suffered, including the 'Turkish' fleet run by Capt. James Williamson's brothers.

PS *Galatea* (1889) operated by the Caledonian Steam Packet Co. for the Gourock to Rothesay service.
Alan Brotchie Collection

PS *Caledonia* (1889) built for the Caledonian Steam Packet Co. for use on the Gourock to Rothesay sailings, post-1903.
McLean Museum & Art Gallery, Inverclyde Council

As the *Caledonia*, *Galatea* and the *Meg Merrilies* were put on the Gourock-Rothesay run, inevitably the Wemyss Bay line and Gillies and Campbell's fleet suffered in consequence even though the fare was the same and the Wemyss Bay crossing shorter. The new boats were faster and more attractive than Captain Campbell's *Lancelot* (1868) and the 12 knot *Adela* (1877). Twenty years earlier, the steamer service at Wemyss Bay had collapsed largely due to inefficiencies on the railway and the running of the boats; once again, the Wemyss Bay line was at risk.

The Wemyss Bay Railway Company sell out

In the autumn of 1888, the G&WBR was bought by the Caledonian Railway, however, in the meantime, it was still managed by Keydens. It was to be some time before the Caley took full control. And things were going badly for Captain Campbell. In July 1889, the Caley rejected his request for a subsidy. He then chartered out the PS *Victoria* to sail at the naval review at Spithead. Philip Keyden objected and John Burns was asked to arbitrate, in accordance with the 1874 Agreement, but declined. Only now did the Caley Board take steps to end Campbell's operation. A letter was drafted, but held back so that the facts could be verified. In October 1889, Captain Campbell again invited the Caley to buy his boats.

The competition from Gourock was disastrous to the fortunes of the Wemyss Bay enterprise which found it could no longer run its line profitably. As observed by J.T. Lawrence in 1905, Gourock while coping with a substantial tourist clientèle, also served the business community, whereas Wemyss Bay was almost entirely dependent upon the summer tourist.

Captain Campbell's Wemyss Bay fleet still received only 8½d. out of the 2s. 6d. fare from Glasgow to Rothesay. This was insufficient to stop him hiring out his boats for excursions and contributed to the deterioration of his steamboat service. Over eight years, his 'take' had not changed. Campbell decided to force the Caley to give him a better deal. On 22nd April, 1890, instead of the stipulated six months' warning, he gave them notice he intended to quit in a week's time, on the 30th. The General Manager of the Caley replied on the 24th April accepting Campbell's withdrawal, reserving the right to any claim the Caley might need to make 'for irregular termination of agreements'. Captain Campbell withdrew his boats.

It seems Captain Campbell had not expected this turn of events. In July 1890, the Traffic Committee considered his claim for compensation for 'having been made to withdraw his steamers from the Wemyss Bay traffic'!

Whether the Caley had been working to a long term plan to take over the whole operation is open to question, but now it was in command, it made the most of it. As previously observed, on 1st May, 1890, the Caley temporarily transferred its smart new boats *Caledonia* and *Galatea* from Gourock to run the Wemyss Bay to Rothesay and Millport routes respectively, without a break in service and Wemyss Bay trains began to run into Central Station. The Wemyss Bay steamboat office was staffed by CSP personnel and a telephone linked the Gourock and Wemyss Bay steamer offices. By summer 1890, the *Caledonia* and the *Galatea* had returned to their Gourock runs, replaced by the *Marchioness of Breadalbane* and the *Marchioness of Bute* built by Messrs John Reid & Co. These new steamers had their bridge in front of the funnel, an innovation on the Clyde.

Trade improved. In the summer, Wemyss Bay saw droves of trippers pouring out of the trains, queuing to board steamers to Largs, Millport and Kilchattan Bay from the south side of the pier, or from the north side or at the end if they were going to Innellan, Rothesay, Arran and the Kyles of Bute.

Caledonian Steam Packet PS *Duchess of Hamilton* (1890), fitted with a Parsons turbine to generate electricity. *Alan Brotchie Collection*

PS *Duchess of Fife* (1903) working hard – she could take 1,100 passengers and travel at 17½ knots. *David Hamilton Collection*

The Railway Steamers

By the end of the 19th century, more boats were dashing across the waters than necessary. Most were railway steamers though some were privately owned, mainly used for the heavy summer tripper trade. Racing was rampant, evidenced by palls of smoke trailing the hard-worked coal-burning steamers. Competition made it seem that steamer captains were keener on racing than carrying passengers. Earlier in the century, Captain Price, captain of the *Ruby* on the Glasgow to Rothesay run, apparently left Dunoon with passengers suspended on the gangway, saying 'What are 10s. worth of passengers compared to spoiling a good race?' Such recklessness eventually forced his resignation but did not go unmatched: in 1890, Captain Morrison of the *Duchess of Hamilton* left Brodick pier with passengers still getting on, the gangway and passengers dangling over the side.

In May 1895, the CSP and the G&SWR agreed to reduce competition and racing as this wasted fuel and led to accidents. By now, the scheduled time by train and the PS *Victoria* from Bridge Street to Rothesay via Wemyss Bay was 85 minutes, though 79 minutes had been achieved at least once (by the 4.35 pm on 10th June, 1889); via Gourock, the journey normally took 100 minutes. Timings were eased, and the public grumbled. The Agreement only lasted five years, after which the companies reverted to competing against each other. In 1898 according to J.F. McEwan, the Caley timetable had at least one train taking only 32 minutes between Glasgow and Gourock. On one occasion, a shaken passenger complained that the train took just 27½ minutes for the entire journey, the part between Port Glasgow and Greenock being 'taken only by the wheels on the outer edge of the carriages'. (Similar complaints were levelled against the G&SWR - the trip downhill to Princes Pier could be hair-raising.)

Good weather and summer brought out the tourists. On 3rd July, 1897, under 'Remarks and Reflections', the *Rothesay Chronicle and Buteshire & West Coast Advertiser* reported that 'The Glasgow and South Western Railway Coy offer some tempting cruises on the *Jupiter* for the coming week. If the *Jupiter* is a relation to Jupiter Pluvius good weather may be assured'. Mind you, sailing could be a bit rough. One detects a degree of gleeful malice about their mainland colleagues in this piece dated 7th January, 1899 under the same caption: 'Some Glasgow pressmen had a stormy passage from Millport to Wemyss Bay yesterday. One of them wrote a description for his paper. He was evidently very sick'.

In 1898, forced by the competition, the Caley omitted calls to Craigmore by its Wemyss Bay steamers to accelerate the timetable to Rothesay. Excursion traffic including MacBrayne's steamers continued to use Wemyss Bay pier for other destinations - Campbelltown by the *Davaar* was 4-4½ hours from Wemyss Bay though faster vessels could do it in 2¾ hours.

This was a period of innovation: paddle steamers were bigger, more luxurious, the promenade deck extended to the bows, more powerful engines were fitted and electricity was generated by steam turbine. The CSP grew as it developed its trade down the coast. Turbine propulsion appeared in 1906 and in 1911 a telemotor to operate the steering gear was fitted for the first time on the Clyde to the Turbine Steamers' boat, the *Queen Alexandra*. By 1910, the *Railway Magazine* reported that paddle steamers were almost extinct, except on the Clyde, where the Caley, the North British Railway Company, the G&SWR and other companies found their manoeuvrability invaluable, and continued to build them.

By 1905, there were well-established sailings to Rothesay, Innellan, Dunoon, the Kyles of Bute, and farther afield to Tarbert, Ardrishaig, Inverary and Oban. Combining rail, coach and steamer, the tourist could cover a substantial number of places of interest on the west coast in three days. J.T. Lawrence wrote, 'The Scotch tourist is constantly on the move. A flat stretch of sandy beach, with a promenade and a band, suffice for the Southron when he goes away for his annual fortnight, but the Scot wants scenery. And, after leaving the Glasgow shipyards, there is little in Great Britain to compare with the succession of magnificent panoramas which meet the eye in whatever direction it be turned'. Some excursion boats had their own itinerant fiddler or a band playing Scottish or popular pieces - not always to music hall standard.

In 1906, the Caley had under its command the following steamers - *Duchess of Argyll*, *Duchess of Hamilton*, *Duchess of Rothesay*, *Ivanhoe*, *Duchess of Fife*, *Duchess of Montrose*, *Marchioness of Lorne*, *Marchioness of Breadalbane*, *Marchioness of Bute*, *Caledonia*, and the *Madge Wildfire*.

Contraction began in 1907 as a result of excessive competition; the G&SWR and the Caley agreed to lay off steamers. The 'Clyde Coast Pool' was introduced in 1909 whereby the CSP, the G&SWR, the North British Railway Company (which sailed from the north bank of the Clyde) and certain private steamers, in so far as they carried passengers travelling with combined rail and boat tickets, would operate the same mileage proportions as in 1906-7 with receipts from the railway and steamer operations being pooled and shared. This lasted for 20 years and saw the CSP and G&SWR boats sharing routes and piers. G&SWR boats started using the Wemyss Bay terminal. Travellers could use the trains or boats of one company and transfer to the boat of another at a changing pier.

Declining trade and companies competing for the same market saw the appearance of Sunday rail and ferry services. Before Sunday sailings, Saturdays had been especially busy. On 6th June, 1909, against fierce opposition, the Caley introduced its first ever Sunday service using the *Duchess of Hamilton* on the Gourock, Dunoon and Rothesay route. The traffic expanded rapidly. Services reached a climax the next year, with more steamers engaged on the morning and evening peak runs. There were 12 sailings daily from Wemyss Bay to Rothesay, Largs and Millport, with more on Saturdays, the last service about 11 pm. But extra steamers did not increase passenger traffic.

The slight improvement in returns in 1910 declined the following year - there was an air of uncertainty. Rothesay was now 80 minutes from Glasgow. Princes Pier traffic declined but trade was slightly better at Gourock and Wemyss Bay. The Frith of Clyde Steam Packet Co. sailed from the Broomielaw, near Central Station - on a much cleaner river. In the summer of 1914, over a dozen steamers sailed from the Broomielaw to the Clyde Coast. Some competition returned as the fortunes of railway companies wavered. Railway fares rose. Local authorities and the public agitated against reducing services and higher fares. But then the Caley had to reduce its fleet to eight vessels. Traffic diminished further against a background of generally rising wages and prices.

During World War I, Clyde services were severely disrupted by requisitioning. The boom across the Clyde from the Cloch lighthouse to Dunoon split services across the Firth; those to Dunoon and places north were served from terminals above the boom but places below were accessible only from Wemyss Bay and terminals further south. First the *Duchess of Montrose*, then the *Duchess of Hamilton* and finally the *Duchess of Fife*, were called away. Wemyss Bay was used by the *Duchess of Rothesay* and the *Caledonia* for the Rothesay run and by the *Marchioness of Lorne* to Millport. In 1916, the *Duchess of Rothesay* and the *Marchioness of Lorne* were also 'called up', forcing the Caley to charter the *Benmore* and the *Ivanhoe* to join the *Marchioness of Breadalbane* out of Wemyss Bay. The next year, the *Marchioness of Breadalbane* and the *Caledonia* went to war. All the Caley steamers now served their country. The Caley was forced to charter the *Fusilier* for the winter runs between Wemyss Bay and Rothesay, the *Benmore* doing the Millport turn.

Captain James Williamson, who had done so much to create the Caley Steamboat Company, died in 1919, prior to the return of the requisitioned boats. The *Duchess of Argyll* and the *Marchioness of Breadalbane* returned to the Wemyss Bay-Rothesay turn in time for summer 1919. Simultaneously, a service was introduced linking Gourock to Dunoon, Wemyss Bay and Rothesay.

The steamer fleet was depleted and needing attention. The Caledonian ships were amalgamated with those of the Glasgow and South Western Railway under the banner of the London Midland and Scottish Railway (LMS), but still trading as the Caledonian Steam Packet Company. The LMS took over the Caledonian Railway Company and the G&SWR on 1st January, 1923, thereby making the CSP a subsidiary of the LMS. While some vessels were owned directly by the LMS, others remained under the CSP flag. The fleet of the combined companies now numbered 11, the CSP being reduced to five. The LMS ran passenger ferry services from seven mainland piers - Greenock (Princes Pier), Gourock, Wemyss Bay, Largs, Fairlie, Ardrossan and Ayr. The LMS steamship companies dominated the Clyde tripper trade, the London and North Eastern Railway share (formerly the North British) being generally limited to piers on the Clyde's northern shores.

Profitability returned to the CSP in the early 1920s. Charles A. Bremner, who succeeded Captain Williamson, became marine superintendent of the LMS steamers in 1924, looking after the CSP, G&SWR and LMS boats for all of Scotland from an office in Gourock. Financial control later moved to the LMS offices in Glasgow (Buchanan Street). Donald Matheson, formerly General Manager of the Caledonian Railway and now Deputy General Manager of the LMS in Scotland, managed to have the CSP retained as an entity. Staff from the rival railway fleets were merged, from Board level downwards.

Between the wars, more paddle and turbine steamers were built, creating a small increase in the number of boats sailing the Clyde. In 1928, the LMS and the coast lines purchased the MacBrayne fleet.

In 1926, the 7.40 am from Glasgow Central to Wemyss Bay enabled connections to be made to Innellan, and to Craigmore and Rothesay on Bute. The intense use of steamers is apparent when one considers the zig-zag trip made by the *Jupiter*. After leaving Greenock Princes Pier at 8.45 am having picked up passengers from the 7.30 am from Glasgow St Enoch, she then sailed to Gourock to take passengers from the 8.00 am out of Glasgow Central, proceeded across to Dunoon, south to Innellan then back to Wemyss Bay to connect with the 8.55 am from Central. Then back she sailed across the firth to Craigmore and Rothesay before turning to Largs, followed by a trip via Millport to Ayr. On certain days, she toured round Bute, Cumbrae and went through the Kyles of Bute to Loch Riddon, Loch Striven, Loch Goil and Loch Long. The return journey included a stop at Wemyss Bay to allow passengers who had embarked at Largs and Millport to get home by another steamer.

A favourite tour was to catch the 8.50 am turbine steamer *Duchess of Argyll* at Princes Pier. This vessel stopped at Gourock, Kirn (north of Dunoon), Dunoon, Largs and Wemyss Bay where passengers who had travelled by the 6.55 am Edinburgh Princes Street train could embark. The boat then crossed to Bute, visiting Craigmore and Rothesay before passing through the Kyles of Bute to Tighnabruaich then down the west coasts of Bute and Arran, calling at various piers. The tour continued back up the Clyde to reach Rothesay at 4.25 pm, Wemyss Bay at 5.00 pm, Gourock at 5.50 pm and Greenock (Princes Pier) at 6.05 pm. If one took the train from Wemyss Bay, Greenock or Gourock, one could be back in Glasgow by 6.14 pm or 7.02 pm. Passengers leaving the boat at Wemyss Bay could be in Edinburgh by 8.12 pm.

Another popular tour was to embark at Wemyss Bay and sail to Largs, Millport and Kilchattan Bay (at the southern end of Bute) and take a coach to Rothesay. People sailing, whether on short or longer trips, had to be fed. Breakfasts, lunches and teas as well as light refreshments were served with different menus for first and second class saloons.

The 1930s was a period of severe unemployment; there was less to spend on holidays. Greenock Princes Pier took less traffic, Gourock and Wemyss Bay being favoured instead. A letter dated 5th January, 1932 from J.W. Johnston, Town Clerk of Clydebank, to the Secretary of State for Scotland at the Scottish Office in Whitehall revealed the severity of the problem. Work had been halted at John Brown's Clydebank yard on Ship No. 534, the 3-funnel liner later named the *Queen Mary*. Many shipbuilders were unemployed. Consequently local businesses and trades farther afield were affected. No other work existed. The Town Clerk pointed to a triple loss - money was having to be found from local authorities' Public Assistance Departments, the stoppage would occasion a depressing effect on the whole UK shipbuilding industry ('and in these times it is desirable that every effort should be made to stimulate and to revive the industry') and the loss of national prestige as a shipbuilding nation. (The time had not yet arrived when he could point out the irony of an island nation

The Cunard White Star liner RMS *Queen Mary* (81,000 gross tons, 1,020 feet in length) on her first trip down the Clyde to Greenock in March 1936.   *Langmuir Collection, Mitchell Library*

Cunard White Star line RMS *Queen Mary* being turned in the upper reaches of the Clyde prior to her cautious 14 mile trip down to Greenock at the tail o' the bank. Note the throng of people on the river side.   *Langmuir Collection, Mitchell Library*

being dependent on outsiders to build its boats.) However, the bureaucratic in-tray eventually processed the request and work recommenced two years later, the enormous hull being launched on 26th September, 1934. With re-employment came better times; holidaymakers arrived by rail from England and the Clyde steamer traffic benefitted to the extent that a record 3 million passengers were carried in 1935. The scenery, the replacement of the fleet and the building of the TSS *Duchess of Montrose* for excursion work, all helped maintain traffic on the Clyde.

By 1935, the CSP fleet numbered eight vessels, the LMS five. The LMS extended its grip on the Clyde steamers by acquiring the Williamson-Buchanan fleet that year and transferring them to the CSP, yet retaining their white funnels and separate identity. The PS *Kylemore* (1897), PS *Eagle III* (1910) and the PS *Queen Empress* (1912), (formerly of the Williamson and Buchanan fleet), were transferred from the Broomielaw trade to the Gourock/Wemyss Bay/Millport and Rothesay services. 1937 saw all the LMS boats transferred to the CSP, bringing the combined fleet up to a total of 26. Some of these 'new' boats began to appear at Wemyss Bay. When Gourock was busy, more of the Rothesay steamers used Wemyss Bay. Sunday services developed resulting in less demand for the early morning Monday sailings.

In the 1930s, limited allowance was made for transporting cars. Initially, they were lifted on to deck by crane, later driven on by a precarious arrangement using planks (two or three cars could be placed aft of a paddle-steamer's funnel), but the intervention of World War II postponed development of this trade on the Upper Clyde.

World War II changed Clyde services drastically. But reductions elsewhere did not affect the (summer only) Wemyss Bay-Largs-Millport-Kilchattan Bay schedule. Instead war passenger services *raised* the need for steamers during winter and imposed all-the-year-round demands on the remaining boats. Because of the reinstated Cloch lighthouse-Dunoon boom, MacBrayne could not use the Upper Clyde ports for all their services; for example, the Ardrishaig service ran from Wemyss Bay.

For a short period at the beginning of the War, boats were painted grey, then repainted in company colours. Grey returned for the later war years. Barrows for handling cargo were introduced, wheeled on planks from the quayside on to the steamers, just as cars were. The ease by which they could be loaded was dependent upon the state of the tide. While this reduced delays, the barrows damaged the decks.

Nationalisation

After the war, once again there was a boat shortage. The service was reduced. The Caledonian Steam Packet Co. now had only 15 boats, mostly coal burners. But the fuel was of indifferent quality and labour and other costs were rising.

As personalised transport took more people to places inaccessible by public transport, tripper traffic 'doon the watter' declined. The style of vessels changed, boats designed for mass people movement being replaced by vehicle ferries. The piers became less associated with railways and more an extension of the road system.

Nationalisation took effect from 1st January, 1948. LMS, LNER and CSP boats came under the British Transport Commission (BTC) as part of British Railways (Scottish Region). The marine superintendent's office moved from Gourock to 50 George Square, Glasgow.

Petrol derationing in 1950 led to a great increase in the number of vehicles on the road and affected the Clyde passenger services. The days of paddle steamers and steam turbines were numbered as the different social perspective anticipated before World War II now prevailed - car ferries were required. Greater spending power had another effect on Clyde traffic - transatlantic traffic picked up sufficiently for Princes Pier to be deepened for small liners at the end of the 1950s. Bigger vessels would anchor out in the roads and small paddle steamers acting as tenders would take passengers ashore.

MV *Cowal* (1954) in the foreground with the turbine steamer *Duchess of Hamilton* (1932) preparing to depart from Wemyss Bay pier in August 1967. Note that the line on to the pier still exists and that the wooden ramp up to the luggage platform is being used by a luggage trolley tug.

W.A.C. Smith

Throughout the west of Scotland, services were curtailed as uneconomic passenger ferry services were withdrawn. Small piers closed despite vociferous protests. But on the main routes - Gourock-Dunoon, Wemyss Bay-Rothesay and Ardrossan-Brodick - sailed small diesel-engined ferries with electric hoists to load cargo and vehicles. These, the 'A, B, C' ferries (so called because they were named *Arran*, *Bute* and *Cowal*) had two side entry doors amidships, between which was an elevating platform incorporating two turntables. On docking, the ramps were lowered and the platform raised. Two cars would be driven from the quay on to the turntables. The platform would then be lowered, the cars turned and driven forwards or aft below decks. There was a third turntable near the bows on to which off-loading cars could be driven and turned to regain the elevating platform. Lorries were too big to be driven below decks and instead were accommodated on the turntable platform. Loading and un-loading was time-consuming.

Direct ownership by the BTC of its last three Clyde paddlers, the *Jeanie Deans*, the *Talisman* and the *Waverley* passed to the CSP on 5th November, 1951 and by so doing, the railway connection with the steamers was severed. The steamer offices returned to Gourock as the Clyde Shipping Services.

On 1st October, 1954, all-the-year-round passenger and car ferry services between Wemyss Bay and Rothesay commenced. Goods were loaded on to 3 ton containers at College Goods Depôt in Glasgow, railed to Gourock or Wemyss Bay where they were transferred to trailers hauled by 'mechanical horses' and towed on to the 'A, B, C' boats. This was the beginning of the roll-on roll-off principle. Even though the journey by roads that were sometimes not very good was lengthy and took longer, the public perception that it was more 'convenient' to go door to door by car or lorry than to load and unload passengers and cargo brought to an end the era of the passenger only ferry served by the railway. Motorised traffic increased dramatically. In 1957, there were 4.3 million passengers and 65,000 vehicles using ferries throughout Scotland. But the Glasgow to Rothesay travelling time had increased to 97 minutes, partly because of the time taken to load the car ferries.

In *The Caledonian Steam Packet Co. Ltd* by Iain McArthur, purser Ian McCrorie recalled the variety that was an almost daily commonplace of Clyde traffic around 1960. On the Gourock-Dunoon route, for example, the first boat was the 6.45 am carrying the bread van and barrowloads of goods for the shops. There would be strawberries on the 12.10, the BRS lorry on the 1.10, families and prams on the 2.00, cleaners on the 5.30, the bowler hats on the 6.10 and the drunks on the 8.35 pm.

He further recalled that on Saturdays up till 1960, there would be great congestion at Wemyss Bay pier between 11.30 am and 12.00 noon with the arrival and departure of five vessels: the TSMV *Cowal* car ferry to Rothesay, the Millport-bound PS *Talisman*, the PS *Waverley* doing the Wemyss Bay-Rothesay run, the TSS *Duchess of Montrose* on the relief sailing from Gourock to Dunoon, Wemyss Bay and Rothesay and the TSMV *Maid of Cumbrae* from Rothesay berthed across the end of the pier.

Passenger traffic dropped suddenly in 1962 when a combination of bad summers and continental holidays drove people away from the Clyde resorts. By 1967, it was clear to the CSP that the days of train and ferry 'doon the watter' were over. The future lay with car ferries as railway-generated traffic was now small. When electric passenger trains arrived in the late 1960s, British Rail's limited interest in freight saw bulk goods transfer to the road. Wemyss Bay station, which in 1957 only shifted 2,700 tons of coal and 1,850 tons of oil, including fuel for the steamers, (compared with Greenock and Gourock which together conveyed over 275,000 tons of coal and other goods) saw this trade disappear. The train plus boat trip to Rothesay from Glasgow Central improved to 85 minutes via Wemyss Bay (as good as at the end of the 19th century). Costs rose as British Railways, trying to improve its finances, levied a charge on passengers using BR piers, collected with the ferry fare. Ferries were rationalised with Wemyss Bay serving Rothesay and Gourock serving Dunoon.

Under the Transport Act 1968, the Secretary of State for Scotland became responsible for the management of the CSP fleet. On 1st January, 1969, the Caledonian Steam Packet Co. ceased to be under railway 'control' and became part of the Scottish Transport Group (STG), an organisation dominated by the Scottish Bus Group Ltd. Later the same year, the STG gained complete control of the red-funnelled fleet and road vehicles of David MacBrayne Ltd. (founded in 1851 as David Hutcheson and Company). The CSP now operated both the Caley and MacBrayne fleets.

New offices were built for the CSP on Gourock pier in 1971, the CSP leaving the station premises they had occupied since 1889. The pier at Wemyss Bay was also transferred to the STG.

The change in transport patterns left the new owners with an ageing fleet and mounting deficits. To correct this, in 1970-71, Clyde excursion fares more than doubled. The STG also concentrated on fewer crossings to the islands and used motor ferries with drive-on drive-off facilities, allowing larger vehicles to be conveyed with quicker turn-arounds. In 1971, the Government allocated £15m [*£116m] over four years to the STG for improvements to road and shipping services.

The roll-on, roll-off ferry *Glen Sannox* appeared on the Wemyss Bay-Rothesay run in May 1970. But at certain tides, the vessel could not unload at Rothesay. In the same year, plans for end loading were considered for Rothesay and Wemyss Bay though Wemyss Bay was thought to be too exposed and constricted a site to develop. (In heavy weather, the Rothesay-Wemyss Bay ferry may have to berth at Gourock.) It was believed Bute might be better (and more economically) served from Gourock, Largs or Fairlie instead. Meanwhile Wemyss Bay's wooden pier was causing concern, resulting in a weight restriction of 7½ tons being imposed.

Trials in 1965 and 1966 with an SR-N6 hovercraft by Clyde Hover Ferries Ltd, resurrecting a pre-war proposal of a fast ferry carrying 12 passengers between Wemyss Bay and Rothesay

CLYDE STEAMER, P.S. "JEANIE DEANS"

The PS *Jeannie Deans* was built in 1931 for the London & North Eastern Railway (LNER) to run between Craigendoran and Arrochar. She was transferred to the Wemyss Bay to Rothesay sailings in the 1960s and sold off river in 1964. Her maximum speed was 18 knots and her passenger complement 1,390.

Alan Brotchie Collection

The former LNER paddle steamer *Waverley* pays a rare visit to Wemyss Bay during a squall on 21st April, 2001, shortly after a major overhaul. Her siling speed was 15 knots, the passenger complement 1,350.

Shonagh Fleming

in 10 minutes, came to nothing. (Walter Smart - *The Story of the Parish consisting of Skelmorlie and Wemyss Bay* - mentioned that Kellybridge harbour beside the present Wemyss Bay Ferry Terminal had been modified to allow hovercraft to be beached.) In 1970, the CSP Co. tried using a hovercraft based at Greenock with existing piers, rather than beaching. With its marine propellers, it could achieve 35 knots but the experiment was not a success and it was withdrawn in September 1971.

The Scottish Transport Group ordered new vessels: the *Pioneer*, *Juno*, *Jupiter* and the *Saturn*, all of which used the Wemyss Bay terminal during the 1992/93 restoration works. The 30-minute crossing is currently served by boats averaging an hourly frequency.

The rise and fall of Steamer Traffic on the Clyde

A paddler could last a very long time. The short-lived few like *Lady Gertrude*, wrecked after only five years, were the exception. Some lasted well over 50 years - the *Iona*, built in 1864, was eventually withdrawn 73 years later. A curious feature is that serviceable machinery was sometimes transferred from one hull to another. It says much of the boats and their robust machinery that they survived and maintained their appeal so long against relentlessly rising costs.

Of the boats that some time in their lives were to berth at Wemyss Bay, three were built between 1840 and 1859, 12 between 1860 and 1869, seven between 1870 and 1879, eight between 1880 and 1889 and 10 between 1890 and 1899. Traffic declined in the 20th century with only seven boats constructed between 1900 and 1929. However, between 1930 and 1939, 12 boats left the slipways to do service on the Clyde including calling at Wemyss Bay.

The graph illustrates the existence at any one time of passenger carrying boats that were to serve Wemyss Bay but by extrapolation, it may also indicate the level of water borne activity on the Clyde, showing a peak round about 1900.

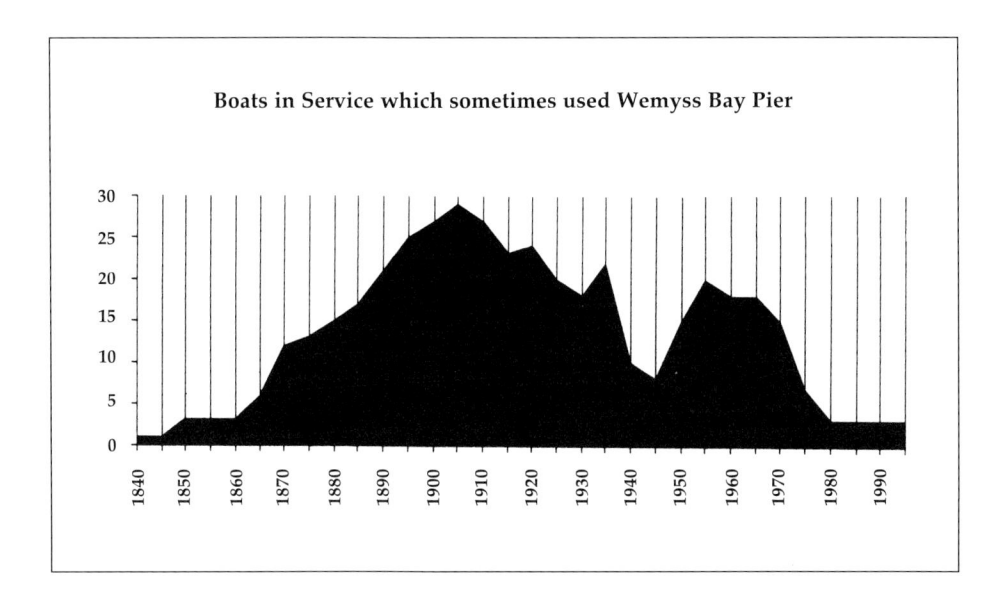

Boats in Service which sometimes used Wemyss Bay Pier

Steamers required about an hour each day to replenish their bunkers at the pierheads, coal being bagged or barrowed on board. At Wemyss Bay, coal trucks used to stand behind the sea wall before being wheeled on to the north side of the pier - possibly pulled by horse or reversed on by a locomotive to minimise the load on the pier. Rothesay was a busy overnight terminal, with moorings in the bay for the Caley's Gourock and Wemyss Bay steamers. During World War I, boats were regularly coaled at Wemyss Bay, even though they might not operate from there. In the 1930s, Wemyss Bay steamers berthed overnight at weekends at Port Bannatyne pier, just north of Rothesay.

Fuel oil was a particular concern. The Petroleum Acts of 1871 to 1881 became enshrined in separate but similar Caledonian Railway Byelaws for Wemyss Bay and Gourock piers in 1905.

The first oil firing experiment was made in 1893 with the *Caledonia*. This improved both steaming and cleanliness, but the fuel cost was too high and the vessel reverted to coal. At this time, the country was in a depression and coal prices were falling (the railways bought theirs for between 6s. 6d. and 7s. [*£16.50-£17.80] per ton). Oil firing on Clyde steamers only became common after 1937.

Liveries

The Wemyss Bay Steamboat Company, which operated briefly between 1865 and 1869 had black hulls, red at the waterline, mahogany superstructure and a white funnel with black cap. The boats flew a blue pennant with a white cross.

Gillies and Campbell's boats on the Wemyss Bay service between 1869 and 1890 carried the same livery as their predecessor.

From 1890 the boats of the Caledonian Steam Packet Company Ltd carried various liveries. Initially the *Meg Merrilees* had a navy blue hull with gold lines below main deck level, white paddle boxes, white water line, green underbody and yellow funnel. Early in their career, the CSP boats adopted a black hull, red at the waterline with a white line above, white superstructure and yellow funnel. A yellow pennant with red lion rampant flew from the masthead. Later, the livery changed to a dark blue hull, green at the waterline, white paddlebox, white band at the top of the hull, red superstructure and orange funnel. The pennant remained unchanged. This was subsequently amended to a black hull, red at the waterline, with a white band at deck level, a white superstructure and a yellow funnel with black cap and lion rampant. The smart liveries were matched by uniformed staff, as in railway practice.

The LMS boats carried a different livery to the CSP vessels - black hull, white at the waterline, red underbody, varnished deckhouses, white paddleboxes and a yellow funnel with black cap (though briefly they had a red separating band between the yellow and black).

Following the takeover of the steamship operations by the STG in 1969, new colours were adopted for the Caledonian Steam Packet Co. and David MacBrayne vessels - black hulls, a red and white band at the waterline, white superstructure, with black topped red funnel carrying the 'lion' badges on yellow roundels. The two companies were united as Caledonian MacBrayne Ltd. in 1973.

Cloch Lighthouse near Gourock. *Author*

Chapter Ten

Clyde River Traffic

Wemyss Bay is less than three miles across the Clyde from the Cowal Peninsula and six from the Isle of Bute. The mind conjures up a picture of fine rugged scenery bordering a smooth river with steamers and sail boats floating like toys on a millpond. It can be like this. But high winds, horizontal sleet, fog and difficult seas are not uncommon in these parts. Man's commercial needs and his quest for speed have endangered boats in foul and fair weather. With ferries crossing trading routes, this area is no stranger to calamity.

Before the advent of railways and good roads, sloops, schooners, sailing coasters and gabbarts carried bulk cargo up and down the Clyde and through to the west coast. Flat-bottomed puffers later took on this rôle, sharing the busy Clyde with newly-built passenger ships and, like the fishing boats, made regular use of the Crinan Canal to get to the west coast, or the Forth and Clyde Canal to sail into central Glasgow and across to Grangemouth. Small vessels fished the Clyde while naval craft and new boats like the 45,647 ton liner *Aquitania* ran the measured mile off Skelmorlie (established by Robert Napier in 1866).

The measured mile, defined by white posts, was much used and responsible for several accidents. Over the last two centuries, in the four miles from Wemyss Point to Largs, several boats have been lost, including the PS *Princess of Wales* while on trial. In one year (1838-39) on the Upper Clyde alone, 69 collisions were recorded. Up to the mid-20th century, the Clyde was a particularly busy thoroughfare.

Over the same period on the other side of the firth near Rothesay, it is known that six vessels were wrecked, including Gillies and Campbell's PS *Lady Gertrude* completing her run from Wemyss Bay. These varied from small vessels to a steamer of 1,217 net tons. The present day ferry route passes to the north of an area marked on the charts as Skelmorlie Bank where at least two other vessels have come to grief.

The year 1897 was a busy one on the Clyde. In May, the torpedo boat destroyer *Earnest*, built by Messrs Laird, Birkenhead, for the British Admiralty, was reported to have carried out a power consumption trial at 30 knots, with very satisfactory results, achieving a mean speed of 30.38 knots during six runs on the measured mile and 30.1 knots for over three hours, the coal consumption per horse power per hour being within specification. Small wonder that accidents happened when vessels were running at such speeds over several hours. Anyone who has tried to stop a canal boat travelling at 4 mph knows that it takes forever. Some details of vessels wrecked or stranded on the coast near Wemyss Bay or Rothesay, are given below.

Some Clyde Casualties

Around the end of the 18th century, in bitterly cold weather, the sloop *Star* transporting troops from Campbeltown ran aground off the 'Cock of Arran', on the island's northern tip. Refloated at high tide, she made for Skelmorlie to inspect the damage. The soldiers were put ashore to walk to Greenock, marching till exhausted in a severe snowstorm through knee-deep snowdrifts.

On Christmas Day 1806, a fierce storm blew the *Elizabeth* ashore at Knock. Then the *Juno* was blown into Wemyss Bay while making her way up the Clyde from Stranraer. Robert Wallace of Kelly, observing the *Juno's* difficulties, organised his staff and the villagers to beach the craft, whereupon she unloaded her cargo of '340 quarters oats ashore at Weems Bay'.

In April 1855, the 94 ton paddle steamer *Mars* was stranded at Largs. Twenty years on, in December 1875, the 476 ton wooden barque *Tovernus* was lost after a collision at Skelmorlie Bank, south of the Wemyss Bay to Rothesay ferry route.

Puffer *Dane* of 1903, renamed *Saxon* and subsequently used in the televised 'Para Handy' series created by Neil Munro where it was christened the *Vital Spark*. *Author's Collection*

On 16th January, 1877, while on her normal run, Gillies and Campbell's Wemyss Bay Steamboat Company's *Lady Gertrude* (1872) was wrecked on the rocks at Toward pier when she failed to engage reverse. The passengers disembarked safely on to the pier from the stern. At first, it seemed she could be refloated but she broke her back and became a total wreck. As previously mentioned her engine was removed and fitted into the *Adela* (1877).

In September 1881, the RMPS *Columba* rammed and holed the Wemyss Bay steamer *Sheila* below the waterline following a race for Innellan Pier. The *Sheila's* passengers disembarked on to the pier then the *Sheila* was beached, patched and towed away for repair. She was sold without returning to Wemyss Bay.

Two months later, the 1,217 ton barque *Ardenlea* was stranded off Toward Point. A much smaller vessel, the 58 ton schooner *John Craich* foundered off Skelmorlie Bank in October 1889. In January 1898, the 37 ton smack *Dolphin* ran ashore at Wemyss Bay and in March 1923, the 131 ton schooner *Reaper* ran aground at Toward Point.

In August 1889, the *Adela* tragically ran down a small sailing boat off Toward Point, killing a young doctor. It seems the pilot's position aft of the funnel prevented him seeing properly ahead.

In February 1893 the small 48 ton lighter *Louise* departed from Rothesay carrying tar and casks of ammoniacal liquor, towing her lifeboat behind her. The cargo could not be entirely contained below decks and consequently the hatch covers were not fully secured. All went well until the vessel reached the Kyles of Bute when the sea became rough. Attempting to return to Rothesay to await calmer weather, she broached to, whereupon the three-man crew got into the lifeboat. Unfortunately, they could not cut the painter attaching the boats resulting in the *Louise* dragging the lifeboat and her crew under.

Shortly after its introduction, the CSP steamer *Caledonia* ran down a small boat with four holidaymakers as it left Craigmore Pier at Rothesay in July 1889. Unhappily in December 1891 the same boat lost her mate. The *Caledonia*, having experienced great difficulty drawing alongside Wemyss Bay pier, cast off, Mr Muir being washed overboard and drowned. Two passengers were lowered in a boat and attempted to find him but narrowly missed sharing his fate, just making it to the shore. In December 1892, the 45 ton ketch *Matchless* was lost following a collision off Wemyss Bay.

The closing years of the 19th century saw two disasters caused by fog at the Rothesay end of the Wemyss Bay ferry route. The first was on 28th December, 1889, when the 444 ton steamship *Ovington* was sailing down the Clyde about midnight in poor weather. When she reached Toward Point, the vessel was hit by fog and snow squalls and the captain decided to anchor and wait till the weather improved. Meanwhile, the homeward bound *Queen Victoria* of 1,500 tons was sailing northwards and appears to have mistaken the *Ovington's* lights for Toward Lighthouse. The *Queen Victoria* rammed into the side of the *Ovington* causing her to sink in five minutes, taking several of her crew with her.

The other accident occurred when 'the fog was so thick the gulls were sitting on it'. With visibility nil, sight and sound become confused and navigation in busy waters is extremely hazardous. In September 1895, the 1,077 ton *Wallachia* set out from Glasgow for Trinidad and Demerara carrying general cargo. Proceeding cautiously, she was hit on her starboard side by the 1406 ton Norwegian steamer *Flos*. The crew were rescued but the boat sank.

A serious accident happened in July 1925, when the TSS *Duchess of Argyll* collided with the TSS *King Edward* (1901) off Largs when the *Argyll* set out to cross the bows of the *King Edward*. The *Argyll* was put hard astern but was hit amidships by the *King Edward*. The latter proceeded on her run to Fairlie but the *Argyll* required repairs costing £2,400 [*£60,000].

Though not on the ferry route, passengers bound for Wemyss Bay may spot a more recent casualty as they climb the hill above Greenock - the Greek registered *Captayannis*, a sugar vessel that capsized in 1974. Moored in Greenock bay, she dragged her anchor and holed herself on a BP tanker undergoing trials. She then turned on her side on a sandbank, where she remains like a beached whale, seaward of where Scott Lithgow's Goliath crane stood.

Accidents on the Measured Mile

As the Measured Mile commenced at Skelmorlie, ships on trial were either running up to speed or slowing down as they crossed the ferry route at Wemyss Bay. Providence ensured that the potential for accidents was guaranteed.

On 16th June, 1888, the 112 ton two-funnel paddle steamer *Princess of Wales* sailed from Barclay Curle's Glasgow yard to commence speed trials. On board were about 50 guests and workmen completing the fitting out. At noon she ran up to full speed and entered the Measured Mile from the north. She completed the run and turned slowly to starboard for her run back. Meanwhile, the *Balmoral Castle* began a high speed run from the north, slightly inshore of the *Princess of Wales*. Her pilot made a slight adjustment to starboard, considering he was too close inshore. The pilot on the *Princess of Wales*, seeing this, made a further starboard adjustment. The distance closed rapidly. The *Princess of Wales* went full ahead but the *Balmoral Castle* sliced through the vessel aft of the engine room bulkhead, causing the stern to sink. The ladies were put into the remaining lifeboat and rowed to Skelmorlie. Those still in the fore part were rescued by rowing boats from the shore. Three workmen in the stern were lost. At the time, the PS *Adela* was in the vicinity and took the still floating bow section in tow intending to beach her at Wemyss Bay. However the bows sank in 30 fathoms of water off the Bay pier.

On 29th January, 1897, in clear calm weather, Torpedo-Boat Destroyer No. 289 HMS *Electra*, on trials, violently struck the stern of the *Meg Merrilies* on her regular ferry trip from Wemyss Bay to Largs. Fearing she might sink, Captain Duncan Smith ran his boat into shallow water. Finding her undamaged below the water line he continued on her run. In two other incidents, a ship on trial over the Measured Mile actually took off the end of Wemyss Bay pier and the destroyer HMS *Laverock* ran aground further south in Blackhouse Burn.

View from the Wemyss Bay line as it climbs from Port Glasgow towards the site of Upper Greenock station. The hull of the *Captayannis*, a sugar vessel which capsized in 1974, lies on a sandbank in the Clyde. Craigendoran is visible on the north bank. *Author*

On 18th September, 1907, the 94 ton steamer *Kintyre*, nicknamed the 'Campbeltown yacht' because of her twin masts, graceful swept lines and clipper bow, was steering close to the Renfrewshire coast on her way to Campbeltown. Built nearly 40 years earlier, she was owned by the Campbeltown and Glasgow Steam Packet Joint Stock Company and skippered by Captain John McKechnie. Meanwhile, the Denny built Union Steamship Company of New Zealand boat *Maori* (3,500 tons), having completed a northward run on the 'Mile' was turning to port prior to a starboard turn for her next run south. At this point, the vessels were about half-a-mile apart. Both sounded their sirens. For some reason, *Kintyre* maintained full speed instead of slowing to allow the bigger vessel to complete her turn in front of her. The *Maori* attempted to avoid a collision by reversing her engines but hit the *Kintyre* at speed in her starboard quarter. For a few moments, the boats were locked together, time enough for all except Captain McKechnie and Chief Engineer William Lennox to board the *Maori*. Though Captain McKechnie tried to beach his vessel, *Kintyre* blew up and sank in five minutes in 25 fathoms of water 400 yards south west of Wemyss Point and only 200 yards off shore. A nearby yacht and the CSP steamers *Marchioness of Breadalbane* and *Marchioness of Bute*, which had just left Wemyss Bay for Bute, put about to render assistance. Captain McKechnie was saved but Lennox's body was never found. Two local children, Ninian Stewart and his sister, rowed out and retrieved the ship's log, which they later handed to Captain McKechnie at the Wemyss Bay Hotel.

The Navy's here

The Clyde has long been associated with British and other countries' navies, most recently with the nuclear submarines of the American fleet. The *Rothesay Chronicle and Buteshire & West Coast Advertiser* of 18th December, 1897 reported that 'a Spanish torpedo boat destroyer which put into Rothesay to replenish her whisky kegs, proceeded south yesterday'.

During World War II, Skelmorlie was the HQ of the 1st Army which landed in Tunisia. Beaches at Wemyss Bay and elsewhere were concreted over to ease loading and unloading of Tank Landing Craft. All the beaches were protected against invasion. Vessels from the Dutch, Norwegian, French and Polish navies appeared in the Clyde. It was such a sensitive area that a decoy village was built at the north end of Bute, lit up at night to attract enemy bombs away from Clydebank and other prime targets.

Because the Clyde was important to the war effort and within reach of German bombers, the Clyde River Patrol, a kind of water-based home guard whose main task was to seek out and flag up stray mines, was busy during the Second World War. Using lightly armed private boats, they sailed under the Royal Navy Volunteer Supplementary Reserve. Huge volumes of goods, both military and consumables, passed through the Clyde to and from the 'Clyde Anchorages Emergency Port' at Greenock to vessels moored in nearby lochs and mid-stream at the Tail o' the Bank. At any time there might be 400 ships of several nationalities at anchor with Catalina flying boats and Sunderland seaplanes flying in and out. Two visits by German bombers did extensive damage to Greenock but no bombs fell on the fleet. Later, troop carriers appeared including the *Queen Mary* and *Queen Elizabeth*. Nearly 2,000 vessels were handled and over 2.3 million tons of goods transferred. A marine first aid unit was set up in a slow paddler with six beds while a fast launch was available to render first aid.

At a crisis point during World War II, the Government decided to ship the nation's reserves to Canada. Thousands of boxes of gold bullion were sent to Plymouth and the Clyde, mostly to the latter. One train hauling bullion worth about £20m [*£438m] in sealed rolling stock was accidentally shunted up a siding at Wemyss Bay instead of the Greenock docks. HMS *Revenge* alone carried gold worth £160m plus stocks and shares. Four other ships departed from the Clyde with destroyer escort. In total, over £440m [*£9,627m] was shipped overseas in two small convoys.

In 1947 a naval review was held on the river. The biggest gathering of the fleet since D-Day saw battleships extending from the Tail o' the Bank as far as the eye could see. Berths were found up and down the Clyde - at Dunoon, Rothesay, Largs and Millport. At the same time, the Clyde, an established 'yachtsman's paradise' was again home to a racing yacht regatta. By 19th July 1947, the *Glasgow Herald* was commenting on the naval arrangements: 17 submarines were berthed in Rothesay Bay around the mother ships HMS *Montclare* and HMS *Maidstone*, and 24 naval vessels including four destroyers had arrived in the Clyde. They would be there for the duration of Clyde Fortnight. Before long, the gathered Home Fleet amounted to over 100 vessels including the battleships HMS *Duke of York* where the C-in-C hoisted his flag, HMS *Anson* and HMS *Howe*, aircraft carriers HMS *Illustrious* and HMS *Vengeance*, the cruisers *Cleopatra*, *Dido* and *Syrius*, destroyers, submarine target vessels and motor torpedo boats. Altogether, a fleet larger than the whole of the British navy in 2001.

On 22nd July, King George VI and Queen Elizabeth (the present Queen Mother) inspected the fleet with Prime Minister and Mrs Atlee, the sounds of a 21-gun salute once again rolling off the hills.

Two days' later, the *Glasgow Herald* described the royal itinerary for the 24th, while continuing to report the on-going Clyde regatta. At 8.58 am, the King and Queen, accompanied by Princess Elizabeth and Lieutenant Philip Mountbatten RN (whose engagement had been announced less than a fortnight earlier) and Princess Margaret, would arrive at Port Glasgow to board the royal train to Wemyss Bay. At 10.23, Lord Inverclyde would receive the royals at Wemyss Bay before they embarked on HMS *Superb*. The ship would take them to Brodick Pier for a visit to Brodick Castle, before continuing to Whiting Bay and Lochranza, returning to Wemyss Bay at 6.55 pm, five minutes before the royal party was due to board the train. The paper added that the train would stop over at Moffat on its way to London.

By 1995, the level of naval traffic was minimal but submarines near the mouth of the Clyde worried the fishing fleet - the *Antares* was dragged under when her nets caught a submerged submarine. While restoration work was being carried out at Wemyss Bay railway station, on a day when there was a flat calm, a sudden swell lasting several minutes left one with the impression that a large vessel was passing rapidly up the firth. But there was no boat on the surface.

Clyde River Traffic to the end of the 20th Century

On the Clyde, big liners are now rare visitors. Occasionally they moor at Greenock to take on passengers or reprovision whereas in the 1920s there were often two liners a week, with additional trains running to carry their passengers. Battleships are only occasionally seen. Paddle steamers have been replaced by motor ferries. By 1955, there were only 17 steamers plying the Clyde whereas there had been 38 in 1914. Recent regular users included the grey and yellow hulled 'banana boats' *Dalmarnock* and *Garroch Head* on their daily trips to dump Glasgow's sewage sludge out at sea - these have since been 'phased out'. There may be a link between the decline of the tripper trade, the improvement in sewage treatment from 1895 and the introduction in 1904 of sludge vessels which effectively eliminated the pong from the Clyde.

Private yachts no longer moor in Wemyss Bay. Instead marinas along the coast packed with a variety of yachts provide the better off with the means to get away from it all.

Beautiful when calm, the Clyde can still be treacherous.

Chapter Eleven

The Kirk Upset and the Perils of Travel

The Kirk and Rail and Steamer Companies

A railway cannot be properly maintained 'between trains'; it requires time which occurs only when traffic is light. In 1852, seven years after the Caledonian Railway Company was formed, some Caley shareholders wanted 'no systematic pre-determined work' done on the Sabbath. The motion was defeated, but the rumblings continued. Greenock people favoured no Sunday traffic, but railway Boards running Sunday mail trains questioned why they should not also carry passengers.

In January 1865, James Lamont, a Director of both the Wemyss Bay Steamboat and Wemyss Bay Railway Companies sought election to Parliament. During close questioning from the burghers of Bute, he was asked if he would use his boardroom influence to deter Sunday travelling on the 'Frith'. He responded (ambiguously) to applause that 'It would not be pleasant for me, on the low ground of my own comfort, to see these quiet shores inundated with a crowd of Sabbath desecrators from Glasgow'. He failed to be elected by 15 votes (from a total vote of 205!) which may have been just as well; commercial considerations concluded that the poor benefited from getting away from it all, thus justifying much weekend travelling.

Resentment to Sunday travel continued, hinted at by *Variorum* in the *Greenock Telegraph and Clyde Shipping Gazette* in January 1897, having recently clearly suffered an unhappy train journey. 'More attention might in future be paid by railway officials to the cleaning out and dusting of the special holiday trains before bringing them into use. The condition of some of the carriages on New Year's Day was enough to soil kirk claes beyond all respectability'.

In June 1897, the *Rothesay Chronicle and Buteshire & West Coast Advertiser* predicted that 'the race to the coast by train and steamer promises to be more headlong than ever this season'. A week later, reflecting on church moves to ban Sunday travel, it added the useful note that 'One of the Caledonian steamers came in to Rothesay on Sunday afternoon, and thus proved conclusively that the engines can be got to work on that day if required'.

One of Rothesay's leading ministers refused to be drawn into the argument. The *Rothesay Chronicle* of 5th June, 1897 reported,

Pulpit Defence of the Sunday Steamer - Rev. A. Hutchison is reported to have spoken thus last Sunday evening in St Brendan's Church: There is a clamour just now for a sane Sunday, for a rational Sunday. The sane Sunday, the rational Sunday, must be a religious Sunday. I have not a word against Sunday steamers, Sunday golf and so on, because I know many fine young people serving in grocers' shops in Glasgow who are behind the counter all week and until midnight on Saturday, to whom the Sunday steamer must be a blessing and the Sunday golf too. It is their one chance of breathing God's direct air and of seeing God's works . . . I don't defend the habitual practice of secular enjoyment on Sunday, but I say that when you secure for all shop assistants a weekly holiday or even a half holiday, when you secure that drunken working men shall return home with their wages early on Saturday afternoon so that their wives can get the marketing done in decent time . . . then I shall join in petitioning the Board of Trade against the Sunday Steamer.'

The needs of the navvies were not forgotten. In October 1901, the Revd J. Bannerman of the Free Church at Inverkip asked the Caley Traffic Committee for permission to erect a small iron building on company ground for the navvies to use as a 'reading room'. Permission was granted for a temporary building, probably because navvies and locals often did not get on with each other. One suspects the 'reading room' was also used for other purposes.

Sunday travel was again opposed in the 20th century. In February 1910, the Kirk Session of the Wemyss Bay and Skelmorlie Free Church petitioned the Chairman and Directors of the Caley against the resumption of Sunday traffic to the coast. In May 1913, a high level delegation led by ex-Provost Neil Maclean of Wishaw, president of the Sabbath Protection Association, met Sir Charles Bine Renshaw, Chairman of the Caley, and other office bearers including Donald Matheson, the General Manager, to put their case. The Sabbath Protectionists said it was all very well for railway companies to say they must meet the demands of the public, but there was a difference between the public's needs and their demands. It was a pity the Caley should give way and allow Sunday to be a day of pleasure; the Sabbath was a Divine institution with which no-one could trifle.

Sir Charles politely acknowledged their point of view but stated that fewer trains ran on Sundays than on any other day of the week and besides, Sunday running had been going on for quite some time. He could have added that competition and balance sheets demanded maximum use of assets. He might have been unaware of the less measured tones of one of his predecessors, who, referring to the battle between his company and the North British to acquire the Edinburgh and Glasgow line, which did not operate on Sundays, commented that the Edinburgh and Glasgow directors deliberately prevented people travelling into the country on their one day of leisure, forcing them to stay indoors and thus 'compelling a large consumption of whisky on the Sabbath'. The Caley, a thoroughly commercial line, saw no reason to contribute, as John Prebble wrote of the Edinburgh and Glasgow [*The High Girders*], 'to that air of melancholy inaction that hangs over Scotland on the seventh day'.

In 1917, with the country at war with Germany, the *Glasgow Herald* printed a letter from R.W. Campbell. Referring to the inevitable amalgamation of the railways, Mr Campbell thought that the church had a part to play in running a railway. 'In Canada, isolated shack communities go to church and pray to God for the railways. Here we apparently desire to strangle and destroy one of the greatest assets for winning the war, and the war after the war'.

Accidents on the Wemyss Bay Branch

Despite various Acts - the Railway Regulation Acts of 1840 and 1844, the Regulation of Railways Acts of 1868 and 1889, etc., technical improvements have been followed by more Regulations as some new weak point in the railway system has been exposed. The press was full of 'Extraordinary' and 'Shocking' accidents, 'Frightful Catastrophes' and 'Melancholy Occurrences' on the railways. Things were so bad that in January 1865, the *Glasgow Herald* printed a letter from Queen Victoria who felt compelled to write to the management of railways with termini in London '. . . to call the attention of the directors . . . to the increased number of accidents which have lately occurred . . . and to express her Majesty's warmest hope that the directors . . . will carefully consider every means of guarding against these misfortunes, which are not at all necessary accompaniments of railway travelling'.

The Wemyss Bay line had been open only months when, on 16th September 1865, the Caley Board learned of a bad accident at the terminus. The *Glasgow Herald* reported that the packed 10-coach 1.10 pm train from Glasgow, had crashed into the buffers at Wemyss Bay station after attempting to recover seven minutes' lost time. Beyond Inverkip, at Mr Cook's hotel, Charles Watson the engine driver had shut off steam and applied the 'breaks', but an earlier shower of rain had left the line slippery. Seeing that the train was going too fast, the fireman clambered into the van behind the tender and screwed down the brake. However, the train sped on and hit the buffers at about 6 mph, momentarily rearing up into the air. The tender ended up nearly vertical and one end of a first class carriage was stove in. The driver, fireman and guard jumped before the impact. One man, a Greenock mason, broke a leg and about 30 were injured. The article stated that Mr Ronaldson, a Wemyss Bay Director, was in the guard's van, a fact which curiously was never mentioned thereafter. Within a short time, four doctors and a professor (Allan Thomson, professor of anatomy) were attending the injured with Mr Elliott the station master doing what he could in front of a large crowd. The paper recorded that Mr Strang 'Secretary of the Company' was also present, which is odd as Mr Keyden of Keyden, Strang and Keyden was the named Secretary.

Captain F.H. Rich, RE of the Board of Trade (Railway Department) reported to the Secretary of his Department on 27th October, 1865. His investigations extracted some significant facts which the *Herald* reporter had not mentioned. The engine was a single wheeler of about 26 tons with 7 ft drivers carrying about 11½ tons and leading and trailing wheels 3 ft 6 in. diameter. The tender weighed about 14 tons. The train had comprised, in order, the engine and tender, guard's van, two first class, one third class, two first and four third class carriages, braking facilities being provided only in the third class vehicles in the middle and end of the train and in the guard's van behind the engine. Captain Rich noted that the train started at 1.11 pm with the guard in the rear carriage brake compartment. As the Caley would not provide a second guard despite the engine driver's previous requests, the driver had become used to asking his fireman to go into the 8-ton brake van behind him to provide the additional stopping power needed for the final steep descent (1:69½) to the entrance to Wemyss Bay station.

As the train *approached* Inverkip, the fireman got into the brake van behind the engine. Just as the train *left* Inverkip, the guard, James Currie, conscious of the large amount of luggage in the front van which needed to be shifted speedily on arrival at Wemyss Bay, without telling the driver, left the rear brake van in charge of a watchman who, though a railway company servant, was not competent to operate the brakes, and went to the front van, no doubt to the fireman's considerable surprise. The train proceeded to descend to Wemyss Bay between 20 and 40 mph. The driver shut off steam, reversed his engine at the hotel half-a-mile from the station, reapplied steam and sanded the rails made slippery by the showers, but while the front brakes were put full on, those left in the charge of the watchman were hardly applied. Captain Rich observed, 'it appears that some passengers applied the breaks [sic] in the centre carriage, but this was probably only done at the last moment'. The train hit the buffers with great violence.

Captain Rich criticised the driver for sending his fireman into the van when he was needed on the engine, the guard for leaving his post, where he might have prevented the accident, and the company for not providing a second guard or gradient boards. What Captain Rich did *not* say was which 'Railway Company' the watchman belonged to, leaving the impression that he was a Caley employee (the party responsible for running the trains) as the Greenock and Wemyss Bay Railway *Company* is nowhere mentioned in his otherwise detailed report - but could this have been Mr Ronaldson, the Wemyss Bay Director mentioned in the *Herald* article? Likewise, by omitting the names of those who gave evidence - the fireman, watchman, the station master and Caley officials who confirmed that the driver had previously requested a second guard but for 'another part of the Wemyss Bay line', suggest that the Board of Trade Inspector had identified the driver and guard as the responsible parties. Nowadays, one might expect the Health and Safety Executive to prosecute the company for not having a safe system of work in place.

Mr Gibson (the Caledonian Secretary) was instructed to settle on the best terms he could. By December 1865, the railway had paid out £4,216 4s. [*£175,000] to over 80 claimants. Settlement averaged £18 [*£750] each, but one was paid £2,000 [*£83,000].

While nowadays we expect continuous braking systems, in 1865, the railway inspectorate was not yet pressing for its introduction or highlighting the hazards to railway staff carrying out their duties on non-corridor rolling stock. Captain Rich's comments reveal how much had been learnt since railways began and how much more safety conscious we have since become:

> The fact that the engine driver habitually parted with his fireman, to fulfil the duties of a second guard proves, how much a second guard was required, and it further proves, how desirable it is for railway companies to adopt some system, by which the proper officers will become aware, of what goes on the lines under their charge, be informed of all cases when drivers put their firemen to do guards' duties, and guards leave their posts to attend to passengers' luggage, thereby endangering the safety of the train.

It probably had to take the report of an accident like this to convince the railway company that the practices it allowed were unsafe and required improvement.

Railway accidents provided regular copy for the newspapers. The story goes that after one accident, a Millport lady asked her doctor for 'a pennyworth of Railway Accident Pills' to help overcome the shock. In its issue of 3rd August, 1866, *Engineering* pointed out the need for improvement, concluding that in 1864, the railway companies killed and wounded more people on British lines than fell [on the British side] in the Battle of the Nile in 1798.

Deaths and injuries on British railway lines

Year	Killed	Injured	Total
1859	245	464	709
1860	255	580	835
1861	284	883	1167
1862	216	600	816
1863	184	470	654
1864	222	793	1015

Battle of the Nile

1798	218	677	895

On 4th April, 1878, the 8.30 am Glasgow to Wemyss Bay passenger train, comprising two locomotives hauling a long train of 21 vehicles, approached the signal at Wemyss Bay Junction at about 4mph having just left Port Glasgow station 17 minutes late. The signal was raised when the train was about three or four engine lengths away and John McCluskey, an engine driver with two years' experience, opened his regulator and proceeded uphill to Upper Greenock station. When he applied steam, the guard, William Johnston, riding in the rear brake carriage, felt the couplings snap between the third and fourth carriages from the rear. He brought the coaches to a stand on the main line then protected his train with fog signals and a red flag. He unsuccessfully attempted to attract the attention of the other train guards, then informed the signalman before running back down the line to Port Glasgow.

Major General C.S. Hutchinson, RE, concluded that the incident was caused by the fracturing of the screw coupling at the front of the 19th vehicle and that the side chains used could not take the extra strain. Despite the assertion of the guard that he had not applied the brake, he thought that as the load at the end of the train would be much less than nearer the front, that the brake had been applied. The Inspector made no observation on the driver's comment that there were continuous brakes on the train 'but my engine was not fitted with the apparatus'.

Less than two months later, on 27th May, 1878, driver McCluskey experienced another incident at the same spot. This time he was driving the 2.15 pm Bridge Street to Wemyss Bay train which comprised engine, tender and 10 vehicles. Leaving Port Glasgow, he whistled several times to the signalman as the Wemyss Bay Junction signal was at danger. He drew up slowly and stopped at the home signal, not needing to use the efficient Westinghouse brake with which this train was fitted. Half a minute after he stopped, he felt a slight shock. This was the pilot engine, which had followed to assist the train up the hill, banging into the back of his train.

The guard was James Grant. He said he gave 'the usual signals' to the pilot engine to come on slowly, commenting that though it was hailing, he could see the signals. Both engine drivers stated the lines were greasy at the time. The pilot engine driver, John Heron, had performed this duty for the previous seven years. He explained that his engine would follow the train out when requested and buffer up, but not couple to it. He asserted that the train came to a stand very suddenly and he bumped into it at about four miles an hour. He said he had difficulty observing the train guard owing to the weather conditions. Major F.A. Marinden concluded that the pilot engine driver should have been more cautious and found the practice of sending out a pilot engine to catch up with the preceding train objectionable.

THE KIRK UPSET AND THE PERILS OF TRAVEL.

Simple part failure can lead to disaster - and J.F. McEwan noted nearly did so on 6th August, 1880. A mixed train of 1st, 2nd and 3rd class coaches hauled by 2-4-0 engine No. 95 from Wemyss Bay was passing Ralston when the carrying straps of the air brake cylinder on the engine parted, the cylinder falling on to the track, derailing every wheel behind the engine. Miraculously, the coaches remained upright and only slight injuries resulted.

On 17th September, 1898, a goods train comprising 21 vehicles, 16 loaded with coal and one with stone, left Wemyss Bay at 1.55 pm. At Upper Greenock, it acquired six wagons of paper from Overton Paper Mills. The engine, provided with a steam brake, could not hold its train on the 1 in 66½ down gradient. The signalman at Wemyss Bay Junction box at Port Glasgow, seeing the train was in danger of entering the main line, switched it to a safety siding 100 yards short of the junction, along which it careered, going through the buffers and continuing another 80 feet before smashing up in spectacular fashion. The signalman's presence of mind saved the 2.55 pm from Glasgow Central, then in Port Glasgow station, from getting into the path of the runaway.

On 5th December, 1902, while the new Wemyss Bay station was being built, John Duffy, a navvy, was injured while leaving the train at Wemyss Bay station. He claimed £259 [*£12,750] against the company in the first division of the Court of Session, stating that he was about to step from the train in which he had travelled from Greenock, when without warning it started and he was thrown between the carriage and the platform. He was dragged some distance and suffered a broken right arm and other injuries. The Caley counter claimed that Duffy was trying to leave the train before it had stopped.

A curious and tragic accident happened on 1st May, 1903. The *Glasgow Herald* recorded that while widening the railway to Wemyss Bay was substantially complete, 'several hundred' men were still working on the new station and pier. Many were brought by special train from Upper Greenock station by Pirie, the main contractor. This train, comprising an engine and four coaches, lay in a siding up the line during working hours. At the end of the day, the workmen boarded the train in its siding. The engine was on the turntable but the guard thought it was attached to the train and released his brake. His mistake was immediately obvious when the four coaches accelerated rapidly down the 1 in 70 grade, and despite screwing the brake down hard, crashed into platform 2 (then the west side of the east island platform) where trucks laden with heavy metals were berthed. Two were killed, seven injured and two of the coaches were severely damaged. The normal train, which was taking on passengers from the ferry, was not affected. Eight claims were lodged against the company, varying from £150 to £1,300 [*£7,400 to *£64,000]. The Caley instructed its officers to settle for between £40 and £400 [*£2,000 and *£20,000], and in the case of two horses killed, they agreed to a settlement of £35 [*£1,750].

At 4 pm on 11th July, 1907, Caledonian pug, 0-4-0 No. 514, conveying three loaded wagons, set off uphill to Overton on a 1 in 19 gradient. At the Old Largs Road level crossing, the train halted and Robert Scott the brakesman descended to open the gate, leaving driver Edward Steel and fireman William McEwan on the footplate. Before he could resume his post, the train started to slip backwards and though he tried to sprag the wheels, he failed. The train rapidly gathered momentum hitting the buffers with such force that it bounced into the air and slid some distance before ending up on its side. Driver Steel was mortally injured.

When demand was high, long trains were divided in two, the first portion departing shortly ahead of the scheduled train. On 17th July, 1911, during the Glasgow Fair, the 8.55 am from Glasgow Central nicknamed the 'Campbeltown Express', connecting with the excursion steamer *Queen Alexandra*, was split into two nine-coach trains, plus a van. The divided train, stopping only at the principal stations, was full of people going to Rothesay and other destinations.

Caledonian 0-4-0 'pug' No. 514 crashes off the line at Overton on 11th July, 1907.
J.B. Scrymgeour/A.J.J. McNeill

As the *Glasgow Herald* put it:

The first portion was despatched from Glasgow Central at 8.50, 5 minutes earlier than the scheduled time. It arrived at Wemyss Bay at 9.53 and was docked at No. 2 platform. The passengers alighted and made their way to the pier to await the arrival of the turbine steamer and the luggage also was got out. 5 minutes from the arrival of the first train, the second, which left Glasgow at 8.55 appeared round the curve, and before it could be brought to a standstill it collided with the empty train. According to an official statement, the signalman seemed momentarily to have overlooked the fact that he had already passed the 8.50 train into No. 2 platform. In accordance with the regulations, however, the speed of the incoming train had been reduced to 10 mph in passing the signal box and the engine driver, on seeing that the dock was already occupied, was able further to slow down, with the result that the impact was not of a very serious nature. It was severe enough, however to cause considerable damage to the stationary train. The first compartment of the composite van which formed the last vehicle was smashed, the centre carriage was buffer-locked, the one next to the engine was also damaged and the buffers of the engine were broken.

J.F. McEwan offers a slightly different description. He suggests that while the points lever was in the correct position, the interlocked point blade may have been jammed open by an obstruction.

Despite the train being crowded with passengers preparing to disembark, only six were slightly injured, the worst case being a woman who had a tooth knocked out. Mr Prentice the station master attended to the injured in his office (Wemyss Bay was equipped with a 'wound box') while the other passengers made their way to the boat, which departed on schedule. Five of the injured boarded the next ferry, the *Duchess of Argyll*, which left at 10.30. The sixth was a man who had boarded the train at Paisley intending to travel to Upper Greenock, but being a non-stop to Wemyss Bay he passed his destination. He caught the next stopping train back. The accident was not too serious as the train involved left with passengers less than a quarter of an hour after the accident.

THE KIRK UPSET AND THE PERILS OF TRAVEL

A unique accident occurred on 11th September, 1911. Under the heading 'Horse traction in railway stations', the *Glasgow Herald* reported the civil proceedings in May 1912 when Mrs Margaret Chalmers of Govanhill sued the Caledonian Railway Company for £100 [*£4,400] for injuries and nervous shock she sustained while waiting with her two children on the platform at Wemyss Bay station for the Glasgow train.

At the time, horses were yoked to a 'lorry' or trailer to convey luggage along the platforms to and from the ferries. Sheriff Fyfe determined that one of these animals became restive and that the pursuer of the claim, taking fright, jumped off the platform on to the railway line. She fell on the rails and collapsed unconscious. For a time after the incident, she suffered from nervous shock, though her health was not permanently affected. The Sheriff assumed her complaint against the company was that in conveying luggage from the steamers to the train, the defenders had adopted a system which was fraught with possible danger to travellers and that on this occasion the possibility became a reality. He presumed she was suggesting that hand barrows be used instead of horse lorries. 'No doubt [the horse] came along the platform at a considerable speed but the impact of the proof was that it was brought to a standstill a considerable distance away from the pursuer and where the other passengers were. If she had remained where she was pursuer would have been perfectly safe'. The case was dismissed.

Under the heading 'Remarkable Accident at Wemyss Bay - Eight men entombed', the *Glasgow Herald* recorded a much more serious accident that happened on 27th October, 1920 just south of the railway bridge over the road to Inverkip, at the north end of the lead into Wemyss Bay station.

In December 1920, Greenock Sheriff Court heard that a section of retaining wall supporting the running line behind the goods depôt was being rebuilt because it was bulging. The wall was 26 ft high, 5 ft 6 in. at its base reducing to 3 ft 6 in. at the top and appeared from a visual inspection to

Wemyss Bay station. The timber floored luggage platform is on the far left with the island platforms 4 and 3 straight ahead. A single coach is parked at the buffers behind a very bored and unattended horse while an empty train stands at platform 1. Note the hanging baskets and the small-wheeled luggage 'lorries'.
Watt Library, Inverclyde Council

have 'headers' or bonding stones at intervals through the full thickness of the wall, binding it together. This turned out not to be the case, the original builders being blamed for defective work.

The repair technique was to 'dig a trench inside the wall' and infill with reinforced concrete bonded back to the original wall. The work urgently needed doing and had been under way for some weeks, trains being restricted to the down line. However around mid-day, the top of the wall collapsed into the excavation trapping the men and killing two labourers. Mr Thomson, the Wemyss Bay station master called the emergency services. Eight doctors arrived and a special train took Mr Mason the Caley's district supervisor to the scene. Under the light of flares, work continued till 8 pm to remove the men and the bodies. The wall was then dismantled and rebuilt, trains being stopped and the Wemyss Bay ferries diverted to Gourock. The Sheriff concluded that '. . . it was impossible for any person by the most careful external examination to come to the conclusion that there was a latent defect'. The railway company was not at fault. 'The accident was just one of those unfortunate occurrences that no human agency could foresee'.

In 1948, a 6 ft rail was placed on the line between Upper Greenock and Port Glasgow. Fortunately, the train was not derailed. (According to J.F. McEwan, in the 1840s a Greenock culprit was whipped through the streets and deported overseas for placing a tree on a line - with the added warning that if he ever returned, he would be hanged.)

An accident with fatal consequences occurred on 25th June, 1994, when the 10.45 pm from Wemyss Bay to Glasgow hit an obstruction, not far from that recorded in 1948. The train had accelerated to about 50 mph after leaving Branchton station. On board were driver Arthur McKee, the ticket examiner and four passengers. The collision was violent. The train was derailed, colliding with Peat Road bridge. The front was staved in, heavy stones killing the driver, and the passenger in the front coach was thrown out to die on impact with the bridge. Two 17-year-old youths were sentenced to 15 years on a charge of culpable homicide for placing the concrete lids of trough covers, each weighing about 80 lb. across the line. The last train of the day, the 10.35 pm from Glasgow to Wemyss Bay, was only seven minutes away, but still on the main line to Port Glasgow.

Accidents down the line from Glasgow

Before the Wemyss Bay line was conceived, a curious accident happened on the Glasgow to Greenock line near Paisley. It is included to show how 'informal' some early arrangements were.

On 10th June, 1845, a certain Mr Nairne missed his train to Ayr. He thereupon requested a special to Paisley to catch his train. He was put in the tender and the locomotive proceeded at full speed to Paisley. Unfortunately, a line had been removed near the town but no warning flags positioned. The engine was derailed, putting him and the crew in hospital. (The hire of a 'special' was not unknown; Sir Arthur Conan Doyle's story, *The Final Problem*, set in 1891, had Professor Moriarty 'engage a special' (a carriage and engine) to pursue Sherlock Holmes' train to Newhaven. Whether fiction was based on fact we leave to others to discover.)

Over the years, quite a number of incidents have been recorded on the line from Glasgow, but few at Wemyss Bay itself. However any interruption to railway services between the termini could have serious consequences to the profitability of the line and the passenger ferries.

Likewise, an incident on the Wemyss Bay branch could have 'knock on' consequences at some remove. For example, the train between Glasgow and Wemyss Bay may be rostered to go elsewhere on its return. In the early part of the 20th century, a train could leave Glasgow, run down to Wemyss Bay and back and then be scheduled to travel to Edinburgh on the Carstairs line.

So accidents on the lines to Greenock, Gourock and Wemyss Bay could see large numbers of people seriously inconvenienced, especially when steamers loaded or discharged passengers by the thousand. Terminus arrangements were designed for rapid throughput and not mass stayput - eating, drinking and toilet facilities were never intended to cater for an hour's delay following an accident up the line.

THE KIRK UPSET AND THE PERILS OF TRAVEL

The following is taken from J.F. McEwan's Notes. On 8th September, 1880, at Penilee, 1¾ miles east of Paisley, a ballast train occupying the up slow (goods) line caused signalman Alex Ewing to divert a G&SWR goods from Kilmarnock on to the up (passenger) line till it could rejoin the slow line at Cardonald. Unfortunately, he moved it instead to the down passenger line and as a result, driver Liddesdale thought he was going to be set back into the adjacent colliery branch. However, as no setting back signal was given, he was about to go to the signal box, 100 yards away, when he noticed that the signal had been put in the 'off' position. He realised this was for the 4.00 pm Glasgow to Greenock 'Sugar Brokers' express passenger train which was now bearing down on him. He promptly reversed his engine, and jumped. The Greenock train hit the goods at 40 mph. Driver Young was thrown clear and his fireman jumped before the smash. Eight were killed and 40 injured, and all four lines were blocked with wreckage. A Caley Director, Hugh Brown, took charge and ordered the smashed coaches, the oldest dating back to 1866, to be thrown down the embankment. Medical attention came from Paisley and Mr Ward, the Caley General Manager and Mr Hay, the traffic manager of the Joint line, came down from Glasgow by special engine. It took five hours to return two of the lines to service. The subsequent investigation found that both engines were in back gear and that the brakes on the tender of the express were hard on. It also found that the signalman on this heavily trafficked line had had only one week's training and had been in the box for less than a month.

In January 1938, the 10.40 pm Fowler 2-6-4 tank locomotive No. 2418 and a carriage fell 10 feet to the foreshore in Greenock having been diverted into a siding opposite signal cabin No. 1. The son of a signalman, Peter Watson, smashed a window in the locked cabin, removed some detonators and ran up the line to warn the oncoming train from Glasgow. The train stopped 300 yards from the accident. Three similar accidents occurred at this spot over 18 months. In one case the LMS diverted its steamer *Caledonia* from Gourock to Greenock's Princes Pier to pick up passengers.

In 1941, two railwaymen were killed in Central Station. In 1942, a train crashed into the buffers at Greenock injuring six servicemen (who were presumably returning from leave) and in the same year four boys were killed by a train at Port Glasgow. This last was a sad accident. It was a Saturday afternoon in September and a group of boys were attempting to catch sweets and coins thrown by returning servicemen from a passing train on the up line when they were caught by a train on the down line. There had been several similar incidents but these were the first fatalities.

In 1943, two women were killed and two injured crossing the line at Hillington. The next year, between Bishopton and Georgetown stations, a 12-year-old boy, travelling with three friends from Port Glasgow, was killed falling from a train. In 1944, a serious mishap to a Greenock to Glasgow train was averted after an embankment collapsed between Greenock West and Greenock Central Stations.

Between 1945 and 1950, trains crashed into the buffers at Central Station and Gourock and injuries were sustained at various places down the line. During this period, after several days of rain and very high winds (which had brought down over 1,200 telephone lines in the Glasgow area), a 68-year-old woman was killed crossing a railway bridge at Hillington to avoid the flooded Hillington Road, two people died at Paisley, a War Department policeman was fatally injured at Wester Rossland Level Crossing at the Royal Ordnance factory at Bishopton and a boy was killed by an engine in Greenock.

A remarkable accident happened in 1949 when a 42-year-old man lost his balance in Greenock Central Station as a train emerged from the tunnel. He was hit by the engine, knocked between the rails and the train passed over him without touching him.

As recently as Easter Monday 1979, seven people were killed when the 6.58 pm passenger train from Ayr to Glasgow, which had just left Paisley Gilmore Street, ran across the path of the incoming 7.40 pm electric train from Glasgow to Wemyss Bay. The cause was the premature departure of the 6.58, which had stopped ahead of a starting signal still set at danger, a problem which at the time of publication, still exercises the railway authorities.

Chapter Twelve

Caledonian Railway Rolling Stock

The GP&GR, authorised under the Glasgow, Paisley and Greenock Railway Act 1837, was engineered by Locke and opened in 1841. The Caley, created under the Caledonian Railway Act of 1845, depended on stretches of other railways to link Edinburgh and Glasgow to London. This was achieved on 15th February, 1848. In time, the Caley absorbed many other lines. Within months of the passing of its Act, the Caley was in discussion with the GP&GR first 'to ascertain the terms on which they will co-operate' and then with a view to amalgamation. The Caley acquired the line in 1851 after years of difficult negotiations though final settlement was not achieved till 1883.

The Caley inherited a variety of locomotives of different manufacture from the various companies but by 1846 it was ordering its own engines and coaches. Those were the days when engines cost £1,850 [*£70,000], their tenders £350 [*£13,500] and wagons came in at £72 [*£2,750] each. Carriages appear to have been ordered from coachbuilders - from Mr Wallace of Perth, Mr Croall of Edinburgh and Mr Dunn of Lancaster - and wagons from a variety of suppliers.

In July 1847, the Caley Directors took a trip to Greenock to see progress on six engines and carriages being built 'in their locomotive establishment at Greenock'.

By September 1851, the Caley possessed the following stock:

58	Passenger Locomotives	38	1st Class Carriages	13	Luggage Vans	738	Ordinary Wagons
50	Goods Locomotives	51	2nd Class Carriages	15	Carriage Trucks	52	Coke Wagons
		71	3rd Class Carriages	15	Horse Boxes	3,533	Mineral Wagons
		19	Composite Carriages	17	Brake Wagons	2	Ale Wagons
		2	Saloons	20	Covered Wagons		
		5	Post Offices	140	Cattle Wagons		
				10	Fish Vans		
				10	Sheep Wagons		

Amalgamations brought other companies' locomotives and rolling stock into the Caledonian stable, including 15 engines from the GP&GR. As Joseph Locke observed, there was a need to rationalise the rolling stock. Old wagons without springs bought from private owners and non-standard classes of engine created maintenance problems for both track and user.

In November 1859, the Caley ordered six engines and tenders at £2,450 [*£102,000] each from Beyer, Peacock and a year later, nine from Neilson at £2,550 each. January 1861 saw the Caley Board deciding to purchase 12 mineral engines with tenders at £2,350 and eight 'Blue Goods' engines and tenders at £2,600 apiece. By September 1862, the Caley stock had risen to 82 passenger locomotives, 151 goods engines, 78 1st class carriages, 159 2nd and 3rd class carriages and 29 composites. There were now 4,056 Mineral Wagons.

Some idea of the huge cost of the railway operations can be gleaned from the purchase price of rolling stock. In December 1865, the mighty Caley accepted various quotations:

20 Goods engines at £2,680	(Neilson)	£53,600	[*£2,220,000]
10 Mineral engines at £2,300	(Neilson)	£23,000	[*£953,000]
20 Mineral engines at £2,307	(Dübs)	£46,140	[*£1,915,000]
88 pig iron wagons at £50	(Dübs)	£4,400	[*£182,000]
125 goods wagons at £61	(Dübs)	£7,625	[*£315,000]
62 goods wagons at £69 10s.	(Dübs)	£4,309	[*£180,000]
50 swivel timber trucks at £59 10s.	(Dübs)	£2,975	[*£123,000]
62 covered cattle trucks at £97 5s.	(Dübs)	£6,029 10s.	[*£250,000]
15 goods break (sic) vans at £122 10s.	(Dübs)	£1,837 10s.	[*£77,000]
400 covered goods vans at £87 15s.	(Dübs)	£35,100	[*£1,455,000]
Total		£185,016	[*£7,670,000]

Further amalgamations added to the disparate collection of rolling stock with little attempt to standardise until Dugald Drummond arrived in 1882. But from then till the 1923 Grouping, rationalisation saw the construction of only about nine new designs of both 4-4-0 and 4-6-0 locomotives.

By absorption and consolidation, the Caley became the most powerful railway company in Scotland.

Roughly half-way through its existence, George Graham, the railway's Engineer in Chief, wrote a piece on the origins of the Caley, concluding with a raft of statistics. By that time, the authorised capital was over £41m [*£2,000m], it owned and operated 703 miles, had joint ownership over a further 144 miles and worked 101 miles (including the Wemyss Bay branch) for others. By this time the Caley incorporated 30 companies and was in some way influenced by 228 Acts of Parliament. It received a substantial income, for example for the 12 months to July 1887, it earned £2,821,287 [*£143m]. To run the system required about 14,700 men, 690 engines, 1,660 passenger vehicles and 44,454 goods vehicles, the annual train engine mileage being approximately 12 million miles and passengers carried not far short of 18 million.

The Men and their Engines

In 1841, the GP&GR erected workshops at Greenock where they constructed some of the early locomotives. Scott Sinclair & Co. of Greenock also built locomotives for the Caledonian Railway Company, *Robert Sinclair*, who had family connections with the firm and who had worked on the GP&GR as Locke and Errington's assistant, being appointed the Caley's first locomotive superintendent and General Manager (1849-1856). Sinclair stayed with the Caley till he had built its new engineering works at St Rollox, the Greenock works having become very congested, then left the company. The Greenock buildings were then modified to engine sheds.

The Caley's earliest passenger engines were 2-2-2s of Alexander Allan's 'Crewe' double frame type, with inclined cylinders between the frames over the front wheels. This type survived till Drummond took over 30 years later. The Vulcan Foundry built some with leading and trailing wheels 3 ft 6 in. diameter, the driving wheels being 6 ft. The boiler barrel was only about 3 ft 7 in. diameter and the working pressure 90 lb. per sq. inch. The tall chimney above the smokebox was balanced by a steam collecting dome above the firebox, the safety valves positioned halfway along the boiler. No protection was offered to the crew. The four-wheel tender carried 800 gallons of water and three tons of coal (or two tons of coke). In working order, the engine and tender weighed 28 tons, the engine being 19 tons. Only the tender had brakes. Yet these engines could exceed 50 miles per hour.

Sinclair's passenger engines included 2-2-2s with 7 ft and 7 ft 2 in. drivers. The goods locomotives were 'Old Crewe pattern', with 5 ft 2 in. coupled driving wheels.

Early in 1857, Sinclair was succeeded by *Benjamin Conner* (1813-1876) from Neilson & Co. During the early part of his career with the Caley, the works at Greenock were closed and construction transferred to St Rollox in Springburn, Glasgow.

Outside frame Caley 2-4-0 locomotive No. 214, one of a batch of 2-cylinder tender engines built with 6 ft 2 in. drivers between 1860 and 1862 to Benjamin Conner's design. The style was typical of the period, however the addition of powered tenders to many of this class showed up the inadequacy of their boilers. Drivers soon found that the tender cylinders could be used as an additional brake.
Mitchell Library

Caley 2-4-0 with 6-wheel tender on the line to the goods shed at Wemyss Bay, around 1902. Reputed to be No. 1339, this locomotive is similar to Benjamin Conner's '417' class introduced in 1866, the last of which was broken up in 1920.
LCGB Ken Nunn Collection

Conner built more 2-2-2 passenger locomotives between 1859 and 1875, with 7 ft 2 in. and 8 ft 2 in. drivers and a working pressure of 120 lb. per sq. inch. These engines weighed between 32 and 30 tons and had a long career, the last being broken up in 1901. He also designed and had built 200 2-4-0 goods engines, constructed at St Rollox, the Beyer, Peacock Works and Neilson & Co. His goods engines had either 5 ft 2 in. or 6 ft 2 in.driving wheels for main line work, unusually large for this class of use. The locomotives were built to the 'Crewe style', with the steam collecting dome just behind the chimney, on the centre of the boiler or over the firebox, a weather shield and trailed a four- or six-wheeled tender. In 1874, he supervised the construction of five 0-6-0 goods locomotives. Conner died in 1876 and was succeeded by George Brittain.

George Brittain's (c. 1820-1882), career as locomotive superintendent was much shorter - he was forced to resign due to ill-health in July 1882. But as Conner's assistant, he held the reins as Conner's career drew to an end. Express engines that would have perpetuated Conner's predilection for 2-4-0s were changed to 4-4-0s on Brittain's instructions, their drivers being 7 ft 2 in., the working pressure 140 lb. The engine and tender together weighed 70 tons 14 cwt, the engine being just over 41 tons. But their poor performance saw them relegated to east coast suburban lines. Dübs & Co. constructed some 0-4-2 goods locomotives, working at 140 lb. per square inch. They also built some 2-4-0 tank engines weighing 41 tons 10 cwt. for Brittain in 1879, to the same boiler pressure. Over the combined careers of Conner and Brittain, from about 1860 to 1880, 257 goods locomotives were built, 124 as 2-4-0s with 6 ft 2 in. or 5 ft 2 in. driving wheels, 94 as 0-4-2s with 5 ft 2 in. driving wheels and 39 0-6-0s with 5 ft 2 in. driving wheels. Locomotives of this period were defined as 'goods' or 'passenger'. There were no mixed traffic engines.

Brittain's successor, *Dugald Drummond* (1840-1912), came from the North British Railway Company in 1882. Drummond was an innovator, putting a proper cab on the locomotives in place of the rudimentary weather board previously common, and introducing gas lighting, automatic continuous brakes and steam carriage heating. He modified earlier designs (not always beneficially) to suit heavier loads. Nevertheless he was one of the prominent railway engineers of the 19th century. By increasing the working pressure of older designs from 130 to 150 lb. per square inch, he improved their tractive effort by something like 12 per cent. He experimented with pressures up to 200 lb. per square inch and the efficient design of his 4-4-0s allowed them to reach 75 mph on express service. He set about standardising the Caley locomotive stock. His inside cylinder locomotive designs set the pattern for years to come. Under him, the St Rollox works expanded and Greenock Bogston Shed was built to take 30 of the largest engines. In 1883, he brought out an 0-6-0 goods locomotive, the 294 class, or 'Jumbos', which had 5 ft drivers and a working pressure of 150 lb. per square inch. Over 15 years, extending into McIntosh's superintendency, 244 engines of this class were built. Some were fitted with Westinghouse brakes (introduced in 1882 to replace the Steel-McInnes air brake) for working passenger trains and were used on the Wemyss Bay line. He also brought out more 4-4-0s with 6 ft 6 in. drivers, working to 160 lb. pressure and in 1887, twelve 4-4-0s (the 'Greenock bogies') with 5 ft 9 in. driving wheels. These latter engines worked well on the Greenock line (which was shortly to be extended to Gourock). They were also used on the Wemyss Bay route though they struggled with the steep grades. These engines, which only weighed a little over 40 tons, could and did make some hair-raising descents from Inverkip into Wemyss Bay.

Drummond resigned in July 1890 and was replaced by *Hugh Smellie* (1840-1891) from the G&SWR on 1st September, 1890. The Scottish Railway strike in December 1890 appears to have told on his already delicate health as he died on 19th April, 1891, aged 51, only having worked nine months for the Caley and not having designed any locomotives for the line.

John Lambie (1833-1895) succeeded Smellie but died in office in February 1895. During his career with the Caley, he built 4-4-0T and 0-4-4T for local Glasgow services, 0-6-0T with small 4 ft 6 in.driving wheels for local shipyard use, express engines working at up to 200 lb. pressure, and generally improved the stock.

Caley 2-4-0 and 6-wheel gas-lit coaches as used between 1860 and 1890.
J.F. McEwan Collection, William Patrcik Library, Kirkintilloch

Caley 'Coast Bogie' No. 91 introduced in 1888 by Dugald Drummond.
Caledonian Railway Association

John Farquharson McIntosh (1846-1918) became chief locomotive engineer of the Caley on 1st February, 1895. He was a practical engineer and a leading locomotive designer who had worked his way up from 'the road'. He improved the boilers, raised the working pressure on some of his new locomotives to 180 lb. per square inch and in 1910, brought superheating to Scottish railways. Between 1895 and 1899, he built 83 more of Drummond's 0-6-0 'Jumbos' before producing 96 of his '812' class, an 'uprated Jumbo' 0-6-0 goods with 5 ft driving wheels and a working pressure of 160 lb. per sq. inch. Some of these had Westinghouse brakes, carriage warming apparatus and were painted in Caledonian blue for Clyde coast passenger services where their 30 per cent extra power over Drummond's 4-4-0s improved timings on the Wemyss Bay line. They were built at St Rollox, by Neilson, Reid, by Dübs and by Sharp, Stewart. (One of these is preserved in Glasgow Museum of Transport.) (Incidentally, the three locomotive builders amalgamated with the Clyde Locomotive Co. in 1903 to form the North British Locomotive Company.)

In 1896, McIntosh introduced the first of four versions of the celebrated 'Dunalastair' 4-4-0s. These big boiler engines generated plenty of steam. In 1906 he brought out his '908' class, a 4-6-0 with 5 ft 9 in. driving wheels, specifically designed for mixed traffic and the Clyde Coast expresses. These engines operated to a boiler pressure of 180 lb. per sq. inch. Engine and tender length was 58 ft 11 in. and the tender capacity was 4½ tons of coal plus 3,572 gallons of water. The total weight of engine and tender came to 102 tons. McIntosh also introduced other 4-6-0s, including the 903 'Cardean' class with 6 ft 6 in. driving wheels, for heavy main line passenger work.

McIntosh stayed with the Caley till February 1914 when he retired aged 68. Of the 0-6-0s constructed during his period in office, four were superheated and used to good effect on Clyde Coast trains. Introduced in 1912, they had 5 ft driving wheels and a working pressure of 160 lb. per sq. inch. These engines were later converted to 2-6-0s. By 1914 the Caley had a good range of efficient 4-4-0s and 4-6-0s, many fitted with superheaters which noticeably reduced coal and water consumption.

In 1914, *William Pickersgill* (1861-1928) arrived from the Great North of Scotland Railway to succeed McIntosh. He built several 4-4-0s and 4-6-0s between 1916 and 1920, with pressures up to 180 lb. per sq. inch, none rated as good as their predecessors. He reintroduced outside cylinders and in 1921 built four 4-6-0s with 6 ft 1 in. driving wheels, three cylinders and a conjugated valve gear worked from the outside valve gear. This was so troublesome that the centre cylinder valve gear was converted to Stephenson Link.

Pickersgill's 1917 'Wemyss Bay Pugs' were arguably his most successful. Twelve of these superheated tanks were built by the North British Locomotive Company to Order No. L672. With a 4-6-2 wheel arrangement, 5 ft 9 in. driving wheels, 3 ft 6 in. leading and trailing wheels, a coal capacity of 3 tons and tanks capable of holding 1,800 gallons, these heavy locomotives weighed 74 tons 11 cwt empty and 91 tons 13 cwt (including an allowance of 5 cwt for sand and 3 cwt for men on the footplate) in full working order (*see illustration*). They were designed to operate at a pressure of 170 lb. per sq. inch. Regularly used on the Gourock and Wemyss Bay lines, they were less successful as bankers at Beattock where their small bunker capacity and propensity for tube leakage caused by extremes of high and low demand caused operational problems. The locomotives had 19½ in. outside cylinders driven by Stephenson's link motion on 9 in. piston valves between the frames. The wheelbase was 33 ft 1 in., length over buffers 43 ft 2½ in. and height to chimney 12 ft 10 in. They were solid and reliable but not especially fast runners.

North British Locomotive Company order No. L672 - Pickersgill 4-6-2 tank for use on the Wemyss Bay line - 1917.

CALEDONIAN RAILWAY ROLLING STOCK

The crew and two of the twelve Wemyss Bay 'pugs' introduced by William Pickersgill in 1917 for service on the Clyde Coast lines. Members of this class were later transferred to banking duties at Beattock, the last being withdrawn in 1952. *Alan Brotchie Collection*

North British Locomotive Company order L672 - Pickersgill 4-6-2 Wemyss Bay 'pug' ex-works, 1917. *Mitchell Library*

Pickersgill 4-6-2T No. 944 on a Gourock train near Ibrox.
Caledonian Railway Association/A.G. Ellis Collection

Locomotives of the first 100 years

In summary, the earliest locomotives included 2-2-2 tender engines from various builders, 2-2-2 well tanks, 2-4-0s and 0-4-2s and 0-6-0s. As the century progressed, heavier locomotives were needed with greater adhesion weight. Driving wheel sizes increased from 6 ft to 8 ft 4 in., especially for the crack 'single driver' express trains from Glasgow to the South and East, but as locomotives became bigger, driving wheel sizes reduced to a maximum of about 6 ft 6 in. by the turn of the century. By 1906, 4-6-0s were common on the Clyde Coast route. Pickersgill's heavy 4-6-2 tank engine was later followed by the big Fowler, Fairbairn, Stanier and British Railways Standard class tanks, all much the same size.

Goods engine wheel sizes were always smaller, the earliest recorded being 4 ft 7 in. diameter, but generally not exceeding 5 ft 2 in. Mixed traffic engines tended to have wheel sizes of 6 ft 2 in. or thereabouts.

The extension of the Caley's line to Gourock caused the company to relocate its locomotive shed at Greenock. This resulted in the development of the Ladyburn site in 1885, half-a-mile west of Wemyss Bay Junction. The shed had nine through tracks leading to a turntable and with Polmadie up in Glasgow, supplied the locomotives for the Wemyss Bay branch. It was extremely busy, providing accommodation for long haul locomotives used to pull trains of sugar, rope and sailcloth to Edinburgh and parts of Scotland and Northern England. Likewise, locomotives were needed for the steel trains going to the shipyards from Lanarkshire. At various times, the locomotives included 0-8-0 goods, Drummond 4-4-0 'Coast Bogies', Drummond '294' class 'Jumbo' 0-6-0 and McIntosh '812' class 0-6-0 goods, McIntosh 4-6-0 '908' class, 0-6-0 class '30' engines and 'Dunalastair' class 4-4-0s. There were also diminutive 0-4-0 dock tanks used at Upper Greenock on the Overton Paper Mill Branch. Many of Pickersgill's 1917 'Wemyss Bay Tanks' were stabled at Greenock. Later, Fowler 2-6-4Ts arrived, replaced in 1954 by Fairbairn tanks, and two 'Crabs' were latterly stationed there. In 1921, there were 23 locomotives, in 1945 forty-five, the same as in 1955. The shed closed in 1966.

Liveries

It is believed that early Caledonian locomotives were coloured blue for passenger traffic and green for goods. About 1870, it is thought passenger engines were coloured green, the goods being black. Thereafter, passenger engines were blue (which varied according to which works applied it, those from St Rollox being a lighter hue), the goods black - both picked out with red, white and in the case of the blue engines, black lining. Shaded gilt lettering, a gilt crest and oval brass number plate adorned locomotive and tender sides.

According to J.F. McEwan, the earliest 1st class coaches were blue and varnished and *may* have had white or cream upper panels. Second class were russet brown, possibly with cream or white upper panels while the third class were dull brown. At some point thereafter, up till about 1895 coaches were painted purple-brown. Later, they had white roofs and were purple-brown below the waist and on the ends, the upper and waist panels being white with yellow lining. Shaded gilt lettering and the Caley coat of arms featured on the sides. The underframe, bogies and buffer castings were all black, tyres on steel and Mansell wheels being painted white.

In the early days, wagons were red oxide, with black ironwork. The letters 'C.R.' were painted in white each side. Roofs were white and brake vans had vermilion ends. Refrigerator vans, fish vans and trucks were painted brown.

Trains

After 20th May, 1884, the Caley introduced a new train of 12 coaches - with four 1st class, six 2nd class and only two brake/3rd class coaches. The train was fitted with Westinghouse brakes and gas lighting.

In July 1913, the Caley identified three different marshalling arrangements for trains running on the Wemyss Bay to Glasgow route, the sets being scheduled to operate also on the Gourock line. With the exception of set 122, the sets were renumbered from day to day and except for a 'swapping' arrangement with a set used on the Ardrossan run, appear to have been allocated to the south Clyde service. These are described in Appendix Six.

If the trains were not long enough, Glasgow and Gourock were enjoined to strengthen the trains for Saturday and holiday traffic. These trains were cleaned and repaired at Wemyss Bay, Gourock or Smithy Lye and gassed at Glasgow Central or Smithy Lye.

In addition, there were three workmen's trains between Port Glasgow and Gourock, one comprising 6-wheeled stock and the other two a 4-coach bogie train. These were cleaned and repaired at Gourock and gassed either at Gourock or Glasgow though curiously the 6-wheeled stock had no gassing arrangements, even though it was used in the dark hours.

There were other complications: Except on Mondays when Glasgow provided its own van, a 6-wheeled brake van from Aberdeen was attached to the 5.35 am Glasgow to Gourock. Both vehicles had to be detached at Greenock Central and returned on the 7.05 pm Gourock to Glasgow. There was also the need to ensure that the third and brake composite attached to the 5.25 pm from Gourock to Glasgow, returned on the 6.30pm Glasgow to Port Glasgow, where it was detached for connection to the 7.15 pm to Wemyss Bay. These vehicles were returned the next day on the 8.50 am Wemyss Bay to Glasgow train. They were then sent down to Gourock on the 10.10 am. The timetable indicates that the brake composite would work the 8.25 pm Wemyss Bay to Port Glasgow train and the 9.22 pm return to Wemyss Bay, a thoroughly complicated arrangement.

In 1902, before Wemyss Bay station was enlarged, Glasgow Central station had to telegraph Wemyss Bay the times of departure and the number of all passenger vehicles on the train, presumably so that Wemyss Bay could make arrangements for extra long trains. Central also had to advise of special trains run in addition to those scheduled. On occasion passenger trains might include vehicles to be transferred to the G&SWR at Paisley. Station masters west of Paisley had to notify the Paisley station master of their destination. At 4.10 am, the newspaper train would leave Polmadie on its way to the coast. This appears to have been entirely separate to the other listed trains.

202 CALEY TO THE COAST

A 12-wheel Caley non-corridor coach in LMS days. *Caledonian Railway Association*

Caledonian first class bogie non-corridor coach. *Caledonian Railway Association*

Pickersgill 4-6-2T No. 947 between Ravenscraig and Dunrod c.1924. *C.J.L. Romanes*

Fairburn 2-6-4T No. 42144 emerges from the 'original' tunnel at Inverkip on the 3.30 pm to Glasgow in April 1964. The tunnel on the left has since been abandoned. *W.A.C. Smith*

Selected 19th Century Timetables

April 1865 — *Departure times - as originally proposed*

Wemyss Bay	8.30 am	9.30 am	4.00 pm	6.00 pm
Glasgow	9.00 am	11.00 am	3.00 pm	5.00 pm

May 12th 1865 — *Departure times - as advertised*

Wemyss Bay	8.10 am	10.00 am	3.45 pm	6.25 pm
Inverkip	8.17	10.07	3.52	6.32
Ravenscraig	-	10.16	-	6.40
Upper Greenock	8.23	10.23	4.08	
Port Glasgow	8.40	10.30	4.15	
Paisley	9.05	10.57	4.42	7.35
Glasgow, Bridge St.	9.21	11.17	5.00	
Running Time	*1.11*	*1.17*	*1.15*	

May 12th 1865 — *Departure times - as advertised*

Glasgow, Bridge St.	8.40 am	10.45 am	3.50 pm	5.00 pm
Paisley	8.56	11.01	4.06	5.16
Port Glasgow	9.23	11.28	4.33	5.43
Upper Greenock	9.33	11.38	4.43	5.53
Ravenscraig	-	11.45	-	6.00
Inverkip	9.46	11.52	4.56	6.07
Wemyss Bay	9.52	12.00 noon	5.05	6.15
Running Time	*1.12*	*1.15*	*1.15*	*1.15*

October 1865 — *Departure times*

Wemyss Bay	8.50	12.30	17.00	19.15*
Glasgow	8.40	11.15	16.10	17.45*

*Withdrawn in November 1865

August 1868 — *Departure times*

Wemyss Bay	8.45 am	10.00 am	11.35 am	4.10 pm	5.30 pm
Glasgow	8.25 am	10.10 am	2.45 pm	4.10 pm	6.00 pm

Summer 1869 — *Departure times*

Wemyss Bay	7.40 am	8.45 am*	10.00 am	11.35 am		4.10 pm	7.00 pm
Glasgow	8.35 am	11.30 am	12.40 pm	2.45 pm*	4.10 pm*	6.00 pm	7.00 pm

* Boat connections

Additional Train

1877 — *Departure time*

Glasgow	4.35 pm
Rothesay by Wemyss Bay	5.55
Travelling Time	*1.20*

Chapter Thirteen

Running the Railway

When the public has a grouse against a large amorphous body, it lets off steam by writing to the press to highlight its concerns and seek change. The following letter, printed in the *Rothesay Chronicle and Buteshire & West Coast Advertiser* in July 1897, feelingly expresses the writer's recent unhappy experience. The fact it was reprinted suggests this was not an isolated instance:

> *The Wemyss Bay Service* - A correspondent in the *Glasgow Herald* writes:
> Sir - The average man, on looking up the Caley time tables, would be apt to believe that there is a train from Wemyss Bay at 5.32. But he is the victim of an illusion. There is no train at that hour. It's all a joke of the railway company's. The humour of the thing will be obvious to the meanest intelligence. You take your passengers aboard at Rothesay at 4.50. You run them across and land them at Wemyss Bay at 5.15. You rush them up to the train waiting - for mark you, there is a train - that's part of the joke. You leave them there for some 15 minutes till the advertised time is approached then in the 2 minutes they have to spare, you bundle them out and put them in another train. With an effort, this is done by 5.32 (advertised time). But the train does not start. You get the whistle blown. The victims heave a sigh of relief. But no, this is only more of the joke . . . You finally start them at 6.15, 1 hour after you have landed them . . . The humour of the thing is further enhanced when one discovers that the steamer which lands the victims at Wemyss Bay proceeds to Kirn, Dunoon and Gourock and after all that sailing has its passengers in Glasgow long before the poor victims of the Wemyss Bay joke. After this who can doubt that the railway official is a humorous beast? Was it not Mark Twain who was a railway guard once upon a time?
> I am, etc., one of sixty victims last Saturday.

Note the ferry took less than half-an-hour for the crossing - there is no hint that the Caledonian Steam Packet Company were not running *their* affairs efficiently.

Brakes and Byelaws

The arrival of rapid rail travel highlighted a new problem - railway safety. In 1825, *Locomotion*, a very early locomotive, weighing just over seven tons yet capable of pulling 90 tons, could maintain 8 mph - jogging speed. Now that a train could move as fast as a mail coach and trail as much as a barge, the next stage was to improve reliability and haul greater loads at higher speeds. At the Rainhill trials in 1829, John Ericsson's *Novelty* proved that 40 mph was achievable. But the following year, the opening of the Liverpool and Manchester railway showed how dangerously silent trains can be. As William Huskisson, a prominent MP, descended from the inaugural train, he stepped into the path of Stephenson's *Rocket* which was running round a train on the adjacent track. His death, following Stephenson's commandeering the *Northumbrian* and racing him to Eccles, emphasised that this new and reliable form of transport brought with it the potential for tragedy. As the years passed, wooden brake blocks only on the tender wheels were replaced by metal shoes, brake blocks appeared on locomotive driving wheels, passenger trains became fully braked with vacuum or air brakes, coach lights lit by gas were replaced by electricity and interlocked signalling replaced the time interval system. While interlocking of points and signals had been patented in 1856, a Bill called 'The Regulation of Railway (Prevention of Accidents) Bill' requiring all railway companies to adopt the Block and Interlock system to points and signals was only introduced in 1873. The Caley had already introduced lock and block in certain areas, but saw it as costly and unnecessary for every situation.

GREENOCK & WEMYSS BAY RAILWAY.

BYE-LAWS AND REGULATIONS

Made by the GREENOCK AND WEMYSS BAY RAILWAY COMPANY with the Approval of the Board of Trade, for regulating the Travelling upon and using of all Railways, belonging to, or leased to, the said Company, and with respect to which that Company have power to make Byelaws.

1. No Passenger will be allowed to enter any Carriage used on the Railway, or to travel therein upon the Railway, unless furnished by the Company with a Ticket specifying the Class of Carriage and the Stations for Conveyance between which such Ticket is issued. Every Passenger shall show and deliver up his Ticket (whether a Contract or Season Ticket or otherwise) to any duly authorized Servant of the Company whenever required to do so for any Purpose. Any Passenger failing or refusing to show or deliver up his Ticket as aforesaid shall be required to pay the Fare from the Station whence the Train originally started to the End of his Journey, and in default of Payment thereof is hereby subjected to a Penalty not exceeding *Forty Shillings.*

2. Any Passenger using or attempting to use a Ticket on any Day for which such Ticket is not available, is hereby subjected to a Penalty not exceeding *Forty Shillings.*

3. Any Passenger using or attempting to use a Ticket for any other Station than that for which it is available will be required to pay the Difference between the Sum actually paid and the Fare between the Stations from and to which the Passenger has travelled, and in default of such Payment is hereby subjected to a Penalty not exceeding *Forty Shillings.*

4. Any Passenger wilfully altering or defacing his Ticket so as to render the Date, Number, or any material Portion thereof illegible is hereby subjected to a Penalty not exceeding *Forty Shillings*, and shall in addition be liable to pay the Fare from the Station whence the Train originally started.

5. At the intermediate Stations the Fares will only be accepted, and the Tickets issued, conditionally; that is to say, in case there shall be room in the Train for which the Tickets are issued. In case there shall not be room for all the Passengers to whom Tickets have been issued, those to whom Tickets have been issued for the longest Distance shall (if reasonably practicable) have the Preference, and those to whom Tickets have been issued for the same Distance shall (if reasonably practicable) have Priority according to the Order in which Tickets have been issued, as denoted by the consecutive Numbers stamped upon them. The Company will not, however, hold itself responsible for such Order of Preference or Priority being adhered to, but the Fare or difference of Fare, if the Passenger travel in a class of Carriage inferior to that for which he has a Ticket, shall be immediately returned to any Passenger for whom there is not room as aforesaid.

6. Every Person smoking Tobacco in any building of the Company, or in any Carriage or Compartment of a Carriage used on the Railway not specially provided for that Purpose, is hereby subjected to a Penalty not exceeding *Forty Shillings.* The Company's Officers and Servants are required to take the necessary Steps to enforce Obedience to this Byelaw; and any Person offending against it is liable in addition to incurring the Penalty above mentioned to be summarily removed, at the first Opportunity, from the Carriage, or from the Company's Premises.

7. Any Person travelling without the special Permission of some duly authorized Servant of the Company in a Carriage or by a Train of a Superior Class to that for which his Ticket was issued, is hereby subjected to a Penalty not exceeding *Forty Shillings;* and shall in addition be liable to pay the Fare, according to the class of Carriage in which he is travelling, from the Station whence the Train originally started.

8. Any Person found in a Carriage, or elsewhere upon the Company's Premises, in a state of Intoxication, using Obscene or Abusive Language, or committing any Nuisance, or otherwise wilfully interfering with the Comfort of other Passengers, is hereby subjected to a Penalty not exceeding *Forty Shillings*, and shall immediately, or, if a Passenger, at the first Opportunity, be removed from the Company's Premises.

9. Any Person who wilfully cuts any Lining or Window Strap, removes or defaces any Number Plate, or breaks or scratches any Window of a Carriage used on the Railway, or who otherwise, except by unavoidable accident, damages or injures any such Carriage, or any Station, or other property of the Company, is hereby subjected to a Penalty not exceeding *Five Pounds*, in addition to the Amount of any Damage for which he may be liable.

10. No Passenger shall be permitted to travel on the Roof, Steps, or Footboard of any Carriage; and any Passenger persisting in doing so, after being warned to desist by the Guard in charge of the Train, or any duly authorized Servant of the Company, is hereby subjected to a Penalty not exceeding *Forty Shillings.*

11. Any Passenger entering or leaving, or attempting to enter or leave, any of the Carriages while the Train is in motion, or elsewhere than at the Side of the Carriage adjoining the Platform, or other Place appointed by the Company for Passengers to enter or leave the Carriages, is hereby subjected to a Penalty not exceeding *Forty Shillings.*

12. Any Passenger entering a Carriage or Compartment of a Carriage containing the full Number of Persons which it is constructed to convey, except with the Consent of the Persons in such Carriage or Compartment, is hereby subjected to a Penalty not exceeding *Forty Shillings.*

13. Dogs and other Animals will not be suffered to accompany Passengers in the Carriages, but will be conveyed separately and charged for, and any Person taking a Dog or other Animal with him into any Passenger Carriage used on the Railway is hereby subjected to a Penalty not exceeding *Forty Shillings.*

14. Loaded Fire Arms, except with the express Permission of some Officer of the Company, are on no account to be taken into or placed upon any Carriage, Waggon, Truck, or other Vehicle forming or intended to form a Train or any portion of a Train on the Railway, and every Person so offending is hereby subjected to a Penalty not exceeding *Five Pounds.*

15. Every Driver or Conductor of an Omnibus, Cab, Carriage, or other Vehicle shall, while in or upon any Station Yard or other Premises of the Company, obey the reasonable Directions of the Company's Officers and Servants duly authorized in that Behalf; and every Person offending against this Regulation is hereby subjected to a Penalty not exceeding *Forty Shillings.*

16. Any Person (not being an Officer or Servant of the Company) using or attempting to use any Carriage, Waggon, or Truck belonging to the Company, except as a Passenger, or with the express Permission or under the Direction of the Company, or one of its Officers, shall be liable to a Penalty not exceeding *Five Pounds.*

17. A Return Ticket is granted solely for the purpose of enabling the Person to whom the same is issued to travel therewith to and from the Stations marked thereon, and is not transferable. Any Person who sells or attempts to sell, or parts or attempts to part with the Possession of the Return Half of any Return Ticket in order to enable any other Person to Travel therewith, is hereby subjected to a Penalty not exceeding *Forty Shillings*, and any Person purchasing such Half of a Return Ticket, or travelling or attempting to travel therewith, shall be liable to pay the Fare which he would have been liable to pay for the Single Journey, and shall, in addition thereto, be subjected to a Penalty not exceeding *Forty Shillings.*

Given under the common seal of the Greenock and Wemyss Railway Company, the sixth day of April, 1872.

James Keyden
Secretary of the Company.

The Board of Trade hereby signify their allowance and approval of the above Byelaws and Regulations.

Signed by order of the Board of Trade
the eleventh day of April 1872
W. R. Malcolm
An Assistant-Secretary to the Board of Trade.

NOTICES.

Penalty for Fraud.

1. Under the 96th and 97th Sections of the Railways Clauses Consolidation (Scotland) Act, 1845, it is provided that if any Person travel or attempt to travel in any Carriage of the Company, or of any other Company or Party using the Railway, without having previously paid his Fare, and with Intent to avoid Payment thereof, or if any Person, having paid his Fare for a certain Distance, knowingly and wilfully proceed in any such Carriage beyond such Distance without previously paying the additional Fare for the additional Distance, and with Intent to avoid Payment thereof, or if any Person knowingly and wilfully refuse or neglect, on arriving at the Point to which he has paid his Fare, to quit such Carriage, every such Person shall for every such Offence forfeit to the Company a Sum not exceeding *Forty Shillings*; and if any Person commit any such Offence, all Officers and Servants and other Persons on behalf of the Company may lawfully apprehend and detain such Person until he can conveniently be taken before the Sheriff or some Justice, or until he be otherwise discharged by due course of Law.

Obstructing Officers of the Company.

2. Under the 102d Section of the Railways Clauses Consolidation (Scotland) Act, 1845, it is provided that if the Infraction or Non-observance of the Company's Byelaws or Regulations be attended with Danger or Annoyance to the Public, or Hindrance to the Company in the lawful Use of the Railway, it shall be lawful for the Company summarily to interfere to obviate or remove such Danger, Annoyance, or Hindrance; and under the 16th Section of the Act 3 and 4 Vict., cap. 97, it is provided that if any Person shall wilfully obstruct or impede any Officer or Agent of the Company in the Execution of his Duty upon the Railway, or upon or in any of the Stations or other Works or Premises connected therewith, every such Person so offending, and all others aiding or assisting therein, may be seized and detained until he can conveniently be taken before a Justice, and shall in the Discretion of such Justice forfeit any Sum not exceeding *Five Pounds*, and in default of Payment thereof be imprisoned for any Term not exceeding Two Calendar Months.

Injuring Notice Boards, &c.

3. Under the 136th Section of the Railways Clauses Consolidation (Scotland) Act, 1845, it is provided that if any Person pull down or injure any Board put up or affixed for the Purpose of publishing any Byelaw or Penalty, or shall obliterate any of the Letters or Figures thereon, he shall forfeit for every such Offence a Sum not exceeding *Five Pounds*, and shall defray the Expenses attending the Restoration of such Board.

Sending dangerous Goods.

4. Under the 98th Section of the Railways Clauses Consolidation (Scotland) Act, 1845, it is provided that no Person shall be entitled to carry, or to require the Company to carry upon the Railway any Aquafortis, Oil of Vitriol, Gunpowder, Lucifer Matches, or any other Goods which in the Judgment of the Company may be of a dangerous Nature, and if any Person send by the Railway any such Goods without distinctly marking their Nature on the Outside of the Package containing the same, or otherwise giving Notice in Writing to the Bookkeeper or other Servant of the Company with whom the same are left at the Time of so sending, he shall forfeit to the Company *Twenty Pounds* for every such Offence, and it shall be lawful for the Company to refuse to take any Parcel that they may suspect to contain Goods of a dangerous Nature, or require the same to be opened to ascertain the Fact.

Using Communication between Passengers and Servants of the Company.

5. Under the 22d Section of the Regulation of Railways Act, 1868, it is provided that any Passenger who makes use of the Means of Communication between the Passengers and the Servants of the Company in charge of a Train without reasonable and sufficient Cause, shall be liable for each Offence to a Penalty not exceeding *Five Pounds.*

Trespassing on Railway.

6. Under the 23d Section of the Regulation of Railways Act, 1868, it is provided that if any Person shall be or pass upon the Railway, except for the Purpose of crossing the same at any authorized Crossing, after having received Warning by the Company which works such Railway, or by any of their Agents or Servants, not to go or pass thereon, every Person so offending shall forfeit and pay any Sum not exceeding *Forty Shillings* for every such Offence.

Omitting to Shut and Fasten Gates.

7. Under the 68th Section of "The Railways Clauses Consolidation (Scotland) Act, 1845," it is provided that if any person omit to shut and fasten any gate set up at either side of the Railway, for the accommodation of the Owners or Occupiers of the adjoining lands, as soon as he, and the carriage, cattle, or other animals under his care have passed through the same, he shall forfeit, for every such offence, any sum not exceeding *Forty Shillings.*

Injuring or Defacing Boards or Milestones.

8. Under the 88th Section of "The Railways Clauses Consolidation (Scotland) Act, 1845," it is provided that no Tolls shall be demanded or taken by the Company for the use of the Railway during any time at which the boards thereinbefore directed to be exhibited shall not be so exhibited, or at which the milestones thereinbefore directed to be set up and maintained shall not be so set up and maintained; and if any person wilfully pull down, deface, or destroy any such board or milestone, he shall forfeit a sum not exceeding *Five Pounds* for every such offence.

G&WBR bye-laws adopted in April 1872, signed by James Keyden, which includes references to Railway Acts of 1845 and 1868. *Scottish Record Office Ref. BLR 1/4*

The lack of good brakes on trains was a recognised cause of serious accidents. Writing to *The Engineer* in 1864, John Clark commented that people would be more confident travelling by rail if they knew the train would stop 'in 20 seconds instead of 2 minutes, as now'. His own system of continuous air brakes was of proven efficiency, but railway companies were reluctant to spend money that would save lives - and reduce the scale of compensation claims.

In March 1872, the Caledonian Railway carried out an experiment using the Westinghouse continuous air brake that had proved very successful in America. An article in the 5th June, 1903 issue of *Engineering* on the American George Westinghouse (1846-1914), commented: 'when [he] . . . first succeeded in getting his air brake tried in this country, he secured the co-operation of Mr Benjamin Conner, the Caledonian Railway Company's Locomotive Superintendent [between 1857 and 1876], and got the use of the Wemyss Bay line to give demonstrations'. Westinghouse used the whole route from Bridge Street station to Wemyss Bay and the train comprised 12 carriages and two vans, all fitted with the brake. The brake was also fitted to the tender, but not to the engine. The locomotive was a 4-year-old Conner 2-4-0 with 7 ft driving wheels. There was a refinement: passengers could pull a handle in each carriage which simultaneously would commence braking and give a short blast on whistles in the engine and (if necessary) the guard's van. *Engineering* published the results, noting that the stops were 'wonderfully prompt':

Place where stop was made	Gradient	Speed of train when brake applied (mph)	Time occupied in making the stop (secs)	Distance run after application of the brake (yards)
Houston Station	Level	50	19	264
Bishopton	1 in 400 up	40	17	188
Langbank	1 in 200 down	58	23	276
Ravenscraig incline	1 in 130 down	50	20	268
Near Inverkip Station	1 in 68 down	60	23	308

This was a more accurate test than one carried out on the London and St Albans line where distance was estimated by counting telegraph poles. It would have been interesting to have had more detail, but it was one of the first tests carried out to assess braking systems. Three years later, the Royal Commission on Railway Operations conducted more scientific tests near Newark on the Midland Railway when different railway companies sent engines and trains with hydraulic, chain, air and vacuum brakes for a series of brake tests - oddly, the Caley contribution was a train using Steel and McInnes's air brake and the description suggests the train was made up of old stock. *Engineering* had no doubt whatsoever that the Westinghouse air brake was the best.

It was not until the Regulation of Railways Act in 1889 that all railways were compelled to introduce interlocking of points and signals and provide automatic continuous (fail-safe) brakes on passenger trains. Formalised rules and Regulations took a long time to be developed, individual branch lines and stations often working under their own local rules. In the case of the Wemyss Bay line, the running was done to Caley rules, though its own printed Byelaws were very similar to the Caley's.

Byelaws were periodically revised during the life of a railway company, usually becoming more prescriptive with time, though some clauses disappeared. In 1866, the Caledonian Railway submitted its proposed Byelaws to the Board of Trade. Forty Shillings [i.e. £2] [*£80] was a common penalty and it may seem surprising that even then, tobacco smoking was regarded as objectionable to the extent that persistent offenders could be ejected from the company's property. Gaming and Games of Chance were equally abhorrent to the railway company.

By 1872, the G&WBR had posters with its own Byelaws, covering items that also featured on the Caley - not surprising when most trips involved Caley trains on Caley metals. The punishment for not possessing a valid ticket or having a dog in the compartment was a penalty not exceeding forty shillings. Defacing a ticket or travelling in a 'superior class' also attracted a penalty not exceeding forty shillings as well as having to pay the fare from the station whence the train originally started. On transferrability, the company frowned on both the seller and the recipient of the return portion of a ticket - both would be liable to the forty shilling penalty and the 'return' traveller would have to pay his fare in addition. (This would not seem to cause any loss to the railway companies so goodness knows why they do it.) Smoking in non-smoking compartments or in non-smoking areas in company buildings, a state of intoxication, using obscene or abusive language, committing a nuisance 'or otherwise interfering with the comfort of other passengers' would result in the inevitable penalty 'not exceeding forty shillings', plus removal.

The company took strong action against those wilfully damaging window straps, scratching windows or defacing railway property - the penalty was £5 [*£200] plus the cost of repair. Loaded Fire Arms (*note: not unloaded*) rendered the offender liable to a similar penalty.

A curious Byelaw referred to intermediate stations - if the train did not have room for all the passengers (*note: not seats*), then those travelling farthest would get preference, in order of the numbers stamped on the tickets. The Byelaw covered the (unlikely) eventuality of a traveller having to travel in a class of carriage inferior to that for which he had a ticket - he would either get his fare, or the difference of the fare, returned to him. A later Byelaw has a sort of Hoffnung reference [when entering a railway compartment, make sure to shake hands with all the passengers] - 'Any passenger entering a Carriage . . . containing the full Number of Persons which it is constructed to convey, except with the Consent of the Persons in such Carriage . . . is hereby subjected to a Penalty . . .' A hangover from the earliest days of travel when carriages looked like stagecoaches, features in the Byelaw which forbade travelling on the roof, steps or footboard of carriages. More serious was where passengers attempted to enter or leave carriages in motion, or exit other than at the platform side.

These Byelaws, signed by James Keyden as Secretary of the G&WBR and given under the common seal of the Greenock and Wemyss Railway Company [sic], were supplemented by similar 'Notices' based on the Railways Clauses Consolidation (Scotland) Act 1845 where officers and servants of the company were given the right to apprehend miscreants. The Penalties were variously spelt out - forty shillings, five pounds, two months' imprisonment. Goods of a dangerous nature - Aquafortis, Oil of Vitriol, Gunpowder or Lucifer Matches - had to be clearly identified to the railway company, on pain of a £20 [*£750] fine.

The Regulation of Railways Act, 1868, introduced the 'communication cord', and inevitably a (£5) penalty for its misuse. The same Act dealt with trespassers on to the railway, the previous (1845) Act having already alerted individuals to the need to shut gates leading on to the railway line. The Act additionally covered financial and legal issues, trains for the Post Office and described how company affairs should be set out for public scrutiny. Schedules were included so that the railway company's Engineer (and similarly the locomotive superintendent) could certify that the whole of the company's permanent way, stations, buildings and other works had been maintained in good order over the previous six months. Reporting procedures clearly lacked consistency. When one considers that the 3rd class return fare from Wemyss Bay to Glasgow at the time was about 2s., the penalties are quite significant.

The Caledonian Railway added another Byelaw in 1887, over 40 years after its creation. 'Any person found upon the Railway, or upon or in any Station, Depot, Works, or Premises, the property of the Caledonian Railway Company, without proper authority, selling or offering for sale newspapers or other literature, or hawking fruits, wares, or goods of any description, or soliciting luggage to carry, is hereby subjected to a penalty not exceeding Forty Shillings [*£100]'. It seems somewhat 'over the top' but provides an insight to what the Caley must have seen as an increasingly unsavoury element detracting from their public image - it probably tells us that the economy was in one of its flat periods when work was not so readily available.

By contrast, the British Railways Board Railway Byelaws introduced in 1965 (modified in October 1990), and which applied to the end of the nationalised railway system up to 1997, were a great deal more complex. Penalties had been increased to maxima of £50 [*£105] and £200 [*£425] before being put on the Standard Scale as described in the Criminal Justice Act 1982.

The comparatively simple 1866 byelaw which stated 'Any person found in a Carriage or Station in a state of intoxication or committing any nuisance, or otherwise interfering with the comfort of other passengers is hereby subjected to a penalty not exceeding forty shillings [£2], and shall immediately, or, if travelling, at the first opportunity, be removed from the company's premises' has now been converted into obscure legal prose seven times longer than the original.

The variety of competitive fares available led to anomalies. Long distance travel could be cheaper than short trips on the same line. So a byelaw was introduced to deal with fare dodgers: 'When the fare to an intermediate station exceeds the fare to a more distant station, no person shall, for the purpose of travelling to such intermediate station, take or use, or attempt to use a ticket for the more distant station with intent to avoid payment of the additional fare to such intermediate station'. The fairness and logic of such a byelaw is unclear.

The Caley's regulations against hawking were elaborated so that in British Rail's day they covered a prohibition on soliciting alms and playing musical instruments, etc., a killjoy enamelled panel in Central Station announcing that: 'No person while on the railway shall to the annoyance of any other person sing, perform on any musical or other instrument or use any gramophone, record player, tape recorder or portable wireless apparatus'.

Some 120 years of progress on the railways has seen the Caledonian's 11 byelaws of 1866 increased to 34 on British Railways by 1990.

The Book of Rules and Regulations

In the Appendix to the Working Time Tables of 1902 the Caley supplemented its February 1898 Book of Rules and Regulations with the following, some of which indicate that the line was undergoing reconstruction:

Tunnel between Upper Greenock and Wemyss Bay Junction (Cartsburn Tunnel)
When it is necessary for a platelayer's Lorry to go through the Tunnel . . ., the Ganger or Leading Man in charge of the Lorry must be in possession of the Tablet (for single line operation); the Lorry must be signalled on the Tablet Instruments in accordance with the authorised Code, and the Signalman at the Tablet Station in advance must, if the Section be clear, as laid down in Rule 5, give permission for the Lorry to approach under the 'Warning' arrangement. Should the Lorry, after passing through the Tunnel, be removed from the rails before reaching the next Tablet Station, the Ganger or Leading Man must take the Tablet to the Signalman at the opposite end of the Section, and he must inform the Signalman that the Lorry is clear of the Line, and hand the Tablet to him. [Construction traffic was therefore treated as a train.]

Vehicles Running Away - Wemyss Bay Junction to Wemyss Bay
The Signalman at the Tablet Station from which the runaway Vehicle or Train has started, or any other Signalman whose Station may be passed by the Runaway Vehicle or Train, must immediately give the 'Obstruction Danger' Signal to the Signalman at the Tablet Station towards which the Runaway Vehicle or Train is travelling before giving the 'Vehicles Running Away' Signal, as prompt action on the part of both Signalmen may prevent a mishap. Should the Signalman receiving the 'Obstruction Danger' Signal succeed in stopping the Train or Engine for which he has given the 'Is Line Clear?' Signal, he must restore the Tablet to the Instrument, and then advise the Signalman in advance by giving the 'Cancel' Signal...

The following are the Sections of Line on which the new type of Instrument is in operation, viz.:-

Wemyss Bay Junction and Berryards.	Until operations
Upper Greenock and Dunrod.	for doubling of
Dunrod and Inverkip.	Line are
Inverkip and Wemyss Bay Engine Sheds.	completed.

The sections between Berryards and Upper Greenock, and from Wemyss Bay Engine Sheds and the station itself, were operated by Block Telegraph instead of by tablet. Overton Paper Mill sidings, between Berryards and the mill, required a train staff (coloured black) and keys for the points and crossings. These were kept at Berryards signal box.

Wemyss Bay was one of a group of stations (which included Gourock, Greenock and Glasgow) where the 1902 Caley Appendix to the Working Timetables required that a first and a third class compartment in trains had to be reserved for 'Ladies only' and that station masters and guards 'must see that the attention of Ladies travelling alone is specially directed to such compartments, and also that Gentlemen do not travel in them'. This was matched by a Byelaw issued in 1905 which stated: 'Except by express permission of a guard of the train, a person of the male sex above, or apparently above, the age of eight years shall not travel or attempt to travel or remain in any compartment of a carriage marked or notified as being reserved or appropriated for the exclusive use of persons of the female sex'. The penalty for this heinous crime was a fine of up to £5 [*£250]. The corresponding byelaw in British Rail's time read: 'No person of the male sex above the age of 12 years shall travel or attempt to travel or remain in any vehicle or place on the railway marked or notified as being reserved or appropriated for the exclusive use of persons of the female sex'. The penalty - £50 [*£105]. And if on a cold winter's night the crossing from Rothesay had been a bit rough, the ladies could obtain a footwarmer at Wemyss Bay station.

Then there were other general rules:

Vehicles not to be moved whilst Lampmen or Others are on the top of them - it seems obvious enough but the Rule Book is full of the obvious.

Travelling with Infectious Disorder - special permission had to be obtained or the person with the infection, and anyone accompanying them, could be liable for a 40 shilling fine. Later British Rail byelaws included a similar prohibition.

Time tables - the Caley was considerate of its clientèle - Station Masters were enjoined to underline the name of their station 'in red ink' on all sheet timetables.

Regulating clocks - to ensure the line ran to time, signal box clocks were set from Edinburgh. Two minutes before 1 o'clock, Edinburgh would signal 'time' to the instruments in its area and the Glasgow Circuits, and Glasgow Central would thereupon warn Wemyss Bay and other instruments in its area of the impending time signal. On the firing of the one o'clock gun in Edinburgh, Edinburgh would signal 'one' and all instruments throughout the Caley would be adjusted to suit.

Out of date excursion bills, handbills, public time tables, and the like - 'not required for lavatory purposes' - had to be returned to store. It is nice to note that after consultation they could still serve one useful final function.

Horse Boxes, Carriage, Fish and Milk Trucks

(h) the Guard must examine Horse Boxes at starting and during the journey, and satisfy himself as to the condition of the Animals.

(i) Station Masters and Foremen must arrange for the internal fittings of each horse box being examined on arrival and report to the Plant Superintendent if anything is found wrong . . . and if found unsuitable for traffic, it must be sent to the Workshops for inspection - if fit to run - unless the defect is such that the Carriage Examiner - if there is one at the Station - can put right.

(j) Station Masters and Foremen must see that the Head Collars and Halters are kept in good order, and that the former are rubbed from time to time with oil to keep them pliable . . . that Horse Boxes are cleansed and disinfected in accordance with the Regulations . . . and that all Carriage, Fish, Milk Trucks, and Horse Boxes are regularly cleaned.

(l) A telegram must be sent to the Plant Superintendent from the Stock Stations daily, at 6.00 pm, giving the total number of Horse Boxes, Carriage Trucks, etc, loaded during the day, stating where to, and how many Vehicles are left in hand. [Wemyss Bay was listed as a Stock Station for Horse Boxes.]

In 1865, a request from the Justices of the Peace in Forfar that cattle should not be moved without a certificate that they were free of the plague (our equivalent of Foot & Mouth disease), was rejected by the Caley as impracticable. By 1902, the railways recognised that they could cause the spread of animal diseases. As a result, higher standards of hygiene were required, as prescribed under the heading 'Railway Traffic horse boxes' which required washing down shavings and sweepings being removed and mixed with quicklime, etc.

It is surprising that Wemyss Bay is *not* listed as a station where water was available for animals, especially as Greenock and Gourock were.

Second class coaches were taken off the Greenock and Wemyss Bay coastal routes and through west coast trains in March 1889, three years after they had been removed from the rest of the Caledonian system. The Caley, finding that people who could well afford to travel first were travelling in lesser accommodation, were losing money. Elimination of the second class removed an option and no doubt led to better use of the coaching stock.

In 1902, the semaphore head code for trains between Wemyss Bay and Glasgow had one long leg pointing horizontally towards the 'six-foot' side of the engine (i.e., facing the engine's smokebox, it pointed left). By the time the 1915 time table appeared, the horizontal arm pointed in the diametrically opposite direction! Gourock trains carried the indicator with the leg pointing vertically upwards.

It was particularly important that when vehicles were detached they could not run away. The short stretch of line from Port Glasgow to Wemyss Bay possessed some stiff grades - 1 in 67½ at Berryards, 1 in 94 at Upper Greenock, 1 in 120 at Ravenscraig, 1 in 69 at Hill Farm, 1 in 168 at Inverkip and 1 in 69 at Wemyss Bay engine shed. The brakesman had to ensure that before the engine was detached from the train, the brake in the brake van was hard on and a sufficient number of others pinned down - with one or more sprags placed in the wheels of the wagons. Catch points to intercept runaways, a particular problem where wagons were not connected to the train braking system, were located on the Wemyss Bay branch on the down line (i.e. that leading to Wemyss Bay) about 150 yards west of Wemyss Bay Junction. The points at Overton Paper Mill Branch also served to deflect runaways from the running line. Hill Farm siding could only be worked by trains going towards Wemyss Bay, the frame being unlocked by the train tablet for the Dunrod to Inverkip section. At Inverkip, in order to tell the driver that his train had cleared the points - the train being in the curving tunnel, a bell was fitted in the tunnel, operated from the signal box. At Wemyss Bay, there were two ground frames, one to work the crossover and the other to allow entry to the goods siding - both of these were 'rod locked' from Wemyss Bay signal box.

Locomotive Matters

In 1902, the rules in the Caley Appendix to the Working Timetable allowed goods trains between Greenock and Polmadie to be made up to a maximum of 50 vehicles. An 8-wheeled coupled goods could manage 50 mineral wagons but a 6-wheel coupled goods was limited to 40, while the 'third class' was restricted to 25 trucks. Empty eight-wheel 'coaching vehicles' were considered the equivalent of two wagons.

Before the advent of more powerful engines, if passenger trains leaving Glasgow Central for Wemyss Bay exceeded 10 vehicles, and were not worked by a six-wheeled coupled engine, Central Station had to advise the Port Glasgow station master, *without delay*, so that the latter could whistle up an engine from the locomotive foreman at Greenock to act as pilot. Likewise, if the train leaving Wemyss Bay was too heavy for the locomotive power available, he could either use an incoming pilot or seek one from Greenock. In those days, when double-heading was common on main line expresses, the maximum number of vehicles which an 'ordinary' engine could take was limited to 13. A six-wheeled coupled engine or double engine arrangement was permitted to take up to 17 vehicles, including vans. The working timetable also makes reference to trains running 'in duplicate', the division being such that each engine could handle its portion without a pilot.

Wemyss Bay engine shed with water tank and turntable taken prior to electrification and singling of the line. The 55 ft turntable was a tight fit for a 'Black 5' which was nearly 64 ft long and which would clearly obstruct the up line when being turned.

W.A. Camwell/J.L. Stevenson Collection

Fairburn 2-6-4T No. 42144 on its way to Glasgow passing the water tank and ash pit at Wemyss Bay engine shed in May 1961.

W.A.C. Smith

Between Wemyss Bay Junction and Upper Greenock, the Caley allowed a banking engine for goods, mineral or empty carriage trains. No shunting was permitted on the main line, trains for Upper Greenock having to enter the loop at Berryards signal box. The signalman was alerted to which of the Berryards sidings the train was to go into by a selection of whistles and 'crows' made by the driver. Whistle codes were used throughout the railway system - a busy intersection like Bridge Street Junction had over 20 different codes to contend with. For example, the train from Wemyss Bay into Central Station would give two whistles, from Gourock one whistle, and so on. At Wemyss Bay Junction, trains going to or from Wemyss Bay would give a double whistle as they passed. In 1902, trains entering or leaving Wemyss Bay Station would give one of five whistle signals dependent on whether they were going into or out of the two platforms, the carriage siding or the goods road.

The 1902 Appendix required trains to be propelled from Berryards on to the Overton Paper Mill line with the brakesman on the front wagon or van. His duties included opening and closing the locked level crossing gates at Berryards Farm and Largs Road and operating two sets of points arranged to protect the line against runaways. This one mile line, with its 1 in 19 approach gradient, was served by a diminutive 0-4-0 saddle tank, which was supposed to take a maximum of two trucks at a time but as has been seen (*page 187*) this was not always adhered to.

Wemyss Bay being the terminus, tender locomotives needed turning. The Rule Book allowed 15 minutes for this exercise. In 1902, Wemyss Bay had a 42 ft diameter turntable, the most common size after the 50 ft diameter. (At that time there were seven sizes from 60 ft to 40 ft. The turntables at Bridge Street, Greenock (Ladyburn) and Gourock were 54 ft, 50 ft and 50 ft diameter respectively. Engines needing turning at Glasgow used the Bridge Street turntable.)

The Wemyss Bay turntable was sandwiched between the running lines and the embankment above the main road. The railway over the turntable extended into a stone engine shed, which from 1927 was only used for a coal or ash wagon. On the Greenock side of the turntable was the water tank (with heater below) and ash clean-out point. In the 1890s the turntable was linked by rodding to a signal box lever to protect the main line. While tank locomotives like the 43 ft long 'Wemyss Bay Pugs' did not need turning, the 'Coast Bogies' were getting on for 52 ft long - and just fitted on to the table. A plan of the layout shows that the buffers of a locomotive on the turntable could foul the running line. In 1915 it was decided to interlock the signals with the turntable to prevent accidents.

In 1924, prompted by the activities of a local land agent, an effort was made to find a site for a larger turntable, but it was not till 1938 that a 55 ft turntable was installed on the site of the old engine shed, the running lines being skewed to accept it. Even so, there was insufficient clearance to allow trains to pass on the up line when the turntable was in use.

Signal Boxes

In 1902, the line between Wemyss Bay and Port Glasgow required the following boxes, each linked by telephone to the next:

Wemyss Bay Station (manned between 5.30 am and 9.00 pm);
Wemyss Bay Engine Shed (manned between 5.30 am and 9.00 pm);
Inverkip (manned between 5.30 am and 8.30 pm);
Dunrod (manned between 5.30 am and 8.25 pm);
Greenock (manned between 5.00 am and 8.25 am);
Berryards (manned between 5.00 am and 8.15 pm);
Wemyss Bay Junction (manned between 5.00 am and 10.45 pm).

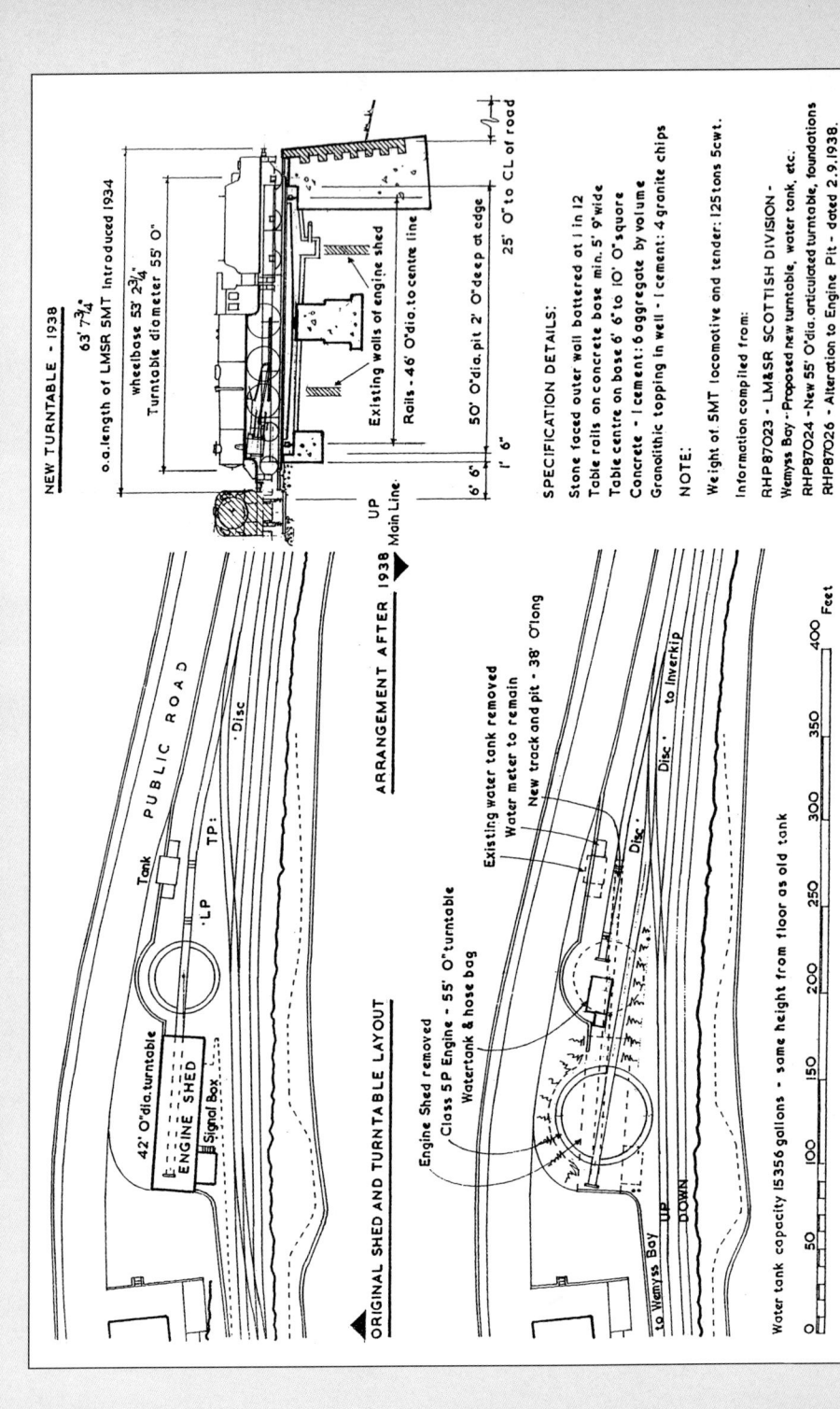

THE WEMYSS BAY TURNTABLES

In every case, working hours ended when the traffic for the day was over. During summer, the signalmen had to remain on duty to serve the extra traffic.

By contrast, the pressing need of the hugely busy Central Station for replacement signalling saw the introduction in May 1908 of a new 374 miniature lever electro-pneumatic box sited above the lines on the bridges over the Clyde. This covered the whole of Central Station and the tracks across the Clyde. Entrance was either by an external staircase at the Bridge Street end or by a gantry and stairs down to platform 13 at the west side of the station.

When the Gordon Street station opened in 1879, it was served by a signal cabin in Ann Street. In turn this was replaced by a much larger Central Station cabin in 1889. The 1908 box replaced both this cabin and another at Clyde Place and only required three signalmen and a train recording boy. The 1908 box has been replaced by a control room at Cook Street, commissioned in January 1961. The semaphore signals were supported from the station roof and on gantries across the tracks.

Railway Organisation

According to J.F. McEwan, in 1909, the footplate staff at Greenock included 31 drivers, 7 passed firemen, 25 Firemen and 11 passed cleaners. The Wemyss Bay staff comprised 3 drivers, 2 passed firemen, 2 firemen and 2 passed cleaners.

In 1902, Wemyss Bay trains were subject to the authority of the chief inspector in the general superintendent's office in Glasgow and the coaching traffic inspector at Eglinton Street station. The engineering aspects involved the divisional engineer in Germiston Street, various superintendents based in Buchanan Street Station and an inspector based in Greenock West whose area extended as far east as Paisley and Linwood. Signalling was organised from Killermont Street in Glasgow, telegraph inspectors from Buchanan Street and telegraph linesmen from Central Station and Greenock.

Discipline could be harsh. Relations between management and employees had polarised by the mid-1860s. Management adopted a tough and unsympathetic line against those who infringed regulations. On 27th June, 1866, the 5.45 Glasgow to Wemyss Bay was detained 'owing to breach of rules on the part of William Grant, the clerk in charge at Wemyss Bay - on the application of the Rev. Mr Boyd'. Despite Mr Boyd writing to Thomas Hill, Deputy Chairman of the Caley and much involved in the Wemyss Bay operations, interceding on behalf of the driver and the clerk, they were both dismissed five days later. It is small wonder that three railway unions were formed in 1865-1866 to represent employees when employers adopted such an approach, reflecting the militaristic origins of railway organisation. The continuing difficult relations resulted in the creation of the Amalgamated Society of Railway Servants (ASRS) in 1871 and the Associated Society of Locomotive Engineers and Firemen (ASLEF) in 1879.

The Caledonian Railway's early years were characterised by vigorous management and rapid expansion. Men who joined the railway as young professionals stayed in the company throughout their lives. Some died in harness. The turn of the 20th century was particularly traumatic with a trade depression and several old hands dying in succession or resigning. J.C. Bolton, Chairman till 1897 died in 1901, his successor J.C. Bunten died a few months later, Irvine Kempt retired as general superintendent in 1902 and the new Chairman Sir James Thompson died in office in 1906 aged 72, the same year as Hugh Brown, a fellow Director. His successor, Sir James King died in 1911. But bright recruits kept the railway moving forwards - Donald Matheson and William Pickersgill to name but two.

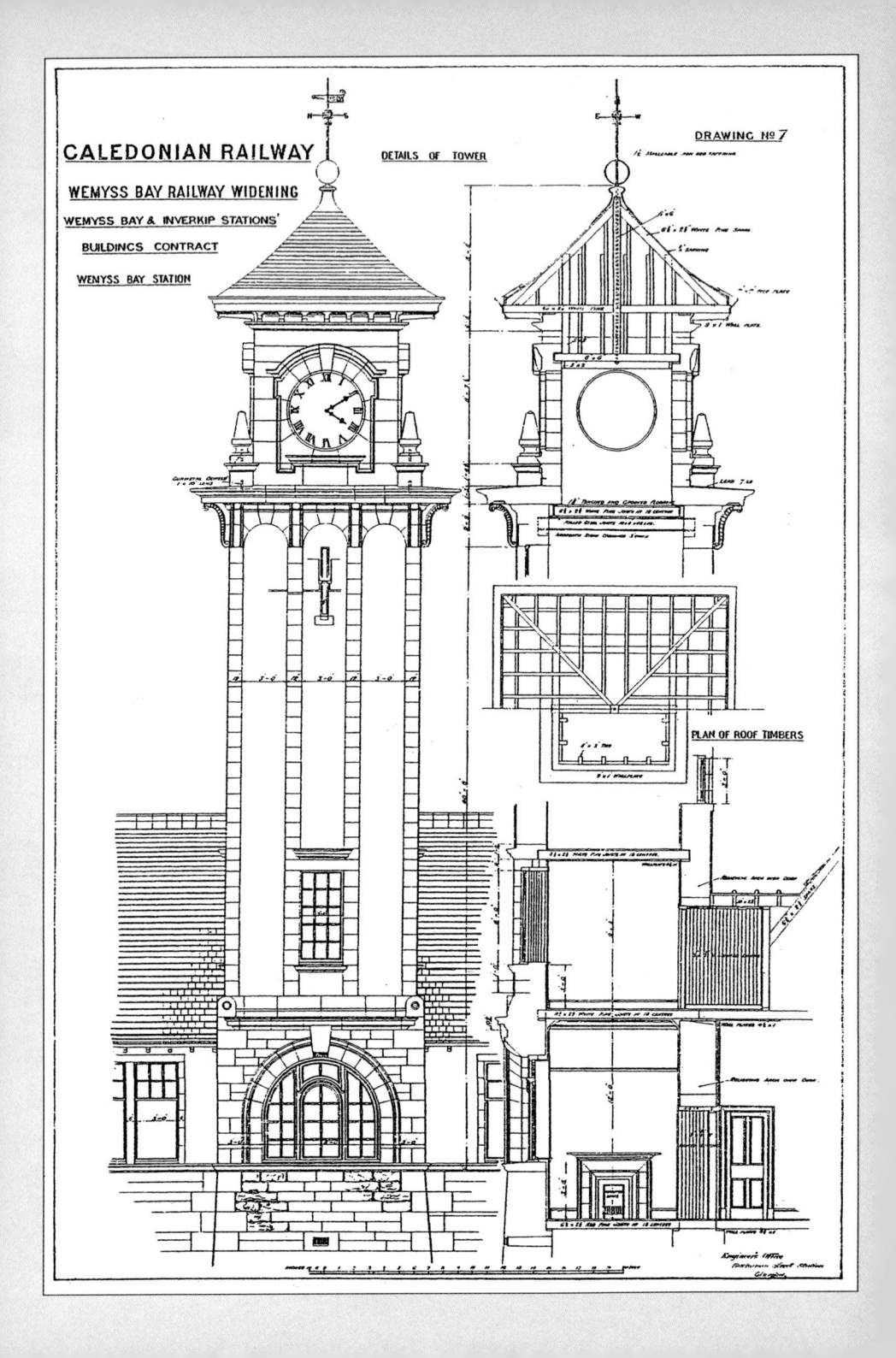

CALEDONIAN RAILWAY

WEMYSS BAY RAILWAY WIDENING
WEMYSS BAY & INVERKIP STATIONS BUILDINGS CONTRACT
WENYSS BAY STATION

DETAILS OF TOWER

DRAWING No. 7

PLAN OF ROOF TIMBERS

Chapter Fourteen

The Second Wemyss Bay Station and Other Works

Soon after the Caley came to control the line in 1893, they commenced reconstruction of the stations and a major upgrading. The Caledonian Railway Company had to enter into an Agreement with the Trustees of the late Alexander Stephen of Kelly before Wemyss Bay station could be enlarged. The Trustees were 'big' in the commercial world, - John, Alexander and Frederick Stephen were the Linthouse shipbuilders and John and James Templeton of Glasgow supplied carpets for Clyde-built liners. The Agreement covered the site boundaries and drainage from the lands and houses of Kelly (a large outfall crosses under the station platforms to discharge into the Clyde). The owner of Kelly obtained the Caley's Agreement to him using the new pier for tying up his yacht and for loading and unloading his household traffic. The signal box at the end of the station platform, an eyesore as far as the Stephens were concerned, would be moved further north by the Caley. (The Specification later drawn up for the new station buildings included a copy of the Agreement.) The Trustees also sold land to the Caley for £1,000 [*£50,000].

The Wemyss Bay pier was extended under section 4 of the Caledonian Railway (General Powers) Act of 1899, ('An Act to authorise [the widening of the Caley's railway line across the Clyde between Central Station and Bridge Street Station] and enlargement of the pier at Wemyss Bay in the County of Renfrew'). The Caley's ownership spread 150 yards into the Firth beyond the pier, in all directions. The Caley had to erect a fog signal on the pier to satisfy the Trustees of the Clyde Lighthouses.

The two men mainly responsible for rebuilding Wemyss Bay station had already made a significant impact on the Scottish scene in the architectural and engineering worlds. They were contemporaries, had gone to school together and, in late Victorian times, had worked together on numerous railway projects. The following biographical details chart their progress to high office in their respective professions.

Donald Alexander Matheson, MICE, (1860-1935) - born at Perth, studied at the Heriot-Watt College in Edinburgh (now the Heriot-Watt University). He joined the London and North Western Railway as assistant engineer in the Lancashire and Yorkshire district between 1884 and 1886 when he moved to R. McAlpine, the contractor for the Lanarkshire & Ayrshire Railway. In 1890, he was appointed Resident Engineer for the Central Low Level Lines, at a time when according to O.S. Nock, the Caley's engineering department was fully committed. The work was so complex that it took six years to complete the four mile section from Dalmarnock to Stobcross, finished in 1896. His competence so impressed the Caley that in 1899, on the death of George Graham, the Engineer-in-Chief of the Caledonian Railway, he was invited to fill the post.

In 1903, he was sent by the Caley Directors to study railway engineering practice in Canada and the USA. His experience in the construction of the underground was to prove invaluable in the early years of the 20th century in the great enlargement and reconstruction of Glasgow Central station.

In 1910 Matheson succeeded Guy Calthrop as General Manager. In 1912, he joined the Communications Board set up by the War Office and the Board of Trade. In 1916, he advised the War Office on the materials and railway expertise needed in France. On 1st January, 1923, the Caledonian was 'Grouped' with the Highland and the Glasgow & South Western to form the Northern Division of the London Midland & Scottish Railway, Donald Matheson being appointed Deputy General Manager for LMS (Scotland) till his retirement in 1926. Other offices he held included the chairmanship of the Railway Engineers' Association of the UK and the position of Vice-President of the Institution of Engineers and Shipbuilders in Scotland.

Matheson was not inclined to spend money unnecessarily. He once commented, 'There should be due regard to engineering economies meaning thereby the science of so spending

Upper Greenock station designed by James Miller c.1903. *Caledonian Railway Association*

Upper Greenock station as viewed looking towards Glasgow. The island platform is accessed from below. *Andrew F. Swan Collection*

money in the acquirement of land and in the design and construction of works as will tend to ensure adequate financial return on commercial enterprise'. He was ultimately responsible for the design of Wemyss Bay station.

Matheson was assisted by the Architect, *James Miller*, Hon. FRIAS ARSA FRIBA (1860-1947), who was born at Auchtergaven near Bankfoot in Perthshire. He attended Perth Academy at the same time as Matheson. He was apprenticed to Andrew Heiton, a Perth Architect who designed stations for several railway companies, including the Caledonian, before moving to the Edinburgh practice of Hippolyte Blanc. In 1888, he joined the Caledonian Railway Co. in Glasgow to work under George Graham on stations for the Gourock extension. While there he is believed to have designed a new frontage for Bridge Street Station in 1889-90 - which still exists. He started his own practice in 1893 on winning a competition for Belmont Parish Church in Glasgow. Between 1889 and 1925, he was responsible, either with the Caley or in his own practice, for nearly 70 stations, including the Caley stations at Gourock Pier (1889), Fort Matilda (1889), Greenock West (1889), Port Glasgow, Upper Greenock (1901-1902), Wemyss Bay (1903-1904), Inverkip (1903-1904) and Stirling (1912-1915), a replacement for Andrew Heiton's earlier construction. He designed the St Enoch subway station (1896 - Glasgow & District Subway Co.) and stations on the West Highland Railway, Princes Pier station Greenock, (1893 - Glasgow & South Western Rly Co.) and the railway hotels at Turnberry (G&SWR) and Gleneagles (Caley). Working with Donald Matheson, Miller was responsible for the architectural work for the new Glasgow Central station, where curving passenger flow lines were combined with function. Somehow, Miller managed not to fall out with the Caley, a misfortune experienced by several other Architects.

Miller's most successful station was Wemyss Bay, combining Matheson's ideas on people flow patterns with functional design - an Italianate clock tower acting as a pivotal landmark for passengers whether they be travelling from Rothesay or approaching from Glasgow. Features used in this station appear elsewhere - for example the concourse at Stirling station and the bellcote at St Andrew's East Church, Dennistoun.

He was a major Architect of his time, moving with the architectural manners of the period from the decorative styles of Sir Robert Lorimer and Sir Robert Rowand Anderson towards more austere functional designs. He was an eclectic, not afraid of using different styles to suit the particular site or building type. Miller once claimed that 'the architecture of the exterior should be an expression of its character and purpose'. His office was successful in many competitions, mostly in Glasgow, but also in London and elsewhere in Scotland and England. His 'portfolio' included restoration of the 1456 Kirk of the Holy Rude in Stirling, the 'Chicago style' offices for the Commercial Bank of Scotland in West Nile Street, Glasgow, Glasgow Royal Infirmary and the English Revival style Kildonan house at Barrhill. In addition to residential and commercial work, he designed the Glasgow International Exhibition (1901), Olympic House (1903) on the corner of Queen Street and George Square, Glasgow, and interior designs for the Cunard steamer *Lusitania*. He was a modest man 'known to prefer to stand in the background, out of the limelight, when attending the opening ceremonies of buildings which he had designed' (Sloan and Murray). His office was at 15 Blythswood Square in Glasgow.

In 1933, by which time Miller was one of the Commissioners of the Royal Fine Art Commission for Scotland and a member of the Scottish Architectural Advisory Committee of the Department of Health for Scotland, he was joined by his son George. The practice was then renamed James Miller and Son. On James Miller's death, the practice was restructured as Miller and Manson and later renamed Frank Burnet Bell and partners.

Upper Greenock station was rebuilt in 1901-1902 as an island station with offices on the platform in ornate style to James Miller's designs. The station was entered through a stone arch where a small verandah carried the company name, up a flight of steps to the station above. The hipped canopies over the platforms were glazed, with a slated roof between. The valance was edged with fretted wooden planks typical of the period. The station stood till 5th June, 1967 when changed commuter demands and electrification saw it replaced by a new station at Branchton, two miles west.

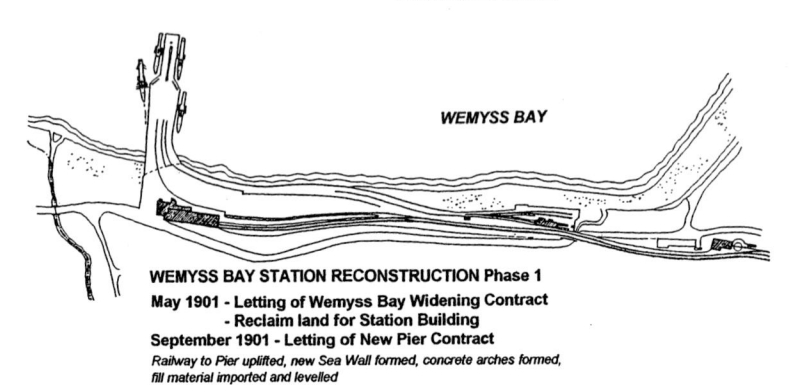

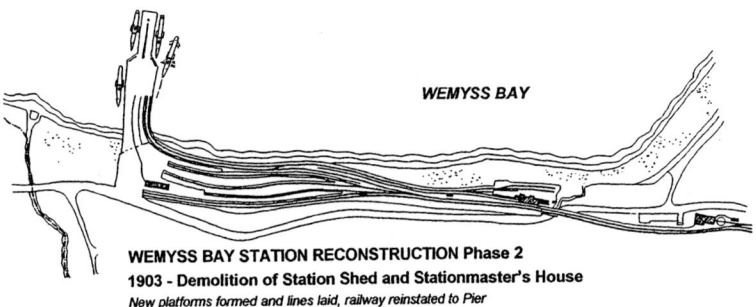

THE FIRTH OF CLYDE

WEMYSS BAY

WEMYSS BAY STATION RECONSTRUCTION Phase 1
May 1901 - Letting of Wemyss Bay Widening Contract
 - Reclaim land for Station Building
September 1901 - Letting of New Pier Contract
Railway to Pier uplifted, new Sea Wall formed, concrete arches formed, fill material imported and levelled

THE FIRTH OF CLYDE

WEMYSS BAY

WEMYSS BAY STATION RECONSTRUCTION Phase 2
1903 - Demolition of Station Shed and Stationmaster's House
New platforms formed and lines laid, railway reinstated to Pier

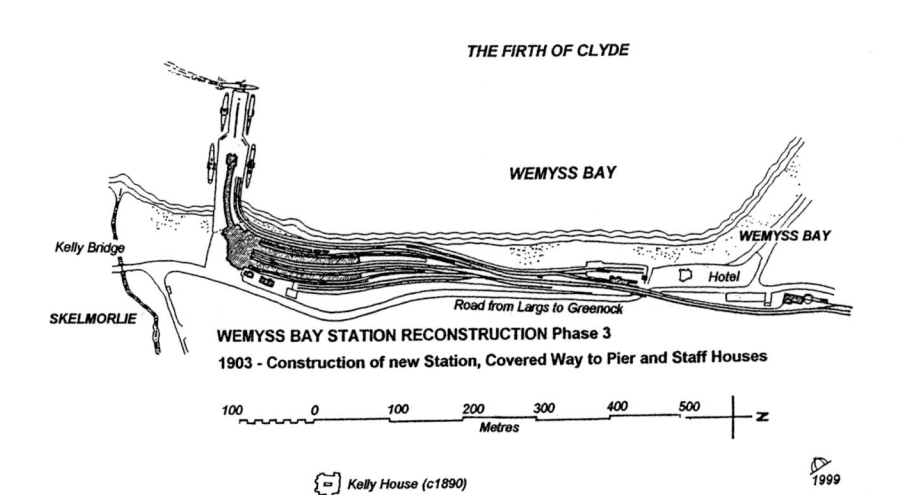

THE FIRTH OF CLYDE

WEMYSS BAY

Kelly Bridge

SKELMORLIE

WEMYSS BAY

Hotel

Road from Largs to Greenock

WEMYSS BAY STATION RECONSTRUCTION Phase 3
1903 - Construction of new Station, Covered Way to Pier and Staff Houses

Metres

Kelly House (c1890)

1999

THE SECOND WEMYSS BAY STATION AND OTHER WORKS

Wemyss Bay Line Widening Works Proceed

Preliminary Works

The widening of the line and the construction of the new (i.e. present) Wemyss Bay station was carried out over a 10-year period. The replacement of the station itself was complex involving simultaneous work by several contractors to a strict sequence:

1. Reclaim land on the seaward side and construct new station foundation walls (May 1901 - widening contract);
2. Construct the new pier (September 1901 - pier contract)
3. Demolish east wall and roof of station shed, station master's house and refreshment rooms (early 1903 - station contract);
4. Construct the western platforms and concourse (these were skewed allowing the old platforms to continue in use, the sinuous curves being aesthetically pleasing and providing more platform space) (May 1903 - station contract)
5. Demolish the old station and relay track on east side of new east island platform (about May 1903 - station and widening contracts)
6. Build the clock tower, adjacent buildings and new eastern platforms (October 1903 - station contract)
7. Construct the covered way on the pier (December 1903 - station contract)

Powers were sought in the 1894/95 Parliamentary session to extend Wemyss Bay pier. In June 1894, the Traffic Committee accepted Goodwin and Jardine's quotation of £707 10s. [*£37,000] for a three-arch bridge at Wemyss Bay Junction in Port Glasgow. In April 1895, the Caley authorised spending £2,800 [*£150,000] doubling the line between Wemyss Bay station and the engine shed plus some (presumably minor) improvements to the station platforms and £1,100 [*£60,000] forming a passing place at Dunrod. Part of this was probably 'enabling works' for the later major construction activity. A proposal to spend £4,700 [*£250,000] on a passing place at Upper Greenock was delayed 'meantime'. In July 1895, the Traffic Committee accepted Alexander Findlay's tender of £775 [*£42,000] to renew and widen a bridge over a public road - presumably that near Wemyss Bay engine shed. The same month, £300 [*£16,300] was authorised for installing train tablet telegraphs between Upper Greenock and Dunrod, between Dunrod and Inverkip and between Inverkip and Wemyss Bay Engine Shed signal box; this was later extended to Wemyss Bay station, the total cost coming to £374 [*£20,000]. In November 1895, the Traffic Committee authorised the relocation of the telegraph poles between Wemyss Bay Engine Shed and the station, at an estimated cost of £50 [*£2,700].

A start was made in April 1893 improving signalling at Wemyss Bay station by providing an electrical repeater (costing £8) to a home signal and transferring the Block and other telegraph apparatus from the old signal box to the new for £10. April 1896 saw £85 spent improving the signalling at Wemyss Bay with electrical repeaters and more signals and June the authorisation of £100 to install a cross-over road inside the station (total £203 -*£10,300). Some of this activity appears to relate to an Agreement between the trustees of the late Alexander Stephen of Kelly and the Caley to have the Wemyss Bay signal box moved north as part of a 'package' of measures drawn up to allow the Caley to enlarge Wemyss Bay station. (This Agreement was incorporated in the Caledonian Railway (General Powers) Act, 1899 and included with the Contract documents for the station rebuilding contract.)

The Caley Directors met on 31st August, 1897 to consider doubling the line and providing a new pier and station at Wemyss Bay. The minute confirmed the action to be taken:

> Approve the doubling of the Wemyss Bay line and enlarging pier, to be proceeded with gradually. Negotiations to be entered into with landowners and Board of Trade. Engineer to arrange for complete survey and submit to Board with the view of proceeding with the works. Doubling of railway from Upper Greenock to Wemyss Bay Junction and pier at Wemyss Bay to have first consideration for execution.

222 CALEY TO THE COAST

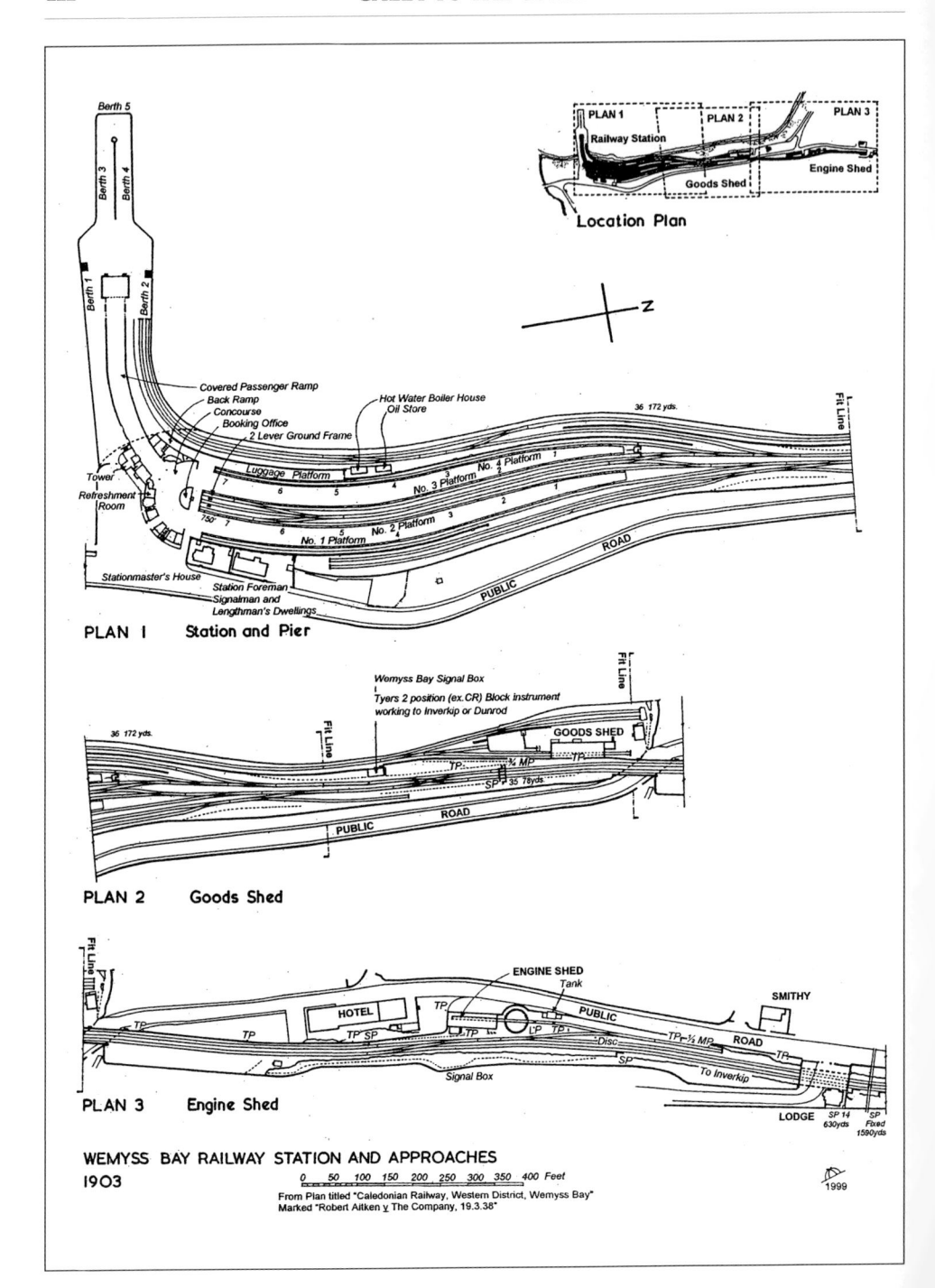

PLAN 1 Station and Pier

PLAN 2 Goods Shed

PLAN 3 Engine Shed

WEMYSS BAY RAILWAY STATION AND APPROACHES
1903

From Plan titled "Caledonian Railway, Western District, Wemyss Bay"
Marked "Robert Aitken v The Company, 19.3.38"

THE SECOND WEMYSS BAY STATION AND OTHER WORKS   223

Though plans were submitted and approved on 2nd November, 1897 for a new station and extended pier at Wemyss Bay, at an estimated cost of £50,000 [*£2.625m] (and quotations were instructed to be obtained), it was five years before the Board's instructions were matched by progress on the ground. The same meeting approved an £11,500 [*£600,000] proposal to alter Upper Greenock station. In May 1898, the Traffic Committee sought tenders for doubling the line at Upper Greenock but again there was a two-year delay before work proceeded. It is possible that the purchase of land from Sir Michael Shaw Stewart for level crossings, etc. may have postponed the commencement date, apart from the need to obtain Parliamentary approval.

In February 1899, the Traffic Committee approved installing gas lighting in the Wemyss Bay engine shed, estimated cost - £20 [*£1,000].

Extension of Wemyss Bay Pier and Wemyss Bay Line Widening Works

In November 1898, the Caley Directors approved the inclusion of further development of the Wemyss Bay line in a Bill to be presented to Parliament the following year. In April 1899, they agreed technical details with the widow of Alexander Stephen of Kelly and the Trustees of the Clyde Lighthouses in order to ease the passage of this, the Caledonian Railway (General Powers) Bill 1899, then being considered by the Parliamentary Bills Subcommittee. The Bill proposed doubling the Wemyss Bay line along its entire length. Subsequently, Clause 4 of the Caledonian Railway (General Powers) Act 1899, approved on 9th August, 1899, referred to 'A railway 10 miles 3.1 chains in length being a widening of the Company's Wemyss Bay Railway commencing by a junction with the Company's Greenock Railway at a point one hundred yards or thereabouts westwards from the centre of the bridge carrying the said Greenock Railway over Mary Street in Port Glasgow and terminating at a point forty-six yards or thereabouts northwards from the South West corner of the Company's station buildings at Wemyss Bay'. Without any reference to possible alterations to the station, it went on to permit '. . . An extension and enlargement of the Company's pier at Wemyss Bay commencing at a point thirty yards or thereabouts westwards from the South West corner of the Company's station buildings at Wemyss Bay and extending thence in a westerly direction to and terminating at a point two hundred yards or thereabouts from the point of commencement'. It is only by reading the schedule referred to in a short Clause (No. 12) in the Act, confirming the Agreement with the trustees of Alexander Stephen of Kelly, that one discovers that Wemyss Bay station is to be rebuilt. The Agreement included a reference to drainage from the Kelly estate to the Clyde (the 1993 restoration works revealed a large oval sewer well below platform level which may relate to this item), the free use by the owners of Kelly of the enlarged pier for their yacht and loading/unloading of household traffic (i.e. for the same traffic as before) and moving the Wemyss Bay signal box as far away from the station northwards as possible so as to be out of view of the Mansion House of Kelly. The owners of Kelly also received £1,000 [*£52,000] for ground acquired by the railway.

Clause 2 of the Act provided that the pier need not be kept open 'upon any days upon which trains shall not be run on the railways of the Company in connexion therewith'.

Because the Glasgow and South Western Railway was considering building a line to connect Greenock to Largs and thence by their recently opened line to Ardrossan, thus making Wemyss Bay less attractive to those destined for Millport and places further south, the Caley decided that as the proposed G&SWR route would bypass Wemyss Bay to join the Caley line at Dunrod for the four mile run to Upper Greenock station, they would keep *that* section single. This would prove to Parliament that while sufficient for the Wemyss Bay traffic, it could not cope with the additional G&SWR trains. (This commercial attitude may be compared with the Caley's pressing request to the G&WBR to extend its line to Largs in 1865.) Nevertheless, the bridges would be wide enough to double the track, even though they never

A view from the footbridge as McAlpine's 1901 contract for doubling the line at Upper Greenock station nears completion. Berryyards Sugar Refinery and sidings are to the north with the station pictured between two signal boxes. The line to the left connects with the steep uphill line to Overton. *National Railway Museum*

1901 and McAlpine's men prepare the formation for a new line and crossover east of Upper Greenock station after a spot of rain. The square chimneys of the Berryyards Sugar Refinery are visible in the distance. *National Railway Museum*

did. The Caley kept its options open, seeking extensions of time in 1904, 1907, 1909, 1913 and 1915 to double the line. According to the *Glasgow Herald* of 5th April, 1922, even after the Act for amalgamating the G&SWR with the Caley had been passed, they sought an extension of time for completing the doubling of the line between Greenock and Wemyss Bay. Only the two miles from Port Glasgow to just beyond Upper Greenock station and the four miles from Dunrod to Wemyss Bay were ever modified. I understand that arrangements for doubling the remaining sections were cancelled in 1928.

At a meeting in Westminster on 1st May, 1900, the Caley Board decided to advertise for tenders for the extension of the pier and widening of the railway from Port Glasgow up to and including Upper Greenock station. In typically cryptic fashion, the minute book states: 'Take in tenders'. The accounts book records payment of £33 7s. [*£1,700] in January 1900 - to James Gillespie of Rothesay - presumably for survey work associated with the pier.

The same month, the Traffic Committee appointed Thomas Stevenson and James Dunbar as inspectors to superintend the widening of the line from Port Glasgow to Upper Greenock and the driving of an additional tunnel at Cartsburn. (This was the one abandoned when the line was returned to single operation in 1967.) They would also supervise the work at Wemyss Bay pier. The wage - £3 per week [*£8,000p.a.]. As Mr Dunbar was momentarily unavailable, Samuel Smith would act as a temporary stand-in.

The Port Glasgow to Upper Greenock Widening

On 29th May, 1900, the Caley Board accepted a tender from Robert McAlpine and Sons of Glasgow for £42,241 16s. 4d. [*£2.15m] to widen the line between Port Glasgow and Upper Greenock. In July, the Traffic Committee approved changed access arrangements to Upper Greenock station recommended by Mr Matheson and allowed McAlpine to build a service railway alongside the proposed new line. In October, the Traffic and Permanent Way Committee 'loaned' McAlpine second-hand rails to lay a further mile of service line. The Wemyss Bay line was too heavily used to allow contractors to bring up materials between trains.

In September 1901, McAlpine claimed £1,500 from the retention monies, indicating the firm considered it had completed its contracted works, however Matheson disagreed and the Board paid £1,000 [*£50,000].

Part of the work was postponed. In November 1901, the permanent signal box at Upper Greenock was allowed to remain unfinished meantime, the signal cabin at the east end of the station being retained in use. A temporary signal cabin was to be fitted out at the west end of the platform. In December, McAlpine sought another £2,500, but was paid £1,500, the residue being paid in May 1902, which presumably covered the permanent signal box. The Wemyss Bay Junction to Upper Greenock section was duly opened as double track on 2nd June, 1902. The next four miles would remain single track.

The Pier

On 29th May, 1900, the Board also accepted an offer from Peter M. McBride of Port Glasgow to extend the Wemyss Bay Pier for £17,324 15s. 11d. [*£880,000]. Work started. Part of the new pier was to be double the width of the old, with piles of greenheart, an extremely strong and very heavy hardwood with proven durability in marine environments. It would be faced with elm, as a fender. Where the previous pier had been of constant width, the enlarged pier was wider at the shore so that viewed end on from the Firth, the bows of four vessels might be visible. This made for easier berthing, quicker departures and provided good crowd control.

George Pirie's contract included the building of the sea retaining wall and underbuilding for the new station. The photograph above shows the original station in use with formwork in place to create a concrete arch under the refreshment room. On the other side of the stone wall is the ramp from the old station down to the pier. Much of this wall probably still exists below ground level. The sea wall is visible on the right in the lower view. Considering the area available for the contractor to work in, reclaiming land from the Clyde and levelling out the site, there is an extraordinary amount of clutter with untidy stacks of timber and stone hampering movement of the cranes and the operation of the pumps. *(Both) Andrew F. Swan Collection*

CALEDONIAN RAILWAY

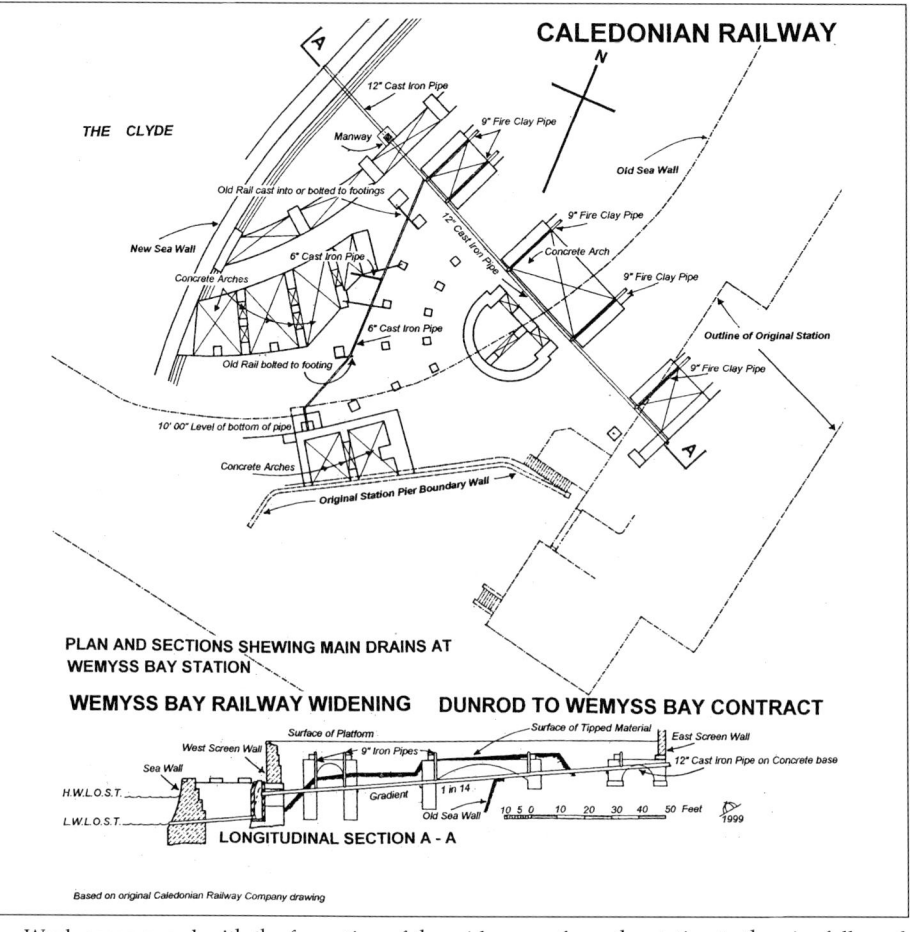

PLAN AND SECTIONS SHEWING MAIN DRAINS AT WEMYSS BAY STATION

WEMYSS BAY RAILWAY WIDENING — DUNROD TO WEMYSS BAY CONTRACT

LONGITUDINAL SECTION A - A

Based on original Caledonian Railway Company drawing

Work commenced with the formation of the wide ramp from the station to the pier followed by reconstruction of the pier, complete with central windbreak. The next we learn is that on 21st September, 1900, part of the pier was destroyed by fire (later pier alterations also suffered fire damage during reconstruction). According to the next day's *Glasgow Herald*, the contractor had deposited oil and other combustibles in a hut at the top of the pier. These had somehow become ignited. At 1.00 am, Mr Robison the station master woke to find the contractor's store ablaze. He called the Greenock and Largs fire brigades and roused his staff to save what they could. The firemen found that while there was an abundance of water, their hoses were too short. So the PS *Caledonia* was dispatched from Gourock with more hoses. When the fire had been quelled, it was found that McBride's portable engine and sawmill had fallen into the sea and two cranes had been partly destroyed. Damage was estimated between £12,000 and £15,000 [*£610,000 - £760,000]; the paper noted that it was covered by insurance. However, the Caley Minute Book records that £1,000 [*£50,000] had to be found (presumably an excess payment). This cost was equally shared between the Caley and McBride which may relate to the form of contract rather than implying that both parties shared responsibility for the fire developing. The damage was serious enough to cause Mr Matheson, Mr Anderson, and the Caley's district engineer and district superintendent, to visit the station next day and for an advertisement to be placed on the front page of the *Glasgow Herald* advising the public that the ferry service was back in operation only hours after the fire had been extinguished. More work was incurred due to minor damage caused just before the new year when the PS *Marchioness of Breadalbane* misjudged her approach.

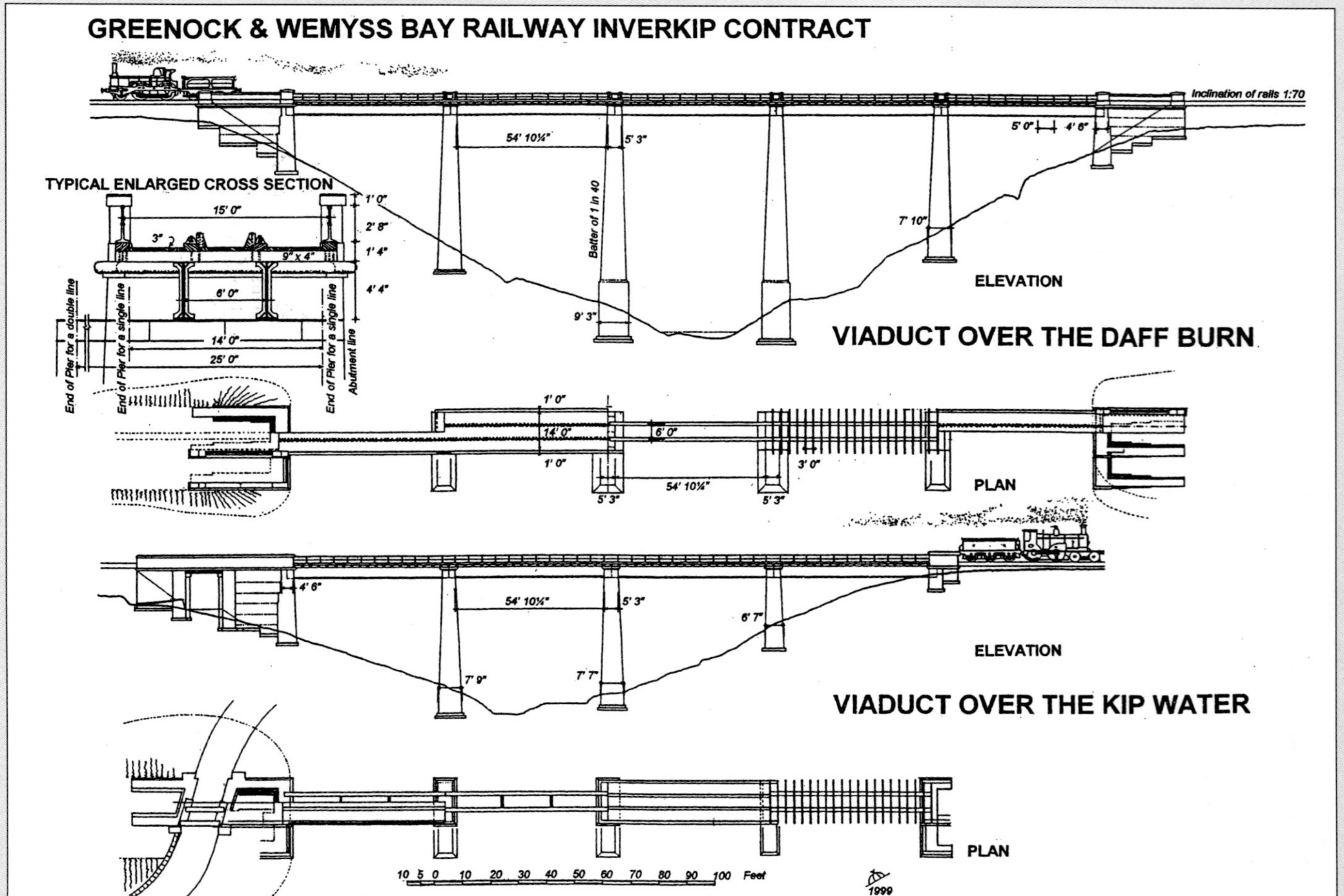

Redrawn from original contract drawings Nos.8 and 14 Ref. Nos.53:SC000234 and SC000235

Doubling the track at one of the Inverkip viaducts required new beams to placed on piers built under A. & K. McDonald's line doubling contract. Considering that there is a drop of up to 90 ft, the workforce seem remarkably relaxed about the need for any kind of safety precautions. *Andrew F. Swan Collection*

Like the original pier works, it seems that permanent lighting was only considered once the pier reconstruction was well under way. Matheson's lighting proposal to the Traffic Committee was approved in March 1901. In May, the Greenock Harbour Trust's tender for dredging the pier was accepted and in June 1901, the Traffic Committee authorised three gangways at £9 [*£460] each.

During the reconstruction, boats continued to deliver passengers and the Traffic Committee found it necessary to spend another £200 [*£10,000] on a temporary gangway - this must have been a substantial affair, possibly a lengthy walkway to reach the steamers while dredging was taking place. In September 1901, the Caley shareholders learnt that the Wemyss Bay pier extension had been completed.

In March 1903, Matheson reported that a sandbank was forming at the inner north berth of the pier, due to the construction activity. The Traffic Committee accepted that the area be dredged and instructed that the cost be borne by the contractor carrying out the Wemyss Bay widening works. Three months later, a similar problem arose at the inner south berth and Matheson instructed dredging at a cost of £200.

The Dunrod to Wemyss Bay Widening

At its meeting on 7th August, 1900, the Board considered Matheson's plans for a further widening - from Dunrod to Wemyss Bay - as well as enlarging Wemyss Bay station. Fortunately, it was not necessary to widen all the bridges as the overbridges had been built to suit double track. However the viaducts over the Rivers Kip and Daff needed doubling. The proposals were approved and Matheson was instructed to obtain quotations and on 1st October, 1900 the Caley advertised for tenders. The foundation walls for an enlarged station at Wemyss Bay, partly on land reclaimed from the foreshore, were included in this contract (but not the station itself) and had to be completed by 31st May, 1901. The whole works had to be finished by 31st May, 1902. The contractor was expected to convey as much as possible on the Caledonian's metals - the Caley was not going to be over generous: 'No clearance, weigh bills or free passes will be granted for materials, plant or persons, and the Contractor shall pay the ordinary rates, fares and charges . . .' He had to pay a toll for each wagon using

Wemyss Bay pier in the 1930s with Upper Skelmorlie village visible beyond the trees.
Crown Copyright - Royal Commission on the Ancient and Historical Monuments of Scotland

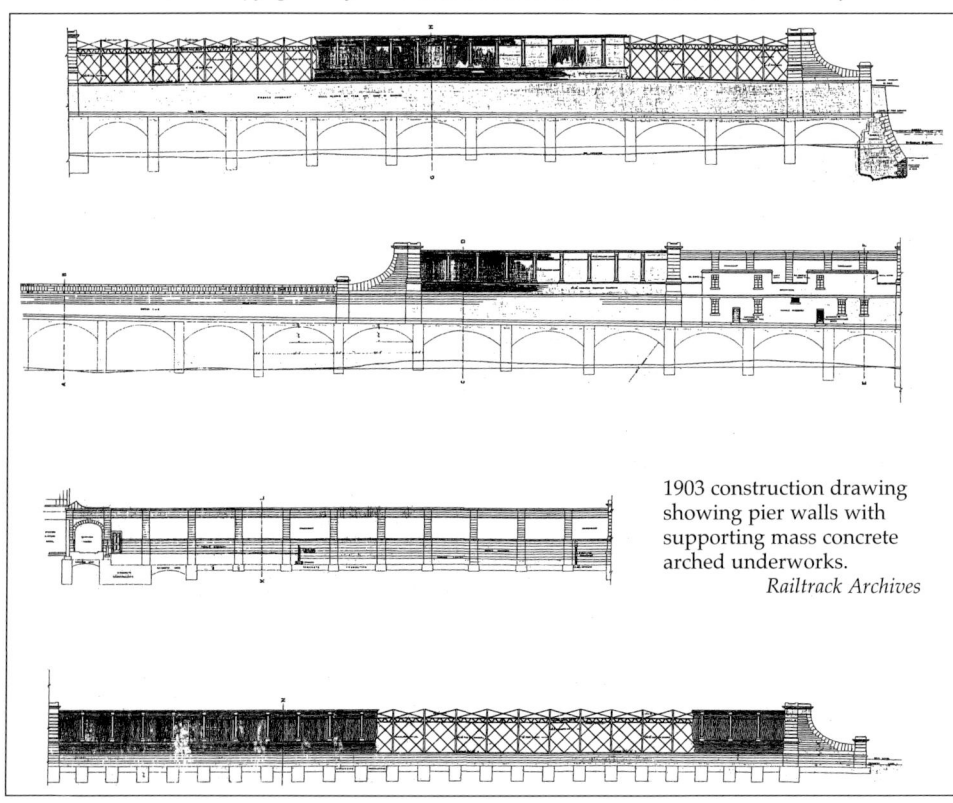

1903 construction drawing showing pier walls with supporting mass concrete arched underworks.
Railtrack Archives

the Company's line. The accommodation for the Caley's Resident Engineer was to be 'a neat and substantial brick and slated office, lined with wood, having two rooms..with fire places, fuel, water supply and lighting, provided with drawing tables, desks, stools, presses . . .' etc. (One assumes this would have been used for the station and pier contracts as well, possibly sited on the forecourt at Wemyss Bay station where it would be near to the railway and serve the later contracts. It could not have been on the site of the present station houses as the train shed was still *in situ* till early 1903. The station houses were actually built after the station was completed.) Renewing existing bridges and new station works was to be carried out at night or on Sundays and, because the foundations of the sea walls had to be constructed under water, skilled divers were required to lay concrete-filled jute bags, tightly abutting and inclined. Diving bells had to be available as well as a boat to allow the Resident Engineer and his Inspectors to examine the foundations and other works. The contractor's life was not going to be made too easy. However, as he had to retain the existing licensed premises on the site, he could always resort to the tavern at the end of the day.

As is usual in construction, the employer imposed conditions. The use and storage of explosives was specially mentioned: no blasting was permitted within half-an-hour of any train (effectively reducing the number of 'blasting opportunities' in the normal week day to four). A temporary line was to be built to avoid disrupting trains on the line, with connections at Dunrod, Inverkip, Kelly Quarry or Wemyss Bay. Where he was instructed to shift hoardings and plant to suit railway operations, he could not expect extra payment. He had to provide locomotives and qualified staff to run them. If it was necessary to go to arbitration, the case would be referred to Sir John Wolfe Barry KCB, FRS, CE or Mr Charles Forman CE (died 1901) 'notwithstanding that they are, or may be, and continue to be, holders of shares in the stock of the Company', a factor which one would have thought would automatically disqualify them.

The railway worked out in detail how the work was to be done and what provisions had to be made for its own staff - 'Allow for a spare set of diving apparatus and clothing.. for use of the Resident Engineer or Inspectors'.

George Pirie of Aberdeen was awarded the contract. According to J.F. McEwan, the accepted tender was £97,337 [*£4.95m]. In the first half of 1902 Pirie submitted a claim for additional payment. It seems surprising that, in May 1902, it ended up being discussed before Sir James Thompson (now the Caley Chairman) and five other Directors, the General Manager, the Chief Engineer, Secretary and Solicitor, Mr Pirie and his advisor. One assumes that all other efforts to settle the claim had failed. Pirie explained that there had been an increase in the price of the work, adding that the method proposed in the contract documents by the Caley's engineers to build the sea wall was impractical - indeed impossible. This seems to be confirmed in a *Glasgow Herald* article written two years later. Sir James would have none of it. He pointed out that Pirie's letter to the Board, written in September 1901, promised that the work would be pushed ahead vigorously to the satisfaction of the Caley's Engineer. The Board expected him to adhere to the specification. Pirie replied that he had no additional resources on which to draw and he was not prepared to borrow to complete the work. Sir James replied that in that case, he was sorry but the Caley would have to take the contract out of Pirie's hands. Perhaps the Caley found no-one else prepared to take the job on because after the meeting, Pirie set out his proposals for continuing the work. It appears that Pirie's claim was left 'on the file' while work continued. The shareholders were only told at their meeting in September 1902 that the work was 'continuing'.

In November 1902, presumably supervision was not to the Caley's liking as it insisted that Pirie appoint one or two engineers to work under its direction while being paid by him. Reading between the lines, Pirie's contract seems to have been less than straightforward as Sir John Wolfe Barry, who was currently involved as engineer on Glasgow Central station, acted as arbiter at one point.

Left: The south side of Inverkip tunnel after the second tunnel had been formed, with a supervisor standing in front of the pier erected after a landslip. Taken about 1903.
Andrew F. Swan Collection

Right: The southern end of Inverkip tunnel around 1903. Note the new tunnel on the right has been affected by a landslip and as a result the tunnel mouth is being extended. The precarious nature of the stonework, the trestle, the lack of lifting gear, scaffolding, temporary restraint or protective headgear, leaves one wondering whether construction safety was ever considered.
Andrew F. Swan Collection

Left: The east side of Inverkip tunnel with a new drift being formed for the second tunnel. This (new) tunnel is no longer in use. *Andrew F. Swan Collection*

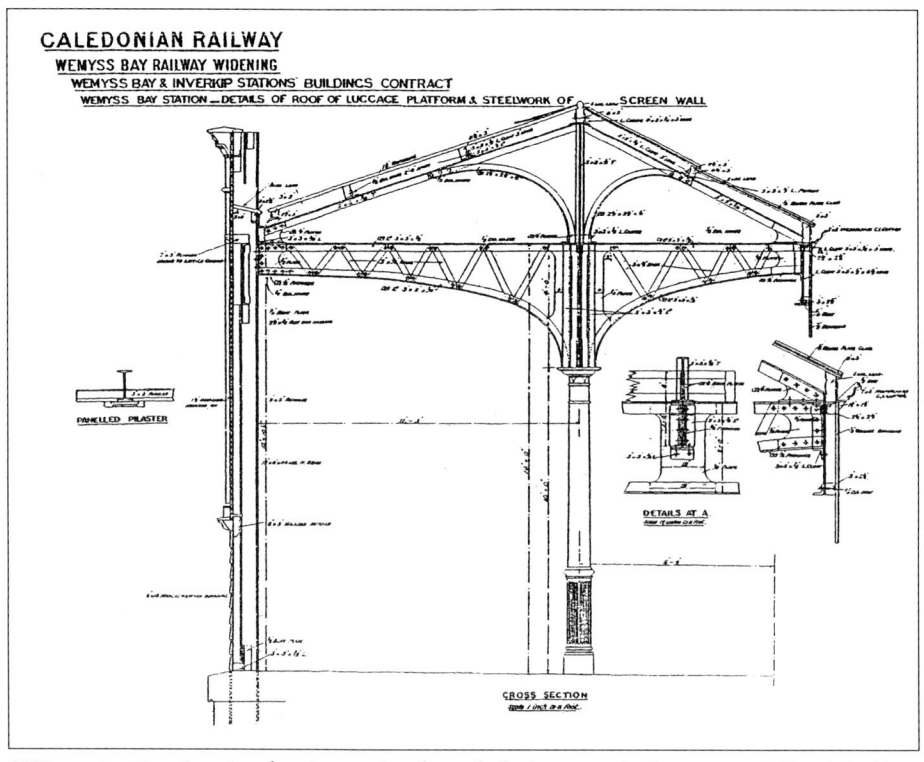

THE SECOND WEMYSS BAY STATION AND OTHER WORKS 233

1903 construction drawing showing section through the luggage platform. Railtrack Archives

The Dunrod to Wemyss Bay widening completed, the section opened on 1st June, 1903. An additional tunnel had been driven through the rock at Inverkip, but the west tunnel mouth, built flush with the existing entrance, had to be reconstructed further out and with heightened retaining walls due to a landslip. (This 'new' tunnel was abandoned when the line was singled in 1967.) The Finnock cutting was widened to suit the wider 'Coast Set' carriages then being built. *Engineering* noted (5th June, 1903) that the speed between Dunrod and Wemyss Bay was 'currently" restricted to 25 mph, indicating that work there was incomplete. In December 1903, the Traffic Committee instructed that Pirie's claim for additional monies be settled for a sum 'not exceeding £10,000'. A fortnight later, it was settled for £9,000 [*£445,000], a 9 per cent uplift on his tender indicating Pirie's claim was at least partly justified.

Wemyss Bay Station Building and Inverkip Station Replacement

With the Wemyss Bay line attracting so much custom, the Caley embarked on upgrading the terminal station. From a drawing signed 'Donald Matheson 1898', showing part of the front elevation, it is clear that much thought had already been applied to enlarging the station. The drawing, which presumably was actually prepared by James Miller, indicates that the concourse design had already been developed as buildings round a semi-circular space. The design is rather flowery - giving the station an 'overdressed' appearance. It is likely that the plan (which has not

CALEDONIAN RAILWAY.
WEMYSS-BAY STATION AND PIER EXTENSION

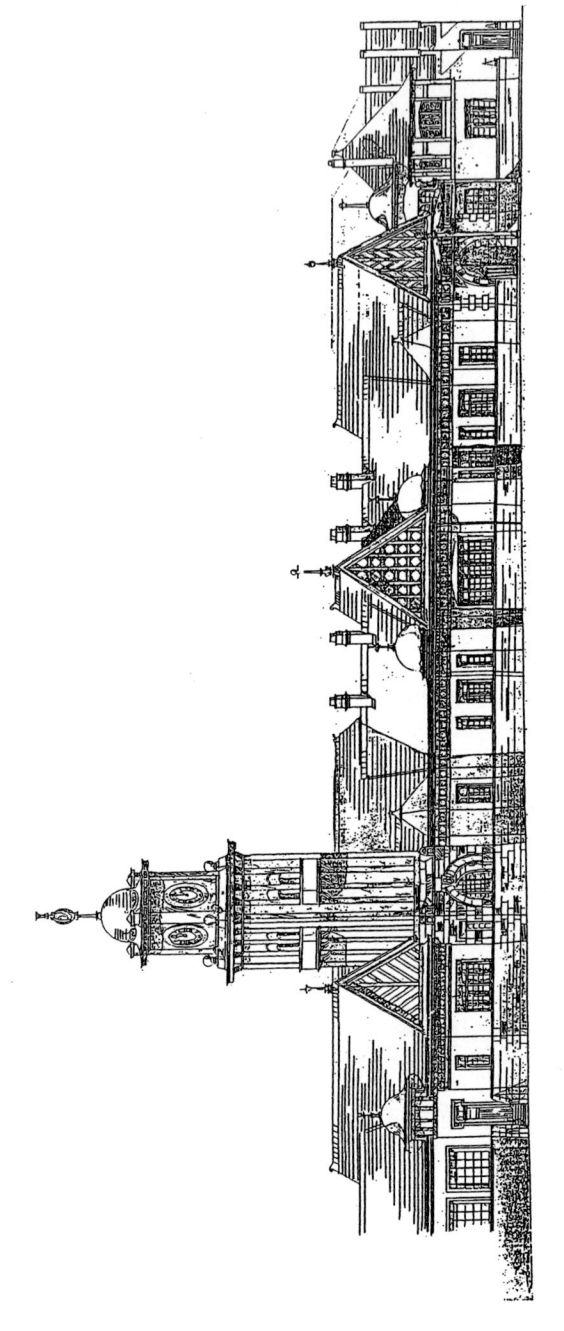

SOUTH ELEVATION OF STATION OFFICES

Donald Matheson
1898.

Drawing No. 2 showing the south elevation of the station offices in flamboyant style. Signed 'Donald Matheson 1898', drawn five years before the station was built.
Author's Collection

George Ferguson's Wemyss Bay station contract shows a cluttered site with the prefabricated painted steelwork miraculously rising through it all. The single planks no doubt used as walkways leaves one wondering what was regarded as an acceptable accident rate.   *Andrew F. Swan Collection*

survived) accompanying the elevation [*see illustration*] would show that the pedestrian flow patterns Matheson is attributed to have introduced five years later following his visit to the United States were already being employed in this design. It is also clear that drawings of the proposed station had been shown to affected local people as the widow and trustees of Alexander Stephen had approved plans for the enlarged station following earlier opposition.

On 21st October, 1902, the Traffic Committee, which was reduced to only two - Hugh Brown and Lord Newlands - with the General Manager and Engineer in attendance, discussed the drawings for Wemyss Bay Station. The new station required that a strip of land 100 to 120 feet wide, bounded by a substantial retaining wall, had to be reclaimed from the river to allow more platforms to be built. Part of this was in Pirie's Contract. The civil works required excavating down to bedrock which had to be terraced to form a flat foundation. On the lowest terrace, the sea wall was to be erected, 1,400 feet long and 16 feet wide, located using short lengths of steel rails inserted into pockets in the rock and backfilled with 8,300 cubic yards of 'selected rock' and spoil from the Finnock cutting, a mile back up the line. By curving the wall on plan, the force of the waves would be dissipated. The station itself would be supported on concrete arches built up off the rock foundation (described in the Bills of Quantities as 'Concrete with rubble in archways under platforms'), the piers for each arch supporting a pair of hollow cast-iron columns to provide a conduit for rainwater to the drainage system. Each column would be kept in place by 1¼ in. diameter bolts 10 ft 6 in. long, bolted through rails buried in the concrete.

Being responsible for so many of the Caley's stations and no doubt under instruction that they should have a distinctive 'Caledonian' appearance, James Miller repeated certain detailing from station to station. The windows might not be consistent in style in any one station but they could be seen elsewhere on the line. The base to dado level tended to be in stone or facing brick with timber panelling above, the roofs would be hipped and covered in red tiles and above the windows there tended to be a white painted frieze.

According to whom you read, the Wemyss Bay station buildings were constructed in Miller's 'Domestic Revival rustic style', 'Bold, muscular Tudor-revival' or 'Queen Anne' style. It had red sandstone footings, rough cast pseudo half-timbered walls above, the Italianate clocktower being clearly visible from many directions. Closer examination reveals that while

Looking down the pedestrian walkway to the pier at Wemyss Bay station, probably taken prior to 1910. The bookstall is operated by John Menzies and the central concourse flower arrangement, common on so many of these pictures, is missing. *Alan Brotchie Collection*

The concourse at Wemyss Bay station taken from near the head of the ramp down to the pier some time before 1910, where a porter makes light work of a lady's trunk. The central floral decoration in the concourse is missing and there appear to be trains standing at both platforms 3 and 4. *Alan Brotchie Collection*

Photograph showing a simplified Caledonian Railway crest carved in the lintol above the ladies' lavatories. *Author's Collection*

there is a similarity in style throughout, the station gables are not to the same pattern. At the main entrance, there was a canopy similar to one recently built at Upper Greenock station though this was not included on the construction elevation drawing. The wooden-sided covered way on the sloping ramp down to the pier ends was built with three arches flanked by a pair of stumpy 'Glasgow Movement' Japanese-style towers. The concourse, situated between pier and platforms, with its glazed curved fan-like roof, gave a sense of cheerful lightness quite different to the gloomy shed that it replaced.

The station was to become admired for its floral decorations round the semi-circular concourse - in pots round the walls, suspended in hanging baskets from the roof girders and in various exotic arrangements on the radiused concourse paving. In 1915, the *Glasgow Herald* reported that the station was among 20 winning 1st Class Premiums for the best kept stations on the Caledonian line. This continued under the Northern Division of the LMS which, in 1923, no doubt wishing to encourage a sense of identity in the much enlarged system, set aside £750 [*£19,000] for prizes for the best kept stations. Prize levels were graded and of the 270 prizewinners, Wemyss Bay station was among the most prominent.

The station houses were constructed in similar style. That nearest the station entrance was for the station master, the one due north being a tenement block housing (from south to north) the station foreman, the signalman and the lengthman (who maintained the track). In terms of architectural merit, the station and houses were later listed Category B, subsequently upgraded to Category A. In front of the station there was a spacious forecourt capable of receiving a large number of carriages and charabancs. This is now divided up to separate the ferry traffic from the railway's.

Although Wemyss Bay station and the station houses were designed by James Miller, the Caley Minute Book does not mention him and remarkably, neither is he mentioned in two detailed accounts of the new station in the *Glasgow Herald* (4th June, 1904) nor in an article in the *Railway Magazine* in 1905. Indeed in the latter, credit is given to Mr D.A. Matheson, 'the chief engineer of the Caledonian Railway [who] made all the plans'. But the Directors were obviously satisfied with the proposals as Matheson was instructed to advertise for tenders. There is also a reference to Sir John Wolfe Barry being involved in the Dunrod to Wemyss Bay, Wemyss Bay station and Port Glasgow to Upper Greenock Contracts in 1904.

To allow the works to be completed while still maintaining the station operational, Matheson advised the Glasgow Central Hotel Committee that the refreshment rooms should be closed for six months from the beginning of 1903. The Board decided that temporary refreshment rooms should not be provided during the closure.

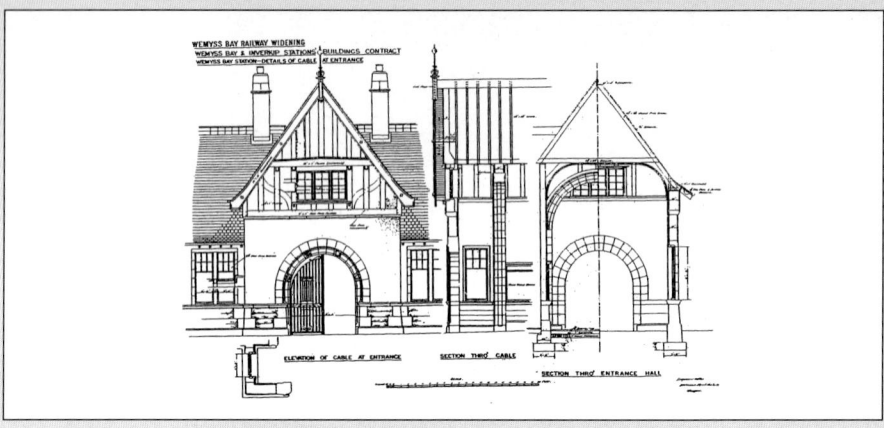

1903 construction drawing showing main entrance (without projecting canopy). *Railtrack Archives*

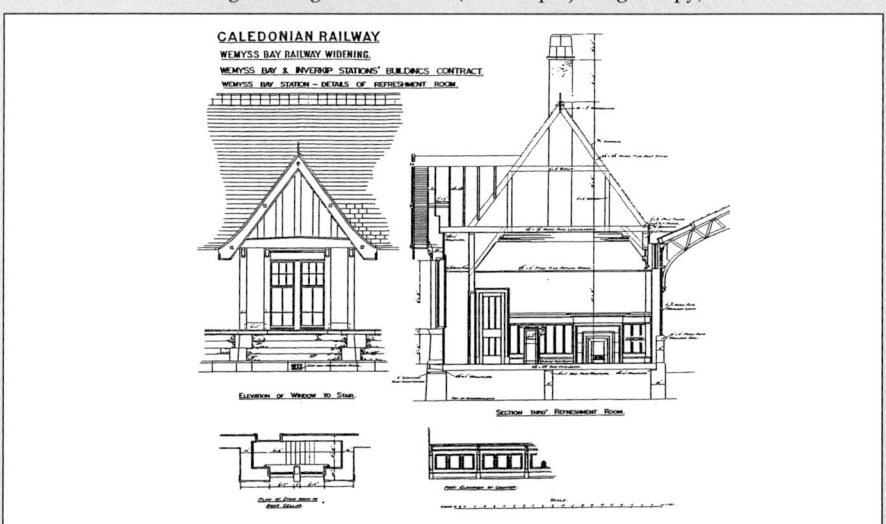

1903 construction drawing showing details of the 'refreshment room'. *Railtrack Archives*

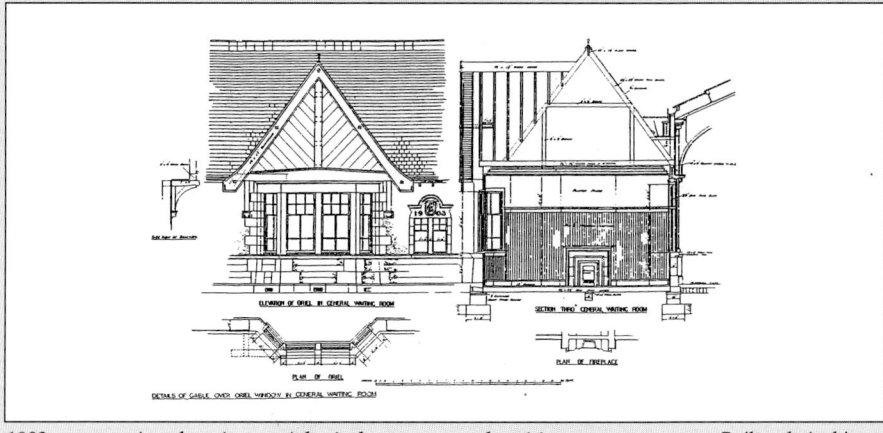

1903 construction drawing - oriel window to general waiting room. *Railtrack Archives*

The new Wemyss Bay station with gas lamp style fittings along the platform. On the north side of the pier is what appears to be the PS *Marchioness of Breadalbane* (1890) while on the other side of the pier and steaming away southwards are the two-funnel turbine steamers, the *King Edward* (1901) and the *Queen Alexandra* (1902).
Andrew F. Swan Collection

The approach to the new Wemyss Bay station taken on 12th August, 1904. The picture is taken from the signal box (note the points rods in the foreground). On the far left, two lines snake behind the east screen wall of the station. The island platforms are numbered 1 and 2 on the left with 3 and 4 on the right, the reversing line running down between the islands. The line serving Platform 4 also runs adjacent to the luggage platform inside the west screen wall. On the right of the 'up' line, a single track runs down and on to the pier, connecting with the goods line beside the sea wall.
Andrew F. Swan Collection

CALEDONIAN RAILWAY

WEMYSS BAY RAILWAY WIDENING

WEMYSS BAY & INVERKIP STATIONS' BUILDINGS CONTRACT

INVERKIP STATION.   PLANS, SECTIONS, & ELEVATIONS OF BUILDINGS

DRAWING Nº 32

OIL & COAL STORE

BUILDINGS ON UP LINE PLATFORM

ELEVATION TO ROAD

ELEVATION TO PLATFORM

PLAN

END ELEVATION

SECTION C-C

END ELEVATION

END ELEVATION

SECTION A-A

SECTION B-B

BUILDINGS ON DOWN LINE PLATFORM

ELEVATION TO ROAD

ELEVATION TO PLATFORM

PLAN

THE SECOND WEMYSS BAY STATION AND OTHER WORKS

Fairburn 2-6-4T No. 42243 pauses at Inverkip station in June 1960 on its way to Wemyss Bay. The down platform and its shelter disappeared with electrification and removal of the line on which the train is travelling. The signal box on the left and the yard have also been removed.

W.A.C. Smith

Inverkip station was considered by the Traffic Committee on 2nd December, 1902 when Matheson and Calthrop were instructed to obtain tenders for their rebuilding. Both Wemyss Bay and Inverkip were to be included in *one* contract.

On 13th December, 1902, tenders were invited for reconstructing both stations. The drawings were 'available to view' at the company Engineer's Office at Buchanan Street station in Glasgow and arrangements had been made to have an Assistant Engineer on site at Wemyss Bay Station on 23rd December to show contractors round and describe the proposals. On 27th January, 1903, (eight days after the advertised date) tenders were received for the building work and only three days later, *two* contracts were let - to George Ferguson & Sons of Glasgow for Wemyss Bay station and to John Miller & Company of Greenock for Inverkip Station. The tender for the latter was £5,138, [*£253,000] but the tendered cost for Wemyss Bay station has not been found. The other contractors concerned with the project included Alex Findlay & Co. of Motherwell (steelwork), George Barlas (masonry) and Messrs Mellowes, (patent glazing). The contracts fell under the authority of Mr Matheson as Engineer-in-Chief of the Caley, with Mr R.W. Gairns of Glasgow as Resident Engineer and Alexander Grant as Superintendent of Works.

The new Inverkip station was constructed generously with two platforms, each with its own offices and glazed canopies over the platforms. The entrance was approached up an open flight of steps under a pleasing sloping slate roof. Sadly, both buildings have been removed, the smaller one and its south platform being first. Similar features appeared in both Wemyss Bay and Inverkip stations - the valance fretwork, chimney stacks and glazed weather screens at the ends of the station buildings being the most obvious.

Wemyss Bay Station Rebuilding

In April 1903, the Traffic Committee was notified by the law agents of the late Alexander Stephen of Kelly that the houses being constructed on the east side of the station were being erected on their land. The matter was referred to the company solicitor. How it was resolved is unclear, but the houses were built. From personal experience of land tenure documentation at Wemyss Bay, it is quite possible the drawings showing land ownership were not precise.

In view of the complexity of the works, it is surprising to read in the minute book of the shareholders' meetings, that by September 1903, less than eight months from commencement, that Inverkip and Wemyss Bay stations 'will be finished shortly'. This was quite inaccurate as six months later, at the next meeting, they were told that 'the new station at Wemyss Bay is nearly complete, the two platforms on the west side having been opened for traffic, and it is expected that all the platforms will be in use by the end of April'. The probable explanation is that the September meeting recorded the imminent completion of the first phase work - the western platforms on the newly reclaimed land. These had to be built first to allow the train shed to be demolished.

A series of small works needed instructing - £75 [*£3,700] for the Wemyss Bay tower clock (the brass plate on the diminutive mechanism is dated 1904 - electrified in 1994), fitted with four 5 ft diameter opal dials 'suitable for illumination by gas or electricity' and £10 15s. [*£530] for a clock (believed to be double-sided) serving the booking office and the station concourse, both provided by Messrs Robert & William Sorley. Then there was £40 [*£2,000] for the piermaster's office, £20 [*£1,000] for a telephone link between the station platform and the Caledonian Steam Packet Co.'s pier and £50 [*£2,500] for accommodation for loading and unloading private carriages (which sounds like a forerunner of Motorail). In May 1904, Matheson and Calthrop's recommendation that the retaining wall be extended at a cost of £45 [*£2,200] was accepted.

So it was not till 1st August, 1904, that the Caley told its shareholders that the station was now 'completely open'. There remained a number of minor items, like the General Post Office pillar box on the kerb beside the carriage entrance to the station that had yet to be considered.

In December 1903, a few days before the new platforms at Wemyss Bay were opened to the public, Variorum reported in the *Greenock Telegraph & Clyde Shipping Gazette*:

> ... A correspondent writes to call attention to what he describes as 'the disgraceful condition of things' at Wemyss Bay Station and Pier. He complains that on arriving at Wemyss Bay Station one day in a drenching rain, passengers had to trudge through mud, water, etc. to the pierhead and there wait, exposed to all the inclemency of the weather, till the steamer arrived and was berthed, there being no shelter provided.'

I suspect a temporary route led through the old station into the new concourse space and that the covered way to the pier was framed up only, the roof glazing not due to commence till demolition of the old building was complete and the pier buildings formed.

Shortly after, on Monday 7th December, 1903, the paper gave the briefest announcement of the opening: '*Opening of New Station at Wemyss Bay* - The new pier station at Wemyss Bay, which has been constructed in consequence of the doubling of the line, was opened this morning by the departure of the eight o'clock train'.

The paper devoted more column inches to the case of Thomas Scullion who pled guilty to travelling between Paisley and Port Glasgow without a ticket. He was fined 7s. 6d. with £1 18s. 2d. expenses [*£110], or seven days' imprisonment. The paper paid almost as much attention to the forthcoming opening of the Caledonian Railway Station Hotel in Edinburgh on 21st December, 1903 as it did to Wemyss Bay station. Prosecution of a delinquent sells more papers than talking about new buildings.

In January 1904, the Caley Board resolved that the Wemyss Bay station refreshment room should be fitted out as a tea room and not licensed. Unnecessary expenditure was to be avoided. This might also have been an attempt to keep the drunks off the platform. The tearoom opened on Saturday 21st May, 1904.

THE SECOND WEMYSS BAY STATION AND OTHER WORKS

Messrs Williamson and Calthrop were convinced that the increase in traffic on the line justified an augmented service and persuaded the Caley Board to add a new train from Glasgow to Wemyss Bay at 11.30 am in July and August.

Two weeks later, on Saturday 4th June, 1904, the *Glasgow Herald* provided a plan and a detailed description of the new station, and what it had replaced. As a contemporary account of what substantially remains, it is worth repeating at length:

Wemyss Bay Line, Station and Pier Extensions

[The] Wemyss Bay section of the Caledonian Railway system, which has for over five years been in a state of transition, is now arrived at a perfected reconstruction, and is fully equipped and prepared for the rising tide of the summer traffic. The Directors of the company have not been letting the grass grow under their feet since the assimilation of the branch in 1893. Three years prior to this date the old Bridge Street terminus, which had subsisted since 1865, was numbered among the things of the past and the trains carried over the Clyde to the Central. Within the expiry of a reasonable period, and while yet weighted with the anxieties attaching to the enormous extensions and outlays on the city stations, the heads of departments were engrossed also with the problem of more adequately providing for the steadily increasing flow of passengers to the coast and of offering with these facilities a greater share of the comforts and conveniences that are now essential to all modes of travelling. The Gourock scheme of adaptation, when the preliminary obstacles had been overcome, was simplicity itself, and now after many years' experiences, pier and station, combined so deftly and so conveniently, may be regarded as almost beyond improvement. At Wemyss Bay, on the other hand, there were difficulties in the way that retarded the initiation of a new order. Directors, managers, and engineers were not less aware than the most observant of the public that the station buildings called out for demolition, or that the pier, while commodious enough in respect of more superficial uses came short of the standard of modern requirements. Had the plans that were in the minds of those gentlemen been capable without hindrance or objection of being at once proceeded with, we should today be looking upon a somewhat different formation of pier and railway terminus, however handsome, spacious, and convenient these undoubtedly are. It was the original aim, as at Gourock, to have the trains run alongside and parallel with the pier, so that the passage to and from the steamers might be rendered as short as possible. This aim was defeated through the failure of negotiations with a neighbouring proprietor [presumably Alexander Stephen of Kelly] with the result that passengers are asked to walk a hundred yards instead of twenty. No-one will feel overtaxed at this demand upon our exertions though doubtless there are some who refuse to regard any system of transit perfect that does not altogether dispense with physical expenditure. Having reached a determinate point in relation to the pier, that extension must proceed on the lines of the existing structure, the directors were enabled to lay the bones of the three-fold scheme in prospect - the doubling of the line between Port Glasgow Junction and Wemyss Bay, the rehabilitation of the stations at Upper Greenock, Inverkip, and Wemyss Bay, and the construction of a new and enlarged landing stage.

The Railway Line

Dealing first with the railway line, the ten miles of which the branch consists have hitherto been laid throughout with a single set of rails only. It need scarcely be said that the need for a double line was even more clamant than that for extended pier or station offices. In the height of the season, and especially during the congestion of the Fair week [the second two weeks in July], the traffic was greatly impeded owing to this limitation. There was not, however, an absolute necessity for laying a double line of rails over the entire section. It was enough, that the uninterrupted passage of trains down and up the line should be secured. To attain this end, over six miles of the ten have been laid down with an additional line, on the down side - from the western limit at Port Glasgow Junction to a point beyond Upper Greenock Station, and

Wemyss Bay station 1903 - general plan superimposed on 1865 station.

THE SECOND WEMYSS BAY STATION AND OTHER WORKS

again from Dunrod, to the west of Ravenscraig, on through Inverkip to Wemyss Bay. The work of excavation proved laborious, and was at portions beset with more than ordinary difficulties on account of the quantity of rock to be blasted and removed. This was particularly the case in connection with the Cartsburn and Inverkip tunnels, at both of which places hard material preponderated. The former tunnel is 380 yards in length, it is 17 feet 6 inches in its greatest width, and from centre to centre of the old and new tunnellings the space is 50 feet. The Inverkip Tunnel is 180 yards in length, and there is a distance of 40 feet between the centres of the old and the new. A few hundred yards to the east of Upper Greenock Station, and near to Wellington Bowling Green, a siding on an exceedingly steep gradient branches off to the Overton Paper Mill over which the trains are drawn by an engine of a specially powerful type. Several other sidings have been formed over the extent of the line, three of which - at Hole Farm, Finnockbog, and Dunrod - are for the convenience of farmers in the district. No great outlay was called for in the way of over-bridging, but two viaducts in the neighbourhood of Inverkip took money and time to complete. In each case the existing bridge was untouched and the new erected alongside with a considerable width from centre to centre. Kip Viaduct has had three new piers of 56 feet added, and Daff Viaduct four piers of 85 feet, the depth here from rail level to the stream below being 95 feet. These viaducts cross streams in a tract of very pretty country amongst the sights of which are the Roman Bridge [an old but not 'Roman' bridge over the Kip], Inverkip Glen, Lady Octavia's Drive, Ardgowan, and the Greenock water cut. The line is laid with rails weighing 90 lb. per lineal yard, and the permanent way is equal in quality to that of a main line.

Stations

The reconstruction and enlargement of the terminal station at Wemyss Bay was in itself a work of considerable magnitude. The old station had only two platforms and a comparatively modest station building with waiting room accommodation. The new station has four lines of rails for passenger traffic adjoining the four edges of two island platforms, each of which is 780 feet in length, with an average width of 34 feet. [What the writer did not mention was that the platform width increased towards the station concourse, reflecting the greater amount of space required for the greater volume of passengers approaching the circulation area simultaneously from the trains and from the boats.] Between the two main roads there is a third road to allow of the engine which brings the train into the station rounding the train to get to the other end. The platforms are protected for a length of 500 feet with glazed awnings of graceful design, and they terminate in a semi-circular concourse about 50 feet in width, and also covered with a glazed roof, similar to these over the platforms. The station waiting room and office accommodation is ranged round the outside of the semi-circular concourse, and consists of station master's room, first class waiting rooms for ladies and gentlemen, third class waiting room for ladies, tea-rooms, bookstall, lavatories, &c, the booking office forming the centre of the semi-circle. There is a covered passage 30 feet in width extending from the concourse to the pier so that passengers travelling to the coast by that route are practically under cover until they arrive at the gangway of the steamers. A feature of the new station is the luggage platform on the extreme west side, and away from the passenger platforms, at which it is proposed that the enormous quantities of luggage which are conveyed to the coast at the beginning and end of each month shall be dealt with without inconvenience to the passengers travelling by the same trains. The luggage platform gives access to the pier by means of an incline alongside the passenger incline, but separated from it by a wall. In front of the station there is a spacious forecourt for the accommodation of private carriages and other vehicles. To the external appearance of the station buildings special attention has been given, with the view to having it in keeping with the handsome private residences in the neighbourhood. The buildings have a red stone base extending to the level of the window cills, and above that level the walls are rough cast with half timber and rough cast gables. The clock tower, which can be seen from all directions, is about 60 feet in height. A house for the station master is in course of construction, as well as houses for other servants of the company, and the design of these is also receiving special attention in view of the prominent position which they will occupy.

1903 construction drawing showing typical platform section. Rainwater discharges down inside the cast-iron columns to pipework below platform level. *Railtrack Archives*

A crowded train arrives at platform 3 behind 0-6-0 No. 817, of the '812' class while a similar locomotive has arrived at platform 4 with a train which includes luggage vans. *Andrew F. Swan Collection*

At Upper Greenock, the station has been reconstructed in the form of an island platform, with access from the street by means of a subway passing under the up line and ascending to the platform by an easy stair.

The station at Inverkip has also been provided with elegant buildings, with all the essential offices, and will be found to meet all the requirements of the village and district.

Wemyss Bay Pier

With regard to Wemyss Bay Pier, that has been extended westwards and widened at the outer end, so that it is now capable of accommodating four river steamers at one time. Considerable difficulties were encountered in the construction of the seawall that was rendered necessary in connection with the extension of the pier and railway lines at Wemyss Bay Station. This wall has been built of freestone on ground reclaimed from the sea; it is laid upon rock, is 1400 feet long, 16 feet wide at the bottom, battered on the face, and shows a fine graceful profile.

Concurrent with the completion of this scheme of extension, the Caledonian Company has overhauled the time-table for the summer service of trains and steamers, which has been augmented and accelerated to the advantage of the public ... It may be noted here that special facilities are given for quick passages to all the principal ports on the firth, to Campbeltown, and to Lochfyne piers. There is also an excellent service of fast express trains to Glasgow in the afternoon and evening, the average time of running between the two points being about forty minutes.

Like almost all contracts, there was work to do after Practical Completion. In July 1904, the Caley's Traffic and Permanent Way Committee decided to spend £50 [*£2,500] getting the dredger *Caledonian* to deepen the berth at the pier. (The job was repeated in 1920 when, I understand, the *Caledonian* was brought through the Caledonian Canal to dredge the Forth and Clyde Canal at Bowling and also the Wemyss Bay pier.) In October 1904, Messrs Ferguson, the Wemyss Bay station contractor, sought and were paid £2,000 [*£98,500] out of the retained percentages. This suggests that the station buildings (but not the preparation works carried out by Pirie) cost at least £80,000 [*£3.95m].

Expenditure

Between 1898 and the end of 1907, the Caley spent over £267,000 [*about £13.5m] upgrading the Wemyss Bay line, adding signals and building Upper Greenock, Inverkip and Wemyss Bay stations. Some 2.15 per cent (£5,745 - *£290,000) of this related to land and compensation costs, and 97.58 per cent (£260,581 - *£13.1m) to construction and materials. The remainder covered legal charges. In 1898, expenditure was £635. This jumped to nearly £21,000 in 1900 (£2,850 on land purchase), rising in 1901 to £63,000, peaking at £87,500 in 1902 before falling in 1903 to £61,300 and in 1904 to £21,300 (approximations). The costs in 1905 were still significant as £1,500 [*£73,830] was paid out. About £9,000 was spent in the next 18 months, partly on land and compensation bills, the remainder probably relating to retentions held by the Caley pending making good defects.

Compensation had had to be paid for land purchase, temporary use of land and disturbance costs. The Finance Committee recorded in 1906 that Sir Michael Hugh Shaw Stewart was claiming £580 [*£30,500] compensation in lieu of restoration of spoil banks at Strone and Craigieknowes, plus £200 [*£10,500] 'for disturbance of game'.

Holiday traffic to the New Station

The new station was much admired. It is recorded that on Rothesay Whole Holiday, boat trains comprised up to 18 coaches. J.T. Lawrence writing in *The Railway Magazine* in 1905, gave a flavour of the times:

> Wemyss Bay is not a suburban residential resort. There are residents, it is true, but they are of the kind who live in castellated mansions, and are clothed in purple and fine linen, and who drive motor cars. Nor - outside the railway station - is there anyone at Wemyss Bay who wants to see the tripper. Probably the feeling is reciprocated, for Wemyss Bay is about the last place the ordinary tripper would think of spending a day in. There are no sands - no band - and very few houses of refreshment. Nine persons out of every ten probably who use the station know it only as the point of transfer from train to steamer.

The walk between train and steamer was only 100 yards 'mostly covered, and all downhill'. The station captivated the writer:

> The graceful curves of the ground plan, . . . the delicate tracery of the steelwork which carries the azure tinted roof of frosted glass, the impression of light and coolth, the semi-circular area bounded by the various offices, the luxurious and dainty tea rooms, the floral decorations, all in turn invite regard . . . Looking down the platforms we notice the suggestion of fan tracery in the spring from the capital of each pillar.

The writer noted that the pillars and the rest of the steel work was painted white 'and, owing to the absence of dust and smoke, they have a chance of remaining so'. There were 35 cream-painted brackets for flowers round the circulating area and more than 12 flower tubs on the floor. 'Mr Robison, the station master, is a horticulturist of no mean order, and takes personal charge of this department, and his own private garden is practically a nursery ground for the station'.

Lawrence noted the complete lack of advertisements. Only railway and steamboat advertisements were permitted. 'It may be possibly that pills and patent medicines are a superfluity in the tonic breezes of Wemyss Bay, but it is quite certain that the absence of such advertisements conduces much to the appearance of the station'. Some time later, an advertisement was painted on one of the cream panels above the bookstall advertising the Glenburn Hotel in Rothesay, but in 1905, only pictorial advertisements from the Caley and connecting railways were displayed. There were other typical station features - the weighing machine near the end of platforms 3 and 4, at the west of the concourse, John Menzies the newsagent's prolific display (continuing their presence from pre-reconstruction days), slatted timber seats with cast-iron ends, simple black and white projecting signs and sweetmeat dispensers.

Signs there were. Lawrence noted that 'the various caution boards which allude to the demeanour of the travelling public are in keeping with the high tone which prevails everywhere. Such notices usually terminate with stringent reference to the rigours of the law, and 40s. and costs. Here passengers' finer instincts are appealed to, and they are "respectfully requested" to do what, elsewhere, they have to be frightened into doing'.

The waiting rooms could only have catered for a fraction of the traffic. But as the train/boat connection was fairly swift, unless there was a delay, it is doubtful whether these rooms were much used. What the writer discreetly failed to mention was that there were few toilets. Gentlemen were well catered for, but first and third class ladies had a ludicrously small provision and the refreshment room (the pub) and the tearoom had nothing whatsoever - a problem when the train/boat connection was delayed. The tea-rooms were 'a powerful counter attraction to the delights of the waiting room'. The first class tea-room, between the general waiting room and the kitchen, was 'enamelled' in white. The second-class waiting room (probably the general waiting room), was painted green. Little basket tables covered with white tea-cloths, were adorned with 'expensive but fragile china ware, out of which ladies seem to prefer to drink their tea' while the sideboard was decorated with shining electro ware displaying 'expensive cakes and comfits'.

Near the head of the passenger ramp to the pier Lawrence found the porters' room, 'luxuriously furnished with easy chairs and couches. Truth, however, compels us to state that much of this furniture had a second-hand look about it. The walls were adorned with the prevailing mural decoration of the station, supplemented by information as to how the frequenters of the room might better their prospects by emigrating'. At the time Lawrence was writing, the semi-circular booking office incorporated a cloakroom and parcels depository as well as issuing (mostly) through tickets.

His comments on the passenger dock, that nearest the Clyde, are interesting but to date, I have seen no photograph or drawing to corroborate his comment that the 250 ft long by 18 ft wide platform had a wall 'pierced at regular intervals along its whole length'. During the 1993 restoration works, this brick and timber wall was dismantled and those working on or visiting the station commented on the splendid views across the river. Consideration was given to provide openings so that the view could be enjoyed - behind glass - but these could not be included in the 'restoration' works. Lawrence noted that the luggage vans were normally marshalled behind the engine so that passengers could descend on to the main platform while their luggage was simultaneously unloaded on to horse-drawn drays and vans on the luggage platform and hauled down to the steamers. The platform was decked in timber to prevent horses slipping, the arrangement allowing passengers to be routed separately to the steamers.

The 30 ft wide ramped passage to the pier was covered by a 'rough plate-glass roof' which followed the curve of the station, completed according to J.F. McEwan in May 1904. The Caledonian Steam Packet Company had its offices at the top of the passage, in accommodation now forming part of Pier House. Suspended from the roof, the hanging baskets of flowers (geraniums in summer) were supplemented by potted plants of some profusion, later mixed with the actual crests and photographs from the paddle boxes of two bygone paddle steamers, the *Caledonia* (1889-1933) and the *Marchioness of Lorne* (1891-c.1923) (the latter now in Caledonian MacBrayne's Gourock offices), and painted advertisements on the panels below the windows. The concourse leading to the ramp may have been devoid of such colourful distractions but the passage to the pier certainly was not.

Provision was made for some goods traffic. Just before the station, a line ran off seawards, connecting with another running back past the signal cabin to the goods shed. Both lines ran on to the pier, allowing coal and goods to be taken to the steamers. The operation of the pier was in the hands of Mr Melrose.

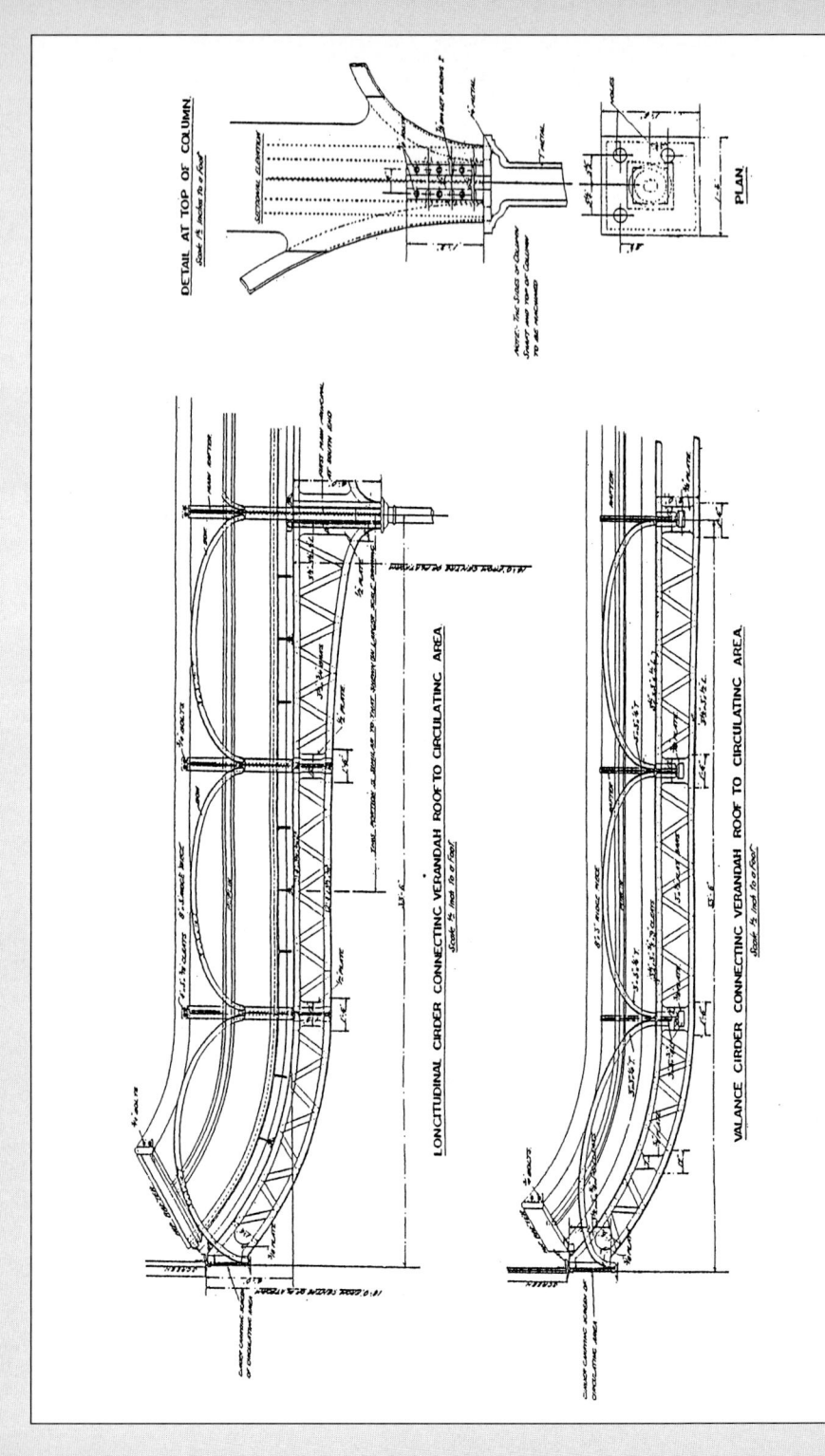

1903 construction drawing showing transitional trusses connecting the platform glazing to the Concourse structure. *Railtrack Archives*

But winter trade was not good. In October 1906, the Caley's Hotel and Refreshment Rooms Committee decided that as expenditure had far exceeded receipts in previous winter months, the tea room should be closed for the winter.

The construction of the 3-stall stable on the seaward side of the station beyond the luggage platform was only authorised in February 1909. Horses were not only used to haul drays loaded with luggage down the luggage platform on to the back ramp from the train to the steamer, they were also used for local deliveries. Whether these stables were used for any length of time is open to doubt as Mr Dallas, the coalman, is noted as stabling the station horses in 1925. Cattle and sheep were also unloaded on to the luggage platform and driven down the ramp to be herded on to boats for Rothesay.

In a few years, not only was there a profusion of plants inside, but ivy was allowed to extend up under the gables either side of the main entrance while the narrow strip of garden round about was covered with shrubs to the height of the window cills. The station has been described as 'Scotland's most beautiful station' and 'the jewel in Inverclyde's architectural crown'.

Traffic in the LMS Period

By 1926, 'Indicator' writing in the *Railway Magazine* could identify five types of traffic on the Clyde Coast lines:

Firstly, during summer there was a considerable amount of daily business travel between Clyde resorts and Paisley and Glasgow, involving inward journeys in the morning and return services in the late afternoon or early evening.
Secondly, there was a large amount of week-end traffic requiring outward services on Friday or Saturday afternoons, with provision for return on Monday mornings, frequently in time to commence business in Glasgow by about 10 am.
Thirdly, there was an extensive day-trip traffic outwards from Glasgow in the morning, returning in the evening.
Fourthly, there was general holiday traffic involving both inwards and outward journeys on Saturdays.
Fifthly, there was the month-end traffic, when whole households moved to or from their holiday homes.

Each summer weekday, one could leave Rothesay at 7.10 am and be in Glasgow by 8.50 am (100 minutes). The 4.30 pm from Glasgow (Central) enabled arrival at Rothesay by 6.00 pm, a travelling time of 90 minutes. On Monday mornings, to meet the requirements of week-end traffic, services were much amplified, boats from Rothesay at 6.45, 7.10 and 8.05 am to Wemyss Bay, giving arrivals in Glasgow before 10.00 am. In the opposite direction summer Saturday arrangements were even more generous. (During World War II, trains to Wemyss Bay were curtailed to seven each way on weekdays and one each way on Sundays.)

At some time the screen walls on the east and west sides were shuttered, except for the Luggage Platform area, filled with lightweight concrete and rendered. It has been suggested that this was done during World War II as a protection against blast damage which might have arisen due to the naval activity on the Clyde.

Photographs show that at the end of the LMS period the pier could still be mobbed with holidaymakers carrying small cases to the ferry. The division along the pier, which provided some shelter, still separated those going to Millport from those embarking for Rothesay. Even in 1956, despite spitting rain, cheery faces peeped out from under umbrellas as they made their way to the ferry berthed across the pier end. The pier master's octagonal hut, surmounted by a light and semaphore signals, reminds one of the racing days though the rail tank wagons show that oil had replaced coal for the ferries.

BR and Beyond

From about 1947 to 1970, goods containers containing luggage were loaded on to flat trucks or vans at Sighthill in Glasgow and off-loaded at the Wemyss Bay station luggage platform on to 5 ft x 8 ft wheeled flats. Twenty-one of these were daily hauled down to the pier and offloaded by a small mobile crane with metal wheels on to the boat for Rothesay. At one stage, there were 72 flats parked on platform 4 (the landward side platform).

In later years, the flats were wheeled round to the front of the station where a larger mobile crane off-loaded the containers on to lorries for local destinations or for Rothesay. This was a noisy operation, especially at night, and not surprisingly local people objected. A 5 ton static electric crane was then erected at the gap in the landward screen wall so that trucks could be emptied in the east yard area. The loss of rail-based goods traffic by 1993 saw Caledonian MacBrayne (CalMac) using a diesel tug to pull two or three flats from its office in the concourse down the passenger ramp to the boats.

In January 1965, the centre road between platforms 2 and 3 was still used, the semaphore signals at the platform ends still controlled from the signalbox at the throat of the station. Rails served both sides of the two island platforms and the carriage/goods yard behind the east screen wall. The valances at the platform edges were the original fretted pattern. In August 1966 the centre road was dismantled as dmus took over the line, still using both island platforms. Cars began to be parked on the east platform.

Electrification arrived in 1967 and with it the 3-car emus. The valances were trimmed. The back ramp from the luggage platform was still used and outside, an (unelectrified) track stopped at a pair of buffers on the pier.

The Caledonian Steam Packet Company kept its offices in the concourse until 1968, when the CalMac staff moved down to the pier end. The accommodation provided there was a mess room, toilets and waiting room. There they stayed till their offices were damaged by fire during renovation work on the pier. They then returned to the concourse.

The platforms were re-numbered in 1974. The west side of the east island became platform 1 while the west island was re-numbered 2 and 3, the luggage platform becoming a 'storage area'. The back ramp to the pier continued in use for parcel traffic and the pier provided five berths - 1 and 3 on the south side, 2 and 4 on the north side and 5 across the pier end.

In 1983, Strathclyde PTE, which contributed to the cost of running the transport network in its area, introduced its 'Strathclyde red' livery - in actuality, orange with a black stripe. I suspect, but have not been able to confirm that the stations along the line, possibly led by Wemyss Bay because of its significance and condition, were painted about the same time.

Between 1983 and 1987, the tracks to platforms 1 and 2 on the east island were lifted and the island itself became a car park.

Pier reconstruction and Clock Tower Restoration

The Wemyss Bay pier was the last on the Clyde to be modified to suit roll on-roll off provision. In recent years, the outer berths would take the *Maid of Skelmorlie* and *Sannox* and the inner the *Cowal* and *Arran* car ferries. It was shortened in 1977 reducing the number of berths available from five to two.

Once again, there was a serious pier fire during the works. It was easy to start a fire as rubbish jammed between the planks of the CalMac ramp could be set alight by dropped matches and cigarette ends. When Bairds were refurbishing the pier, a fire started in a contractor's hut on the pier, caused by clothes over a heater getting alight. As a result, the bottom of the pier was badly burnt. The fire brigade had difficulty extinguishing the blaze because of lack of pressure in the hydrants and they had to resort to seawater.

The 20-year-old *Glen Sannox* inaugurated the new facility on 20th May, 1977. It took two more years to complete the work, at a total cost of £220,000 [*£750,000].

Wemyss Bay station pier round about 1913 - Kelly House dominates the skyline to the left of the picture.
Alan Brotchie Collection

Autumn 1987 saw further major work when Lilley Construction shortened the pier. Temporary props had to be kept in place while work was done underneath creating new foundations, piling and reinstating the greenheart timbers. The result was that only the berth on the south side could be used for Caledonian MacBrayne's roll-on/roll-off ferries. The staging and the inclined platform on the north side of the pier, which allowed trucks laden with coal or vans with goods to be run up beside the steamers was demolished so that the back ramp from the luggage platform now terminates abruptly and incongruously at the sea wall.

In 1988 repairs were carried out on the clock tower. It was found that the steel joists supporting the clock platform had eroded to one-third of their thickness, from ¾ in. thick to ¼ in. In 1989, the clock tower restoration won a commendation from the Glasgow Institute of Architects, the jury expressing the hope 'that similar remedial work would be carried out to the rest of the 1903 station building'.

Some time prior to 1993, the platforms on the west and east sides respectively of the west island platform were renumbered Nos. 1 and 2, platform 3/4 continuing as a car park along most of its length, despite the lack of any edge protection. The most noticeable change in the use of the station accommodation was that Caledonian MacBrayne used spare accommodation in the concourse area for offices and incidental storage, its previous offices at the foot of the ramp being used as a waiting space and trolley park.

Wemyss Bay station concourse in BR days (probably in the 1960s) when hanging baskets and flower decorations could still be maintained.
Alex Boyd Collection

Fairbairn 2-6-4T No. 42241 in the Finnock Cutting travelling from Wemyss Bay to Inverkip in July 1960.
Hamish Stevenson Collection

Chapter Fifteen

From Caley Times to British Rail

Under the Railways Act of 1921 dated 19th August, 1921, ('An Act to provide for the reorganisation and further regulation of Railways and the discharge of liabilities arising in connection with the possession of Railways, and otherwise to amend the law relating to Railways . . .'), the London Midland and Scottish Railway Company emerged to take over the Caledonian Railway under the North Western, Midland and West Scottish Group Amalgamation Scheme. This was the third of four groupings covered by the Act, the others being the Southern Group, the Western Group, and the North Eastern, Eastern and East Scottish Group. Schemes had to be submitted to the Minister of Transport by 1st January, 1923 to enable implementation by 1st July, 1923.

At yet another time of transportation change and reorganisation we might note the purpose of the Act as described in Clause 1 with a sense of amusement: 'With a view to the reorganisation and more efficient and economical working of the railway system of Great Britain, [the] railways shall be formed into groups in accordance with the provisions of this Act, and the principal railway companies in each group shall be amalgamated, and other companies absorbed in manner provided by this Act'.

When British Railways took control of the station and pier, they did not anticipate there would be any change to the situation obtaining between the war years. 'The pier serves the main purpose of a railhead for passenger and goods traffic to and from Clyde coast places' says a note in the Railway Executive's brief history of the development of Scotland's lines. With electrification of the line, goods traffic has ceased and the railway now handles only a comparatively small passenger traffic. How times have changed!

The age of steam may have passed, but the memories linger, like smoke. We can imagine passenger trains hauled by Robert Sinclair's 1850s cabless 2-2-2s with their 7 ft drivers toiling up the 1 in 69 out of Wemyss Bay station, or pulled by the 1890 Drummond 5 ft 9 in. 4-4-0 'Coast Bogies' hooting their twin organ pipe whistles. Some may recall coastal expresses pulled by McIntosh's blue liveried 1900 period 0-6-0 '812' class with their whirling 5 ft driving wheels, or the heavy 1917 vintage Pickersgill 4-6-2Ts, the 'Wemyss Bay Pugs', thundering along the line. In more recent times, we might have seen Fowler, Stanier and Fairburn 2-6-4 tank engines in LMS red and black liveries and latterly the British Railways 2-6-4 '4MT' tank engines. Some of these, especially the tank engines, were used for goods as well as passenger traffic.

Since the line opened, coal trucks have been hauled to the steamers and fish vans collected from the quayside, pulled by a variety of early 0-6-0s, 2-4-0s, 0-4-2s, or by Drummond's ubiquitous blue and black liveried 5 ft 0-6-0 'Jumbos'. From LMS days the Hughes 'Crab', an unattractive but powerful 2-6-0 tender engine with 5 ft 6 in. driving wheels, and Stanier 6 ft 4-6-0 tender engines found their way to Wemyss Bay.

In the early years of the line, trainspotters would have observed an 0-4-2 or a 2-4-0 chugging along the Dunrod Quarry line, trailing a string of trucks under clouds of smoke, while at Upper Greenock Station, another Drummond product, the tiny 1890s class '611' 0-4-0 saddle tank, struggled up the 1 in 17 'puggie line' to Overton Paper Mills, pushing a couple of trucks.

Some, like Hugh Cantlay and Jim Clanaghan, remember driving the route. Hugh's career was complicated by the fact that when he joined in 1937, there had been two periods (in 1925 and 1935/6) when the LMS had not recruited new locomotive staff. Almost as soon as he began work at St. Rollox, he was laid off. He was re-employed and worked his way up, firing and driving on the footplate of express engines to Carlisle, Manchester and Crewe.

The motion of Fairburn 4MT 2-6-4T No. 42276 is closely inspected as sister tank engine No. 42246 lets off steam. The engines head the 8.25 and 8.30 pm. trains to Glasgow in August 1954.
W.A.C. Smith

Hughes 6P 2-6-0 'Crab' No. 42740 standing at Wemyss Bay station with the 2.15 pm to Glasgow in April 1960.
W.A.C. Smith

Jim joined the railway in the early 1940s and served it for 40 years. He began as an engine cleaner at Ladyburn engine shed in Greenock before qualifying in turn as a passed cleaner, fireman, passed fireman and then driver at the end of World War II. To become a 'passed cleaner', thereby qualifying for fireman's duties, the applicant had to sit a 2-day exam when he was tested on the Rule Book and how to carry out running repairs on the road. Normally, it took about five years from starting as a cleaner to becoming a passed fireman. There was more security for the more experienced - where redundancies were necessary, a driver might 'drop a stage' to fireman, and so on, so the least qualified tended to suffer most.

By 1945, locomotives were very run-down following lowered war time maintenance. Nevertheless, every 12 days, the engines were taken in for examination and a boilerwash. As the local water is soft, there was never a problem with pipes furring up. Occasionally, flue pipes would be replaced at Ladyburn, but more significant repairs would be carried out at St Rollox in Glasgow.

Drivers were responsible for ensuring their engines were properly lubricated. At the end of each shift, the driver would fill in a repair card advising the fitters of repairs needed, or steaming problems - these were usually attended to quickly.

Before a driver could take a train over a given route, he had to sign a card indicating he was familiar with the gradients and other features of the line. Tablet operation applied on the single track section between the west end of Upper Greenock station and Dunrod signal box, east of the doubled track. There were three watering points between Wemyss Bay and Glasgow Central: at the water tank near the turntable beside the road bridge north of Wemyss Bay station, at the east end of Upper Greenock station on the up line and at Bridge Street in Glasgow, on the south side of the Clyde from Glasgow Central.

At Wemyss Bay station, once the locomotives had pulled their trains into the middle platforms, numbered 2 (east side) and 3 (west side) (platform numbering being the reverse of 1990s numbering), the engines would be uncoupled and transferred to the middle road, the points being operated from a ground frame near the buffers. The points at the north end of this line were worked from the signal box on the sea wall outside the station. Tender engines were reversed up to the 45 ft turntable north of the road bridge near Wemyss Bay Hotel, the turntable being operated from the engine's vacuum brake pipe. Nearby was the water tank and a place where the fires could be cleaned. Such was the traffic that three locomotives once used to be stabled at Wemyss Bay engine shed.

Carriages were stored on two of the roads east of the station, just beyond the screen wall that encloses the station platforms. It was the duty of station staff to clean out the carriages in the station. While two tracks led down to the pier, only one ran on to it, allowing coal trucks to be taken down to the steamers. Engines were not allowed on to the wooden pier, so trucks had to be backed down the line, as at Gourock.

Locomotives for Wemyss Bay were shedded at Ladyburn and Princes Pier (on the old Glasgow and South Western line). There they would have their smokeboxes and grates cleaned out and be marshalled in order of use.

A typical shift would involve taking the 5.30 am freight from Port Glasgow goods yard to Wemyss Bay. This mostly comprised vans containing fruit and perishables for Wemyss Bay, Rothesay and for a time, Innellan. The vans would be left in the 'dock' platform at Wemyss Bay station while the engine went back up the line to be turned on the turntable, watered and have its fire cleaned over the ash pit. (The platelayers had to clean out the pit.) The engine would later back down into another platform and be coupled to the coaches for the 8.25 express to Glasgow Central, due there at 9.23 am. On reaching Glasgow, the engine would be uncoupled and reversed to Bridge Street where it would take on water, be turned and sent back into Central Station to take the 10.35 to Gourock, stopping at Bogston (just west of Port Glasgow and not a scheduled stop) to allow the crews to be changed. The old crew would then proceed to Ladyburn to sign off.

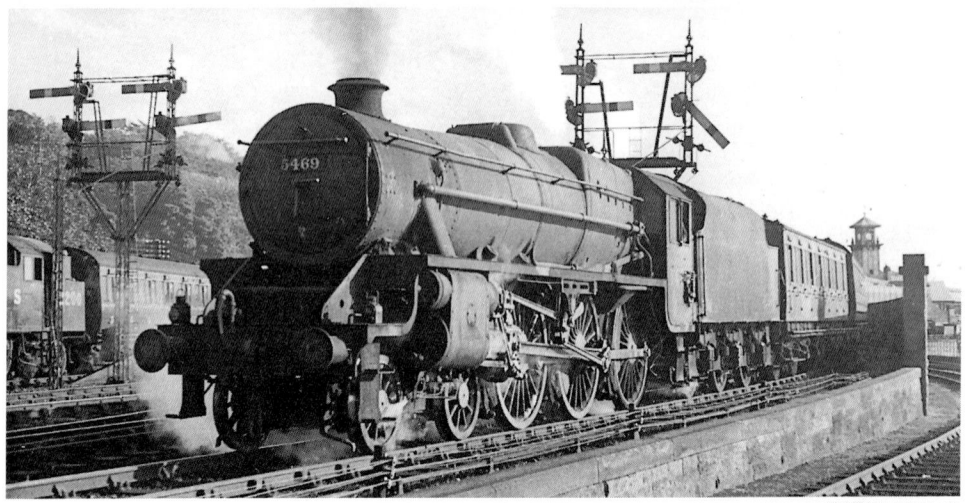

Above: Stanier 'Black 5' (5MT) 4-6-0 No. 5469 in LMS days, with an LMS period tank engine in the background, at Wemyss Bay in September 1946.
J.L. Stevenson Collection

Right: Pickersgill Wemyss Bay 'pug' in the carriage yard on the east side of Wemyss Bay station.
C.J.L.Romanes - Railway Magazine - 1931

The west end of the Ladyburn engine shed in Greenock in June 1963.
Hamish Stevenson Collection

The line was particularly busy during summer and Trades Holidays, especially during the Glasgow Fair. Eight coaches was the maximum size of train in steam days. These were of the normal suburban type - compartmented non-corridor stock with doors at each side. Hugh would do the 'summer short rest' turn. This involved taking an excursion train down from Glasgow to Wemyss Bay. There it stayed till it returned in the evening. Not being required to run the engine up and down the line, the crew could join their families for an outing on the beach.

Engine driver Dan Morris, was also Provost of Greenock. He would drive passenger trains until his favourite paper, the *Daily Herald*, came out, when his fireman would find that his share of the work running the train suddenly increased.

Skidding on autumn leaves is not a modern phenomenon affecting diesels and electric trains - steam locomotives had the same problems, though their greater adhesion weight gave them better grip. The train crew would take sand dried by a heater in the engine shed and pour it into the engine's sand boxes before setting out. The sand was ejected using steam but if the sanders did not work or conditions were sufficiently adverse, the driver had to scatter sand on the line ahead of the engine to get going. This was particularly important for the stiff climb up from Wemyss Bay station.

Hugh found the most economical setting was with the regulator fully open and a short cut-off (the smaller the cut-off, the less steam enters the cylinders). When taking trains up the steep grade out of Wemyss Bay, he managed with only 10 per cent cut-off. This saved water, but produced more vibration. One driver he fired for used half-regulator and 25 per cent cut-off which was less economical but gave a smoother ride.

Once Jim was delayed leaving Glasgow Central and had to make up lost time. His train, the 5.35 pm, was hauled by a tank engine. A friend of his, not a footplateman, cadged a lift from Paisley. Jim was in a hurry. The engine was a rough rider, but the first opportunity his much shaken friend got to leave the bucking engine was Port Glasgow, 13 miles on. On another occasion, his engine broke a connecting rod on the stiff climb up from Wemyss Bay Junction. Sometimes, drivers could manage on only one cylinder, but this was not possible on a steep gradient. The train had to be protected by detonators on the line behind while help was sought from the nearest signal box.

At one time Jim drove the smallest engines on the line - the diminutive 0-4-0 saddle tanks built in 1895. While used on the Overton Paper Mill branch, they also trundled through Greenock, delivering steel plates made at Dalmarnock. His little train of three or four flat trucks with its 27 ton engine would rumble down Carsdyke Street and Arthur Street to Victoria Harbour behind a policeman waving a red flag. There his load would be lifted on to a boat and conveyed to Belfast and the shipbuilding yards. These 'pugs' were draughty, rough-riding and carried so little coal that a small 4-wheeled wooden wagon had to be attached as a 'tender'. Numbers 56028-31 were stationed at Greenock. They frequently jumped the tracks, requiring outside assistance to re-rail them.

Two Johnson compound class 4-4-0 locomotives were stabled at Ladyburn, No. 41149 being one. These '4P' engines were introduced in 1924 and ran expresses on the west coast main line till the increasing weight of trains forced their retirement on to lesser duties. Jim recollected they would be started using the two outside high pressure cylinders before the centre (larger) low pressure cylinder was connected up. There was a knack in getting a successful changeover, but with all three cylinders working, the engines could show a fine turn of speed.

Jim drove 'Black Fives' (a numerous class of 2-cylinder 4-6-0 tender engine) and No. 46107 *Argyll and Sutherland Highlander*, which weighed nearly 140 tons. This was a 3-cylinder 4-6-0 tender engine of the 'Royal Scot' class shedded at Polmadie (Glasgow). These engines regularly hauled 15-coach expresses of over 400 tons on the West Coast main line. It was rebuilt in 1950 and withdrawn in 1962 after 35 years' service. Several of these engines ran over 2 million miles.

Photograph taken in August 1966 showing a dmu at platform 3 and the middle road being taken up as part of the rationalisation process prior to electrification of the line. Porters' trolleys are evident on platforms 1 and 2 while a tractor and trolley stand alongside the train. It seems that cars are beginning to be parked on platform 4.   *J.A.Vallance - Railway Magazine - August 1966*

Looking up the passenger ramp towards the concourse at Wemyss Bay station. On opposite sides in the foreground are the decorations that once adorned the paddle boxes of the PS *Lorne* and the PS *Caledonia*. The photograph possibly dates from the late 1930s.   *J.L. Stevenson Collection*

Two 1927 Fairbairn '4MT' 2-cylinder 2-6-4 tank locomotives, Nos. 42175 and 42176 were allocated to Greenock Ladyburn and Princes Pier. They had drop grates making Jim's job as fireman to driver David McNaughton much easier. They only carried 2,000 gallons so long delays could cause problems if an engine was 'caught short' between the watering points at Upper Greenock and Bridge Street. It was normally possible to travel from Greenock to Glasgow and back on one fill of water.

Glasgow Central station was electrified around 1961/62. At that time, Hugh went to Hyndeland to learn to drive electric trains. The changeover from steam to electric traction suited him as he was beginning to need glasses. Men who wore glasses could not drive steam engines though they were allowed to drive diesel or electric locomotives. He was the first of 60 Glasgow drivers to qualify to run electric trains. At that time no electric trains ran to Wemyss Bay or Largs.

Three weeks were allowed for training on diesels. Dmus were stabled at Gourock. In Jim's opinion, the removal of the 'second man' (formerly the fireman working his way up the promotion ladder) brought about after the changeover from steam to diesel, lost the railway a lot of good railwaymen. These were younger men than the drivers but with single manning there was no place for them in the cab. The railway therefore lost a generation of competent men with working knowledge, leaving a wide gap between experienced and novice drivers.

Six weeks was allowed for training on emus. In the event of failure, the driver cannot do anything, unlike the steam locomotive where there might be some prospect of keeping the engine going. Electric locomotives might have better acceleration than steam engines, but due to their light weight (the central motor car weighs 56 tons against the 86 tons of a '5MT' tank locomotive), their traction is not as good, especially on damp or greasy lines.

During the 1993/1994 alterations, I had several conversations with Frank Chandler who had retired as inspector (chargeman) at Wemyss Bay station in 1987 and Alex Boyd, a former CalMac employee. Frank lived in the Pier House flat, in the base of the clock tower, and Alex in the former signalman's house. They provided some of the more recent historical footnotes.

There has been a remarkable change in staff levels at Wemyss Bay station. Figures are only available for recent years but the 1966 staffing levels, when Frank came to Wemyss Bay, provide a clue to earlier arrangements. It was at that time that the positions of station master and pier master were discontinued when the previous incumbent, Bob Kinaird, retired to live in the station master's house. The new regime resulted in a downgrading with two inspectors appointed to look after both Wemyss Bay and Inverkip stations.

Nevertheless, in 1966, there were:

1 inspector for each shift (total 2);
1 foreman for each shift (total 2);
1 booking clerk on front, back and middle shifts (total 3);
1 ticket collector on each shift (total 2);
2 leading porters on each shift (total 4);
1 porter on each shift (total 2);
1 middle shift porter (total 1);
1 cleaner who looked after the station and four camping coaches - three on the foreshore and one at Inverkip.

There was also Dick Johnson, once gardener to Sir Hugh Fraser and then to Inverclyde District Council, who could be seen in porter's uniform tending the flowers which made the station so well known, as well as acting as car park attendant. The flowers won prizes for years, till staff reductions made it impossible to continue this feature. The total station staff on the middle shift was therefore 10.

On the pier were one foreman, two porters, a man to look after the queuing of cars for each vessel during each shift, plus five joiners who looked after the pier - total nine. Additional staff would be brought in to cope with holiday demands, so at a peak, over 20 staff would serve the trains and the boats. By 1993, this had been reduced to about seven, only two being employed per shift on the railway 'side'.

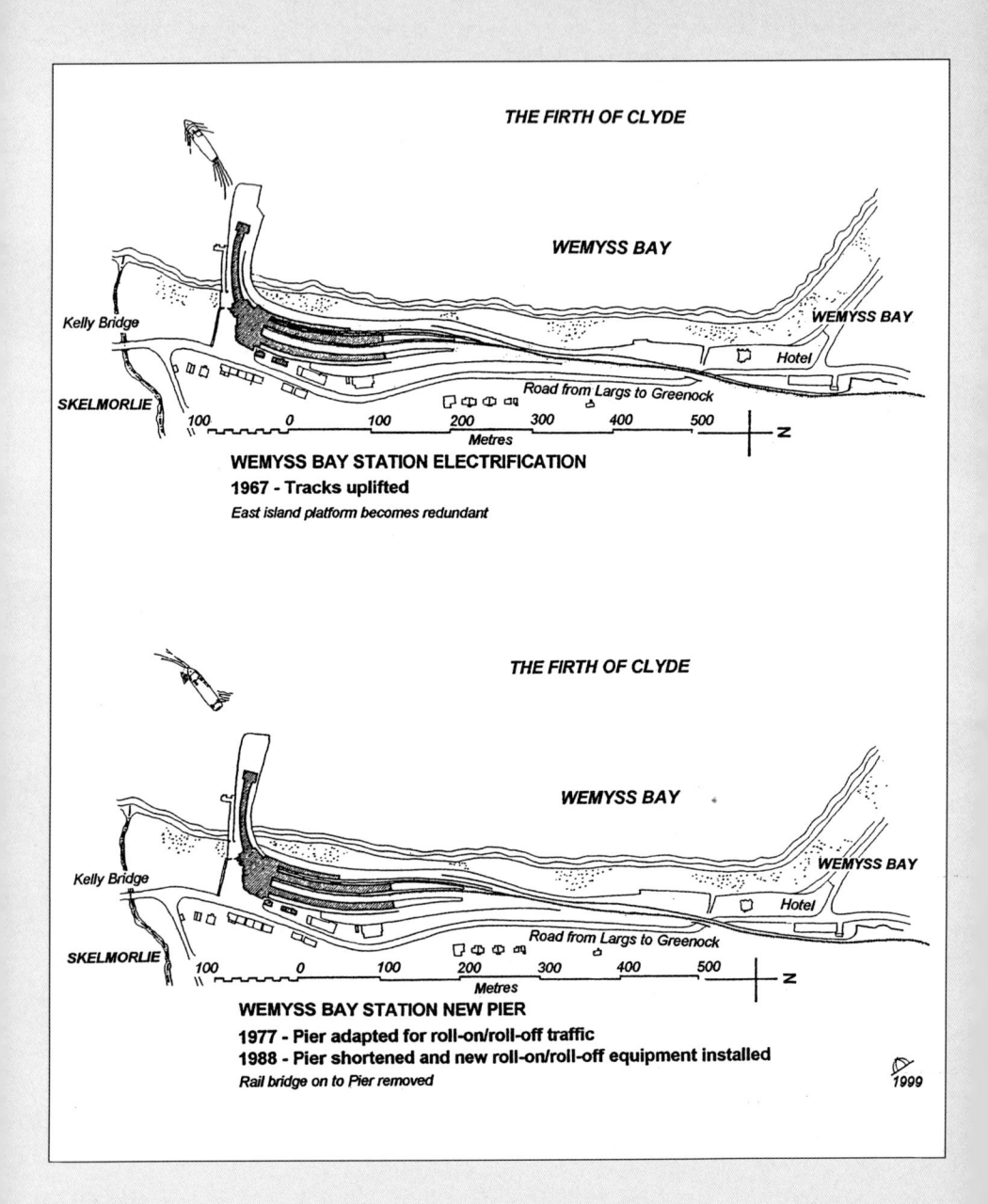

WEMYSS BAY STATION ELECTRIFICATION
1967 - Tracks uplifted
East island platform becomes redundant

WEMYSS BAY STATION NEW PIER
1977 - Pier adapted for roll-on/roll-off traffic
1988 - Pier shortened and new roll-on/roll-off equipment installed
Rail bridge on to Pier removed

In the 1960s, first dmus then 3-car emus took over the passenger traffic. Normally, the boat trains required 6-car sets. On Saturdays, especially during the Glasgow Fair or on Edinburgh or Fife holidays, trains would arrive with boatloads of people for Rothesay. The most popular boat was the 12 o'clock. On these occasions, up to five boats would be berthed and there would be huge queues as people scrambled between boat and train. These major holidays required 9-car train sets from Glasgow. One train would travel direct from Glasgow, another would stop only at Paisley Gilmour Street and a third would stop only at Paisley (Gilmour Street) and Port Glasgow. Up to 18 coaches might be needed to convey passengers. However, the brisk trade of the early 1960s fell away to the end of the decade.

Wemyss Bay used to have a station fire brigade with Frank as Firemaster assisted by six members of staff. Practices were held weekly. After the start of the electric trains, it was disbanded on safety grounds. (Electricity and water are a lethal combination!) Porters' duties included looking after the paraffin lamps in the signals. In the 1960s, trains were not cleaned by the Wemyss Bay station staff - that was done at Gourock. When a train came in, the porters would check for left luggage and only do incidental cleaning.

One of BR's standing rules was that drinking on duty was forbidden. On one occasion, Willie Miller, a porter of large proportions and a bit of a boozer, was spotted by Mr Angus, the Area Manager, coming out of the Station Bar, somewhat under the influence. He was lucky; Mr Angus took him for an Irishman celebrating his birthday and St Patrick's Day and let him off. It may have been St Patrick's Day, but Jimmy was no Irishman.

Pier House has two apartments plus kitchen and toilet on its two floors. It seems surprising, but in the 1960s, the only way to get a body wash was to drag out a tin bath. The access to the clock tower is by a 'ladder' of D-shaped cut-outs in a hidden panel in the upper room. These lead to a timber stair which climbs round the wall to the clock platform where the tiny mechanism rotates the hands on the four dials. Every week till the summer of 1993, Frank climbed the stairs to wind the clock. The clock was electrified just before Christmas 1993.

Alex Boyd came to Wemyss Bay in 1965 as a station foreman. He then became pier foreman. He continued under railway pay till 1968 when he joined Caledonian MacBrayne when they became 'independent' as CalMac. In the 1960s, the pier foreman's job was to ensure that passengers were in the right queues. At that time, the seaward end of the passenger ramp had three wide openings - the northern one for Millport on Great Cumbrae, the southern for Rothesay on the Isle of Bute and the centre one for passengers going from the boats to the trains. One of Alex's jobs was to ensure that the berthing lamp at the pier end was always lit - in stormy conditions, the wind sometimes blew it out. When there were strong winds, frail and elderly people found it impossible to make their way along the pier without assistance from his staff, especially after the 8 ft wall down the centre of the pier, a feature from the earliest days, was removed.

One of the last 'characters' at Wemyss Bay station retired shortly after the 1993 renovation work was completed. This was John Maher, a stocky little chap with a pleasant smiling countenance, white haired, a purposeful walk and possessed of a penetrating Irish brogue that could be heard above the rattle of machinery. Some 38 years previously, he came across from Ireland to work as a freight shunter at Greenock Regent Street before moving to Ladyburn and Gourock. Later he was promoted to freight guard and sometimes came down to Wemyss Bay on the freight from Ladyburn. There were two freight trains a day, one in the morning and one in the afternoon, with an empty return train in the late afternoon. Occasionally, he was guard on the passenger train from Port Glasgow - there were some short haul trains in steam days. In 1983 he was made a chargeman at Wemyss Bay, graded a 'ROG2SRP', which stands for 'Retail Operating Grade 2 Supervisor Personnel'.

John could be seen patrolling the concourse when he was not in his office, keeping a watchful eye on the people in the station, and passing the time of day with the other station users. Apart from dispensing tickets, his most obvious duties were as train starter and advising the public when the next train was due up to Glasgow.

June 1907 Weekdays — UP

Station	Goods	Exp. Pass.[1]	Exp. Pass.[2]	Exp. Pass.[2]	Exp. Pass.[1]	Exp. Pass.	Goods	Empty C'rgs	Exp. Pass.	Goods	Goods	Goods	Pass.	Exp. Pass.[3]	Exp. Pass.	Exp. Pass.[2]	Exp. Pass.	Pass.[5]	Exp. Pass.	Exp. Pass.[5]	Exp. Pass.[5]
Wemyss Bay	7.00 arr.	6.50	7.55	8.00	8.10	10.00	11.42	12.05 pm	1.00 pm	1.57	-	-	2.15 dep.	3.30	5.32	5.45	6.15	7.20 pm	7.23	7.35	7.50	9.50
Inverkip	-	6.57	-	(8.05)	8.17	10.07	11.49	-	-	2.03	-	-	-	3.37	(5.37)	5.52	-	7.27	7.30	7.42[7]	7.59	9.59
Dunrod	-	(7.00)	(8.03)	(8.09)	8.20	(10.10)	(11.53)	(12.16)	(1.09)	(2.06)	-	(2.40)	-	(3.40)	(5.40)	(5.55)	(6.23)	-	(7.34)	(7.45)	-	(10.03)
Ravenscraig	-	-	-	-	-	-	11.56	-	1.15	(2.08)	-	-	-	(3.43)	(5.45)	5.59[4]	-	-	7.37	7.49[7]	8.08	-
Upper Greenock	-	7.11	(8.09)	8.15	8.30	10.19	12.03	12.25	-	2.13	3.35 arr.	2.30 dep.	3.05	3.50	-	6.06	(6.31)	(7.37)	7.44	7.54[7]	8.16	10.15
Lower Greenock	-	-	-	-	-	-	-	-	-	-	-	-	-	3.50 arr.	-	-	-	-	-	-	-	-
Greenock Central	5.15 dep.	-	-	-	-	-	-	-	-	2.25 dep.	-	-	-	-	-	-	-	-	-	-	-	-
Greenock Ladyburn	-	-	-	-	-	-	-	-	-	-	-	2.50 arr.	-	-	-	-	-	-	-	-	-	-
Bogston	-	-	-	-	-	-	-	-	-	2.35	-	-	-	-	-	-	-	-	-	-	-	-
Wemyss Bay Jctn.	-	-	-	-	-	-	-	-	(2.18)	2.42	2.38	3.12	(3.55)	5.50	(6.11)	(6.36)	-	-	-	-	-	-
Port Glasgow	5.25	7.19	(8.13)	(8.19)	8.38	(10.24)	12.10	-	(1.22)	2.20	-	-	3.15	3.57	-	6.13	-	(7.44)	7.52	8.00[7]	8.22	10.25
Langbank	-	-	-	-	-	-	-	-	-	-	-	-	-	(4.04)	-	-	-	-	-	-	-	-
Bishopton	-	(MO)	(MO)	-	-	-	-	-	(SO)	(SO)	-	-	-	4.10	-	-	-	-	(SO)	(SX)	-	(SO)	(SO)
Houston	-	-	-	8.53	-	-	-	-	-	-	-	-	-	4.15 (SO)	-	-	-	-	-	-	-	-
Paisley St.James	-	•	-	-	-	-	-	-	-	→	-	-	-	-	-	-	-	-	•	-	-	-
Paisley Gilmore St.	-	8.42	8.32	(8.36)	9.00	10.40	12.28	-	(1.45)	2.40	-	-	-	4.22	6.05	6.32	6.54	8.01	-	8.19	8.44	10.47
Paisley (Goods)	-	-	-	-	-	-	-	-	-	-	-	-	-	-	-	-	-	-	-	-	-	-
Cardonald	-	-	-	-	-	-	-	-	-	-	-	-	-	-	-	-	-	-	-	-	-	-
Ibrox	-	-	-	-	-	-	-	-	-	-	-	-	-	-	-	-	-	-	-	-	-	-
Shields Junction	-	(7.51)	(8.40)	(8.43)	(9.07)	(10.48)	(12.36)	-	(1.57)	(2.49)	-	-	-	(4.32)	(6.14)	(6.40)	(7.02)	(8.09)	-	(8.28)	(8.52)	(10.56)
Pollokshields	-	(7.52)	(8.41)	(8.45)	9.11	10.52	12.39	-	-	(2.52)	-	-	-	4.34	6.18	6.43	7.06	(8.14)	-	8.32	8.57	(10.57)
Glasgow Central	-	7.55	8.43	8.48	9.14	10.55	12.43	-	2.02	2.56	-	-	-	4.38	6.21	6.46	7.09	8.17	-	8.36	9.00	11.00
Running Time	-	1.05	0.48	0.48	1.04	0.55	1.01	-	1.02	0.59	-	-	-	1.08	0.49	1.01	0.54	0.57	-	1.01	1.10	1.10

June 1907 Weekdays — DOWN

Station	E'pty C'ges	Goods	Exp. Pass.	Exp. Pass.[1]	Exp. Pass.[3]	Exp. Pass.	Exp. Pass.	Goods	Exp. Pass.	Exp. Pass.	Exp. Pass.	Exp. Pass.	Exp. Pass.	Exp. Pass.[1]	Exp. Pass.	Exp. Pass.	Pass.	Pass.[5]	Pass.[6]	Exp. Pass.[5]
Glasgow Central	-	-	7.50	9.00	9.45	10.30	11.45	-	12.42 pm	1.07	1.50	2.20	2.21	4.07	4.30	4.30	5.12	6.00	-	-	8.20
Pollokshields	4.30	-	7.53	9.03	-	10.33	(11.48)	-	12.46	(1.10)	1.54	2.24	(2.24)	4.11	(4.33)	4.33	-	(6.03)	-	-	8.24
Shields Junction	(4.33)	-	(7.54)	(9.04)	(9.48)	(10.34)	(11.49)	-	(12.48)	(1.11)	(1.55)	(2.25)	(2.26)	(4.12)	(4.34)	(4.35)	(5.16)	(6.04)	-	-	(8.25)
Ibrox	-	-	-	-	-	-	-	-	-	-	-	-	-	-	-	-	-	-	-	-	-
Cardonald	-	-	-	-	-	-	-	-	-	-	-	-	-	-	-	-	-	-	-	-	-
Paisley (Goods)	-	-	-	-	-	-	-	-	-	-	-	-	-	-	-	-	-	-	-	-	-
Paisley Gilmore St.	(4.50)	-	8.04	9.14	9.57	10.44	11.59	-	12.57	1.21	2.05	2.34	2.36	4.20	4.43	4.43	5.25	6.18	-	-	8.35
Paisley St.James	-	-	-	-	-	-	-	-	-	-	-	-	-	-	-	-	-	-	-	-	-
Houston	-	-	-	-	-	-	-	-	(SO)	(SX)	(SO)	-	(SO)	-	(Z)	(SX)	-	-	-	(SO)
Bishopton	(MO)	-	-	-	-	-	(SO)	-	(SO)	-	2.14	-	-	-	-	-	-	-	-	-	-
Langbank	-	-	-	-	-	-	-	-	-	-	2.22	-	-	-	-	-	-	-	-	-	-
Port Glasgow	(5.10)	5.50	8.23	(9.29)	10.13[9]	11.03	(12.15)	11.23	1.15	(1.37)	2.30	2.52	(2.54)	4.38	(4.59)	5.01	(5.40)	6.33	7.22	8.00	8.54
Wemyss Bay Jctn.	-	(5.53)	(8.24)	-	-	-	-	(11.25)	(1.17)	-	-	-	-	-	-	-	-	-	-	-	-
Bogston	-	-	-	-	-	-	-	-	-	-	-	-	-	-	-	-	-	-	-	-	-
Greenock Ladyburn	-	-	-	-	-	-	-	-	-	-	-	-	-	-	-	-	-	-	-	-	-
Greenock Central	-	-	-	-	-	-	-	-	-	-	-	-	-	-	-	-	-	-	-	-	-
Lower Greenock	-	5.15 dep.	-	-	-	-	-	10.05 dep.	-	-	-	-	-	-	-	-	-	-	-	-	-
Upper Greenock	(5.20)	6.22	(8.31)	9.33	10.20[8]	11.11	12.21[10]	12.35	1.24	(1.42)	2.39	-	-	-	-	-	-	-	-	-	-
Ravenscraig	-	6.32	-	-	-	11.17	-	12.50	(1.27)	-	(2.44)	(3.05)	-	-	-	-	-	(6.47) (SO)	7.34	8.12	-
Dunrod	5.28	6.40	(8.36)	-	(10.27)	(11.20)	(12.27)	12.58	(1.29)	(1.48)	(2.46)	(3.07)	(3.06)	-	(5.11)	(5.16)	(5.52)	(6.49)	(7.37)	(8.18)	(9.10)
Inverkip	-	6.48	8.42	-	-	11.25	-	1.05	1.35	(1.51)	2.54	(3.12)	(3.09)	(4.59)	-	5.21	-	6.53	7.42	(8.20)	9.15
Wemyss Bay	5.40	7.00 arr.	8.49	9.45	10.35	11.33	12.33	1.20 arr	1.42	1.57	3.00	3.19	3.15	5.05	5.17	5.27	6.00	7.00	7.50	8.28	9.23
Running Time	-	-	0.59	0.45	0.50	1.03	0.48	-	1.00	0.50	1.10	0.59	0.54	0.58	0.47	0.57	0.48	1.00	-	-	1.03

FOOTNOTES:
[1] Introduced on 3rd June 1907
[2] Prior to 3rd June 1907, this service took 10 minutes longer
[3] Commenced on 15th June 1907
[4] Ceases calling at Ravenscraig on 1st June 1907
[5] Commenced 1st. June 1907
[6] During May 1907 only
[7] Ran SO in May and daily in June 1907. Commencing Sat. 1st June 1907, only called at Paisley and Pollockshields on Saturdays.
[8] From Smithy Lye
[9] Does not carry pass. for Port Glasgow or Upper Greenock
[10] Does not carry passengers for Upper Greenock
[11] Does not carry passengers for Upper Greenock. Does not convey any luggage for the coast.

CODES:
MO — Runs on Mondays only
FO — Fridays only
SO — Runs on Saturdays only
SX — Does not run on Saturdays
ASX — Except Saturdays and Glasgow Public Holiday Mondays
Su — Sundays only
D — Calls at Ravenscraig when required to take up
Z — Available for Workmen's tickets daily

Timetable comparisons in the 20th century.

1993 UP

1993 UP	Weekdays													Miles
Wemyss Bay	7.10	7.36(ASX)	8.38	10.14	10.44		16.44	17.48	18.18	18.44	19.37		22.37	0
Inverkip	7.14	7.40	8.42	10.18	10.48	And at	16.48	17.52	18.22	18.48	19.41	And at	22.41	2.25
[Dunrod]	-	-	-	-	-	same	-	-	-	-	-	same	-	
IBM (authorised only)	7.22	7.45	8.47	10.26	10.53	minutes	16.53	18.00	18.30	18.53	19.46	minutes	22.46	
[Ravenscraig]	-	-	-	-	-	past the	-	-	-	-	-	past the	-	5.75
Branchton	7.24	7.48	8.50	10.28	10.56	hour,	16.56	18.03	18.33	18.56	19.49	hour,	22.49	
[Drumfrochar]	Station not yet built					every						every		
[Upper Greenock]	-	-	-	-	-	hour till:	-	-	-	-	-	hour till:	-	8
Whinhill	7.26	7.50	8.52	10.30	10.58		16.58	18.05	18.35	18.58	19.51		22.51	
Port Glasgow	7.33	7.57	8.59	10.37	11.05		17.05	18.12	18.45	19.05	19.58		22.58	10.75
Woodhall	7.36	-	-	-	11.07		17.07	18.14	18.47	19.07	20.00		23.00	
Langbank	7.40	-	-	-	11.11		17.11	18.18	18.51	19.11	20.04		23.04	14.75
Bishopton	7.45	8.06	9.08	10.46	11.17		17.17	18.24	18.57	19.17	20.10		23.10	18.75
[Houston/G'getown]	-	-	-	-	-		-	-	-	-	-		-	20.75
Paisley St James	7.50	-	-	-	11.22		17.22	18.29	19.02	19.22	20.15		23.15	23
Paisley Gilmore St.	7.54	8.16	9.16	10.54	11.25		17.25	18.32	19.05	19.25	20.18		23.18	23.75
Hillington West	7.58	8.20	-	-	11.29		17.29	18.36	19.09	19.29	20.22		23.22	
Hillington East	8.00	8.22	-	-	11.31		17.31	18.38	19.11	19.31	20.24		23.24	26.5
Cardonald	8.01	8.23	-	-	11.33		17.33	18.40	19.13	19.33	20.26		23.26	27.25
[Ibrox]	-	-	-	-	-		-	-	-	-	-		-	28.5
[Shields Road]	-	-	-	-	-		-	-	-	-	-		-	29.75
Glasgow Central	8.09	8.32	9.29	11.06	11.41		17.41	18.48	19.22	19.41	20.34		23.34	31
Running Time	0.59	0.56	0.51	0.52	0.57		0.57	1.00	1.04	0.57	0.57		0.57	

On Sundays, there were 12 up trains on an hourly service except for the last. The first train departed from Wemyss Bay at 9.20 hours and the last at 20.38 hours. The scheduled travelling time to Glasgow Central was 53 minutes, the first arriving at 10.13 hours.

1993 DOWN

1993 DOWN	Weekdays													Miles
Glasgow Central	6.03	6.35	7.35	8.37	9.35		16.35	17.15	17.40 (ASX)	18.35			22.35	0
[Shields Road]	-	-	-	-	-	And at	-	-	-	-	And at		-	1.25
[Ibrox]	-	-	-	-	-	same	-	-	-	-	same		-	2.5
Cardonald	-	6.42	7.42	8.44	9.42	minutes	16.42	17.22	17.47	18.42	minutes		22.42	3.75
Hillington East	6.11	6.44	7.44	8.46	9.44	past the	16.44	17.24	17.49	18.44	past the		22.44	4.5
Hillington West	6.13	6.46	7.46	8.48	9.46	hour,	16.46	-	17.51	18.46	hour,		22.46	
Paisley Gilmore St.	6.17	6.50	7.50	8.52	9.50	every	16.50	17.29	17.55	18.50	every		22.50	7.25
Paisley St.James	-	-	7.52	8.54	9.52	hour till:	16.52	-	17.57	18.52	hour till:		22.52	8
[Houston/G'getown]	-	-	-	-	-		-	-	-	-			-	10.25
Bishopton	6.23	6.56	7.57	8.59	9.57		16.57	17.35	18.02	18.57			22.57	12.25
Langbank	-	-	8.03	9.05	10.03		17.03	-	18.08	19.03			23.03	16.25
Woodhall	6.30	7.03	8.07	9.09	10.07		17.07	-	18.12	19.07			23.07	
Port Glasgow	6.33	7.06	8.09	9.11	10.09		17.09	17.44	18.14	19.09			23.09	20.25
Whinhill	6.36	7.09	8.12	9.14	10.12		17.12	17.47	18.17	19.12			23.12	
[Upper Greenock]	-	-	-	-	-		-	-	-	-			-	23
[Drumfrochar]	Station not yet built													
Branchton	6.42	7.15	8.18	9.20	10.18		17.18	17.53	18.23	19.18			23.18	
[Ravenscraig]	-	-	-	-	-		-	-	-	-			-	25.25
IBM (authorised only)	6.44	7.17	8.21	9.23	10.21		17.21	17.55	18.26	19.21			23.21	
[Dunrod]	-	-	-	-	-		-	-	-	-			-	
Inverkip	6.49	7.22	8.26	9.26	10.26		17.26	18.00	18.31	19.26			23.26	28.75
Wemyss Bay	6.56	7.29	8.32	9.34	10.32		17.32	18.07	18.37	19.32			23.32	31
Running Time	0.53	0.54	0.57	0.57	0.57		0.57	0.52	0.57	0.57			0.57	

On Sundays, there were 12 down trains on an hourly service. The first train departed from Glasgow Central at 8.20 hours and the last at 19.20 hours. The scheduled travelling time to Wemyss Bay was 51 minutes, the first arriving at 9.11 hours.

Timetable comparisons in the 20th century.

At various points round the concourse there were wooden seats with cast-iron ends, flower tubs, a luggage weighing machine, refuse bins, hanging flower baskets and flowers on ledges round the ticket office and the concourse perimeter (these last appearing on a very early photograph). There was also a central flower display over a green painted circle on the grano in the concourse. There were Cadbury's and Fry's chocolate machines as well as a Malcolm Campbell machine dispensing fruit pastilles. At the top of the ramp to the ferries, on the seaward end, was a drinking fountain.

On one occasion, a passenger, not knowing the station's famed displays, reputedly asked, 'What's on today, mister?' On the other hand, a pair of German tourists made a detour to visit the station in the early 1990s - and were disappointed to see no flowers. Such was their pride in the station that plants were provided by the station staff from their own gardens and from the glasshouse in the garden of the station master's house next door. Dick Johnson was well-known in the 1950s-80s for his gardening skills and produced splendid displays to fill the concourse area. From about 1968 to 1988, there was a glass house within the station concourse, alongside the gentlemen's toilet. The glasshouse was subsequently dismantled and reassembled by an hotelier in Rothesay. Its foundations were only finally removed in 1994. At Christmas time, Lord Inverclyde used to donate a Christmas tree which was sited between the Station Bar and the ladies' waiting room.

The ramp down to the steamers was flanked by potted plants between which could be seen the crests from the paddleboxes of two former paddle-steamers, with pictures of the boats themselves. Throughout the station and at the head of the ramp, were it the property of the Caledonian Railway, the LMS, British Rail or ScotRail, there were posters or station information on framed notice boards.

Wemyss Bay concourse around the time of electrification. The middle road has disappeared, the valances have had their decorative fretwork removed, platform 3 has been renumbered platform 1, a railing (which did not seem to last many years) has been erected and cars are now parked at the end of what had been platform 4.

Crown Copyright - Royal Commission on the Ancient and Historical Monuments of Scotland

Chapter Sixteen

Restoring Wemyss Bay Station

Late in November 1992, my firm, Reiach and Hall, was invited to prepare documents for restoring Wemyss Bay station. Five months previously, we had carried out feasibility studies for revitalising the whole station or alternatively for a partial restoration which would have seen the demolition of much of the outer platform canopies and part of the east and west screen walls. Historic Scotland insisted that the whole Category A listed building be restored. ScotRail then set about arranging the necessary finance. I was asked to take charge as Project Architect under Bob Steel as Partner in Charge. The timing was propitious, as I had just completed a two-year stint as Resident Architect on a central Edinburgh office block.

My colleague Bill Sutherland introduced me to the station and for the first time, I discovered what a gem it was. The day was sunny and bright, the Clyde sparkled and the occasional train discharged its passengers to the waiting ferry. The only difficulty was it took two hours to get there - and two hours back! That day, we met Tommy Thomson our ScotRail 'client', Richard Gardner, our Civil Engineer, and the Quantity Surveyor, Nigel Walker of Davis Langdon and Everest.

Bill had done a lot of spade work, acquired copies of the original Caley drawings and was already progressing the specifications. Assisted by Andy Law and George Douglas, we set to work in earnest, as yet uncertain of the scope of the project. The surveyor and I walked along the lead and cast iron gutters as far as we could, carefully going where only thieves and temporary roof repairers had gone before, to find that almost all the lead had been stripped off and that the glazing was in sore need of replacement.

The weather was not always kind and it was soon obvious why the station needed so much attention. On one occasion, the fierceness of the bitter snow-laden blast at the seaward end of the luggage platform forced us to change our survey plans. I had arranged for a ScotRail PICOW (Person in Charge of Work) to conduct me across the tracks so that I could identify areas of stone on the seaward wall needing replacing. When we got there, it was impossible to record anything on paper. The waves crashed against the sea wall, sending spray over the old low level track, and us. It was bitterly cold and the wind was gale force. However, I got enough to put down on a drawing. I chipped away some old mortar and removed a flake of stone so that we could find a match. That night, my train to Edinburgh was an hour late and the roads so slippery that few buses on my route were running.

Our notional budget was reduced to £750,000, then to £610,000 - creating uncertainty as to whether the project would actually proceed. But on 23rd December, just as the office closed for a fortnight's holiday, Tommy Thomson rang to say the *full* restoration scheme would go ahead - on a budget of £1.2m!

January 1993. A shortened break was followed by hectic work getting drawings and specifications prepared and cost checked, contractors selected, tender documents out and a contractor appointed to allow work to start early in March 1993. My train trips to Wemyss Bay were spent writing and checking piles of contract documents. In the lull while contractors prepared their tenders, I did some research, conscious that in our haste, we might have overlooked something important. That is how this story came to be written and how I found there had been an earlier station. The reason for inconsistencies became clearer, for example why fretted valances in one corner of the station contrasted with the cropped valances along the platform edges, cut at the time of electrification.

February 1993. Even as tenders were being obtained, the budget was reduced as monies were allocated for light fittings and other ScotRail works. We learned that ScotRail's Business Architect was investigating colour schemes. I went down to Wemyss Bay with Tommy Thomson and met the tenants to describe what was proposed. The licensee was happy that something was going to happen soon. We discussed matters that concerned him - could he have a toilet accessed off his tea room, could we suggest security measures for the 9 metre 'keg' drop from the concourse into his cellar, and was the dampness coming through the basement walls from 'the drains'? I was surprised to find that the long-established refreshment rooms had no toilets - patrons shared the facilities accessible from the concourse. Tommy Thomson suggested that as I was to be based on site as Resident Architect, the licensee could approach the planners and ScotRail through me. This promising suggestion might see us being commissioned to refurbish the whole station!

While I was on the platform taking some paint scrapings for colour matching, I met Neil Pirrit, a planner from Inverclyde District Council. We discussed the proposals and site access for contractors' vehicles taking account of future parking needs.

I could not find much information on the station's colour schemes and the paint scrapings revealed surprisingly little. It is possible that Wemyss Bay station may have included some individualistic features. What was eventually discovered can be summarised in the table shown on page 306.

On the train back to Glasgow, Tommy and I considered the station's potential. There was a lot of unused space. For example, one vacant room might be a florist, another a bookshop for Caley/Steamboat memorabilia and the area at the end of the luggage platform might be a glasshouse. Perhaps the missing track along platform 3 could be relaid, with Egon Ronay meals served in an old restaurant car which could be hauled up to Inverkip to enjoy the splendid views, and back. Tommy pointed out that the £150,000 cost of laying points off the line would be a substantial commitment. The theme developed with the thought that ScotRail could run an evening restaurant car from Glasgow non-stop to Wemyss Bay, even connecting up with the *Waverley* paddle steamer. (I later met Professor Dugald Cameron, the Director of Glasgow School of Art who warmed to the idea of an evening diner from Glasgow.) Pipe dreams!

The tenders arrived in Derby on a Friday. The following Wednesday, Bob Steel and I delivered our report to Tommy. We then awaited completion of the approvals procedure. On 26th February, we were given the go ahead. As ScotRail had to make a rapid start because of conditions attached to the European Regional Development Fund grant, we made immediate contact with the successful contractor, Tarmac Construction. Meanwhile, I got a safety briefing from ScotRail.

Phase I - March 1993. At the beginning of March, we had our first site meeting with ScotRail and Tarmac representatives. Tom Osborne was to be Tarmac's Site Agent and Bruce Milne would keep an eye on site safety for ScotRail. ScotRail expected me to produce a 'Safety Plan', a document which was then a novelty to me. (I have since become thoroughly familiar with Health & Safety Plans under legislation introduced a couple of years later.) On 12th March, the site hut was in place and Tom and I moved into our new offices. I put a message on my answering machine advising callers that as the Resident Architect was out trainspotting, would they please leave their telephone number . . . (I changed it to something more conventional later.) As I represented ScotRail as their Site Safety Officer, supported in the evenings and at weekends by my colleague David Thomson, I had to be on site during the working day, starting at 8.30 am. As Safety Officer, I had to read the relevant sections of the 45-page Track Safety Handbook to every man Tarmac employed on site. By the end of the contract, we had read the same bits to 283 men and handed out as many copies of the Handbook. I do not believe ScotRail expected so much of my time to be spent on inductions. I certainly had not.

At this time, it seemed a development plan might be prepared for the under-utilised station, so I collected illustrations and photos and passed them back to the office to be drawn up. Unhappily, despite a fair amount of good will, there was a greater degree of inertia.

Quite unexpectedly, an 'analyst' appeared to check some rusty roofing sheets on the east island platform that I had assumed to be corrugated iron. They were metal, but coated with bitumen containing some asbestos. Then Tarmac opened up a trap door on the timbered luggage platform to enable the steelwork supporting the deck to be inspected. A number of beams were so corroded that bits of the flanges were actually missing - plainly a dangerous situation. We immediately told Tarmac not to walk or drive on parts of the platform.

Things started moving on the 'asbestos front'. The BR area scientist came down with ScotRail's asbestos advisor and Tommy, and the Health and Safety Executive's Railway Inspector appeared with his assistant. It was decided the only way to remove the asbestos sheets was to construct a high level polythene tent on trestles so that the asbestos could be removed in a totally enclosed environment.

The demolition contractor was now dismantling the brickwork on the luggage platform and the roofer was removing the slates for re-use. The Clyde became visible from inside the station, and how beautiful it looked on calm days! We saw a submarine creating waves half way across the water as it made its way up river - several minutes later, to our surprise we saw that the still sea was now heaving.

April 1993. Holes were dug round the foot of the cast iron columns on the platforms to allow them to be properly painted. Six were cracked right round their bases, mostly at the exposed northern extremities of the island platforms. Ricky Gardner got hold of a specialist who drilled a series of holes and 'stitched in' pieces of high strength steel across the cracked sections (a bit like putting in staples) without moving the columns from their locations. The stitches were roughly 1 inch (25-30 mm) apart and further holes were drilled along the cracks and filled with tapped screws set in a bonding agent.

May 1993. The asbestos removal contractor appeared on site with his decontamination hut and erected a small polythene tent on a sample section of the roof. ScotRail's scientist took background readings before the sample section was removed, on the day of the test and after the test was completed. We later learned that the only readings of any significance were on the personal monitors on the workmen's clothing - and these were barely borderline. However, the Railway Inspectorate insisted that the work was carried out in an enclosure which travelled the length of the roof as work progressed.

In order that the steel could be fully inspected and repainted, it was necessary to gritblast all the paint off it. This is a horribly messy operation and because grit flies everywhere, the operatives had to work in an illuminated enclosed space wearing full protective clothing, goggles and masks. Their method was to erect a tent of tarpaulins, tied to the steelwork at the top and anchored with poles and planks at the bottom. Track 1 (nearest the Clyde) had been isolated with trains using the east side of the island platform (track 2). The grit blasters started at the extremity of platform 1. Owing to the tarpaulins and the curve on the platform, it was not possible for train drivers leaving the station to see the signals when they parked their trains against the buffers as was normal. It was suggested to ScotRail that the drivers stopped their trains further out so that they could see the signals. However no change occurred.

The grit blasters got one day's work done then stopped for the weekend. At 4.30 pm on the Saturday, the booking office staff contacted Operations and advised that the canvas was blowing about a bit. Operations sent down a crew to 'make it safe' and as a result seven good new tarpaulins were damaged beyond reasonable repair. It took some time to get tempers to cool and sort out a workable new method.

We found many of the 12 in. by 3 in. (300 mm x 75 mm) decking planks on the luggage platform had rotten ends and the timber joists supporting them were in poor shape too. But almost all the steel girders carrying the joists were so weakened where they entered the walls that the luggage platform should have collapsed long ago. Rust had attacked the flanges, building up to three times the original steel thickness and the ends of the webs connecting the top and bottom flanges were completely rotted away. Clearly safety checks had missed this area.

Sitting in my office dealing with paperwork, I was interrupted by a ScotRail official, dressed in a suit and sporting a bright new orange waistcoat and hard hat. 'Where's the gaffer?' he demanded. I told him the Site Agent was next door. He said he was a safety officer and had just stopped two men working because they were using an unsafe method. I mentioned that *I* was the Site Safety Officer, and would he please sign the visitors' book before showing me the problem? He did, then indicated a mobile scaffold being erected on two planks over the track 1 void. The matter was easily solved. By the end of the month, something like 20 people had visited the site from ScotRail. I guessed we were conveniently located for safety training.

Two days of incessant rain found us opening up floors to check the drains only to find that some had been blocked for years. I advised ScotRail they had a problem that wouldn't go away. Grit blasting fell badly behind schedule and so therefore did the follow on trades.

As if we had not enough to contend with, at 9 o'clock one morning, a joiner, working with his mate removing battens from the steel on platform 3 to allow the structure to be cleaned, fell off a plank he was shifting along the girders and broke his pelvis. The ambulance was called and came accompanied by the civil police. Statements were taken. The Railway Inspectorate was informed, although the accident had happened well away from the running line, and their Inspector arrived to spend a day viewing the site and taking interviews. People appeared from ScotRail. Tommy Thomson, an Operations Manager, the British Rail transport police, Tarmac's Project Manager and their Safety Officer came down along with the man's employer. It was not a happy day. Next day was not much better - more people appeared from ScotRail House. The only bit of light relief occurred when the Railway Inspector forgot his notebook. As I went through Glasgow that night, I posted it off to him. The following month, the Railway Inspectorate appeared on site for two days of interviews. In the following months I had to produce statements for ScotRail, our office insurers and others.

June 1993. Following a meeting in the tearoom with Trevor Scott (the ScotRail Architect), Historic Scotland, Inverclyde District Council Planning Department, Bob Steel and myself, two sample panels were painted on the exterior of the ticket office - an 'historical' one and something more modern. The one I thought was 'historical', because it incorporated the purple theme common to the Caley, turned out to be the majority favourite however the ScotRail 'historical' version, a mixture of lime green girders, browns and white, was eventually selected.

Lack of progress preparing the steelwork saw the labour force dwindling. After trying canvas tarpaulins and seeing them blown away, a plywood hoarding was erected along the platform, roofed over with heavy tarpaulins secured down to the ground.

The discovery of lead in the original paint gave cause for concern. Under the Control of Lead at Work Regulations 1980, the whole workforce likely to be affected - including myself - had to have blood tests to determine lead levels. Some of the grit blasters who were to be directly involved removing paint had to have subsequent checks because of the higher level of lead in their bodies. As a regular cyclist, perhaps I should not have been surprised to find my blood lead level higher than Tom Osborne, who drove to work.

The new steel beams for the luggage platform were laid in and the roof repairs on the station buildings were completed prior to retiling. Lightning protection, which existed on the tower, was added to the chimney stacks. I wondered why a 90-year-old building now required an enhanced lightning protection system.

Grit blasting recommenced, but was temporarily halted when grit dust escaped from the enclosure. At the time the grit blasting was restarting, the asbestos removal was getting fully under way. A larger tented enclosure was erected to do this. The scientific test arrangements were set up. In sweltering heat, three men wearing special protective clothing bagged the asbestos sheets, changed into different clothing to dispose of the materials into a locked skip and then changed into their everyday clothing in the 'decontamination unit'. The scientist set up his microscope on my drawing board and announced that the air samples in the tent revealed a very low fibre count. I was startled to learn that the fibres he had counted under his 'scope were not necessarily asbestos - they could have been off the men's clothing.

Masons appeared and started repairs to the chimney stacks, that over the pier building having to be substantially rebuilt in Locharbriggs sandstone. The steel fixers returned to continue repairs to the seaward columns. A dense 'birdcage' scaffold was built in the concourse to access the roof steelwork so that glass could be removed, timber repaired and decoration carried out.

I had not anticipated preparing the colour scheme for the project, however, it landed on my plate. At odd moments, and when I was away in a friend's caravan on the Solway Firth, I coloured up prints based on the ScotRail 'palette'. I decided it would be nice to add a little 'Caley blue' to brighten up the scheme, so I put a couple of thin bands on the collars on the column heads. The drawings were then sent to ScotRail for approval.

July 1993. Because the site office was too small, project team meetings were held in the station tearoom, thanks to the kindness of Brian Monaghan, the pub licensee and tearoom proprietor. I used to type up these meetings and compose letters and Architect's Instructions on my lap top computer in the train on the way home. If I was due a day off, I would sign them and leave the documents to be faxed or posted out from the office the next day.

Roofing work continued reusing old tiles on the front of the building mixed with second-hand tiles of about the same vintage from a nearby site. There were not enough tiles to do the whole project so we put new tiles on the roof of the pier building. By mid July, about a third of the steel columns on the luggage platform had been cut in two, the rusted bottom portions replaced with new steel.

The grit blasting was now getting into its stride and as a result, we found that some of the old steel that had looked sound from ground level was wafer thin or rotted through in places. Ricky had a look at it and the necessary instructions began to make a hole in our sum for contingencies.

August 1993. Clients expect regular progress reports and the one I prepared for the August project team meeting suggested that the contractor was running late on the grit blasting and in other areas. It looked as though the project would not be completed on time. I left David in charge as I took the train back up to Glasgow, returning to Wemyss Bay at the end of the meeting.

On one occasion, my homeward bound train from Wemyss Bay failed to arrive because children had thrown a rope over the overhead line at Woodhall. The rope got caught in a train's pantograph resulting in 400 metres of overhead line being pulled down. So we three intending passengers boarded a bus to Gourock there to take the Gourock-Glasgow train. This train in turn was held up by signals before it eventually parked behind three other 3-coach sets in Central Station. To add insult to injury, I saw the 7.30 pm Glasgow-Edinburgh train glide smoothly out the opposite side of the station.

Tom shifted the tented enclosure from platform 3 across to the end of platform 1 nearest the ticket office. By this time, the scaffold in the concourse area had been completely dismantled on the east side and re-erected on the west side. The last of the glass over the concourse started to be removed, lowered by chute to platform level into a dumper truck.

The grit blasting on platform 1 was proceeding apace. David and I inspected the bared steel to enable the painters to apply the first protective coating. Old-fashioned riveting of the steel braces on the luggage platform was now nearing completion and the luggage platform timbers were beginning to go down to provide a working platform for grit blasting work there. But the improvement in progress in my view was not going to meet the deadline dates in Tarmac's programme. Out of site over the seaward wall, the stonemasons patched up inspection holes made to allow Ricky to check the condition of the buried steel posts.

The joiners had replaced much of the damaged roof sarking so lead work was now progressing, large sheets being dressed around the roofs and upstands at the concourse. Lead is a nice material to work with. It is comparatively soft and in the hands of a good leadworker, which we had, the pipes and rolls and welted joints were smoothly formed. We found some most peculiar detailing on parts of the original roof which must have given rise to many of the past problems. For example, normally, one would expect a gutter to have at least a 3 inch (75 mm) upstand. But here we found considerable volumes of water were being channelled into significantly undersized down pipes via gutters and channels with less than 1½ inch (35 mm) upstands. We did what we could to improve the flow characteristics, adding a new pipe here and an overflow there, but expenditure limits curtailed what could be achieved.

Major expense was something Tommy Thomson had to avoid. His budget declined as demands were made on it by ourselves and railway staff. Early in August, we reached a point where instructions needed in the light of some new-found discovery had to be costed and approved by Tommy before they could be issued. Things we would like to do, like restoring the fretted valances along the platforms, had to be rejected and where new castings should have replaced damaged cast-iron gutters, we had to weld broken sections together instead, a job requiring special skills; fortunately we had a young welder who was interested in this difficult work.

One place where we managed to improve on the original detailing was where diagonal steel bracing above the luggage platform roof had been exposed to the atmosphere. Old sarking boards which would otherwise have been scrapped provided a new lining which was subsequently given a coat of 'lead' coloured paint. I reckoned that the lack of protection to the steel had contributed significantly to the rotting away of the structural steelwork on the screen wall below.

Tommy saw an opportunity to obtain more finance and asked me to include *all* the items I thought would need to be covered. I don't think he expected quite such a detailed list. I added in alterations to the toilets and other things I thought should be done and Nigel costed them. It came to a tidy sum and Tommy seemed rather taken aback. However other things were happening off-stage which we knew nothing about and Tommy managed to persuade the sponsors to part with most of the money needed. There was even the possibility of more work to follow the present contract, though this could not be confirmed yet.

A BR photographer appeared on site to take pictures for a talk that Cyril Bleasdale, then the Director of ScotRail, was scheduled to give. He must have run off four reels in quick succession. It is a very photogenic station.

The front roof of the station building was largely completed though some of the tile-laying left something to be desired. Following an early morning meeting in Glasgow, Ricky and I took the train to Wemyss Bay to make a close assessment of the steelwork repairs still needing doing. Back in the office in the afternoon, a head popped round the door. Cyril Bleasdale had just come down from Stirling station and was curious to see the progress. We spent an hour going round the site. He said that next month, there would be a meeting of the various sponsoring groups on site and asked me to make up some display boards to explain the work in hand. Later that afternoon, Bob Hislop from Historic Scotland dropped in so I was able to show him the proposed colour scheme.

The grit blasting was once again going at a reduced pace, this time on the luggage platform. The weather was fine, the *Waverley* paddle steamer and a nuclear submarine could be clearly seen on the far side of the Clyde, but the workforce was diminished. The programme was slipping. My progress report was not hopeful that the work could be finished by the contract completion date.

By this time, others had become aware of my interest in the station. Ian Smith, a retired engineer who had worked on ships and in the railway offices, showed me a marvellous collection of old photographs and picture postcards covering both the present station and its predecessor. The prints he later obtained were used in a presentation to the Railway Heritage Trust.

The lead drainage pipes from the platform canopies looked all right on the outside but were perforated at concealed bends. We had to replace the lot with something acceptable to Historic Scotland for this listed building. We thought of using copper before Nigel told me that his company had been dealing with a lead worker who might be worth approaching. The upshot was that though the number of outlets were reduced (on cost grounds), we were able to use the traditional materials. The result was quite satisfying.

The seaward concrete screen wall proved to be another 'nasty'. The cope was found to be in very bad shape and panels of render had failed due to rusting of the steelwork behind or to poor adhesion. All that could be done within our budget was to patch the worst and ask ScotRail to put the rest on to an inspection rota.

September 1993. My research material was developed by my colleagues to produce two 'then and now' presentation panels for display to the sponsors at Wemyss Bay, ScotRail showing an interest in items that had once graced their own archives! The panels were amplified with items I had discovered in the Watt Library in Greenock and in the J.L. Stevenson collection.

Heavy rain found its way past the temporary tarpaulins over the roof of the ticket office. Water poured in, pulling down ceiling tiles and filling up the light fittings. Inspection revealed that the existing gutters and outlets were woefully under-sized and that some of the pipes and overflows were either clogged up or had never been properly connected. Two 3 inch (75 mm) downpipes had to cope with the water from the ticket office roof *and* from half the concourse *and* from the glazed concourse gables *and* from part of the platform canopies! Small wonder the station had always had a problem draining the storm water. We heard stories that station staff used to move their desks in heavy weather. Later inspection led us to conclude that the main drains themselves had never been large enough and that when they were running full bore, the stacks in the ticket office and elsewhere, unable to discharge, filled up with water till a weak joint was reached and water would leak out. Exploring for leaks revealed birds' nests in the warm space above the ticket office. (Incidentally, a Mr Walter Halliday rescued a jackdaw from a nest in the Bishopton tunnel and brought it to Skelmorlie during World War II. It used to perch on a tree in Moreland overlooking Station Hill and greet those rushing to the train with the cry, 'Hullo! Come on, come on'. Perhaps its descendants are those that came to occupy the station.)

After the rain, we had days when the sunlight off the Clyde had us walking around wearing sunglasses, bemoaning the fact that the bricklayers were now rebuilding the wall on the luggage platform and removing the view. The painters now progressed down platform 1 followed by the roof glaziers on their mobile elevating platforms.

The budgetary problems left us wondering how to tackle the badly cracked main platform. When we prepared the documents, we assumed the grano topping was on top of concrete. We now knew that there was concrete, but it was of variable thickness and unsuitable for re-use. We rejected an asphalt finish as this would be out of character. Paving flags would be very expensive. Tom Osborne suggested laying half the platform width from one end of the canopy to the other, a distance of about 150 metres, in a constant pour, thereafter saw-cutting the concrete into bays. After a morning faxing proposals and counter-proposals getting costs and approval, this proposal was instructed.

As the columns holding up the canopies acted as rainwater conduits, they were therefore subject to erosion from inside. It was important to prove they still had enough metal in them to support the structure. The results of electronic testing suggested they were sound. Later we found rust stains from small holes in some columns and presumed that the grit blasting had removed filler applied during manufacture. We knew that 'Beaumont Egg', a mixture of lead and iron filings, had been used on the 1878 Tay Bridge castings and presumably something similar was used for this 25 years later. We filled the pitted areas with a 20th century filler.

Many of the distinctive ridge tiles off the station building had been damaged beyond repair in dismantling. This was most unfortunate, however, after a search through various suppliers' catalogues, we eventually found a local clayware manufacturer who could make new tiles in the style of the original.

Tarmac stopped grit blasting on the seaward side and started to erect a large enclosure over platforms 3 and 4. The roofers were nowhere to be seen.

Small things in life can sometimes be most debilitating. I was at home when something got into my left eye. Nothing I could do that evening would get it out. But I couldn't cancel arrangements for the next day. My wife drove me to the station where I caught the train, a big white patch over one eye. Keeping both eyes open was a struggle, so I didn't. I dozed most of the way.

On site, my eye was no better. Tom McDougall, the temporary site agent and first-aider tried flushing out my eye. It didn't work. I rang the local surgery and arranged an appointment for 11.00 am. I had to induct another two roofers who had just arrived on site. The ¾ hour read-in was not too easy - no doubt they wondered what they were letting themselves in for when the Safety Officer had a patch over his eye. At a quarter to eleven, another new guy appeared. He got the swiftest induction ever, then I was driven to the surgery. Once the doctor removed the remains of the midge, there was instant relief! A prescription and I was back in the van being carted down the road to the chemist and back to site. It had only taken an hour.

Above: August 1993 - re-roofing the gents' toilet showing the glass removed from the top of the ramped walkway to the pier. The chimney capping stones were replaced by new Locharbriggs sandstone. *Author*

Right: Reglazing above platform 1 in October 1993 where the difficulties of safe working in a Victorian structure become evident. *Author*

Below: Over 90 years, parts of the steel columns and the light steel bracing behind the west screen's timber lining had rotted away. The photograph illustrates how new steel was patched in while a motor launch from Bute closes in to inspect. Had the budget allowed, a few windows inserted into the screen walls could have brought attractive views to observers on the luggage platform. *Author*

On 30th September, the two display posters were pinned up in the tea-room. Promptly at 12.05, the last 3-car blue train on ScotRail metals arrived and a party of 18 decanted, donned their hard hats and orange vests and made their way to the tea-room. The Railway Heritage Trust included Sir William McAlpine, Leslie Soane (a former Director of BR), and John Cameron (formerly from the Scottish Region). After a general description of the history of the station and its importance as a local landmark, a point emphasised by John Hume from Historic Scotland, Cyril Bleasdale expressed the view that a static coach display alongside platform 3 might be worth considering. However, all ideas need money and someone to get the action going.

The tour commenced. There was now enough completed paintwork to give an impression of what the station would look like. Sir William volunteered the view that the concrete screen walls either side of the station might have been blast deflection panels erected during World War II, which seemed plausible considering the huge wartime traffic carried on the Clyde and the possibility that the station could have been used for troop embarkation. This was subsequently corroborated by a long time resident of Largs.

I later heard that many of the party were not convinced with the green colour of the steelwork. But it looked as though additional work might come for new car parking, a toilet redesign, windows off the luggage platform, the addition of fretwork to the valances and refurbishment of the tearoom. The only problem was that the money never appeared to allow this to happen.

October 1993. The weather deteriorated. The grit blasters finished off platforms 1 and 2 and moved over to platforms 3 and 4. The demolition contractor appeared and broke up the concrete on platform 1. The glaziers made steady progress down Platform 1 to the ticket office. The roofers' performance remained poor, their workforce inconstant. ScotRail now had difficulty financing the project and wanted a four-month break in the contract to take the remaining work into the next financial year.

Ricky needed to inspect the two girders spanning between platforms 2 and 3. As this would require temporary isolation of the overhead line to the station, obtaining a Permit to Work and ensuring that adequate railway supervision was in place, all of which takes time to organise, Tarmac decided to wait till track 2 was taken out of use. This would allow inspection to be carried out safely as the girders would be in the 'dead' area.

It had been decided that trains would transfer to platform 1 on Friday 15th October, however, while most of the old granolithic on the platform 1 side had been removed the previous week, the concrete had yet to be laid. Curiously, we did not come across any buried services except the cables serving the train starter buttons so we concluded that the original gas lighting to the platform beyond the canopy must have been served by some other route.

That week was very busy with joiners, glaziers, plumbers and painters working on top of each other, the concretors casting a continuous strip of concrete saw-cut into bays to get platform 1 back into operation. The steelfixers replaced recently discovered rotten steel at the valances and the labourers rodded the pipes from the columns and broke open the trackside drains at the side of platform 1 where they had been found to be silted up.

Wednesday started cold, the temperature just above the point when concrete should not be poured. Concreting started at 8.30am with dumper trucks running up to the top of Platform 1, under the canopy. We were only doing half the width of the platform, but on a 150 metre-long platform, that was a lot of concrete. Using a bunnion roller, a sort of powered rolling pin, held by a man at each end, the concrete was smoothed down. The weather improved steadily and Tom Osborne began to smile. Two-thirds of the platform was done that day, the men forming the pattern with a studded roller working on till 9.00pm. By noon on Thursday, the whole platform had been laid. The electrician struggled to fit the new lights above the 'green' concrete.

Over the weekend, ScotRail buffed up the rusted rails of track 1 so that the track circuits would register correctly, re-energised the dead overhead line to platform 1, isolated the power to track 2 and locked the points to serve platform 1 only. The site boundaries were adjusted to suit the new arrangement and a temporary bridge was built across from platform 2 to platform

The 'Blue Train' pays a visit to Wemyss Bay station in September 1993 with a party from the Railway Heritage Trust, Historic Scotland and other sponsors. Grit blasting is in progress on platform 1. *Author*

The curved stone retaining wall deflects the waves. Viewed from the roof over the luggage platform, one can imagine how the tracks leading on to the pier would have snaked along the top of the sea wall. *Author*

3 - saving a deal of walking. Now platform 2 valances could be stripped and we found the steelwork was no better than elsewhere. A working platform was created by stripping out the platform 2 concrete and replacing it using the same techniques as for platform 1.

The seaward side of the luggage platform timber screen was painted white with a plum coloured fascia and black lining out. To cut costs, as much sound old boarding had been used as possible.

November 1993. One morning, Tom Osborne failed to appear. On the drive to work, he had suffered a heart attack. He was taken to hospital and found to be needing a triple heart bypass. Tom McDowall took charge.

More enclosures were erected and more grit-blasters appeared. A sample roof ridge tile was delivered to site which was close to the style needing replacing (only 20 of the original 300 were actually reusable). It was now getting difficult to access some of the more out-of-the-way places on the job. Checking that some of the rainwater outlets were properly made was quite challenging.

Keen to see a solution to another problem, I had been in contact with the licensee of the station pub, ScotRail and CalMac regarding toilet provision. Present day rules meant that the pub and tearoom required their own toilets. Currently, men would use the ScotRail toilets and ladies those provided by CalMac. I suggested to ScotRail that minor alterations to the building would see the situation rectified. We were asked to develop the ideas and someone was later engaged to prepare working drawings, but nothing came of it.

Occasionally, I found time to walk along the pier and watch the ferries come in. At this time of year, it was quite dramatic watching the boats berthing. The big ferries would rise and fall several feet as the swell rose and fell. The days were getting distinctly shorter. The weather deteriorated. Calm bright days gave way to dull days with strong winds made more unpleasant by a sharp drop in temperature. Steel cleaning was held up when water froze in the tanks and pipes supplying water and grit to the grit blasters, till the sun crawled up over the rim of the concourse.

But the grit-blasting was nearing the end. There were only a few bays to complete on platforms 2, 3 and 4 and the roofers were now replacing the slates over the platforms. I remonstrated with one (allegedly) time-served painter who was painting boards where it was pouring with rain - he moved to a more protected area.

The steelwork was nearly complete when we discovered a truss on the east side needed replacing. It could not be checked earlier as the area had been used as a contractor's store. This was awkward as Tommy Thomson had already been advised what the expected total cost was to be but the work was unavoidable. It was immediately instructed, then cancelled when we found it was going to cost £20,000 to replace. A cost check to find savings elsewhere showed we were in for a £50,000 overspend. The overspend had arisen partly because some work had turned out to be more complex than first estimated. With high cost items such as steelwork, for which no billed rates existed, late presentation of priced dayworks by a contractor could lead to things suddenly going astray.

December 1993. Out of the blue, five ScotRail personnel appeared to discuss access arrangements, especially to awkward roof areas. I offered suggestions which I hoped could be afforded from some other budget. Next day another two railway people came to discuss the drains, a subject of some concern as a new main sewer for the area was being laid in the road outside, but as the station's sewers discharged directly into the Clyde, this would entail a redirection of part of the system under the concourse. Our surveys had revealed that there was also a large drain running deep east-west under the platforms which matched the description in the Bill of Quantities for the 1903 station where 100 linear yards of '2 foot egg-shaped brick main sewer, with sills and concrete haunching complete, on top of existing sea wall at Wemyss Bay' was specified, probably to serve Kelly House.

'Final' inspections revealed areas of work still to be done - parapet timbers above the luggage platform had to be fitted, sealed and painted. In the same area, defective seals in the flat laid gutters needed attention and the slating had to be finished off.

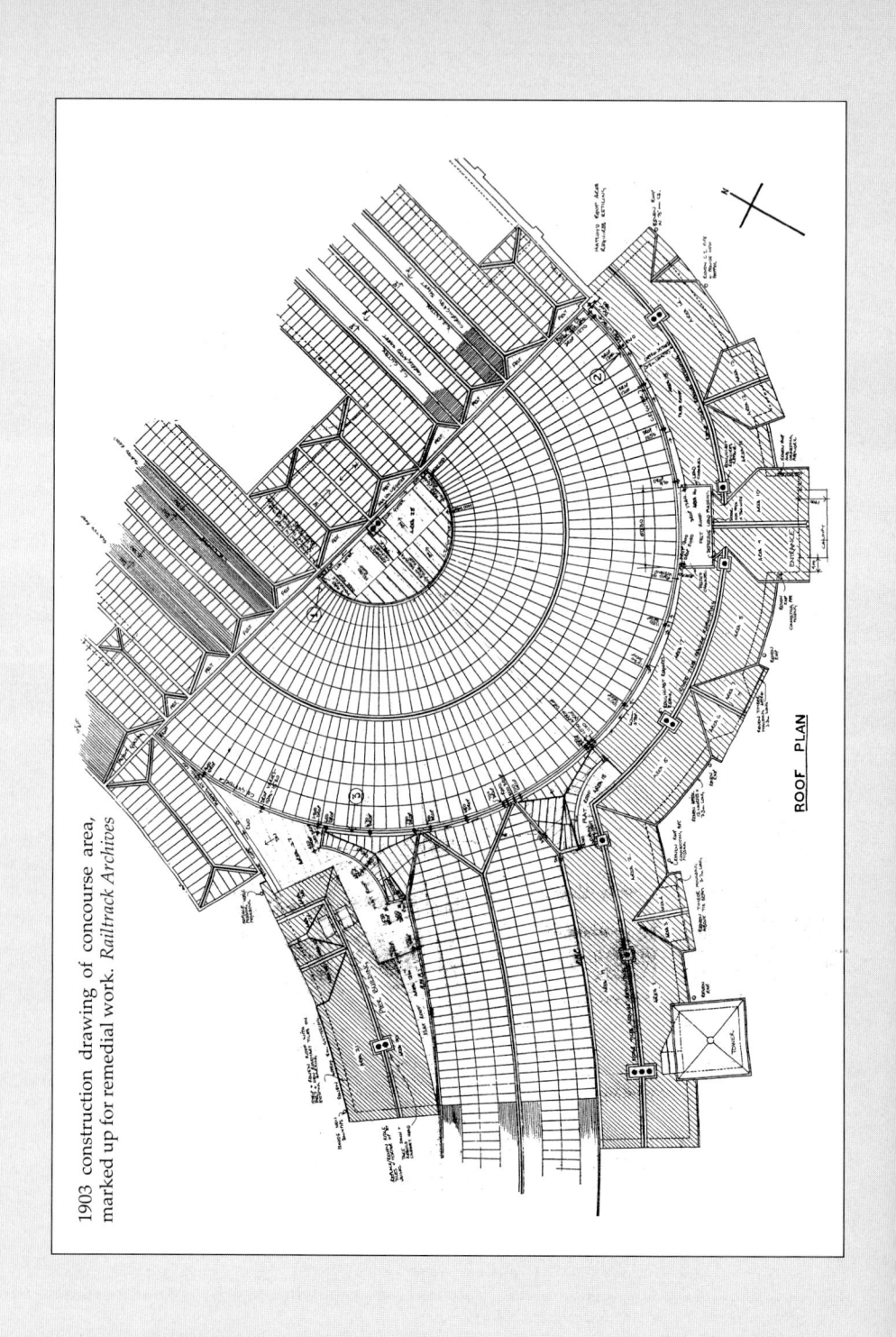

1903 construction drawing of concourse area, marked up for remedial work. *Railtrack Archives*

Grit blasting is a dirty process and the residue had to be bagged and regularly removed off site to an approved dump; 500 bags would appear and be quickly filled. Their removal was another problem. Sometimes I wondered whether the skips would disintegrate under the weight of grit they contained. One truck trying to lift a skip instead found itself with its front wheels in the air.

The weather turned against us. Strong winds and rain battered the site. Rain leaking into the ticket office showed up defects in the building which we had not managed to eliminate. Under the canvases, the grit blasters carried on for as long as the sheets were securely anchored. On the roof, the slaters stopped when the chalk guide lines they 'pinged' on to the underlay were washed away and likewise the painters were limited in what they could achieve. The glaziers working on the roof came close to quitting site, and during one heavy downpour, the welder repairing the cast-iron gutters received an electric shock.

We still didn't know when Phase II was going to happen or indeed the full scope of what it would include. The amount of work found necessary had drilled a hole through our enlarged budget for Phase I, mainly because of the additional steelwork. Nigel and I searched for items that could be cut out - there weren't many. Till the position was clearer, Tommy Thomson was not able to decide if Phase II could start in January or had to wait till April 1994 as programmed. Political rumblings about selling off ScotRail in April was an encouragement to keep the project going.

The tearoom kitchen flooded, as did the ticket office and a drain cover lifted in the concourse. Now that the roof gutters had been improved, the down pipes were clearly undersized. David contacted ScotRail to have the drains pressure cleaned to remove the silt.

Assuming that Phase II was most likely to follow on the heels of Phase I, I carried out a survey to see how much stonework on the seaward wall actually needed replacing. It was very difficult to judge as it seemed that whole areas should be replaced. I gave Tarmac an indication of the work that would be needed to ascertain material ordering or sequencing problems.

Progress was more obvious as the electrician fitted the lights along the remaining section of platform 1 to the end of the canopy. Foul weather stopped the grit-blasters, their plant broke down and their hoses froze, but they finished and their decontamination cabin was removed. The wind got stronger and enthusiasm diminished by the same degree. Neither the glazing work nor the paintwork was going to be complete by Christmas. Fierce winds blew down a mobile scaffold and slowed progress further.

However progress was being made off site - the ridge tiles had been formed and were going to be put in the kiln at the beginning of the New Year, except for a dozen end ridges which had to be made by hand.

Tommy Thomson then indicated that Phase II had been let to Tarmac. I produced a revised Schedule of Work to allow a start after the Christmas break and sent it off to Tommy for clarification. He returned it marked 'in', 'out' and 'maybe'. I was now able to issue Tarmac with an Architect's Instruction describing the scope of the work. Tarmac prepared Method Statements for critical activities for comment and submitted an application to close track 1 again to allow stone and render repairs to be progressed.

In the last few days before Christmas, the site was tidied up, grit and surplus materials removed, the broken stone on the seaward side of the west screen wall removed and waste timbers burnt. The workforce declined. Tom Osborne returned, looking healthier, slightly slimmer and in good humour. Despite his serious operation, he expected to rejoin the construction team in the New Year.

We had just packed our bags when Nigel rang to say that the window repairs, which formed a large part of the works, was going to be twice as costly as previously estimated. The work had already been instructed on the basis of the estimated cost; I arranged for the window work to be placed 'on hold' till it could be discussed in the New Year.

There was one bright note: the tower clock, which had been stopped for some months, was now illuminated from within and reading the correct time, driven by an electric motor instead of by clockwork. At least Frank Chandler, who had the job of winding it up, would be spared his weekly climb up the ladder from his bedroom.

Phase II - January 1994. I found the going hectic during that first week back 'in the office'. I was no longer 'Safety Officer' and was expected to run the job as a normal Project Architect would. I asked Nigel to obtain a price for a revised amount of window repairs. Meanwhile I heard at second-hand that our client was wanting work done that had not yet been discussed.

On that first Friday, Tommy Thomson and Bob Hislop from Historic Scotland came to site. We noted that the clocktower, which had never been scheduled for repainting, needed sprucing up, at least on the three sides accessible by mobile elevating platform. Tommy agreed.

Another deadline was looming. The date for the grand 'opening' had been fixed for 25th March. Tommy had not told me yet, but it was common knowledge on site.

The content of Phase II was still uncertain though I tried hard to get details clarified. The problem was mainly because Tarmac had lodged a claim but without being reasonably sure what it would amount to, Tommy could not confirm a schedule of work. It seemed that £130,000 was available nevertheless, so we drew up a priority list.

Some hastily concocted sketches of stonework needing replacing were given to contractors for tendering purposes. We reduced the scope of window repairs even more. But still there was no instruction to proceed though the budget had been pegged at £110,000.

An Architect's job is never done till the last bit of snagging has been ticked off. While waiting for things to happen, I inspected and identified areas which wanted attention. The ridge tiles to the station buildings, for example, still had to be delivered and fixed. It took several days, and was mixed with general site supervision. In the midst of all this, Tommy Thomson arrived with Cyril Bleasdale and Willie Caldwell. Willie was organising a big celebration to be held on the 25th March to celebrate the completion of the restoration. It was clear that this was going to be no ordinary event.

Cyril Bleasdale was retiring at the end of March and had taken a particular interest in this project. Invited guests would come down on the 'blue train' for the opening at 12.00 noon. Willie had arranged for a tented enclosure to be erected on platforms 3 and 4 to accommodate up to 100 guests; there was to be an orchestra made up of 70 Greenock school children who would sit and play in the concourse and then be fed in the station restaurant. There would be speeches, a walk-around, a video of an old film of travel 'doon the watter' in the former bookstall and then the various parties would depart their separate ways.

Tommy and I felt that the number of plank signs 'needed' for the station could be reduced to a level which would enhance the appearance of the station. Looking at my growing collection of historical photographs, the ScotRail Director agreed; if the station had survived with only a few signs before, there was no need to change things. The signs should also be 'period' rather than 'current'.

The arrival of the Director helped to release the purse strings a little further. While this was going on, Willie cast covetous glances at my photos - could he borrow them to see whether there were any that he could use for his publicity exercise? I lent them to him. (Years later, making enquiries for this book, I found these photos had become part of the Strathclyde Passenger Transport Archive!)

February 1994. I revised the signage plan and Tommy organised a sign contractor to put the work in hand. Bruce made periodic visits to site to check on site safety, not that there was much to check. Now we learned that the grand 'opening' *would* be on 25th March.

There were loose ends to tie up - the signage (as near to Caledonian format as we could make it) in 'Transport Heavy' white lettering on a black background (though a more authentic colour might have been Prussian Blue), litter bins, the landward screen wall and the extent of stonework repairs. The most difficult problem was the screen wall, where the cement fill had deteriorated to such an extent that the proposed repairs - render patching on one side and sprayed concrete on the other - were likely to improve the appearance but not give a very long-lasting finish. Ricky had always been worried about the wall, and had a whole series of tests carried out for sulphate and chloride content before the wall was repaired. By mid-February, between some cold snaps, the render patching got done. The inner face of the seaward screen wall was painted the creamy off-white used on the column shafts.

The replacement ridge tiles arrived at last - a perfect match to the originals. But the installation work was not good enough. When I pointed out that the ridge tiles rose and fell like the waves on the Clyde outside, the roofers protested that the curve of the roof caused the problem. I disagreed and said they should take the lot off (they had put on about 20) and give them a thicker bed to eliminate the variation in height. The men then left the site, never to be seen again. There had now been over 45 roofers on the job.

Site meetings were now more biased to the opening event. The 'temporary' goods yard car park looked likely to become permanent, with cars banned from the platform. Tommy had persuaded the sponsors to put more money into the project to allow resurfacing of platforms 3 and 4 as well as the remainder of platforms 1 and 2 to the signal gantry at the throat of the station. After a lot of difficulty, he acquired funds to form a concrete ramp to replace the rotten timber planks at the rear of the Pier Building, though the timber storm gates which I wanted to reinstate were excluded, at least meantime.

All the electric lights had been installed along the platforms and cables had been re-routed round the concourse, though not without some difficulty. The stonework contractor arrived and I explained what I wanted done.

After all the problems finding money for essential repairs, I was surprised that ScotRail approved my recommendation for two expensive cast-iron litter bins, with the words 'Wemyss Bay' on them. Tommy found more money, £90,000, with the possibility of another £30,000. Bob Steel congratulated Tommy on his skill. The monies would be used for platform concrete works, painting the clock tower, redecorating the gents' toilets and the entrance porch, reconstructing the entrance canopy and miscellaneous minor works. Perhaps it was made easier because ScotRail was ceasing to trade as such from the end of March (when the buildings and railways would be run by Railtrack) and it was the end of the financial year when sponsoring bodies needed to use up their excess funds. With the Director of ScotRail retiring, it looked as though the station was going to feature in the politicking.

Willie Caldwell had the celebrations well under control. Reiach and Hall, Tarmac and Davis Langdon and Everest clubbed together and ordered hanging flower baskets. By the end of February, the most recently instructed platform work was under way. Red sandstone bottoming, presumably either broken stone from the original station or waste material from the early 1900s alterations, was uncovered. The stonemasons worked away on the bookend at platform 1 where severe weather conditions had not only eroded the stonework in a wall 2 ft (600 mm) thick but had created voids several inches deep between the massive stones. The metal gates at the main entrance had been repaired and two new shields had been made to replace the existing. We found a painter willing to paint 'CR - 1903' on them. He made a nice job.

Heavy snow arrived to hamper the work and the thaw resulted in a lot of water entering the ticket office ceiling. The outlet pipes were incapable of taking the load. (Later we discovered a bottle jammed in an overflow.) The now rejuvenated overflow was working hard pouring water on to the platform - just over the entrance door to the ticket office. Needless to say, I got the blame. The roofers continued making a poor job fitting the ridges. I remonstrated and another squad of men downed tools and left site.

March 1994. I now had another contractor to deal with on site, Europa Construction. Their work included the building of a new entrance canopy, the painting of the clock tower and the decoration of the public toilets. But other work, especially the roofing and the gunite spray concrete repairs to the landward screen wall was getting delayed by bad weather. The concreting of the platforms at the far end of platforms 1 and 2 had to be done with a ScotRail lookout, between squalls. The frequency of rain showers meant that cement work done was likely to get washed away. And the long range weather forecast was not promising. The landward screen wall was falling behind and it became clear that the work could not be completed by the 'opening' day. Tom Osborne and I discussed how to make the building look presentable. A more experienced roofing squad appeared and there was a noticeable improvement in the quality of the ridge tile work. The entrance porch was redecorated at night so as not to affect the general public.

The two rooks banished from the roofspace over the ticket office reappeared and so far as we could see, failed to re-establish themselves. I was mildly irritated to find that with days to

Right: In March 1994, a new entrance canopy was built. The tiles had been stripped off the roofs and those that were reusable were fixed to the roof over the front elevation, however, new ridge tiles had to be cast from moulds made from the original clayware.
Author

Below: March 1994 and the restoration work is virtually complete. In the foreground, the semi-circular glazed roof over the concourse embraces the lower roof (with chimney) above the booking office. The graceful sweep of the roofs is very evident. *Author*

go before the ceremony, ScotRail engineers arrived expecting labour to be waiting for them without pre-arrangement. Without any noticeable pre-planning or sense of aesthetic judgement, they then hacked away pieces of station we had just restored to feed cables into the ticket office. If they had made one hole, that would have been bad enough, but their first effort was in the wrong place. This now had to be repaired. I asked ScotRail to get someone to co-ordinate the cable routing affecting ScotRail, the telephones, the Tannoy system and ScotRail's Signals and Telecommunication department.

A cherry picker arrived so that the tower could be painted. I managed to get the use of it with the ScotRail photographer to take some 'aerial' shots. One of the first things we saw was a submarine out in the Clyde.

ScotRail now prepared line 1 for re-use. Their grinding equipment appeared to buff down the rails. The engineers' blue train came and went more frequently, only stopping long enough for the driver to run out of his cab to the opposite end and drive away again.

The week of the ceremony dawned overcast with a weather forecast promising rain and gale force winds. Overnight the newly painted landward screen wall on the station side lost 20 per cent of its new paintwork in the rain, in the same squall that watered down the new paint on the entrance door of Pier House. But on the 'bright side', Inverclyde District Council's gardeners turned over the soil at the front of the building and spent the rest of the week planting flowers and shrubs. Electricians appeared and fitted the new clock over the ticket office. CalMac produced a cover for their extract fan - rather than wait for an electrician to fit it, I got a ladder and did the job myself. ScotRail's men appeared and spent a couple of days painting the platform edges, removing cables and tidying up the track. The hanging baskets arrived and got slung up in the concourse. The place was really looking quite smart.

The men spraying concrete on to the east side of the landward screen wall were struggling against the elements. It was little short of miraculous that they managed to finish the wall, remove their full height scaffolding and clean up the night before the opening.

On 25th March, 1994, ScotRail's original 3-car electric 'Blue Train', left platform 12 in Glasgow with a party of invited guests, including Bob Steel and my recent assistant, David Thomson. John Hume, Chief Inspector for Historic Scotland, gave a description of places of interest as we travelled down. The weather improved as we approached Wemyss Bay and the sun shone through as we arrived.

The station looked smart, the 'WEMYSS BAY' lettering was fixed to the entrance canopy, the painted shields stood proudly on the gates. Inverclyde District Council had completed the external restoration with an attractive display of flowers and shrubs. Two old wooden 'WEMYSS BAY' signs (one of which I had spirited out of Pier House whence it had lain for 30 years), were centred above the notice boards in the porch. These, I suspected had been used in the 1865 station as they were definitely older than the traditional Caley signs. Inside the concourse, the new signs - white lettering on a black background, framed in white - looked 'right' amid the hanging baskets. The station looked complete.

Cyril Bleasdale recalled his 40 years on the railway and how 25 years previously he had first seen Wemyss Bay. When he came to ScotRail in the mid-1980s, he decided that Wemyss Bay, then very run-down, should be restored. He had managed to winkle money out of various bodies and now the station showed the results. Tarmac got a 'thank you' for getting the job done in advance of programme and the sponsors were thanked for the money, without which the project would not have happened.

Malcolm Waugh, Chairman of Strathclyde's Roads and Transportation committee emphasised the local authority's commitment to public transport and Sir Bob Reid, the outgoing Chairman of the British Railways Board also spoke. He was followed by an unannounced guest, the Hon. John MacGregor, MP and Minister of Transport, who gave an upbeat gloss to the changeover, which was not entirely shared by the pessimists and railwaymen who wondered how much longer they would be working on the railways. Finally, the Hon. Sir William McAlpine, Chairman of the Railway Heritage Trust, presented Cyril Bleasdale with an original painting by Professor Dugald Cameron (another was given to him later) and unveiled a plaque in the centre of the station.

Period lights, flowers in baskets, cast-iron litter bins and 'Caley' period signs appear for the ceremonial 'reopening' of the station on 25th March, 1994. *Author*

Restoration Day - 25th March, 1994. John MacGregor (Minister of Transport) speaking, with a front row (*left to right*) comprising The Hon. Sir William McAlpine (Chairman of the Railway Heritage Trust), Sir Bob Reid (Chairman of the British Railways Board), Cyril Bleasdale (retiring Chairman of ScotRail) and Chris Green (incoming Director of Railtrack's train operating division). Malcolm Waugh (Chairman of Strathclyde Roads and Transportation committee) stands in front of the plaque which was unveiled by Sir Bob Reid. *Author*

March 1994 - new canopy with the 'shields' on the entrance gates picked out in blue with gold lettering. *Author*

The 70-strong Greenock High School Orchestra played to the 300 assembled throng before the guests were shoe-horned into the marquee on platform 3/4. An 'Edwardian' style lunch was followed by more speeches when the sponsors were once again thanked (but not the Design Team!) and the party adjourned to the 'Blue Train' and the trip back to Central Station. I doubt whether many of the guests saw much of the station - but it was a lunch worth travelling for.

Work did not end with the celebrations, but from now on, nothing happened fast. The rainwater problem did not go away - if anything, restoration had served to emphasise the drainage difficulties. Various solutions were attempted and some did seem to improve matters. On my occasional visits to Wemyss Bay, I was pleased to see that, since privatisation, the Wemyss Bay service had been changed to an 'express' and the train stopped at fewer stations *en route*. More like the old days. There were still occasions that ScotRail probably would rather forget, like when the tannoy cheerfully announced that the reason the train had not arrived was because the driver hadn't either!

Early in July 1994, the station won the International Brunel Award for intermediate size stations. The letter to Railtrack read:

> The Foundation for Railway Transportation Excellence, Ltd. (FoRTE), the US Federal Administration (FRA), Amtrak and the Watford Group of European Railway Architects and Designers are pleased to announce that Railtrack Property Board Scotland has been chosen as a distinguished recipient of the 1994 Brunel Award in the category 'A5 - Transformed or renovated medium size stations' for your entry entitled 'Wemyss Bay Station Reconstruction'.

The award was presented to Trevor Scott of ScotRail by Jolene Molitoris of the Federal Railroad Administration in Washington on 18th October, 1994.

Pier works in progress in 1988. At this stage, the luggage ramp and the line on to the pier were severed where the station abutted the pier. The 'roll-on roll-off' pier nearest the camera appears complete.

Crown Copyright - Royal Commission on the Ancient and Historical Monuments of Scotland

On 13th December, 1994, another ceremony took place at Wemyss Bay station. A day earlier and it would not have happened as the track to Wemyss Bay was closed. For over 48 hours, Scotland, and the west coast in particular, suffered extremely heavy rainfall, to the extent that parts of Paisley had to be evacuated as flood waters rose. At the same time, the busy low level lines under Central Station were out of use, flooded to a depth of 8 ft (2.4 m), engulfing one of ScotRail's newest trainsets. The previous day, the Lord Mayor of London, Christopher Walford, had presented the Ian Allan award plaque to Railtrack, Trevor Scott representing Railtrack and Bob Steel, Reiach & Hall. The award was given for the fine restoration of a unique and rather special station.

The proceedings were opened by Jim Berry, Property Manager, Railtrack Scotland who expressed the hope that other Clyde stations would be upgraded also. Councillor Charles Gordon, chairman of the roads and transportation committee of Strathclyde Regional Council, Malcolm Waugh's successor, recalled his childhood memories, notably seeing the water far below as he peered through the planks on the ramp to the ferry. In his view, this type of high quality restoration, which had cost £1.68m, made commercial sense.

Councillor Gordon then unveiled a brass plate set on a stone column in front of the ticket office. This read:

1994
Brunel Award
WASHINGTON, D.C.

The prestigious international Brunel Award for a Renovated Medium Sized Station was received from the Watford Conference of Railway Architects and Designers by Railtrack Property on behalf of the Scottish railways and their partners in the Wemyss Bay Project: Strathclyde Regional Council, Historic Scotland, the Railway Heritage Trust, the European Union and Inverclyde District Council. The award ceremony was held by the Foundation for Railway Transportation Excellence Limited (FORTE), the US Federal Administration and Amtrak in Washington DC on October 18, 1994.

1993 Restoration Work

The major restoration work carried out in 1993 and 1994 cost £1.68m [*£1.86m] and involved replacing the platform glazing, roof works, new leadwork, stone repairs and exterior decoration. The work was funded in part by the Railway Heritage Trust, (a body set up in April 1985 with an initial budget of £1m to assist in the maintenance of British Rail's listed buildings, which now number over 1,000). Part of the Trust's function was to act as a catalyst between outside bodies and the BR Property Board to preserve non-operational listed buildings and structures, with a view to their transfer to local trusts or other interested parties. Historic Scotland, Strathclyde Regional Council, Inverclyde District Council and the European Union were other major contributors to the work.

The End?

The vision that brought the Caley to the Coast will be reflected for a while in the polish applied to the Wemyss Bay gem. Most of those involved, including Tom Osborne who died in December 1996, have moved on. As we have seen, railways need constant attention, replacement of track, stock and systems. So too does railway property. To keep this jewel sparkling in its Clyde setting will require increasing attention and the vision to adapt it to suit new circumstances. The potential is there; one hopes the vision is not far behind.

Driving Forward

Railways have an innate fascination for many local historians – they played an important part in shaping the communities and built environment we inherited from the nineteenth century, and the Wemyss Bay line is a good example of this. But this particular railway's role in land transport is complemented – and largely explained – by its place in the equally evocative story of the development of Clyde ferry services. In bringing these two elements together, and relating them so clearly to their local and national context, Archie Clark has crafted a book with a broad appeal both to students of transport history and to those with a more general interest in the development of the west of Scotland. I have enjoyed meeting with Archie and discussing his text and superb drawings while the book was in preparation.

As the author is able to remind us from his personal involvement in the restoration of the magnificent terminal at Wemyss Bay, some of the history of the line is very recent – it is barely a decade since serious consideration had to be given to cutting the branch short because of the conflicting financial demands of maintaining a modern public transport network and preserving the railway's architectural heritage. Fortunately this threat is now behind us, and the railway to Wemyss Bay continues to perform its traditional function of maintaining an essential link with the Rothesay ferry. Indeed, the terminal building and the linked pier and station are a firm reminder that the concept of integrated transport is not a modern invention.

But the branch's wider role, as part of the Strathclyde Passenger Transport network, is not simply rooted in history. Its continuing evolution, symbolised by the replacement of the original 'Blue Trains' by the new 'Juniper' class '334' electric units, is also shown by the new stations on the line – IBM halt, and more recently Whinhill and Drumfrochar. SPT is committed to developing the contribution which the railway network makes to serving the transport needs of west central Scotland, and the Wemyss Bay line remains a key component of that network.

Malcolm Reed
Director General, Strathclyde Passenger Transport Executive
September 2001

Dr Malcolm Reed, Director General of Strathclyde Passenger Transport Executive, flags away a new Juniper trainset from Central Station in April 2001.

Appendix One

Chronology

1175	Glasgow - on the map.
c.1480	James III granted Kelly estate to James Bannatyne.
1600s	Greenock develops as a transatlantic port.
1665	Rothesay Harbour in existence.
1667	Founding of Port Glasgow.
1707-1710	Sir John Shaw funded Greenock Harbour construction.
1747	Travel between Edinburgh and Glasgow took 9 hours.
1748	Travel from Glasgow to London via Edinburgh took 12 days.
1750s	Wemyss Bay named.
1755	Smeaton proposes damming the Clyde to raise water from 1 ft 3 in.-3 ft 8 in. to suit larger vessels.
1763	Glasgow to Greenock coach inaugurated, taking 9 hours for the journey.
1767	First Turnpike Act for Ayrshire passed permitting construction of various roads.
1773	Training wall built from Dumbarton upstream to encourage natural scouring and deepening of the channel.
1775	Clyde navigable to vessels with a draft of over 6 ft.
1775-1783	American Revolution which resulted in larger vessels being constructed on the Clyde.
1779	Cotton Industry develops on Bute.
1780	Glasgow well established as a major manufacturing city.
1780s	Road from Saltcoats via Largs to Skelmorlie completed.
1790	Glasgow connected to Port Glasgow by a new road.
1791	Wheeled road transport in general use.
1792	John Wallace, West Indian Trader, acquired the Kelly Estate.
1800	Glasgow population about 74,000. Glasgow to Greenock by coach took 3½ hours.
1801	William Symington built steam powered paddle boat *Charlotte Dundas*.
1803	Robert Wallace inherited Kelly.
1812	Henry Bell's steam boat *Comet* built by John Wood. Four mansions built at 'New Glasgow'
1820	Glasgow population about 100,000.
1825	*Locomotion* achieved 8 mph hauling 90 tons.
1829	*Novelty* achieved 40 mph at the Rainhill Trials.
1831	*Fairy Queen*, the first iron steamer built.
1834	May - Publication of proposals for a 'Marine Village' at Wemyss Bay in the *Scots Times*.
1835	Road Network well established. London to Glasgow took 44 hours.
1837	15th July - Glasgow & Paisley Joint Railway and Glasgow, Paisley & Greenock Railway authorised.
1837-1839	'Commercial panic' when money was difficult to raise.
1839-1844	Years of Depression.
1840	14th July - Glasgow & Paisley Joint Railway opened.
1841	30th March - Glasgow, Paisley & Greenock Railway opened.
1841	6th April - Bridge Street Station, Glasgow, opened. London reached by train to Ardrossan, boat to Liverpool and thereafter train to London in 24 hours.
1844	Beach House built by George Arbuthnot, the first Villa in Skelmorlie.
1845	July - The Caledonian Railways Act passed.
1845	15th October - The Renfrew and Ayr Counties Railway submitted proposals for a line between Greenock, Gourock & Largs.
1846-1847	Irish potato harvest failure drove families to factories and railways on the mainland.
1847	Caley takeover of the GP&GR sanctioned. Collapse of the economy.
1848	15th February - Glasgow and Edinburgh linked by Caledonian Railway to London - Glasgow to London achieved in 13 hours.

1850	28th October - formation of the Glasgow and South Western Railway.
1850	Glasgow population 300,000.
1850s	Development of Skelmorlie Village.
1851	Caley take over the GP&GR.
1852	Railway Steam Packet Company formed by Caley - relinquished in 1854.
1855	Thirty-six buildings in 'New Glasgow'.
1856	St Rollox Works built. Whiting Bay Pier (Wemyss Bay) blown down.
1857	Pier constructed at Skelmorlie and used by Captain Duncan McKellar till 1869.
1858	Wemyss Bay line first proposed.
1860	9th October - George Bruce asks Caley to consider a line to Wemyss Bay. John Burns bought Castle Wemyss.
1861	James Keyden and James Forman appointed Secretary and Engineer to the Greenock and Wemyss Bay Railway Company. Caley supports proposal to build Wemyss Bay line.
1861	9th May - Wemyss Bay Line Prospectus published.
1862	Greenock business men consider a line between Port Glasgow and Wemyss Bay.
1862	7th March - Caledonian Railway confirms support for proposed Wemyss Bay line.
1862	31st March, 1st and 2nd April - Contract signed between G&WBR and the Caley to construct and run the line.
1862	17th July - The Greenock and Wemyss Bay Railway Act, 1862 obtained.
1863	James Keyden made Secretary of the Wemyss Bay Steamboat Company.
1863	PS *Victory* built. Later purchased by Wemyss Bay Steamboat Company.
1863	8th June - Greenock and Wemyss Bay Railway Extension Act passed.
1863	October - G&WBR propose extending line to Gourock.
1863	23rd December - Wemyss Bay Steamboat Company (Ltd) Prospectus published.
1864	29th April - Wemyss Bay Steamboat Company Limited incorporated under the Companies' Act 1862. Skelmorlie electorate numbers 20.
1864	PS *Largs* built for the Wemyss Bay Steamboat Company.
1864	1st June - Original completion date for the Greenock and Wemyss Bay Railway Line.
1865	13th April - Directors travel the Wemyss Bay branch for the first time.
1865	Greenock and Ayrshire Railway Bill approved.
1865	12th May - Wemyss Bay branch opens with first excursion train carrying invited guests.
1865	13th May - Wemyss Bay Branch opened - The Caledonian Railway Co. runs the trains.
1865	15th May - Regular service starts on the Wemyss Bay line.
1865	PS *Kyles* and PS *Bute* built for the Wemyss Bay Steamboat Company.
1865	September - G&WBR suggest the company run its own steamers.
1865	7th July - Finnoch cutting collapse.
1865	16th September - Glasgow train collides with buffers in Wemyss Bay station.
1866	March - The Greenock and Wemyss Bay Railway Company formed an agreement with the Wemyss Bay Steamboat Company, Gillies and Campbell and the Caledonian Railway Company. Railway projects shelved due to high bank rates.
1866	PS *Argyle* built, and subsequently purchased by the Wemyss Bay Steamboat Company.
1866	March - Caley propose extending a line to Gourock and purchase Gourock Pier.
1866	May - Villa Tickets introduced.
1867	Rothesay Pier extended for steamer traffic. Dr James 'paraffin' Young purchased the Kelly estate. November - G&WBR proposal to Caley to allow connections to Greenock and places in Ayrshire.
1868	Skelmorlie Hydropathic erected by Dr Ronald Currie
1869	Mortimer Evans, CE, takes over from James Forman as Engineer for the Greenock and Wemyss Bay line.
1869	Failure of the Wemyss Bay Steamboat Company.
1869	2nd August - Capt. Campbell of Gillies & Campbell contracts to run the Wemyss Bay Steamboat Company.
1869	GSWR opens line to Princes Pier, Greenock
1870	May - Second class carriages introduced on to the Wemyss Bay line.
1871	Glasgow's population approaches 500,000. Skelmorlie residents number 404.

APPENDIX

1872	PS *Lady Gertrude* built for Gillies & Campbell. Foundered five years later.
1872	Act introduced to abolish turnpike trusts. New platform to be provided at Wemyss Bay station.
1873	Act obtained to build Gordon Street station on site of later Central Station.
1873	Scott & Son's Greenock Sugar Works connected to the G&WBR line. Caley and G&WBR decide to introduce the Block signalling system.
1874	6th October - Landslip at Inverkip viaduct.
1875	12th October - Partial tunnel collapse at Upper Greenock station.
1876	The telephone was invented. St Enoch station, Glasgow, opened by GSWR.
1877	Depression - G&WB Railway affected by extremely low fares on the GSWR route via Princes Pier. Further platform or access improvements proposed at Wemyss Bay.
1877	16th January - *Lady Gertrude* runs aground at Toward pier and becomes a total wreck.
1877	PS *Adela* built for Gillies & Campbell.
1878	Clyde bridged for new Central Station. Greenock and Wemyss Bay line pays its first dividend (5½ per cent).
1879	Introduction of Williams Patent points. Quarrying ceases in Wemyss Bay, though continues in Skelmorlie.
1879	Rothesay Tramways Company commenced service.
1879	December - Gordon Street station (north of the Clyde) opened.
1880s	Tracks widened from 2 to 4 from Cardonald to Paisley Gilmour Street
1881	Gas installed and telegraph wire extended to Wemyss Bay station. Thomas Weir, CE takes over from Mortimer Evans as the Greenock and Wemyss Bay Co.'s. Engineer. Skelmorlie residents number 757.
1881	December - Captain Campbell threatens to withdraw boats from 1st January 1882.
1881-1882	Winter - serious damage to sea wall and Pier at Wemyss Bay.
1882	Line opened to Fairlie pier by GSWR.
1882	Branch proposed from Wemyss Bay line to Gourock.
1883	Strike on the Caley for shorter hours and better pay. Abolition of Turnpike Trust in Ayrshire. G&WBR suggest extending line from Inverkip to Largs.
1884	28th July - Caley obtain Parliamentary approval to extend its line to Gourock.
1884	Installation of Williams Patent Points at Upper Greenock and Berryards.
1885	Central Station Hotel, commenced in 1878, opened. Ladyburn Engine Shed built at Greenock. The GSWR extends a line to Largs.
1886	February - Captain Campbell's contract renewed.
1886	PS *Victoria* built for Gillies & Campbell. 2nd Class abolished on all Caley lines except the through and coast lines.
1886	December - G&WBR request Campbell's contract be terminated.
1886	Work commenced on Greenock to Gourock extension
1887	31st May - Death of James Keyden, Secretary of the Wemyss Bay Line.
1887	Gourock Pier Station opened. Period of depression.
1887	Mr Weir, CE of the G&WBR line left and was replaced by T.O. Niven, CE.
1888	Autumn - The G&WBR arranged for the Caley to take over. November - PS *Galatea* and PS *Caledonia* ordered by the Caledonian Steam Packet Co.
1888	Parliament debates nationalisation of the railways.
1889	1st March - Second Class dropped on through and coast trains.
1889	6th May - PS *Caledonia* launched for the Caledonian Steam Packet Company. (In service from 10th June.) 8th May - Caledonian Steam Packet Company (Ltd) formed with offices at Gourock Pier station.
1889	Captain James Williamson appointed first marine superintendent of the Caledonian Steam Packet Company Ltd. Died 1919.
1889	31st May - PS *Galatea* launched for the Caledonian Steam Packet Company. (Speed trials on 3rd July.)
1889	1st June - opening of line from Greenock to Gourock.
1889	October - Captain Campbell offers his boats to the Caley.
1889	Alexander Stephen, Shipbuilder, acquired the Kelly estate.

A photograph included in an album of McAlpine progress pictures probably taken in 1901 on the Port Glasgow to Upper Greenock contract. Presumably they show the supervising engineer and his assistants outside the works office.

National Railway Museum

1889	Regulation of Railways Act 1889 introduced continuous braking and interlocking of points and signals. 26th September - Overton paper mill line Agreement signed.
1890	PS *Marchioness of Breadalbane* and PS *Marchioness of Bute* built for the Caledonian Steam Packet Company. PS *Duchess of Hamilton* built for the Caledonian Steam Packet Company (with electric lighting).
1890	22nd April - Captain Campbell gave notice of intention to quit the Wemyss Bay route. The Caley accept.
1890	1st May - Wemyss Bay trains gain access to Central Station and the Caledonian Railway commence running their new steamboats *Caledonia* and *Galatea* from Wemyss Bay.
1890	Wemyss Bay pier rebuilt.
1891	Skelmorlie residents number 951.
1892	Greenock and Wemyss Bay Railway Absorption Bill introduced.
1893	1st August - G&WB Railway Line amalgamated with the Caledonian Railway Company under the Caledonian Railway Act of 1893.
1893	Commencement of alterations to signalling system on parts of the Wemyss Bay line.
1894	January - G&WBR valued at £134,731 10s. 8d.[*£7.1m]. Scottish miners' strike.
1894-1895	Powers sought from Parliament to extend the Pier at Wemyss Bay.
1897	November - The Caley Board approve plans for a new station and extended pier for Wemyss Bay. Reconstruction of two gateways into one at Wemyss Bay Pier.
1898	Wemyss Bay to Rothesay scheduled to take 78 minutes.
1899	Wemyss Bay Pier extended and enlarged. Rothesay pier extended for steamer traffic. Gas lighting installed at Wemyss Bay engine shed. GSWR considering a line from Largs to Greenock.
1899	9th August - The Caledonian (General Powers) Act 1899 passed permitting doubling of the Wemyss Bay line, extension of the pier and the reconstruction of Wemyss Bay station.
1899-1903	Widening of sections of Wemyss Bay line.
1900	Glasgow population 750,000.
1901	Wemyss Bay pier extension completed.

APPENDIX

1901-1902	Upper Greenock station reconstructed to James Miller's designs.
1901-1906	Enlargement of Central Station including second bridge across the Clyde.
1902	2nd June - Wemyss Bay Junction to Upper Greenock doubled line opened.
1903	1st June - Doubled track from Dunrod to Wemyss Bay opened.
1903	Inverkip station reconstructed.
1903	7th December - Wemyss Bay station reopened.
1904	21st May - Wemyss Bay station tearoom reopens - unlicensed.
1906	Turbine propulsion introduced for steam ships.
1907	Extension to Central Station Hotel opened.
1908	3rd May - Bridge Street signal box, Glasgow, commissioned.
1909	Clyde Coast Pool introduced to share income.
1909	6th June - Caley introduce Sunday Service to Gourock, Dunoon and Rothesay routes.
1910	Glasgow to Rothesay travelling time possible in 80 minutes.
1913	4th December - Kelly House destroyed by fire.
1914	26th June - Wemyss Bay Pier fire extinguished by staff and local people.
1916	Georgetown sidings laid down for use by the ordnance factory.
1919	February - 8-hour working day introduced by Government.
1920s	Shops built at Wemyss Bay Station Square and Anderson & Conner's Garage (now Pearson's) constructed.
1923	1st July - LMSR takes over the Caley and G&SWR.
1924	Rothesay Winter Garden constructed.
1930s	Rothesay Pavilion erected. Car ferries arrive. Roads 'cluttered with cyclists'.
1934	Launch of RMS *Queen Mary*.
1935	LMS take over the Williamson-Buchanan fleet.
1936	Rothesay Tramways Company ceased trading.
1941	May - Germans bomb Greenock. 800 evacuated to Wemyss Bay and Skelmorlie.
1944	Ravenscraig station closed.
1945	Woodhall station opened.
1946	Skelmorlie population 1,540.
1947	22nd July - Review of Home Fleet - King George VI and Queen Elizabeth visit Wemyss Bay.
1948	1st January - Nationalisation day of the rail and steamer services under British Railways (Scottish Region), a subsidiary of the British Transport Commission.
1950s	Kelly estate sold as a caravan site. Petrol de-rationing brings more cars on to the roads.
1951	5th November - Severance of railway from steamer operations.
1954	1st October - daily car ferry service introduced from Wemyss Bay to Rothesay.
1955	Glasgow to Rothesay travelling time - 97 minutes.
1960s	Electrification using emus results in freight being diverted from rail to road.
1966	Bob Kinaird, the last station master at Wemyss Bay station, retires.
1966-1967	Electrification of line to Gourock and Wemyss Bay. Removal of two of four lines between Glasgow and Paisley and line singled from Port Glasgow to Wemyss Bay.
1967	5th June - Upper Greenock Station closed and Branchton opened.
1968	Caledonian Steam Packet Co. move their Wemyss Bay office from the concourse to the foot of the Pier ramp.
1969	1st January - Caledonian Steam Packet Co. transferred from the BTC to the bus-dominated STG.
1973	Caledonian Steam Packet Co. and David MacBrayne Ltd united as Caledonian MacBrayne Ltd.
1977	May - Introduction on Wemyss Bay-Rothesay route of *Glen Sannox* to provide drive-on, drive-off facility. Wemyss Bay pier fire. CalMac move staff back up to concourse.
1978	8th May - IBM station opened.
1987	Autumn - start of piling work on Wemyss Bay pier.
1988	Wemyss Bay pier rebuilt and clock tower restored.
1990	14th May - Whinhill station opened.
1994	25th March - Restored Wemyss Bay station celebrations.
1994	1st April - ScotRail privatised.
1998	24th May - Drumfrochar station opened.

Appendix Two

Noteworthy Personalities on the Local Scene

Hugh Montgomerie, 3rd Lord Eglinton - soldier and MP, became *12th Earl of Eglinton* in 1796 when his marriage coupled Eglinton (south of Kilwinning) to his own estates of Skelmorlie and Coilsfield. He served in America during the Seven Years' War. Later, he became Inspector of Military Roads in Scotland, surveying and selecting the best routes. He rebuilt Eglinton Castle in the gothic style, laid out Ardrossan town and built Ardrossan harbour, and proposed a canal from Ardrossan to provide a short cut to the Clyde near Glasgow. However the Burgh Council of Glasgow set about improving the river access to the city and his scheme was never completed. He spent a considerable amount of his own money on the harbour and canal schemes, public or government finance not being made available. Later titles included that of Baron Ardrossan and Lord Lieutenant of the County of Ayr.

Archibald William Montgomerie, the 13th Earl of Eglinton (1812-1861) - owned, but did not live in North Skelmorlie. He inherited the title at the age of seven. He was generous to a fault, in the end having to dispose of parts of his estate to pay for his extravagance. He was known as the 'Tournament Earl' on account of an immense spectacle held at Eglinton, which lasted from 28th to 30th August, 1839. At the time, Medieval fashions were popular, and it was decided to hold a tournament, with tents, marquees, jousting, banqueting and period amusements. Many came in fancy dress and among the guests were Benjamin Disraeli and Prince Louis Napoleon. Some 150,000 people arrived, including, it is believed, Charles Dickens, reporting for a London paper. They came by train from London to Liverpool, thence by steamer to Ardrossan and by a rudimentary railway to Eglinton. However, the weather was unkind; starting fine and ending fine, it poured solidly in between. The £2,000 estimated cost was wildly out - it cost £40,000 (*£1.37m).

Eglinton was a successful horse owner winning the St Leger in 1842 and the Derby in 1849. In 1859, Queen Victoria created him Earl of Winton in recognition of his services as Lord Lieutenant of Ireland. He also was also elected Lord Rector of Glasgow University and Marischal College in Aberdeen.

Archibald William Montgomerie, 17th Earl of Eglinton - a District Councillor, lived in the Castle at Skelmorlie from 1945. His wife Ursula was a descendent of the Bannatynes of Kelly.

George Burns (1795-1890) - The Burns family moved from Stirlingshire to Glasgow in 1767. George was the youngest son of Dr John Burns, minister of the Barony Church in Glasgow. After a period in the New Lanark Cotton Spinning Company, he and his brother James began trading as G. & J. Burns, developing a substantial steamship trade. George Burns, created a Baronet in 1889, was a co-founder of the Cunard Steamship line in 1839. Both Burns and James Donaldson, competitors on the Glasgow to Liverpool steamship run, were brought together by Napier, the shipbuilder, who had been approached by Samuel Cunard to build two boats to carry mails to America. Napier had considered the proposed vessels too small and obtained Cunard's agreement to seek additional capital to enable larger vessels to be contemplated. Cunard agreed, and 32 subscribers, including Burns and Donaldson, provided £215,000 on top of Cunard's £55,000 [*a total of £9.25m], enabling four paddle steamers to be built. The first voyage from Liverpool to Boston began on 4th July, 1840 taking 14 days 8 hours at an average speed of 8½ knots. George Burns built Wemyss House and in 1879 the Episcopal Church in Whiting Bay, next to Ferncliffe. The church remained open until 1956. It is now the burial ground of the Inverclyde family.

John Burns - son of George Burns, bought Castle Wemyss in 1860 and was created Baron Inverclyde in 1897. He entertained many famous people, including Anthony Trollope, General Sherman (C-in-C of the US Army), H.M. Stanley and possibly Dr Livingstone, either at the Castle or on board his yachts, the *Mastiff* or the *Capercailzie*.

Lord Inverclyde - was host to Emperor Haile Selassie of Abyssinia at Castle Wemyss in 1936. The Emperor planted a maple tree in the Castle grounds to commemorate his visit. A year later, he returned to await the end of World War II. In 1943, Lord Inverclyde was host to the exiled King Peter of Yugoslavia. In 1947, he received King George VI and Queen Elizabeth at Wemyss Bay during the review of the Home Fleet. In 1957, Alan, 4th Baron Inverclyde died with no direct heir.

Alexander Stephen of Linthouse - a major shipbuilder, purchased Kelly estate in 1889, demolished Kelly House and built a new one in red sandstone higher up the hill. His widow, Mary Templeton or Stephen and other trustees (which included John, Alexander and Frederick Stephen (Shipbuilders at Linthouse, Govan), John and James Templeton (carpet manufacturers in Glasgow), George Moffat (Chartered Accountant) and James Smith Napier (Iron merchant)), entered into an Agreement with the Caledonian Railway Company to allow the Caley to build the replacement Wemyss Bay railway station on Kelly estate land.

King George VI and Queen Elizabeth - stayed overnight in Wemyss Bay in February 1940. The only previously recently recorded visit by royalty was when Edward VII passed through Wemyss Bay station. Later, in July 1947, accompanied by Princess Elizabeth, her fiancée Lieutenant Philip Mountbatten and Princess Margaret, King George and Queen Elizabeth were met by Lord Inverclyde at Wemyss Bay station during a review of the Home Fleet in the Clyde in 1947. Since that date HRH Prince Charles, Duke of Rothesay, has passed through the station.

Prime Minister *Earl Attlee* stayed at Skelmorlie Hydro in the 1950s. *Donald Currie Caskie*, OBE, (1902-1983) - minister of the Scots Kirk in Paris from 1935, assisted the French Resistance movement during World War II and latterly was called to the North Church Skelmorlie and Wemyss Bay.

Local personalities included *Mr Dallas* the coalman, who also stabled the station horses. In 1925, he lost three children when his house, Birchburn Cottage was demolished by the bursting of the lower reservoir above Skelmorlie. In 1916, *Mr Paton* the butcher and *Ure Young* the baker bought petrol driven delivery vans, though horses were used for many years to come. *Doctor Mearns Taylor* (d.1932) - contributed much to local life, encouraging the setting up of the Tennis Club and supporting the golf club.

Engineers, Architects and Railway Staff

John Miller (1805-1883) - was the most prominent of the early railway engineers and architects, involved in the construction of many of Scotland's early railway lines. He joined Thomas Grainger's office in 1823 and by 1825 was in partnership with him. Miller designed the first Bridge Street Station. Among others, he planned the Glasgow, Paisley, Kilmarnock and Ayr lines, in this case assisted by his nephew George M. Cunningham (who later joined Benjamin Hall Blyth). Miller and Grainger prepared initial designs for the Glasgow, Paisley & Greenock Railway before the commission was taken from them and given to Locke and Errington.

Joseph Locke (1807? - 1860) - was a prominent English railway engineer who had worked as an assistant to George Stephenson on the Liverpool & Manchester Railway in the early part of the 19th century. At the request of the Greenock committee for the Glasgow, Paisley & Greenock Railway, he took over the design and construction of the line with his partner John Errington from Thomas Grainger, most probably to attract English finance for a line that was not receiving support from the wealthy Glasgow merchants. The line was very costly, largely because of land acquisition costs and the failure of two contractors. Even though Locke came in for severe criticism for his cost control (to some extent unjustifiably as he had a reputation for being more accurate in his costings than many of his contemporaries), nevertheless for a short time he was a Board member on the opening of the line. John Errington drew up an exemplary code of regulations for running the line. It is probably no coincidence that Locke and Errington were subsequently employed as the Caledonian's civil engineers for the main line to Carlisle. Their assistant, Robert Sinclair, was to become the manager and locomotive superintendent of the Caledonian Railway.

Robert Sinclair (1817-1898) - was born in London and educated at Charter House till he was 15. He served as an apprentice in his uncle's firm, Scott Sinclair & Co. of Greenock. When he was about 20, he went to work for Robert Stephenson on the Manchester and Birmingham Railway and was subsequently appointed to work for Locke on what was to become the London & North Western Railway. After a period working on French railways, he was employed by Errington to supervise the construction of the running shed and repair works of the Glasgow, Paisley & Greenock Railway. In July 1846, he became mechanical superintendent of the GP&GR, a post he held until February 1848 when he was made locomotive superintendent of the Caledonian Railway. By 1851, he also held the appointments of General Manager and Civil Engineer on the line. He set up the new St

The Caledonian Railway Co.

CR Chairmen
William Lockhart, MP	1844
The Rt Hon.Lord Belhaven	1844-1845
John James Hope Johnstone	1845-1850
Capt. The Hon. Edward Plunkett RN	1850-1850
John Duncan	1850-1852
William Baird	1852-1854
William Johnston	1854-1859
Lieut Col Thomas Salkeld	1859-1868
Thomas Hill	1868-1880
J.C. Bolton, M.P.	1880-1897
J.C. Bunten	1897-1901 (d)
Sir James Thompson	1901-1906 (d)
Sir James King, Bart.	1906-1908
Sir C. Bine Renshaw of Barochan, Bart., MP	1908-1918 (d)
Henry Allan	1918-1923

CR General Managers
James Butler Williams	1847 (d)
Capt.Joshua William Coddington, R.E.(& Sec)	1847-1852
Robert Sinclair	1852-1856
Christopher Johnstone	1856-1867
James Smithells	1867-1882
Sir James Thompson	1882-1900
William Patrick	1900-1901 (d)
Robert Millar	1901-1908 (d)
Guy Calthrop	1908-1910
Donald A. Matheson, M.I.C.E.	1910-1926

CR Secretaries
Lt-Col John Hambly Humfry, AICE	1844
David Rankine (Secy and Treasurer)	1844-1846
James Butler Williams	1846-1847 (d)
Capt.Joshua William Coddington, R.E.(& GM)	1847-1852
Archibald Gibson (Asst Secy & Secy)	1847-1890 (d)
George Jackson (Solicitor)	1890-1891
John Blackburn	1891-1920
John Johnston Haining	1920-1926

Locomotive Superintendents:
Robert Sinclair (till 1849 representing Locke and Errington)	1846-1856
Benjamin Conner	1857-1876 (d)
George Brittain	1876-1882
Dugald Drummond	1882-1890
Hugh Smellie	1890-1891 (d)
John Lambie	1891-1895 (d)
John McIntosh	1895-1914
William Pickersgill	1914-1923

Note: (d) - died in office

The Caledonian Steam Packet Co. Ltd

CSP Chairmen
Marquis of Breadalbane (CR Co.)	1889-1898
James Neilson (CR Co.)	1898-1903
David Tod (CR Co.)	1903-1910
H.E. Gordon (CR Co.)	1910-1923
Sir Alexander Gracie (LMSR Co.)	1925-1930

CSP Managers/General Managers/Managing Directors
Capt. James Williamson	1888-1919
Charles A. Bremner	1919-1946
Robert D. Kerr	1946-1947
Capt. Harry J.B. Perry	1948-1951
Lawrence E. Marr	1952-1955
Alexander Stewart	1955-1970
N. John D. Whittle	1970-1973

CSP Secretaries
James Williamson	1889-1919
Charles A. Bremner	1919-1931
Thomas H. Moffat	1932-1953
Alexander Stewart	1953-1956
James Geddes	1956-1959
H.M. Hunter	1959-1962
John A. Gunn	1962-1965
David P. Knighton*	1966-1968
John Reid*	1968-1969
James Kirkwood	1969-1973

Caledonian MacBrayne Ltd (CSP merged with David MacBrayne in 1973)

CalMac Secretaries
Thomas G. Moore	1973-1985
James Kirkwood	1985-1992
Gordon W. McKenzie	1993-

CalMac Managers/General Managers/Managing Directors
N. John D. Whittle	1973-1983
Colin S. Paterson	1983-1997
Capt. Jab Simkins	1997-

Note: * Finance and administration officer

Rollox works before leaving in July 1856 to join the Eastern Counties Railway from which he retired in 1868 due to ill health. He survived for another 30 years.

Benjamin Hall Blyth (1819-1866) - was among the principal railway engineers of the time. He joined the railway and civil engineering practice of Grainger & Miller in 1834 and was subsequently engaged on the Glasgow & Ayrshire Railway, Kilmarnock & Carlisle Railway and the North British Railway. In 1848, he set up on his own. In 1854 he was joined by his brother Edward. Practising from their office at 135 George Street, Edinburgh, their clients included the Caledonian, the Glasgow & South Western Railway, the Scottish Central, the Dundee & Perth, the Great North of Scotland, and the Portpatrick railways. Railway construction was a major part of the firm's business up to 1900 though little railway work was done after 1918. Their office provided designs for the first Glasgow Central station, the rail bridge over the Clyde to Central Station (1876-1878), Perth General, Waverley Station and the Balerno line *(see Oakwood Press - The Balerno Branch by Donald Shaw, 1989).* In 1867 George Miller Cunningham, (see John Miller), principal assistant, was assumed into the partnership and the firm's name changed to Blyth and Cunningham. It was later renamed Cunningham, Blyth & Westland and now trades as Blyth & Blyth Associates.

Christopher Johnstone joined the Caledonian Railway around December 1847 as goods manager. In July 1856, he was promoted to General Manager. According to J.F. McEwan he resigned in July 1868 due to ill-health. Other records suggest that his successor, James Smithells, was in post in 1867.

James Collie, (died about 1870) - Architect of the first Bridge Street Station (1841) which included an impressive classical façade. This station was jointly owned by the Glasgow & Paisley Joint Line Committee, the Glasgow, Paisley, Kilmarnock & Ayr Railway and the Glasgow, Paisley & Greenock Railway. This was Glasgow's first major railway terminus. The companies subsequently became part of the Glasgow & South Western Railway and the Caledonian Railway.

Sir Robert Rowand Anderson LLD, FRIBA (1834-1921) - an Edinburgh Architect, first president of the Institute of Architects in Scotland, (later the Royal Incorporation of Architects in Scotland) designed offices for Glasgow Central station (1878-1883) (his only railway commission) with Blyth & Cunningham of Edinburgh as engineers. Before the offices were completed, they were converted to provide hotel accommodation with nearly 400 rooms. The corner tower dominates the Gordon Street/Hope Street corner. Rowand Anderson was also responsible for the construction between 1877 and 1900 of the present Mount Stuart House for the 3rd Marquess of Bute.

Some Wemyss Bay Station Masters and Staff

Mr Elliott was station master at Wemyss Bay station in 1865 while *Mr. Hughes* was station master there in 1870. In 1863 *Thomas Pettigrew* was clerk at New Galloway station on the Portpatrick Railway. In 1868, he moved to the office of the general superintendent of the Caledonian Railway in Glasgow. He was promoted in 1877 to station master at Wemyss Bay station where he stayed 5½ years. He returned to Glasgow as chief clerk in the general superintendent's office where he remained for 20 years before being made outdoor assistant to Guy Calthrop. He later became General Superintendent.

Mr Robison - entered service with the Caley in 1865 and served as station master at Shotts and Upper Greenock before becoming station master at Wemyss Bay from about 1885. He was present at the pier fire on 21st September, 1900. A 'horticulturist of no mean order', he decorated the new station with hanging baskets and flower displays. In 1905, his office is reputed to have had 130 photographs of celebrities who had used the station, from Sir James Thompson (Chairman from 1901-1906) downwards. About the same time (1884), *Mr Melrose* was piermaster at Wemyss Bay, and was still there when the alteration work was completed in 1904. *Mr Prentice* was station master at Wemyss Bay in 1911; his successor *John Thomson* held the post in 1920 at the time when the collapse of a defective retaining wall occurred near the goods depôt. In 1929, engine driver *William Cunninghame* and guard *James Halliday* retired after 50 years' service. A 'committee of travellers' raised £275 (*£7,300), an astonishing sum, as a farewell gift, handed over in the office of *Mr Toward*, the station master. In BR days, porter *Dick Johnston* maintained the flower arrangements in Wemyss Bay station.

Appendix Three

Fares Compared

Road Tolls

Date	Item	Toll	
1767 (20 miles)	Coach and six horses	4s.	*£11.54
Saltcoats to	Wagon and six	6s.	*£17.31
Kelly Bridge	Drove of sheep (20 No.)	5d.	*£1.20

Road Fares

Date	From	To	Inside Coach		Outside Coach		Time
1835	Glasgow	Greenock	5s.	*£10.65	3s.	*£6.40	3½ hours

Fares permitted under The Greenock and Wemyss Bay Railway Act, 1862

The Act fixed maximum rates by rail per mile (figures in brackets are charges for using Company vehicles), for example: Passengers, each 2d. (4d.) [*34p (*68p)].

In addition, a rate of up to 1d. [*17p] per mile was chargeable for each passenger. The normal maximum charges for express and ordinary trains, inclusive of carriage and locomotive charges, would be 3d./passenger/mile for 1st class, 2d./passenger/mile for 2nd class carriage and 1½d./passenger/mile for 3rd class carriage [*51p, *34p and *25p/mile respectively]. Special train rates were subject to charge under the maximum scale.

Train Fares

Date	Down from Glasgow to	1st (single)		3rd (single)		1st (return)		3rd (return)	
15th May, 1865	Paisley (See Note)	-	-	-	-	-	-	-	-
	Port Glasgow	1s. 6d.	*£3.11	1s.	*£2.07	2s. 6d.	*£5.18	1s. 6d.	*£3.11
	Upper Greenock	1s. 6d.	*£3.11	1s.	*£2.07	2s. 6d.	*£5.18	1s. 6d.	*£3.11
	Ravenscraig	2s.	*£4.15	1s. 6d.	*£3.11	3s.	*£6.22	2s. 3d.	*£4.66
	Inverkip	2s.	*£4.15	1s. 6d.	*£3.11	3s. 6d.	*£7.25	2s. 9d.	*£5.70
	Wemyss Bay	2s.	*£4.15	1s. 6d.	*£3.11	3s. 6d.	*£7.25	2s. 9d.	*£5.70

Date	Up from Wemyss Bay to	1st (single)		3rd (single)		1st (return)		3rd (return)	
15th May, 1865	Inverkip	4d.	*70p	2d.	*35p	6d.	*£1.04	3d.	*52p
	Ravenscraig	1s.	*£2.07	5½d.	*95p	1s. 6d.	*£3.11	9d.	*£1.55
	Upper Greenock	1s.	*£2.07	6d.	*£1.04	1s. 6d.	*£3.11	9d.	*£1.55
	Port Glasgow	1s. 9d.	*£3.63	10½d.	*£1.81	2s. 6d.	*£5.18	1s. 6d.	*£3.11
	Paisley (See Note)	2s.	*£4.15	1s. 6d.	*£3.11	3s. 6d.	*£7.25	2s. 9d.	*£5.70
	Glasgow	2s.	*£4.15	1s. 6d.	*£3.11	3s. 6d.	*£7.25	2s. 9d.	*£5.70

NOTE from contemporary rules: Passengers will not be booked from Glasgow to Paisley, nor vice versa nor will holders of return or season tickets between these two stations be conveyed by the Wemyss Bay trains.

Caledonian PS *Duchess of Fife* faces the Firth while the PS *Marchioness of Breadalbane* berths on the south side of Wemyss Bay pier. Note Kelly House on the ridge behind and the semaphore signals at the end of the pier.   David Hamilton Collection

Boat Fares

Date	From-To	single with cabin	steerage (single only)	return with cabin
15th May, 1865	Wemyss Bay-Innellan, Toward, Rothesay, Largs, Millport	4d. *70p	2d. *35p	6d. *£1.04

Train and Boat Fares

Date	From (via Wemyss Bay)	To	1st with cabin (single)	3rd with cabin (single)	1st with cabin (return)	3rd with cabin (return)
15th May, 1865	Glasgow	Rothesay, Toward, Largs, Millport	2s. 4d. *£4.84	1s. 9d. *£3.63	3s. 9d. *£7.77	3s. *£6.22
	Glasgow	Innellan	2s. *£4.15	1s. 6d. *£3.11	3s. 3d. *£6.74	2s. 6d. *£5.18
	Glasgow	Arran	3s. *£6.22	2s. 6d. *£5.18	5s. *£10.36	3s. 9d. *£7.77
	Glasgow	Tarbert and Ardrishaig	3s. 6d. *£7.25	2s. 6d. *£5.18	6s. *£12.44	4s. *£8.29
	Glasgow	Kyles	2s. 9d. *£5.70	2s. *£4.15	4s. 6d. *£9.33	3s. 3d. *£6.74

Fares at the end of the 19th century

Round about 1890, fares on the Wemyss Bay line were such that few people bought season tickets - the first class return was 3s. 6d. [*£8.60]. To make the £25 [*£1,230] pa season ticket pay, the holder had to travel nearly three times a week.

Train Fares

Date	From Glasgow to	1st (single)	3rd (single)	Standard (single)	1st (return)	3rd (return)	Standard (return)
15th May, 1865	Wemyss Bay	2s. *£4.15	1s. 6d. *£3.11	-	3s. *£7.25	2s. 9d. *£5.70	-
1st Jan., 1867	Wemyss Bay	2s. 4d. *£4.38	1s. 9d. *£3.28	-	4s. *£7.50	2s. 6d. *£4.69	-
c.1885	Wemyss Bay	2s. *£4.77	1s. 2d. *£2.78	-	3s. 6d. *£8.35	2s. *£4.77	-
c.1903	Wemyss Bay	-	-	-	3s. *£7.38	2s. 2d. *£5.33	-
1st Jan., 1999	Wemyss Bay			£3.90			£6.60
1st Jan., 1999	Rothesay via Wemyss Bay			£6.15			£10.85

Appendix Four

Land Purchase and Other Agreements

Miles from Port Glasgow	Parish	Cal. Ref.	Land Owner	Description	Features
0	East Parish of Greenock	3963	Sir Michael Robert Shaw Stewart Bart	Chapelton Farm Gibshill Bogston Fencewood	Port Glasgow Station. Double line to Upper Greenock added 1902 - now removed.
		3964 3965	John Jeffray		
1	East Parish of Greenock	3963	Sir Michael Robert Shaw Stewart Bart	Bridgend Maukinhill Upper Ingleston	Lady Octavia Public Park. Ex-GSWR line connection to Princes Pier.
		3959	Thomas King		G&SWR crosses over the
		5902	Sir Michael Hugh Shaw Stewart		Carts Burn tunnel.
		3960	Thomas MacKnight Crawfurd	At Cartsburn tunnel	Whinhill station
2	East Parish of Greenock	3969 3973	Board of Police of Greenock		Wellington Park. Overton Paper Mill railway junction.
		3967	Messrs Alex Scott & Sons		
		3961	Sir Michael Robert Shaw Stewart Bart	East Berryards	[Upper Greenock station]
		6454	The Westburn Sugar Refineries Ltd		[Drumfrochar station] Sugar Refinery sidings to north.
		5902	Sir Michael Hugh Shaw Stewart		Rope and woollen works to south.
		3970	James Young		
		3976	Sir Michael Robert Shaw Stewart Bart	West Berryards (part) Cornhaddock Murdieston	Single line to Dunrod Aqueduct.
	West Parish of Greenock	3971	Trustees for Hugh McCormick and Co.		HM Prison to north.
3		3963	Sir Michael Robert Shaw Stewart Bart	West Berryards (part) Hole	Overton Paper Mill uphill; siding to North Smithston.
	Parish of Inverkip	3965	Duncan Darroch		Poorhouse to south.
4		3966	Duncan Darroch		Branchton station.
		4586	Duncan Darroch		[Ravenscraig station]
		3962	Sir Michael Robert Shaw Stewart Bart		Ravenscraig Farm.
5		3962	Sir Michael Robert Shaw Stewart Bart	Spango Kingston	IBM Halt.
		5902	Sir Michael Hugh Shaw Stewart		
6		3962	Sir Michael Robert Shaw Stewart Bart	Dunrod Bogside Leap	Dunrod Siding doubled to Wemyss Bay in 1903 - now single line.
		5902	Sir Michael Hugh Shaw Stewart		Kip Viaduct.
7		3962	Sir Michael Robert Shaw Stewart Bart	Inverkip	Daff Viaduct. Hill farm siding.
		5902	Sir Michael Hugh Shaw Stewart		Inverkip station. Inverkip tunnel.
8		3962	Sir Michael Robert Shaw Stewart Bart		
		5902	Sir Michael Hugh Shaw Stewart	Finnockbog	Kelly Quarry siding.
9	Parish of Skelmorlie	3974 3975	James Scott (with consent)		Wemyss Bay station.
		5668	Board of Trade		

APPENDIX

Principal Land Purchase Agreements formed by The Greenock and Wemyss Bay Railway Company

	Acres	Area Roods	Poles
Sir Michael Robert Shaw Stewart Bart (Agreement dated 25th February, 1862, signed by A.S. Finlay and James Scott of Kelly. A further Agreement was made on 11th and 18th April, 1866).	73	1	0 ¼
Duncan Darroch of Gourock (Minute of Agreement dated 5th and 28th May 1862, signed by James Scott and others)	17	0	20 ½
James Scott (Agreement dated 12th and 15th May and 21st July, 1862 and signed by the provisional Directors, and Minute of reference dated 1865)	15	2	30 ¼

1 acre = 4,840 sq. yds, 1 rood = ¼ acre (1,210 sq. yds), 1 pole = ¹⁄₄₀ rood (30¼ sq. yds)

Main Agreements formed by the Greenock and Wemyss Bay Railway Co.

Caledonian Railway Company (Contract dated 31st March and 1st and 2nd April, 1862 and signed by the Greenock and Wemyss Bay Railway Co.).
Caledonian Railway Company (Agreement as extract of Minutes of the Caledonian Railway Company Directors dated 28th March, 1862 - presumably confirming the Caley's initial contribution of £30,000).
The Shaws Water Joint Stock Co. (1825) (Agreement signed by James Scott of Kelly on 4th April, 1862) - the Shaws provided water for driving mills and machinery near Greenock and also water for the town.
Wemyss Bay Steamboat Company and the Caledonian Railway Company (Agreement dated 14th, 20th and 21st March, 1866)
Caledonian Railway Company and Sir Michael R.S. Stewart (dated 1867)
James Gillies and Alexander Campbell (Agreements dated 1869).

CALEDONIAN RAILWAY

BYE-LAW.

Any person found upon the Railway, or upon or in any Station, Depot, Works, or Premises, the property of the Caledonian Railway Company, without proper authority, selling or offering for sale newspapers or other literature, or hawking fruits, wares, or goods of any description, or soliciting luggage to carry, is hereby subjected to a penalty not exceeding Forty Shillings.

Given under the common seal of the Caledonian Railway Company, this Nineteenth day of January, 1887.

ARCH. GIBSON,
Secretary.

Caledonian Railway bye-law - conduct that could lead to a 40s. penalty.

Scottish Record Office Ref. BLR(S)1/1/8

Appendix Five

The Specification for the 1903 Wemyss Bay Station

The Specification stated that the new station buildings 'and relative works' at Wemyss Bay and Inverkip were authorised under the Caledonian Railway (General Powers) Act, 1899, which is stretching a point as only Wemyss Bay station is mentioned in the Act, and that in a passing reference hidden away in a Schedule. On 1st October, 1900, The Caledonian Railway Company sought tenders for widening the Wemyss Bay Railway from Dunrod to Wemyss Bay, advising that an 'Assistant Engineer will attend at Inverkip Station on Monday, the 8th current, at 11.22 am, to accompany contractors over and point out the line of the works'. Presumably such precise timing related to when his train was due in. Tenderers were only allowed to the 22nd of the month to place their bids.

Two years later, on 13th December, 1902, the Caley published the following Advertisement:

Wemyss Bay Railway Widening
Wemyss Bay and Inverkip Stations' Buildings Contract

The Directors of the Caledonian Railway Company are prepared to receive Tenders for the Works to be executed in the construction of new Station Buildings at Wemyss Bay and at Inverkip.

As well as building and relative work, the Contract will include the supply, delivery and erection, of about 600 tons of steel work in platforms' verandah and other roofing.

Drawings may be seen, on and after Friday the 19th instant, at the office of the Company's Engineer, Buchanan Street Station, Glasgow, where copies of the Specification and Schedule may be obtained on payment of Two Guineas, which will be returned to Contractors who make a bona-fide Tender.

An Assistant Engineer will attend at Wemyss Bay Station, on Tuesday 23rd instant, at 11.30 am, to accompany Contractors over and point out the sites of the Works.

Sealed Tenders, endorsed 'Tender for Construction of Wemyss Bay and Inverkip Stations' Buildings,' to be lodged with the undersigned, on or before, Monday the 19th January, 1903.

The Directors do not bind themselves to accept the lowest or any Tender.

(Signed) J. Blackburn,
Secretary

With preparatory works at an advanced stage, the Caley Directors were keen to see building begin. Tenderers had a calendar month to complete and submit their bids, even though Christmas and New Year fell within the tender period. But then, the building trade did not take a fortnight's holiday as it does now. Note that the drawings were only available to *view* (even although 'photographic' reproduction was possible). When bids were sought for the restoration works in 1993, the usual practice of issuing drawings (without charge) to all tendering contractors applied.

The tender documents revealed that work on Wemyss Bay station was to start immediately. The western side was to be complete by 31st May, 1903, the remaining buildings by 31st October, 1903 and the whole contract by 31st December, 1903. At Inverkip, an immediate start was needed to allow completion by 31st May, 1903. Once finished, the buildings were to be maintained for a year. 30 drawings described Wemyss Bay station and the houses, and five Inverkip. (Most of these were still available for the restoration work 90 years later.) At Wemyss Bay, the existing station was to be demolished, priority being given to dismantling the roof and east wall of the station shed, the station master's house and refreshment rooms. The contractor was expected to build a temporary timber refreshment room for use while the works were in progress. A new station 'shed', booking and parcels offices, refreshment rooms, waiting rooms both in the station and on the pier were to be constructed in their place. The work also comprised offices for railway and steamboat staff, a steel and glass verandah and other roofing, connecting passages between the station and the pier, and staff houses in their own grounds outside the station. To allow materials to be delivered, the contractor could make arrangements through the company's Engineer to access the pier or the railway on Sundays or by night. But he would have to bear half the cost of flagmen or signalmen on these occasions.

At Inverkip, the existing structures on the up (Glasgow) side would be replaced and a new building constructed on the down side.

The specification noted that foundations had been built on reclaimed land on the west side of Wemyss Bay station, but the founds on the east side were to be carried out under this contract. The station work on the west side had to be executed first so that train operations were not interfered with. Great emphasis was made on the need to ensure that railway and steamboat traffic was maintained - safely.

In both buildings, stone was to be re-used, and iron, timber, lead and slate would be taken down and put in railway wagons for future use (not necessarily on these stations) at the discretion of the railway's engineer. Movable furnishings and fixings in the refreshment rooms would be retained. Re-used stone was not to be mixed with new facing stone. At Wemyss Bay, it was permissible to use it on surfaces to be rendered and on exposed portions of the screen walls of the new station shed. When repairing platforms in the 1990s, old stone was found under the surface of the eastmost platform, suggesting that some of the upfill for that platform may have come from the original buildings. Likewise at Inverkip, existing stone could be reused. Gas fittings were to be provided as before. While electric light was referred to for the temporary works, it does not seem to have been considered for the permanent installation even although electric light had been installed in Central Station in the mid-1880s. An Appendix to the Specification outlines the Agreement reached with the trustees of Alexander Stephen of Kelly respecting land purchase and other matters.

The workmen had to be provided with sanitary and other facilities (unspecified), as required by the Local Authorities and the Caley's Inspector had to be furnished with a 'substantial office', 15 feet square, built in brick, with a slated roof and a fireplace. The powers of the Caley's Resident Engineer and Inspectors were technically limited as only the company's Engineer was empowered to instruct - in other words, instructions by the Resident Engineer had to be confirmed in writing by Donald Matheson back in Glasgow, though in practice authority was no doubt delegated to site officials.

Details of the Specification

Downtakings - At Wemyss Bay, buildings to be dismantled included the station master's house 'and other dwelling houses'. Existing timber was not to be reused. Some trees had to be axed on the site of the staff houses.

Masonry - Freestone (fine-grained easily-sawn sandstone) was to come from quarries such as Corncockle or Corsehill, and used either as ashlar (i.e. flat faced) or square rubble (rough hewn). The Corncockle Quarry could have supplied the stone for the original station as it was working by 1824. Corsehill Quarry opened in 1880. Both quarries were operational in 1997 though they had been closed between 1955 and the early 1980s.

Corsehill Quarry produced a deep red tight grained sandstone which was much sought after. Corncockle stone is pale red with an open texture and may be streaked with black lines. It is noteworthy that James Miller, the architect of the new Wemyss Bay Station, specified 'the famous red corncockle sandstone from Dumfriesshire' for the present Peebles Hydro, rebuilt about two years after the 'new' Wemyss Bay station was completed. As the Caley built the new Caledonian station and hotel in Edinburgh, using stone from Corncockle, at the same time as the second Wemyss Bay station was under construction, it is quite possible that Corncockle stone was the current favourite and used at Wemyss Bay. Locharbriggs Quarry, near Corncockle, was active from 1858 and produces a stone similar to Corncockle and this was used in restoration work in 1993. The lack of any mention of Locharbriggs may have no significance; it was more important to define the acceptable colour range.

These three quarries are close to each other and transported stone on the Caledonian Railway, but which stone was used is not known.

Stone was either to be well-chiselled ashlar or 'rock-face'. Some pieces were particularly large - 3 ft 6 in. minimum depth for cross bonding, 2 ft 6 in. wide on the visible face. The specification for the separate widening contract similarly required that the sea wall was to be in 'rock-faced freestone or granite ashlar facing', courses below mean water level being up to 18 inches high and those above between 16 inches and 14 inches high. Arbroath stone would be used for stairs (as at the entrance to the tower at Wemyss Bay). Mortar was to be a 1:2 mix of cement to sand. While this may have been sound for engineering works, it produced such a hard material, no lime being added to 'soften' the mixture, that by the 1990s, the stone in the more exposed parts of the station had eroded more rapidly than the mortar thus leaving projecting mortar 'picture framing' round individual stones. Sand had to have the same characteristics as that from Dunduff Quarry and cement was to be English Portland, a specification still used today. Cement was to be delivered to site 'at least six weeks before it is required to be used' and there was always a requirement that a two month supply should be available.

Concrete - was to be made from cement mixed with ballast (small pieces of whinstone and broken freestone or clinker bricks) as aggregate. Granolithic concrete (for platforms and round the concourse) would be in the proportions of 1:2, cement to crushed granite. The build-up for this last item was quite considerable - a formation layer of 7 in. of dry stones, 4 in. of concrete topped by 1½ in. of granolithic concrete, cast in small bays and patterned. Certain areas where the station had been built on reclaimed ground (notably west of the present concourse) were found during the 1993 restoration work to incorporate roughly formed concrete arches - the earth profiled to a curve and mass concrete poured over. Pirie carried out this work for the new tracks on the west side and may also have done similar work on the east side once Ferguson had demolished the old station. The specification identified certain locations, especially the circulating area and the passage to the pier as requiring this detail. It called for the concrete build up to be formed 'with a versed sine of 4 inches on a span of 5 ft, formed by dressing the earth core to proper curvature before the broken stone bottoming is laid, and the thickness of the concrete paving [which included the granolithic topping] shall be 5 inches and 10 inches at the centre and springing respectively'.

Steel and Iron - had to be made in Britain, with the manufacturer's name stamped on it - foreign steel being unacceptable. (Some steel might have come from Glengarnock steelworks 'over the hill'.) Wrought steel had to be smooth and 'entirely free from rust, scales, blisters, indentations, laminations, cracked edges' etc. and of such quality as to be free from fracture after work involving punching, bending or riveting when it was either hot or cold. The description of steel plates even gave the rolling process from the initial ingot. The strength of steel was to be further checked - tensile strength between 28 and 32 tons per square inch, elasticity not less than 14 tons per square inch, bending tests to show no signs of fracture and cold punching of closely-spaced holes to be fracture free. Wrought iron had to achieve a tensile strength with the grain, and across it, of 22 and 18 tons per square inch respectively. Rivets were similarly tested. Broken test pieces of steel had to exhibit at the point of fracture 'a tough silky fibrous appearance of uniform colour without any indication of being crystalline', all of which indicates a developed scientific approach to steel analysis. The temperatures for bending were closely defined and shaping by hammering was not allowed but had to be 'carefully executed under hydraulic pressure' using suitable dies.

Wrought steel and iron plates had to be formed so 'that the fibres of the material shall run in the direction of the greatest strain'. Bolts and nuts were to have Whitworth threads, with hexagonal heads for steelwork, square heads for timber work, bolts, nuts and washers being dipped into boiled linseed oil while hot. Fitting steel plates together and riveting was precisely specified, overlarge holes being fitted with larger diameter rivets, the diameter of the hole being no greater than rivet diameter plus $\frac{1}{32}$ in. Riveting would not be permitted in wet weather, but plates had to be 'closed or riveted while the rivet is at red heat' using hydraulic power 'both in the bridge building yard and at the sites of the works'.

'All steel work shall be executed under cover, be protected from the weather, and be built and erected vertically, that is in the position it will occupy in the finished work'. Steelwork was expected to be fabricated off site and the engineer was to be offered the opportunity of seeing it fitted up in the builder's yard before dispatch to site.

The bedding of girders on stonework (each with an imparted camber of $\frac{1}{60}$ in. per foot run), was to be on three layers of well tarred hair felt. Installation had to be integrated with the railway's normal traffic requirements. 'In the erection of the steel work precautions shall be taken to ensure the safe and regular working of traffic; and for this purpose it shall, where necessary, be placed in position during the cessation of traffic by night and between such hours on Saturday night and Monday morning as the Engineer will determine and direct.'

Cast-iron columns had to have an ultimate tensile strain of 6½ tons per square inch, achieving 2½ tons per square inch without loss of elasticity. Columns were to be cast vertically, and to check their thickness, small holes were to be drilled at intervals then made good with steel filling pieces. (Restoration work uncovered the nameplate of MACKENZIE BROS - IRONFOUNDERS - EDINBURGH screwed to a column base.) Cast-iron gutters, rhone pipes and heads were to be painted internally with tar. The susceptibility of cast iron to cracking was recognised: stopping and plugging to conceal defects would result in that section being immediately broken up. The presence of 'Beaumont's Egg' filler in the cast iron work of the first Tay Bridge and its contribution to the bridge's disastrous failure less than 25 years earlier - within living memory - was no doubt etched in the minds of the fabricators. The thickness of the walls of the cast-iron columns was tested in 1993 with sophisticated electronic equipment; it was not thought wise to drill into the columns.

Cleaning, painting and protecting - In the highly corrosive atmosphere of the Clyde, particular attention was paid to protecting steelwork against rusting. All steel and iron work, both wrought and cast, 'shall be thoroughly coated with boiled linseed oil and be afterwards painted with four coats of paint'. First the steel had to be cleaned of loose particles by brushing, hammering or sand blasting then immediately coated with linseed oil, and after riveting up, primed with a mixture of red and white lead paint with pure linseed oil, 'well worked on'. After erection, three coats of lead paint mixed with linseed oil were to be applied, 'of such colours as will be approved'. Columns and ornamental cast iron work were to receive 'one coat of the purest and best varnish of a prime cost value of not less than twelve shillings per gallon'.

Carpenter and Joiner work - White pine was specified for interior work where it would be less affected by moisture: flooring, ceiling joists, rafters, sarking and roof timbers generally, as well as any general framing work. A more robust specification of best Quebec red pine was selected for timbers bedded in stonework - beams, dooks, dwangs, grounds, joists, planking, door frames, window cases and sashes, outside doors and windows, gable framing and barge boards. Pitch pine was to be used where a strong timber was needed in the presence of a high moisture laden atmosphere - for roof trusses and sarking. American yellow pine was proposed for all inside doors, linings, pilasters, friezes, cornices, skirtings and fixed furniture, except pitch pine would be used where a varnished finish was called for. Baltic split lath was specified behind the plasterwork to walls and ceilings. There was also a reference to snow boards in selected areas, few of which were evident when restoration work was done in 1993.

The pier extension - A small extension was required between the pier and the newly constructed sea wall, on the north side. Greenheart or pitch pine piles were specified. Piles were to be driven 12 inches into rock (where this existed). The pier surface planking was to be in creosoted pitch pine 4 inches thick in planks between 10 in. and 12 in. wide. A gap of ¾ in. was to be left between each plank - these were the days before stiletto heels. The planking of the luggage passage and main (enclosed) passage was to be carried out in a similar fashion. An interesting detail was that any timber in contact with the ground should be properly *charred* and painted two coats of hot coal tar.

Slater work - Ballachulish or Welsh slates were equally acceptable, machine bored, double-nailed every third course in the Scottish fashion, otherwise single-nailed. The roofing of the pier gangway was to a lesser specification - second quality Welsh slates 'or American terra cotta slates'. In the event, the gangway was slated over.

Roof tile work - Strawberry red pressed Broseley tiles were selected for the station buildings and houses. Generally, they would be 10½ in. x 6½ in., though 'tile-and-a-half' tiles were also required. The ridge tiles, finials and chimney pots, which add character to the station, were not as closely described. The tiles would be laid on 'best brown sheathing felt'. Broseley tiles were designed for English roofs where timber battens support two projecting nibs on the rear of each tile. Probably owing to the curvature of the Wemyss Bay roofs as much as to Scottish practice, these nibs had to be broken off - why a special run could not be organised where tiles were manufactured without nibs is not recorded as the labour involved in removing the nibs must have been considerable.

Glazier work - All glass was to be British made - windows of 32 oz. sheet glass. 'Muraneze' and other special patterned glasses would be used, and some samples are still visible where obscure glass was called for.

Typical Caledonian Schemes
(Information prepared by George Russell and John Paton and featured in *The True Line*)

Purple brown	Stone and brick buildings: - All external woodwork and ironwork except window sashes and astragals.
	Timber buildings: Framing, doors and external ironwork.
	Timber footbridges: Vertical and diagonal framing.
Brown	Timber buildings: All external timbering (other than framing), verandah valances. Dark brown may have been used for panel framing and lighter brown for infill woodwork.
White	Window sashes, astragals, top panel [frieze] (excluding framing) on station buildings, undersides of awnings and verandahs, girderwork and brackets supporting verandahs.

Wemyss Bay Station in Caledonian Days
(Information taken from old photographs and 1905 *Railway Magazine* report)

Brown	Cills, cornice round ticket office, dado cill timber, fluted bases to columns.
Light Green	Woodwork above dado level, timber pilasters, cornice round concourse, infill panels between pilasters.
White	Columns above fluted base, girderwork, panels below cornices.
Cream	Flower brackets round the concourse.

LMS Schemes in Scotland up to 1939
As typical Caledonian Schemes above, but with some use of cream with brown framings.

Wemyss Bay Station in LMS Days
(Information taken from old photographs)

Brown	Column bases below fluting and column shaft above fluting, dado cill timber, framing to windows and pilasters in concourse, cornices.
Light Green	Roof girders and steelwork.
Cream	Panels below cornices and centre portion of pilasters.
White	Window sashes, fluted portions of column bases.

Wemyss Bay Station in Early BR Days
(Information taken from old photographs)
As LMS but probably with whole column base, including fluting, coloured brown.

Wemyss Bay in 1983
(Information taken from photographs)

Brown	dado cill timber, cornices.
Cream	Panels below cornices and centre portion of pilasters.
White	Roof girders and steelwork, window sashes.
Grey	Framing to windows.

Strathclyde Scheme c. 1984
(Information taken from survey photographs)

Brown	Dado cill, column bases.
Orange	Columns above fluting.
Vellum	Steel girders and rear of valances.
Red	Doors.
Ochre	Panels below cornice.
Mushroom	Pilasters, Framing to windows.
White	Window sashes.

Wemyss Bay Restoration Scheme 1993
(As instructed during the course of the restoration works)

Dark Brown	Beading, column bases.
Light Buff	Upper pilasters, sarking and internal lining.
Buff	Frieze, notice board border.
Ochre	Pilasters, window mouldings.
Vellum	Wall panelling below cornice, columns above fluted bases.
Cream	Fascia.
Purple	Doors.
White	Window sashes, infill panels on seaward wall.
Turquoise	Rings on columns.
Lime Green	Steelwork generally.
Black	Framing to external windows, Gable timbers.
Plum	Fascia and Pilasters on seaward wall.

Platform verandahs, the concourse and the pier enclosure where substantial quantities of glass were needed, were to have rough rolled plate glass 'without lines' with inverted T-shaped steel astragals, fully resistant to corrosion. These astragals were in surprisingly good condition when removed in 1993. The maximum size of glass was set at 1 ft 9 in. x 4 ft 6 in.-5 ft 3 in. The glass actually used in the canopies had a slightly greenish tinge, with a light combing of lines on the underside. The specification also required that the glazing should take account of vibrations caused by the trains, as well as making allowance for expansion and contraction. A 10-year guarantee was called for in the complete installation.

Plumber work - English soft-milled lead and zinc were used for roofing work. Curiously, the weight of lead was not specified - however, it was described on the drawings. An odd feature is that the lead piping 'shall meet the requirements of the standard of the Glasgow Corporation, and the Local Authorities' which suggests that the Caley had adopted Glasgow city building regulations as the standard the design team should adopt.

All piping that might be exposed to freezing conditions was to be 'carefully covered and packed with asbestos and canvas fixed with copper wire fastenings'.

There is a surprising lack of specification for piping to gas light fittings and to sanitaryware - perhaps the details were standardised or still to be developed. One might expect the Caley to adopt standard components to reduce the need to carry a wide range of spares.

Plaster work - Three coat work was specified, the first containing Scotch lime shells, the third incorporating Irish lime 'with as much stucco mixed with it as will ensure the plaster being perfectly white'. The lime was to be mixed with sand and 'long and fresh curled cow hair, free from grease and all impurity'. External surfaces would be rendered in cement plaster with a dashing coat incorporating white pea gravel or crushed granite chips in Arran sand. Once the render had been applied, it was to be finished with 'three coats of Duresco and be finished in white, cream, buff or other colour, as will be directed'.

Painter work - The paints available at the end of the 20th century present a bewildering range to the specifier. In 1902, the choice was simpler: old white lead paint with linseed oil, best quality copal varnish and American turpentine. Woodwork, steelwork and ironwork would receive four coats of paint. Distemper on a priming coat was acceptable on plaster in place of the 'Duresco'.

Unfortunately, a colour schedule does not seem to exist.

All in all, the 70-odd page Specification is similar to present day specs, the principal difference being that by the end of the 20th century, much more is wrapped up in words with a legal significance.

The picture on this postcard was taken in LMS days, perhaps about 1930, though the card was sent in 1939. Neither the porter nor the bus driver appear unduly harrassed and the shadows seem to suggest that the picture was taken during the summer holidays. *Alan Brotchie Collection*

Sample service (Mondays only)

Underlined Diagrams represent standard train sets; others are 12-wheeled stock.

Diagram	115C	107A	115	116D	123	123	112A	115	115	124aH	115	114	116	107	124
Smithy Lye	-	4.50	-	5.00	-	-	-	-	-	-	-	¶	7.46	-	-
Glasgow C.	4.45	-	5.30	-	-	-	5.35	5.42	6.34	6.45	7.08	7.40	-	8.07	-
	v	v	^	v	-	-	v	v	^	v	v	v	^	^	-
Paisley	5.00	-	5.10	-	-	-	-	6.02	6.10	-	-	-	-	-	-
Port Glasgow	-	-	-	-	5.45	5.55	-	-	-	-	-	-	-	-	8.26
Wemyss Bay	-	6.00	-	-	^	v	-	-	-	-	-	8.46	-	7.05	v
Gourock	-	-	-	6.00	5.20	6.15	6.29	-	-	7.55	8.15	-	6.40	-	8.50
Next Diagram													108		

Diagram	116	112	121E	124	112	119F	109A	111A	121	108A	109	122G	122	110A	113B
Smithy Lye	-	-	-	-	-	#	-	CR	-	-	-	-	-	-	-
								^		^					
Glasgow C.	8.15	8.24	8.31	-	8.35	8.41	8.48	8.54	8.55	8.59	9.03	9.11	9.30	9.33	9.28
	v	^	^	-	v	^	^	v	^	v	^	v	v	^	^
Paisley	-	-	-	-	-	-	-	-	-	-	-	-	-	-	-
Port Glasgow	-	-	-	9.18	-	-	-	-	-	-	-	-	-	-	-
Wemyss Bay	-	-	-	^	-	7.47	7.55	-	9.46	-	-	8.06	10.25	8.42	-
Gourock	9.05	7.15	7.38	8.54	9.19	-	-	8.10	-	8.15	10.09	-	-	-	8.38
	v														
Next Diagram					96										

Diagram	113	117E	110	117	120E	115	108	114	115C	109	124a	124	124	124a	114
Smithy Lye	-	-	-	-	-	-	-	-	-	-					-
Glasgow C.	9.50	9.57	10.00	10.10≠	10.30	10.32	10.40	10.47	11.00	11.21					12.15
	v	^	v	v	v	^	v	^	^	^					v
Paisley	-	-	-	-	-	-	-	-	-	-					-
Port Glasgow	-	-	-	-	-	-	-	-	-	-	12.40	12.20	13.28	12.50	-
Wemyss Bay	-	8.50≠	11.13	-	11.33	-	-	9.45	-	-	^	v	^	v	-
Gourock	10.30	-	-	11.21	-	9.20	11.34	-	11.43	10.25	12.20	12.43	13.02	13.13	13.31
					v										
Next Diagram				117											

Diagram	112	110	117	108	124	124a	124a	124	108	110	116	124	116	117	114
Smithy Lye	-	-	-	-	-	-	-	-	-	-	-	-	-	-	-
Glasgow C.	12.34	12.52	13.15	13.40	-	-		-	14.00	14.15	14.33	-	14.55	15.00	15.16
	^	^	^	^					v	v	^		v	v	^
									-	-	-		-	-	-
Port Glasgow	-	-	-	13.20	14.00	14.10	14.55	-	-	-	-	15.03	-	-	-
Wemyss Bay	-	11.45	-	-	v	^	v	^	-	-	15.18	-	v	-	-
Gourock	11.20	-	12.05	12.45	13.55	13.40	14.33	14.35	15.00	-	13.35	15.24	15.46	16.14	14.05
Next Diagram														121/120	

Diagram	124a	114	112	124a	112	118F	109	124aJ	111	110	108	110	108	118	116
Smithy Lye	-	-	-	-	-	-	-	-	-	-	-	-	-	-	-
Glasgow C.	-	15.45	15.46	-	16.05	16.07	16.30	-	16.35	16.46	16.50	17.12	17.20	17.25	17.32
		v	^		v	v	v		v	^	^	v	v	^	^
Paisley	-	-	-	-	-	16.28	-	-	-	-	-	-	-	16.56	-
Port Glasgow	-	-	-	17.26	-	-	-	18.08	-	-	-	-	-	-	-
Wemyss Bay	v	-	-	^	17.06	-	17.27	^	-	15.35	-	18.03	-	-	-
Gourock	16.35	16.45	14.50	17.05	-	-	-	17.46	17.52	-	15.55	-	18.05	-	16.40
		v							v			v			CR
Next Diagram						110/107					109				

Diagram	118	113B	113	116	114	123	107	123	114C	112	107	115	113	124
Smithy Lye	-	-	-	-	-	-	-	-	-	-	-	-	18.50	-
Glasgow C.	17.40	17.41	17.58	18.08	18.12	-	18.20	-	18.25	18.29	18.30	18.41	EC	19.07
	v	^	v	v	^		^		v	^	v	^	^	^
Paisley	-	-	18.24	-	-	-	-	-	-	-	-	18.30	-	-
Port Glasgow	-	-	-	-	-	17.19	-	18.01	-	-	≠	-	-	-
Wemyss Bay	-	-	-	19.07	-	EC ^	-	v	-	17.25	-	-	-	-
Gourock	18.50	16.50	-	-	17.00	17.08	17.25≠	18.22	19.15†	-	19.33	17.45	-	18.10
		^							v		v			
Next Diagram					115§				111/112	108		114		

Diagram	115	121	111	116	108	≠	≠	111	118	118	≠	115	115	111
Smithy Lye	-	-	-	-	-	-	-	-	-	-	-	-	-	-
Glasgow C.	19.10	19.15	20.17	20.26	20.32	-	-	20.35	20.46	21.30	-	22.17	23.15	23.18
	v	^	^	^	^	v	^	v	v			^	v	^
Paisley	-	-	-	-	-	-	-	-	-	-	-	-	-	-
Port Glasgow	-	-	-	-	-	19.15≠	20.50*	-	-	-	21.22	-	-	-
						v	^				v			
Wemyss Bay	-	18.10	-	19.20	-	19.40*	20.25	-	-	-	21.47*	-	-	-
Gourock	20.21	-	19.05¶	-	19.40	-	-	21.46	19.50	22.40	-	21.10	0.21	22.10
		v						v	v					
Next Diagram		120/116		118/121	107/110			112/111	116/118					

Appendix Six

Marshalling of Trains for use on the Wemyss Bay and Gourock Routes

According to the *CALEDONIAN RAILWAY - MARSHALLING OF TRAINS, JULY 1913*, there were three different marshalling arrangements - a 5-coach 12-wheeled bogie train (2 No.), a 6-coach 12-wheeled bogie train as the 5-coach plus an additional Brake Van (4 No.), and an 8-coach bogie train (9 No.). If the trains were not long enough, Glasgow and Gourock were enjoined to strengthen the trains for Saturday and holiday traffic.

Set No.115 (configured as No. 113) while deployed on the Gourock line was not used on the Wemyss Bay line. No. 123 was a 'Workman's' train between Gourock and Port Glasgow made up of 6-wheeled stock - 1 first, 1 composite, 3 thirds and 2 brake thirds - total 7 vehicles. Nos. 124 and 124a were bogie trains running on alternate days between Gourock and Port Glasgow, and Glasgow and Ardrossan each comprising 1 first, 1 third and 2 brake thirds - total 4 vehicles.

No. 107	12-wheeled bogie train comprising 1 first, 1 composite, 1 third, 1 7-compartment brake third, 1 9-compartment brake third. Cleaned and repaired at Smithy Lye.	5 *Vehicles*
No. 108	as No. 107. Cleaned and repaired at Smithy Lye.	5 *Vehicles*
No. 109	12-wheeled bogie train comprising 1 first, 1 composite, 1 third, 1 7-compartment brake third, 1 9-compartment brake third, 1 brake van. Cleaned and repaired at Smithy Lye.	6 *Vehicles*
No. 110	as No. 109. Cleaned and repaired at Smithy Lye.	6 *Vehicles*
No. 111	as No. 109. Cleaned and repaired at Smithy Lye.	6 *Vehicles*
No. 112	as No. 109. Cleaned and repaired at Smithy Lye.	6 *Vehicles*
No. 113	Bogie train comprising 2 Firsts, 4 Thirds, 1 Brake Third, 1 Brake Van Cleaned, gassed and repaired at Gourock.	8 *Vehicles*
No. 114	as No. 113. Cleaned and repaired at Gourock, gassed at Glasgow Central.	8 *Vehicles*
No. 116	as No. 113. Cleaned and gassed at Smithy Lye, repaired at Gourock.	8 *Vehicles*
No. 117	as No. 113. Cleaned and gassed at Smithy Lye, repaired at Wemyss Bay.	8 *Vehicles*
No. 118	as No. 113. Cleaned, repaired and gassed at Smithy Lye.	8 *Vehicles*
No. 119	as No. 113. Cleaned and repaired and gassed at Smithy Lye.	8 *Vehicles*
No. 120	as No. 113. Cleaned and gassed at Smithy Lye, repaired at Wemyss Bay.	8 *Vehicles*
No. 121	as No. 113. Cleaned and gassed at Smithy Lye, repaired at Wemyss Bay.	8 *Vehicles*
No. 122	as No. 113. Cleaned and repaired at Wemyss Bay and gassed at Glasgow Central. Cleaned and repaired at Wemyss Bay and gassed at Glasgow Central.	8 *Vehicles*

Notes for table opposite

A   Cleaned and repaired at Smithy Lye.
B   Cleaned, gassed and repaired at Gourock.
C   Cleaned and repaired at Gourock; gassed at Glasgow Central.
D   Cleaned and gassed at Smithy Lye; repaired at Greenock.
E   Cleaned and gassed at Smithy Lye; repaired at Wemyss Bay.
F   Cleaned, repaired and gassed at Smithy Lye.
G   Cleaned and repaired at Wemyss Bay; gassed at Glasgow Central.
H   Extra Third Class on Mondays.
J   Empty carriages to Port Glasgow Junction.

CR = cleaned and repaired.
Direction of travel is indicated by v and ^.
EC = empty carriages.
* = Approximate times.

† Returned attached to 9.10 pm or 10.10 pm train (other weekdays).
# Changes train with No. 96 (Ardrossan set) which comprises 1 first, 1 third and 2 brake thirds.
§ Changes train with No. 115 (Glasgow to Paisley and Gourock set) which has same composition.
¶ On Mondays, a 6-wheeled brake van is attached to the 5.35 am and other weekdays a brake van arriving from Aberdeen at 12.25 am. Both vehicles to be detached at Greenock Central and returned on the 7.5 pm to Glasgow.
≠ Third and brake composite attached to 5.25 pm ex Gourock to Glasgow, returning on the 6.30 pm Glasgow to Port Glasgow and thence by the 7.15 pm to Wemyss Bay. The vehicles will be returned from Wemyss Bay to Glasgow attached to the 8.50 am from Wemyss Bay. They will then be sent by the 10.10 am Glasgow Central train to Gourock. The timetable indicates that the brake composite would work the 8.25 pm Wemyss Bay to Port Glasgow train and the 9.22 pm return to Wemyss Bay.

Appendix Seven

A Selection of Engines known to have run on the Greenock and Wemyss Bay Lines

Over the lifespan of the Caledonian, locomotives were built by various companies as well as by the Caley itself at its Greenock and St Rollox works. Joseph Locke's experience of railway construction in England led to the early purchase by the Glasgow, Paisley & Greenock line of engines from Sharp & Roberts of Manchester. Other builders included the Vulcan Foundry, Jones & Potts, Scott Sinclair & Co., Neilson & Co., Beyer, Peacock & Co., Dübs and Co., Andrew Barclay & Sons, Sharp Stewart & Co., the North British Locomotive Co., and Armstrong Whitworth. Locomotive style developed from the earliest 2-2-2s through 0-4-2s and 2-4-0s to 4-4-0s (introduced in 1876), the 0-6-0 being a favourite goods style from early days. The early years of the 20th century saw 4-6-0s, 4-6-2s, 2-6-0s and 2-6-4s being built for heavier traffic. Neilson's order book shows that the majority of locomotives they built had driving wheels between 5 ft and 5 ft 6 in., with batches of engines with 6 ft 2 in. to 6 ft 6 in. drivers and a few with drivers of 7 ft and over. These wheel sizes were all established by 1867. Early passenger locomotives are believed to have been coloured blue while goods engines were coloured green. About 1870, it seems that passenger locomotives were painted green, the goods being black. The principal colour schemes of the later Caledonian era were as described below. Engines were rich in colour and extensively lined out in red, black and white.

Passenger Locomotives

The Caley engines were famed for their attractive blue colour, however it is well recorded that there was no single shade of blue. It appears that the 'official' shade of blue took many coats to obtain the required 'body', and while outside contractors did achieve this, the St Rollox painters looked for quicker results. Accordingly, engines built in the Caley workshops were covered in a lighter shade of blue which owed much to the amount of white paint added to thicken up the coat. It seems that engines repaired at Perth were painted an even lighter shade of blue. The chimney, smokebox, cab roof and frames were black, the boiler blue, cab sides and tender being lined out. Wheels were blue with black axle ends and tyres. Buffer beams and stocks were crimson lake, but between the buffers was a vermilion panel, the front one carrying the letters 'C.R.' to the left and the engine number to the right of the coupling hook. The engine number was painted in red shaded gilt figures on the upper part of the rear of the tender. The side panels of the tenders carried the initials 'C.R.' (gilt painted with red shading), either side of the company's coat of arms (borrowed without the authority of the Lord Lyon King of Arms). The engine number featured on an oval brass plate on the cab or bunker side.

Goods Locomotives

Goods engines were generally black with splashers, cab roof and sides and tender side sheets lined out. The wheels were also black. The tender side panels carried the letters 'C.R.' either side of the coat of arms, the letters being shaded as on the passenger locomotives. Buffer beams were vermilion, the lettering being as on the passenger locomotives. The numbers on the backs of the tenders were similarly located to the passenger engines. Many goods engines had red coupling rods which tended to hide blemishes in the metal. Goods engines fitted for passenger service were liveried as the passenger locomotives.

Tractive Effort

Where published figures are not available, I have calculated tractive effort using the formula:

$$TE = \frac{d^2 \times s \times p \times 85}{w \times 100}$$

where d is the cylinder diameter in inches, s is the cylinder stroke in inches, p is the boiler pressure in lb./square inch (psi) and w is the driving wheel diameter in inches. The calculation assumes a working pressure of 85 per cent capacity and applies to two-cylinder locomotives. For 3-cylinder simple locomotives, multiply by 1½.

APPENDIX

Class: 2-2-0 tender (Named *Lucifer*, *Zamiel* and *Hecate* - Caledonian Nos. 1, 2 and 3)
Origin: Glasgow Paisley & Greenock Railway
Introduced: 1840
Purpose: Mixed traffic
Designer: Rothwell & Co.
Driving wheel: 5 ft 0 in.
Leading and Trailing Wheels: 3 ft 6 in.
Cylinders: 13 in. x 18 in.
Boiler Pressure: 55 psi
Tractive Effort: 2,370 lb.
Locomotive Weight: 12½ tons
Historical Notes: *Zamiel* ran with *Hawk* pulling the first train on the Glasgow and Paisley line in 1840. In 1844, *Zamiel's* boiler blew up and was subsequently replaced by that from *Hawk*. These locomotives were modified to 2-2-2 in 1841. All had been withdrawn by 1854.

Class: 2-2-2
Origin: Caledonian Railway (probably Greenock works)
Introduced: c.1847-1856
Designer: Robert Sinclair
Purpose: Express
Driving Wheel: 7 ft 0 in.
Cylinders: 16 in. x 20 in.
Historical Notes: A locomotive matching this description with 3 ft 6 in. leading and trailing wheels and weighing 26 tons (40 tons with tender) was involved in a crash at Wemyss Bay station on 16th September, 1865.

Class: 2-4-0 Nos. 98-102, 108-112, 117-122
Origin: Caledonian Railway (Neilson & Co. and St Rollox)
Introduced: 1867-1868
Designer: Benjamin Conner
Purpose: Passenger
Driving Wheel: 7 ft 2 in.
Cylinders: (2) 17 in. x 24 in.
Boiler Pressure: 140 psi
Tractive Effort: 9,825 lb.
Historical Notes: Sixteen built for main line work. Subsequently rebuilt by Lambie and lasted until 1913-1915. An illustration of No. 101 featured in an article in the 24th May, 1872 issue of *Engineering* with a description of Westinghouse air brake trials held on the Wemyss Bay line in March 1872.

Class: 0-6-0, '294' 'Jumbo' class
Introduced: 1883-1897
Designer: Dugald Drummond
Purpose: Goods and passenger
Driving Wheel: 5 ft 0 in.
Cylinders: 18 in. x 26 in.
Boiler Pressure: 150 psi
Tractive Effort: 17,900 lb.
Coal Capacity: 4 tons 10 cwt.
Water Capacity: 2,500 and 2,840 gallons
Length: 49 ft 10¾ in.
Locomotive Weight: 41 tons 6 cwt. (Westinghouse locomotives 40 tons 6 cwt. and condensing locomotives 42 tons 4 cwt.)
Tender Weight: 31 tons 19 cwt-33 tons 19 cwt.
Historical Notes: 244 built, provided with new 'Drummond cab'. Initial engines painted in Caledonian blue. Early locomotives had steam brakes, some fitted with Westinghouse brakes for passenger trains and five fitted with condensing apparatus to work on Glasgow Central (Underground) Railway. These locomotives did high mileages, ranging from 1,364,674 for No. 567 to 2,067,787 for No. 539. The first engines cost £2,900 [*£125,000], reducing to £1,700 [*£86,500] four years later. Used widely, including on the Greenock line, until post-Nationalisation. The design was developed for 96 engines of the '812' class.

Class: 4-4-0 class 80 - 'Coast' or 'Greenock Bogies'
Origin: Caledonian Railway (St Rollox)
Introduced: 1888-1891
Designer: Dugald Drummond
Purpose: Passenger
Driving Wheel: 5 ft 9 in.
Bogie Wheel: 3 ft 6 in.
Cylinders: 18 in. x 26 in.
Boiler Pressure: 150 psi (later 160 psi and 170 on No. 85)
Tractive Effort: 15,566 lb.
Water Capacity: 2,840/3,130 gallons
Length: 51 ft 7 in.
Locomotive Weight: 42 tons 7¼ cwt, 43 tons 9¾ on No. 85).
Tender Weight: 34 tons 17 cwt.
Historical Notes: Twelve built. Intended for Clyde Coast services and also for general excursion work. For a short time, some were painted dark blue with yellow lining. Their motion was similar to the 'Jumbo' ('294' class). They had a Westinghouse pump, train heating gear and compressed air sanding. The locomotives were fitted with twin organ pipe whistles. Cost varied from £1,667 in 1887 to £1,994 in 1891 [*£85,000-*£98,000] per locomotive. Four were allocated to Polmadie, two to Greenock and later engines went to Perth, Edinburgh and St Rollox shed. They were used on coastal traffic until about 1917. It is reputed that in 1898 these locomotives were scheduled to run non-stop express trains between Glasgow and Gourock in 32 minutes, some apparently doing it in 27½ minutes.

Class: 0-4-0ST class '264'
Origin: Caledonian Railway
Introduced: 1885
Designer: Dugald Drummond, with later development by J.F. McIntosh
Purpose: Dockyard shunting
Driving Wheel: 3 ft 8 in.
Cylinders: (2) 14 in. x 20 in.
Boiler Pressure: 140 psi
Tractive Effort: 10,601 lb.
Coal Capacity: 1¼ tons (see note)
Water Capacity: 800 gallons
Length: 22 ft 3¾ in.
Locomotive Weight: 27 tons 7½ cwt.
Historical Notes: 34 built. No normal coal bunker provided - only a small amount carried in the cab. Where necessary, a small truck was attached as a tender, coal being shovelled in using a waist-high door in the cab rear sheeting. At least two locomotives seem to have been allocated to Greenock at any one time. No. 514 ran back downhill to Upper Greenock when its brakes failed in 1907, killing the driver.

Class: 0-6-0T '782' class - (including class '29')
Origin: Caledonian Railway
Introduced: 1895
Designer: John Farquharson McIntosh
Purpose: Freight and shunting
Driving Wheel: 4 ft 6 in.
Cylinders: (2) 18 in. x 26 in.
Boiler Pressure: 150 and 160 psi
Tractive Effort: 19,890 lb. and 21,215 lb.
Water Capacity: 1,300 gallons
Coal Capacity: 2½ tons
Length: 30 ft 10 in.
Locomotive Weight: 47 tons 15 cwt
Historical Notes: 147 built for short distance passenger and mineral trains. The class became the second largest on the Caledonian Railway. The first locomotives were fitted with condensing gear and Westinghouse brakes. Later locomotives were mostly fitted with steam brakes. Original cost was £1,502 [*£82,000].

Pickersgill 4-6-2T No. 15357 stands at the head of platform 3 about 1923. Note the coaches parked behind at platform 4.
J.L. Stevenson Collection

Fairburn 2-6-4T No. 2201 running on to a train on platform 2 in September 1946. Note Wemyss Bay signal box in the middle distance. The locomotive is crossing the reversing line between platforms 2 and 3. Carriage sidings are to the right and the goods and pier lines run off at far left.
J.L. Stevenson Collection

APPENDIX

Class: 0-6-0 class '30'
Origin: Caledonian Railway (St Rollox)
Introduced: 1912
Designer: John Farquharson McIntosh
Purpose: Goods
Driving Wheel: 5 ft 0 in.
Cylinders: (2) 19½ in. x 26 in.
Boiler Pressure: 160 psi
Tractive Effort: 22,409 lb.
Coal Capacity: 4 tons 10 cwt
Water Capacity: 3,000 gallons
Length: 53 ft 6 in.
Locomotive Weight: 51 tons 2 cwt
Tender Weight: 37 tons 6 cwt.
Historical Notes: Four built, painted blue and used on Clyde Coast trains, including the Wemyss Bay route. Fitted with Westinghouse gear and painted blue for use on the Glasgow Central-Wemyss Bay route for passenger work. Locomotives cost £2,312 [*£101,000] to build.

Class: 4-6-2T class '944' - 'Wemyss Bay Pugs'
Origin: Caledonian Railway (North British Locomotive Company - Order No. L672)
Introduced: 1917
Designer: William Pickersgill
Purpose: Suburban traffic
Driving Wheel: 5 ft 9 in.
Bogie Wheel: 3 ft 6 in.
Trailing Wheel: 3 ft 6 in.
Cylinders: 2 - outside - 19½ in. x 26 in.
Boiler Pressure: 170 psi
Tractive Effort: 20,704 lb.
Coal Capacity: 3 tons
Water Capacity: 1,800 gallons
Length: 43 ft 2½ in.
Total Weight: 74 tons 11 cwt empty and 91 tons 13 cwt in working order.
Historical Notes: 12 built for Clyde Coast traffic to Gourock and Wemyss Bay and for banking duty at Beattock (for a short time in 1917). Based on Pickersgill's 62 ft long class '60' tender locomotive but with smaller drivers and a shorter wheelbase. Fitted with Westinghouse brake gear and train heating gear. Steam sanding gear fitted for forward and backward running. Locomotives cost £5,250 [*£129,000] each. They were painted blue. The locomotives were withdrawn between 1946 and 1952, the remaining engines being transferred to Beattock in 1948.

Class: 4-4-0 '4P'
Origin: Midland Railway
Introduced: 1924
Designer: R.M. Deeley
Purpose: Passenger express
Driving Wheel: 6 ft 9 in.
Bogie Wheel: 3 ft 6½ in.
Cylinders: Compound - 2 outside - 21 in. x 26 in., 1 inside - 19 in. x 26 in.
Boiler Pressure: 200 psi
Tractive Effort: 22,649 lb.
Coal Capacity: 5 tons 10 cwt
Water Capacity: 3,500 gallons
Length: 56 ft 8 in.
Total Weight: 104 tons 8 cwt
Historical Notes: An outstanding class. In 1953, there were 186 extant.

Class: '6P/5F' 2-6-0 'Crab'
Origin: LMS
Introduced: 1926
Designer: George Hughes & Sir Henry Fowler
Purpose: Mixed Traffic
Driving Wheel: 5 ft 6 in.
Pony Wheel: 3 ft 6½ in.
Cylinders: (2 outside) 21 in. x 26 in.
Boiler Pressure: 180 psi
Tractive Effort: 26,580 lb.
Coal Capacity: 5 tons
Water Capacity: 3,500 gallons
Length: 59 ft 3 /8 in.
Total Weight: 66 tons (engine) 108 tons 4 cwt total.
Historical Notes: 245 built. An unattractive looking but very sound engine.

Class: 4-6-0 class '5MT'
Origin: LMS
Introduced: 1934
Designer: Sir William Stanier
Purpose: Mixed traffic
Driving Wheel: 6 ft 0 in.
Bogie Wheel: 3 ft 3½ in.
Cylinders: (2 outside) 18½ in. x 28 in.
Boiler Pressure: 225 psi
Tractive Effort: 25,455 lb.
Coal Capacity: 9 tons
Water Capacity: 4,000 gallons
Length: 63 ft 7¼ in.
Total Weight: 125 tons 5 cwt
Historical Notes: 842 built. The ubiquitous 'Black Five' class.

Class: 2-6-4T '4MT' class
Origin: LMS
Introduced: 1935
Designer: Stanier and Fairburn
Purpose: Suburban passenger
Driving Wheel: 5 ft 9 in.
Pony Wheel: 3 ft 3½ in.
Trailing Wheel: 3 ft 3½ in.
Cylinders: (2 outside) 19¾ in. x 26 in.
Boiler Pressure: 200 psi
Tractive Effort: 24,670 lb.
Coal Capacity: 3 tons 10 cwt
Water Capacity: 2,000 gallons
Length: 47 ft 2¾ in.
Total Weight: 85 tons 5 cwt
Historical Notes: 287 built. Development of Fowler '4MT' class of 1927. Later developed as the BR '80000' class.

Class: 303 Electric 3-car multiple units - the original 'Blue trains'
Introduced: 1959-1961
Weight: Driving trailers 34.4 and 38.4 tonnes each, non-driving motor coach 56.4 tonnes.
Transmission: Four AEI (M.V.) 155 kW traction motors.
Maximum speed: 75 mph
Length: 63 ft 11¾ in. + 63 ft 6¼ in. + 63 ft 11¾ in.
Historical Notes: 48 train sets survive in the current Strathclyde livery but the 'Blue Train' No. 303 048 is the last remaining in original Strathclyde colour scheme. That unit has 236 open seats in three units without communicating gangway doors and is used for special occasions only. All the other train sets are gangwayed stock providing 160 seats. Sliding doors are air-operated.

Class: '318' Electric 3-car multiple units
Introduced: 1985-1987
Transmission: Four Brush motors rated at 268 kW
Maximum speed: 90 mph
Length: 65 ft 0¾ in. + 65 ft 4¼ in. + 65 ft 0¾ in.
Historical Notes: 21 train sets built.

Appendix Eight

A Selection of Paddle Steamers known to have visited Wemyss Bay and some other vessels

Key
PS   Paddle Steamer   TSMV   Turbine Screw Motor Vessel
SS   Steam Ship   DEPV   Diesel Electric Paddle Vessel
RMPS   Royal Mail Paddle Steamer   MV   Motor Vessel
TSS   Turbine Screw Steamer

Dimensions are taken from various sources and should be regarded as indicative rather than accurate.

PS *Venus* (1852) 100 tons, 139 ft 3 in. x 17 ft 2 in. x 8 ft 3 in. draught, twin stack, built by J. & G.Thomson of Clydebank. Entered service with McKellar fleet on the Millport run, sold to Gillies & Campbell. Scrapped 1875 at Port Glasgow.

PS *Largs* (1864) 87 tons, 161 ft 5 in. x 19 ft 1 in. x 7 ft 11 in. draught, 86 nominal horse power, twin stack, built by T. Wingate and Co. of Glasgow, for the Wemyss Bay Steamboat Company, launched 17th September, 1864. First used between Glasgow and Millport (on Cumbrae) then transferred on the opening of the line to Wemyss Bay to run from Wemyss Bay to Millport and Lamlash (Isle of Arran) and Largs. Later transferred to Millport, Wemyss Bay, Rothesay and Kyles ports. Continued the service under Gillies & Campbell until sold off the Clyde in 1877.

PS *Kyles* (1865) 171 tons, 219 ft 5 in. x 20 ft 3 in. x 8 ft 5 in. draught, 120 nominal horse power, 17 knots after modification, twin stack, built and engined by Caird of Greenock for the Wemyss Bay Steamboat Company to run on the routes to Rothesay, Kyles piers and Ardrishaig. In May 1865, it reportedly achieved 19 knots but only as a result of some 'persuasion'. Sold in 1866 and broken up in 1888. The PS *Bute* (1865), a replacement for the *Hattie*, which was sold on the stocks for blockade running, was of similar dimensions. She was sold off the Clyde in 1866.

PS *Argyle* (1866) 177ft 3 in. x 17 ft 5 in. x 7 ft 6 in. draught, haystack boiler, single stack, built by Barclay Curle & Co. for Captain Duncan Stewart, sold to Wemyss Bay Steamboat Co. in 1866, then to Gillies & Campbell who sold her in 1890. Broken up 1908.

SS *Kintyre* (1868) 299 tons, 184 ft 8 in. x 22 ft 11 in. x 11 ft 6 in. draught, screw steamer, half passenger and half cargo, (fish crates, sheep, bullocks, whisky, etc.), single stack, built by Robertson and Co. of Port Glasgow for Campbeltown & Glasgow Steam Packet Joint Stock Co. and calling at Glasgow, Greenock, Wemyss Bay, West Arran, the Kintyre coast and Campbeltown. Rammed and sunk by the *Maori* off Skelmorlie on 18th September, 1907.

PS *Lancelot* (1868) 142 tons, 191 ft 2 in. x 18 ft x 6 ft 9 in. draught, 40 lb. haystack boiler, single stack, built by R. Duncan for Graham Brymner for the Glasgow to Largs and Millport run. In 1869, the G&WBR asked Brymner to include a stop at Wemyss Bay but the service proved unreliable and was dropped when Gillies & Campbell took over. The boat was later acquired by Gillies & Campbell for the Wemyss Bay sailing. Disposed off the Clyde in 1890.

PS *Adela* (1877) 206 tons, 207 ft 7 in. x 19 ft 2 in. x 7 ft 4 in. draught, speed 12 knots, 50 lb. Haystack boiler, single stack, built by Caird & Co. for Gillies & Campbell, used on Wemyss Bay route till 1891 when she was sold off the Clyde. Believed to have been broken up in 1898. Engine was taken from the wrecked and uninsured *Lady Gertrude* and built into the boat. It had a tendency to stick in top dead centre when travelling slowly. This happened approaching Wemyss Bay pier and nearly brought her to grief in her latter days.

PS *Sheila* (1877) 225 tons, 205 ft 6 in. x 20 ft x 7 ft 8 in. draught, built by Caird & Co. of Greenock, acquired by Gillies & Campbell for the Rothesay route. Fitted with 50 lb. haystack boiler, single stack. Reputedly 'very fast' - over 17 knots. Rammed and holed by PS *Columba* in 1881 at Innellan Pier following a race. Sold 1882 to the N.B. Steam Packet Co. and renamed *Guy Mannering*. Later named PS *Isle of Bute*. Scrapped 1913.

RMPS *Columba* (I) (1878), 602 tons, 301 ft 5 in. x 27 ft 1 in. x 9 ft 5 in. draught, speed originally 18, later 19½ knots, capacity 2,000 passengers. Built by J. & G. Thomson, Clydebank, for David MacBrayne on the Glasgow and Ardrishaig run. Originally built with four navy type boilers, reboilered with two 50 lb. haystack boilers and provided with two stacks. Accommodation included a Post Office. Rammed and holed the PS *Sheila* in 1881 at Innellan Pier following a race. Sailed from Wemyss Bay during World War I because of the anti-submarine boom from Cloch to Dunoon. Scrapped in 1935.

PS *Victoria* (1886), 300 tons, 222 ft 4 in. x 23 ft 1 in. x 8ft draught, built by Blackwood & Gordon for Gillies & Campbell. Fitted with two haystack boilers, two-stacks. Sold off the Clyde in 1890. Withdrawn 1897. Provided with an early electric light generator.

PS *Caledonia* (1889) 244 tons, 200 ft 5 in. x 22 ft x 7 ft 6 in. draught, speed 16½ knots, capacity 1,093 passengers. Launched 6th May, 1889. Two navy 90lb. boilers, single stack, built by John Reid & Co. at Port Glasgow for the Caledonian Steam Packet Co. Ltd. and worked on the Gourock-Rothesay route. Her first Captain, Duncan Bell, had previously worked for the Wemyss Bay Co. Cost £14,000 [*£690,000] to build. Experiments made with oil burning in 1893 and 1897, but due to the expense, returned to coal firing. Used to bring hoses from Gourock to quell a fire on Wemyss Bay Pier in 1900. Between 1917 and 1919 served away from the Clyde as a minesweeper or transport vessel. Scrapped at Barrow in 1933. The PS *Marchioness of Breadalbane* (1890) was similar and marginally faster.

PS *Galatea* (1889) 331 tons, 230 ft 1 in. x 25 ft 1 in. x 7 ft 10 in. draught, speed 17 knots, capacity 1,307 passengers. Launched 31st May, 1889. Fitted with four Navy 109 lb. boilers, twin stack. Built by Caird & Co. at Greenock for the Caledonian Steam Packet Co. and worked the Gourock-Rothesay route. Involved in collision with the 306 ton G&SWR PS *Minerva* (1893) in 1894 during racing. Cost £18,000 [*£885,000] to build. Withdrawn 1904, sold off the Clyde in 1906. Broken up 1913. (According to O.S. Nock in *The Caledonian Railway*, Galatea was rarely run all-out as the engines were more powerful than the hull could stand.)

PS *Duchess of Hamilton* (1890) 553 tons, 250 ft x 30 ft 1 in. x 10 ft 1 in., speed 18 knots, capacity 1,780 passengers, built by William Denny & Bros. of Dumbarton for the Caledonian Steam Packet Co. and provided with the first ever Parson's turbine to generate electric lighting. Fitted with three Navy 120 lb. boilers. Single stack. In 1909 she was put on the first Sunday railway connections. First paddle steamer to have promenade deck carried right forward. Requisitioned in World War I and sunk in 1915 off Harwich.

PS *Marchioness of Lorne* (1891) 295 tons, 200 ft x 24 ft x 8 ft 3 in. draught, speed 16 knots, capacity 1,159 passengers. Built by Russell & Co. of Port Glasgow, for the Caledonian Steam Packet Co., and used on the Wemyss Bay and Millport runs in the summer while in the winter she ran the Arran (Brodick) to Ardrossan route. Fitted with two Navy 140 lb. boilers. Involved in collision with the G&SWR 20 knot, 610 ton PS *Glen Sannox* (1892). Requisitioned for naval duties in 1916 and served in the Mediterranean. Disposed of in 1923 for £740 [*£18,500] 'in a very dilapidated condition' and broken up.

PS *Duchess of Rothesay* (1895) 338 tons, 225 ft 7 in. x 26 ft 1 in. x 8 ft 7 in. draught, speed 17¼ knots, capacity 1,382 passengers. Cost £20,000 [*£1.09m] to build. Fitted with double-ended 150 lb. boiler, single stack. Coal capacity 30 tons. Built by J. & G. Thomson, Clydebank for the Caledonian Steam Packet Co. for the Arran run, used to convey Queen Victoria from Rothesay to the Broomielaw in 1897, George V in 1914 and again in 1920. She was requisitioned during World War I for work as a minesweeper, renamed *Duke of Rothesay*. On returning in 1919 for refitting by Barclay Curle & Co. Ltd, she sank at her moorings but was refloated some weeks later. Between the two wars, she sailed from Gourock and Wemyss Bay. Served as a minesweeper and accommodation vessel in World War II. Broken up in 1946.

PS *Duchess of Fife* (1903) 336 tons, 210 ft 4 in. x 25 ft x 8 ft 6 in. draught, speed 17½ knots, capacity 1,101 passengers, built Fairfield Shipbuilding & Engineering Co. of Govan for the Caledonian Steam Packet Co., capacity 1,101 passengers. Two navy boilers, single stack. Cost £20,500 [*£1.001m]. Requistioned during both World Wars for minesweeping and other purposes. Ran on the Wemyss Bay to Rothesay, and Largs and Millport runs as well as from Gourock. Broken up in 1953.

TSS *Duchess of Hamilton* (1932) 795 tons, 262 ft x 32 ft 1 in. x 10 ft 1 in. draught, speed 19 knots, capacity 1,918 passengers, triple turbines, twin stack, built by Harland & Wolff of Govan for the Caledonian Steam Packet Co. for the Ayr, Troon and Ardrossan excursions. Requisitioned during World War II for transport purposes. Resumed Clyde sailings, including trips from Wemyss Bay after the War. Converted to oil burning in 1956. Withdrawn 1972. The TSS *Duchess of Montrose* (1930) was of similar size and slightly faster.

DEPV *Talisman* (1935) 450 tons, 215 ft x 27 ft 8 in. x 8 ft 11 in. draught, speed 14 knots on two engines, 17 at full power, capacity 1,252 passengers and a few cars on the rear promenade deck, single stack. Powered by four diesel engines driving an electric motor. Built by A. & J. Inglis Ltd of Glasgow for the LNER Craigendoran service. Requisitioned for war service as HMS *Aristocrat*. After World War II, returned to the Craigendoran-Dunoon-Kirn and Rothesay run. Operated on the Wemyss Bay-Millport route from 1954 to 1967. Broken up at Dalmuir in 1967.

PS *Waverley* (1947) 693 G.R.T., 239 ft 7 in. x 30 ft 2 in. x 8 ft 7 in. draught, speed 15 knots, twin stack, capacity 1,350 passengers, built by A. & J. Inglis of Pointhouse for the LNER, taken over by the Caledonian Steam Packet Co. Ltd. in 1951. Around 1960, it is recorded that the *Waverley* used the Wemyss Bay pier. Withdrawn from service in 1973, sold to the Paddle Steamer Preservation Society for £1 and thereafter used for excursions by Waverley Steam Navigation Ltd. Still sailing in 2001.

TSMV *Arran* (1953) 568 tons, 178 ft 10 in. x 35 ft 1 in. x 7 ft 4in. draught, speed 15½ knots, squat single stack, capacity 360 passengers and 35 cars. Built for the Gourock to Cowal peninsula route by William Denny & Bros Ltd of Dumbarton for the Caledonian Steam Packet Co. Ltd, the first boat built to carry cars on the Clyde using an electrically-operated lift. Ran on Wemyss Bay and Gourock services until mid-1970s. Also sailed on MacBrayne's Islay route from 1970-1974. Laid up in 1979. (One of the similarly-sized 'A, B, C' ferries, the others being the *Bute* and the *Cowal*.)

TSMV *Glen Sannox* (1957), 1,107 tons, 243 ft 11 in. x 44 ft 1 in. x 9 ft 5 in. draught, speed 17 knots, 2,330 shp, squat single stack, capacity 1,100 passengers and 45-50 vehicles, built by Ailsa Shipbuilding Co. Ltd of Troon for the Caledonian Steam Packet Co. Ltd Ardrossan-Brodick (Arran) trade. Below-deck garage served by (rather slow) hydraulic hoist of capacity 5 vehicles. In 1970 converted to stern loading (while retaining the lift). Inaugurated Wemyss Bay to Rothesay roll on-roll off service in 1977 before being transferred to other duties.

MV *Jupiter* (1972), 848 tons, 227 ft x 45 ft x 8 ft draught, speed 15½ knots (later 12 knots), two Mirrlees Blackstone diesel engines each 1,000 shp coupled to Voith Schneider propellers (1 forward, 1 aft), two stacks, capacity 694 passengers and 36 cars (later revised to 510 passengers and 40 cars), built for CalMac (Caledonian Steam Packet Co. amalgamated with MacBrayne) Gourock-Dunoon service by James Lamont, Port Glasgow. From 1978 replaced the *Glen Sannox* on the Wemyss Bay-Rothesay run. The MV *Juno* (1974) is of similar specification.

MV *Pioneer* (1974), 1,071 tons gross, 221 ft 6 in. x 45 ft x 8 ft draught, speed 15½ knots, two Mirrlees Blackstone diesel engines each 1,700 shp, two stacks, capacity 273 passengers and 30 cars (later altered to 356 passengers and 32 cars), built for the CalMac West Loch Tarbet to Islay service by Robb Caledon, Leith. From 1978 replaced the *Glen Sannox* on the Wemyss Bay-Rothesay run.

TSMV *Saturn* (1977), 851 tons, 227 ft x 46 ft x 8 ft draught, speed 14 knots, two squat stacks, capacity 694 passengers and 36 vehicles (later altered to 510 passengers and 40 cars), built by the Ailsa Shipbuilding Co. Ltd of Troon for CalMac for the Wemyss Bay to Rothesay service. Terminals were modified at each end to accommodate the new service.

Other Vessels mentioned in the text

Capercailzie (1883) 526 tons, 194 ft x 24 ft x 13 ft draught, built for Sir John Burns, (Lord Inverclyde of Castle Wemyss, Bart. Hon. Lieut RNR), coal-fired, 600 hp, built by Barclay Curle & Co. of Whiteinch. Two masted with single stack and three deck houses in line. Sold about 1891 to the Admiralty as the port admiral's yacht and renamed *Vivid*. Purchased 1918 by the Directors of the Royal Technical College, Glasgow for £1,800 [*£36,000]. Foundered on a rock in July 1918 near Colonsay.

Aquitania (1913) 45,647 gross tons, 868 ft x 97 ft x 49 ft draught, speed 24 knots, passenger liner built by John Brown for Cunard line. Four funnels, four propellers, turbine propulsion. Broken up in 1949.

Queen Mary (1936) 81,235 tons, 1,020 ft x 118 ft 6 in. x 68 ft 5 in. four screw, speed 32 knots, 2,100 passengers, 1,100 crew, 3 stack, turbine propulsion. Built for the merged Cunard and White Star line in the Depression years commencing in 1930 for use between Southampton and New York. Sold to a US company in 1967.

MV *Dalmarnock* (1970), 2,266 gross tons, 312 ft x 51 ft 2 in. x 14 ft 6 in. draught, service speed 12 knots, motor sludge vessel built by James Lamont & Co. Ltd of Port Glasgow for Glasgow Corporation. Cost £647,000 [*£5.5m]. Single stack, two diesel engines. Capacity 3,000 tons. Transferred to West of Scotland Water in 1996 and disposed of off the Clyde in 1998. The MV *Garroch Head* (1977) is slightly larger and was sold off the Clyde in 1999.

Selected References

General and Local History
The Third Statistical Account of Scotland - The Counties of Renfrew & Bute, edited by A.C. Somerville and W. Stevenson, Collins, 1962
Guide to Wemyss Bay, Skelmorlie, Inverkip, Largs and Surrounding Districts by Alexander Gardner, Paisley, 1879
The South Clyde Estuary - An Illustrated Architectural Guide to Inverclyde and Renfrew by Frank Arneil Walker, Royal Incorporation of Architects in Scotland, 1986
The Story of the Parish consisting of Skelmorlie and Wemyss Bay by Walter Smart, Skelmorlie & Wemyss Bay Community Centre, 1968
An Illustrated History of Skelmorlie and Wemyss Bay 1750-1980 by WEA Local History Class, Skelmorlie, Spring 1980
Greenock, Inverkip and Wemyss Bay in Old Picture Postcards, by Wilson Holland, Parish Historian, Inchinnan, Renfrewshire
Greenock from Old Photographs, by Matt Anderson & Joy Monteith, Inverclyde District Libraries, 1980
Notes from 'Gourock, Inverkip and Wemyss Bay' from old photographs by Joy Monteith & Sandra MacDougall, March 1981
Images of Greenock, by Anthony McNeill, Argyll Publishing, 1998
History of Bute by Dorothy N. Marshall, 1992

Personalities
Montgomeries of Eglington, by Elizabeth M.B.L. Cousins
From Royal Stewart to Shaw Stewart, by J.S. Bolton, Nenufra Publications, 1989
James Miller, by Audrey Sloan with Gordon Murray, Royal Incorporation of Architects in Scotland, 1993
Scottish Architects' Papers - A Source Book, by Rebecca M. Bailey, Rutland Press, 1996
Personal Diaries of George Graham, Engineer in Chief of the Caledonian Railway, 1864

Water Power
'Robert Thom and his work on Water Power for the Rothesay Cotton Mills', by Arnold Earls, from the *Transactions of the Buteshire Natural History Museum, Vol. XIII*, (1945)
'Robert Thom's Cuts on the Island of Bute', by Ian Maclagan, from the *Transactions of the Buteshire Natural History Museum, Vol. XXIV*, (1996)
'A History of Public Water Supply in Rothesay', by Graeme Connor from the *Transactions of the Buteshire Natural History Museum, Vol. XXIV*, (1996)

Trains and Trams
The Origins of the Scottish Railway System 1722-1844, by C.J.A. Robertson, John Donald, Edinburgh, 1983
A Regional History of the Railways of Great Britain Vol. 6, Scotland, The Lowlands and the Borders, by John Thomas, revised J.S. Paterson, David & Charles, 1984
The Caledonian Railway - Account of its Origin and Completion, by George Graham, Engineer, McCorquordale & Co. Ltd, 1888
Caledonian Railway Centenary (1847-1947), The Stephenson Locomotive Society, September 1947
The Caledonian Railway, O.S. Nock, Ian Allan, 1963
Scottish Locomotive History 1831-1923, by Campbell Highet, Allen & Unwin Ltd, 1970
Forty Years of Caledonian Locomotives, by H.J. Campbell Cornwell, David & Charles, 1974
The Observer's Book of Railway Locomotives, H.C. Casserley, Frederick Warne & Co. Ltd, 1960, 1962 and 1974 editions
Manuscript notes prepared by J.F. McEwan, William Patrick Library, Kirkintilloch
LMS Engine Sheds, Volume 5, The Caledonian Railway, by Chris Hawkins & George Reeve, Wild Swan Publications Ltd, 1987
Glasgow Stations, by Colin Johnston & John R. Hume, David & Charles, 1979
Caledonian Railway - Appendix to Working Time Tables, 1st May 1902. (Supplementary to the *Book of Rules and Regulations*, dated 1st February, 1898)
Caledonian Railway - Marshalling of Trains, July 1913
Caledonian Railway - Wemyss Bay Railway Widening - Specification 1902
Some notes on the Wemyss Bay Railway (unpublished) by Ian B. Smith, 1994
'Rothesay Tramways - A Brief History 1882-1936', by Allan Leach, from the *Transactions of the Buteshire Natural History Museum, Vol. XVII*, (1969)

Roads
Road Developments in Ayrshire 1750-1835 (including the Tale of a Road), from a thesis by Alexander K Godwin attending the Department of Economic History of the University of Strathclyde, 1970

Boats and Piers
Clyde Piers, A Pictorial Record, by Joy Monteith & Ian McCrorie
The Clyde Passenger Steamer - Its rise and progress during the 19th Century, by Captain James Williamson, James Machelhose & Sons, Glasgow, 1904
The Clyde Passenger Steamers, by Kenneth Davies, Kyle Publications, Ayr, 1980
To the Coast - 100 years of the Caledonian Steam Packet Co., by Ian McCrorie, Fairlie Press, 1989
The Caledonian Steam Packet Co. Ltd., Iain Charles MacArthur, Clyde River Steamer Club, Glasgow, 1971
'In the Track of the Comet on the Clyde', *The West Coast and the Channel Vol. XXX*, by James Wotherspoon
The Story of Henry Bell's Comet, Scottish Maritime Museum
Yacht Racing on the Clyde 1893-1890, by W.J. Finlayson, Maclure Macdonald & Co.
The British Seaman, by Christopher Lloyd, Paladin, 1970
Clyde Shipwrecks, by Peter Moir & Ian Crawford
Echoes of Old Clyde Paddle Wheels, by Andrew McQueen, Gowans & Gray, 1924
Clyde River & Other Steamers, by C.E. Duckworth & G.E.Langmuir, Brown, Son & Ferguson, 1937
The Golden Years of the Clyde Steamers (1889-1914), Alan J.S. Paterson, David & Charles, 1969
The Victorian Summer of the Clyde Steamers (1864-1888), Alan J.S. Paterson, David & Charles, 1972
Classic Scottish Paddle Steamers, by Alan J.S. Paterson, David & Charles, 1982
The Clyde, by John Riddell, The Fairlie Press, 1988
The Clyde - The Making of a River, by John Riddell, John Donald, 2000

Magazines
The Railway Magazine
Herapeth's Railway & Commercial Journal, 1851-1875
Engineering
The Engineer
The True Line, Journal of the Caledonian Railway Association

Newspapers
The Glasgow Courier
The Glasgow Herald
Rothesay Chronicle and Buteshire & West Coast Advertiser
The Greenock Telegraph & Clyde Shipping Gazette
The Largs and Millport Weekly News
The Evening Times

Information Sources
The Scottish Record Office.
Glasgow University Archives.

Index

Accidents -
  At Wemyss Bay (1865)(1911), 184,189
  Finnoch cutting collapse (1865), 110
  Irish labourer killed (1865), 103
  Peat Bridge derailment (1994), 190
  Port Glasgow (train parted 1878), 186
  Runaway Train (1898), 187
  Workman falls off roof at W. Bay (1993), 270
  Workers entombed (1920), 189
  Workers' train collision at W. Bay (1903), 187
Acts -
  Caledonian Railway Act 1845, 80, 192
  Caledonian Railway Act 1893, 124
  Caledonian Railway (General Powers) Act 1899, 113, 221, 223
  Glasgow, Paisley and Greenock Rlwy Act 1837, 192
  Greenock & Wemyss Bay Rlwy Act 1862, 87
  Greenock & W. Bay Rlwy Ext. Act 1863, 92
Anderson, Sir Robert Rowand 45, 136, 139, 219, 297
Ardgowan, 29, 52, 54, 63, 71, 147
Ardrossan, 135, 147
Arran, Brodick and Lamlash, 109, 122, 155, 182
Barlas, George, Stonemason, 241
Berryards Junction, 27
Berryards, Sugar Works at, 95
Bill proposed to extend line to Largs 79, 111
Bill, Greenock and Wemyss Bay Absorption, 123
Blue trains introduced (Electrification), 252
Board of Trade -
  Maj. Gen. C.S. Hutchinson, RE (1878), 47, 122, 141, 186
  Maj. F.A. Marinden, RE (1878), 141
  Captain F.H. Rich, RE (1865), 185
  Captain Reid, RE (1865), 107
Brakes, continuous 185, 207
Bridge Street Station, Glasgow, 11, 79, 119, 134, 139
Broomielaw, 11, 139, 168
Broun, Charles Wilsone, 55
Burns, George and John, 55, 58, 60, 85, 150, 152, 157, 165, 294
Bute Industry - cotton and tiles, 45
Bute, Marquess of, 29, 43
Byelaws, 207
Caledonian Railway 7, 80, 135
  Locomotive Superintendents 193
  Conner, Benjamin 115,193,207
  Drummond, Dugald 163,193,195,255
  McIntosh, John F. 197,255
  Pickersgill, William 197,215,255
  Sinclair, Robert (First Loco. Super. & GM), 193, 255, 295
  Gibson, Archibald (Secy 1852-1890), 77, 103, 134, 185
  Gilchrist, James 152, 155
  Graham, George (Eng. in Chief)(1853-1899), 76, 103, 107, 111, 122, 135, 140, 193, 219
  Hill, Thomas 77, 81, 215
  Matheson, Donald, 139, 169, 184, 215, 217
  Smithells, James (General Manager), 115, 118, 155
  Thompson, James (GM & Chairman), 77, 132, 134, 159, 215, 231
  Ward, Henry (Gen. Sup. 1857-), 77, 103, 107, 111, 191
Caledonian takes over the G&WBR, 27, 124, 135, 165
Caledonian Steam Packet Company, 162, 176
  Capt. James Williamson (Sup'dent), 77, 162
  CSP commences Wemyss Bay service, 165
Caledonian MacBrayne (CalMac), 252, 263
Caley proposes line to Gourock, 123
Campbell, Alexander, Captain of WB Steamers, 60, 128, 137, 156

Canal proposed to Glasgow, 147
Car ferries, 171, 172, 252
Central Station, 7, 123, 135, 136, 215
Churches, Skelmorlie & Wemyss Bay, 53, 59, 63
Cloch lighthouse, boom at, 168, 171
Clyde Coast Pool, 168
Clyde, deepening the (John Golbourne), 147
Clyde Fortnight, 182.
Clyde Navigation Bill 1887, 140
Clyde River Patrol, The, 181
Clyde, stench of the, 182
Coghill, Mr, Dunrod Quarry, 115
Colm Fair (St Columba's Day), 53
Craigendoran, 47
Cromwell, 43
Cunard Steamship line, 85, 148, 151
Dallas, Mr, Coalman, 62, 67, 251, 295
Darroch, Duncan, of Gourock, 79,97
Decoy village built on Bute, 50, 181
Discipline, Railway, 79, 215
Doubling the line, 27
Dumbarton, 21, 52, 147
Dunlop's bus service, 67, 77
Dunoon, 47, 152, 167
Dunrod and Dunrod Works, 33, 71, 115, 117, 128, 141, 229
Electrification of Coast Line, 173, 252, 261
English tourists arrive, 149, 171
Fairlie, 69, 136, 156
Fares, and complaints of high fares, 105, 110, 114, 118, 299
Ferguson, Messrs George (Contractor) 241, 247
Firework display at Kelly, 60
Findlay, Alexander, bridge and WB station steelwork, 241
Fishing for salmon, 45, 53, 147
Forman & McCall, J.R. Forman, 75, 76, 81, 109, 117, 128, 231
Fourth class fare, 118
Gas Co., Skelmorlie & Wemyss Bay, 60, 117
German Air Force bomb Greenock, 63, 181
Gillies and Campbell, 94, 155, 165
Glasgow & Paisley Joint Railway, 7
Glasgow, St Enoch Station (GSWR), 136, 137
Glasgow Fair, 47, 243
Glasgow Paisley & Greenock Railway, 7, 15, 57, 68, 71, 79, 192
Glasgow, Paisley, Kilmarnock & Ayr Railway, 7, 11, 68, 79
Glasgow & South Western Railway, 7, 79, 135
Gold Run, the (reserves sent to Canada), 181
Gourock Railway & Quay Bill, 113
Grainger & Miller, 15, 295
Greenock & Ayrshire Co., 95
Greenock & Wemyss Bay Railway Co., 7 Directors, 82
  Broun, Charles Wilsone Swinfen, 80, 82, 103
  Christie, G. Fyffe, 82, 103, 155
  Finlay MP, Alexander Struthers, of Castle Toward, 82
  Hadaway, Thomas Spark, Glasgow, 82, 134, 140, 143
  Lamont, James, of Knockdow, 82, 103, 104, 131, 183
  Ronaldson, Alexander, of Glasgow, 57, 82, 103, 184
  Scott, James, of Kelly, 55, 73, 82, 103
  Stewart, James of Garvocks, 82, 103, 118
  Turner, James William, WS, Greenock, 82, 112, 134, 143
  Evans, Mortimer (CE 1869-1881), 77, 117, 121, 125, 128, 140
  Niven, T.O., (CE 1870-), 77, 121, 130
  Weir, Thomas D. (CE 1881-1887), 77, 117, 128, 130, 131, 141
Connections proposed to G&WBR Co. line, 223

Dividends, 104
Land transactions, 93, 300
Line for sale, 103, 118, 121
Line opened, 69, 107
Prospectus, 81
Start of operations, 104, 107
Viaducts, the Daff and Kip Viaducts, 97, 122, 126, 128, 140, 245
Working Agreement, 120
Greenock Central Station, 162
Greenock Custom House Quay, 161
Greenock Cut (Robert Thom), 29
Greenock, Cathcart Street Station, 79, 140, 161, 162
Greenock, Princes Pier, 27, 136, 157, 161
Herring Industry, Fishing Screws 45,147,151
Holiday Homes (Houses used in summer only), 47, 61, 70
Horse Boxes, 210
Housing at Wemyss Bay and Skelmorlie, growth in 59, 61
Hutcheson & Company, David, 152
Hydropathic Hotels, Skelmorlie and Rothesay, 37, 47, 59, 63, 123, 248
Innellan, 47, 77, 109, 167
Inverclyde, Lord, 55, 58, 74, 182, 266, 294
Inverkip, 33, 37, 94, 97, 144, 241
Irish labour, availability of, 57, 69, 92
Jamieson, Mr., Manager of Dunrod Quarry, 115, 118
Joint Management Committee (Caley and G&WBR Co.), 104
Kelly and Kelly House, 51, 54, 58, 60, 73, 150, 217
Kellybridge and Kelly Burn, 51, 52, 69,1 47
Kelly Quarry Siding, 130
Kennedy, Hugh, Contractor, 92, 97
Keydens, W.S., James, Philip, 69, 74, 81
Kilchattan Bay, Bute, 45, 47
Kilcreggan, 47, 59, 152
Kilmarnock and Troon Railway, 68
King Robert II of Scotland, 43, 52
King Robert III of Scotland, 29, 43, 52
Kintyre, steamer, sunk in collision with *Maori*, 181
Knock, 51, 54, 57
Kyles of Bute, 33, 37, 45, 167
Ladyburn Engine Shed, 257
Largs, 47, 51, 69, 154, 156
Largs, proposed lines from Greenock to (1845) (1899), 55, 69, 75, 79
Largs, proposed line from Wemyss Bay to, 111
Largs Steamboat Company, 156
Leith to London, carriage of goods between, 65
Livingstone, Dr, 73
Loch Long and Loch Fyne, 37,45,47
Loch Thom and Robert Thom, 29, 45, 97
Locke, Joseph, and John Errington, 15, 68, 76, 192, 297
London rail link to Glasgow & Edinburgh, 69, 192
Luggage allowance, 116, 145
McAdam, John Loudon, 65
McAlpine, Robert, Contractor, 132, 225
MacBrayne, David, 152, 159, 162, 169, 173
McBride, Peter, Contractor, 225
McDonald, A. & K., Contractors, 92, 97
Mail conveyance, 64, 114
Measured Mile, 177, 179
Miller, James, Architect, 136, 139, 219, 235
Miller, John, Architect and Engineer, 134, 295
Miller, John, Contractor, 241
Millport, 47, 69, 152, 156, 153
Montgomerie, Hugh, 12th Earl of Eglinton, 65, 147, 294
Montgomerie, James, of Wrighthill, MP, 57
13th Earl of Eglinton (Tournament Earl), 57, 294

319

Mount Stuart House, Bute, 45
Mundegumbri, Robert de, 52
Music on the steamers, 109, 149, 167
Naval Review, 182
Omnibus service - Largs to Wemyss Bay, 110
Overton Paper Mills (Puggie Line), 27, 97, 187, 210, 213, 245, 259
Peile, Horatio R.B., Lawyer, Mansion House, 113, 128, 132, 133
Pennyfern (or Penny Farm), 27, 97, 113
Pier Lights and Signals, 93, 111, 121, 132, 163, 221
Pirie, George, Contractor, 231, 235
Port Bannatyne, Bute, 37, 47, 162
Port Glasgow, 23, 147, 221
Postal Service, 115
Press Gangs (the Impress Service), 148
Private carriages, 133
Quarries, 57, 60
Queen Victoria, 69, 184, 150
Rail weights and rails, 125, 127, 132
Railway Accident Pills, 186
Railway Steamboat Packet Company formed, 152
Railways, Parliament debates nationalisation of, 69
Rates and Taxes, 144
Redesdale, Lord, 87, 103
Regattas, Yachting, 150, 161, 182
Renfrew & Ayr Counties Railway, 79
Reservoir disasters, 62, 95
Reverend Gentlemen, 59, 101, 114, 183, 215
Roman occupation, forts, 21, 51
Rothesay, 37, 152, 167, 248
Rothesay Tramways Company, 47
Rothesay Water Supply, 45
Royal Train, 33
Royalty visits Wemyss Bay, 63, 70, 182, 295
Rules and Regulations, 84, 205
Scott and Son's Siding, 94, 121, 130
Scottish Transport Group, 173
Second Class Carriages introduced, 118
Second Class Abolished, 145, 211
Sewage treatment for Glasgow, 182
Shares in the G&WBR Co., purchasing, 121
Shaw, Sir John, 71, 95, 147
Shaw Stewart, Sir John, 65, 71
Shaw Stewart, Sir Michael Hugh, 63, 73, 248
Shaw Stewart, Sir Michael Robert, 21, 68, 71, 115, 144
Shaws Water Co., 29,94,147
Sheep cartage, 132
Shipbuilders, 21, 23, 148
Skelmorlie, 51, 53, 54, 57
Skelmorlie Castle, 51, 57, 63
Slavery, 153
Smuggling, 54, 74, 148
Steamboat Co., The Wemyss Bay, 154
Steamboat Quay, Wemyss Bay, 57
Steamer fuelling, 176
Steamer regulation at piers, 140
Steamer sailings, 69, 110, 150
Steamer companies try to collapse Wemyss Bay trade, 155
Steamers (including diesel powered vessels) -
 Adela (1877), 157, 161, 165, 178, 179
 Argyle (1866), 155, 157, 161
 Arran, TSMV (1953), Bute (1954), Cowal (1954), 172
 Britannia (Royal yacht), 50
 Bute (1865), 154, 155
 Caledonia (1889), 60, 138, 162, 165, 178, 227, 249
 Comet and Charlotte Dundas, 151
 Duchess of Argyll (1906), 179
 Duchess of Hamilton (1890), 60
 Duchess of Rothesay (1895), 151
 Fairy Queen, 151

Galatea (1889), 60, 138, 162, 165
Glen Sannox (1957), 173, 252
Ivanhoe (1880), 60, 158, 163
Jeanie Deans (1931), 172
Juno (1974), Jupiter (1972) and Pioneer (1974), 175
King Edward (1901), 179
Kyles (1865), 109, 153, 155
Lancelot (1868), 157, 161, 165
Lady Gertrude (1872), 157, 175, 178
Largs (1864), 109, 153, 157
Lord of the Isles (1877), 122, 158
Madge Wildfire (1886), 60, 162
Marchioness of Breadalbane (1890), 165, 180, 227
Marchioness of Bute (1890), 60, 165, 180
Marchioness of Lorne (1891), 249
Meg Merrilies (1883), 60, 162, 165, 179
Rothesay Castle, 151
Queen Alexandra (1902), 167
Queen Mary and Queen Elizabeth, 169, 181
Saturn (1977), 175
Sheila (1877), 157, 178
Talisman (1935), 172, 173
Venus (1852), 156
Victoria (1886), 160, 161
Victoria and Albert, 50, 150
Victory (1863), 155
Waverley (1947), 151, 172, 173
Steamers withdrawn from Wemyss Bay 138, 157
Stephen of Kelly, Alexander 217, 221, 295
Stewards of Bute/Stewart/Stuart, 43, 52
Strikes, Long Hours, 144, 195
Sugar Works, Scott & Son's, Tate & Lyle, 94, 121, 130
Sunday Services, 137, 159, 171, 183
Tail o' the Bank, 37, 51, 95, 150, 181
Telegraph arrives on Bute, 47
Telephones, 131, 145, 165
'Terminals' (Railway charges), 91, 116, 121
Third Class, seats in the, 116
Tickets - Season, Villa, Week-end Facilities, 70, 114, 119
Titanic disaster, 151
Toward Point and Lighthouse, 37, 178, 179
Track, double and single, 221
Train composition and subdivision, 123, 135, 201
Trains between Wemyss Bay and Edinburgh, 70
Tramcar from Wemyss Bay proposed, 67
Transfer time between train and boat, 161, 162
Travel time comparison, 55, 64, 68, 135
Tunnels - Inverkip & Cartsburn, 27, 33, 92, 95, 97, 128, 140, 209, 211, 225, 233,2 45
Turf, cutting the first, 92, 95
Turnpike Trusts (introduced and abolished), 65,67
Upper Greenock station, 27, 116, 123, 132, 140, 219, 245, 247
Upper Greenock Works, 225
Waggonways, 67
Wallace, Robert, MP for Greenock, 55, 73, 177
Watt, James. 67, 97
Wellington Park and Bowling Green, 71, 94, 245
Wemyss Bay -
 Bathing Bay, 54
 Beach concreted for tank landing craft, 181
 Bob Wemyss, fisherman, 54
 Castle Wemyss, 55, 60
 Hotel, 89,129, 257
 Marine Village, 55, 73
 New Glasgow, 54
 Proposals for development, 55
 Rail proposed to Wemyss Bay, 81
 Trains run into Central, 165

Watering Place, a rising, 85
Whiting Bay (Wemyss Bay), 53, 55, 69, 150
Wemyss Bay station, 36
 Advertising, 123, 248
 Asbestos, 268
 Bookstall, 101, 249
 Carriage/Goods yard, 257
 Clock in tower, 242, 253, 263, 279
 Contracts ,92
 Engine Shed, 97, 221, 257
 Flats/Container traffic, 252
 Flower decorations, 237, 249, 261,2 66, 281
 Gas lighting proposed, 117, 129
 Goods Shed, 101, 249
 Holiday Traffic, 248, 251
 Horse drawn drays, 249, 251
 Luggage Platform, 268
 Cranes, 252
 New platform provision, 114, 122, 128
 Paddle Box crests, 249, 266
 Paint colours, 306
 Phased re-construction, 221
 Pier damaged by fire, 227, 252
 Pier House, 249, 263
 Pier rebuilt, 123, 225, 247, 252
 Pier repairs, 122, 125, 127
 Platform Numbering, 252, 257
 Porters' Room, 249
 Refreshment room, 110, 134, 145, 242, 249
 Replacement station opened, 242
 Retaining wall extended, 247
 Screen Walls, 251, 272, 283
 Sea Wall, 122, 125, 128, 231, 235
 Signal Boxes, 213, 217
 Stables at, 125, 132, 251
 Staffing levels, 215,2 61
 Station Houses, 101, 237
 Ticket Platform, 97
 Turntable, 129, 213, 257
 Undersized drains, 279
 Valances trimmed back, 252
 Wagons lost, 127
 Water for engines at Wemyss Bay, 116, 131, 257
 Water for Wemyss Bay station, 128
 Wemyss Bay station staff, 297
 Elliott Mr (Station Master W. Bay in 1865), 185
 Hughes Mr (Station Master at WB 1870), 119, 134
 Melrose Mr (WB Piermaster 1884-1904?), 249
 Prentice Mr (Station Master at WB 1911), 188
 Robison Mr (Station Master at WB 1885-), 227, 248
Wemyss Bay Steamboat Company (Ltd), 109, 154, 176
 Agreements-1866, 1874-1877, 1881 etc., 93, 94, 157
 Intention to quit (1881 and 1890), 158, 165
 Failure of, 118,1 55
 Directors, 154
 Captain Alexander Campbell, 156
 Prospectus, 154
Westinghouse, George 207
Widening Works, 133, 225
Williams Patent points, 129
Williamson, Captain James, 140 et seq., 162, 168
Witch, the last, 53, 97
Wolfe Barry, Sir John, 139, 231
Yachts - Capercailzie, Mastiff and Beryl, 58, 150
Young & McCall, Contractors, 92, 95
Young, Dr James of Kelly, 58, 73, 116
Young, James, of Sunderland, Contractor, 92, 101